You can reach Coronado by taking the ferry across the bay, but I get a little thrill every time I drive across the **SAN DIEGO–CORONADO BAY BRIDGE (left).** Its graceful, sweeping design offers a panoramic vista incorporating downtown, the island-like peninsula of Coronado, the Navy shipyards, and—on a clear day—Mexico. Roll down your windows and let the wind blow through your hair—just be sure to keep your eyes on the road, too.

San Diego boasts several easily accessible places where you can commune with nature. None is more spectacular than **TORREY PINES STATE RESERVE (above),** home to the rarest pine tree in North America and located just minutes from downtown. With its wind-swept sandstone cliffs, ocean-view trails, and fabulous beach, this fragile coastal environment offers the best of natural San Diego. In winter you might catch sight of migrating whales; in spring, wildflowers put on a colorful show; while year-round, you can watch dolphins patrol the coast.

© John Warden/Getty Images

The San Diego Zoo may be world famous, but it's the **WILD ANIMAL PARK (above)** that many people end up celebrating as their favorite animal attraction. It features vast open areas where various species roam freely, interacting much as they would on the plains of Africa. There's also room for some human and animal interaction, including a petting station and a special photo caravan that shuttles visitors out into the heart of the enclosures on a mini-safari.

If you're looking for an immersion in Southern California beach lifestyle, you've come to the right place. From surfing to **BEACH VOLLEYBALL (right)**, to just plain old sun worshipping, San Diego has elevated seaside fun to a science. To get a taste of it, just walk, roll, or pedal along the Mission and Pacific Beach boardwalk, where a nonstop parade of characters makes for some great people watching.

© Brett Shoaf/Artistic Visuals

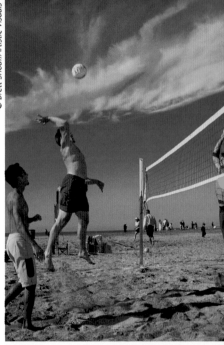

Frommer's®
San Diego

My San Diego

by Mark Hiss

HIGH-END NIGHTCLUBS. ADVENTUROUS DINING. HYPERMODERN ARCHITECTURE.
What's going on here? What happened to that sleepy Navy town, that nice little city of San Diego? What about that killer whale?

Well, folks, that sleepy burgh has woken up and it wants to party. Over the last decade, growth has been fast and furious—and at times awkward, as growth can be—but San Diego now finds itself with a new skyline and a new attitude. With its 70 miles (112.6 km) of coastline and its array of theme parks and attractions (and yes, killer whales), it's still a family-friendly destination, but the nearly nightly bacchanalia in the Gaslamp Quarter is evidence of something young, exciting, and new.

I spent 5 years as the editor of a visitor magazine here, and I was lucky enough to play tourist in my own town. During that time I came to realize there is no easy way to sum up San Diego—whatever you're interested in, from astronomy to zebras, it's here. It's an embarrassment of riches, really (and that's not even taking into account we have the country's best weather).

At the turn of the millennium, the city was riding the crest of a wave unlike anything it had seen since its rootin'-tootin' boomtown days in the 1880s, and that most recent boom has left behind a legacy that includes more than just new hotels, bars, and restaurants. The San Diego Museum of Contemporary Art opened its third space, a sleek downtown annex at the historic Santa Fe Depot; The New Children's Museum debuted its architecturally striking downtown facility; two historic theaters have been restored to their Roaring '20s glory; and swords are being sculpted—not beaten—into ploughshares at NTC Promenade, a former Navy base that is on track to become one of the country's most exciting cultural districts.

Of course, that boom in the 1880s was followed by an inevitable bust, which cast a pall over downtown San Diego for nearly 100 years. Historically, San Diego has always risen and deflated in spasms of growth and bust, usually tied to real estate ventures; it's pretty obvious where we are in the cycle right now. A recent weekend in the Gaslamp Quarter proved as boisterous as ever, though … the good times soldier on. So my advice to you? Come now while the party is still rolling. This is not your father's San Diego. It's more like your great-great-grandfather's San Diego.

© Brett Shoaf/Artistic Visuals

San Diego's coastal environment runs from wide, sandy beaches to rocky shorelines where **TIDE POOLS (right)** beg for exploration. These shallow, low-tide pools are little worlds unto themselves, populated by hermit crabs, sea anemones, and starfish. The wonders of the deep come tantalizingly close for budding marine biologists.

Originally established in 1769 (and relocated to its present site in 1774), **MISSION BASILICA SAN DIEGO DE ALCALÁ (below)** is California's oldest mission and an active Catholic Parish where mass is conducted daily. The lovely grounds exude calm and serenity—a far cry from the mission's early days when things were a little more strained between the friars and the indigenous population.

© Brett Shoaf/Artistic Visuals

© Brett Shoaf/Artistic Visuals

Each spring desert wildflowers burst into full bloom at **CABRILLO NATIONAL MONUMENT (above),** home to prehistoric fossils, ancient Native American sites, sandstone canyons, and granite mountains. This is California's largest state park, featuring trails to satisfy any level of hiker— the best route leads to an honest-to-goodness palm tree oasis. Also keep an eye out for the endangered bighorn sheep that navigate the steep canyon walls.

Finding a parking space downtown can be frustrating (and expensive), but riding the **SAN DIEGO TROLLEY (right)** is an easy option for exploring the Gaslamp Quarter, Little Italy, and Old Town; it's also a convenient way to head south of the border to Tijuana.

The **HOTEL DEL CORONADO** is one of the region's most iconic structures. Built in 1888, it has hosted kings, presidents, literary giants, and movie stars. Even if you don't stay here, the grounds are worth a tour.

Each spring, desert wildflowers burst into bloom in **ANZA-BORREGO DESERT STATE PARK (above)** home to prehistoric fossils, ancient Native American sites, sandstone canyons, and granite mountains. This is California's largest state park, featuring trails to satisfy any level of hiker—the best route leads to an honest-to-goodness palm tree oasis. Also keep an eye out for the endangered bighorn sheep that navigate the steep canyon walls.

The historic Gaslamp Quarter offers a dazzling array of restaurants, clubs, and shopping opportunities, as well as numerous Victorian architectural masterpieces. **The LOUIS BANK OF COMMERCE (right)** once housed an oyster bar frequented by Wild West lawman Wyatt Earp.

BALBOA PARK is the nation's largest urban cultural park, filled with museums, theaters, and gardens, as well as recreational facilities and walking trails. Many of the park's structures were built in a florid Spanish Colonial Revival style for two world's fairs, making a stroll down the pedestrian thoroughfare a must. You could spend all day in Balboa Park (and I have) and only see a fraction of what's here.

San Diego's North County towns of Carlsbad and Encinitas make up a noted commercial flower-growing region. The most vibrant palette of blossoms comes alive in March and April at the **FLOWER FIELDS AT CARLSBAD RANCH (left)**.

San Diego's skyline has gone through an amazing transformation over the years, with a slew of new, burnished skyscrapers helping to erase the city's reputation as a sleepy Navy town. Set right on the edge of the bay, **DOWN-TOWN SAN DIEGO (above)** includes a convention center, a baseball stadium, and the historic Gaslamp Quarter, the city's main entertainment district. Hugging downtown along the water-front is the pedestrian-friendly Embarcadero, lined with attractions and eateries.

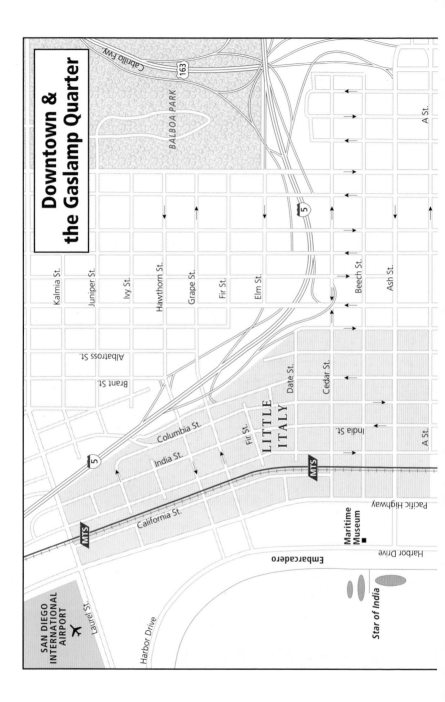

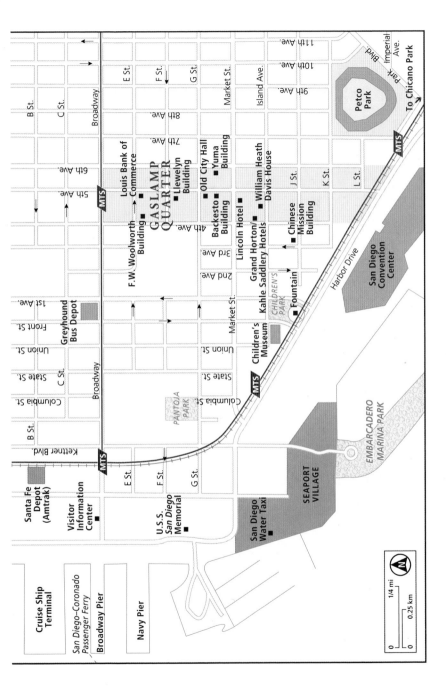

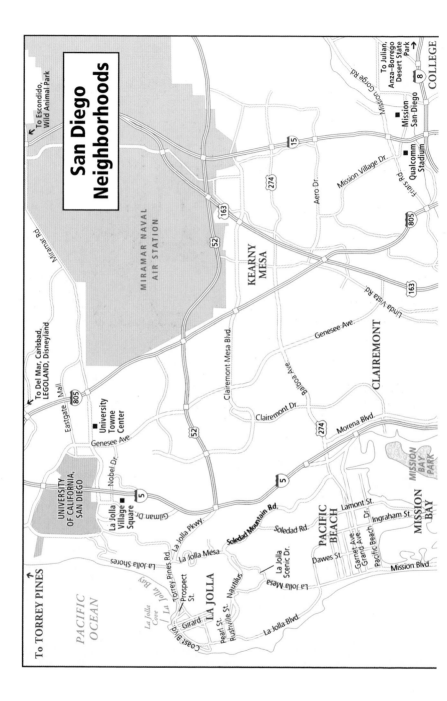

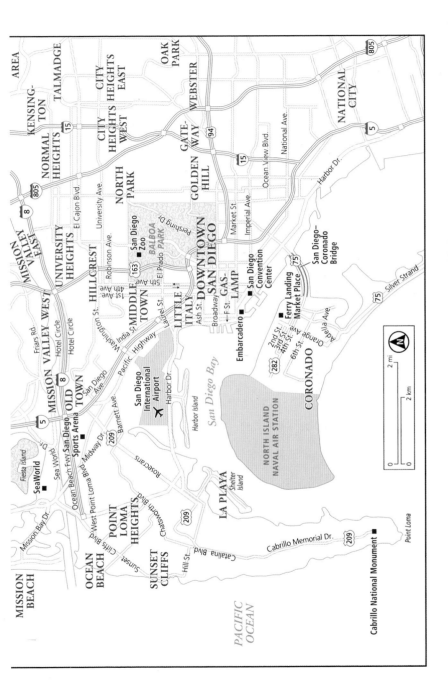

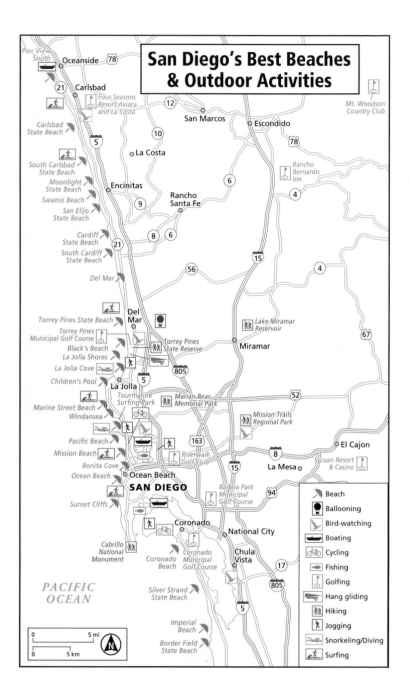

San Diego's Best Beaches & Outdoor Activities

Pier View South
Oceanside 78
Carlsbad 21
Four Seasons Resort Aviara and La Costa
12
Mt. Woodson Country Club
San Marcos
Escondido
Carlsbad State Beach
5
10
78
La Costa
South Carlsbad State Beach
Rancho Bernardo Inn
Moonlight State Beach
Encinitas
6
4
Swamis Beach
9
Rancho Santa Fe
San Elijo State Beach
Cardiff State Beach
8   6
South Cardiff State Beach
21
15
56
4
Del Mar
Del Mar
Lake Miramar Reservoir
67
Torrey Pines State Beach
Torrey Pines Municipal Golf Course
Torrey Pines State Reserve
Miramar
Black's Beach
La Jolla Shores
805
La Jolla Cove
Children's Pool
5
La Jolla
Tourmaline Surfing Park
Marian-Bear Memorial Park
52
Marine Street Beach
Mission Trails Regional Park
Windansea
Pacific Beach
163
El Cajon
Mission Beach
Riverwalk Golf Club
8
Bonita Cove
15
La Mesa
Sycuan Resort & Casino
Ocean Beach
Ocean Beach
SAN DIEGO
Balboa Park Municipal Golf Course
94
Sunset Cliffs
Coronado
National City
Cabrillo National Monument
Coronado Beach
Coronado Municipal Golf Course
Chula Vista
17
PACIFIC OCEAN
Silver Strand State Beach
805
5
Imperial Beach
0   5 mi
0   5 km
Border Field State Beach

Beach
Ballooning
Bird-watching
Boating
Cycling
Fishing
Golfing
Hang gliding
Hiking
Jogging
Snorkeling/Diving
Surfing

Frommer's®

San Diego 2010

by Mark Hiss

Here's what the critics say about Frommer's:

"Amazingly easy to use. Very portable, very complete."
—BOOKLIST

"Detailed, accurate, and easy-to-read information for all price ranges."
—GLAMOUR MAGAZINE

"Hotel information is close to encyclopedic."
—DES MOINES SUNDAY REGISTER

"Frommer's Guides have a way of giving you a real feel for a place."
—KNIGHT RIDDER NEWSPAPERS

WILEY
Wiley Publishing, Inc.

ABOUT THE AUTHOR

Mark Hiss is a third-generation Southern Californian who has spent more than 25 years in San Diego. He was founding editor of both the visitor guide *Where San Diego* and *Performances*, the playbill magazine for the city's leading performing arts venues. He is also author of *Frommer's San Diego Day by Day* and contributes to *Frommer's California*. In a previous life he was a publicist who worked for several of San Diego's top theater companies.

Published by:

WILEY PUBLISHING, INC.

111 River St.
Hoboken, NJ 07030-5774

ISBN 978-0-470-48725-9

Editor: Anuja Madar
Production Editor: Jana M. Stefanciosa
Cartographer: Tim Lohnes
Photo Editor: Richard Fox
Production by Wiley Indianapolis Composition Services

Front cover photo: Coronado Beach: Boogie body boarders playing in surf at dusk.
©VisionsofParadise.com/Alamy Images
Back cover photo: SeaWorld: Girl watching killer whales from glass enclosure.
©Chad Ehlers/Alamy Images

For information on our other products and services or to obtain technical support, please contact our Customer Care Department within the U.S. at 877/762-2974, outside the U.S. at 317/572-3993 or fax 317/572-4002.

Wiley also publishes its books in a variety of electronic formats. Some content that appears in print may not be available in electronic formats.

Manufactured in the United States of America

5 4 3 2 1

CONTENTS

LIST OF MAPS	vi

WHAT'S NEW IN SAN DIEGO	1

1 THE BEST OF SAN DIEGO   3

1 The Most Unforgettable Travel Experiences.....................3

2 The Best Splurge Hotels...........5

3 The Best Moderately Priced Hotels 5

4 The Best Dining Experiences 6

5 The Best Things to Do for Free 6

2 SAN DIEGO IN DEPTH   8

1 San Diego Today 8

2 Looking Back at San Diego.........9

3 Eating & Drinking in San Diego....14

4 San Diego in Pop Culture: Books, Film, TV, Theater, Music, Art & Sports................16

3 PLANNING YOUR TRIP TO SAN DIEGO   18

1 When to Go......................18

   San Diego Calendar of Events.......19

2 Entry Requirements 25

3 Getting There & Getting Around . .26

4 Money & Costs...................37

   What Things Cost in San Diego...........................38

5 Health 39

6 Safety...........................39

7 Specialized Travel Resources 40

8 Sustainable Tourism..............46

9 Special-Interest Trips & Escorted General-Interest Tours............47

10 Staying Connected...............48

   The Best of San Diego Online 50

4 SUGGESTED SAN DIEGO ITINERARIES   51

   The Neighborhoods in Brief.........51

   Off the Beaten Path: North Park & Beyond 54

1 The Best of San Diego in 1 Day.....56

2 The Best of San Diego in 2 Days....57

3 The Best of San Diego in 3 Days....57

5 WHERE TO STAY   59

1 Tips on Accommodations........59
2 Best Hotel Bets...................61
3 Downtown, the Gaslamp
& Little Italy......................62
4 Hillcrest & Uptown................71
5 Old Town & Mission Valley........74

6 Mission Bay & the Beaches........76
7 La Jolla...........................82
*The Road to Wellness—
Healthful Havens*...................87
8 Coronado..........................89
9 Near the Airport 93

6 WHERE TO DINE   94

1 Best Bets for Dining 94
2 Restaurants by Cuisine 96
3 Downtown, Gaslamp Quarter
& Little Italy......................99
Attack of the Killer Burgers 104
4 Hillcrest & Uptown 105
5 Old Town & Mission Valley....... 109

6 Mission Bay & the Beaches 112
Baja Fish Tacos.....................114
7 La Jolla........................... 117
Appetizing Views...................122
8 Coronado........................ 123
9 Off the (Tourist) Beaten Path 125

7 WHAT TO SEE & DO   127

1 The Three Major Animal Parks.... 127
2 San Diego's Beaches 132
3 Attractions in Balboa Park 136
Balboa Park Guided Tours..........141
4 More Attractions 143
5 Free of Charge & Full of Fun 155

6 Especially for Kids 157
7 Special-Interest Sightseeing..... 159
8 Organized Tours................. 162
9 Outdoor Activities............... 166
10 Spectator Sports 176

8 CITY STROLLS   179

*Walking Tour 1: The Gaslamp
Quarter* 179
*Walking Tour 2:
The Embarcadero*...................185

Walking Tour 3: Old Town..........189
Walking Tour 4: Balboa Park 193

9 SHOPPING   199

1 The Shopping Scene............ 199
2 The Top Shopping
Neighborhoods................. 199

3 Shopping A to Z 208

10 SAN DIEGO AFTER DARK · 215

1 The Performing Arts............. 216

2 Live Entertainment.............. 219

3 The Bar & Coffeehouse Scene 221

Brewpubs & Wine Bars 224

4 Gay & Lesbian Nightlife 226

5 More Entertainment 227

Running with the Grunion 228

6 Only in San Diego............... 229

11 SIDE TRIPS FROM SAN DIEGO · 230

1 North County Beach Towns: Spots to Surf & Sun 230

2 North County Inland 245

Grape Escape: Temecula Wineries............................249

3 The Disneyland Resort & Knott's Berry Farm 251

The Art of the (Package) Deal 253

4 Julian: Apple Pies & More........ 263

5 Anza-Borrego Desert State Park....................... 269

6 Tijuana: Going South of the Border 274

FAST FACTS, TOLL-FREE NUMBERS & WEBSITES · 290

1 Fast Facts: San Diego............ 290

It's Easy Being Green 291

2 Toll-Free Numbers & Websites.... 297

Long-Haul Flights: How to Stay Comfortable.......................298

INDEX · 302

General Index................... 302

Accommodations Index 308

Restaurant Index................ 309

LIST OF MAPS

Suggested Itineraries 53

Where to Stay in Downtown
San Diego 63

Where to Stay in Hillcrest
& Uptown 73

Where to Stay in Old Town
& Mission Valley 75

Where to Stay in Mission Bay
& the Beaches 77

Where to Stay in La Jolla 83

Where to Stay in Coronado 91

Where to Dine in Downtown
San Diego .101

Where to Dine in Hillcrest
& Uptown .107

Where to Dine in Old Town 111

Where to Dine in Mission Bay
& the Beaches 113

Where to Dine in La Jolla 119

Where to Dine in Coronado 125

What to See & Do in
San Diego .129

Balboa Park .137

What to See & Do in Downtown
& Beyond .145

What to See & Do in Old Town
& Mission Valley 149

What to See & Do in La Jolla 151

Walking Tour 1: The Gaslamp
Quarter 181

Walking Tour 2: The
Embarcadero 187

Walking Tour 3: Old Town 191

Walking Tour 4: Balboa Park 195

Downtown San Diego
Shopping 201

Hillcrest & Uptown
Shopping 203

La Jolla Shopping 206

Northern San Diego County 231

Eastern San Diego County 265

Tijuana 275

HOW TO CONTACT US

In researching this book, we discovered many wonderful places—hotels, restaurants, shops, and more. We're sure you'll find others. Please tell us about them, so we can share the information with your fellow travelers in upcoming editions. If you were disappointed with a recommendation, we'd love to know that, too. Please write to:

Frommer's San Diego 2010
Wiley Publishing, Inc. • 111 River St. • Hoboken, NJ 07030-5774

AN ADDITIONAL NOTE

Please be advised that travel information is subject to change at any time—and this is especially true of prices. We therefore suggest that you write or call ahead for confirmation when making your travel plans. The authors, editors, and publisher cannot be held responsible for the experiences of readers while traveling. Your safety is important to us, however, so we encourage you to stay alert and be aware of your surroundings. Keep a close eye on cameras, purses, and wallets, all favorite targets of thieves and pickpockets.

Other Great Guides for Your Trip:

Frommer's San Diego Day by Day

Frommer's Los Angeles Day by Day

Frommer's California

Frommer's Los Angeles

Frommer's Mexico

Frommer's Los Cabos & Baja

The Unnoficial Guide to California with Kids

The Unofficial Guide to Disneyland

FROMMER'S STAR RATINGS, ICONS & ABBREVIATIONS

Every hotel, restaurant, and attraction listing in this guide has been ranked for quality, value, service, amenities, and special features using a **star-rating system.** In country, state, and regional guides, we also rate towns and regions to help you narrow down your choices and budget your time accordingly. Hotels and restaurants are rated on a scale of zero (recommended) to three stars (exceptional). Attractions, shopping, nightlife, towns, and regions are rated according to the following scale: zero stars (recommended), one star (highly recommended), two stars (very highly recommended), and three stars (must-see).

In addition to the star-rating system, we also use **seven feature icons** that point you to the great deals, in-the-know advice, and unique experiences that separate travelers from tourists. Throughout the book, look for:

Finds	Special finds—those places only insiders know about
Fun Facts	Fun facts—details that make travelers more informed and their trips more fun
Kids	Best bets for kids, and advice for the whole family
Moments	Special moments—those experiences that memories are made of
Overrated	Places or experiences not worth your time or money
Tips	Insider tips—great ways to save time and money
Value	Great values—where to get the best deals

The following **abbreviations** are used for credit cards:

AE	American Express	DISC	Discover	V	Visa
DC	Diners Club	MC	MasterCard		

TRAVEL RESOURCES AT FROMMERS.COM

Frommer's travel resources don't end with this guide. **Frommers.com** has travel information on more than 4,000 destinations. We update features regularly, giving you access to the most current trip-planning information and the best airfare, lodging, and car-rental bargains. You can also listen to podcasts, connect with other Frommers.com members through our active-reader forums, share your travel photos, read blogs from guidebook editors and fellow travelers, and much more.

What's New in San Diego

Ah, the contact sport that is California politics.

In November 2008, California voters narrowly passed a constitutional amendment banning gay marriage. Proposition 8 had been added to the ballot in response to the California Supreme Court's legalization of same-sex marriage in May 2008. With thousands of marriages in legal limbo (and millions of dollars in potential revenue remaining untapped), the matter is heading back to the courts. As of this writing, the outcome is uncertain. Interestingly, although San Diego is an extremely gay-friendly destination with one of the largest annual Pride celebrations in the country, one-third of the money raised by Prop 8 supporters came from San Diego donors. Most notable among them was developer Doug Manchester, who ponied up $125,000. This has led a group called Californians Against Hate to organize a boycott of Manchester's two hotel properties: downtown's bayside **Manchester Grand Hyatt** and the luxurious **Grand Del Mar** in the North County. Check www.boycottmanchesterhotels.com for more information.

After a bruising battle that finally came to an end in February 2009, state legislators hammered out a budget that addresses California's projected $42-billion deficit. It will be residents who take it on the chin, of course, but visitors may note reduced services or higher fees at some parks, beaches, and other state-run facilities. The state has also raised the sales tax by 1%.

Currently, San Diego's sales tax is 7.75% (the figure varies from county to county)—it's unknown if the local tax will be increased in response to the state's action.

What *is* known is the fate of alcohol at city beaches—it's out. Voters made permanent a 1-year trial ban of booze from all 17 miles of San Diego beaches, as well as coastal parks and bay shores. Fines max out at $250.

WHERE TO STAY Another style-conscious hotel is added to the downtown mix with the **Hotel Indigo,** 950 Island Ave. (© 877/846-3446 or 619/727-4000; www.hotelindigo.com). Located near PETCO Park in the East Village, the 12-story, 210-room property will open in August 2009. Look for the rooftop terrace to be a real sweet spot.

Towering above the bay and offering killer views is the new 30-story **Hilton San Diego Bayfront,** 1 Park Blvd. (© 619/564-3333; www.sandiegobayfront.hilton.com). Opened in December 2008, it's literally just steps from the water and the convention center. The severe architecture is all business, but the location encourages pleasure.

Another downtown property opened in December '08 is **Sé San Diego,** 1047 Fifth Ave. (© 877/515-2211 or 619/515-3000; www.sesandiego.com). This lavish, Asian-inspired hotel features all the high-tech amenities you would expect, plus such simple pleasures as floor-to-ceiling windows that open wide.

On the opposite end of the spectrum, a new hostel opened in downtown's East Village, **Lucky D's,** 615 Eighth Ave. (© **619/595-0000;** www.luckyds.com). It offers a host of freebies, including Wi-Fi, telephone calls anywhere in the U.S. or Canada, meals three times a week, and Gaslamp Quarter walking tours. You don't have to go far to find a good time, either—Lucky D's operates a bar right downstairs.

WHERE TO DINE Urban sophistication reigns at downtown's **Crescent Heights Kitchen & Lounge,** 655 W. Broadway (© **619/450-6450;** www.crescentheights sd.com). Chef David McIntyre, a protégé of Wolfgang Puck, serves California modern cuisine in a chic setting. It's located outside of the tourist zone, between the Embarcadero and the Gaslamp, and is definitely worth seeking out.

Diet? What diet? You're on vacation. That's the handy rationale you'll use when you see sleek, modern, and oh-so-sweet **Mille Feuille Chocolates & Pattiseries,** 3896 Fifth Ave. (© **619/295-5232;** www. millefeuillechocolates.com). Besides temptations such as the cappuccino mocha éclair or the Pop Rocks–encrusted macaroons, this Hillcrest pastry shop also serves lunch.

How much juice does Bing Crosby have today? The folks behind **Bing Crosby's Restaurant and Piano Lounge,** 7007 Friars Rd. (© **619/295-2464;** www.bing crosbysrestaurant.com), hope plenty. For you kids out there, think of Bing as the Justin Timberlake of his day; and as a crooner and Academy Award–winning actor, Der Bingle's day lasted for decades. If you're a fan, you'll love this place; if not, this upscale Fashion Valley eatery can be enjoyed on its own merits for its "country club" cuisine (or at least for a martini after a hard day of shopping).

Casual Oceanside has been given a shot of style with the opening of **333 Pacific,** 333 N. Pacific St. (© **760/433-3333;**

www.cohnrestaurants.com). Operated by San Diego's most successful restaurant group, this steak and seafood spot sits right across from the Oceanside Pier, and diners are treated to 180-degree views of the Pacific.

WHERE TO GO The **San Diego Zoo** in Balboa Park (© **619/234-3153;** www. sandiegozoo.org) will unveil its newest habitat in June 2009. The $44-million Elephant Odyssey features a herd of Asian elephants, and also includes an endangered California condor, sloths, snakes, and rodents. Additionally, the exhibit highlights the region's prehistory, with life-size replicas of animals that wandered these parts 10,000 years ago. Visitors can walk through the herd via a tunneled pathway and get a behind-the-scenes look at keepers and veterinarians as they interact with the animals; kids can participate in a fossil dig, too.

The natural treasure-trove that is the San Elijo Lagoon Ecological Reserve can now be explored more thoroughly thanks to the newly opened **San Elijo Nature Center,** 2710 Manchester Ave. (© **760/ 634-3026;** www.sanelijo.org). This interpretive center gives an overview of the reserve's history, flora, and fauna, as well as information on the 7.5 miles of hiking trails available. This 1,000-acre coastal wetland, located between Solana Beach and Encinitas, was nearly lost to development—like 90% of the rest of California's wetlands—and is now home to some 700 species of plants and animals.

AFTER DARK One of San Diego's coolest venues is located in a warehouse district in the Middletown neighborhood. Various nightclubs have come and gone from the space, but there's real buzz over the latest, **Spin,** 2028 Hancock St. (© **619/294-9590;** www.spinnightclub.com). The tri-level, industrial-fun-house setting, featuring an open-air, bay-view rooftop, hosts DJs doing their thing into the wee after-hours.

The Best of San Diego

Over the last 2 decades, San Diego has evolved past its old reputation as a slow-growth, conservative Navy town graced with 70 miles of fabulous sandy coastline. Amid all the change, San Diego is still first and foremost a big outdoor playground. You can swim, snorkel, windsurf, kayak, bicycle, in-line skate, and partake of other diversions in or near the water, as well as in the mountains and desert. But if you think this place is just about wiggling your toes in the sand or cooing over panda bears at the justly famous zoo, prepare to be surprised by San Diego's big-city style. Beyond the stunning natural beauty, you'll find high-octane nightlife, world-class cultural organizations, family-friendly attractions, and sophisticated dining. And the city is perched on the world's busiest international border, with the sights, sounds, and tastes of Mexico just a Chihuahua's length away. Welcome to San Diego—California's grown-up beach town.

1 THE MOST UNFORGETTABLE TRAVEL EXPERIENCES

- **Zipping Across the San Diego–Coronado Bay Bridge:** The first time or the 50th, there's always an adrenaline rush as you follow this engineering marvel's dramatic curves and catch a glimpse of the panoramic view to either side. Driving west, you can easily pick out the distinctive **Hotel del Coronado** (p. 89) in the distance.

- **Escaping to Torrey Pines State Reserve:** Poised on a majestic cliff overlooking the Pacific Ocean, this state park is set aside for the rarest pine tree in North America. The reserve has short trails that immerse hikers in a delicate and beautiful coastal environment. See p. 153.

- **Communing with Seals at the Children's Pool:** This tiny La Jolla cove was originally named for the young bathers who could safely frolic behind a man-made seawall. These days, seals and sea lions sunning themselves on the sand are the main attraction. The beach had

been off-limits to humans since 1997, but following much public debate was reopened to swimmers in 2005. Keep a safe distance—these are wild animals—and you'll be rewarded with a unique wildlife experience. See p. 134.

- **Taking in the City's Best Panorama:** Cabrillo National Monument at the tip of Point Loma offers an unsurpassed 360-degree view that takes in downtown, the harbor, military bases, Coronado, and, in the distance, Mexico and San Diego's mountainous backcountry. It's also a great vantage point from which to watch migrating Pacific gray whales in the winter. See p. 144.

- **Renting Bikes, Skates, or Kayaks at Mission Bay:** Landscaped shores, calm waters, and paved paths make Mission Bay Park an unsurpassed aquatic playground. Encompassing 4,600 acres and featuring 27 miles of bayfront beaches and picnic areas, there's plenty to explore on both land and water. See p. 133.

- **Strolling Through the Gaslamp Quarter:** You'll be convinced you've stepped back in time when you walk through this 16¹/₂-block area lined with Victorian commercial buildings. The beautifully restored structures, in the heart of downtown, house some of the city's most popular shops, restaurants, and nightspots. See "Walking Tour 1: The Gaslamp Quarter," on p. 179.

- **Spending an Idyllic Day in Balboa Park:** This is San Diego's crown jewel and the largest urban cultural park in the nation. The buildings that grew out of Balboa Park's two world's fairs (1915–16, 1935–36) create a vision of Spanish Golden Age splendor and provide a home for 15 of the city's best museums. The park also features gardens, walking trails, theaters, and recreational facilities, and is the location of the San Diego Zoo. See p. 136.

- **Being a Groundling:** You won't have to stand as they did in William Shakespeare's day, but you can see the Bard's work alfresco at the Old Globe Theatre's Summer Shakespeare Festival. The Tony Award–winning Old Globe hosts performances of Shakespeare's work in repertory, alternating three productions at its open-air theater in Balboa Park. See p. 22.

- **Floating Up, Up, and Away over North County:** Sunset hot-air-balloon rides carry passengers over the golf courses and luxury homes north of the city. Do it while you can—open space for landings has been fast disappearing—making ballooning an endangered species here. See p. 166.

- **Witnessing the Desert's Spring Fling:** Anza-Borrego Desert State Park, California's largest state park, attracts most of its visitors during the spring wildflower season, when a kaleidoscopic carpet of blooms blankets the desert floor. Others come year-round to hike more than 100 miles of trails. See p. 269.

- **Paddling With the Fishes:** The calm surfaces and clear waters of the San Diego–La Jolla Underwater Park are the ultimate spot for kayaking, snorkeling, or scuba diving. This ecological reserve features sea caves and vibrant marine life, including California's state fish, the electric-orange garibaldi. See p. 150.

- **Teeing off at Torrey Pines Golf Course:** These two 18-hole championship courses in La Jolla overlook the ocean and provide players with plenty of challenge. In January, the Buick Invitational Tournament is held here. The rest of the year, these popular municipal courses are open to everybody. See p. 171.

- **Spending a Day at the San Diego Zoo, Wild Animal Park, or SeaWorld:** At the zoo, animals live in naturalistic habitats; at the Wild Animal Park, most of the 3,500 animals roam freely over an 1,800-acre spread. SeaWorld is an aquatic wonderland of pirouetting dolphins and 4-ton killer whales with a fetish for drenching visitors. See p. 127.

- **Making a Run for the Border:** What a difference a line makes. Once you cross it, you're instantly immersed in the chaotic vibrancy of Mexico's fourth-largest city. Just a 20-minute drive from downtown, Tijuana has a raucous tourist zone with plentiful shopping, as well as an array of cultural and culinary delights. See p. 274.

- **Toasting the Good Life:** Just across the county line in Temecula, about 60 miles north of downtown San Diego, are some two-dozen wineries. They range from mom-and-pop operations with minimal amenities to slick commercial ventures with fancy tasting rooms, retail boutiques, and restaurants. See p. 249.

- **Buying Some Peanuts and Cracker Jack:** San Diego's Major League Baseball team, the Padres, plays at PETCO Park, a state-of-the-art ballpark that opened in 2004. Incorporating seven buildings that date as far back as 1909,

PETCO's clever design and downtown location have made it a fan favorite. See p. 176.

- **Getting in Touch With Your Pioneer Spirit:** The mountain hamlet of Julian was founded as a gold-mining town in the 1860s, but it eventually gained fame for a different kind of mother lode: apples. Today, this rustic community has a distinctly Victorian, Old West charm, redolent of hot apple pies. See p. 263.

2 THE BEST SPLURGE HOTELS

- Resembling an ornate Tuscan villa, the **Grand Del Mar,** 5300 Grand Del Mar Way (© **888/314-2030** or 858/314-2000), is an aptly named resort tucked into the foothills of Del Mar. Opened in 2007, it features exquisite terraces, fountains, gardens, and amenities galore. Its stand-alone restaurant, Addison, is the first San Diego dining establishment to receive a AAA 5 Diamond Award. See p. 232.
- **Ivy Hotel,** 600 F St. (© **877/489-4489** or 619/814-1000), exudes warmth, modern style, and class, and features such amenities as a personal butler and luxury cars to tool guests around downtown at no charge. The Ivy knows how to party, too—not only is there a jamming nightclub on-site, but one of the suites also includes a stripper pole. See p. 64.
- **Four Seasons Resort Aviara,** 7100 Four Seasons Point (© **800/819-5053** or 760/603-6800), is a AAA 5 Diamond resort in Carlsbad that pulls off the hat trick of encompassing one of the best restaurants, spas, and golf courses in the county. See p. 240.
- San Diego's other AAA 5 Diamond property is the **Lodge at Torrey Pines,** 11480 N. Torrey Pines Rd. (© **800/656-0087** or 858/453-4420). Painstakingly designed in the Craftsman style, the Lodge features an elegant restaurant and a blissful spa, and elbows up against renowned Torrey Pines Golf Course in La Jolla. See p. 85.

3 THE BEST MODERATELY PRICED HOTELS

- You won't find a better location than the **Horton Grand,** 311 Island Ave. (© **800/542-1886** or 619/544-1886). This historic Victorian beauty has called the Gaslamp Quarter home since 1886, and some otherworldly guests have reputedly been hanging around since then, too. See p. 68.
- In San Diego's Little Italy, **La Pensione Hotel,** 606 W. Date St. (© **800/232-4683** or 619/236-8000), feels like a small European hotel and offers tidy lodgings at bargain prices. There's an abundance of great dining in the surrounding blocks, and you'll be perfectly situated to explore the rest of the city by car or trolley. See p. 70.
- Like some other recent hotel projects around town, the **Hotel Occidental,** 410 Elm St. (© **800/205-9897** or 619/232-1336), is a refurbished old beauty, built around 1923, and has a great location (near Balboa Park). Unlike those other properties, though, the Occidental is incredibly affordable. See p. 70.

- Supper clubs have proliferated in San Diego, but none have matched the panache and sophistication of **Anthology,** 1337 India St. (© **619/595-0300**). It's hard to say what takes center stage here—culinary pooh-bah Bradley Ogden's excellent new American fare or the live music performed by an eclectic lineup of international artists. See p. 100.

- **Blanca,** 437 S. Hwy. 101 (© **858/792-0072**), may be located in a strip mall blocks away from an ocean view, but this Solana Beach restaurant flies its foodie flag high. It's one of the best upscale establishments in the county. See p. 242.

- If you want to know what San Diego tastes like, you can find out at **Market,** 3702 Via de la Valle (© **858/523-0007**). Native son Carl Schroeder finds the best local ingredients, creates his menu daily, and serves it all in a casually elegant space in Del Mar. See p. 236.

- At the **Marine Room,** 2000 Spindrift Dr. (© **866/644-2351**), executive chef Bernard Guillas's creative, modern French cuisine provides ample evidence of how far the city's invigorated dining scene has come. See p. 117.

- **Jack's La Jolla,** 7863 Girard Ave. (© **858/456-8111**), is a three-story epicurean fun house featuring a trio of restaurants and five lounges. Chef/owner Tony DiSalvo, a veteran of Jean-Georges in New York City, oversees the menus, which range from Italian fare to sushi. See p. 118.

- **Georges California Modern/Ocean Terrace,** 1250 Prospect St. (© **858/454-4244**): These two longtime favorites in La Jolla share an *aah*-inspiring ocean view. Georges underwent a $2.5-million renovation and re-imagining (and a slight name change), but powerhouse chef Trey Foshee is thankfully still working his magic here. See p. 118.

- **Addison,** 5200 Grand Del Mar Way (© **858/314-1900**), is San Diego County's one and only AAA 5 Diamond restaurant. This sumptuous dining destination is grandly European, offering daily tasting menus of modern French cuisine and featuring a jaw-dropping wine list that's more like a wine book. See p. 234.

- You can't visit San Diego without trying a **fish taco.** If the city has an official food, this is it. See p. 114 for suggestions on where to get one.

5 THE BEST THINGS TO DO FOR FREE

- **Timken Museum of Art:** It's a small collection, and the museum's modern architecture is distinctly out of place in Balboa Park, but the always-free Timken (© **619/239-5548**) houses 600 years of art history. Masterpieces by Rembrandt and Rubens, as well as works by such seminal American painters as Eastman Johnson and John Singleton Copley, are among the holdings. See p. 143.

- **Organ Pavilion Concerts:** Organ recitals have been staged at the **Spreckels Organ Pavilion** (© **619/702-8138**) in Balboa Park almost without interruption since 1915. With 4,530 pipes, this is one of the world's largest outdoor organs. Free concerts are presented every Sunday at 2pm. See p. 143.

- **Chicano Park Murals:** More than 70 works of art grace the support structure of the Coronado Bridge in **Barrio**

Logan's Chicano Park, National Avenue at Crosby Street (© **619/563-4661**). The images celebrate and honor Latino culture, and are considered the largest and most important collection of outdoor murals in the country. See p. 155.

- **Self-Realization Fellowship Hermitage and Meditation Gardens:** This retreat in Encinitas, 215 W. K St. (© **760/753-2888**), with its distinctive lotus-shaped towers, was built by a yogi in 1937. Its cliff-side meditation gardens overlook the Pacific and offer incredible vistas. Visitors are welcome free of charge, and no one will give you a spiritual sales pitch. See p. 239.

2

San Diego in Depth

by Maya Kroth

Locals call it the Sunshine Tax: the willingness we all have to make certain concessions for the privilege of living in what many still deem the finest city in America, if not on earth.

Baseball players and corporate executives accept less money for jobs that might pay more handsomely in places such as Boston or Minneapolis, figuring that a minor salary reduction is a reasonable price to pay for never, ever having to shovel another driveway.

The Sunshine Tax hints at the ethos lying at the heart of San Diego. With 70 miles of pristine coastline and plenty of sunny days, this is a place where play comes first, makin' a buck second.

Sure, there's industry here. In fact, this is one of the country's leading centers for manufacturing, defense, bio-science, and high-tech. But it's the fun stuff that really gets us going, and that's not limited to our most famous attractions (the beach, SeaWorld, the Zoo, and Balboa Park).

Due in part to its diverse topography, with canyons and mesas slicing the area into dozens of discrete pockets, San Diego's identity is hard to sum up in a word. It's a city of villages, as civic planners like to say, and each neighborhood has its own style.

There are the coastal enclaves that could only be found in Southern California, from tony La Jolla by the sea to funky, counterculture Ocean Beach to sleepy Encinitas in North County.

Then there's San Diego's urban side. Though they may not have been much 25 years ago, today downtown's Gaslamp Quarter and East Village vibrate with big-city buzz, while hip uptown spots such as Hillcrest and North Park deliver edgier fashion and culture.

Thanks to growing cultural and dining scenes, unparalleled outdoor activities, sports franchises, and other entertainment options, urban San Diego can now go toe-to-toe with any American metropolis.

1 SAN DIEGO TODAY

San Diego is a place of many identities and perhaps defines itself most strongly in terms of what it *isn't*: namely, Los Angeles. Home to Hollywood and much of California's industry, Los Angeles casts a long shadow over its kid sister to the south, a city that once hoped to be Southern California's dominant metropolis. Today, many natives have come to dislike the City of Angels and all that it stands for. Where career-minded Angelenos have a reputation for wheeling and dealing and superficiality, San Diegans are a laid-back lot who seldom ask, "So, what do you do?"

San Diego's redheaded stepchild identity can trace its roots at least as far back as the 1880s, when the city's sudden and dramatic boom hinged on its hope of becoming the West Coast terminus of the Santa Fe Railway's transcontinental railroad. The city's subsequent cataclysmic bust coincided with the Santa Fe's decision to reroute its line through L.A., making San Diego the end of a spur line and squashing dreams of transforming the city's promising port into the seat of commerce and industry in the Southland.

Just as San Diego is defined, in part, by its northern neighbor, so, too, is it shaped by its sibling to the south. With the world's busiest land-border crossing, San Ysidro, located less than 20 miles south of downtown, San Diego is heavily influenced by Tijuana, and vice versa. Despite nearly 600 miles of fencing and concertina wire running along the southwestern border, language, food, and culture fly back and forth. (People, too: Visitors are often surprised by the yellow freeway signs that caution drivers to watch for families running across the highway.) In fact, the Mexican flag flew over Old Town for a few decades before the Mexican-American War, and for nearly a quarter-century, San Diego was the unofficial capital of Upper (Alta) and Lower (Baja) California.

Since virtually the beginning, San Diego's climate and natural endowments have been her principal attractions; today the region's nearly three million residents partake in outdoor activities like they're going out of style. Dramatic topography allows for skiing in the morning and surfing in the afternoon, making San Diego a haven for board sports enthusiasts. Skateboarder Tony Hawk and Olympic snowboarder Shaun White are but a few who

cut their teeth—and other parts—in San Diego.

And let's not forget about those legendary waves. Always battling other coastal California towns for the title of "Surf City, USA," San Diego wholeheartedly embraces the surfing lifestyle. The sport's local roots go back as far as 1910; some 50 years later, Tom Wolfe famously documented the scene in his essay, *The Pump House Gang*, which chronicled a group of surfers at La Jolla's **Windansea Beach** (p. 134). Windansea remains a coveted—and crowded—surf break, along with the mellow **Swami's** (p. 239), which gets its name from the **Self-Realization Fellowship Hermitage** (p. 239), an ashram housed on the bluff above the beach.

Today, San Diego's top industries are defense, manufacturing, tourism, and agriculture, which are bolstered by growing biotechnology and telecommunications sectors. While locally based companies such as Qualcomm put San Diego's people to work, the city has many other attributes that attract those who love to play. The temperate climate and nearly 100 golf courses have lured retirees; the numerous colleges and universities—more than a dozen—and raucous nightlife are magnets for students; and attractions including **SeaWorld** (p. 130), **LEGO-LAND** (p. 237), and the **San Diego Zoo** and **Wild Animal Park** (p. 127) draw children and families from all over the globe. It all adds up to a quality of life deemed worthy of a little Sunshine Tax.

2 LOOKING BACK AT SAN DIEGO

It's been called the Plymouth Rock of the West Coast, the Naples of America, and America's Finest City. San Diego is a city shaped by individuals, from the Spanish explorers who first "discovered" it to the prescient businessmen who envisioned the booming seaside metropolis it was to

become, and the many colorful characters that came in between.

FROM NATIVE TIMES TO THE SPANISH CONQUEST Excavators recently unearthed a mammoth skull in downtown San Diego estimated to be 500,000 years old, but the human hunters who followed those mammoths over the Bering Straight into North America probably didn't get here until about 20,000 years ago. The area's earliest cultural group, dated to around 7500 B.C., is the San Dieguito Paleo-Indian, followed a millennium later by the La Jollan, Yuman, and Shoshonean tribes.

By A.D. 1500, some 20,000 Indians were living in thatched huts or caves in about 90 settlements, comprising five tribes: the Luiseño, Cahuilla, Cupeño, Ipai, and Kumeyaay, many of which persist today on reservations, some operating **casinos** (p. 228). These are the people that the Spaniard Juan Rodríguez Cabrillo encountered when he became the first European to set foot on what is now the West Coast of the United States.

In 1542, Cabrillo sailed from Mexico into what he called "a very good enclosed port"; he named it San Miguel and declared it a possession of the king of Spain. Despite this news, Spain didn't send another explorer back to San Miguel until 1602, when Sebastián Vizcaíno led a 200-man expedition from Acapulco, arriving at a port he called "the best to be found in all the South Sea." Not recognizing he had stumbled upon Cabrillo's San Miguel, Vizcaíno renamed the spot San Diego, after his flagship and also in honor of a popular 16th-century saint, San Diego de Alcalá de Henares.

Apparently easily impressed, Vizcaíno went on to discover Monterey Bay, declaring *it* "the best port that could be desired," but Spain again failed to act on its explorers' discoveries, leaving California alone for almost another hundred years.

FROM THE MISSION ERA TO THE MEXICAN-AMERICAN WAR Concerned about protecting its New World territories from a potential Russian encroachment from the North, the Spanish in 1697 authorized the construction of Jesuit missions in Baja California, with designs on employing the assimilated Indians as a defense force against foreign interests.

In 1767, the Jesuits were expelled by California's new governor, Gaspar de Portolá, who sent the Franciscans to take over mission building in Alta California. The Franciscans' leader, Father Junípero Serra, arrived in San Diego in 1769 and founded Alta California's first mission, **Mission Basilica San Diego de Alcalá** (p. 147), on July 16 at what is now called **Presidio Hill,** above present-day **Old Town** (p. 147). Five years later, Father Serra moved the mission to an inland site, closer to fresh water and fertile soil, and despite being damaged in an Indian revolt in 1775, the mission remains there to this day.

Meanwhile, a military presidio at the mission's original site housed a population of soldiers, civilians, and children that numbered 200 by 1790. By 1800, ships from France, America, and Britain had come to trade for cowhide, otter skins, and beef tallow (later they would make the whalers rich by buying tons of whale oil, along with local wool and honey). In 1821, Mexico won independence from Spain, and California swore its allegiance to the newly formed state. The new government began distributing land grants as compensation for soldiers, who left the presidio to raise cattle on sprawling backcountry ranchos.

Back in town, the presidio went into precipitous decline, while epidemics of smallpox and malaria vanquished much of the remaining Indian population. Mexico, realizing it could no longer afford to support the missions as the Spanish had done, passed the Secularization Act of 1833, which resulted in the closure of Mission San Diego and the sale of its lands.

The Mexican-American War arrived on San Diego's doorstep in December 1846, when the Mexican Californios met General Stephen Kearny's Army troops in a valley northeast of San Diego. Historians disagree about which side actually won the bloody Battle of San Pasqual, as both claimed victory, but the end result is the same: California was eventually ceded to the Americans in the 1848 treaty of Guadalupe Hidalgo, which relinquished the southwest to the union for $15 million.

FROM OLD TOWN TO NEW TOWN Having outgrown and then abandoned the presidio in 1835, settlers began building adobe houses at the foot of Presidio Hill. A few of the original adobes remain, including **Casa de Estudillo** and others that have been restored and preserved in **Old Town State Historic Park** (p. 148). By mid-century, Old Town's diverse population of about 650 included Filipinos, Chinese, East Indians, and Afro-Hispanics, and the community showed early signs of modernity: An overland mail route was established; the *San Diego Herald* newspaper began printing; the first public schoolhouse opened; and in 1856, New York–born businessman and sometime brick-maker Thomas Whaley built the first brick structure in Southern California. The still-standing (and certifiably haunted) **Whaley House** (p. 149) functioned not only as the Whaley family residence but also variously as a general store, granary, courthouse, school, and the town's first theater.

But some had a different vision for the city that was developing in Old Town. The British explorer George Vancouver was, in 1793, perhaps the first to wonder why San Diegans had situated their settlement so far away from what most agreed was a rather wonderful port. In 1850, San Francisco merchant William Heath Davis had a similar idea and purchased 160 acres of bayside land in what was then called "New Town" (present-day **downtown**), about 4 miles south of Old Town. In hopes of luring people and businesses, Davis built a wharf, ordered a handful of prefab salt-

boxes houses shipped in from Maine, and oversaw the opening of two hotels. New Town didn't take off, however, and the experiment was dubbed "Davis's Folly."

NEW TOWN BOOM & BUST Less than 2 decades later, another San Francisco businessman, Alonzo Horton, swooped in and picked up 800 acres in New Town for $265. Within 2 years he rebuilt Davis's previously destroyed wharf and opened a theater; thanks to aggressive promotion, his downtown lots were selling like hot cakes.

The decision to move county records from Old Town to New Town in 1871 signaled the direction the city was moving. Old Town's fate was sealed when it was swept by a devastating fire in 1872, followed 2 years later by a massive flood.

San Diego's population had already quadrupled (to about 2,300) by 1870, but that was nothing compared to the boom that was coming. Gold was discovered in the nearby **Julian** (p. 263) hills in 1870, and in 1873 construction began on an eastward transcontinental railroad line from San Diego. A stock market panic put the kibosh on that project, but by 1885 the first train from the east finally reached the city.

This touched off "the great boom," as speculators realized the commercial potential of combining San Diego's unparalleled port with the railroad's ability to transport goods eastward. A rate war broke out between rival rail lines in 1887, bringing the cost of a westward ticket down from $125 to $1. This brought even more boomers out west, not only to speculate on land but also to partake of the fresh air and whatever it was in the water that was making the local Indians live to 135, as reports of the day claimed.

The 1880s were, by all accounts, a wild time in San Diego. New Town filled with traveling circuses and minstrel shows, with gambling halls and at least 60 saloons, plus more than 100 houses of ill repute, employing hundreds of painted ladies in the "**Stingaree**" district. (The present-day Stingaree nightclub [p. 223] pays homage to the old red-light zone.) The boom years brought a variety of notable characters to town, including Wild West lawman Wyatt Earp, who ran three gambling parlors, "Buffalo" Bill Cody, and Ulysses S. Grant, Jr., the president's son.

New Town wasn't the only neighborhood to develop; enclaves such as **La Jolla** (p. 150), **Ocean Beach** (p. 133), and **Pacific Beach** (p. 134) also began to take shape. The northern village of **Carlsbad** (p. 236) boomed, too, when former sea captain John Frazier dug a freshwater well and began touting the healing powers of the mineral water. Midwesterners Elisha S. Babcock and H. L. Story bought and developed the peninsula across the bay from New Town, renaming it Coronado and opening the storybook **Hotel del Coronado** (p. 89) in 1888. The $1.5-million lodge became the world's largest resort hotel, famous for its now-iconic red turrets.

When a San Francisco sugar baron named John D. Spreckels began investing in San Diego—notably in public transit—it became clear that Alonzo Horton's New Town was growing into a full-fledged city. Population soared to 50,000 that decade, but by 1888 the real estate boom had ended, and a nationwide depression sent more than half those fortune-seekers back home. The railroads, meanwhile, had quietly moved their operations northward, leaving San Diego merely the end of a spur line from L.A. rather than the transcontinental terminus it had hoped to

be. Ironically, in 1919 San Diego would finally get its railroad—just in time for the rising popularity of the automobile to make it nearly obsolete.

EMBRACING TOURISM Perhaps resigned to the notion that it had lost the battle to become California's industrial capital, San Diego turned its attention to tourism. Capitalizing on the completion of the Panama Canal, the city organized the **Panama-California Exposition** of 1915 in its newly flowering crown jewel, **Balboa Park** (p. 136), the 1,400-acre parkland plot designated by Alonzo Horton back in 1868 and later developed by botanist Kate O. Sessions. The iconic **Botanical Building** (p. 138) was constructed, along with a Japanese temple, an outdoor pipe-organ pavilion, and many other buildings. The animals brought in for the exposition remained even after the fair closed, becoming the first residents of the **San Diego Zoo** (p. 128).

A second fair in 1935 showcased curiosities including a nudist colony (now the Zoro Garden butterfly habitat) and "Midget Village," which advertisements described as a display "built on doll-house scale, where more than one hundred Lilliputians will work and play." Meanwhile, the fair also showed off the newly built Fine Arts Gallery (now **San Diego Museum of Art,** p. 142), **Natural History Museum** (p. 142), and **Old Globe Theatre** (p. 217).

The park's Spanish Revival architecture seen today was conceived in an effort to present San Diego as a place with a romantic European heritage. Promotional literature dubbed the city the "Naples of

Trivia: Segregated No More

On January 5, 1931, trustees at Lemon Grove Grammar School instructed principal Jerome Green to turn Mexican children away at the door, resulting in a lawsuit. The "Lemon Grove Incident" became the first successful school desegregation court decision in U.S. history.

Trivia: Fourth Time's the Charm

It was from a naval base in San Diego that President Franklin D. Roosevelt gave a radio address accepting the Democratic nomination to run for a fourth term in 1944.

America" and exalted its fine Mediterranean climate.

The fairs showed the world that San Diegans were living the good life. Not even Prohibition could dampen spirits in the newly minted Shangri-La, for all the legal drinking one desired could be had just south of the border in Tijuana. With a new racetrack, golf course, resort hotel, casino, and spa, Tijuana became a playground for the Hollywood set—and San Diego its gateway.

By the 1930s, booze was back in vogue and San Diego had its own world-class horse racing facility in the **Del Mar Racetrack** (p. 178). Founder Bing Crosby himself was there to greet the track's first guests at the gate on opening day in 1937.

THE MILITARY BUILDS A HOME Military defense, a leading industry in San Diego for more than a half-century, began at least as far as back 1796, with the Spaniards' construction of Fort Guijarros (at present-day Point Loma) to defend the port from foreign ships.

In 1911, Aviator Glenn Hammond Curtiss established a flight school on Coronado's **North Island** and invited the Army and Navy there to train for free. With the onset of World War I in 1917, the government purchased North Island, which by then had already been in use by the Army, Navy, and Marines. The Navy relocated its Pacific Fleet to San Diego in 1919.

North Island's aviation activity continued after the war, too, most famously when a young pilot named **Charles Lindbergh** hired San Diego's Ryan Aeronautical Company to manufacture a special plane of his own design, called the Spirit of St. Louis.

On May 10, 1927, Lindbergh left North Island for New York on a test flight, setting a transcontinental record in the process. Ten days later, he flew from New York to Paris, becoming the first pilot to make a solo nonstop flight across the Atlantic. San Diego's airport, **Lindbergh Field** (p. 27), pays homage to the flying legend.

San Diego became a key part of U.S. military strategy after the bombing of Pearl Harbor during World War II underscored the Pacific Coast's vulnerability to attack. Giant underwater nets crisscrossed the bay to ward off Japanese subs, while nearly 2,000 Japanese-Americans from San Diego were held at internment camps such as Manzanar, at the foot of the Sierra Mountains.

Today, military history is honored at the **USS *Midway*** (p. 146), an aircraft carrier museum stationed on the waterfront. Commissioned in 1945 and still active during Desert Storm in 1991, the *Midway* is the world's longest-serving aircraft carrier.

THE RISE OF THE SUBURBS & THE MALL THAT CHANGED EVERYTHING With suburbanization taking root in America in the wake of the war, neighborhoods with names such as Clairemont Hills flourished outside the center of the city, while San Diego's downtown core was left to decay.

When a few national magazines suggested San Diego had again gone bust, the city renewed its attempts to restore its former glory. The next decade saw several big-city developments, including the construction of new downtown high-rises and the addition of a **symphony** (p. 218), **opera** (p. 218), and major-league sports franchises. By the late

'60s, the American Football League's **Chargers** (p. 177) and Major League Baseball's **Padres** (p. 176) were playing at a shiny new stadium in Mission Valley, and **SeaWorld** (p. 130) had opened on Mission Bay.

The postwar years also saw the flowering of new education and research institutes, including the public **University of California, San Diego;** the Catholic **University of San Diego;** and the **Salk Institute** (p. 152), founded by polio vaccine developer Jonas Salk. These joined the already-established **Scripps Institution of Oceanography** (p. 152) and San Diego's State Teachers' College (later renamed **San Diego State University**).

Despite civic and cultural improvements, downtown—still overrun with porn theaters, strip clubs, flophouse hotels, and dive bars—was decidedly unbefitting of California's second-largest city. But the 1984 construction of the kaleidoscopic, carnivalesque **Horton Plaza** (p. 200) shopping center, named for founding father Alonzo Horton, kicked off urban renewal in San Diego. Downtown's seedy elements were eradicated, and the quirky, colorful, multilevel mall now anchors the vibrant and family-friendly **Gaslamp Quarter** (p. 99) entertainment district.

The construction of a new baseball stadium east of the Gaslamp Quarter further invigorated downtown. When **PETCO Park** (p. 176) opened in 2004, the surrounding neighborhood (dubbed the **East Village,** p. 52) began to gentrify, with restaurants, galleries, and boutiques replacing industrial warehouses.

Another downtown real estate boom spurred the construction of thousands of apartments and condos, but when the bubble burst a few years ago, developers found themselves with a surplus inventory. Though San Diego was among the economies hit hardest by the crash, it's hard not to sense the opportunity in today's downtown air, and ponder for a moment what someone like Alonzo Horton might do in this situation.

3 EATING & DRINKING IN SAN DIEGO

Some time ago, "San Diego cuisine" meant tacos, burgers, and whatever else could be scarfed at the beach without utensils and washed down with a can of beer. But the city's culinary scene has come a long way in recent years, and modern San Diego boasts fine restaurants and sophisticated food.

Increasing numbers of young, ambitious chefs have set up shop here, attracted by the plentiful, high-quality local produce and fresh seafood. Some find the more laid-back, less cutthroat culinary landscape a great place to experiment with anything from molecular gastronomy to nouvelle French. Throughout the city you'll also find traditional Italian trattorias, old-school steakhouses, lavish Indian buffets, incredible sushi bars, and Spanish tapas restaurants, not to mention spots offering authentic Afghan, Ethiopian, Russian, and, of course, Mexican food. As for home-grown cuisine, here's a look at what you'll find on the menu in San Diego.

FRUITS OF THE SEA Though much restaurant seafood comes from other places, this town still manages to turn out some of the freshest, whether it be from Alaska or Australia. Local waters produce a variety of fish and shellfish, including **halibut, yellowtail tuna, swordfish, prawns,** and **uni.** In wintertime, **spiny lobster** pops up on menus up and down the coast; local lobster differs from its East Coast cousins in that it's smaller and doesn't have claws. The **fish taco,** rumored to have been imported from Mexico by local surfers, is the city's unofficial signature dish; it's practically criminal to leave town without sampling at least one. The fish can be any variety, often mahi-mahi, which is grilled or deep-fried, topped with shredded cabbage and a creamy sauce, and tucked inside a corn tortilla with a lime wedge. Perfection.

FROM THE FARM TO THE TABLE

Don't be surprised to see many restaurant menus crediting farms by name for everything from the pork loin to the baby lettuce. The provenance of produce, meat, and other edibles is taken seriously in this town, especially given the growing "locavore" movement. Eating locally is a pleasure in agriculturally blessed San Diego, whose soil has historically produced excellent **strawberries, grapes, walnuts, corn, tomatoes,** and other crops. Today, we're one of the nation's leading producers of **avocados.** Chefs in the burgeoning farm-to-table movement have taken note, and even California Cuisine icons such as Alice Waters and Wolfgang Puck are known to source some ingredients from San Diego. In addition to fruits and veggies, many chefs are also using **pork, beef,** and **dairy** products from local ranches.

COMIDA DE MEXICO, OLD & NEW

Without a doubt, what's missed most by those who've left San Diego is the Mexican food. It's hardly an exaggeration to say that there's a taco shop on every corner, serving traditional dishes such as **tacos, burritos, tortas** (Mexican sandwiches), **tostadas,** and **quesadillas.** Among the regional favorites are *carnitas,* delectable chunks of slow-cooked pork, and the unusual **California burrito,** a giant flour tortilla stuffed with *carne asada* (beef), cheese, guacamole, and french fries. South of the border, chefs are developing an elevated fusion cuisine known as **"Baja Med."** Bearing little resemblance to the familiar food of mainland Mexico, Baja Med, as its name implies, combines Baja ingredients such as tomatoes, olives, and tuna with Mediterranean techniques and flavor profiles.

WHAT TO WASH IT ALL DOWN WITH

Outside of brewery circles, it's a little-known fact that San Diego is one of the **craft brewing** (p. 224) capitals of the world. The birthplace of "double IPA" (a strong, hoppy India Pale Ale), the region is home to at least half a dozen boutique breweries that churn out a variety of beers, from no-nonsense, hops-filled brews to delicate fruit-flavored ones. Some San Diego breweries have tasting rooms and offer tours of their facilities; others merely distribute their suds to the many **beer bars** (p. 224) around town. Just across the border, the **Tecate brewery** in the town of the same name brews a lighter quaff and also offers tours and tastings.

There are also two **wine regions** within an hour's drive of downtown. The **Temecula Valley** (p. 249) northeast of San Diego grows more than 40 different varietals and is home to 20 wineries. South of the border, northern Baja's wine country is tucked into the **Guadalupe Valley** (p. 286) east of Ensenada. Baja produces 90% of Mexico's wine, notably at large-scale producers such as L.A. Cetto, but there are more than 20 smaller wineries that produce anywhere from 500 to 40,000 cases per year. Top varietals in the valley include Tempranillo, Cabernet Franc, Nebbiolo, chenin blanc, and more.

Back in central San Diego, a new **wine bar** (p. 224) seems to crop up weekly, each offering convenient and often affordable ways to sample local and international wines by the glass.

Trivia: Fast-Food Fact

In 1951, Robert Oscar Peterson founded the fast-food chain Jack In the Box here, opening a drive-through restaurant at 63rd Street and El Cajon Boulevard, near San Diego State University. A hamburger cost 18¢.

4 SAN DIEGO IN POP CULTURE: BOOKS, FILM, TV, THEATER, MUSIC, ART & SPORTS

LITERATURE San Diego's sparkling shores have stirred many a scribe, dating back at least to 19th-century novelist **Helen Hunt Jackson,** whose *Ramona* many agree was inspired by her stay at Rancho Guajome, near Oceanside. It's often cited as the first novel about life in Southern California.

L. Frank Baum, author of *The Wizard of Oz,* began wintering on Coronado in the early 20th century and wrote a few of his *Oz* stories there. Though unnamed, some of the fictional villages in his stories are thought to be thinly veiled depictions of La Jolla.

Later, La Jolla was home to pulp novelist **Raymond Chandler.** His last novel, 1958's *Playback,* finds his hero, Philip Marlowe, tracking Betty Mayfield to the fictional town of Esmeralda, another La Jolla stand-in. (The crime novel continues to be a popular form for San Diegans: Contemporary authors Don Winslow and Joseph Wambaugh both work in the genre.)

Around the same time Chandler was writing *Playback,* another La Jolla resident, Theodore Seuss Geisel, better known simply as **Dr. Seuss,** published the legendary children's book *The Cat in the Hat.* Geisel later skewered his uppity neighbors in *The Sneetches.*

In the 1960s, **Tom Wolfe** showed a different side of La Jolla in *The Pump House Gang.* Written in Wolfe's "New Journalism" style, the piece offered a portrait of the surf scene centered at Windansea Beach.

MUSIC San Diego's musical tradition was greatly enriched by the closing of New Orleans's red-light district Storyville in 1917; that brought many Big Easy jazz cats out west, including composer and pianist **Jelly Roll Morton,** who had a regular gig at the US Grant hotel until he quit upon learning his group was being paid less than the house white band.

Tom Waits and **Frank Zappa** were two of the bigger hits to come out of San Diego in the '60s and '70s; Waits even spent some time working as a doorman of a Mission Beach nightclub before moving to Los Angeles and releasing *Closing Time* in 1973. During that era, San Diego–based hard rock band **Iron Butterfly** released *In-A-Gadda-Da-Vida,* which was given the industry's first platinum award. Down in Mexico, a young **Carlos Santana** was sharpening his guitar chops in the bars of Tijuana.

In the 1990s, San Diego talents were represented in genres as diverse as folk, grunge, and punk rock. One-named songstress **Jewel** famously lived in a van while gigging at local coffeehouses, while **Eddie Vedder** lived in San Diego before moving to Seattle to front Pearl Jam. Poway's **blink-182** got famous on the back of skate-rock anthems such as "What's My Age Again?" and "All the Small Things."

Contemporary mainstream artists include pop singer **Jason Mraz,** bluegrass trio **Nickel Creek,** and soulful surf-rockers **Switchfoot.**

FILM & TELEVISION One of the first big features to be shot in San Diego was Billy Wilder's 1959 film *Some Like it Hot,* which starred Jack Lemmon, Marilyn

---

Trivia: Heavy Petting

For the cover photo of their 1966 album *Pet Sounds,* the Beach Boys posed with goats at the San Diego Zoo's petting zoo.

Trivia: The Curse of the Bambi

Talk to San Diego sports fans for any length of time, and you'll quickly notice a certain commonality: pessimism. This is an outgrowth, no doubt, of the sad reality that no local sports team has ever won a major league title, leading some to believe in a **San Diego sports curse.** This doesn't just apply to the Padres and the Chargers, who've gone 0-fer in championships since their beginnings in the 1960s. When you factor in the now-departed Clippers and Rockets basketball teams, San Diego clubs have gone nearly 90 seasons without one. To make matters worse, all four teams have losing records overall.

In a story that sounds a lot like the Boston Red Sox's 86-year "Curse of the Bambino," some blame the jinx on the Chargers' decision to trade Lance "Bambi" Alworth to the Dallas Cowboys in 1970, after which the Cowboys recorded several Super Bowl appearances while the Chargers languished.

Monroe, and Tony Curtis, and was filmed at the Hotel Del Coronado.

In 1986, *Top Gun* told the story of Lieutenant Pete "Maverick" Mitchell (played by Tom Cruise), a hotshot pilot at the flight school at Miramar. Downtown restaurant Kansas City Barbeque was the backdrop for several scenes; despite suffering a fire in 2008, restaurant owners managed to salvage the piano used by Goose and Maverick to sing "Great Balls of Fire."

Writer/director Cameron Crowe based his rock-'n'-roll coming-of-age picture *Almost Famous* on his own experiences as a 15-year-old rock critic in San Diego. The cross-border drug trade has inspired many set-in–San Diego productions, including *Traffic,* which won an Oscar for director Stephen Soderbergh, and the TV series *Weeds,* starring Mary-Louise Parker. Will Ferrell's 1970s-newscaster spoof *Anchorman* remains one of the most often-quoted films among a certain generation of San Diegans. (Demure types are advised to cover their ears should someone start explaining what "San Diego" means in German.)

The list of actors who were born or lived in San Diego includes Annette Bening, Cameron Diaz, Ted Danson, Robert Duvall, Dennis Hopper, Whoopi Goldberg, Gregory Peck, and Raquel Welch, among many others.

THEATER It may not be Broadway or the West End, but San Diego's theater scene is surprisingly sophisticated, having produced several plays and musicals that went on to success on the Great White Way and beyond. Among these are *Thoroughly Modern Millie,* **The Who's** *Tommy,* Billy Crystal's *700 Sundays,* and *Jersey Boys,* which all originated at the La Jolla Playhouse (p. 216). The Old Globe Theatre (p. 217) has also staged several productions on their way to New York, including *Into the Woods,* August Wilson's *Two Trains Running,* a 1993 revival of *Damn Yankees,* and holiday favorite **Dr. Seuss'** *How the Grinch Stole Christmas.*

SPORTS One of the most legendary baseball players ever, **Ted Williams,** was a product of San Diego's Hoover High School. Williams played for the minor-league precursor to today's San Diego Padres in 1936 before moving on to the Boston Red Sox and becoming one of the best hitters in history. Hall of Famer **Tony Gwynn** was a Padre throughout his 20-year career. Phillies pitcher and 2008 World Series MVP **Cole Hamels** was also born in San Diego.

Olympic swimmer **Greg Louganis** hails from here, as does champion golfer **Phil Mickelson.** Famous footballers include **Marcus Allen, Reggie Bush,** and **Marshall Faulk,** among others.

Planning Your Trip to San Diego

This chapter contains all the practical information and logistical advice you need to make your travel arrangements a snap: from deciding when to go to finding the best airfare. For additional help in planning your trip and for more on-the-ground resources in San Diego, please see "Fast Facts, Toll-Free Numbers & Websites" on p. 290, or log on to www.frommers.com.

1 WHEN TO GO

San Diego is blessed with a mild climate, low humidity, and good air quality. In fact, *Pleasant Weather Rankings,* published by Consumer Travel, ranked San Diego's weather no. 2 in the world (behind Las Palmas, in the Canary Islands). It's worth keeping in mind, though, that San Diego County covers more than 4,500 square miles and rises in elevation from sea level to 6,500 feet. It can be a pleasant day on the coast but blisteringly hot on the inland mesas; or conversely, it can be a foggy day at the beach but gloriously sunny just minutes away downtown.

With its coastal setting, the city of San Diego maintains a moderate climate. Although the temperature can change 20° to 30°F between day and evening, it rarely reaches a point of extreme heat or cold; daytime highs above 100°F (38°C) are unusual, and the mercury dropping below freezing can be counted in mere hours once or twice each year. San Diego receives very little precipitation (just 10 in. of rainfall in an average year); what rain does fall comes primarily between November and April, and by July, our hillsides start to look brown and parched. It's not unusual for the city to go without measurable precipitation for as long as 6 months in the summer and fall.

My favorite time of year in San Diego is the fall. The days are still warm (even hot), and the cool nights remind you that yes, even in Southern California, we have a change of seasons. February and March are also beautiful periods when the landscapes are greenest and blooming flowers at their peak, although it's still too cold for all but the heartiest people to go into the ocean without a wet suit. Beachgoers should note that late spring and early summer tanning sessions are often compromised by a local phenomenon called **May Gray** and **June Gloom**—a layer of low-lying clouds or fog along the coast that doesn't burn off until noon (if at all) and returns before sunset. Use days like these to explore inland San Diego, where places such as the Wild Animal Park are probably warm and clear.

A more unpredictable Southern California phenomenon is the hot, dry winds known as **Santa Anas.** They usually hit a couple times a year, typically between September and December, and can last for several days. These desiccating winds heighten wildfire danger and can be a backcountry firefighter's worst nightmare, but Santa Anas invariably bring warm temperatures and crystal-clear skies.

Occurring irregularly every 2 to 7 years, the **El Niño** weather pattern—storms created by a warming of Pacific Ocean waters—can cause unusually heavy winter rains. A 1988 El Niño storm even toppled a research platform off Mission Beach (it can now be explored by divers as part of San Diego's Wreck Alley—p. 174).

San Diego is busiest between Memorial Day and Labor Day. The kids are out of school and *everyone* wants to be by the seashore; if you visit in summer, expect fully booked beachfront hotels and crowded parking lots. The week of the July 4th holiday is a zoo at Mission Beach and

Pacific Beach—you'll either love it or hate it. But San Diego's popularity as a convention destination and its temperate year-round weather keep the tourism business steady the rest of the year, as well. The only slow season is from Thanksgiving to early February. Hotels are less full, and the beaches are peaceful and uncrowded; the big family attractions are still busy on weekends, though, with residents taking advantage of holiday breaks. A local secret: Although they're in the coolest, rainiest season (relatively speaking, anyway), November through February are also the sunniest months of the year.

Average Monthly Temperatures (°F & °C) & Rainfall (in.)

		Jan	Feb	Mar	Apr	May	June	July	Aug	Sept	Oct	Nov	Dec
High	(°F)	65	66	66	68	69	72	76	77	77	74	71	66
	(°C)	18	18	18	20	20	22	24	25	25	23	21	18
Low	(°F)	48	50	52	55	58	61	65	66	65	60	53	49
	(°C)	8	10	11	12	14	16	18	18	18	15	11	9
Rainfall		2.2	1.6	1.9	0.8	0.2	0.1	0	0.1	0.2	0.4	1.1	1.4

SAN DIEGO CALENDAR OF EVENTS

You might want to plan your trip around one of these annual events in the San Diego area (including the destinations covered in chapter 11, "Side Trips from San Diego"). For an exhaustive list of events beyond those listed here, check http://events.frommers.com, where you'll find a searchable, up-to-the-minute roster of what's happening in cities all over the world.

JANUARY

San Diego Restaurant Week encourages diners to check out some of San Diego's best eateries. For 6 days, more than 150 restaurants offer special three-course prix-fixe meals. For details, go to www.sandiegorestaurantweek.com. Mid-January.

The **Carlsbad Marathon & Half Marathon** takes place along a scenic coastal route in San Diego's North County. For more information, call © 760/692-2900, or visit www.carlsbadmarathon.com. Late January.

FEBRUARY

Buick Invitational, Torrey Pines Golf Course, La Jolla. Since 1952, this PGA Tour classic has drawn more than 100,000 spectators each year and features 150 of the finest professional golfers. For information, call © 619/281-4653, or see www.buickinvitational.com. Early February.

USA Sevens Rugby Tournament and International Festival is North America's largest rugby event. Downtown's PETCO Park hosts 2 days of matches featuring teams from around the world.

The Fan Festival promises the "ultimate rugby experience." Call ☏ 888/784-2977, or go to www.usasevens.com. Mid-February.

Mardi Gras in the Gaslamp Quarter is downtown's largest event. This "Fat Tuesday" party features a Mardi Gras parade, live bands and DJs, and plenty of special deals from participating clubs and restaurants. This is a ticketed event for ages 21 and older. For more information, call ☏ 619/233-5227, or visit www.gaslamp.org. February 16, 2010.

Wildflowers bloom in the desert between late February and the end of March, at Anza-Borrego Desert State Park. Timing varies from year to year, depending on the winter rainfall (see "Anza-Borrego Desert State Park," in chapter 11). For details, call ☏ 760/767-4684, or go to www.theabf.org.

March

Kiwanis Ocean Beach Kite Festival. For more than 60 years the skies over the Ocean Beach Recreational Center have gotten a brilliant shot of color during this kite-flying contest. Festivities include a grand finale parade down to the beach. For more information, call ☏ 619/531-1527. First Saturday in March.

The **San Diego Latino Film Festival,** one of the largest and most successful Latino film events in the country, features more than 100 movies from throughout Latin America and the United States. Call ☏ 619/230-1938, or surf to www.sdlatinofilm.com. Mid-March.

St. Patrick's Day Parade, Hillcrest. A tradition since 1980, the parade starts at Sixth Avenue and Juniper Street. An **Irish Festival** follows in Balboa Park. Call ☏ 858/268-9111, or check www.stpatsparade.org. March 13, 2010.

Flower fields in bloom at Carlsbad Ranch. One of North County's most spectacular sights is the yearly blossoming of a sea of bright ranunculuses during March and April. Visitors are welcome to tour the fields off I-5 (at the Palomar Airport Rd. exit). For more information, call ☏ 760/431-0352, or go to www.theflowerfields.com.

April

San Diego Crew Classic, Crown Point Shores, Mission Bay. Since its launch in 1973, this has grown into one of the great rowing events in the country, drawing collegiate teams and clubs from throughout the U.S. Call ☏ 619/225-0300, or check out www.crewclassic.org. First weekend in April.

Adams Avenue Roots Festival, Normal Heights. Blues, folk, Cajun, Celtic, bluegrass, and international music festival held on six stages along Adams Avenue, between 34th Street and Wilson Avenue. Free to the public and features food, beer gardens, and arts-and-crafts vendors. Call ☏ 619/282-7329, or stop by www.normalheights.org. Late April.

Coronado Flower Show weekend, Spreckels Park. Organizers claim this is the largest tented flower show in the Western United States. The weekend-long event, now in its 8th decade, includes a book sale, art show, and a lineup of classic cars. Go to www.coronadoflowershow.com for more details. Late April.

ArtWalk, Little Italy, along Kettner Boulevard and India Street. This 2-day festival is now the largest art event in the San Diego/Tijuana region. For more information, call ☏ 619/615-1090, or visit www.missionfederalartwalk.org. Late April.

Day at the Docks, Harbor Drive and Scott Street, Point Loma. This sport-fishing tournament and festival features food, entertainment, and free boat rides. Call ☏ 619/234-8793, or see www.sportfishing.org. Usually the last Sunday of April.

Del Mar National Horse Show. This is the first event in the Del Mar racing season and is held at the famous Del Mar Fairgrounds. The field at this show includes Olympic-caliber and national championship horse-and-rider teams. Call ⓒ **858/793-5555,** or visit www. sdfair.com. Mid-April to early May.

Lakeside Rodeo. You won't forget you're way out West at this down-home rodeo held in East County. From barrel racing to bull riding, this is the real deal. For information, call ⓒ **619/561-4331,** or go to www.lakesiderodeo.com. Late April.

MAY

Fiesta Cinco de Mayo, Old Town. Uniformed troops march and guns blast to mark the 1862 triumph of Mexican soldiers over the French at the battle of Puebla. The festivities include a battle reenactment. (*Hint:* Take the trolley and make dining reservations well in advance.) Admission is free. Call ⓒ **619/291-4903,** or visit www.old townsandiegoguide.com. Weekend closest to May 5.

Carlsbad Spring Village Faire, Grand and State streets. This event is billed as the biggest and best arts-and-crafts fair in Southern California. Call ⓒ **760/931-8400** for more details, or go to www.carlsbad.org. Early May (a fall festival is also held in Nov).

Gator by the Bay, Harbor Island. Let the good times roll at this annual zydeco and blues music festival. In addition to the music, the festival features Cajun food and cooking demonstrations, dances, and a variety of exhibitors and vendors. Call ⓒ **619/234-8612,** or go to www.sandiego festival.com for more details. Mid-May.

Mainly Mozart Festival. Presenting the work of Mozart and his contemporaries, this acclaimed classical-music festival features concerts on both sides of the border. An all-star orchestra draws players from around the world. For information, call ⓒ **619/239-0100,** or go online at www.mainlymozart.org. Performances throughout the month.

The **Rock 'n' Roll Marathon** not only offers runners a unique course through Balboa Park, downtown, and around Mission Bay, but it also pumps them (and spectators) up with live bands on 26 stages along the course. There is a pre-race fitness expo and post-race concert, featuring big-name talent. Call ⓒ **800/311-1255,** or go online at www.rnrmarathon.com. Early June.

Indian Fair, Museum of Man, Balboa Park. Native Americans from dozens of tribes across the United States gather to demonstrate tribal dances and sell arts, crafts, and edibles. Call ⓒ **619/239-2001,** or check www.museumofman. org. Mid-June.

San Diego County Fair. Referred to by locals as the Del Mar Fair, this is the *other* major happening—besides horse racing—at the Del Mar Fairgrounds. In addition to livestock competitions, thrill rides, flower-and-garden shows, and more, there are also grandstand concerts by name performers (some require a separate admission). The fair lasts more than 3 weeks. Call ⓒ **858/793-5555,** or visit www.sdfair.com. Mid-June to early July.

Twilight in the Park Concerts, Balboa Park. These free concerts at the Spreckels Organ Pavilion take place on Tuesday, Wednesday, and Thursday evenings. Call ⓒ **619/239-0512.** Mid-June to August.

Old Globe Summer Shakespeare Festival, Balboa Park. The Bard takes center stage with three different works staged at the Tony Award–winning Old Globe's open-air theater. Produced in true repertory style, shows alternate each night, performed by the same company of actors. Call ✆ 619/234-5623, or visit www.theoldglobe.org. Mid-June through September.

JULY

San Diego Symphony Summer Pops, downtown. The symphony's summer pops series features lighter classical, jazz, opera, Broadway, and show tunes, all performed under the stars and capped by fireworks. Held most summer weekends at the Embarcadero downtown. For details, call ✆ 619/235-0804, or visit www.sandiegosymphony.com. Early July to early September.

U.S. Open Sandcastle Competition, Imperial Beach Pier. Here's the quintessential beach event: A parade and children's sand-castle contest occur on Saturday, followed by the main competition Sunday. *Note:* The castles are usually plundered right after the award ceremony. For details, call ✆ 619/424-6663, or visit www.usopensandcastle.com. Mid-July.

World Championship Over-the-Line Tournament, Mission Bay. This popular event is a San Diego original—a beach softball tournament dating from 1953. It's renowned for boisterous, beer-soaked, anything-goes behavior, with a total of 1,200 three-person teams competing and more than 50,000 fans in attendance. It takes place on 2 consecutive weekends, on Fiesta Island in Mission Bay, and admission is free. For more details, call ✆ 619/688-0817, or visit www.ombac.org. Mid-July.

Thoroughbred Racing Season. The "turf meets the surf" in Del Mar during the thoroughbred racing season at the Del Mar Race Track. Post time is 2pm most days; the track is dark on Tuesdays. For this year's schedule of events, call ✆ 858/755-1141, or visit www.dmtc.com. Mid-July to early September.

San Diego LGBT Pride Parade, Rally, and Festival. This event is one of San Diego's biggest draws, celebrating the lesbian, gay, bisexual, and transgender community. It begins Friday night with a rally at the Organ Pavilion in Balboa Park, and reconvenes at 11am on Saturday for the parade through Hillcrest, followed by a massive festival—held at the park's Marston Point—that continues Sunday. For more information, call ✆ 619/297-7683, or visit www.sdpride.org. Third or fourth weekend in July.

Comic-Con International, downtown. Upwards of 60,000 people attend America's largest comic-book convention each year when it lands at the San Diego Convention Center for a long weekend of auctions, dealers, autographs, and seminars focusing on graphic novels, fantasy, and sci-fi. *Note:* Single-day tickets often sell out; preregistration is encouraged. Call ✆ 619/491-2475, or check www.comic-con.org. Late July.

AUGUST

La Jolla SummerFest is perhaps San Diego's most prestigious annual music event. It features a wide spectrum of classical and contemporary music. SummerFest also offers master classes, open rehearsals, and workshops. It's presented by the La Jolla Music Society; call ✆ 858/459-3728, or visit www.ljms.org for more information. Early to mid-August.

Julian Weed & Craft Show, Julian. This is one event that's better than its name. Artwork and arrangements culled from the area's myriad woods, rocks, wildflowers, and indigenous plants (okay, weeds) are displayed and sold. The Julian Chamber of Commerce (✆ 760/765-1857; www.julianca.com) has further details. Second half of August.

Surfing Competitions. Oceanside's pier-side surfing spot attracts several competitions, including the **World Bodysurfing Championships** and the **Longboard Surf Club Competition.** Call the Oceanside Visitors Bureau at ✆ 800/350-7873 or 760/721-1101, or visit www.worldbodysurfing.org and www.oceansidelongboardsurfingclub. org. Mid- or late August.

SEPTEMBER

La Jolla Rough Water Swim, La Jolla Cove. The country's largest rough-water swimming competition began in 1916 and features masters, men's and women's, junior, and amateur heats. Spectators don't need tickets. For information, call ✆ 858/456-2100. Downloadable entry forms are available at www.ljrws. com. Sunday after Labor Day.

Ocean Beach Jazz Festival. This day-long outdoor concert features a wide spectrum of jazz. Call ✆ 619/388-3037, or go to www.objazz.org. Early September.

Julian fall apple harvest. The popular apple harvest season runs for 2 months in early fall. For more information, contact the chamber of commerce at ✆ 760/765-1857; www.julianca.com. Mid-September to mid-November.

Festival of Beer, downtown. San Diego's local breweries (along with guest brewers from around California and beyond) strut their stuff at this outdoor festival. Some 150 different beers are on tap, along with live music and food at this 21-and-up-only event. For more information, go to www. sdbeerfest.org. Mid-September.

San Diego Bayfair. You'll need a good pair of earplugs for this world series of powerboat racing on Mission Bay (they don't call them thunderboats for nothing). This family-friendly event also features a beach festival. For information, call ✆ 619/225-9160, or go to www.sandiegobayfair.org. Mid-September.

Street Scene. This alternative music festival has bounced around to various venues over the last few years, but now finds itself back on the streets of downtown where it began. It's looking to regain the luster it had in years past as one of the country's top music fests. Get info at www.street-scene.com. Mid-September.

San Diego Film Festival, downtown. More than 70 features, documentaries, shorts, and music videos from around the world are screened over 4 days. There are also educational panels and nightly soirees. Call ✆ 619/582-2368 for more information, or log onto www. sdff.org. Late September.

OCTOBER

Fleet Week is a bit of a misnomer. It's the nation's largest military appreciation event and lasts the entire month. It features Navy ship tours, a college football game, an auto race of classic speedsters, an air show, and more. Check out www.fleetweeksandiego.org for more information.

Little Italy Festa. One of the largest celebrations of Italian culture in the West, the Festa draws some 100,000 people to the streets of Little Italy for a day of traditional food, music, and entertainment. Highlights include stickball and chalk-art street painting competitions. For information, call ✆ 619/233-3898, or visit www.little italysd.com. Mid-October.

Carlsbad Fall Village Faire. Billed as the largest 1-day street fair in California, this festival features more than 850 vendors on 24 city blocks. The epicenter is the intersection of Grand Avenue and Jefferson Street. Call © **760/931-8400,** or visit www.carlsbad.org. First Sunday in November (a spring festival is held in May, as well).

San Diego Bay Wine & Food Festival. Held at various venues over several days, this is Southern California's largest wine and culinary event. More than 200 wineries and restaurants participate. For details, call © **619/342-7337,** or log onto www.worldofwine events.com. Mid-November.

Dr. Seuss' *How the Grinch Stole Christmas!,* Balboa Park. San Diego was the adopted hometown of Theodor Geisel, aka Dr. Seuss, and since 1998 the Old Globe Theatre has been transformed into Whoville each holiday season. This musical has become a family tradition, with discounted seats for kids. For more information, call © **619/234-5623,** or check www.the oldglobe.org. Mid-November through December.

San Diego Thanksgiving Dixieland Jazz Festival. More than 20 bands perform at this annual festival, held over Thanksgiving weekend. Call © **619/297-5277,** or visit www.dixielandjazz festival.org. Late November.

Fall Flower Tour and the **Poinsettia Festival Street Fair,** Encinitas. These two events celebrate the quintessential holiday plant and other late-flowering blooms. The 1-day street fair takes place in late November. For the flower tour, make reservations by early October; the nursery tours take place in early December. For poinsettia information, call the Encinitas Visitors Center at © **800/953-6041** or 760/753-6041; for the street fair, call © **760/943-1950,** or see www.kennedyfaires.com.

DECEMBER

Ocean Beach Christmas Parade and Tree Festival. This parade is a family affair (Santa Claus is on hand, of course), but with entries such as the Off-Key Choir and the Geriatric Surf Team, it's definitely quirky. Call © **619/224-4906,** or see www.oceanbeachsandiego. com. First Saturday in December.

Balboa Park December Nights. San Diego's wonderful urban park is decked out in holiday splendor for this 2-night event. The event is free and lasts from 5 to 9pm both days; the park's museums are free during those hours. For more information, call © **619/239-0512,** or visit www.balboapark.org. First Friday and Saturday in December.

Whale-watching season takes place during the winter months along the San Diego County coast. More than 20,000 Pacific gray whales make the annual trek from chilly Alaskan seas to the warm-water breeding lagoons of Baja California, and then back again with calves in tow. Cabrillo National Monument, on the panoramic Point Loma peninsula, offers a glassed-in observatory from which to spot the whales, examine whale exhibits, and listen to taped narration describing these popular mammals. Various companies offer whale-watching tours throughout the season, as well. For more information, call © **619/557-5450** or 236-1212, or visit www.sandiego.org. Mid-December to mid-March.

Mission Bay Boat Parade of Lights, from Quivira Basin in Mission Bay. Held on a Saturday, the best viewing is around Crown Point, on the east side of Vacation Island, or the west side of Fiesta Island; it concludes with the lighting of a 320-foot tower of Christmas lights at SeaWorld. Call

℃ **858/488-0501.** For more vessels dressed up like Christmas trees, the **San Diego Boat Parade of Lights** is held in San Diego Bay on two Sundays, with a route starting at Shelter Island and running past Seaport Village and the Coronado Ferry Landing Marketplace. Visit www.sdparadeoflights.org for more information. Mid-December.

College bowl games. San Diego is home to two college football bowl games: the **Holiday Bowl** and the **Poinsettia Bowl,** both held in late December. The Holiday Bowl pits top teams from the Pac 10 and Big 12 conferences, and the Poinsettia Bowl pairs a team from the Mountain West Conference against an at-large opponent. The Poinsettia Bowl (℃ **619/285-5061;** www.poinsettiabowl.net) was inaugurated in 2005; the Holiday Bowl (℃ **619/283-5808;** www.holidaybowl. com) has been around since 1978, and features several special events, including the nation's biggest balloon parade of giant inflatable characters. Late December.

2 ENTRY REQUIREMENTS

PASSPORTS
Virtually every air traveler entering the U.S. is required to show a passport. All persons, including U.S. citizens, traveling by air between the United States and Canada, Mexico, Central and South America, the Caribbean, and Bermuda are required to present a valid passport. As of June 1, 2009, this rule is scheduled to be implemented for travel by sea and land, as well. (As of this writing, U.S. and Canadian citizens entering the U.S. at land and sea ports of entry from within the Western Hemisphere need to present government-issued proof of citizenship, such as a birth certificate, along with a government-issued photo ID, such as a driver's license.)

VISAS
The U.S. State Department has a **Visa Waiver Program (VWP)** allowing citizens of the following countries to enter the United States without a visa for stays of up to 90 days: Andorra, Australia, Austria, Belgium, Brunei, Czech Republic, Denmark, Estonia, Finland, France, Germany, Hungary, Iceland, Ireland, Italy, Japan, Latvia, Liechtenstein, Lithuania, Luxembourg, Malta, Monaco, the Netherlands, New Zealand, Norway, Portugal, San Marino, Singapore, Slovakia, Slovenia, South Korea, Spain, Sweden, Switzerland, and the United Kingdom. (*Note:* This list was accurate at press time; for the most up-to-date list of countries in the VWP, consult www.travel.state.gov/visa.)

As of January 12, 2009, all VWP travelers will be required to obtain **Electronic System for Travel Authorization (ESTA)** clearance. This free, automated system is used to determine the eligibility of visitors under VWP. ESTA applications may be completed online at https://esta.cbp.dhs. gov. An ESTA authorization is generally valid for up to 2 years and is good for multiple entries. It's recommended you submit an application as soon as you begin making your travel plans.

Note: Any passport issued on or after October 26, 2006, by a VWP country must be an **e-Passport** for VWP travelers to be eligible to enter the U.S. without a visa. Citizens of these nations also need to present a round-trip air or cruise ticket upon arrival. E-Passports contain computer chips capable of storing biometric information, such as the required digital photograph of the holder. (You can identify an e-Passport by the symbol on the bottom of the cover of your passport.) If your passport doesn't have this feature, you can still travel without a visa if it is a valid passport issued before October 26, 2005, and includes a machine-readable zone, or between October 26, 2005, and October 25, 2006, and includes a digital photograph. For more information, go to **www.travel. state.gov/visa**. Canadian citizens may enter the United States without visas; they will need to show passports and proof of residence, however.

Citizens of all other countries must have (1) a valid passport that expires at least 6 months later than the scheduled end of their visit to the U.S., and (2) a tourist visa.

CUSTOMS
What You Can Bring into the U.S.

Every visitor at least 21 years of age may bring in, free of duty, the following: (1) 1 liter of wine or hard liquor; (2) 200 cigarettes, 100 cigars (but not from Cuba), or 3 pounds of smoking tobacco; and (3) $100 worth of gifts. These exemptions are offered to travelers who spend at least 72 hours in the United States and who have not claimed them within the preceding 6 months. It is forbidden to bring into the country almost any meat products (including canned, fresh, and dried meat products such as bouillon, soup mixes, and so forth). Generally, condiments, including vinegars, oils, spices, coffee, tea, and some cheeses and baked goods, are permitted. Avoid rice products, as rice can often harbor insects. Bringing fruits and vegetables is not advised, though not prohibited. Customs will allow produce depending on where you got it and where you íre going

after you arrive in the U.S. International visitors may carry in or out up to $10,000 in U.S. or foreign currency with no formalities; larger sums must be declared to U.S. Customs on entering or leaving, which includes filing form CM 4790. For details regarding U.S. Customs and Border Protection, consult your nearest U.S. embassy or consulate, or U.S. Customs (www.customs.gov).

What You Can Take Home from San Diego

For information on what you íre allowed to take home, contact one of the following agencies:

Canadian Citizens: Canada Border Services Agency (✆ **800/461-9999** in Canada, or 204/983-3500; www.cbsa-asfc. gc.ca).

U.K. Citizens: HM Customs & Excise at ✆ **0845/010-9000** (from outside the U.K., 020/8929-0152), or consult its website at www.hmce.gov.uk.

Australian Citizens: Australian Customs Service at ✆ **1300/363-263**, or log on to www.customs.gov.au.

New Zealand Citizens: New Zealand Customs, The Customhouse, 17ñ21 Whitmore St., Box 2218, Wellington (✆ **0800/428-786** or 04/473-6099; www. customs.govt.nz).

MEDICAL REQUIREMENTS

Unless you're arriving from an area known to be suffering from an epidemic (particularly cholera or yellow fever), inoculations or vaccinations are not required for entry into the United States.

---

3 GETTING THERE & GETTING AROUND

GETTING TO SAN DIEGO
By Plane

San Diegans have a love-hate relationship with **San Diego International Airport**

(✆ 619/231-2100; www.san.org), also known as Lindbergh Field. The facility (airport code: SAN) is just 3 miles northwest of downtown, and the landing approach is right at the edge of the central business district. Pilots thread a passage between high-rise buildings and Balboa Park on their final descent to the runway—you'll get a great view on either side of the plane. The best part: We usually count the time from touchdown to gate-park in seconds, not minutes, and departures are rarely delayed for weather problems.

Lindbergh Field is the nation's busiest single-runway commercial airport—all 600 daily arrivals and departures use just one strip of asphalt. And while its dainty size makes it easy for travelers to navigate, its truncated facilities make it virtually unusable for international travel. Most overseas visitors arrive via Los Angeles or points east (**Air Canada** and **AeroMéxico** are the only international carriers flying into San Diego). Domestically, the city is served by most national and regional airlines, although none utilize Lindbergh Field as a connecting hub. City officials are well aware of the critical need to enlarge or move the airport. Plans have ranged from a floating airport-at-sea (yes, really) to setting it in the Anza-Borrego Desert to conscripting Miramar Naval Air Station. The latest plan calls for a build-out of the current site.

Planes land at Terminal 1 or 2, while the Commuter Terminal, a half-mile from the main terminals, is used by regional carriers **American Eagle** and **United Express** and for connecting flights to Los Angeles (for flight info, contact the parent carriers). The Airport Flyer ("red bus") provides free service from the main airport to the Commuter Terminal, or there's a footpath. General **information desks** with visitor materials, maps, and other services are near the baggage claim areas of both terminals 1 and 2. You can exchange foreign currency at **Travelex** (⊘ **619/681-1941;** www.travelex.com) in Terminal 2 on the second level (*inside* the security area, near the gates); **hotel reservation** and **car-rental courtesy phones** are in the baggage-claim areas of terminals 1 and 2.

If you are staying at a hotel in Carlsbad, Encinitas, or Rancho Santa Fe, the McClellan-Palomar Airport in Carlsbad (CLD) may be a more convenient point of entry. The airport is 42 miles north of downtown San Diego and is served by **United Express** from Los Angeles.

Overseas visitors can take advantage of the APEX (Advance Purchase Excursion) reductions offered by all major U.S. and European carriers. In addition, some large airlines offer transatlantic or transpacific passengers special discount tickets under the name **Visit USA,** which allows mostly one-way travel from one U.S. destination to another at very low prices. Unavailable in the U.S., these discount tickets must be purchased abroad in conjunction with your international fare. This system is the easiest, fastest, and cheapest way to see the country.

For airline contact information, see p. 296.

Arriving at the Airport

IMMIGRATION & CUSTOMS CLEARANCE International visitors arriving by air, no matter what the port of entry, should cultivate patience and resignation before setting foot on U.S. soil. U.S. airports have considerably beefed up security clearances in the years since the terrorist attacks of September 11, 2001, and clearing Customs and Immigration can take as long as 2 hours.

Getting Into Town from the Airport

BY BUS The **Metropolitan Transit System** (**MTS;** ⊘ **619/233-3004;** www.transit.511sd.com) operates the San Diego Transit Flyer—bus route no. 992—providing service between the airport and downtown San Diego, running along Broadway. Bus stops are at each of Lindbergh Field's three terminals. The one-way fare is $2.25, and exact change is required.

If you're connecting to another bus or the San Diego Trolley, you'll need to purchase a Day Pass; free transfers are no longer given. A 1-day pass starts at $5 and is available from the driver or online. The ride takes about 15 minutes, and buses come at 10- to 15-minute intervals.

At the **Transit Store,** 102 Broadway, at First Avenue (© 619/234-1060), you can get information about greater San Diego's mass transit system (bus, rail, and ferry) and pick up passes, free brochures, route maps, and timetables. The store is open Monday to Friday, 9am to 5pm.

BY TAXI Taxis line up outside terminals 1 and 2. The trip to a downtown location, usually a 10-minute ride, is about $10 (plus tip); budget $20 to $25 for Coronado or Mission Beach, and about $30 to $35 for La Jolla.

BY SHUTTLE Several airport shuttles run regularly from the airport to points around the city; you'll see designated pickup areas outside each terminal. The shuttles are a good deal for single travelers; two or more people traveling together might as well take a taxi. The fare is about $8 per person to downtown hotels; Mission Valley and Mission Beach hotels are $12; La Jolla, $31 ($9 for each additional person); and Coronado hotels, $16. Rates to a residence are about $8 more than the above rates for the first person. One company that serves all of San Diego County is **Super Shuttle** (© 800/974-8885; www.supershuttle.com).

BY CAR If you're driving to downtown from the airport, take Harbor Drive south to Broadway, the main east-west thoroughfare, and turn left. To reach Hillcrest or Balboa Park, exit the airport toward I-5, and follow the signs for Laurel Street. To reach Mission Bay, take I-5 north to I-8 west. To reach La Jolla, take I-5 north to the La Jolla Parkway exit, bearing left onto Torrey Pines Road. For complete information on rental cars in San Diego, see "Getting Around San Diego," later in this chapter.

GETTING TO SAN DIEGO
By Bus

Greyhound buses serve San Diego from downtown Los Angeles, Phoenix, Las Vegas, and other Southwestern cities, arriving at the downtown terminal, at 120 W. Broadway (© **800/231-2222** or 619/239-3266; www.greyhound.com). A number of hotels, Horton Plaza, and the Gaslamp Quarter are within walking distance, as is the San Diego Trolley line. Buses from Los Angeles are as frequent as every hour, and the ride takes about $2^{1}/_{2}$ hours. One-way fare is $22 and round-trips are $35. You can whittle the price down by purchasing nonrefundable tickets or by getting them in advance online.

Greyhound is the sole nationwide bus line. International visitors can obtain information about the **Greyhound North American Discovery Pass.** The pass can be obtained from foreign travel agents or through www.discoverypass.com for unlimited travel and stopovers in the U.S. and Canada.

By Train

Trains from all points in the United States and Canada will take you to Los Angeles, where you'll need to change trains for the journey to San Diego. You'll arrive at San Diego's Santa Fe Station, downtown at the west end of Broadway, between India Street and Kettner Boulevard. It's within walking distance to many downtown hotels and the Embarcadero. Taxis line up outside the main door, the trolley station is across the street, and a dozen local bus routes stop on Broadway or Pacific Coast Highway, 1 block away.

Amtrak (© **800/872-7245**; www. amtrak.com) trains run between downtown Los Angeles and San Diego about 11 times daily each way. They stop in Anaheim (Disneyland), Santa Ana, San Juan Capistrano, Oceanside, and Solana Beach. Two trains per day also stop in San Clemente. The travel time from Los Angeles to San

Diego is about 2 hours and 45 minutes (for comparison, driving time can be as little as 2 hr., or as much as 4 hr. during rush hour). A one-way ticket to San Diego is $29, or $43 for a reserved seat in business class.

International visitors can buy a **USA Rail Pass,** good for 15, 30, or 45 days of unlimited travel on Amtrak. The pass is available online or through many overseas travel agents. See Amtrak's website for the cost of travel within the Western, Eastern, or Northwestern United States. Reservations are generally required and should be made as early as possible. Regional rail passes are also available.

By Boat

San Diego's **B Street Cruise Ship Terminal** is at 1140 N. Harbor Dr., right at the edge of downtown (© **800/854-2757** or 619/686-6200; www.sandiegocruiseport. com). Carnival Cruise Lines (© **888/227-6482;** www.carnival.com) counts San Diego as a year-round home port, while several others, including Holland America Line (© **877/932-4259;** www.holland america.com), Royal Caribbean (© **866/562-7625;** www.royalcaribbean.com), and Celebrity (© **800/647-2251;** www. celebritycruises.com) make seasonal stops here.

By Car

Three main interstates lead into San Diego. **I-5** is the primary route from San Francisco, central California, and Los Angeles; it runs straight through downtown to the Tijuana border crossing. **I-8** cuts across California from points east such as Phoenix, terminating just west of I-5 at Mission Bay. **I-15** leads from the deserts to the north through inland San Diego; as you enter Miramar, take **Hwy. 163** south to reach the central parts of the city.

If you're planning a road trip, being a member of the **American Automobile Association (AAA)** offers helpful perks. Members who carry their cards with them not only receive free roadside assistance,

but also have access to a wealth of free travel information (detailed maps and guidebooks). Also, many hotels and attractions throughout California offer discounts to AAA members—always inquire. Call © **800/922-8228** or your local branch, or visit www.aaa-calif.com, for membership information.

Visitors driving to San Diego from Los Angeles and points north do so via coastal route I-5. From points northeast, take I-15 and link up with Hwy. 163 S. as you enter Miramar (use I-8 W. for the beaches). From the east, use I-8 into the city, connecting to Hwy. 163 S. for Hillcrest and downtown. Entering the downtown area, Hwy. 163 turns into 10th Avenue. If you are heading to Coronado, take the San Diego–Coronado Bay Bridge from I-5. Maximum speed in the San Diego area is 65 mph, and many areas are limited to 55 mph.

San Diego is 130 miles (2–3 hr.) from **Los Angeles;** 149 miles from **Palm Springs,** a 2^1/$_2$-hour trip; and 532 miles, or 9 to 10 hours, from **San Francisco.**

We complain of increasing traffic, but San Diego is still easy to navigate by car. Most downtown streets run one-way, in a grid pattern. However, outside downtown, canyons and bays often make streets indirect. Finding a parking space can be tricky in the Gaslamp Quarter, Old Town, Mission Beach, and La Jolla, but parking lots are often centrally located. Rush hour on the freeways is generally concentrated from 7 to 9am and 4:30 to 6pm. Be aware that San Diego's gas prices are often among the highest in the country. Also note that, generally speaking, we're not the best drivers in the rain—vehicles careening out of control during the first couple of winter dousings keep the Highway Patrol and local news channels very busy. For up-to-the-minute traffic info, dial © **511.**

Note on driving to Mexico: If you plan to drive to Mexico, be sure to check with your insurance company at home to verify

(Tips) Curb Appeal

Street-parking rules are color-coded throughout the city. A **red curb** means no stopping at any time. **Blue curbs** are used to denote parking for people with disabilities—the fine for parking in these spaces without a distinguishing placard or a disabled license plate is $400 (out-of-state disabled plates are okay). A **white-painted curb** signifies a passenger loading zone; the time limit is 3 minutes, or 10 minutes in front of a hotel. A **yellow curb** is a commercial loading zone—which means that between 6am and 6pm Monday through Saturday, trucks and commercial vehicles are allowed 20 minutes to load or unload goods, *and* passenger vehicles can unload passengers for 3 minutes (from 6pm–6am and all day Sun, anyone can park in a yellow curb zone, though some yellow zones are in effect 24 hours—be sure to check any nearby signage). A **green curb** designates short-term parking only—usually 15 or 30 minutes (as posted). Unpainted curbs are subject to parking rules on signs or meters.

exactly the limits of your policy. Even if your insurance covers areas south of the border, you may want to purchase Mexican car insurance because of the two countries' different liability standards. Mexican car insurance is available from various agencies (visible to drivers heading into Mexico) on the U.S. side of the border.

Car Rentals

I'd love to tell you that public transportation is a good way to get around, as in New York City or London, but the distances between attractions and indirect bus routings usually make it inefficient. Those staying downtown will find plenty to see and do within easy reach (including Balboa Park and Old Town), but otherwise, if you don't drive to San Diego with your own car, you'll probably want to rent one. You *can* reach virtually all sights of interest using public transportation, but having your own wheels is a big advantage.

All the major car-rental firms have an office at the airport, and several have them in larger hotels. For listings of the major car-rental agencies in San Diego, please see "Toll-Free Numbers & Websites" (p. 296). *Note for Mexico-bound car renters:* Some companies, including Avis, will allow their

cars into Mexico as far as Ensenada, but other rental outfits won't allow you to drive south of the border.

If you're visiting from abroad and plan to rent a car in the United States, keep in mind that foreign driver's licenses are usually recognized in the U.S., but you should get an international one if your home license is not in English. International visitors should also note that insurance and taxes are almost never included in quoted rental-car rates in the U.S. Be sure to ask your rental agency about additional fees for these. They can add a significant cost to your car rental.

Check out **Breezenet.com,** which offers domestic car-rental discounts with some of the most competitive rates around. Also worth visiting are Orbitz, Hotwire.com, Travelocity, and Priceline.com, all of which offer competitive online car-rental rates. For additional car-rental agencies, see "Toll-Free Numbers & Websites" on p. 296.

Saving Money on a Rental Car

Car-rental rates vary even more dramatically than airline fares. Prices depend on the size of the car, where and when you pick it up and drop it off, the length of the rental period, where and how far you drive it, whether you buy insurance, and a host of other factors. A few key questions could save you hundreds of dollars:

- Are weekend rates lower than weekday rates? Ask if the rate is the same for pickup Friday morning, for instance, as it is for Thursday night.
- Does the agency assess a drop-off charge if you don't return the car to the same location where you picked it up?
- Are special promotional rates available? If you see an advertised price in your local newspaper, be sure to ask for that specific rate; otherwise, you may be charged the standard cost.
- Are discounts available for members of AARP, AAA, frequent-flyer programs, or trade unions?
- How much tax will be added to the rental bill? Local tax? State use tax?
- How much does the rental company charge to refill your gas tank if you return with the tank less than full? Though most rental companies claim these prices are competitive, fuel is almost always cheaper in town.

Demystifying Renter's Insurance

Before you drive off in a rental car, be sure you're insured. Hasty assumptions about your personal auto insurance or a rental agency's additional coverage could end up costing you tens of thousands of dollars, even if you're involved in an accident that was clearly the fault of another driver.

If you already hold a **private auto insurance** policy, you're most likely covered in the United States for loss of or damage to a rental car and liability in case of injury to any other party involved in an accident. Be sure to find out whether you're covered in the area you're visiting, whether your policy extends to everyone who will be driving the car, how much liability is covered in case an outside party is injured in an accident, and whether the type of vehicle you are renting is included under your contract. (Rental trucks, SUVs,

and luxury vehicles or sports cars may not be covered.)

Most **major credit cards** (especially gold and platinum cards) provide some degree of coverage as well, provided they're used to pay for the rental. Terms vary widely, however, so be sure to call your credit card company directly before you rent.

If you're **uninsured,** your credit card will probably provide primary coverage as long as you decline the rental agency's insurance and as long as you rent with that card. This means that the credit card will cover damage or theft of a rental car for the full cost of the vehicle. (In a few states, however, theft is not covered; ask specifically about state law where you will be renting and driving.) If you already have insurance, your credit card will provide secondary coverage, which basically covers your deductible.

Note: Though they may cover damage to your rental car, *credit cards will not cover liability,* or the cost of injury to an outside party, damage to an outside party's vehicle, or both. If you do not hold an insurance policy, you may seriously want to consider purchasing additional liability insurance from your rental company, even if you decline collision coverage. Be sure to check the terms, however. Some rental agencies cover liability only if the renter is not at fault; even then, the rental company's obligation varies from state to state.

The basic insurance coverage offered by most car-rental companies, known as the **Loss Damage Waiver (LDW)** or **Collision Damage Waiver (CDW),** can cost as much as $20 a day. It usually covers the full value of the vehicle with no deductible if an outside party causes an accident or other damage to the rental car. Liability coverage varies according to the company policy and state law, but the minimum is usually at least $15,000. If you are at fault in an accident, you will be covered for the full replacement value of the car, but not for liability. Some states allow you to buy additional liability coverage for such cases. Most rental companies will require a police report to process any claims you file, but your private insurer will not be notified of the accident.

Driving Rules

San Diegans are relatively respectful drivers, although admittedly we often speed and sometimes lose patience with those who don't know their way around. We also have a tough time driving in the rain—watch for spinouts and hydroplaning vehicles when traveling in our rare wet weather.

California has a **seat-belt law for both drivers and passengers,** so buckle up before you venture out. State law requires drivers to use **hands-free cellphone technology** (drivers age 17 and under cannot use a cellphone at all); **text messaging while driving** is also illegal. The first-offense fine for both is $20. **Smoking in a car with a child** age 17 and under is punishable by a $100 fine; an officer cannot pull you over for this, but can tack it onto another infraction. You may **turn right at a red light after stopping** unless a sign says otherwise; likewise, you can turn left on a red light from a one-way street onto another one-way street after coming to a full stop. **Pedestrians have the right of way at all times,** not just in crosswalks, so stop for pedestrians who have stepped off the curb. Penalties in California for **drunk driving** are among the toughest in the country. Speed limits on freeways, particularly Hwy. 8 through Mission Valley, are aggressively enforced after dark, partly as a pretext for nabbing drivers who might have imbibed. Also beware of main beach arteries (Grand Ave., Garnet Ave., and Mission Blvd.). Traffic enforcement can be strict—random checkpoints set up to catch drunk drivers are not uncommon.

Parking

Metered parking spaces are found in downtown, Hillcrest, and the beach communities, but demand outpaces supply.

Posted signs indicate operating hours—generally Monday through Saturday from 8am to 6pm. Be prepared with several dollars in quarters—some meters take no other coin, and 25¢ usually buys only 12 minutes, even on a 2-hour meter. Most unmetered areas have signs restricting street parking to 1 or 2 hours; count on vigilant chalking and ticketing during the regulated hours. Three-hour meters line Harbor Drive opposite the ticket offices for harbor tours; even on weekends, you have to feed them. If you can't find a metered space, there are plenty of hourly lots downtown. Parking in Mission Valley is usually within large parking structures and free, though congested on weekends and particularly leading up to Christmas.

Downtown parking structures on Sixth Avenue (at Market and K sts.) have helped ease parking woes, but it's still a challenge. Of special concern are game nights—and days—at PETCO Park (Apr–Sept). Unless you're staying downtown or want to attend the game, it's best to avoid the baseball traffic and head elsewhere for dining or nightlife.

Street Maps

The Convention & Visitors Bureau's **International Visitor Information Center,** 1040¹/₃ W. Broadway, along the downtown Embarcadero (© **619/236-1212;** www.sandiego.org), provides an illustrated pocket map. Also available are maps of the 59-mile scenic drive around San Diego, the Gaslamp Quarter, Tijuana, San Diego's public transportation, and a "Campgrounds and Recreation" map for the county.

The **Automobile Club of Southern California** has 10 San Diego offices (© **619/233-1000;** www.aaa-calif.com). It distributes great maps, which are free to AAA members and to members of many international auto clubs, and it sells auto insurance for those driving within Mexico.

Car-rental outfits usually offer maps of the city that show the freeways and major streets, and hotels often provide complimentary maps of the downtown area. You can buy maps of the city and vicinity at the retail stores listed under "Travel Accessories," in chapter 9 (p. 213). The **Transit Store,** 102 Broadway, at First Avenue (⟨C⟩ **619/234-1060**), is a storehouse of bus and trolley maps, with a friendly staff on duty to answer specific questions.

If you're moving to San Diego or plan an extended stay, I recommend the *Thomas Guide,* available at bookstores, drugstores, and large supermarkets for $25 (www.thomasmaps.com). This all-encompassing book of maps deciphers San Diego County street by street.

GETTING AROUND SAN DIEGO
By Car
Main Arteries & Streets

It's not hard to find your way around downtown San Diego. Most streets run one-way, in a grid pattern. First through Eleventh avenues run north and south—odd-number avenues are northbound, even numbers run south; A through K streets alternate running east and west. Broadway (the equivalent of D St.) runs both directions, as do Market Street and Harbor Drive. North of A Street, the east-west streets bear the names of trees, in alphabetical order: Ash, Beech, Cedar, Date, and so on. Harbor Drive runs past the airport and along the waterfront, which is known as the Embarcadero. Ash Street and Broadway are the downtown arteries that connect with Harbor Drive.

The Coronado Bay Bridge leading to Coronado is accessible from I-5, south of downtown, and I-5 N. leads to Old Town, Mission Bay, La Jolla, and North County coastal areas. Balboa Park (home of the San Diego Zoo), Hillcrest, and Uptown areas lie north of downtown San Diego. The park and zoo are easily reached by way of Park Boulevard (which would otherwise be 12th Ave.), which leads to the

parking lots. Fifth Avenue leads to Hillcrest. Hwy. 163, which heads north from 11th Avenue, leads into Mission Valley.

CORONADO The main streets are Orange Avenue, where most of the hotels and restaurants are clustered, and Ocean Drive, which follows Coronado Beach.

DOWNTOWN The major thoroughfares are Broadway (a major bus artery), Fourth and Fifth avenues (which run south and north, respectively), C Street (the trolley line), and Harbor Drive, which curls along the waterfront and passes the Maritime Museum, Seaport Village, the Convention Center, and PETCO Park.

HILLCREST The main streets are University Avenue and Washington Street (both two-way, running east and west), and Fourth and Fifth avenues (both one-way, running south and north, respectively).

LA JOLLA The main avenues are Prospect and Girard, which are perpendicular to each other. The main routes in and out of La Jolla are La Jolla Boulevard (running south to Mission Beach) and Torrey Pines Road (leading to I-5).

MISSION VALLEY I-8 runs east-west along the valley's southern perimeter; Hwy. 163, I-805, and I-15 run north-south through the valley. Hotel Circle is an elongated loop road that parallels either side of I-8 to the west of Hwy. 163; Friar's Road is the major artery on the north side of the valley.

PACIFIC BEACH Mission Boulevard is the main drag, parallel to and 1 block in from the beach, and perpendicular to it are Grand and Garnet avenues. East and West Mission Bay drives encircle most of the bay and Ingraham Street cuts through the middle of it.

By Train

San Diego's express rail commuter service, the **Coaster,** travels between the downtown Santa Fe Depot station and the

(Tips) Money-Saving Bus & Trolley Passes

Day Passes allow unlimited rides on MTS (bus) and trolley routes. Passes are good for 2, 3, and 4 consecutive days, and cost $9, $12, and $15, respectively. Day Trippers are for sale at the Transit Store, all trolley station automated ticket vending machines, and online at www.transit.511sd.com. Call (619/234-1060 for more information.

Oceanside Transit Center, with stops at Old Town, Sorrento Valley, Solana Beach, Encinitas, and Carlsbad. Fares range from $5 to $6.50 each way, depending on how far you go, and can be paid by credit card at vending machines at each station. Eligible seniors and riders with disabilities pay $2.50 to $3.25. The scenic trip between downtown San Diego and Oceanside takes 1 hour. Trains run Monday through Friday from about 6:30am (5:30am heading south from Oceanside) to 7pm, with four trains in each direction on Saturday; call (800/262-7837 or 511 (TTY/TDD 888/722-4889) for the current schedule, or log on to **www. transit.511sd.com**.

Amtrak ((**800/872-7245**; www. amtrak.com) trains head north to Los Angeles about 11 times daily each way. They stop in Solana Beach, Oceanside, San Juan Capistrano, Santa Ana, and Anaheim (Disneyland). Two trains per day also stop in San Clemente. A one-way ticket to Solana Beach is $9; to Oceanside, $13; to San Clemente or San Juan Capistrano, $15; and to Anaheim, $20.

The **Sprinter** rail service runs west to east alongside Hwy. 78, from Oceanside to Escondido. The Sprinter operates Monday through Friday from about 4am to 9pm daily, with service every 30 minutes in both directions. On weekends, trains run every half-hour from 9:30am to 5:30pm (westbound) and 10:30am to 6:30pm (eastbound). There is hourly service before and after those times. Basic one-way fare is $2; $1 for seniors and travelers with disabilities.

By Public Transportation
By Bus

The **MTS Transit Store,** 102 Broadway at First Avenue ((**619/234-1060**), dispenses passes, tokens, timetables, maps, brochures, and lost-and-found information. It issues ID cards for seniors 60 and older, as well as for travelers with disabilities—all of whom pay $1.10 per ride. Request a copy of the useful brochure *Fun Places by Bus & Trolley,* which details the city's most popular tourist attractions and the public transportation that will take you to them. The office is open Monday through Friday from 9am to 5pm.

San Diego has an adequate bus system that will get you to where you're going—eventually. Most drivers are friendly and helpful; on local routes, bus stops are marked by rectangular red, white, and black signs every other block or so, farther apart on express routes. Most bus **fares** are $2.25. Buses accept dollar bills and coins, but drivers can't give change. Transfers are no longer issued, so if you need to make a connection with another bus or trolley, purchase a $5 day pass from the driver, at the Transit Store, trolley station ticket vending machine, or online. It gives you unlimited use of most bus and trolley routes for the rest of the service day.

For assistance with route information from a living, breathing entity, call MTS at (**619/233-3004.** You can also view timetables, maps, and fares online—and learn how the public transit system accommodates travelers with disabilities—at **www. transit.511sd.com**. If you know your route and just need schedule information—or automated answers to FAQs—call **Info Express** (© **619/685-4900**) from any touch-tone phone, 24 hours a day.

Some of the most popular tourist attractions served by bus and rail routes are

- Balboa Park west entrance: Routes 1, 3, and 120
- Balboa Park east entrances and San Diego Zoo: Route. 7
- SeaWorld: Routes 8 and 9
- Cabrillo National Monument: Route 84
- Seaport Village: San Diego Trolley Orange Line
- Qualcomm Stadium: Route 14 and San Diego Trolley Blue and Green lines
- Tijuana: San Diego Trolley Blue Line
- San Diego International Airport: Route 992
- Wild Animal Park: Route 386 (Mon–Sat only)
- Convention Center: San Diego Trolley Orange Line
- PETCO Park: Routes 3, 4, 5, 11, 901, 929, 992; San Diego Trolley Orange and Blue lines
- Coronado: Routes 901 (or Bay Ferry)
- Gaslamp Quarter and Horton Plaza: most downtown bus routes and San Diego Trolley Blue and Orange lines
- Old Town: Routes 8, 9, 10, 14, 28, 30, 35, 44, 105, 150; San Diego Trolley Blue and Green lines; and the Coaster

The Coronado Shuttle, bus no. 904, runs between the Marriott Coronado Island Resort and the Old Ferry Landing, and then continues along Orange Avenue to the Hotel del Coronado, Glorietta Bay, and back again. It costs $1 per person. No. 901 goes all the way to Coronado from San Diego and costs $2.25.

When planning your route, note that schedules vary and most buses do not run all night. Some stop at 6pm, while other lines continue to 9pm, midnight, or 2am—ask your bus driver for more specific information.

The privately owned bus tours operated by **Old Town Trolley Tours** (p. 163) and City Sightseeing (p. 164) are also an excellent way to get around much of the city during a short visit. Both are narrated sightseeing tours, but you can disembark at various points and join up later with the next passing group.

By Trolley

Although the system is too limited for most San Diegans to use for work commutes, the San Diego Trolley is great for visitors, particularly if you're staying downtown or plan to visit Tijuana. There are three routes. The **Blue Line** is the one that is the handiest for most visitors: It travels from the Mexican border (San Ysidro) north through downtown and Old Town, with some trolleys continuing into Mission Valley. The **Orange Line** runs from downtown east through Lemon Grove and El Cajon. The **Green Line** runs from Old Town through Mission Valley to Qualcomm Stadium, San Diego State University, and on to Santee. The trip to the border crossing takes 40 minutes from downtown; from downtown to Old Town takes 10 to 15 minutes. For a route map, see the inside front cover of this guide.

Trolleys operate on a self-service fare-collection system; riders buy tickets from machines in stations before boarding (some machines require exact change). There is a $1.25 fare for 2 hours of travel in the downtown area; otherwise it's a flat fare of $2.50 for travel between any two stations. A $5 day pass is also available, good for all trolley trips and most bus routes. Fare inspectors board trains at random to check tickets.

The lines run every 15 minutes during the day and every 30 minutes at night; during peak weekday rush hours the Blue Line runs every 10 minutes. There is also expanded service to accommodate events at PETCO Park and Qualcomm Stadium. Trolleys stop at each station for only 30 seconds. To open the door for boarding, push the lighted green button; to open the door to exit the trolley, push the lighted white button.

For recorded transit information, call © **619/685-4900.** To speak with a customer service representative, call © **619/233-3004** (TTY/TDD 619/234-5005) daily from 5:30am to 8:30pm. For wheelchair lift info, call © **619/595-4960.** The trolley generally operates daily from 5am to about midnight; the Blue Line provides limited but additional service between Old Town and San Ysidro throughout the night from Saturday evening to Sunday morning; check the website at **www.transit.511sd.com** for details.

By Taxi

Half a dozen taxi companies serve the area. Rates are based on mileage and can add up quickly in sprawling San Diego—a trip from downtown to La Jolla will cost about $30 to $35. Other than in the Gaslamp Quarter after dark, taxis don't cruise the streets as they do in other cities, so you have to call ahead for quick pickup. If you're at a hotel or restaurant, the front-desk attendant or concierge will call one for you. Among the local companies are **Orange Cab** (© 619/291-3333), **San Diego Cab** (© 619/226-8294), and **Yellow Cab** (© 619/234-6161). The **Coronado Cab Company** (© 619/435-6211) serves Coronado.

By Water

BY FERRY There's regularly scheduled ferry service between San Diego and Coronado (© **800/442-7847** or 619/234-4111; www.sdhe.com). Ferries leave from the Broadway Pier (1050 N. Harbor Dr., at the intersection with Broadway) and the Fifth Avenue Landing (located behind the Convention Center). Broadway Pier departures are scheduled Sunday through Thursday on the hour from 9am to 9pm, and Friday and Saturday until 10pm. They return from the Ferry Landing in Coronado to the Broadway Pier Sunday through Thursday every hour on the half-hour from 9:30am to 9:30pm and Friday

and Saturday until 10:30pm. Trips from the Convention Center depart about every 2 hours beginning at 9:25am, with the final departure at 8:25pm (10:25pm Fri and Sat); return trips begin at 9:17am, then run about every 2 hours thereafter until 8:17pm (10:17pm Fri and Sat). The ride takes 15 minutes. The fare is $3.50 each way; buy tickets at the San Diego Harbor Excursion kiosk on Broadway Pier, the Fifth Avenue Landing, or at the Ferry Landing in Coronado. The ferries do not accommodate cars.

BY WATER TAXI Water taxis (© 619/235-8294; www.sdhe.com) will pick you up from any dock around San Diego Bay and operate Friday through Sunday from 3 to 10pm, with extended hours in summer. If you're staying in a downtown hotel, this is a great way to get to Coronado. Boats are sometimes available at the spur of the moment, but reservations are advised. Fares are $7 per person to most locations.

By Bicycle

San Diego is ideal for exploration by bicycle, and many roads have designated bike lanes. Bikes are available for rent in most areas; see "Outdoor Activities" in chapter 7 for suggestions.

San Diego RideLink publishes a comprehensive map of the county detailing bike *paths* (for exclusive use by bicyclists), bike *lanes* (alongside motor vehicle ways), and bike *routes* (shared ways designated only by bike-symbol signs). The free **San Diego Region Bike Map** is available online at **www.511sd.com**, or by calling © **511** or 619/699-1900. It can also be found at visitor centers.

It's possible to take your two-wheeler on the city's **public transportation.** For buses, let the driver know you want to stow your bike on the front of the bus, then board and pay the regular fare. The trolley also lets you bring your bike on the trolley for free. Bikers can board at any entrance *except* the first set of doors behind the driver; the bike-storage area is at the back of each car. The cars carry two bikes except during weekday rush hours, when the limit is one bike per car. For more information, call the **Transit Information**

Line (② 619/233-3004). Bikes are also permitted on the ferry connecting San Diego and Coronado, which has 15 miles of dedicated bike paths.

3

4 MONEY & COSTS

The Value of the Dollar vs. Other Popular Currencies

US$	Can$	UK £	Euro €	Aus$	NZ$
1	C$1.22	68p	€.73	A$1.43	NZ$1.75

The currency conversions quoted above were correct at press time. However, rates fluctuate, so before departing consult a currency exchange website such as www. oanda.com/convert/classic to check up-to-the-minute rates.

The cost of living is not cheap in San Diego, but it's still a moderately priced destination compared with New York, London, or San Francisco.

It's always advisable to bring money in a variety of forms on a vacation: a mix of cash, credit cards, and traveler's checks. You should also exchange enough petty cash to cover airport incidentals, tipping, and transportation to your hotel before you leave home, or withdraw money upon arrival at an airport ATM.

The most common bills are the $1 (a "buck"), $5, $10, and $20 denominations. There are also $2 bills (seldom encountered), $50 bills, and $100 bills (the last two are usually not welcome as payment for small purchases).

Coins come in seven denominations: 1¢ (1 cent, or a penny); 5¢ (5 cents, or a nickel); 10¢ (10 cents, or a dime); 25¢ (25 cents, or a quarter); 50¢ (50 cents, or a half-dollar); the gold-colored Sacagawea coin, worth $1; and the rare silver dollar.

ATMS

Nationwide, the easiest and best way to get cash away from home is from an ATM (automated teller machine), sometimes referred to as a "cash machine," or "cashpoint." The

Cirrus (② 800/424-7787; www.mastercard. com) and **PLUS** (② 800/843-7587; www. visa.com) networks span the country; you can find them even in remote regions. Go to your bank card's website to find ATM locations at your destination. Be sure you know your daily withdrawal limit before you depart.

Note: Many banks impose a fee every time you use a card at another bank's ATM, and that fee is often higher for international transactions (up to $5 or more) than for domestic ones (where they're rarely more than $2). In addition, the bank from which you withdraw cash may charge its own fee. To compare banks' ATM fees within the U.S., use **www. bankrate.com**. Visitors from outside the U.S. should also find out whether their bank assesses a 1% to 3% fee on charges incurred abroad.

CREDIT CARDS & DEBIT CARDS

Credit cards are the most widely used form of payment in the United States: **Visa** (Barclaycard in Britain), **MasterCard** (Eurocard in Europe, Access in Britain), **American Express, Diners Club,** and **Discover.** They also provide a convenient record of all your expenses, and offer relatively good exchange rates. You can withdraw cash advances from your credit cards at banks or ATMs, but high fees make credit card cash advances a pricey way to get cash.

What Things Cost in San Diego	US$
Taxi from the airport to downtown	12.00
Bus from the airport to downtown	2.25
Local telephone call	0.50
Double at the Hotel del Coronado (very expensive)	300.00
Double at the Sofia Hotel (expensive)	215.00
Double at the Park Manor Suites (moderate)	159.00
Double at La Pensione Hotel (inexpensive)	90.00
Breakfast or lunch for one at the Mission (inexpensive)	11.00
Lunch for one at Casa de Guadalajara (moderate)	16.00
Two-course dinner for one at Filippi's Pizza Grotto (inexpensive)	15.00
Two-course dinner for one at Caffé Bella Italia (moderate)	25.00
Two-course dinner for one at Thee Bungalow (expensive)	36.00
Two-course dinner for one at Baleen (very expensive)	50.00
Pint of beer at Karl Strauss Brewery	5.95
Large coffee at Claire de Lune Coffee Lounge	2.25
All-day adult ticket aboard Old Town Trolley Tours	32.00
SeaWorld adult admission	65.00
Best seat at the Old Globe Theatre	79.00

It's highly recommended you travel with at least one major credit card. You must have a credit card to rent a car, and hotels and airlines usually require a credit card imprint as a deposit against expenses.

ATM cards with major credit card backing, known as **debit cards,** are now a commonly acceptable form of payment in most stores and restaurants. Debit cards draw money directly from your checking account. Some stores enable you to receive cash back on your debit-card purchases as well. The same is true at most U.S. post offices.

TRAVELER'S CHECKS

Though credit cards and debit cards are more often used, traveler's checks are still widely accepted in the U.S. Foreign visitors should make sure traveler's checks are denominated in U.S. dollars; foreign-currency checks are often difficult to exchange.

You can buy traveler's checks at most banks. Most are offered in denominations of $20, $50, $100, $500, and sometimes $1,000. Generally, you'll pay a service charge ranging from 1% to 4%.

The most popular traveler's checks are offered by **American Express** (© 800/807-6233; © 800/221-7282 for cardholders—this number accepts collect calls, offers service in several foreign languages, and exempts Amex gold and platinum cardholders from the 1% fee); **Visa** (© 800/732-1322)—AAA members can obtain Visa checks online (www.aaa.com) for a $9.95 fee (for checks up to $1,500) or by calling © 866/339-3378; and **MasterCard** (© 800/223-9920).

Be sure to keep a copy of the traveler's check serial numbers separate from your checks in the event they are stolen or lost. You'll get a refund faster if you know the numbers.

Another option is **prepaid traveler's check cards;** these are reloadable cards that work much like debit cards but aren't linked to your checking account. With the **Visa TravelMoney Card** you can withdraw money from an ATM, or use the card for shopping, dining, or hotels—anywhere

Visa debit cards are accepted. Funds can be added to the card by phone, online, or at the point of purchase (banks, AAA, several major grocery store chains). If you lose the card, your available funds will be refunded within 1 business day. Check www.visa. com for more information.

5 HEALTH

STAYING HEALTHY

Contact the **International Association for Medical Assistance to Travelers** (© **716/754-4883** or 416/652-0137 in Canada; www.iamat.org) for tips on travel and health concerns, and for lists of local doctors. The United States **Centers for Disease Control and Prevention** (© **800/ 232-4636;** www.cdc.gov) provides up-to-date information on health hazards by region or country and offers tips on food safety. The website **www.tripprep.com**, sponsored by a consortium of travel medicine practitioners, **Travel Health Online,** may also offer helpful advice on traveling abroad. You can find listings of reliable clinics overseas at the **International Society of Travel Medicine** (www.istm.org).

WHAT TO DO IF YOU GET SICK AWAY FROM HOME

San Diego has several good hospitals with emergency rooms. Near downtown San Diego, **UCSD Medical Center-Hillcrest,** 200 W. Arbor Dr. (© **619/543-6222**), has the most convenient emergency room. In La Jolla, **UCSD Thornton Hospital,**

9300 Campus Point Dr. (© **858/657-7000**), has a good emergency room, and you'll find another in Coronado, at **Sharp Coronado Hospital,** 250 Prospect Place (© **619/522-3600**), opposite the Marriott Resort.

If you suffer from a chronic illness, consult your doctor before your departure. Pack **prescription medications** in your carry-on luggage, and carry them in their original containers, with pharmacy labels—otherwise they won't make it through airport security. Visitors from outside the U.S. should carry generic names of prescription drugs. Medications are readily available throughout San Diego at various chain drugstores such as Long's, Rite-Aid, and CVS, which sell pharmaceuticals and nonprescription products. Some branches are open 24 hours (p. 291). Local hospitals also sell prescription drugs.

For U.S. travelers, most reliable healthcare plans provide coverage if you get sick away from home. Foreign visitors may have to pay all medical costs upfront and be reimbursed later. See "Insurance," in "Fast Facts" in the appendix on p. 291.

6 SAFETY

STAYING SAFE

Fortunately, San Diego is a relatively safe destination, by big-city standards. Of the 10 largest cities in the United States, it historically has had the lowest incidence of

violent crime, per capita. Still, it never hurts to take some precautions.

Virtually all areas of the city are safe during the day. In Balboa Park, caution is advised in areas not frequented by regular foot traffic (particularly off the walkways on the Sixth Ave. side of the park). Transients are common in San Diego—especially downtown, in Hillcrest, and in the beach areas. They are rarely a problem, but can be unpredictable when under the influence. Downtown areas to the east of PETCO Park are sparsely populated after dusk, and poorly lit.

Parts of the city that are usually safe on foot at night include the Gaslamp Quarter, Hillcrest, Old Town, Mission Valley, Mission Beach, Pacific Beach, La Jolla, and Coronado.

Avoid carrying valuables with you on the street, and keep expensive cameras or electronic equipment bagged or covered when not in use. If you're using a map, try to consult it inconspicuously—or better yet, study it before you leave your room. Hold on to your pocketbook, and place your billfold in an inside pocket. In theaters, restaurants, and other public places, keep your possessions in sight.

Always lock your room door—don't assume that once you're inside the hotel, you are automatically safe and no longer need to be aware of your surroundings. Hotels are open to the public, and security may not be able to screen everyone who enters.

Note: Tijuana has seen a dramatic rise in violence. For information on staying safe south of the border, see p. 276.

DRIVING SAFETY Driving safety is important too, and carjacking is not unprecedented. Question your rental agency about personal safety, and ask for a traveler-safety brochure when you pick up your car. Obtain written directions—or a map with the route clearly marked—from the agency, showing how to get to your destination. San Diego's airport area, where most car-rental firms are based, is generally safe.

If you drive off a highway and end up in a dodgy-looking neighborhood, leave the area as quickly as possible. If you have an accident, even on the highway, stay in your car with the doors locked until you assess the situation or until the police arrive. If you're bumped from behind on the street or are involved in a minor accident with no injuries, and the situation appears to be suspicious, motion to the other driver to follow you. Never get out of your car in such situations. Go to the nearest police precinct, well-lit service station, or 24-hour store.

Whenever possible, always park in well-lit and well-traveled areas. Always keep your car doors locked, whether the vehicle is attended or unattended. Never leave packages or valuables in sight. If someone attempts to rob you or steal your car, don't try to resist the thief/carjacker. Report the incident to the police department immediately by calling © **911.**

7 SPECIALIZED TRAVEL RESOURCES

In addition to the destination-specific resources listed below, please visit Frommers.com for additional specialized travel resources.

TRAVELERS WITH DISABILITIES

Most disabilities shouldn't stop anyone from traveling in the United States. There are more options and resources out there than ever before, and San Diego is one of the most accessible cities in the country. Most of the city's major attractions are wheelchair friendly, including the walkways and museums of Balboa Park, the San Diego Zoo (which has bus tours to navigate the steep canyons), SeaWorld, the Wild Animal Park, and downtown's Gaslamp Quarter. Old Town and the beaches require a little more effort, but are generally accessible.

Manual wheelchairs with balloon tires are available free of charge daily at the main lifeguard stations in Ocean Beach, Mission Beach, Pacific Beach, and La Jolla. Beach conditions permitting, the Mission Beach lifeguard station also has four electric wheelchairs available daily (except Tues) 11:30am to 4:30pm from May through October, and Friday to Sunday, 11:30am to 3:30pm, from November through April (℃ **619/525-8247** or 619/221-8852).

Obtain more specific information from **Accessible San Diego** (℃ **619/325-7550;** www.asd.travel), the nation's oldest center for information for travelers with disabilities. The center has an info line that helps travelers find accessible hotels, tours, attractions, and transportation. The annual *Access in San Diego* pamphlet, a citywide guide with specifics on which establishments are accessible for those with visual, mobility, or hearing disabilities can be ordered online for $7.50; a downloadable version can be purchased for $5.

On buses and trolleys, riders with disabilities pay a fixed fare of $1.10. Because discounted fares are subsidized, *technically* you must obtain a Transit Travel ID from the **Transit Store** (℃ **619/234-1060**); the ID card certifies that a rider is eligible for the discount, but most drivers use visual qualifications to establish criteria. All MTS buses and trolleys are equipped with wheelchair lifts; priority seating is available on buses and trolleys. People with visual impairments benefit from the white reflecting ring that circles the bottom of the trolley door to increase its visibility. Airport transportation for travelers with disabilities is available in vans holding one or two wheelchairs from **Super Shuttle** (℃ **800/974-8885** or 858/974-8885, TDD 866/472-4497; www.supershuttle.com).

The **America the Beautiful—National Parks and Federal Recreational Lands Pass—Access Pass** (formerly the **Golden Access Passport**) gives visually impaired travelers or travelers with permanent disabilities (regardless of age) free lifetime entrance to federal recreation sites administered by the National Park Service, including the Fish and Wildlife Service, the Forest Service, the Bureau of Land Management, and the Bureau of Reclamation. This may include national parks, monuments, historic sites, recreation areas, and national wildlife refuges.

The America the Beautiful Access Pass can be obtained only in person at any NPS facility that charges an entrance fee. You need to show proof of a medically determined disability. Besides free entry, the pass also offers a 50% discount on some federal-use fees charged for such facilities as camping, swimming, parking, boat launching, and tours. For more information, go to www.nps.gov/fees_passes.htm, or call the United States Geological Survey (USGS), which issues the passes, at ℃ **888/275-8747.**

Organizations that offer a vast range of resources and assistance to travelers with disabilities include **MossRehab** (℃ **800/225-5667;** www.mossresourcenet.org), the **American Foundation for the Blind** (℃ **800/232-5463;** www.afb.org), and the **Society for Accessible Travel & Hospitality** (℃ **212/447-7284;** www.sath.org). **Air Ambulance Card** (℃ **877/424-7633;** www.airambulancecard.com) is now partnered with SATH and allows you to preselect top-notch hospitals in case of an emergency.

Many travel agencies offer customized tours and itineraries for travelers with disabilities. Among them are **Flying Wheels Travel** (℃ **877/451-5006** or 507/451-5005; www.flyingwheelstravel.com) and **Accessible Journeys** (℃ **800/846-4537** or 610/521-0339; www.disabilitytravel.com).

British travelers should contact **Holiday Care** (℃ **0845-124-9971** in the U.K. only; www.holidaycare.org.uk) to access a wide range of travel information and resources for seniors and those with disabilities.

GAY & LESBIAN TRAVELERS

Despite the conservative local politics, San Diego is one of America's gay-friendliest destinations. Over the years, the city has had several openly gay politicians and public officials, including the country's first openly gay district attorney, Bonnie Dumanis. San Diego also has one of the nation's oldest gay and lesbian theater companies, Diversionary Theatre.

Gay and lesbian visitors might already know about Hillcrest, near Balboa Park, the city's most prominent "out" community. Many gay-owned restaurants, boutiques, and nightspots cater to both a gay and straight clientele, and the scene is lively most nights of the week. In the 1990s, the community's residential embrace spread west to Mission Hills, and east along Adams Avenue to Kensington.

The **San Diego Gay Rodeo** is one of the largest rodeos on the International Gay Rodeo Association circuit, drawing cowboys and cowgirls from across the country for bronco riding and two-stepping. It's held in early summer at the rodeo grounds in the East County city of Lakeside; call © **619/298-4708,** or see www.sandiegorodeo.com for more info.

For information on the **Annual San Diego LGBT Pride Parade, Rally, and Festival,** see "San Diego Calendar of Events," earlier in the chapter.

The free *San Diego Gay and Lesbian Times* (www.gaylesbiantimes.com), published every Thursday, is the most information-packed of several local out publications, and available at the gay and lesbian **Obelisk** bookstore, 1029 University Ave., Hillcrest (© **619/297-4171;** www.obeliskbookstore.com), along with other businesses in Hillcrest and neighboring communities. And check out the **San Diego Gay & Lesbian Chamber of Commerce** online at www.gsdba.org. You can search the business directory with its 800-plus members and find a variety of restaurants, cafes, hotels, and other establishments that welcome gay and lesbian clients. The **San Diego Convention and Visitors Bureau** also publishes a pamphlet, *San Diego from Gay to Z,* with information on gay accommodations and events. For more information or to order the free pamphlet, go to www.sandiego.org. The CVB also has touring suggestions for gay and lesbian visitors on its cultural website, www.sandiegoartandsol.com.

The **International Gay & Lesbian Travel Association** (© 954/630-1637; www.iglta.com) is the trade association for the gay and lesbian travel industry, and offers an online directory of gay- and lesbian-friendly travel businesses and tour operators.

Gay.com Travel (© 415/834-6500; www.gay.com/travel or www.outandabout.com) is an excellent online successor to the popular *Out & About* print magazine. It provides regularly updated information about gay-owned, gay-oriented, and gay-friendly lodging, dining, sightseeing, nightlife, and shopping establishments in every important destination worldwide.

The Canadian website **GayTraveler** (www.gaytraveler.ca) offers ideas and advice for gay travel all over the world.

SENIOR TRAVEL

Nearly every attraction in San Diego offers a senior discount; age requirements vary, and prices are discussed in chapter 7 with each individual listing. Public transportation and movie theaters also have reduced rates. Don't be shy about asking for discounts, but always carry identification, such as a driver's license, that shows your date of birth.

Members of **AARP,** 601 E St. NW, Washington, DC 20049 (© **888/687-2277;** www.aarp.org), get discounts on hotels, airfares, and car rentals. AARP offers members a wide range of benefits, including *AARP The Magazine* and a monthly newsletter. Anyone over 50 can join.

The U.S. National Park Service offers an **America the Beautiful—National Parks and Federal Recreational Lands Pass—Senior Pass** (formerly the **Golden Age Passport**), which gives seniors 62 years or older lifetime entrance to all properties administered by the National Park Service—national parks, monuments, historic sites, recreation areas, and national wildlife refuges—for a one-time processing fee of $10. The pass must be purchased in person at any NPS facility that charges an entrance fee. Besides free entry, the American the Beautiful Senior Pass also offers a 50% discount on some federal-use fees charged for such facilities as camping, swimming, parking, boat launching, and tours. For more information, go to www.nps.gov/fees_passes.htm or call the United States Geological Survey (USGS), which issues the passes, at © **888/275-8747.**

Many reliable agencies and organizations target the 50-plus market. **Elderhostel** (© **800/454-5768;** www.elderhostel.org) arranges worldwide study programs for those age 55 and over. **ElderTreks** (© **800/741-7956,** 0808-234-1514 in the U.K., or 416/558-5000 anywhere else in the world; www.eldertreks.com) offers small-group tours to off-the-beaten-path or adventure-travel locations, restricted to travelers 50 and older.

FAMILY TRAVEL

With its plethora of theme parks, animal attractions, and beaches and parks, San Diego is an ideal family vacation destination. And, of course, Disneyland is right up the road, too.

To locate accommodations, restaurants, and attractions that are particularly kid-friendly, refer to the "Kids" icon throughout this guide. Also, keep in mind some hotels offer free or discounted lodging for children who share a room with a parent or guardian—be sure to ask.

Recommended family travel websites include **Family Travel Forum** (www.family

travelforum.com), a comprehensive site that offers customized trip planning; **Family Travel Network** (www.familytravelnetwork.com), an online magazine providing travel tips; and **TravelWithYourKids.com** (www.travelwithyourkids.com), a site written by parents for parents offering sound advice for long-distance and international travel with children.

You might also consider checking out *The Unofficial Guide to California with Kids* (Wiley Publishing, Inc.).

Parents who don't want the added stress and hassle of lugging along items such as strollers, cribs, car seats, or toys on their trip can contact **Go Baby Go!** (© **760/832-1353;** www.gobabygosandiego.com). The company will deliver directly to your destination or even the airport.

MULTICULTURAL TRAVELERS

Although San Diego has a reputation as a predominantly white, middle-class, conservative-leaning metropolis, a closer look reveals a more diverse picture: 25% of the city's inhabitants are Hispanic, 14% are Asian, and 8% are African American. The **San Diego Art + Sol** website (www.sandiegoartandsol.com) is an excellent place to get additional information on the city's contemporary cultural attractions; it also features a variety of touring itineraries.

The **San Diego Museum of Man** covers 4 million years of hominid history, with a particular focus on the native heritage of the Americas (p. 142). The history of San Diego's indigenous peoples is related at **Mission Trails Regional Park** (p. 148) and the **Junípero Serra Museum.**

With the Mexican border just 16 miles from downtown San Diego, Mexico's influence is unmistakable, and Spanish street and place names are prevalent. The **Mission Basilica San Diego de Alcalá** (p. 147), **Junípero Serra Museum,** and **Old Town** (p. 147) showcase Spanish-Mexican history, while contemporary culture is reflected in the murals of **Chicano Park** (© **619/563-4661;** www.chicano-park.org) under the San Diego–Coronado Bay Bridge. **Voz Alta,** 1754 National Ave. (© **619/230-1869;** www.vozalta.org), is a gathering spot in Barrio Logan for writers, artists, and musicians with a Chicano bent that hosts concerts, art exhibits, poetry slams, and other events. The **Centro Cultural de la Raza** (© **619/235-6135;** www.centroculturaldelaraza.org) in Balboa Park offers classes, live entertainment, and exhibits.

Cinco de Mayo (May 5) is a huge celebration in Old Town, but any day is great for shopping for Latin American handicrafts at **Bazaar del Mundo** or **Plaza del Pasado** (p. 204). Americanized Mexican food is ubiquitous, but for a taste of the real Mexico, try **El Agave Tequileria** (p. 109), or head south of the border. While in Tijuana, be sure to visit the excellent **Centro Cultural Tijuana** (p. 279), which covers the history, contemporary art, culture, and performing arts of Baja California and the rest of Mexico.

Initially lured by the California gold rush in the 1850s, a small Chinese community came to live in San Diego and controlled much of the fishing industry until 1890; Chinese also helped build (and later staff) the Hotel del Coronado. Chinatown—downtown, south of Market Street—eventually merged with the rough-and-tumble Stingaree, San Diego's red-light district. At the turn of the last century, the area was a hub of gambling, prostitution, and opium dens, and Chinese families ran notorious bars such as the Old Tub of Blood Saloon and the Seven Buckets of Blood Saloon.

Today, an **Asian/Pacific Historic District** is beginning to materialize, concentrated between Market and J streets, and between Third and Fifth avenues. Eighteen buildings in this area have strong historical ties to the Asian/Pacific-American community. Also here is the **San Diego Chinese Historical Museum,** which offers walking tours of the old Chinatown the second Saturday of the month (p. 146).

An African presence has also been felt in small but important ways throughout San Diego history. Black slaves were part of Juan Cabrillo's expedition along the California coast in 1542, and Pío Pico, a San Diegan who became the last Mexican governor of California before it was annexed by the United States, was of African descent. The Clermont Hotel, 501 Seventh Ave., is nondescript but socially significant—it was built in 1887 and was one of the city's first black-owned businesses. A segregated hotel "for colored people" until 1956, it may be the oldest surviving historically black hotel in the nation and was designated an African-American landmark in 2001.

The **Black Historical Society of San Diego,** 740 Market St. (© **619/232-1480;** www.blackhistoricalsociety.org), offers a variety of downtown tours focusing on San Diego's black history; it also has a gift store and genealogy resources. In Old Town, the ramshackle **Casa del Rey Moro African Museum,** 2471 Congress St. (© **619/220-0022;** www.ambers.com), provides a scholarly look at black history, with a special emphasis on how it has played out in San Diego and California. The **WorldBeat Cultural Center** (© **619/230-1190;** www.worldbeatcenter.org) in Balboa Park produces reggae and African music concerts, has a variety of classes, a gift shop, and even runs its own radio station. In the mountains east of San Diego, you'll find the **Julian Gold Rush Hotel** (p. 268), built in 1897 by freed slave Albert Robinson. The town itself was founded after gold was discovered in 1869 by another freed slave, Frederick Coleman. The **Julian Black Historical Society,** 2024 Third St. (© **760/765-1120;** www.julianblackhistoricalsociety.org), offers its "Soul of Julian" walking tour every Saturday and Sunday.

Soul of America (www.soulofamerica. com) is a comprehensive website, with travel tips, event and family-reunion postings, and sections on historically black beach resorts and active vacations. The section on San Diego is fairly detailed and has a calendar of events.

STUDENT TRAVEL

Check out the **International Student Travel Confederation** (www.istc.org) website for comprehensive travel services information and details on how to get an **International Student Identity Card (ISIC),** which qualifies students for substantial savings on rail passes, plane tickets, entrance fees, and more. It also provides students with basic health and life insurance and a 24-hour help line. The card is valid for a maximum of 18 months. You can apply for the card online or in person at **STA Travel** (✆ 800/781-4040 in North America, 134-782 in Australia, or 0871/2-300-040 in the U.K.; www. statravel.com), the biggest student travel agency in the world; check out the website to locate STA Travel offices worldwide. If you're no longer a student but are still under 26, you can get an **International Youth Travel Card (IYTC)** from the same people; it entitles you to some discounts. **Travel CUTS** (✆ 800/592-2887, or 866/246-9762 in Canada; www.travelcuts. com) offers similar services for both Canadians and U.S. residents. Irish students may prefer to turn to **USIT** (✆ 01/602-1906; www.usit.ie), an Ireland-based specialist in student, youth, and independent travel.

SINGLE TRAVELERS

On package vacations, single travelers are often hit with a "single supplement" to the base price. To avoid it, you can agree to room with other single travelers or find a compatible roommate before you go, from one of the many roommate-locator agencies.

TravelChums (✆ 212/787-2621; www.travelchums.com) is an Internet-only travel-companion matching service with elements of an online personals-type site, hosted by the respected New York–based Shaw Guides travel service.

Many reputable tour companies offer singles-only trips. **Singles Travel International** (✆ 877/765-6874; www.singles travelintl.com) offers singles-only escorted tours. **Backroads** (✆ 800/462-2848; www. backroads.com) offers "Singles + Solos" active-travel trips to destinations worldwide.

For more information, check out Eleanor Berman's classic *Traveling Solo: Advice and Ideas for More Than 250 Great Vacations,* 5th Edition (Globe Pequot).

TRAVELING WITH PETS

Many of us wouldn't dream of going on vacation without our pets. And these days, more and more lodgings and restaurants are going the pet-friendly route. In chapter 5, I've noted which hotels accept pets; the **Loews Coronado Bay Resort** (p. 91), **W San Diego** (p. 67), and **Hotel Solamar** (p. 64), in particular, go out of their way to welcome pets. Many San Diegans congregate with their canine friends at **Dog Beach,** at the north end of Ocean Beach, where dogs can swim, play, and socialize. After your pooch is thoroughly coated in seawater and sand, take him to the do-it-yourself **Dog Beach Dog Wash,** 2 blocks away at 4933 Voltaire St. (✆ 619/523-1700; www.dogwash.com). **Nate's Point** in Balboa Park is another favored place to let your pooch run loose. It's at the west end of the park, on the south side of Cabrillo Bridge.

Good resources include **www.pets welcome.com**, which dispenses medical tips, names of animal-friendly lodgings and campgrounds, and lists of kennels and veterinarians; **www.pettravel.com**; and **www.travelpets.com**. Also check out *The Portable Petswelcome.com: The Complete Guide to Traveling with Your Pet* (Howell Book House), which features the best selection of pet travel information anywhere.

Another resource is *Pets-R-Permitted Hotel, Motel & Kennel Directory: The Travel Resource for Pet Owners Who Travel* (Annenberg Communications).

If you plan to fly with your pet, a list of requirements for transporting live animals is available at **http://airconsumer.ost.dot.gov/publications/animals.htm**. You may be able to carry your pet on board a plane if that pet is small enough to put inside a carrier that can slip under the seat. Pets usually count as one piece of carry-on luggage. The ASPCA discourages travelers from checking pets as luggage at any time, as storage conditions on planes are loosely monitored, and fatal accidents are not unprecedented. Your other option is to ship your pet with a professional carrier, which can be expensive. Ask your vet whether you should sedate your pet on a plane ride or give it anti-nausea medication. Never give your pet sedatives used by humans.

8 SUSTAINABLE TOURISM

In San Diego, and throughout the Western United States in general, perhaps the biggest environmental concern can be summed up in one word: water. Drought conditions have pushed supply to the limit, and mandatory water conservation looms for San Diego. Mayor Jerry Sanders has already announced proposals that will attempt to curtail water usage by 20% citywide. Golf courses (which lap up some 12 billion gallons annually in San Diego) and resorts with lush landscaping will definitely feel the impact—businesses are being asked to cut water consumption by 45% outside and 3% inside. For more information, go to www.sandiego.gov/water.

Barona Creek Golf Club (p. 169) is leading the way for the county's golf courses in adapting to the water emergency. Barona has reconfigured its course to include less turf and more bunkers, and has also installed a computerized sprinkler system. **Steele Canyon Golf Club** (p. 169) has responded, as well, investing in its own weather station that constantly monitors how much water the course requires.

Two overlapping components of sustainable travel are **ecotourism** and **ethical tourism.** The **International Ecotourism Society (TIES)** defines ecotourism as responsible travel to natural areas that conserves the environment and improves the well-being of local people. TIES suggests that ecotourists follow these principles:

- Minimize environmental impact.
- Build environmental and cultural awareness and respect.
- Provide positive experiences for both visitors and hosts.
- Provide direct financial benefits for conservation and for local people.
- Raise sensitivity to host countries' political, environmental, and social climates.
- Support international human rights and labor agreements.

You can find some eco-friendly travel tips and statistics, as well as touring companies and associations—listed by destination under "Travel Choice"—at the TIES website, www.ecotourism.org. Also check out **Ecotravel.com,** which lets you search for sustainable touring companies in several categories (water-based, land-based, spiritually oriented, and so on).

While much of the focus of ecotourism is about reducing impacts on the natural environment, ethical tourism concentrates on ways to preserve and enhance local economies and communities, regardless of location. You can embrace ethical tourism by staying at a locally owned hotel or shopping at a store that employs local workers and sells locally produced goods.

Responsible Travel (www.responsible travel.com) is a great source of sustainable travel ideas; the site is run by a spokesperson for ethical tourism in the travel industry. **Sustainable Travel International** (www.sustainabletravelinternational.org) promotes ethical tourism practices, and manages an extensive directory of sustainable properties and tour operators around the world.

In the U.K., **Tourism Concern** (www.tourismconcern.org.uk) works to reduce social and environmental problems connected to tourism. The **Association of Independent Tour Operators** (www.aito.co.uk) is a group of specialist operators leading the field in making holidays sustainable.

Volunteer travel has become increasingly popular among those who want to venture beyond the standard group-tour experience to learn languages, interact with locals, and make a positive difference while on vacation. Volunteer travel usually doesn't require special skills—just a willingness to work hard—and programs vary in length from a few days to a number of weeks. Some programs provide free housing and food, but many require volunteers to pay for travel expenses, which can add up quickly.

For general info on volunteer travel, visit **www.volunteerabroad.org** and **www.idealist.org**. Before you commit to a volunteer program, it's important to make sure any money you're giving is truly going back to the local community, and that the work you'll be doing will be a good fit for you. **Volunteer International** (www.volunteerinternational.org) has a helpful list of questions to ask to determine the intentions and the nature of a volunteer program.

Animal-Rights Issues

For information on animal-friendly issues throughout the world, visit **Tread Lightly** (www.treadlightly.org). For information about the ethics of swimming with dolphins, visit the **Whale and Dolphin Conservation Society** (www.wdcs.org).

9 SPECIAL-INTEREST TRIPS & ESCORTED GENERAL-INTEREST TOURS

ADVENTURE & WELLNESS TRIPS

Surrounded by ocean, mountains, and desert, San Diego's prime location makes quick getaways to commune with nature a snap. For organized tours of the region, two great resources are the **San Diego Natural History Museum** (p. 142) and the **Birch Aquarium at Scripps** (p. 152). Each offers guided outings, such as day hikes or grunion hunts (p. 228), as well as multiday excursions, including trips to the desert or to the Pacific gray whale breeding lagoons in Baja California.

In the Anza-Borrego Desert, **California Overland** (p. 271) will guide you through otherworldly landscapes on trips lasting anywhere from a few hours to 2 days. They provide all the gear and do all the cooking on the overnight trips—all you have to do is sit back and enjoy the campfire and the spectacular display of stars overhead.

For an unforgettable immersion in Baja wilderness, check out **Baja Airventures** (© 800-221-9283; www.bajaairventures.com), which will fly you in a small plane from San Diego to remote parts of the Baja peninsula for personalized tours that can encompass fishing, surfing, snorkeling, kayaking, or just snoozing in a hammock.

Stateside, **Hike Bike Kayak** (p. 168) is a one-stop shop for outdoor activities in San Diego. You can arrange everything from a surfing lesson to exploring La Jolla's sea caves via kayak (you can even set up a full-day, three-sport combo package).

The region is also home to a number of wellness spas, including **Rancho La Puerta,** which was founded in 1940 just across the border in Tecate, Mexico. This groundbreaking venture pioneered the concept of the destination spa, where feel-good massages take a back seat to mind-and-body workouts. Holistic guru Deepak Chopra has also set up shop in San Diego with his **Chopra Center for Wellbeing,** located at La Costa Resort and Spa. Here you'll find an array of classes and treatments, as well as a gift shop. At **Warner Springs Ranch** in the Cleveland National Forest, you can soak in the healthful mineral water, and also enjoy horseback riding, golf, and hiking (all at a fraction of the cost of the upscale wellness resorts). For more information on San Diego's healthful havens, see p. 87.

FOOD & WINE TRIPS

San Diego is adjacent to two prolific wine regions: Temecula Valley to the north, just across the Riverside County line, and to the south, the Valle de Guadalupe, where you will find Mexico's most important wineries. Either makes for an easy day trip, with plenty of overnight options, as well. For more information on Temecula, see p. 249; for tours to Mexico's wine country, see p. 277.

San Diego's rising foodie profile can be experienced firsthand via wine and cooking classes at the **Balboa Park Food & Wine School** (© 619/557-9441; www. balboafoodwine.com). This top-notch operation is located at the gorgeous House of Hospitality in the heart of Balboa Park

and is operated by the folks who run the **Prado** restaurant (p. 198). If things get too hot in the kitchen for you here, you can just step out onto the terrace with its wonderful views of the park.

The **San Diego Wine & Culinary Center,** 200 Harbor Dr., Ste. 120 (© 619/231-6400; www.sdwineculinary. com), is conveniently located just across the trolley tracks from the Convention Center. It offers a variety of classes, as well as food and wine excursions—including to **Julian** (p. 263) and Baja wine country. To top it off, there are a wine bar and jazz club here, as well.

Great News!, 1788 Garnet Ave., Pacific Beach (© 888/478-2433 or 858/270-1582; www.great-news.com), has been a fixture in San Diego since 1977. Cooking classes in the state-of-the-art kitchen run the seasonal and ethnic gamut; plus they sell just about any piece of cookware or food gadget you could ever want.

ESCORTED GENERAL-INTEREST TOURS

Escorted tours are structured group tours, with a group leader. The price usually includes everything from airfare to hotels, meals, tours, admission costs, and local transportation.

Collette Tours (© 800/340-5158; www. collettevacations.com), **Globus** (© 866/755-8581; www.globusjourneys.com), and **Tauck World Discovery** (© 800/788-7885; www.tauck.com) each offer California coastal tours that hit the state's highlights, from San Francisco to San Diego.

---

10 STAYING CONNECTED

TELEPHONES

Generally, hotel surcharges on long-distance and local calls are astronomical, so you're better off using your **cellphone** or a **public pay telephone.** Many convenience

groceries and packaging services sell **prepaid calling cards** in denominations up to $50; for international visitors these can be the least expensive way to call home. Many public phones at airports now accept American Express, MasterCard, and Visa credit cards. **Local calls** made from public pay phones in most locales cost either 35¢ or 50¢. Pay phones do not accept pennies, and few will take anything larger than a quarter.

Most long-distance and international calls can be dialed directly from any phone. **For calls within the United States and to Canada,** dial 1 followed by the area code and the seven-digit number. **For other international calls,** dial 011 followed by the country code, city code, and the number you are calling.

Calls to area codes **800, 888, 877,** and **866** are toll-free. However, calls to area codes **700** and **900** (chat lines, bulletin boards, "dating" services, and so on) can be very expensive—usually a charge of 95¢ to $3 or more per minute, and they sometimes have minimum charges that can run as high as $15 or more.

For **reversed-charge** or **collect calls,** and for person-to-person calls, dial the number 0 then the area code and number; an operator will come on the line, and you should specify whether you are calling collect, person-to-person, or both. If your operator-assisted call is international, ask for the overseas operator.

For **local directory assistance** ("information"), dial 411; for long-distance information, dial 1 and then the appropriate area code and 555-1212.

Most hotels have **fax machines** available for guest use (be sure to ask about the charge to use them). Many hotel rooms are even wired for guests' fax machines. A less expensive way to send and receive faxes may be at stores such as the **UPS Store.**

CELLPHONES

Just because your cellphone works at home doesn't mean it'll work everywhere in the U.S. (thanks to our nation's fragmented cellphone system). It's a good bet your phone will work in major cities, but take a look at your wireless company's coverage map on its website before heading out; T-Mobile, Sprint, and Nextel are particularly weak in rural areas. If you need to stay in touch at a destination where you know your phone won't work, **rent** a phone that does from **InTouch USA** (✆ 800/872-7626; www.intouchglobal.com) or a rental car location, but beware that you'll pay $1 a minute or more for airtime.

If you're not from the U.S., you'll be appalled at the poor reach of the **GSM (Global System for Mobile Communications) wireless network,** which is used by much of the rest of the world. Your phone will probably work in most major U.S. cities; it definitely won't work in many rural areas. To see where GSM phones work in the U.S., check out www.t-mobile.com/coverage. And you may or may not be able to send SMS (text messaging) home.

In a worst-case scenario, you can always rent a phone; in San Diego, **Four Points Communications,** 3956 First Ave., Hillcrest (✆ 800/237-3266 or 619/234-6182; www.fourpointscom.com), and **BearCom,** 4506 Federal Blvd. (✆ 800/585-2159 or 619/263-2159; www.bearcom.com), deliver to hotels within the Metro area.

VOICE-OVER INTERNET PROTOCOL (VOIP)

If you have Web access while traveling, consider a broadband-based telephone service (in technical terms, **Voice-over Internet Protocol,** or **VoIP**) such as Skype (www.skype.com) or Vonage (www.vonage.com), which allow you to make free international calls from your laptop or in a cybercafe. Neither service requires the people you're calling to also have that service (though there are fees if they do not). Check the websites for details.

The Best of San Diego Online

- **www.sandiego.org** is maintained by the San Diego Convention & Visitors Bureau and includes up-to-date weather data, a calendar of events, and a hotel booking engine.
- **www.sandiegoartandsol.com** is the link for cultural tourism. You'll find a list of art shows and music events, plus intriguing touring itineraries that delve into the city's culture.
- **www.sandiegomagazine.com** is the online site for *San Diego Magazine*, offering feature stories and dining and events listings.
- **www.sdreader.com**, the site of the free weekly *San Diego Reader*, is a great resource for club and show listings. It has printable dining and other coupons, plus opinionated arts, eats, and entertainment critiques.
- **www.signonsandiego.com** is where CitySearch teams up with the *San Diego Union-Tribune*, catering as much to locals as to visitors. It offers plenty of helpful links, plus reviews of restaurants, music, movies, performing arts, museums, outdoor recreation, beaches, and sports.
- **www.wheresd.com** provides information on arts, culture, special events, shopping, and dining for San Diego, Orange County, and Los Angeles. You can also make hotel reservations through the site.
- **www.voiceofsandiego.org** is an excellent online news source that offers information on what's happening in the city politically and culturally.
- **www.sezio.org** is a hip spot where you can check in with the local art and music scene and learn about the latest openings and shows.

INTERNET & E-MAIL
With Your Own Computer

More and more hotels, resorts, airports, cafes, and retailers are going Wi-Fi (wireless fidelity), becoming "hotspots" that offer free high-speed Wi-Fi access or charge a small fee for usage. Wi-Fi is found in campgrounds, RV parks, and even entire towns. Most laptops sold today have built-in wireless capability. To find public Wi-Fi hotspots at your destination, go to **www.jiwire.com**; its Hotspot Finder holds the world's largest directory of public wireless hotspots.

For dial-up access, most business-class hotels in the U.S. offer dataports for laptop modems, and thousands of hotels in the U.S. and Europe now offer free high-speed Internet access.

Wherever you go, bring a **connection kit** of the right power and phone adapters, a spare phone cord, and a spare Ethernet network cable—or find out whether your hotel supplies them to guests.

Without Your Own Computer

To find cybercafes in your destination, check **www.cybercaptive.com** and **www.cybercafe.com**. Neighborhoods such as Hillcrest, North Park, and the beach areas are good spots to find coffee and computers.

Most major airports have **Internet kiosks** that provide basic Web access for a per-minute fee that's usually higher than cybercafe prices. You might also check out copy shops such as **FedEx Office** (formerly FedEx Kinko's).

Suggested San Diego Itineraries

If 1 to 3 days is all you have in San Diego, maximize your time with our ready-made itineraries. Rent a car and hit the beach—at sunset or under the almost-always-shining sun. Stroll the vibrant Gaslamp Quarter, cruise across the San Diego–Coronado Bay Bridge, head up to La Jolla for upscale shopping and dining, or explore dramatic Torrey Pines State Reserve. Whatever you do, dress in layers and bring a sweater or light jacket—Southern California mornings are often cool and foggy (especially near the ocean), and it can get chilly after sundown.

THE NEIGHBORHOODS IN BRIEF

Tucked into the sunny and parched southwest corner of the United States, San Diego is situated in one of the country's most naturally beautiful metropolitan settings. Learning the lay of the land is neither confusing nor daunting, but it helps to understand a few geographical features. Two major characteristics give San Diego its topographical personality: a superb and varied coastline; and a series of mesas bisected by inland canyons inhabited by coyotes, skunks, and raccoons.

San Diego's downtown—16 miles north of the Mexico border—sits at the edge of a large natural harbor, the San Diego Bay. The harbor is almost enclosed by two fingers of land: flat Coronado "Island" on one side, and peninsular Point Loma on the other. Both of these areas hold important military bases, bordered by classic neighborhoods dating to the 1890s and 1920s, respectively.

Heading north from Point Loma is Mission Bay, a lagoon that was carved out of an estuary in the 1940s and is now a watersports playground. A series of communities is found along the beach-lined coast: Ocean Beach, Mission Beach, Pacific Beach, La Jolla, and, just outside San Diego's city limits, Del Mar. To the south of downtown, you'll find National City, which is distinguished by shipyards on its bay side, then Chula Vista, and San Ysidro, which ends abruptly at the border (and where the huge city of Tijuana begins, equally abruptly).

Inland areas are perhaps best defined by Mission Valley, a mile-wide canyon that runs east-west, 2 miles north of downtown. Half a century ago, the valley held little beyond a few dairy farms, California's first mission, and the San Diego River (which is more like a creek for about 51 weeks a year). Then I-8 was built through the valley, followed by a shopping center, a sports stadium, another shopping center, and lots of condos. Today, Mission Valley is perhaps the most congested—and least charming—part of the city.

In spite of this, residents all use the valley, and many live along its perimeter: On the southern rim are desirable older neighborhoods such as Mission Hills, Hillcrest, Normal Heights, and Kensington; to the north are Linda Vista and Kearny Mesa—bedroom communities that emerged in the 1950s—and Miramar Naval Air Station. Just outside and to the north of the city limits is Rancho Bernardo, a quiet, clubby suburb.

The city of San Diego possesses one other vital (if man-made) ingredient: Balboa Park. Laid out in a 1,400-acre square between downtown and Mission Valley, the park contains the San Diego Zoo, many of the city's best museums, theaters (including the Tony Award–winning Old Globe), wonderful gardens, recreational facilities, and splendid architecture.

CORONADO Locals refer to Coronado as an island, but it's actually on a peninsula connected to the mainland by a long, sandy isthmus known as the **Silver Strand.** It's a wealthy, self-contained community inhabited by lots of retired Navy brass living on quiet, tree-lined streets. The northern portion of the city is home to **Naval Base Coronado** (also referred to as **U.S. Naval Air Station, North Island**) in use since World War I. The southern part of Coronado, with its architecturally rich neighborhoods, features some of the region's priciest real estate, and has a long history as an elite playground for snowbirds. Shops line the main street, Orange Avenue, and you'll find several ritzy resorts, including the landmark **Hotel del Coronado,** referred to locally as the "Hotel Del." Coronado has a lovely dune beach (one of the area's finest), plenty of restaurants, and a downtown reminiscent of a small Midwestern town.

DOWNTOWN After decades of intense development and restoration, downtown San Diego has emerged as a vibrant neighborhood with attractions that last long after banking hours. The city center is now a magnet for travelers, conventioneers, and locals. The business, shopping, dining, and entertainment heart of the city, the downtown area encompasses Horton Plaza, the Gaslamp Quarter, the Embarcadero (waterfront), the Convention Center, and Little Italy, sprawling over eight individual "neighborhoods." The **Gaslamp Quarter** is the center of a massive redevelopment kicked off in the mid-1980s with the opening of the Horton Plaza shopping complex; now, it's a cluster of renovated historic buildings housing some of the city's top restaurants and clubs. Immediately east of the Gaslamp is the **East Village,** where you'll find **PETCO Park,** home of the San Diego Padres Major League Baseball team since 2004. Also having undergone a renaissance is **Little Italy,** a bustling neighborhood along India Street and Kettner Boulevard, between Cedar and Laurel streets, at the northern edge of downtown. It's a great place to find a variety of restaurants (especially Italian) and boutiques.

HILLCREST & UPTOWN Part of Hillcrest's charm is the number of people out walking, shopping, and just hanging out. As the city's first self-contained suburb in the 1920s, it was also the desirable address for bankers and bureaucrats to erect their mansions. Now, it's the heart of San Diego's gay and lesbian community, but it's an inclusive neighborhood, charming everyone with an eclectic blend of shops and cafes. Despite the cachet of being close to **Balboa Park** (home of the **San Diego Zoo** and numerous **museums**), the area fell into neglect in the 1960s. By the late 1970s, however, legions of preservation-minded residents began restoring Hillcrest. Centrally located and brimming with popular restaurants and boutiques, Hillcrest also offers less expensive and more personalized accommodations than any other area in the city. Other old Uptown neighborhoods of interest are **Mission Hills** to the west of Hillcrest, and **University Heights, Normal Heights, North Park, South Park,** and **Kensington** to the east.

MISSION BAY & THE BEACHES *Casual* is the word of the day here. Come here when you want to wiggle your toes in the sand, feel the sun warm your skin,

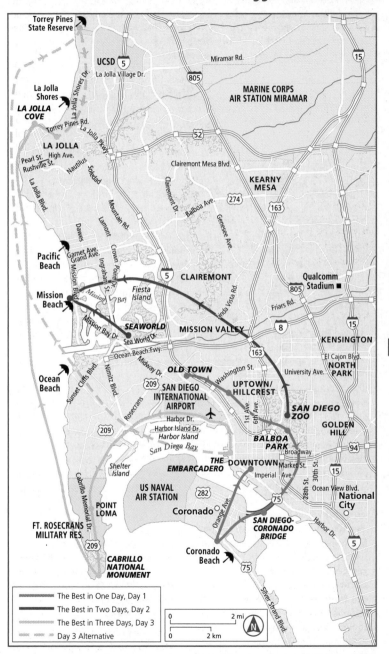

Off the Beaten Path: North Park & Beyond

To the northeast of Balboa Park is North Park, one of San Diego's original suburbs. Established in 1911, this mixed-use residential and commercial district was scraped out of a lemon grove, and thrived until the 1970s and 1980s. The neighborhood then went into decline, but recent gentrification has brought it roaring back to life. North Park was also the site of the worst aviation disaster in California history. On September 25, 1978, PSA Flight 182 collided in mid-air with a small plane over the community, killing 144 people, including 7 on the ground, and destroying or damaging 22 homes.

North Park's turnaround is best exemplified by the 2005 renovation of the fabulous **North Park Theatre** (p. 215), a 1928 vaudeville house where a variety of performing arts groups now strut their stuff. **Eveoke Dance Theatre** (p. 218) has established a permanent home nearby, as well. The area's lively scene gets a monthly showcase with **North Park Nights** (www.northparknights.org), held the second Saturday of every month from 6 to 11pm.

Dining makes a strong showing here, too, with **Hawthorn's** (p. 108), the **Mission** (p. 117), **Spread** (p. 126), **Urban Solace** (p. 126), **Jayne's Gastropub** (p. 126), and **Ranchos Cocina** (p. 126). There are great tacos and 135 tequilas available at **Cantina Mayahuel** (2934 Adams Ave.; ✆ **619/283-6292;** www.cantinamayahuel.com), while meat lovers will have a field day with the quality sausages at the **Linkery** (p. 126) and the gourmet burgers (more than 30) at **Tioli's Crazee Burger** (p. 104). And don't forget to save room for something sweet from **Heaven Sent Desserts** (3001 University Ave.; ✆ **619/793-4758;** www.heavensentdesserts.com). New arrivals making noise on the dining front include **Sea Rocket Bistro** (3382 30th St.; ✆ **619/255-7049;** www.searocketbistro.com) and **Farm House Café** (2121 Adams Ave.; ✆ **619/269-9662;** www.farmhousecafesd.com).

exert yourself in recreational activities, and cool off in the blue ocean waters. Mission Bay is a watery playground perfect for water-skiing, sailing, kayaking, and windsurfing. The adjacent communities of **Ocean Beach, Mission Beach,** and **Pacific Beach** are known for their wide stretches of sand, active nightlife, and informal dining. If you've come for the SoCal beach lifestyle, this is where you'll find it. The boardwalk, which runs from South Mission Beach to Pacific Beach, is a popular place for in-line skating, bike riding, people-watching, and sunsets.

LA JOLLA Mediterranean in design and ambience, La Jolla is the Southern California Riviera. This seaside community of about 25,000 is home to an inordinate number of wealthy folks who could probably live anywhere. They choose La Jolla for good reason—it features gorgeous coastline, outstanding restaurants, shops, galleries, and some of the world's best medical facilities, as well as the **University of California, San Diego (UCSD).** The heart of La Jolla is referred to as the **Village,** roughly delineated by Pearl Street to the south, Prospect Street to the north, Torrey Pines Road to the

By day there's shopping at places such as **Vintage Religion** (p. 203), specializing in art, jewelry, and apparel inspired by world religions; and the cool **Kate Ross** boutique (p. 203). By night, check out a few of the hipster dives, such as **Bar Pink** (3829 30th St.; ☏ 619/564-7194; www.barpink.com), **U-31** (3112 University Ave.; ☏ 619/584-4188; www.myspace.com/u31sandiego), and **Live Wire** (2103 El Cajon Blvd.; ☏ 619/291-7450; www.livewirebar.com). The **Toronado** (4026 30th St.; ☏ 619/282-0456; www.toronadosd.com) has 50 beers on draft, and the **Red Fox Steak House** (2223 El Cajon Blvd.; ☏ 619/297-1313) has an old-school piano bar.

And if you really need your morning edition of *Le Monde,* you can find it at **Paras Newsstand,** the city's best (3911 30th St.; ☏ 619/296-2859).

Despite its name, South Park is actually east of Balboa Park, and it blends into Golden Hill at the park's southeastern corner. Both neighborhoods have architectural gems including meticulously preserved Victorian mansions and Craftsman bungalows. And both areas have a crop of bars and restaurants worth investigating. The pack is led by **Vagabond** (2310 30th St.; ☏ 619/255-1035; www.vagabondkitchen.com), an intimate bistro that enjoys cult-status popularity; there's also the retro **Turf Supper Club** (p. 225), the **Whistle Stop Bar** (2236 Fern St.; ☏ 619/284-6784; www.whistlestopbar.com), and **Influx Cafe** (1948 Broadway; ☏ 619/255-9470; www.influxcafe.com), with its minimalist-chic decor and home-baked goods. And the funky breakfast spot known as the **Big Kitchen** (3003 Grape St.; ☏ 619/234-5789; www.bigkitchencafe.com) is a local institution—it's where a pre-fame Whoopi Goldberg once worked.

east, and the rugged coast to the west. This is a picturesque neighborhood, which makes it perfect for simply strolling about. It's uncertain whether "La Jolla" (pronounced La-*hoy*-ya) is misspelled Spanish for "the jewel" or a native people's word for "cave," but once you see it, you'll no doubt go with the first definition.

OLD TOWN & MISSION VALLEY
These two busy areas wrap around the neighborhood of Mission Hills. On one end are the Old Town State Historic Park (where California "began") and several museums that document the city's

beginnings. Old Town is said to attract more visitors than any other site in San Diego—it's where you can steep yourself in history while eating and shopping to your stomach's and heart's content. Not far from Old Town lies the vast suburban sprawl of Mission Valley, a tribute to the automobile and to a more modern style of prosperity. Its main street, aptly named Hotel Circle, is lined with a string of moderately priced hotels as an alternative to the ritzier neighborhoods. In recent years, condo developments have made the valley a residential area and a traffic nightmare.

1 THE BEST OF SAN DIEGO IN 1 DAY

To get an overview of San Diego in just 1 day, you'll have to dart around town a bit. Begin with a taste of the area's Hispanic heritage, then embrace San Diego's dazzling beaches, and end the day in the spirited downtown Gaslamp Quarter.

❶ Old Town

Old Town State Historic Park is the most visited state park in California (and it's free). This is San Diego's original downtown, and history comes to colorful life here, especially at **Plaza del Pasado,** a once-dilapidated 1930s motel converted into shopping and dining arcades, replete with mariachi players echoing the sounds of Mexico around an inner courtyard. See p. 204.

❷ Hillcrest

Hillcrest, San Diego's equivalent of L.A.'s West Hollywood or New York's West Village, is an urban, pedestrian-friendly neighborhood. Its tolerant attitude fosters a large gay community and a hip, eclectic vibe. Pop into trendy boutiques, second-hand clothing stores, and an array of restaurants and cafes. Check out the '40s-era Art Deco neighborhood sign dangling above University Avenue (at Fifth Ave.).

❸ BREAKING BREAD

Bread & Cie., 350 University Ave. (✆ 619/683-9322), is perfect for a quick shot of java and a fresh scone or muffin. Lunch fare features hearty Mediterranean sandwiches served on delectable homemade bread, such as a rosemary and cheese baguette or olive focaccia. Relax at one of the bistro tables or take your bite to go for a picnic at your next stop, Balboa Park. See p. 108.

❹ Balboa Park

Balboa Park, the nation's largest urban cultural park, contains a cluster of diverse museums and theaters, as well as San Diegans lolling about in the grass on any given pristine 70°F (21°C) sunny day (which is pretty much every day). Wander past the Spanish Golden Age–style buildings along the pedestrian mall, El Prado, then take in the sublime beauty of the Botanical Building's lily pond or explore the meandering park trails. See p. 136.

❺ The San Diego–Coronado Bay Bridge

Drive across the 2-mile-long, curved San Diego–Coronado Bay Bridge with the salty wind whistling in your ears. If you've rented a convertible, put the top down *now.* In a word: invigorating. See p. 154.

❻ Hotel del Coronado & Coronado Beach

Nicknamed by locals as the "Hotel Del," this Victorian landmark, with its spiky red turrets and gingerbread trim, is a San Diego gem. Stroll through the elegant lobby (perhaps you'll meet the resident ghost, Kate Morgan), meander along the sprawling decks facing the Pacific, and take a leisurely walk along Coronado Beach. This is a great place to watch a sunset. See p. 89 and 133.

❼ The Gaslamp Quarter

Finish the day in the historic Gaslamp Quarter, which always promises a lively evening street scene. Pick from dozens of restaurants (many housed in restored Victorian commercial buildings), and stick around for live music or dancing after dinner—if you have the energy. See p. 99, 179, and 219.

2 THE BEST OF SAN DIEGO IN 2 DAYS

Your second full-day tour starts with a famous San Diego theme park, but you'll need to choose which one: SeaWorld or the San Diego Zoo. You could spend the entire day at either one, but if you need a change of scenery halfway through the afternoon, spend a few active hours at the public aquatic park, Mission Bay, or on the Mission Beach boardwalk. If you have no desire to bike or kayak, chill out on the beach and embrace a lazy afternoon under the sun.

❶ A Theme Park: SeaWorld or San Diego Zoo

You'll get a dose of animals at both places, but do yourself a favor and choose *either* SeaWorld *or* the San Diego Zoo; don't try to do both in 1 day. Get there when the gates open to maximize your touring time, and spend a little more than half of the day exploring. Plan to leave by early afternoon for a late lunch.

At **SeaWorld,** Shamu may be the star, but there's a whole lot more to see and do here. You'll find Journey to Atlantis (a roller coaster), Shipwreck Rapids (a splashy river ride), lovable penguins at the Penguin Encounter, and, of course, animal shows—including one featuring a certain killer whale. There's also a passel of *Sesame Street*–related attractions, including rides, a musical production *(Big Bird's Beach Party)*, and a "4-D" interactive movie experience. See p. 130.

More than 4,000 creatures reside at the world-renowned **San Diego Zoo,** known not only for its giant pandas, gorillas, and tigers housed in naturalistic environments, but also for its successful animal preservation efforts. The Children's Zoo petting area is perfect for little ones (and any adult who loves animals). See p. 128.

❷ A POST-THEME-PARK BREAK
If you're coming from SeaWorld and don't mind a little irony, try the fresh-off-the-boat seafood at **❷ᴬ** the **Fishery,** 5040 Cass St. (✆ **858/272-9985**)—a casual Pacific Beach fish market. See p. 114. If you spent the morning at the San Diego Zoo, pick up a gourmet taco at colorful **❷ᴮ Mamá Testa,** 1417 University Ave. (✆ **619/298-8226**), a local favorite. See p. 114.

❸ Mission Bay Park & Mission Beach

Outfitters such as **Mission Bay Sportcenter** and **Mission Beach Surf & Skate** (p. 174 and 167) rent gear including bikes, in-line skates, kayaks, and catamarans to better make your way through and around Mission Bay Park, a 4,600-acre aquatic playground. You can also enjoy unparalleled people-watching along the Mission Beach boardwalk, which hugs the wide swath of sandy beach. Or just grab a blanket, plop down on the sand, catch some rays, and ponder the volleyball players' sun-tanned muscles. See p. 133.

3 THE BEST OF SAN DIEGO IN 3 DAYS

After you've followed the previous two itineraries, spend your third day touring the Embarcadero, contemplating the ocean vistas from Point Loma or Torrey Pines, and exploring another spectacular beach (as well as a bevy of outdoor dining venues and high-end boutiques) in La Jolla. If you have kids in tow, consider visiting the theme park you didn't choose on Day 2.

4

❶ The Embarcadero

Along the Embarcadero, downtown San Diego's waterfront, you'll find harbor tours, a ferry to Coronado, and historic vessels such as the aircraft carrier USS *Midway* and the *Star of India,* the world's oldest active ship. Both are now floating museums (p. 146 and 144); also close by are the downtown spaces for the **Museum of Contemporary Art San Diego** (p. 144). There are also plenty of restaurants and shops at **Seaport Village,** a maritime-themed retail area (p. 201).

❷ The Great Outdoors: Cabrillo National Monument or Torrey Pines State Reserve

You don't have to go far to find stunning natural environments in San Diego. The two best and closest are Cabrillo National Monument and Torrey Pines State Reserve. Hours can easily melt away at either of these magical spots, so you'll have to select just one.

You'll find **Cabrillo National Monu-ment** at the end of Point Loma, a slice of land jutting into the Pacific just southeast of downtown San Diego. This 144-acre park features a statue of Juan Rodríguez Cabrillo, the Portuguese explorer who landed in San Diego in 1542; a restored 1855 lighthouse; museum installations and a bookstore; bayside trails; tide pools; and a 422-foot-high lookout. This is an excellent vantage point to see migrating Pacific gray whales in winter; year-round, you'll enjoy awesome views of San Diego's harbor and skyline, and the rocky Pacific coastline. When skies are clear, you can also see Mexico in the distance. See p. 144.

Just north of La Jolla, **Torrey Pines State Reserve** is one of San Diego's most treasured spots. The 1,000-acre reserve is home to the distinctively gnarled tree that gives the place its name (and which is found only here and on an island off the coast). Trails range from flat and easy to steep and narrow, but all provide utterly breathtaking views of the ocean, lagoon, canyons, sandstone formations, and the famed Torrey Pines Golf Course. Take a hike or just head down to the beach. See p. 153.

---

❸ FISH TACOS & DESSERTS

Stop for a snack or lunch at the harborside **3A** **Point Loma Seafoods,** 2805 Emerson St. (☏ **619/223-1109**), a fish market (with a few outdoor picnic tables) offering sandwiches, sushi, salads, and tasty fish tacos. See p. 114. In La Jolla, sweet and savory options are available at **3B** **Michele Coulon Dessertier,** 7556 Fay Ave., Ste. D (☏ **858/456-5098**). If you need something more substantial than sweets, the menu at this small restaurant goes way beyond amazing desserts. Try the onion soup, Belgian endive salad, or a quiche, along with a slice of flourless chocolate Cognac cake. See p. 117.

---

❹ La Jolla

End your day in La Jolla, San Diego's swanky neighbor to the north. This town is upscale, exclusive, and home to some of the area's priciest real estate. Take one look at the pristine coastline, and you'll instantly understand the allure. The main shopping and dining venues are clustered along or near Prospect Street, but La Jolla's most spectacular spot is the bluff above La Jolla Cove. Stroll along Coast Boulevard for the most scenic views. With its calm, crystal-clear water, the cove is also great for swimming. In the tide pools at its small, sandy beach, you can glimpse marine life such as starfish, sea anemones, and sea urchins. See p. 150.

Where to Stay ·

San Diego offers a variety of places to stay, ranging from hip high-rises to spa- and golf-blessed resorts, from inexpensive cookie-cutter motels to out-of-the-ordinary B&Bs.

This chapter explores all the options within the city proper. Lodging recommendations for Del Mar, Encinitas, and Carlsbad (all beautifully situated along the coast and within 40 min. of the city) are found in chapter 11, as are hotels for the Disneyland area, south of the border, and inland regions.

High season is vaguely defined as the summer period between Memorial Day and Labor Day—some hotels inch rates higher still in July and August. Because San Diego is a very popular convention destination,

however, you'll find that rates for the larger downtown hotels and a few of the Mission Valley hotels are largely determined by the ebb and flow of conventions in town during the week—which means that weekend and holiday rates can be good bargains. On the other hand, leisure-oriented hotels along the coast and in Mission Valley are generally busier on weekends, especially in summer, so midweek deals are easier to snag. Here's an idea to maximize your discounts: Spend the weekend at a downtown high-rise and duck into a beach bungalow on Monday. And keep in mind—in the current economic conditions *everybody* is making deals. You might be able to wrangle a room in one of the city's finest hotels for a pittance.

---

1 TIPS ON ACCOMMODATIONS

SAVING ON YOUR HOTEL ROOM

A hotel's "rack rate" is the official published rate, and those are the prices quoted here. They will help you make an apples-to-apples comparison. The truth is, though, *hardly anybody pays rack rates,* and with the exception of smaller B&Bs, you can usually pay quite a bit less than the rates shown below. Here's how the price categories are organized:

- **Very Expensive:** $275 and up
- **Expensive:** $190 to $274
- **Moderate:** $120 to $189
- **Inexpensive:** under $120

These are all high-season prices, with no discounts applied. And keep in mind that the rates given in this chapter do not include the hotel tax, which is an additional 10.5%, or 12.5% for lodgings with 70 or more rooms. But *always* peruse the category above your target price—you might just find the perfect match, especially if you follow the advice below.

- Dial direct.
- Ask about special rates or other discounts.
- Book online at the hotel's website.
- Remember the law of supply and demand.

- Look into group or long-stay discounts.
- Avoid excess charges and hidden costs (such as minibar charges).
- Book an efficiency.
- Investigate reservations services such as **Quikbook** (© **800/789-9887;** www.quik book.com); **Hotel Locators** (© **858/581-1315;** www.hotellocators.com); **Accommodations Express** (© **800/950-4685;** www.accommodationsexpress.com); and **Hotel Discounts** (© **800/715-7666** in the U.S. and Canada, 00800/1066-1066 in Europe, or 1214/369-1264 elsewhere; www.hoteldiscount.com).

BED & BREAKFASTS
Travelers who seek bed-and-breakfast accommodations will be pleasantly surprised by the variety and affordability of San Diego B&Bs (especially compared with the rest of California). Many B&Bs are traditional, strongly reflecting the personality of an on-site innkeeper and offering as few as two guest rooms; others accommodate more guests in a slickly professional way. More than 10 B&Bs are part of the close-knit **San Diego Bed & Breakfast Guild** (© **800/619-7666;** www.bandbguildsandiego.org), whose members work actively at keeping prices reasonable; many good B&Bs average $100 to $125 a night.

HOSTELS
Those in search of less expensive accommodations should check into San Diego's collection of hostels. You should have your own sack sheet or sleeping bag (or plan to rent one) and be prepared for shared dorm-style rooms, although private rooms are also found at most. Communal kitchens are also available at most hostels. Reservations are a good idea *any* time of year, and overbooking is not uncommon.

USAHostels (© **800/438-8622** or 619/232-3100; www.usahostels.com) is in the heart of the Gaslamp Quarter at 726 Fifth Ave. in a historic building; private rooms cost $75, four-bed rooms are $29, and six-bed rooms run $26 per person (online reservations receive a discount). Also in the Gaslamp is **HI Downtown Hostel** (© **888/464-4872,** ext. 156, or 619/525-1531; www.sandiegohostels.org), at 521 Market St. This facility has 4-, 6-, and 10-person rooms, with or without en suite bathrooms; and double, twin, and family-size private rooms, with or without bathroom. Reception is open 24 hours. Private rooms start at $47 and dorm rooms start at $19. **Hostelling International** also has a 53-bed location in Point Loma (© **888/464-4872,** ext. 157, or 619/223-4778), at 3790 Udall St., which is about 2 miles inland from Ocean Beach; rates start at $17 per person, and private rooms that sleep two or three start at $42 and $48, respectively. The **Ocean Beach International Hostel,** 4961 Newport Ave. (© **800/339-7263** or 619/223-7873; www.californiahostel.com), has more than 60 beds and is just 2 blocks from the beach. Bunk rates start at $15 per person, and they offer free pickup from the airport, train, or bus station. There's an extensive collection of DVDs for guests, and free barbecues are held Tuesday and Friday. U.S. residents must show current student ID, proof of international travel within the last 6 months, or be a member of a hostelling organization in order to stay. You can truly embrace your inner beach bum at **Banana Bungalow,** 707 Reed Ave. (© **858/273-3060;** www.bananabungalowsandiego.com). Even the finest hotel won't get you any closer to the beach than this place—it's right on the raucous Pacific Beach boardwalk. In summer, dorm rooms are $25 and private rooms are $105.

- **Best Historic Hotel:** The **Hotel del Coronado,** 1500 Orange Ave. (© **800/468-3533** or 619/435-6611), positively oozes history. Opened in 1888, this Victorian masterpiece had some of the first electric lights in existence, and over the years has hosted kings, presidents, and movie stars. Meticulous restoration has enhanced this glorious landmark, whose early days are well chronicled in displays throughout the hotel. See p. 89.
- **Best for a Romantic Getaway:** At the **Lodge at Torrey Pines,** 11480 N. Torrey Pines Rd. (© **800/566-0087** or 858/453-4420)—one of only two AAA 5-diamond hotels in the county—you can enjoy a fireplace in your room, sunset ocean views from your balcony, and superb meals at the hotel's A.R. Valentien restaurant. See p. 85.
- **Best for Families:** The **Paradise Point Resort & Spa,** 1404 Vacation Rd. (© **800/344-2626** or 858/274-4630), is a tropical playground offering enough activities to keep family members of all ages happy. In addition to a virtual Disneyland of on-site options, the aquatic playground of Mission Bay surrounds the hotel's private peninsula. See p. 78.
- **Best Moderately Priced Hotel:** The **Horton Grand,** 311 Island Ave. (© **800/542-1886** or 619/544-1886), is a Victorian landmark full of creature comforts that belie its friendly rates. You'll also be smack-dab in the heart of the trendy Gaslamp Quarter. See p. 68.
- **Best Budget Hotel:** In San Diego's Little Italy, **La Pensione Hotel,** 606 W. Date St. (© **800/232-4683** or 619/236-8000), feels like a small European hotel and offers tidy lodgings at bargain prices. There's an abundance of great dining in the surrounding blocks, and you'll be perfectly situated to explore the rest of town by car or trolley. See p. 70.
- **Best Bed-and-Breakfast:** The picture-perfect **Heritage Park Bed & Breakfast Inn,** 2470 Heritage Park Row (© **800/995-2470** or 619/299-6832), has it all: an exquisitely maintained Victorian house, lively and gracious hosts who delight in creating a pampering and romantic ambience, and an Old Town location equally close to downtown, Hillcrest, and Mission Bay. See p. 75.
- **Best Boutique Inn:** Smartly located in the center of La Jolla, the 20-room **Hotel Parisi,** 1111 Prospect St. (© **877/472-7474** or 858/454-1511), has the composed, quiet feel of a Zen garden, with feng shui–inspired suites, modern furnishings, and first-class amenities. See p. 82 .
- **Best Place to Stay on the Beach:** Although the Hotel Del is the grande dame of West Coast seaside resorts, if you really want to be in the heart of San Diego's beach culture, no place is better than **Tower 23,** 723 Felspar St. (© **866/869-3723**). This sleek, modernist hotel—which takes its name from a nearby lifeguard station—sits right on the Pacific Beach boardwalk. See p. 79.
- **Best Hotel for Travelers with Disabilities:** While many of San Diego's hotels make minimal concessions to wheelchair-accessibility codes, downtown's **Manchester Grand Hyatt San Diego,** 1 Market Place (© **800/233-1234** or 619/232-1234), goes the distance. There are 23 rooms with roll-in showers and lowered closet racks and peepholes. Ramps are an integral part of all the public spaces, rather than an afterthought. The hotel's Braille labeling is also thorough. See p. 65.

• **Best Hotel Pool:** The top-floor pool, sun deck, and lounge at the **Ivy Hotel,** 600 F St. (📞 **877/489-4489** or 619/814-1000), collectively make up downtown's largest rooftop space. Although the pool is shallow, the video-enhanced cabanas, Gaslamp Quarter vistas, and clubby vibe attract the beautiful people (some of whom are also shallow). See p. 64. For a more private, guests-only experience, the pool at **La Valencia Hotel,** 1132 Prospect St. (📞 **800/451-0772** or 858/454-0771), is oh-so-special, with its spectacular setting overlooking Scripps Park and the Pacific. See p. 84.

3 DOWNTOWN, THE GASLAMP & LITTLE ITALY

San Diego's downtown is an excellent place for leisure travelers to stay. The nightlife and dining in the Gaslamp Quarter and Horton Plaza shopping are close at hand; Balboa Park, Hillcrest, Old Town, and Coronado are less than 10 minutes away by car; and beaches aren't much farther. It's also the city's public-transportation hub, and thus very convenient for car-free visitors.

Many downtown hotels seem designed for the expense-account crowd, but there are more moderately priced choices. There's the colorful, modern **Bristol Hotel,** 1055 First Ave. (📞 **800/662-4477** or 619/232-6141; www.thebristolsandiego.com), adjacent to the Gaslamp Quarter. In the budget category, you can't beat the 259-room **500 West,** 500 W. Broadway (📞 **866/315-4251** or 619/234-5252; www.500westhotel.com). It offers small but comfortable rooms for $89 to $129 a night in a seven-story building dating to 1924. It has contemporary style, history, and a good location, but bathrooms are down the hall. Cheaper still are downtown's hostels; see p. 60.

VERY EXPENSIVE

Embassy Suites Hotel San Diego Bay-Downtown ★★   If you can snag a room when a big convention isn't forcing up downtown rates, this business hotel can be a good deal for families. This spot provides modern accommodations with lots of room for families or claustrophobes. Built in 1988, the neoclassical high-rise is topped with a distinctive neon bull's-eye that's visible from far away. Every room is a suite, with a king or two doubles in the bedroom, plus a sofa bed in the living/dining area; each has convenient features such as a kitchenette and a dining table that converts into a work area. All rooms open onto a 12-story atrium filled with palm trees, koi ponds, and a bubbling fountain; each also has a city or bay view. It's located 1 block from Seaport Village and 8 blocks from the Gaslamp Quarter.

601 Pacific Hwy. (at N. Harbor Dr.), San Diego, CA 92101. 📞 **800/362-2779** or 619/239-2400. Fax 619/239-1520. www.embassysuites.com. 337 units. $279–$389 suite. Extra person $20. Rates include full breakfast and cocktail hour. Children 17 and under stay free in parent's room. AE, DC, DISC, MC, V. Valet parking $30. Trolley: Seaport Village. **Amenities:** 2 restaurants; babysitting; children's programs; concierge; exercise room; Jacuzzi; indoor pool; tennis court. *In room:* A/C, TV, hair dryer, Internet, kitchenette.

Hilton San Diego Gaslamp Quarter ★★★   At the foot of the Gaslamp Quarter and across the street from the convention center, this hotel is ideally situated for business travelers. The Hilton is a great place for guests who want to be close to the action (which includes loads of restaurants, nightlife, and the ballpark within a few blocks), but not get lost in the shuffle. This nonsmoking hotel opened in 2001 on the site of the old Bridgeworks building—part of San Diego's original wharf a century ago; much of the brick

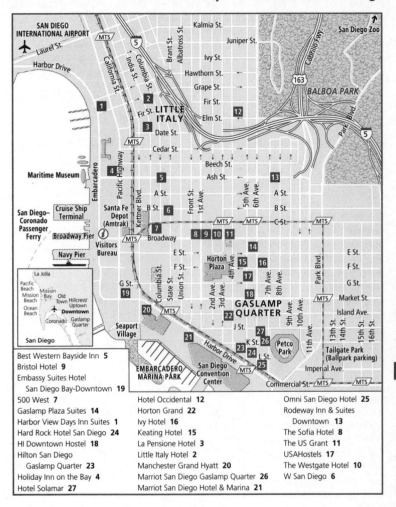

SAN DIEGO INTERNATIONAL AIRPORT [MTS]
Laurel St.
Harbor Drive
California St.
India St.
Columbia St.
Brant St.
Albatross St.
Kalmia St.
Juniper St.
San Diego Zoo
Cabrillo Fwy.
Ivy St.
Hawthorn St.
Grape St.
163
BALBOA PARK
Fir St. LITTLE ITALY
Elm St.
Park Blvd.
5
Date St.
Cedar St.
[MTS]
Maritime Museum
Embarcadero
Pacific Highway
Beech St.
Ash St.
A St.
Front St.
1st Ave.
5th Ave.
6th Ave.
A St.
B St.
Kettner Blvd.
Santa Fe Depot (Amtrak)
Cruise Ship Terminal
San Diego–Coronado Passenger Ferry
Broadway Pier
Navy Pier
Visitors Bureau
Broadway
E St.
F St.
Horton Plaza
4th Ave.
7th Ave.
8th Ave.
Park Blvd.
E St.
F St.
G St.
Market St.
La Jolla
Pacific Beach
Mission Beach
Mission Bay
Old Town
Hillcrest/Uptown
Downtown
Ocean Beach
Coronado
Gaslamp Quarter
San Diego
Columbia St.
State St.
Union St.
2nd Ave.
3rd Ave.
GASLAMP QUARTER
9th Ave.
10th Ave.
11th Ave.
J St.
Seaport Village
Harbor Drive
K St.
L St.
Petco Park
13th St.
14th St.
15th St.
16th St.
Island Ave.
Tailgate Park (Ballpark parking)
Imperial Ave.
EMBARCADERO/ MARINA PARK
San Diego Convention Center
Commercial St.

Best Western Bayside Inn **5**	Hotel Occidental **12**	Omni San Diego Hotel **25**
Bristol Hotel **9**	Horton Grand **22**	Rodeway Inn & Suites
Embassy Suites Hotel	Ivy Hotel **16**	Downtown **13**
San Diego Bay-Downtown **19**	Keating Hotel **15**	The Sofia Hotel **8**
500 West **7**	La Pensione Hotel **3**	The US Grant **11**
Gaslamp Plaza Suites **14**	Little Italy Hotel **2**	USAHostels **17**
Harbor View Days Inn Suites **1**	Manchester Grand Hyatt **20**	The Westgate Hotel **10**
Hard Rock Hotel San Diego **24**	Marriot San Diego Gaslamp Quarter **26**	W San Diego **6**
HI Downtown Hostel **18**	Marriot San Diego Hotel & Marina **21**	
Hilton San Diego		
Gaslamp Quarter **23**		
Holiday Inn on the Bay **4**		
Hotel Solamar **27**		

facade was incorporated into the hotel's polished design. Standard rooms boast upmarket furniture. There are also suites and an executive floor, but the really snazzy picks are rooms in the Lofts at 5th Avenue, a hotel within the hotel that features 30 oversize guest rooms with towering ceilings, custom furnishings, and lavish tubs. These are some of the most handsome hotel rooms downtown.

401 K St. (at Fourth Ave.), San Diego, CA 92101. (© **800/445-8667** or 619/231-4040. Fax 619/231-6439. www.hilton.com. 282 units. $389 double; from $424 suite. Children 11 and under stay free in parent's room. AE, DC, DISC, MC, V. Valet parking $30. Trolley: Gaslamp Quarter or Convention Center. Pets less than 75 lb. accepted with $75 fee. **Amenities:** Restaurant; 2 bars; babysitting; concierge; health club; Jacuzzi; outdoor pool; room service; full-service spa. *In room:* A/C, TV, hair dryer, Internet, minibar.

Hotel Solamar ★★ This Kimpton property is stylishly urban and sophisticated, and provides excellent Gaslamp Quarter digs, just around the corner from PETCO Park. There are the usual high-end amenities such as plush beds and flatscreen TVs, as well as more thoughtful ones including complimentary yoga accessories, art supplies, and condoms. You don't even have to leave the hotel for fine dining—Solamar's **JSix** restaurant, serving coastal California cuisine, is a creative space with lots of interesting architectural features and decor, including a wall of fezzes. Up on the fourth-floor pool deck, you'll find **Lounge Six,** featuring fire pits and cabanas. It used to be quite a scene here, but management has attempted to chill things down a bit. Just in case, though, if you plan to go to bed early, ask for a room away from the pool. This nonsmoking hotel also offers an evening wine hour in the lobby "living room."

435 Sixth Ave. (btw. J St. and Island Ave.), San Diego, CA 92101. ✆ **877/230-0300** or 619/819-9500. Fax 619/819-9539. www.hotelsolamar.com. 235 units (16 suites). $329 double; $429 suite. Children 16 and under stay free in parent's room. Packages available. AE, DC, DISC, MC, V. Valet parking $32. Bus: 3 or 120. Trolley: Gaslamp Quarter. Pets accepted (no limits, no fees). **Amenities:** Restaurant; bar; concierge; fitness center; outdoor pool; room service. *In room:* A/C, TV/DVD, CD player, hair dryer, minibar, Wi-Fi.

Ivy Hotel ★★★ The Maryland Hotel, a dowdy old property built in 1914, has been magically transformed into a world-class, high-style luxury destination called the Ivy Hotel. Its unbeatable Gaslamp Quarter address assures a steady stream of beautiful people making their way into **Envy,** the hotel's four-level nightclub. The Ivy also boasts downtown's largest rooftop pool and entertainment area, a 17,000-square-foot playground known as **Ivy Rooftop.** *Note:* These are very popular weekend nightspots; if you don't care to play along, you may want to look for other accommodations. The $75-million renovation at this nonsmoking property was overseen by a design team that has not only worked on various W Hotels, but also made a name for itself in Hollywood, art-directing projects for directors including Ridley Scott. The fashionable rooms are modern but warm, featuring 42-inch flatscreen TVs, glass-enclosed bathrooms, and high-tech workspaces; the signature suite is a split-level affair with a spiral staircase that leads to a private poolside cabana. Be sure to take advantage of a blissful soak prepared in-room by your personal Bath Butler.

650 F St. (btw. Sixth and Seventh aves.), San Diego, CA 92101. ✆ **877/489-4489** or 619/814-1000. Fax 619/531-7955. www.ivyhotel.com. 159 units. $349–$449 double; from $549 suite. Children 12 and under stay free in parent's room. Packages available. AE, DC, DISC, MC, V. Valet parking $30. Bus: 3 or 120. Pets less than 35 lb. accepted with $150 fee. **Amenities:** Restaurant; bar; nightclub; free local transportation; 24-hr. concierge; fitness center; outdoor pool; room service; spa services. *In room:* A/C, TV/DVD, CD player, MP3 docking station, full bar, hair dryer, Wi-Fi.

Keating Hotel ★ Pininfarina, the Italian design group that is the driving force behind Ferrari and Maserati, made its first foray into hotel design right here in San Diego. The Keating Hotel is located in the heart of the Gaslamp Quarter in a gorgeous Romanesque-style structure built in 1890. Boutique in size with 35 rooms, this non-smoking property features sleek, ultramodern interiors and luxury amenities, such as goose-down beds, Frette linens, Bang & Olufsen electronics, and even in-room espresso machines (gotta love those Italians). The rooms (or *"stanzas,"* as they say in Italy and at the Keating) are highly contemporary—some may find them cold—and feature an interior design that does away with walls between the bed and bathroom areas. The hotel's **Minus 1 Lounge** is a Gaslamp hot spot (the pricey cover charge is waived for guests), while the new **MerK Bistro Italiano** keeps the style quotient high. Hotel packages are available that include the use of a Ferrari. *Note:* If you're not interested in partaking of the Gaslamp's loud and late revelry, you might want to look for quieter digs elsewhere.

432 F St. (btw. Fourth and Fifth aves.), San Diego, CA 92101. *(C)* **877/753-2846** or 619/814-5700. Fax 619/814-5750. www.keatinghotel.com. 35 units. From $279 double; from $779 suite. One child 11 and under stays free in parent's room. Packages available. AE, DC, DISC, MC, V. Valet parking $30. Bus: 3, 120, or 992. Pets less than 20 lb. accepted with $150 fee. **Amenities:** Restaurant; bar; babysitting; 24-hr. concierge; room service; spa services. *In room:* A/C, TV/DVD, CD player, hair dryer, minibar, MP3 docking station, free Wi-Fi.

Manchester Grand Hyatt San Diego ★

If you're looking for a room with a view, you can't do better than this twin-towered behemoth. The shorter structure, a 33-story expansion completed in 2003, stands alongside the original 40-story hotel, built in 1992. The tallest waterfront building on the West Coast, it's crowned by the **Top of the Hyatt** lounge—definitely worth a visit whether you are staying here or not. The hotel is adjacent to the convention center and Seaport Village shopping complex. These facilities and attractions create a neatly insular, if touristy, little world, complete with bayside parks, restaurants, a marina, and a walking path. In the other direction, busy Harbor Drive separates the hotel from the rollicking Gaslamp Quarter. *Note:* Gay rights activists have called for a boycott of this property in response to the owner's $125,000 contribution to Proposition 8 which, as of this writing, has outlawed same-sex marriage in California; see www.boycottmanchesterhotels.com.

1 Market Place (Market St. at Harbor Dr.), San Diego, CA 92101. *(C)* **800/233-1234** or 619/232-1234. Fax 619/233-6464. www.manchestergrand.hyatt.com. 1,625 units (95 suites). $289–$364 double; from $500 suite. Children 17 and under stay free in parent's room. Packages available. AE, DC, DISC, MC, V. Valet parking $32; self-parking $22. Trolley: Seaport Village. Pets accepted. **Amenities:** 3 restaurants; 3 bars; concierge; exercise room; 2 Jacuzzis; outdoor pool; room service, spa; 2 tennis courts. *In room:* A/C, TV, hair dryer, minibar, Wi-Fi.

Marriott San Diego Gaslamp Quarter ★

The Marriott chain took control of a 22-story eyesore hotel and in 2004 turned it into something worthy of this happening Gaslamp Quarter location. A massive renovation transformed the property into a stylish, nonsmoking destination with a boutique feel, despite its 300-plus rooms. A sleek, street-level restaurant and bar, **Soleil@K,** complements an even hipper outdoor bar on the top floor. With its fire pits and direct views into nearby PETCO Park, **Altitude** is worth a visit even if you're staying elsewhere. The hotel has no pool, though, so if that's important to you, stay elsewhere (although guests here do have access to the pool a few blocks away at the Marriott San Diego Hotel & Marina, below).

660 K St. (btw. Sixth and Seventh aves.), San Diego, CA 92101. *(C)* **888/800-8118** or 619/696-0234. Fax 619/231-8199. www.sandiegogaslamphotel.com. 306 units. $335–$485 double; from $575 suite. AE, DC, DISC, MC, V. Valet parking $30. Trolley: Gaslamp Quarter. **Amenities:** Restaurant; 2 bars; concierge; concierge-level rooms; exercise room; access to pool at Marriott San Diego Hotel & Marina; room service. *In room:* A/C, TV, CD player, hair dryer, Wi-Fi.

Marriott San Diego Hotel & Marina ★★

Well before the San Diego Convention Center was even a blueprint, the Marriott's stylish, mirrored towers, with their banquet rooms and ballrooms, *were* a convention center. Today they merely stand next door, garnering a large share of convention attendees who are drawn to the scenic 446-slip marina, lush grounds, waterfall pool, and breathtaking bay-and-beyond views. This nonsmoking property competes with the newer Grand Hyatt next door, so guests benefit from constantly improved facilities and decor. Leisure travelers can also take advantage of greatly reduced weekend rates and enjoy a free-form tropical pool area (at the edge of downtown, no less). Note that all rooms in the north tower have a small balcony, but only the suites in the south tower do. Because the Marriott tends to focus on public features and business services, guest quarters are well maintained but plain, and standard rooms are on the small side. **Roy's Hawaiian Fusion** restaurant operates on-site, perched alongside the marina.

333 W. Harbor Dr. (at Front St.), San Diego, CA 92101. 𝄐 800/228-9290 or 619/234-1500. Fax 619/234-8678. www.marriott.com. 1,362 units. $335–$459 double; from $765 suite. Children 17 and under stay free in parent's room. AE, DC, DISC, MC, V. Valet parking $30; self-parking $21. Trolley: Convention Center. Pets accepted with $75 fee. **Amenities:** 3 restaurants; bar; bikes; concierge; concierge-level rooms; exercise room; Jacuzzi; 2 lagoonlike outdoor pools; room service; sauna; 6 lighted tennis courts; watersports equipment/rentals. *In room:* A/C, TV, hair dryer, Internet, minibar.

Omni San Diego Hotel ★★   This downtown property has a fourth-floor "sky-bridge" that connects it with PETCO Park—it's the only hotel in the United States that's directly linked to a major-league ballpark. Twelve rooms even have (limited) views of the field. A signature suite is decked out in baseball collectors' items (trimmed in the Padres' team colors), and the hotel's common areas are decorated with baseball memorabilia, such as Babe Ruth's 1932 contract with the Yankees and Joe DiMaggio's cleats from his record-setting 1941 season. Packages that include tickets to a Padres game are available. Outside of baseball season, this 32-story high-rise caters to the business crowd, luring convention-eers with more than 27,000 square feet of meeting space and an up-to-the-minute business center. The hotel's street-level function space is fronted by a surprisingly adventurous art gallery that focuses on the work of California artists; while **McCormick & Schmick's Seafood Restaurant** adds name recognition to the on-site dining offerings.

675 L St. (at Sixth Ave.), San Diego, CA 92101. 𝄐 888/444-6664 or 619/231-6664. Fax 619/231-8060. www.omnihotels.com. 511 units. $389 double; from $500 suite. Children 11 and under stay free in parent's room. Packages available. AE, DC, DISC, MC, V. Valet parking $30. Trolley: Gaslamp Quarter. Pets under 40 lb. accepted with $50 nonrefundable fee. **Amenities:** 2 restaurants; 2 bars; concierge; exercise room; Jacuzzi; outdoor pool; room service. *In room:* A/C, TV/DVD, hair dryer, minibar, MP3 docking station, Wi-Fi.

The US Grant ★★★   Following a 20-month, $56-million renovation, one of San Diego's most historic properties reopened in the fall of 2006. Originally built in 1910 by the son of two-term United States president and Civil War general Ulysses S. Grant, this grandiose 11-story property sits at the northern edge of the Gaslamp Quarter. An impressive Beaux Arts beauty, the Grant is part of the Starwood Hotel & Resorts' Luxury Collection and is owned by the Sycuan Band of the Kumeyaay Nation. In a nice touch of irony, the tribe was given its sovereignty in 1875 by President Grant. Guest rooms all have 9-foot ceilings, plush wool carpets, ornate moldings, custom furniture, Italian linens, and Native American artwork in the foyer. Over each bed is an original abstract painting created on-site by a commissioned artist. In-room spa services incorporating local herbs and plants are also available. The **Grant Grill,** long a clubby spot for power lunches and dinners, has been given an Art Deco modern makeover, with plenty of curves, creamy white leather booths, rich mahogany, and iron filigrees. The restaurant serves regional, seasonal cuisine complemented by local and international wines and beers.

326 Broadway (btw. Third and Fourth aves., main entrance on Fourth Ave.), San Diego, CA 92101. 𝄐 800/237-5029 or 866/837-4270. Fax 619/239-9517. www.usgrant.net. 270 units (47 suites). From $341 double; from $519 suite. Children 17 and under stay free in parent's room. Packages available. AE, DC, DISC, MC, V. Valet parking $28. Bus: Numerous downtown routes, including 2, 3, 7, 20, 120, 923, 929, and 992. Trolley: Civic Center. Most dogs less than 40 lb. accepted with $150 fee. **Amenities:** Restaurant; 2 bars; babysitting; 24-hr. concierge; exercise room; room service. *In room:* A/C, TV, CD player, hair dryer, minibar, Wi-Fi.

W San Diego ★★   With its dynamic restaurant and lounges, the W took San Diego by storm when it opened in 2003, delivering swanky nightlife beyond the Gaslamp Quarter. Rooms are bright and cheery—like mod beach cabanas beamed into downtown, replete with beach ball-shaped pillows, cozy window seats, and sexy showers. For those who want to go all out, the WoW suite on the 19th floor is a 1,250-square-foot luxury accommodations with a host of state-of-the-art features and killer skyline views. The restaurant, **Rice,** has an adventurous and playful menu featuring contemporary global cuisine. The adjoining lounge, **Magnet,** has a menu of creative cocktails, while the airy lobby bar, **Living Room,** has turntables and board games (good luck concentrating on your chess match). **Beach,** on the third floor, is where the developers let it rip: The open-air bar has a sand floor (heated at night), a fire pit, and cabanas. Drinks are served in plastic, allowing you to safely roam the terrace barefoot. Pets feel the love here, too—the hotel offers "peticure" nail and paw treatments and doggie happy hours (last Tues of the month, from 5–7pm).

421 W. B St. (at State St.), San Diego, CA 92101. © **619/398-3100.** Fax 619/231-5779. www.whotels.com/sandiego. 259 units. From $360 double; from $599 suite. Children 11 and under stay free in parent's room. AE, DC, DISC, MC, V. Valet parking $28. Bus: 810 or 820. Trolley: American Plaza. Dogs accepted, usually under 40 lb., with $100 fee plus $25 extra per night. **Amenities:** Restaurant; 3 lounges; free local transportation; 24-hr. concierge; exercise room; pool; room service; spa. *In room:* A/C, TV/DVD, CD player, hair dryer, minibar, Wi-Fi.

EXPENSIVE

Hard Rock Hotel San Diego ★★   A far cry from the tired burger-and-memorabilia joint over on Fourth Avenue, this 12-story condo-hotel has a sweet location—right at the gateway to the Gaslamp Quarter—and plenty of star power. The Black Eyed Peas weigh in with a million-dollar "doped-out" suite specially designed by the group. It's one of 17 "Rock Star" suites, some of which include private decks, fire pits, outdoor hot tubs, and 270-degree city views. Standard rooms are hip and modern, with sophisticated furnishings and 42-inch TVs; accommodations are also well soundproofed from the Gaslamp hubbub. Master chef Nobuyuki Matsuhisa, who has partnered with actor Robert De Niro on restaurants around the world, adds San Diego to the list with **Nobu,** the hotel's signature eatery (p. 99). The Hard Rock, which opened in late 2007, also features two music venues (**Folsom,** a 500-person-capacity indoor space, and **Woodstock,** a 9,000-sq.-ft. area next to the pool), a full-service spa, and a retail boutique.

207 Fifth Ave. (btw. K and L sts.), San Diego, CA 92101. © **866/751-7625** or 619/702-3000. Fax 619/702-3007. www.hardrockhotelsd.com. 420 units. From $250 double; from $389 suite. AE, DC, DISC, MC, V. Valet parking $30. Trolley: Gaslamp Quarter. **Amenities:** 2 restaurants, 2 bars; 2 music venues; concierge; exercise room; pool; room service; spa. *In room:* A/C, TV, hair dryer, minibar, MP3 docking station, Wi-Fi.

The Westgate Hotel ★★   It may look like a 1970s office building from the outside, but the interior of the Westgate Hotel is positively Palace of Versailles. With its lush and lavish decor, which includes plenty of baroque furnishings, antiques, chandeliers, a sweeping grand staircase, and gorgeous floral displays, this is about as "Old World" as San Diego gets. This nonsmoking property is a hub of cultural and culinary activities, including afternoon teas, wine dinners, and special events. It has a great downtown location across the street from the Horton Plaza shopping center and the beginning of the Gaslamp Quarter. Behind the hotel is the San Diego Concourse, featuring convention spaces, the Civic Theatre, and the seat of city government. There's even a trolley stop right on the corner. International foods including wine, cheese, and chocolates are available at the **Gourmet Wine and Delicatessen,** and there's a sumptuous Sunday brunch (10am–2pm); the cozy piano bar is a great spot for a nightcap.

1055 Second Ave. (btw. Broadway and C St.), San Diego, CA 92101. ⓒ **800/522-1564** or 619/238-1818. Fax 619/557-3737. www.westgatehotel.com. 223 units. From $245 double; from $500 suite. Children 13 and under stay free in parent's room. Packages available. AE, DC, DISC, MC, V. Valet parking $27. **Bus:** Numerous downtown routes, including 2, 3, 7, 20, 120, 923, 929, and 992. Trolley: Civic Center. **Amenities:** 2 restaurants; 2 bars; babysitting; 24-hr. concierge; exercise room; room service; spa services. *In room:* A/C, TV/DVD, hair dryer, free Internet, minibar, MP3 docking station.

MODERATE

Best Western Bayside Inn   This high-rise representative of reliable Best Western offers quiet lodgings, even though this corner of downtown has been a hotbed of rede-velopment. Although calling it "bayview" would be more accurate than "bayside," rooms in the 14-story hotel reveal nice city and harbor views. Rooms and bathrooms are basic chain-hotel issue, but they are well maintained and have balconies overlooking the bay or downtown (ask for the higher floors). The accommodating staff makes this a mecca for budget-minded business travelers, and this Best Western is also close to downtown's tourist sites. It's an easy walk to the Embarcadero, a bit farther to Horton Plaza, and just 3 blocks to the train station.

555 W. Ash St. (at Columbia St.), San Diego, CA 92101. ⓒ **800/341-1818** or 619/233-7500. Fax 619/239-8060. www.baysideinn.com. 122 units. $174 double. Extra person $10. Children 11 and under stay free in parent's room. Rates include continental breakfast. AE, DC, DISC, MC, V. Parking $10–$17. Bus: 83, 810, or 820. Trolley: American Plaza. **Amenities:** Restaurant (breakfast daily, dinner Mon–Fri only, no lunch); free airport transfers (7am–11pm); Jacuzzi; outdoor pool. *In room:* A/C, TV, fridge, hair dryer, free Internet, microwave.

Holiday Inn on the Bay ★★ (Kids)   This better-than-average Holiday Inn is reliable and nearly always offers great deals. The three-building high-rise complex is on the Embarcadero across from the harbor and the Maritime Museum. This scenic spot is only 1¹⁄₂ miles from the airport (you can watch planes landing and taking off) and 2 blocks from the train station and trolley. Rooms, while basic and identical, always seem to sport clean new furnishings and plenty of thoughtful comforts. The only choice you have to make is whether you want marvelous bay views or a look at San Diego's still-evolving skyline. In either case, request the highest floor possible.

1355 N. Harbor Dr. (at Ash St.), San Diego, CA 92101-3385. ⓒ **800/972-2802** or 619/232-3861. Fax 619/232-4924. www.holiday-inn.com/san-onthebay. 600 units. From $180 double; from $360 suite. Children 17 and under stay free in parent's room. AE, DC, DISC, MC, V. Valet parking $28; self-parking $22. Bus: 2, 210, 810, 820, 850, 860, 923, or 992. Trolley: American Plaza. Pets accepted with $25 nightly fee and $100 deposit. **Amenities:** 3 restaurants; 2 bars; babysitting; bikes; concierge; exercise room; outdoor heated pool; room service. *In room:* A/C, TV, hair dryer, Wi-Fi.

Horton Grand ★ (Finds)   A cross between an elegant hotel and a charming inn, the Horton Grand combines two hotels that date from 1886: the Grand Horton (once an infamous red-light establishment) and the Brooklyn Hotel (which sat above a saddlery). Both were saved from demolition, moved to this spot, and connected by an airy atrium lobby filled with white wicker. The facade, with its graceful bay windows, is original (see p. 183 for more on the Horton Grand's history). Each room at this nonsmoking property is unique, containing vintage furnishings and gas fireplaces; bathrooms are lush with reproduction floor tiles, fine brass fixtures, and genteel appointments. Rooms overlook either the city or the fig tree–filled courtyard; they're divided between the clubby and darker "saddlery" side and the pastel-toned and Victorian "brothel" side. The suites (really just large studio-style rooms) are in a newer wing; choosing one means sacrificing historical character for a sitting area/sofa bed and minibar with microwave. If you're lonely, request room no. 309, where the resident ghost, Roger, likes to hang out. The **Palace Bar** serves afternoon tea Saturdays from 2:30 to 5pm.

311 Island Ave. (at Fourth Ave.), San Diego, CA 92101. **℗ 800/542-1886** or 619/544-1886. Fax 619/239-3823. www.hortongrand.com. 132 units. From $179 double; from $279 suite. Extra person $20. Children 17 and under stay free in parent's room. AE, DC, MC, V. Valet parking $25. Bus: 3, 11, or 120. Trolley: Convention Center. **Amenities:** Restaurant (breakfast only); bar. *In room:* A/C, TV, hair dryer, Wi-Fi.

The Sofia Hotel ★   Built in 1926 and originally known as the Pickwick, this gorgeous Gothic Revival brick structure was once one of the city's luxury properties, offering the city's first "en suite" bathrooms. Following an 18-month, $16-million renovation, the Sofia Hotel opened with renewed charm and sparkle in 2007. Centrally located on the edge of the Gaslamp Quarter and a short distance from the Embarcadero and Little Italy, the Sofia has a comfortably chic design scheme and features modern amenities. This nonsmoking property keeps things humming 24/7: A concierge is available day and night, a 24-hour yoga studio features audio and video programming and an on-call instructor, and the complimentary business center is open round-the-clock. Worth a visit is the Sofia's restaurant, **Currant.** This American-style bistro has a romantically baroque design and serves breakfast, lunch, and dinner. It was also the first San Diego establishment to reintroduce absinthe cocktails, which until recently were illegal in the U.S.

150 W. Broadway (btw. Front St. and First Ave.), San Diego, CA 92101. **℗ 800/826-0009** or 619/234-9200. Fax 619/544-9879. www.thesofiahotel.com. 211 units. From $169 double; from $269 suite. Children 17 and under stay free in parent's room. Packages available. AE, DC, DISC, MC, V. Valet parking $28. Bus: Numerous downtown routes including 2, 7, 15, 30, 150, 923, and 992. Trolley: Civic Center. Small pets accepted with $50 fee. **Amenities:** Restaurant; bar; 24-hr. concierge; exercise room; spa services. *In room:* A/C, TV, fridge, hair dryer, Internet, microwave, MP3 docking station.

INEXPENSIVE

Inexpensive motels line Pacific Highway between the airport and downtown. The **Harbor View Days Inn Suites,** 1919 Pacific Hwy. at Grape Street (℗ **800/329-7466** or 619/232-1077; www.daysinn.com), is within walking distance of the Embarcadero, the Maritime Museum, and the Harbor Excursion. Rates start around $100. Also see "Hostels," earlier on p. 60.

Gaslamp Plaza Suites ★★ (Value)   This restored Edwardian beauty is right in the center of the vibrant Gaslamp Quarter. Built in 1913, its 11 stories made it San Diego's first skyscraper. Crafted (at great expense) of Australian gumwood, marble, brass, and exquisite etched glass, the splendid building originally housed San Diego Trust & Savings. Various other businesses (jewelers, lawyers, doctors, photographers) set up shop here until 1988, when the elegant structure was placed on the National Register of Historic Places and reopened as a boutique hotel. Timeless elegance abounds at this nonsmoking property, from the wide corridors to the guest rooms furnished with European flair. Most rooms are spacious and offer luxuries rare in this price range, such as pillow-top mattresses and premium toiletries; microwaves and dinnerware; and impressive luxury bathrooms. Beware of the cheapest rooms on the back side—they are uncomfortably small (although they do have regular-size bathrooms) and have no view. The higher floors boast splendid city and bay views, as do the rooftop patio and breakfast room. And despite noise-muffling windows, don't be surprised to hear a hum from the street below when things gets rockin' on the weekends.

520 E St. (corner of Fifth Ave.), San Diego, CA 92101. ✆ **800/874-8770** or 619/232-9500. Fax 619/238-9945. www.gaslampplaza.com. 64 units. From $119 double; from $189 suite. Extra person $15. Rates include continental breakfast. AE, DC, DISC, MC, V. Valet parking $26. Bus: 3 or 120, plus numerous downtown routes. Trolley: Fifth Ave. **Amenities:** Concierge; room service. *In room:* A/C, TV, fridge, hair dryer, microwave, Wi-Fi.

Hotel Occidental ★ (Finds)   Located in Bankers Hill and conveniently situated between Hillcrest and downtown, the Hotel Occidental is also just a block from Balboa Park. Built as a Knights of Columbus meeting place in 1923, the attractive mission-style architecture has been restored to its original glory. The hotel features kitchenettes in all rooms, free wireless Internet, free use of bicycles, and a daily continental breakfast. Rooms are available with both shared and private bathrooms. Other nice touches at this nonsmoking property include a business center, laundry service, and a garden patio.

410 Elm St. (btw. Fourth and Fifth aves.), San Diego, CA 92101. ✆ **800/205-9897** or 619/232-1336. Fax 619/232-1331. www.hoteloccidental-sandiego.com. 54 units. From $69 double; $139 suite. Rates include continental breakfast. AE, MC, V. Limited self-parking $10; street parking. Bus: 3 or 120. **Amenities:** Bikes; concierge. *In room:* A/C, TV/DVD, hair dryer, kitchenette, free Wi-Fi.

La Pensione Hotel ★ (Value)   This place has a lot going for it: up-to-date amenities, remarkable value, a convenient location in Little Italy within walking distance of the central business district, a friendly staff, and free parking (a rare perk for hotels in San Diego). The Pensione is built around a courtyard and feels like a small European hotel. The decor throughout is contemporary and streamlined, with plenty of sleek black and metallic surfaces, crisp white walls, and modern wood furnishings. Each moderately sized but comfortable room offers a ceiling fan and minifridge; some have a small balcony. None have air-conditioning; you can open your window, but keep in mind that street cafes stay busy till midnight on weekends. If you're sensitive to noise, request a room away from the street, though this means no bay or city view. La Pensione is within walking distance of eateries (two restaurants are directly downstairs), nightspots, and a trolley station.

606 W. Date St. (at India St.), San Diego, CA 92101. ✆ **800/232-4683** or 619/236-8000. Fax 619/236-8088. www.lapensionehotel.com. 75 units. $90 double. AE, DC, DISC, MC, V. Limited free underground parking. Bus: 83. Trolley: Little Italy. *In room:* TV, fridge, hair dryer, Internet.

Little Italy Hotel ★   Originally a boardinghouse for Italian fishermen, this renovated 1910 property is a boutique bed-and-breakfast just steps from the galleries, delightful eateries, and hip boutiques of Little Italy. It's also just a short distance from the Gaslamp Quarter and Balboa Park. While preserving the building's historic architecture, the owner has added the latest in guest comforts, such as wireless Internet and a healthful, filling continental breakfast. The accommodations are cozy, romantic, and tastefully appointed with antiques, but are not fussy or precious; every room is unique and smoke-free (smoking is allowed on the outdoor patio only). Some feature bay views, in-room Jacuzzi tubs, or kitchenettes (one has a full kitchen), as well as oversize closets, wood floors, and spacious bathrooms with plush bathrobes; some rooms have shared bathrooms. And though the inn is located at an intersection of planes, trains, and automobiles, the rooms are well insulated from the sound.

505 W. Grape St. (at India St.), San Diego, CA 92101. ✆ **800/518-9930** or 619/230-1600. Fax 619/230-0322. www.littleitalyhotel.com. 23 units. From $99 double; from $199 suite. Extra person $15. Rates include continental breakfast. AE, DISC, MC, V. Street parking only. Bus: 83. *In room:* A/C, TV/DVD, fridge, hair dryer, free Wi-Fi.

Rodeway Inn & Suites Downtown   Set in the northern corner of downtown, this place is good for business travelers without expense accounts and vacationers who just need reliable, safe accommodations. This humble chain motel must be surprised to find itself in a quickly gentrifying part of town: The El Cortez Hotel across the street has been transformed into upscale condos and shops, and new residential construction has blossomed nearby. The Rodeway is designed so rooms open onto exterior walkways surrounding the drive-in entry courtyard, lending an insular feel in this once-dicey part of town. *Note:* The hilltop location gives thighs a workout on the walk to and from the Gaslamp Quarter, but third-floor rooms offer the best chance of a view.

719 Ash St. (at Seventh Ave.), San Diego, CA 92101. © **877/424-6423** or 619/232-2525. Fax 619/687-3024. www.rodewayinn.com. 67 units. From $79 double; from $109 suite. Extra person $15. Children 17 and under stay free in parent's room. Rates include continental breakfast. AE, DISC, MC, V. Parking $14. Bus: 850 or 860. Pets less than 35 lb. accepted, one-time $25 fee. *In room:* A/C, TV, fridge (in some), hair dryer, microwave (in some), free Wi-Fi.

4 HILLCREST & UPTOWN

The gentrified historic neighborhoods north of downtown are something of a bargain; they're convenient to Balboa Park and offer easy access to the rest of town. Filled with casual and upscale restaurants, eclectic shops, and percolating nightlife, the area is also easy to navigate. All of the following accommodations cater to the mainstream market and attract a gay and lesbian clientele, as well.

A note on driving directions: You can reach all of these accommodations from I-5.

VERY EXPENSIVE

Britt Scripps Inn ★★★   One of San Diego's most glorious Victorian houses was lovingly restored in 2005 into what is now known as the Britt Scripps Inn. Built around 1887, the property was occupied for more than 45 years by one of San Diego's most prominent families: the Scripps. The home and surrounding grounds have been converted into a nine-room "estate hotel"—part B&B, part luxury hotel. Offering first-class amenities such as 1,000-thread-count sheets, flatscreen TVs, free Wi-Fi, and heated towel racks, this gracious lady lays on the personal charm as well, with gourmet breakfasts including homemade pastries and breads, late-afternoon wine and cheese, and a vintage Steinway piano in the music alcove. Staff is always on-site, but usually out of sight. The inn has a list of striking architectural elements—seven gables, a dramatic turret, wraparound porch, twisting oak staircase, and a two-story, three-paneled stained-glass window. And it's all just a block away from Balboa Park.

406 Maple St. (at Fourth Ave.), San Diego, CA 92103. © **888/881-1991** or 619/230-1991. Fax 619/230-1188. www.brittscripps.com. 9 units. From $375 double. Rates include full breakfast and afternoon wine and hors d'oeuvres. AE, DC, MC, V. Bus: 3 or 120. Take the Laurel St. exit off I-5, make a left on Laurel, a left on Fifth Ave., and a left on Maple St. *In room:* A/C, TV/DVD, CD player, hair dryer, MP3 docking station, free Wi-Fi.

MODERATE

The Cottage   Tucked behind a homestead-style house at the end of a residential cul-de-sac is this romantic hideaway. Built in 1913, the Cottage is surrounded by gardens growing herbs and climbing roses, and has its own private entry. More of a vacation rental than a B&B (breakfast is not included), the Cottage is filled with walnut and oak antique furnishings—the proprietor used to run an antiques store, and it shows. There's a wood-burning stove in the living room as well as a queen-size sofa bed; the bedroom has a king-size bed. This charming space also has a fully equipped kitchen and a full bathroom. The Cottage is 5 blocks from the cafes of Mission Hills and Hillcrest and a short drive from Balboa Park. Book early for this find.

3829 Albatross St. (off Robinson Ave.), San Diego, CA 92103. ℂ **619/299-1564.** Fax 619/299-6213. www. sandiegobandb.com. 1 unit. $125–$149. Extra person $10. 2-night minimum stay. AE, DISC, MC, V. Bus: 10. Take Washington St. exit off I-5, exit at University Ave., right on First Ave., right on Robinson Ave. *In room:* TV, hair dryer, kitchen.

Crone's Cobblestone Cottage Bed & Breakfast ★ (Finds)

Artist and bookmaker Joan Crone lives in the architectural award-winning addition to her 1913 Craftsman bungalow, a designated historical landmark. Her warmly welcomed guests have the run of the entire house, including a book-filled, wood-paneled den and antiques-filled living room. Both cozy guest rooms are nonsmoking and have antique beds, goose-down pillows and comforters, and eclectic bedside reading. They share a full bathroom; the Eaton Room also has a private half bathroom. You can rent the entire house (two bedrooms plus the den), to sleep five or six. Mission Hills, the neighborhood a half-mile west of Hillcrest, is one of San Diego's treasures, and lots of other historic homes can be explored along quiet streets.

1302 Washington Place (4 blocks west of Goldfinch St. at Ingalls St.), San Diego, CA 92103. ℂ **619/295-4765.** www.cobblestonebandb.com. 2 units. $150 double. Rates include continental breakfast. 3-night minimum stay. No credit cards (checks accepted). Bus: 10. From I-5, take the Washington St. exit east uphill. Make a U-turn at Goldfinch, and then keep right at the Y intersection onto Washington Place. *In room:* No phone.

Park Manor Suites ★ (Value)

This eight-story property was built as a full-service luxury hotel in 1926 and sits on a prime corner overlooking Balboa Park. Although dated, guest rooms are huge and very comfortable, featuring full kitchens, dining rooms, living rooms, and bedrooms with a separate dressing area. A few have glassed-in terraces; request one when you book. The overall feeling is that of a prewar East Coast apartment building, complete with steam heat and lavish moldings. Park Manor Suites does have its weaknesses, particularly bathrooms that have mostly original fixtures and could use some renovation. There's an old-world restaurant on the ground floor (with piano bar), and lunch is served weekdays in the penthouse banquet room (the view is spectacular). On Friday evenings, the penthouse bar becomes the launching pad for the gay party scene, drawing big crowds.

525 Spruce St. (btw. Fifth and Sixth aves.), San Diego, CA 92103. ℂ **800/874-2649** or 619/291-0999. Fax 619/291-8844. www.parkmanorsuites.com. 74 units. From $169 studio; from $199 1-bedroom suite; $309 2-bedroom suite. Extra person $15. Children 11 and under stay free in parent's room. Rates include continental breakfast. AE, DC, DISC, MC, V. Free parking. Bus: 3 or 120. Take Washington St. exit off I-5, right on Fourth Ave., left on Spruce. **Amenities:** Restaurant; bar; access to nearby health club ($5); room service. *In room:* TV, hair dryer, kitchen, free Wi-Fi.

Sommerset Suites Hotel ★

This all-suite hotel on a busy street was originally built as apartment housing for interns at the nearby hospital. This nonsmoking property retains a welcoming, residential ambience and features unexpected amenities such as huge closets, medicine cabinets, and fully equipped kitchens in all rooms (even dishwashers). Rooms are oversize and comfortably furnished, and each has a private balcony; be prepared for noise from the busy thoroughfare below, though. Poolside barbecue facilities encourage warm-weather mingling, while just across the street you'll find several blocks'

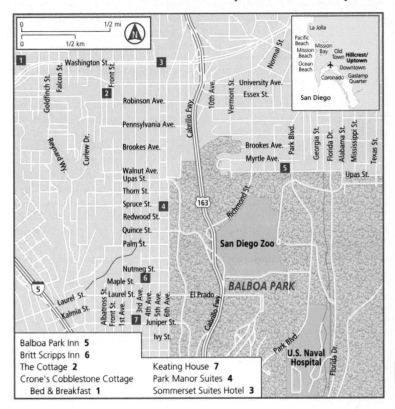

Balboa Park Inn **5**
Britt Scripps Inn **6**
The Cottage **2**
Crone's Cobblestone Cottage
  Bed & Breakfast **1**

Keating House **7**
Park Manor Suites **4**
Sommerset Suites Hotel **3**

WHERE TO STAY

5

HILLCREST & UPTOWN

worth of restaurants and shops, plus a multiplex cinema. Package deals and extended stays add bang to your buck here.

606 Washington St. (at Sixth Ave.), San Diego, CA 92103. (Ⓒ) **800/962-9665** or 619/692-5200. Fax 619/692-5299. www.sommersetsuites.com. 80 units. From $159. Extra person $10. Children 15 and under stay free in parent's room. Rates include continental breakfast. AE, DC, DISC, MC, V. Parking $6. Bus: 3 or 83. Take the Washington St. exit off I-5. Pets less than 35 lb. accepted with $50 nonrefundable fee. **Amenities:** Jacuzzi; outdoor pool. *In room:* A/C, TV, hair dryer, kitchen, Wi-Fi.

INEXPENSIVE

Balboa Park Inn ★   Insiders looking for unusual accommodations head straight for this small pink inn at the northern edge of Balboa Park. This cluster of four Spanish Colonial–style former apartment buildings lies in a mostly residential neighborhood a half-mile east from the heart of Hillcrest; the hotel has long been popular with gay travelers drawn to the area's restaurants and clubs. All the rooms and standard suites are themed (and nonsmoking), some evoking Victorian or Art Deco sensibilities, others reaching for a more elaborate fantasy, such as the "Orient Express" room with its red hues and Chinese wedding bed. Seven of the rooms have Jacuzzi tubs, and most have kitchens—all have private entrances, though the front desk operates 24 hours. From here, you're close enough to walk to the San Diego Zoo and other Balboa Park attractions.

3402 Park Blvd. (at Upas St.), San Diego, CA 92103. *C* **800/938-8181** or 619/298-0823. Fax 619/294-8070. www.balboaparkinn.com. 26 units. $99 double; from $149 suites. Extra person $10. Children 11 and under stay free in parent's room. Rates include continental breakfast. AE, DC, DISC, MC, V. Parking available on street. Bus: 7. From I-5, take Washington St. east, follow signs to University Ave. E., and turn right at Park Blvd. *In room:* TV, fridge, microwave, Wi-Fi.

Keating House ★★ (Finds)   This grand 1880s Bankers Hill mansion, between downtown and Hillcrest and 4 blocks from Balboa Park, has been meticulously restored by two energetic innkeepers. Even the overflowing gardens that bloom on four sides of this local landmark are authentically period. The house contains a comfortable hodgepodge of antique furnishings, and the downstairs entry, parlor, and dining room all have cozy fireplaces. Bathrooms—all private—are gorgeously restored with updated period fixtures. There are six rooms in the main house, with three additional rooms in the restored carriage house, which opens onto an exotic garden patio (all rooms are nonsmoking). Breakfast is served in a sunny, friendly setting; special dietary needs are cheerfully considered. In contrast to many B&Bs in Victorian-era homes, this one eschews dollhouse frills for a classy, sophisticated approach.

2331 Second Ave. (btw. Juniper and Kalmia sts.), San Diego, CA 92101. *C* **800/995-8644** or 619/239-8585. Fax 619/239-5774. www.keatinghouse.com. 9 units. From $115 double. Rates include full breakfast. AE, DISC, MC, V. Bus: 11. From the airport, take Harbor Dr. toward downtown, turn left on Laurel St., and then right on Second Ave. *In room:* A/C, hair dryer, no phone, Wi-Fi.

5 OLD TOWN & MISSION VALLEY

Old Town is a popular area for families because of its proximity to Old Town State Historic Park and other attractions that are within walking distance. SeaWorld and the San Diego Zoo are within a 10-minute drive. Around the corner is Mission Valley, where you'll find the city's largest collection of hotels offering rooms under $100 a night. Mission Valley lacks much personality—this is the spot for chain restaurants and shopping malls, not gardens or water views. But it caters to convention groups, families visiting the University of San Diego or San Diego State University, and leisure travelers drawn by the lower prices and competitive facilities. *A note on driving directions:* All Old Town and Mission Valley hotels are reached from either I-5 or I-8.

MODERATE

Crowne Plaza San Diego ★   Formerly known as the Red Lion Hanalei, this Mission Valley hotel has a Polynesian theme and comfort-conscious sophistication. Most rooms are split between two eight-story towers, set back from the freeway and positioned so that the balconies open onto the tropically landscaped pool courtyard or the attractive links of an adjacent golf club; a few rooms are found in a third structure, which is a little too close to the freeway. The heated outdoor pool and the oversize Jacuzzi are large enough for any luau, and there's even a waterfall in an open-air atrium. The **Islands** restaurant serves breakfast, lunch, and dinner, bringing out the sushi and pupu platters in the evening to go along with the specialty tropical cocktails. Hotel services include a free shuttle to Old Town and the Fashion Valley Shopping Center.

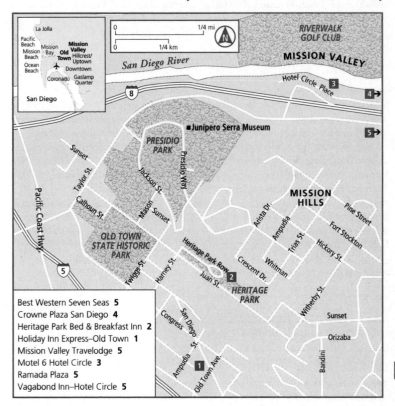

La Jolla
Pacific Beach
Mission Bay
Mission Beach
Ocean Beach
Coronado
San Diego

Mission Valley
Old Town
Hillcrest/Uptown
Downtown
Gaslamp Quarter

0   1/4 mi
0   1/4 km

San Diego River

RIVERWALK GOLF CLUB

MISSION VALLEY

Hotel Circle Place **3**

4→

■Junipero Serra Museum

5→

PRESIDIO PARK

Presidio Way

Sunset
Taylor St.
Jackson St.
Calhoun St.
Mason
Sunset

Pacific Coast Hwy.

OLD TOWN STATE HISTORIC PARK

Heritage Park Row

MISSION HILLS

Arista Dr.
Ampudia
Trias St.
Pine Street
Fort Stockton
Hickory St.

Crescent Dr.
Whitman

Twiggs St.
Harney St.
Juan St.

2

HERITAGE PARK

Witherby St.

Sunset

Congress
San Diego
Orizaba

Ampudia St.
Old Town Ave.

Bandini

1

Best Western Seven Seas **5**
Crowne Plaza San Diego **4**
Heritage Park Bed & Breakfast Inn **2**
Holiday Inn Express–Old Town **1**
Mission Valley Travelodge **5**
Motel 6 Hotel Circle **3**
Ramada Plaza **5**
Vagabond Inn–Hotel Circle **5**

2270 Hotel Circle N., San Diego, CA 92108. ☎ **800/227-6963** or 619/297-1101. Fax 619/297-6049. www.cp-sandiego.com. 417 units. From $152 double; from $300 suite. AE, DC, DISC, MC, V. Parking $12. Bus: 14. From I-8, take Hotel Circle exit, follow signs for Hotel Circle N. **Amenities:** 2 restaurants; bar; exercise room; nearby golf course (packages available); Jacuzzi; outdoor pool; room service; spa. *In room:* A/C, TV, hair dryer, Internet.

Heritage Park Bed & Breakfast Inn ★★   This exquisite 1889 Queen Anne mansion is set in a Victorian park—an artfully arranged cobblestone cul-de-sac lined with historic buildings saved from the wrecking ball and assembled here as a tourist attraction. Most of the rooms at this nonsmoking property are in the main house, with a handful of equally appealing choices in an adjacent 1887 Italianate companion. Surrender to the pampering of breakfast by candlelight, afternoon tea, or watching the sunset from a veranda rocking chair. Like the gracious parlors and porches, each room is meticulously outfitted with period antiques and luxurious fabrics; the small staff provides turndown service and virtually anything else you might require. Although the fireplaces are all ornamental, some rooms have whirlpool baths. In the evenings, classic films on DVD are shown in the Victorian parlor, complete with popcorn.

2470 Heritage Park Row, San Diego, CA 92110. ☎ **800/995-2470** or 619/299-6832. Fax 619/299-9465. www.heritageparkinn.com. 12 units. From $125 double. Extra person $20. Rates include full breakfast and afternoon tea. AE, DC, DISC, MC, V. Free parking. Bus: Numerous Old Town routes, including 10, 14, and 30. Trolley: Old Town. Take I-5 to Old Town Ave., turn left onto San Diego Ave., and then turn right onto Harney St. *In room:* Ceiling fan, DVD player, hair dryer, free Wi-Fi.

Holiday Inn Express–Old Town ★   Just a couple of easy walking blocks from the heart of Old Town, this Holiday Inn has a Spanish Colonial exterior that suits the neighborhood's theme. Inside you'll find better-than-they-have-to-be contemporary furnishings and surprising small touches that make this hotel an affordable option favored by business travelers and families alike. The hotel is smartly oriented toward the inside; request a room whose patio or balcony opens onto the pleasant courtyard. Rooms are thoughtfully and practically appointed, with extras such as microwaves and writing tables. The lobby, surrounded by French doors, features a large fireplace, several sitting areas, and a TV. Although the address is listed as Old Town Avenue, the hotel entrance is on Jefferson Street, which runs perpendicular to Old Town Avenue.

3900 Old Town Ave., San Diego, CA 92110. ☎ **800/972-2802** or 619/299-7400. Fax 619/299-1619. www. hiexpress.com/ex-oldtown. 125 units. From $162 double; from $184 suite. Extra person $10. Children 17 and under stay free in parent's room. Rates include continental breakfast. AE, DC, DISC, MC, V. Parking $12. Bus: 10 or 30. Trolley: Old Town. Take I-5 to Old Town Ave. exit. **Amenities:** Jacuzzi; outdoor pool. *In room:* A/C, TV, fridge, microwave, Wi-Fi.

INEXPENSIVE

Room rates at properties on Hotel Circle are significantly cheaper than those in many other parts of the city. You'll find a cluster of inexpensive chain hotels and motels, including **Best Western Seven Seas** (☎ **800/328-1618** or 619/291-1300; www.bestwestern.com), **Mission Valley Travelodge** (☎ **800/578-7878** or 619/297-2271; www.travelodge.com), **Ramada Plaza** (☎ **800/272-6232** or 619/291-6500; www.ramada.com), and **Vagabond Inn-Hotel Circle** (☎ **800/522-1555** or 619/297-1691; www.vagabondinn.com).

Motel 6 Hotel Circle   Yes, it's a Motel 6, so you know the drill: no mint on the pillow and you have to trundle down to the front desk to retrieve a cup of coffee in the morning. On the other hand, these budget hotels—now part of the mammoth Accor chain, one of the world's largest hotel companies—know how to provide a consistent product at dependably inexpensive rates, and this one is very central to San Diego's sightseeing. The modern, four-story motel sits at the western end of Hotel Circle. Rooms are sparingly but adequately outfitted, with standard motel furnishings; bathrooms are perfunctory. Stay away from the loud freeway side—rooms in the four-story structure in back overlook a scenic 18-hole golf course and river.

2424 Hotel Circle N., San Diego, CA 92108. ☎ **800/466-8356** or 619/296-1612. Fax 619/543-9305. www. motel6.com. 204 units. From $80 double. Extra person $3. Children 17 and under stay free in parent's room. AE, DC, DISC, MC, V. Free parking. Bus: 14. From I-8, take Taylor St. exit. Pets accepted. **Amenities:** Outdoor pool. *In room:* A/C, TV, Wi-Fi.

6 MISSION BAY & THE BEACHES

If the beach and aquatic activities are front-and-center on your San Diego agenda, this part of town may be just the ticket. Although the beach communities don't offer much in the way of cultural or upscale attractions, downtown and Balboa Park are only a

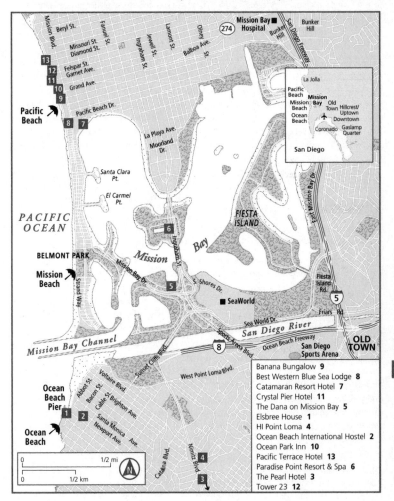

Banana Bungalow **9**
Best Western Blue Sea Lodge **8**
Catamaran Resort Hotel **7**
Crystal Pier Hotel **11**
The Dana on Mission Bay **5**
Elsbree House **1**
HI Point Loma **4**
Ocean Beach International Hostel **2**
Ocean Park Inn **10**
Pacific Terrace Hotel **13**
Paradise Point Resort & Spa **6**
The Pearl Hotel **3**
Tower 23 **12**

WHERE TO STAY

5

MISSION BAY & THE BEACHES

15-minute drive away. Some hotels are right on Mission Bay, San Diego's water playground; they're usually good choices for families. Ocean Beach is more neighborhood-oriented and easygoing, while Mission Beach and Pacific Beach provide a taste of the beach-bum lifestyle—they can be a bit raucous at times, especially in summer. If you're looking for a more refined landing, head to La Jolla or Coronado.

Accommodations here tend to book up solid on summer weekends and even some weekdays (rates shown are for summer). But discounts can be found, especially for those who try walk-up bookings on the afternoon of arrival—admittedly, a risky proposition on a Friday or Saturday in July and August. *A note on driving directions:* All directions are provided from I-5.

Crystal Pier Hotel ★★ (Finds) (Kids)   If historical charm is higher on your wish list than hotel-style service, head to this unique cluster of cottages sitting literally over the surf on the vintage Crystal Pier in Pacific Beach. You'll get a separate living room and bedroom, a fully equipped kitchen, and a private patio with breathtaking ocean views—all within the whitewashed walls of carefully renovated cottages from 1936 (the pier itself dates to 1927). Each of the Cape Cod–style cottages has a deck; the more expensive units farthest out have more privacy. Six less expensive units are not actually on the pier, but still offer sunset-facing sea views. Guests drive right out and park beside their cottages, a real boon on crowded weekends. This nonsmoking operation is strictly BYOBT (beach towels), and the office is open only from 8am to 8pm. These accommodations book up fast; reserve at least 4 to 6 months in advance. Or with luck, you might be able to nab someone's canceled reservation.

4500 Ocean Blvd. (at Garnet Ave.), San Diego, CA 92109. © **800/748-5894** or 858/483-6983. Fax 858/483-6811. www.crystalpier.com. 29 units. From $300 double; $500 for larger unit sleeping 6. 3-night minimum in summer, 2-night minimum in winter. DISC, MC, V. Free parking. Bus: 8, 9, 27, or 30. Take I-5 to Grand/Garnet exit; follow Garnet to the pier. **Amenities:** Beach equipment rental. In room: TV, kitchen.

Pacific Terrace Hotel ★   This modern hotel on the boardwalk swaggers with a heavy-handed South Seas–meets–Spanish Colonial ambience. Rattan fans circulate in the lobby and hint at the sunny Indonesian-inspired decor in guest rooms. More upscale than most of the casual places nearby, it's at the north end of the Pacific Beach boardwalk. Large, comfortable guest rooms each come with balconies or terraces and fancy wall safes; bathrooms, designed with warm-toned marble and natural woods, have a separate sink/vanity area. About half the rooms have kitchenettes, and top-floor rooms in this three-story hotel enjoy particularly nice views. Management keeps cookies, coffee, and iced tea at the ready throughout the day. The lushly landscaped pool and hot tub are literally 15 feet from the boardwalk, overlooking a relatively quiet stretch of beach. Four nearby restaurants allow meals to be billed to the hotel, but there's no restaurant on the premises.

610 Diamond St., San Diego, CA 92109. © **800/344-3370** or 858/581-3500. Fax 858/274-3341. www.pacificterrace.com. 73 units. From $359 double; from $490 suite. Children 12 and under stay free in parent's room. Extra person $15. 2- to 4-night minimums apply in summer. AE, DC, DISC, MC, V. Parking $20. Bus: 30. Take I-5 to Grand/Garnet exit and follow Grand or Garnet west to Mission Blvd., turn right (north), and then left (west) onto Diamond. **Amenities:** Concierge; exercise room; Jacuzzi; pool; room service; spa services. In room: A/C, TV/DVD, fridge, hair dryer, microwave (in some), minibar, Wi-Fi.

Paradise Point Resort & Spa ★★ (Kids)   Smack-dab in the middle of Mission Bay, this hotel complex is almost as much a theme park as its closest neighbor, SeaWorld (a 3-min. drive away). Single-story accommodations are spread across 44 tropically landscaped acres of duck-filled lagoons, lush gardens, and swim-friendly beaches; all have private verandas and plenty of thoughtful conveniences. The resort was updated with refreshingly colorful beach-cottage decor, while still retaining its low-tech 1960s charm. Standard "lanai" rooms range considerably in price, based solely on view; despite daunting high-season rack rates, though, you can usually get a deal here. An upscale waterfront restaurant, **Baleen,** offers fine dining in a contemporary, fun space. A stunning Indonesian-inspired spa offers cool serenity and aroma-tinged Asian treatments; this spa is a vacation in itself.

1404 Vacation Rd. (off Ingraham St.), San Diego, CA 92109. © **800/344-2626** or 858/274-4630. Fax 858/581-5924. www.paradisepoint.com. 462 units. From $329 double; from $495 suite. Extra person $20.

Children 17 and under stay free in parent's room. AE, DC, DISC, MC, V. Parking $22. Bus: 8 or 9. Follow I-8 west to Mission Bay Dr. exit; take Ingraham St. north to Vacation Rd. **Amenities:** 2 restaurants; 2 bars; bikes; concierge; exercise room; 18-hole miniature golf course; Jacuzzi; 5 outdoor pools; room service; tennis/basketball courts; full-service spa; marina w/watersports equipment/rentals. *In room:* A/C, TV, fridge, hair dryer, Internet.

Tower 23 ★★   Named for a lifeguard station that once pulled duty nearby, Tower 23 is a modernist beach resort that opened in 2005. Sitting on the Pacific Beach (aka P.B.) boardwalk, the hotel enjoys a sky-high people-watching quotient matched only by its first-class contemporary amenities, including wireless Internet access right on the beach. Featuring clean lines and glass-box architecture, Tower 23's rooms all have private balconies or patios (though not all with ocean views); a guest-only second-story deck with industrial fire pit overlooks the beach. The hotel's **Tower Bar,** which has indoor/outdoor seating along the boardwalk, and **JRDN** restaurant, serving contemporary steak and seafood (there's also an eight-seat sushi bar), are worth checking out whether you're staying here or not. Although it's the most chic bar/restaurant in the area—check out the hypnotic, 75-foot-long "wave wall" and its morphing color scheme—the P.B party atmosphere still pervades. Don't be surprised if the folks at the table next to you start playing a drinking game.

723 Felspar St., San Diego, CA 92109. ✆ **866/869-3723.** Fax 858/274-2333. www.t23hotel.com. 44 units. From $309 double; from $689 suite. Children 17 and under stay free in parent's room. AE, DC, DISC, MC, V. Valet parking $20. Bus: 8, 9, 27, or 30. Take I-5 to Grand/Garnet exit, left on Grand Ave., right on Mission Blvd., left on Felspar St. Pets less than 25 lb. accepted with $150 fee. **Amenities:** Restaurant; bar; room service; spa services. *In room:* A/C, TV/DVD, CD player, hair dryer, minibar, MP3 docking station, free Wi-Fi.

EXPENSIVE

Best Western Blue Sea Lodge   Looking something like a Mediterranean resort designed by a Soviet architect, the squat, three-story Blue Sea Lodge is a reliable choice in a prime location that keeps up with the other properties in the Best Western chain. Despite the rates listed, this nonsmoking property can be a bargain; ask about possible discounts. Aesthetically, the original rooms are a snore, but nevertheless boast a balcony or patio and a handful of necessary comforts. Rooms with full ocean views overlook the sand and have more privacy than those on the street, but the Pacific Beach boardwalk has never been known for quiet or solitude. If an ocean view is not important, save a few bucks and check in to one of the units in an expansion building that opened in 2003; the decor is brighter, more enticing. The lobby offers a cafe for guests in the morning, and its heated pool and Jacuzzi are steps from the beach.

707 Pacific Beach Dr., San Diego, CA 92109-5094. ✆ **800/258-3732** or 858/488-4700. Fax 858/488-7276. www.bestwestern-bluesea.com. 128 units. From $229 double; from $409 suite. Children 17 and under stay free in parent's room. AE, DC, DISC, MC, V. Parking $12. Bus: 8 or 9. Take I-5 to Grand/Garnet exit, follow Grand Ave. to Mission Blvd. and turn left; then turn right onto Pacific Beach Dr. **Amenities:** Jacuzzi; outdoor pool. *In room:* A/C, TV, fridge, hair dryer, microwave, Wi-Fi.

Catamaran Resort Hotel ★★ (Kids)   Right on Mission Bay, the Catamaran has its own beach, complete with watersports facilities. Built in the 1950s, the hotel has been fully renovated to modern standards without losing its trademark Polynesian theme. The atrium lobby holds a 15-foot waterfall and full-size dugout canoe; koi-filled lagoons meander through the property; and torches blaze after dark. Guest rooms—in a 13-story building or one of the six two-story buildings—have subdued South Pacific decor, and each has a balcony or patio. High floors of tower rooms have commanding views, and studios and suites have kitchenettes. A 9,300-square-foot spa was added in 2005, featuring a menu of South Pacific and Asian-inspired treatments. The Catamaran is within a few blocks of Pacific Beach's restaurant-and-nightlife scene; the resort's **Moray's Lounge** features live music nightly, as well. During the summer, the Bahia Belle, a Mississippi River–style stern-wheeler boat plies Mission Bay nightly (weekends only the rest of the year); guests board free of charge. Luaus are also a part of the summer fun.

3999 Mission Blvd. (4 blocks south of Grand Ave.), San Diego, CA 92109. ✆ **800/422-8386** or 858/488-1081. Fax 858/488-1387. www.catamaranresort.com. 311 units. From $249 double; from $429 suite. Children 11 and under stay free in parent's room. AE, DC, DISC, MC, V. Valet parking $17; self-parking $13. Bus: 8 or 9. Take Grand/Garnet exit off I-5 and go west on Grand Ave., and then south on Mission Blvd. **Amenities:** Restaurant; 2 bars; bikes; children's programs; concierge; exercise room; Jacuzzi; outdoor pool; room service; full-service spa; watersports equipment/rentals. *In room:* A/C, TV, fridge (in most), hair dryer, MP3 docking station, Wi-Fi.

Ocean Park Inn ★   This oceanfront motor hotel offers simple, attractive, spacious rooms with contemporary furnishings. Although this nonsmoking property has sophistication uncommon in this surfer-populated area, you won't find much solitude with the boisterous scene outside. You can't beat the sand access and the view—both are directly onto the beach. Rates vary according to view, but most rooms have at least a partial ocean view; all have a private balcony or patio. Units in front are most desirable; but take note, it can get noisy directly above the boardwalk. Go for the second or third floor, or pick one of the junior suites, which have huge bathrooms and pool views.

710 Grand Ave., San Diego, CA 92109. ✆ **800/231-7735** or 858/483-5858. Fax 858/274-0823. www.oceanparkinn.com. 73 units. From $199 double; from $229 suite. Rates include continental breakfast. AE, DC, DISC, MC, V. Parking $10. Bus: 8, 9, or 30. Take Grand/Garnet exit off I-5; follow Grand Ave. to ocean. **Amenities:** Jacuzzi; outdoor pool; room service; spa services. *In room:* A/C, TV, fridge, hair dryer, microwave, free Wi-Fi.

MODERATE

The Beach Cottages   This family-owned operation has been around since 1948 and offers a variety of guest quarters, most of them geared to the long-term visitor. Most appealing are the 17 cute, little detached cottages just steps from the sand, though some of them lack a view. Each has a patio with tables and chairs. Adjoining apartments are perfectly adequate, especially for budget-minded families who want to log major hours on the beach—all cottages and apartments sleep four or more and have full kitchens. There are also standard motel rooms that are worn but cheap (most of these sleep two). The property features shared barbecue grills, shuffleboard courts, and table tennis, and is also within walking distance of shops and restaurants. The cottages themselves aren't pristine, but they have a rustic charm—reserve one well in advance.

4255 Ocean Blvd. (1 block south of Grand Ave.), San Diego, CA 92109-3995. ✆ **858/483-7440.** Fax 858/273-9365. www.beachcottages.com. 61 units, 17 cottages. From $140 double; from $285 cottages and apts for 4 to 6. Extra person $10. 2-night minimum on weekends. AE, DC, DISC, MC, V. Free parking. Bus: 8 or 9. Take I-5 to Grand/Garnet exit, go west on Grand Ave. and left on Mission Blvd. *In room:* TV, fridge, kitchen (in some).

The Dana on Mission Bay ★   The Dana completed a $20-million renovation and expansion in 2004, which added 74 contemporary rooms in a three-story arc wrapping around an infinity pool. Some rooms on this 10-acre property overlook bobbing sailboats in the recreational marina; others face onto the original kidney-shaped pool whose surrounding Tiki torch-lit gardens offer shuffleboard and Ping-Pong. You'll pay a little extra for bay and marina views; every one of the old rooms is the same size, with plain but well-maintained furnishings. The new rooms are bigger and feature water views and reclaimed redwood beam ceilings. Beaches and SeaWorld are a 15-minute walk away; there's also a complimentary shuttle that can take you to the theme park.

1710 W. Mission Bay Dr., San Diego, CA 92109. ℂ **800/345-9995** or 619/222-6440. Fax 619/222-5916. www.thedana.com. 270 units. From $161 double; from $259 suites. AE, DC, DISC, MC, V. Parking $12. Bus: 8 or 9. Follow I-8 west to Mission Bay Dr. exit; take W. Mission Bay Dr. **Amenities:** 2 restaurants; bikes; concierge; exercise room; 2 Jacuzzis; 2 outdoor heated pools; room service; spa services; marina w/ watersports equipment/rentals. *In room:* A/C, TV, fridge, hair dryer, microwave (in some), wet bar (in some), Wi-Fi.

Elsbree House ★ Katie and Phil Elsbree turned this modern Cape Cod–style building into an immaculate, exceedingly comfortable B&B, half a block from the water's edge in Ocean Beach. Each of the five guest rooms has a patio or balcony, as well as a private entryway and full, private bathroom. Guests share the cozy living room (with a fireplace and TV), breakfast room, and kitchen. There is also a fully furnished condo unit with private entrance; it rents for a 4-day minimum (breakfast not included in condo rental) and sleeps from two to six people. This Ocean Beach neighborhood is eclectic, occupied by ocean-loving couples, dedicated surf bums, and the occasional contingent of punk skater kids who congregate near the pier. Its strengths are proximity to the beach, a casual-but-pleasing selection of eateries and bars that attract mostly locals, and San Diego's best antiquing (along Newport Ave.).

5054 Narragansett Ave. (at Bacon St.), San Diego, CA 92107. ℂ **800/607-4133** or 619/226-4133. www. bbinob.com. 6 units. From $150 double; $1,800 per week or $350 per night 3-bedroom condo (lower rates if only 1 or 2 rooms used). 3-night minimum for advance guest room reservations in summer; 4-night minimum for condo. Rates include continental breakfast (except condo). MC, V. Bus: 35 or 923. From airport, take Harbor Dr. west to Nimitz Blvd. to Lowell St., which becomes Narragansett Ave. *In room:* Hair dryer, no phone.

The Pearl Hotel ★ (Finds) The Pearl Hotel designers took a run-down motel property and let fly with the vintage cool—the lounge area features high-style furniture and light fixtures, exposed stone, and shag carpet and throw pillows that encourage guests to relax on the floor and play a board game. Accommodations are modest in size but have been refreshed with amenities such as Internet radios and contemporary chrome bathroom fixtures; thoughtful design touches include custom mosaic artwork and a pet fish in each room. The Pearl's restaurant and lounge area is snug and features outdoor dining spaces alongside the saltwater pool (where "dive-in" movies are screened weekly). Although there are no beaches in the immediate area (the closest is over the hill in Ocean Beach), this is a nautical neighborhood, with the marinas, bars, and restaurants of Shelter Island nearby. The airport and Cabrillo National Monument are also just minutes away. This is a smoke-free property, both in rooms and common areas.

1410 Rosecrans St. (at Fenelon St.), San Diego, CA 92106. ℂ **877/732-7573** or 619/226-6100. Fax 619/226-6161. www.thepearlsd.com. 23 units. From $149 double; "Play & Stay" rate $79 after midnight (must be booked on-site, subject to availability). AE, DISC, MC, V. Parking $15. Bus: 28. Take I-5 S. to Rosecrans St. exit. **Amenities:** Restaurant; bar; bikes; outdoor saltwater pool; spa services. *In room:* A/C, TV, hair dryer, MP3 docking station, Wi-Fi.

7 LA JOLLA

"La Jolla" is thought by many to be misspelled Spanish for "the jewel," while others believe the name is derived from an indigenous word meaning "cave." One look at La Jolla's beautiful coastline and upscale downtown village, and you'll be firmly in the Spanish camp. Bargain accommodations aren't easy to find in this wealthy, conservative community. But remember, most hotels—even those in the "Very Expensive" category—have occupancy-driven rates.

If a modern business hotel is more your style, chain hotels farther afield include the **Hyatt Regency** ★★, 3777 La Jolla Village Dr. (© **888/591-1234** or 858/552-1234; www.hyatt.com). It's a glam, business-oriented place with several good restaurants next door. The **Residence Inn by Marriott** ★, 8901 Gilman Dr. (© **888/236-2427** or 858/587-1770; www.marriott.com/residenceinn), is a good choice for those who want a fully equipped kitchen and more space. Both are near the University of California, San Diego.

A note on driving directions: From **I-5 N.,** use the La Jolla Parkway exit or from **I-5 S.,** take the La Jolla Village Drive West exit, both of which merge with Torrey Pines Road.

VERY EXPENSIVE

The Grande Colonial ★★★ (Finds)
Possessed of an old-world European flair that's more London or Georgetown than seaside La Jolla, the Grande Colonial has earned accolades for its meticulous restorations over the past decade. The most recent involves the 2007 renovation of two adjacent properties, the **Little Hotel by the Sea** and the **Garden Terraces,** which add 18 more suites to the Grande Colonial fold. Some of the new suites feature ocean views, fireplaces, and full kitchens. The Little Hotel is also crowned with a way-cool rooftop loft and deck area from which you can watch the seals at play at the nearby Children's Pool. In the main hotel lounge, guests gather in front of the fireplace for drinks—often before enjoying dinner at the hotel's excellent **Nine-Ten** restaurant (p. 118). Guest rooms at this nonsmoking property are quiet and elegantly appointed, with beautiful draperies and traditional furnishings; many rooms in the original building have sea views, as well. Relics from the early days include oversize closets and meticulously tiled bathrooms. Numerous historical photos illustrate the fascinating story of the hotel, which started as a full-service apartment hotel in 1913.

910 Prospect St. (btw. Fay and Girard aves.), La Jolla, CA 92037. © **888/530-5766** or 858/454-2181. Fax 858/454-5679. www.thegrandecolonial.com. 93 units. From $295 double; from $375 suite. Children 11 and under stay free in parent's room. AE, DC, MC, V. Valet parking $18. Bus: 30. Take Torrey Pines Rd. to Prospect Place and turn right. Prospect Place becomes Prospect St. **Amenities:** Restaurant; bar; concierge; access to nearby health club; outdoor pool; room service. *In room:* A/C, TV, hair dryer, kitchen (in some), MP3 docking station, free Wi-Fi.

Hotel Parisi ★★★ (Finds)
This intimate hotel is on the second floor overlooking one of La Jolla's main intersections (street-facing rooms are well insulated from the modest din). Parisi's nurturing, wellness-inspired vibe first becomes evident in the lobby, where elements of earth, wind, fire, water, and metal blend according to feng shui principles. The Italy-meets-Zen composition is carried into the guest rooms, where custom furnishings are modern yet comfy. Parisi calls the spacious accommodations "suites" (some are more like junior suites), and each has an ergonomic desk, dimmable lighting, goosedown superluxe bedding, and creamy, calming neutral decor. Less expensive rooms at this

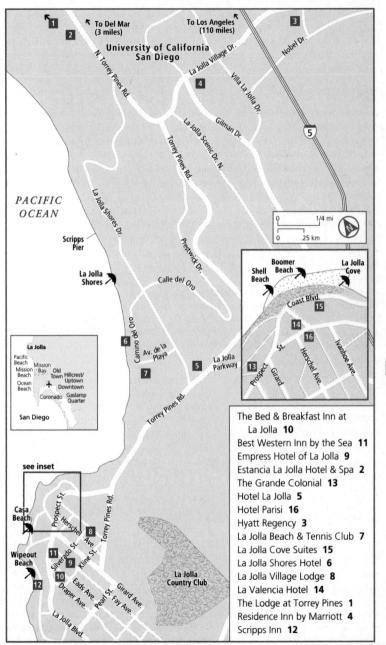

The Bed & Breakfast Inn at La Jolla **10**
Best Western Inn by the Sea **11**
Empress Hotel of La Jolla **9**
Estancia La Jolla Hotel & Spa **2**
The Grande Colonial **13**
Hotel La Jolla **5**
Hotel Parisi **16**
Hyatt Regency **3**
La Jolla Beach & Tennis Club **7**
La Jolla Cove Suites **15**
La Jolla Shores Hotel **6**
La Jolla Village Lodge **8**
La Valencia Hotel **14**
The Lodge at Torrey Pines **1**
Residence Inn by Marriott **4**
Scripps Inn **12**

nonsmoking property are smaller with little or no view; across the street from the hotel is **Parisi Apart**—seven luxury units (one- and two-bedrooms) available for extended stays. The personal service stops at nothing—there's even a menu of 24-hour in-room holistic health services (from yoga to psychotherapy).

1111 Prospect St. (at Herschel Ave.), La Jolla, CA 92037. ⓒ **877/472-7474** or 858/454-1511. Fax 858/454-1531. www.hotelparisi.com. 28 units. From $295 double; from $495 suite; extended stay from $350, 7-day minimum. Rates include continental breakfast. AE, DC, DISC, MC, V. Parking $15. Bus: 30. Take Torrey Pines Rd. to Prospect Place and turn right; Prospect Place becomes Prospect St., turn left on Herschel Ave. **Amenities:** Room service; spa services. *In room:* A/C, TV/DVD, CD player, hair dryer, minibar, Wi-Fi.

La Jolla Shores Hotel ★ (Kids)   Formerly known as the Sea Lodge, this three-story 1960s hotel in a mainly residential enclave is under the same management as the La Jolla Beach & Tennis Club next door. It has an identical on-the-sand location, minus the country-club ambience. About half the rooms at this nonsmoking property have some view of the ocean, and the rest look out on the pool or a tiled courtyard. Priced by view and size, the rooms are pretty basic but were outfitted with new furniture, carpeting, and flatscreen TVs in 2008. Bathrooms feature separate dressing areas with large closets; balconies or patios are standard, and some rooms have fully equipped kitchenettes. From the beach you can gaze toward the top of the cliffs, where La Jolla's village hums with activity (and relentless traffic). Like the LJB&TC, this property is popular with families but also attracts business travelers looking to balance meetings with time on the beach or the tennis court.

8110 Camino del Oro (at Av. de la Playa), La Jolla, CA 92037. ⓒ **866/392-8762** or 858/459-8271. Fax 858/456-9346. www.ljshoreshotel.com. 128 units. From $309 double; from $769 suite. Extra person $20. Children 11 and under stay free in parent's room. AE, DC, DISC, MC, V. Parking $14. Bus: 30. Take La Jolla Shores Dr., turn left onto Av. de la Playa, turn right on Camino del Oro. **Amenities:** Restaurant; babysitting; concierge; exercise room; Jacuzzi; 2 pools (including a wading pool for kids); room service; sauna; 2 tennis courts. *In room:* A/C, TV/DVD, fridge, hair dryer, free Internet.

La Valencia Hotel ★★★   This bastion of gentility does a fine job of resurrecting the elegance of Hollywood's golden age, when celebrities such as Greta Garbo and Charlie Chaplin vacationed here. The bluff-top hotel, which looks much like a Mediterranean villa, has been the centerpiece of La Jolla since opening in 1926. Brides still pose in front of the lobby's picture window against a backdrop of the cove and Pacific Ocean, and neighborhood cronies quaff libations in the clubby **Whaling Bar.** La Valencia is famous for its history and unbeatably scenic location, but you won't be disappointed by the old-world standards of service and style. Most rooms are quite comfortable, each boasting lavish appointments and all-marble bathrooms with signature toiletries. Because rates vary wildly according to view (from sweeping to *nada*), get a cheaper room and enjoy the scene from one of the many lounges, serene garden terraces, or the amazing pool, which fronts the Pacific and nearby Scripps Park. Room decor, layouts, and size (starting at a snug 250 sq. ft.) are all over the map, too. If you've got the bucks, spring for one of the newer villas featuring fireplaces and butler service. And—budget permitting—don't miss the hotel's 11-table **Sky Room,** one of the city's most exclusive and romantic dining rooms.

1132 Prospect St. (at Herschel Ave.), La Jolla, CA 92037. ⓒ **800/451-0772** or 858/454-0771. Fax 858/456-3921. www.lavalencia.com. 113 units. From $295 double; from $595 suites and villas. Minimum stays may be required in summer and on weekends. Pets accepted. AE, DC, DISC, MC, V. Valet parking $17. Bus: 30. Take Torrey Pines Rd. to Prospect Place and turn right. Prospect Place becomes Prospect St. **Amenities:** 3 restaurants; 2 bars; babysitting; concierge; exercise room; Jacuzzi; outdoor pool; room service; sauna; spa services. *In room:* A/C, TV/DVD, hair dryer, minibar, Wi-Fi.

The Lodge at Torrey Pines ★★★ Ten minutes north of La Jolla proper, you'll find this triumphant Craftsman-style creation at the edge of the Torrey Pines Golf Course. The Lodge brims with clinker-brick masonry, art glass windows and doors, Stickley furniture, and exquisite pottery. The less expensive rooms are an unstinting 520 square feet and lavished with Tiffany-style lamps, period wallpaper, framed Hiroshige prints, and lots of wood accents; views face a courtyard carefully landscaped to mimic the rare seaside environment that exists just beyond the hotel grounds. More expensive rooms overlook the golf course and the ocean in the distance; most of these have balconies, fireplaces, and giant bathrooms with separate tub and shower. The 9,500-square-foot spa specializes in treatments utilizing coastal sage and other local plants, and there's an elegant pool area with an elevated Jacuzzi sheltered under a gazebo from where you can gaze out to the golf course's first tee. An excellent restaurant named after painter A. R. Valentien features top-quality seasonal offerings; Valentien's wildflower watercolors line the walls. This is the only AAA 5-diamond property within the San Diego city limits.

11480 N. Torrey Pines Rd., La Jolla, CA 92037. ℭ 800/656-0087 or 858/453-4420. Fax 858/453-7464. www.lodgetorreypines.com. 171 units. From $325 double; from $800 suite. Children 17 and under stay free in parent's room. AE, DC, DISC, MC, V. Valet parking $27; self-parking $22. Bus: 101. From I-5 take La Jolla Village Dr. west, bear right (north) onto N. Torrey Pines Rd. **Amenities:** 2 restaurants; bar; concierge; exercise room; preferential tee times at the golf course; Jacuzzi; outdoor pool; room service; spa. *In room:* A/C, TV, hair dryer, minibar, Wi-Fi.

Scripps Inn ★★ ⒻⒾⓃⒹⓈ This meticulously maintained inn is hidden behind the Museum of Contemporary Art, offering seclusion even though the attractions of La Jolla are just a short walk away. Only a small, grassy park comes between the inn and the beach, cliffs, and tide pools; the view from the second-story deck can hypnotize guests, who gaze out to sea indefinitely. Rates vary depending on ocean view (all have one, but some are better than others). Rooms have a pleasant pale cream/sand palette with new bathroom fixtures and appointments. All rooms have sofa beds; two have wood-burning fireplaces, and four have kitchenettes. The inn supplies beach towels, firewood, and French pastries each morning. Repeat guests return for their favorite rooms, so book early for the best choice.

555 Coast Blvd. S. (at Cuvier), La Jolla, CA 92037. ℭ 866/860-6318 or 858/454-3391. Fax 858/456-0389. www.scrippsinn.com. 14 units. From $295 double; from $325 suite. Extra person $10. Children 4 and under stay free in parent's room. Rates include continental breakfast. AE, DC, DISC, MC, V. Parking $10. Bus: 30. Take Torrey Pines Rd., turn right on Prospect Place; past the museum, turn right onto Cuvier. *In room:* Ceiling fans, TV, fridge, hair dryer, Wi-Fi.

EXPENSIVE

Estancia La Jolla Hotel & Spa ★★★ This California rancho-style property was built on the remains of a horse farm in 2004, and shortly thereafter was named one of the world's hottest new hotels by *Condé Nast Traveler.* The 9½-acre spread has some pretty cool neighbors: the Louis I. Kahn–designed Salk Institute, UC San Diego, the Torrey Pines Gliderport, and Blacks Beach. You won't see any of those things from this self-contained retreat, but the romance created by the hacienda flavor and the meticulously maintained gardens with their native flora and bubbling fountains is diversion enough. Guest rooms face a central courtyard, and many rooms have balconies or patios. All rooms are tastefully appointed with comfy furnishings that would be at home in an upscale residence. With its old *Californio* exterior, outdoor fireplace, and live Spanish guitar music, the **Mustangs & Burros** lounge and bar is a great place to chill out. There's also an award-winning restaurant on the premises. The full-service spa offers organic-based signature treatments such as the red rose hydrating treatment and the garden vegetable wrap.

9700 N. Torrey Pines Rd., La Jolla, CA 92037. ℂ **877/437-8262** or 858/550-1000. Fax 858/550-1001 www. estanciajolla.com. 210 units. From $229 double; from $399 suite. Bed-and-breakfast packages available for an additional $20. AE, DC, DISC, MC, V. Valet parking $25; self-parking $20. Bus: 101. From I-5 take the Genesee Ave. exit westbound, go left on N. Torrey Pines Rd. **Amenities:** 2 restaurants; 2 bars; babysitting; concierge; exercise room w/yoga and personal training; Jacuzzi; outdoor pool; room service; full-service spa. *In room:* A/C, TV, hair dryer, minibar, Wi-Fi.

Hotel La Jolla   As of this writing, the hotel is still in the midst of a longtime renovation, attempting to up its style points with some contemporary flair. Although not in the village, it is within walking distance to the restaurants and the beach at La Jolla Shores (the hotel also offers a complimentary shuttle to both the village and the Shores). Many of the rooms at this nonsmoking property have balconies; if you want a room with an ocean view, try to get something above the fourth floor. The top floor is occupied by **Clay's La Jolla,** a pricey restaurant and lounge that serves breakfast, lunch, and dinner and offers spectacular views and live jazz. This is a smoke-free property.

7955 La Jolla Shores Dr. (at Torrey Pines Rd.), La Jolla, CA 92037. ℂ **800/666-0261.** Fax 858/459-7649. www.hotellajolla.com. 108 units. From $225 double; from $389 suite. Children 17 and under stay free in parent's room. Packages available. AE, DISC, MC, V. Parking $15. Bus: 30. From I-5 merge onto La Jolla Pkwy., which becomes Torrey Pines Rd., and turn right on La Jolla Shores. Dogs less than 60 lb. accepted with $75 fee. **Amenities:** Restaurant; bar w/live jazz (Wed–Sun); concierge; exercise room; Jacuzzi; outdoor heated pool; room service; spa services. *In room:* A/C, TV, fridge, hair dryer, Wi-Fi.

La Jolla Beach & Tennis Club ★ ⓞverrated   The location is unbeatable—right on La Jolla Shores beach. Standard guest rooms are plain, but most have full kitchens that are appropriate for families or longer stays. Beachfront rooms are tiny, but they're brighter, and the wide ocean panorama at the foot of your bed is undeniably splendid. A variety of suites are available, ranging from one-bedroom street-side digs to deluxe two- and three-bedroom accommodations facing the ocean; the 35 beachfront suites have been updated with new paint, carpets, and furnishings. The beach is popular and staff stays busy shooing away nonguests—in California, all beaches are public up to the median high-tide line, and the property strictly enforces its boundaries. Kayaks and watersports equipment can be rented; there are a 3-par pitch-and-putt golf course and lighted tennis courts; and you can even make arrangements for your own private beach barbecue in the evening. The hotel's distinctive **Marine Room** restaurant is one of San Diego's very best. All told, though, you get better room value for your money at the club's sister hotel next door, the La Jolla Shores Hotel (p. 84).

2000 Spindrift Dr., La Jolla, CA 92037. ℂ **800/640-7702** or 858/454-7126. Fax 858/456-3805. www.ljbtc. com. 98 units. From $259 double; from $409 suite. 3-night minimum in summer. Extra person $20. Children 11 and under stay free in parent's room. AE, DC, MC, V. Free parking. Bus: 30. Take La Jolla Shores Dr., turn left on Paseo Dorado, and follow to Spindrift Dr. **Amenities:** 2 restaurants; seasonal beach snack bar; babysitting; children's programs; exercise room; 9-hole pitch-and-putt golf course; 75-ft. heated, outdoor pool; room service; 12 lighted tennis courts; spa services; watersports equipment/rentals. *In room:* A/C, TV/DVD, movie library, CD player, hair dryer, free Internet, MP3 docking station.

La Jolla Cove Suites   Tucked beside prime oceanview condos across from Ellen Browning Scripps Park, this family-run 1950s-era catbird seat actually sits closer to the ocean than its pricey uphill neighbor, La Valencia. The to-die-for ocean view is completely unobstructed, and La Jolla Cove—one of California's prettiest swimming spots—is steps away. The property is peaceful at night, but village dining and shopping are only

The Road to Wellness—Healthful Havens

Health-conscious San Diego is home to a collection of some of the finest fitness spas in the country. These aren't pedicure-and-a-sauna resort spas, but places where you will engage in regimented mind-and-body workouts that just might change your life.

The **Golden Door** ★★★, 777 Deer Springs Rd., Escondido (✆ **800/424-0777** or 760/744-5777; www.goldendoor.com), is a Zen-influenced sanctuary in the North County where a maximum of 40 people engage in a weeklong program of massage, beauty treatments, and fitness activities such as yoga, tennis, and hiking. Most weeks are same-sex, but coed stays are also available; a four-to-one ratio of staff (including a fitness guide, dietician, and esthetician) to guests helps explain the $7,495 price tag (some 3- and 4-day programs are also available). Accommodations and gourmet spa-cuisine meals, featuring products grown on-site, are included.

Rancho La Puerta ★★★, Carretera A Km 5, Tecate, Mexico (✆ **800/443-7565** or 858/764-5500; www.rancholapuerta.com), is the Golden Door's sister property, located about an hour from San Diego, just across the border in Baja California. Opened in 1940, it lays claim to being the world's first fitness spa. This elegant, beautifully landscaped resort is set on some 3,000 acres and encompasses part of a mountain held sacred by the indigenous Kumeyaay people. Weeklong residences are encouraged, but a limited number of partial stays are available. More than 70 classes and activities are held each week. All-inclusive rates range start at $2,890.

Cal-a-Vie ★★★, 29402 Spa Havens Way, Vista (✆ **866/772-4283** or 760/842-6831; www.cal-a-vie.com), sits on 200-plus acres in San Diego's North County, offering 3-, 4-, and 7-night packages. A maximum of 30 guests enjoy exceptional spa cuisine, fitness classes, hiking, lectures, and spa treatments. A nearby golf course provides a golf option. Three-night plans start at $3,995.

Chopra Center for Wellbeing ★★, 2013 Costa del Mar Rd., Carlsbad (✆ **888/424-6772** or 760/494-1600; www.chopra.com), is located on the grounds of the La Costa Resort and Spa (p. 240). Founded by holistic guru Deepak Chopra, the center has yoga and meditation classes daily (including a free group meditation held every day), spa treatments based on 5,000-year-old Ayurvedic principles, multiday healing programs, and a gift store with books, jewelry, and more. An overnight stay is not required, but a special rate is offered.

Warner Springs Ranch, 31652 Hwy. 79, Warner Springs (✆ **760/782-4200;** www.warnersprings.com), was established in 1844, but Spanish explorers and Native Americans had long known about the area's rejuvenating mineral springs. Located in the Cleveland National Forest, about 90 minutes from San Diego, the ranch features three large pools of hot mineral or fresh water; there are also an equestrian center, golfing, and hiking trails. Overnight accommodations and packages start at $80.

a short walk away. You'll pay according to the quality of your view; about 80% of guest quarters gaze upon the ocean. Most rooms are wonderfully spacious, each featuring a fully equipped kitchen, plus a private balcony or patio; they have functional but almost institutional furnishings. An oceanview rooftop deck offers lounge chairs and cafe tables; breakfast is served there each morning.

1155 Coast Blvd. (across from the Cove), La Jolla, CA 92037. ℂ 888/525-6552 or 858/459-2621. Fax 858/551-3405. www.lajollacove.com. 90 units. From $242 double; from $341 suite. Extra person $25. Children 12 and under stay free in parent's room. Rates include continental breakfast. AE, DC, DISC, MC, V. Parking $15. Bus: 30. Take Torrey Pines Rd. to Prospect Place and turn right. When the road forks, veer right (downhill) onto Coast Blvd. Pets accepted with $25 nightly fee. **Amenities:** Access to nearby health club; Jacuzzi; heated outdoor pool. *In room:* A/C (in some), TV, kitchen.

MODERATE

The Bed & Breakfast Inn at La Jolla ★★ (Finds)

This 1913 house designed by San Diego's first important architect, Irving Gill, is the setting for this cultured and elegant B&B. Reconfigured as lodgings, the house—which was the family home of composer/conductor John Philip Sousa in the 1920s—has lost none of its charm. This nonsmoking inn features lovely enclosed gardens and a cozy library and sitting room. Some rooms have a fireplace or ocean view; each room has a private bathroom, most of which are on the compact side. The period furnishings are tasteful and cottage-style, with plenty of old photos of La Jolla adding to the sense of history. A gourmet breakfast is served wherever you desire—dining room, patio, sun deck, or in your room. There is afternoon wine and cheese offered daily in summer; an evening nightcap of sherry and sweets is provided in the off season.

7753 Draper Ave. (near Prospect), La Jolla, CA 92037. ℂ 888/988-8481 or 858/456-2066. Fax 858/456-1510. www.innlajolla.com. 15 units. From $174 double; from $329 suite. 2-night minimum on weekends. Rates include full breakfast; afternoon wine and cheese is served daily in summer. AE, DISC, MC, V. Limited free parking. Bus: 30. Take Torrey Pines Rd. to Prospect Place and turn right. Prospect Place becomes Prospect St.; proceed to Draper Ave. and turn left. *In room:* A/C, hair dryer, Wi-Fi.

Best Western Inn by the Sea ★

The Best Western (and the more formal Empress, a block away; below) offers a terrific alternative to pricier digs nearby. Occupying an enviable location at the heart of La Jolla's charming village, this independently managed, nonsmoking property puts guests just a short walk from the cliffs and beach. The low-rise tops out at five stories, with the upper floors enjoying ocean views (and the highest room rates). Rooms here are Best Western standard issue—freshly maintained, but nothing special. All rooms do have balconies, though, and refrigerators are available at no extra charge; in addition, the hotel offers plenty of welcome amenities.

7830 Fay Ave. (btw. Prospect and Silverado sts.), La Jolla, CA 92037. ℂ 800/526-4545 or 858/459-4461. Fax 858/456-2578. www.bestwestern.com/innbythesea. 129 units. From $169 double; from $249 suite. Children 17 and under stay free in parent's room. Rates include continental breakfast. AE, DC, DISC, MC, V. Parking $12. Bus: 30. Take Torrey Pines Rd. to Prospect Place and turn right. Prospect Place becomes Prospect St.; proceed to Fay Ave. and turn left. **Amenities:** Restaurant; airport shuttle; access to nearby health club; outdoor heated pool. *In room:* A/C, TV, hair dryer, Internet.

Empress Hotel of La Jolla ★

The Empress Hotel offers spacious, nonsmoking quarters with traditional furnishings a block or two from La Jolla's main drag and the ocean. It's quieter here than at the premium cliff-top properties, and you'll sacrifice little other than direct ocean views (many rooms on the top floors afford a partial view). If you're planning to explore La Jolla on foot, the Empress is a good base; it exudes a class many comparably priced chains lack, with warm service to boot. Rooms are tastefully decorated and well equipped; four "Empress" rooms have sitting areas with full-size sleeper sofas. Breakfast is set up next to a serene sun deck; you can grab dinner at the hotel's **Manhattan** restaurant, a loungey, old-school Italian spot.

7766 Fay Ave. (at Silverado), La Jolla, CA 92037. (✆ **888/369-9900** or 858/454-3001. Fax 858/454-6387. www.empress-hotel.com. 73 units. From $169 double; from $329 suite. Rates include continental breakfast. AE, DC, DISC, MC, V. Valet parking $13. Bus: 30. Take Torrey Pines Rd. to Girard Ave., turn right, and then left on Silverado St. **Amenities:** Restaurant; bar; exercise room; room service; spa services. *In room:* A/C, TV, fridge, hair dryer, Wi-Fi.

INEXPENSIVE

Wealthy, image-conscious La Jolla is really *not* the best place for deep bargains, but if you're determined to stay here as cheaply as possible, you won't do better than the **La Jolla Village Lodge,** 1141 Silverado St., at Herschel Avenue (✆ **877/551-2001** or 858/551-2001; www.lajollavillagelodge.com). This 30-room motel is standard Americana, arranged around a small parking lot with cinder-block construction and small, basic rooms. Rates vary wildly by season and day of the week—a room that costs $90 midweek in February doubles in price for a summer weekend.

8 CORONADO

The "island" (really a peninsula) of Coronado is a great escape. It has quiet, architecturally rich streets; a small-town, Navy-oriented atmosphere; and one of the state's most beautiful and welcoming beaches. Coronado's resorts are especially popular with Southern California and Arizona families for weekend escapes. Although downtown San Diego is just a 10-minute drive or 15-minute ferry ride away, you may feel a bit isolated in Coronado, so it isn't your best choice if you're planning to spend lots of time in more central parts of the city.

A note on driving directions: To reach the places listed here, take I-5 to the Coronado Bridge, and then follow individual directions.

VERY EXPENSIVE

Hotel del Coronado ★★★   Opened in 1888 and designated a National Historic Landmark in 1977, the "Hotel Del" is the last of California's stately old seaside hotels. This monument to Victorian grandeur boasts tall cupolas, red turrets, and gingerbread trim, all spread out over 28 acres. Even if you don't stay here, be sure to stroll through the sumptuous, wood-paneled lobby or along the pristine, wide beach. Rooms run the gamut from compact to extravagant, and all are packed with antique charm. The least expensive rooms are snug and have views of a roof or parking lot; the best are junior suites with large windows and balconies fronting one of the state's finest white-sand beaches. Almost half the hotel's rooms are in the renovated, seven-story tower—it has more living space, but none of the historical ambience. The Del's signature restaurant, **1500 Ocean,** opened to rave reviews in 2006. Distinctive and contemporary, it serves a sophisticated "Southland Coastal" cuisine. And don't miss the Sunday brunch in the amazing **Crown Room.** Since 2001, the Del has done nonstop restoration and upgrading, with recent additions including a state-of-the-art spa and the creation of **Beach Village,** a collection of 78 "coastal cottages." These privately owned two- and three-bedroom condos feature fireplaces and oceanview balconies or terraces, and are available for rental.

1500 Orange Ave., Coronado, CA 92118. ℂ **800/468-3533** or 619/435-6611. Fax 619/522-8238. www.
hoteldel.com. 757 rooms. From $340 double; from $465 suite; from $950 cottage. Extra person $25.
Children 17 and under stay free in parent's room. Minimum stay requirements apply most weekends.
$25/day resort fee. AE, DC, DISC, MC, V. Valet parking $33; self-parking $25. Bus: 901 or 904. From Coro-
nado Bridge, turn left onto Orange Ave. **Amenities:** 5 restaurants; 4 bars; airport transfers; babysitting;
bikes; children's programs; concierge; health club; 2 Jacuzzis; 2 outdoor pools; room service; full-service
spa. *In room:* A/C, TV, hair dryer, Internet, minibar.

Marriott Coronado Island Resort ★★ Elegance and luxury here are understated.
Although the physical property is generic, the staff goes out of its way to provide upbeat
attention. Guests just seem to get whatever they need, be it a lift downtown (by water
taxi from the private dock), a tee time at the neighboring golf course, or a prime appointment at the spa. Despite its mostly business clientele, this nonsmoking hotel offers many
enticements for the leisure traveler: a prime waterfront setting with a sweeping view of
the San Diego skyline, a location within a mile of Coronado shopping and dining, walking distance from the ferry landing, and a wealth of sporting and recreational activities.
Guest rooms are generously sized and attractively furnished in colorful French Country
style, and all feature balconies or patios. The superbly designed bathrooms hold an array
of fine toiletries. In terms of room size and amenities, your dollar goes farther here than
at the Hotel Del.

2000 Second St. (at Glorietta Blvd.), Coronado, CA 92118. ℂ **888/236-2427** or 619/435-3000. Fax
619/435-3032. www.marriotthotels.com/sanci. 300 units. From $379 double; from $479 suite. Children 11
and under stay free in parent's room. AE, DC, MC, V. Valet parking $28; self-parking $22. Bus: 901 or 904.
Ferry: From Broadway Pier. From Coronado Bridge, turn right onto Glorietta Blvd., take 1st right to hotel.
Amenities: 2 restaurants; bar; babysitting; bikes; concierge; exercise room; 2 Jacuzzis; 3 outdoor pools;
room service; spa; 6 lighted tennis courts; watersports equipment/rentals. *In room:* A/C, TV, hair dryer,
minibar, MP3 docking station, Wi-Fi.

EXPENSIVE

El Cordova Hotel ★ This Spanish hacienda across the street from the Hotel del
Coronado began life as a private mansion in 1902. By the 1930s, it had become a hotel.
Shaped like a baseball diamond and surrounding a courtyard with meandering tiled
pathways, flowering shrubs, a swimming pool, and patio seating for **Miguel's Cocina
Mexican** restaurant, El Cordova hums pleasantly with activity. Each room is a little different—some sport a Mexican Colonial ambience, while others evoke a comfy beach
cottage. Most rooms in this nonsmoking hotel have kitchenettes with gas stoves; all feature ceiling fans and brightly tiled bathrooms, but lack much in the way of frills. El
Cordova's prime location makes it a popular option; reserve several months in advance
for summer months. Facilities include a barbecue area with picnic table.

1351 Orange Ave. (at Adella Ave.), Coronado, CA 92118. ℂ **800/229-2032** or 619/435-4131. Fax 619/435-
0632. www.elcordovahotel.com. 40 units. From $225 double; from $325 suite. Children 11 and under stay
free in parent's room. Extra person $10. AE, DC, DISC, MC, V. Parking in neighboring structure $8. Bus: 901
or 904. From Coronado Bridge, turn left onto Orange Ave. **Amenities:** 3 restaurants; bikes; Internet in
lobby; Jacuzzi; outdoor pool; watersports equipment/rentals. *In room:* A/C, TV.

Glorietta Bay Inn ★★ Right across the street from the Hotel Del, this pretty, white
hotel consists of the charmingly historic John D. Spreckels mansion and several
younger—and decidedly less charming—motel-style buildings. Only 11 rooms are in the
mansion, which dates from 1908, and it boasts original fixtures, a grand staircase, and
music room with a player piano. The guest rooms are decked out in antiques and have a
romantic and nostalgic ambience. Rooms and suites in the 1950s annexes are much less

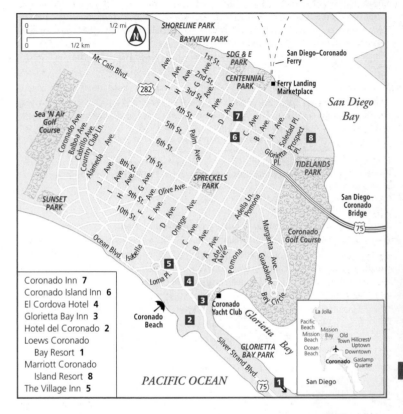

Coronado Inn **7**
Coronado Island Inn **6**
El Cordova Hotel **4**
Glorietta Bay Inn **3**
Hotel del Coronado **2**
Loews Coronado
Bay Resort **1**
Marriott Coronado
Island Resort **8**
The Village Inn **5**

expensive but were upgraded from motel-plain to better match the main house's classy vibe; some have kitchenettes and marina views. The least expensive units are small and have parking-lot views. Wherever your room is, you'll enjoy the inn's excellent customer service. Glorietta Bay, with its boat rentals and excursions, is right outside your door, and the hotel is within easy walking distance of the beach, golf, tennis, watersports, shopping, and dining. Rooms in the mansion are booked early, but are worth the extra effort and expense; this is a nonsmoking hotel.

1630 Glorietta Blvd. (near Orange Ave.), Coronado, CA 92118. © **800/283-9383** or 619/435-3101. Fax 619/435-6182. www.gloriettabayinn.com. 100 units. From $185 double; from $260 suite. Extra person $10. Children 17 and under stay free in parent's room. Rates include continental breakfast and afternoon refreshment. AE, DC, DISC, MC, V. Self-parking $10. Bus: 901 or 904. From Coronado Bridge, turn left on Orange Ave. After 2 miles, turn left onto Glorietta Blvd.; the inn is across the street from the Hotel del Coronado. **Amenities:** Babysitting; concierge; access to nearby health club; Jacuzzi; outdoor pool; spa services. *In room:* A/C, TV/DVD, CD player, fridge, hair dryer, free Wi-Fi.

Loews Coronado Bay Resort ★★ (Kids   Located on its own private 15-acre penin- sula 4 miles south of downtown Coronado, across the highway from the Silver Strand State Beach, the Loews is an all-inclusive resort destination. It offers a plethora of water-related activities such as sailing and jet-skiing from its private 80-slip marina; it also has direct, private access to the beach. It's a family-friendly place with special (healthy) kids' menus, supervised children's activities, and teen-themed DVDs and Gameboys to borrow; pets are always welcome—and catered to—at Loews, as well. Adult pleasures include romantic gondola rides through the canals of the adjacent Coronado Cays, an exclusive waterside community; fine dining at the excellent **Mistral** restaurant (ask for table 61 or 64 for best vistas); and a full-service spa, one of the few in Southern California to offer *watsu*, the shiatsu-influenced massage that is given as you float in a pool heated to body temperature.

4000 Coronado Bay Rd., Coronado, CA 92118. © **866/563-9792** or 619/424-4000. Fax 619/424-4400. www.loewshotels.com. 440 units. From $240 double; from $475 suite. Up to 2 children 17 and under stay free in parent's room. Extra person $25. Packages available. AE, DC, DISC, MC, V. Valet parking $28; self-parking $22. Bus: 901. From Coronado Bridge, turn left on Orange Ave., left on Coronado Bay Rd. Pets accepted with $25 fee. **Amenities:** 2 restaurants; 2 bars; babysitting and pet-sitting; children's programs; concierge; exercise room and classes; 2 Jacuzzis; 3 outdoor pools; room service; spa; 3 lighted tennis courts; marina w/watersports equipment/rentals. *In room:* A/C, TV/DVD, CD player, hair dryer, Internet, minibar.

MODERATE

Coronado Inn ★ Centrally located and terrifically priced, this renovated 1940s courtyard motel has such a friendly ambience, it's like staying with old friends. A continental breakfast is served poolside in the morning; iced tea, lemonade, and fresh fruit are provided in the lobby each afternoon. It's still a motel, though, so rooms are pretty basic. There are six rooms with small kitchens at this nonsmoking hotel; microwaves are available in the rest. Rooms close to the street are noisiest, so ask for one toward the back. The Coronado shuttle stops a block away; it serves the shopping areas and Hotel Del. The Coronado Inn's sister property, the **Coronado Island Inn,** 301 Orange Ave. (© **888/436-0935** or 619/435-0935), is a block away and offers some of the cheapest digs on the island.

266 Orange Ave. (corner of 3rd St.), Coronado, CA 92118. © **800/598-6624** or 619/435-4121. www.coronadoinn.com. 30 units. From $104 double; from $249 suite. Children 16 and under stay free in parent's room. Extra person $15. Rates include continental breakfast. AE, DISC, MC, V. Free parking. Bus: 901 or 904. From Coronado Bridge, stay on 3rd St. Pets accepted with $15 nightly fee. **Amenities:** Outdoor pool. *In room:* A/C, TV, fridge, hair dryer, microwave, Wi-Fi.

INEXPENSIVE

The Village Inn Ⓥalue Its location a block or two from Coronado's main sights is this inn's most appealing feature. Historical charm runs a close second; a plaque outside identifies the three-story brick-and-stucco hotel as the once-chic Blue Lantern Inn, built in 1928. The vintage lobby sets the mood in this European-style hostelry; each simple but well-maintained room holds a four-poster bed and antique dressers and armoires, plus lovely Battenberg lace bedcovers and shams. Front rooms enjoy the best view, and the communal full kitchen is available day and night for guest use. The inn's only Achilles' heel is tiny (but private) bathrooms, though some have been updated with Jacuzzi tubs.

1017 Park Place (at Orange Ave.), Coronado, CA 92118. © **619/435-9318.** www.coronadovillageinn.com. 15 units. $85–$95 double. Rates include continental breakfast. AE, MC, V. Parking available on street. Bus: 901 or 904. From Coronado Bridge, turn left onto Orange Ave., and then right on Park Place. **Amenities:** Kitchen. *In room:* TV.

San Diego's airport has the unusual distinction of being virtually in the downtown area. This is good news for travelers: The accommodations reviewed in the downtown, Hillcrest, and Old Town/Mission Valley sections are only 10 to 15 minutes from the airport.

For those who wish to stay even closer, there are two good airport hotels, both bayside properties. The 1,044-room **Sheraton San Diego Hotel & Marina,** 1380 Harbor Island Dr. (*©* **800/325-3535** or 619/291-2900; www.starwoodhotels.com), offers rooms from $249. At the 211-room **Hilton San Diego Airport/Harbor Island,** 1960 Harbor Island Dr. (*©* **800/445-8667** or 619/291-6700; www.hilton.com), rooms start at $189. Both hotels offer a marina view, a pool, and a 10-minute drive to downtown San Diego—as always, hefty discounts are usually available.

Where to Dine

Thanks to an influx of creative, young chefs—often incorporating the bounty of local farms and ranches into their menus—San Diego's fine-dining scene has come into its own during the past decade.

You'll find terrific seafood, frequently featured in California cuisine and Italian fare, which dominate the scene; while eclectic fusion food has carved out a substantial niche, as well. Of course, San Diego still has plenty of clubby steak-and-potato stalwarts and no shortage of chain eateries.

Number one on most visitors' list of culinary priorities is Mexican food—a logical choice given the city's history and location. You'll find lots of Americanized, fairly satisfying interpretations of Mexican fare (that is, combo plates heaped with melted cheddar cheese) along with a few hidden gems. And don't miss our humble fish taco, perhaps the city's favorite fast food.

In this chapter, restaurants in San Diego proper are indexed by location and price category. Note, however, that some of San Diego's best dining venues lie 30 to 40 minutes to the north, in the communities of Rancho Santa Fe, Del Mar, and Carlsbad. These are found in chapter 11, as are dining options for the Disneyland area and south of the border.

For diners on a budget, the more expensive San Diego restaurants are usually accommodating if you prefer to order a few appetizers instead of a main course, and many offer reasonably priced lunch menus. And now, more than ever, restaurants are seeking ways to drive business—look for a plethora of two-for-one deals, bargain-priced prix-fixe meals, or happy hour specials, even at the city's top dining destinations. *Note:* In keeping with our beach culture, even in the more pricey places, dress tends to be casual.

Discount coupons are also found in the *San Diego Weekly Reader,* available free on Thursdays (and known as the *Weekly* in an edited version distributed at local hotels). Quite a few restaurants offer "early bird" specials, as well—discounted dining for those who don't mind being seated by 6pm or so.

Restaurants are categorized by price, which includes the average cost of one entree, an appetizer (if the entree does not come with a side dish or appetizer), one *nonalcoholic* drink, tax, and tip. **Very Expensive** means a meal averages $50 per person and up; **Expensive** means it costs $30 to $50; **Moderate** means it's $15 to $30; and **Inexpensive** means it's less than $15.

A note on parking: Unless a listing specifies otherwise, drivers can expect to park within 2 or 3 blocks of the restaurants listed here. If you can't find a free or metered space on the street, you can seek out a garage or lot; most Gaslamp Quarter and La Jolla venues offer valet parking.

1 BEST BETS FOR DINING

- **Best Spot for a Business Lunch: Dobson's Bar & Restaurant,** 956 Broadway Circle, downtown San Diego (© **619/231-6771**), has been mixing business and pleasure for more than 20 years. You'll literally rub shoulders (thanks to the restaurant's cozy setup) with power brokers and politicos. See p. 101.

- **Best View:** Many restaurants overlook the ocean, but only from **Brockton Villa,** 1235 Coast Blvd., La Jolla (✆ 858/454-7393), can you see sublime La Jolla Cove. See p. 121.

- **Best Value:** The word "huge" barely begins to describe the portions at **Filippi's Pizza Grotto,** 1747 India St. (✆ 619/232-5094), where a salad for one is enough for three, and an order of lasagna must weigh a pound. There's a kids' menu as well. Filippi's has locations all over, including Pacific Beach, Mission Valley, and Escondido. See p. 105.

- **Best Seafood:** Matt Rimel, owner of **Zenbu,** 7660 Fay Ave., La Jolla (✆ 858/454-4540), loved fishing so much he bought a commercial fishing boat. Then he opened a restaurant so he could do something with the catch. Zenbu is also an excellent spot for sushi. See p. 121.

- **Best Contemporary American Cuisine:** With **Market,** 3702 Via de la Valle, Del Mar (✆ 858/523-0007), the category should be best contemporary *San Diego* cuisine. Native son Carl Schroeder scours local farms and ranches for the best possible products, prints his menu daily, and serves regional cuisine in a comfortably elegant setting. See p. 236.

- **Best Mexican Cuisine:** Rather than the typical "combination plate" fare, **El Agave Tequileria,** 2304 San Diego Ave., Old Town (✆ 619/220-0692), offers memorable recipes from Veracruz, Chiapas, Puebla, and Mexico City—along with a massive selection of boutique and artisan tequilas and mescals. See p. 109.

- **Best Supper Club:** It's hard to say what deserves the most attention at **Anthology,** 1337 India St., downtown (✆ 619/595-0300)—celebrity chef Bradley Ogden's new American cuisine or the eclectic lineup of top-name musical talent onstage. See p. 100.

- **Best Pizza:** You just might mistake San Diego for New York at **Bronx Pizza,** 111 Washington St., Hillcrest (✆ 619/291-3341). Don't even think about asking for a salad—this tiny pizzeria makes nothing but thin-crust pizzas and calzones. See p. 108.

- **Best Desserts:** You'll forget your diet at **Extraordinary Desserts,** 2929 Fifth Ave., Hillcrest (✆ 619/294-2132), and 1430 Union St., Little Italy (✆ 619/294-7001). Heck, it's so good you might forget your name. Proprietor Karen Krasne has a *Certificat de Patisserie* from Le Cordon Bleu in Paris and makes everything fresh on the premises daily. See p. 109.

- **Best Late-Night Dining:** When nothing will satisfy your dance-weary bones like a 2am taco, **Calaco Grill,** 732 Fourth Ave. (✆ 619/269-8032), has you covered. Staying open until 3am Thursday through Saturday, this casual Mexican spot in the Gaslamp Quarter isn't just convenient for late-night clubbers, it's tasty, too. See p. 104.

- **Best Fast Food:** A fish taco may sound strange to the uninitiated, but once you taste one, you'll know why locals line up for them. See p. 114 for suggestions on the best places to become a believer.

- **Best People Watching:** The food is nothing to write home about, but **The Green Flash,** 701 Thomas Ave. (✆ 858/270-7715), is the place to take in the Pacific Beach scene: the good, the bad, and the ugly. The boardwalk is just inches from the tables. See p. 115.

- **Best Picnic Fare:** Pack a superb sandwich from the **Bread & Cie.,** 350 University Ave., Hillcrest (✆ 619/683-9322), where the hearty breads are the toast of the city; see p. 108. Or head to one of several locations of **Whole Foods,** where the deli houses a smashing selection of delicious hot and cold items, a great cheese collection, and a crisp salad bar. You'll find one outpost in Hillcrest at 711 University Ave. (✆ 619/294-2800) and another in La Jolla at 8825 Villa La Jolla Dr. (✆ 858/642-6700).

2 RESTAURANTS BY CUISINE

American

Anthology ★★★ (Downtown, $$$, p. 100)

Bertrand at Mister A's ★★★ (Hillcrest/Uptown, $$$, p. 105)

The Brigantine (Coronado and other locations, $$$, p. 123)

Burger Lounge (Coronado, Kensington, La Jolla, $, p. 104)

Clayton's Coffee Shop (Coronado, $, p. 124)

Corvette Diner (Point Loma, $, p. 116)

Cowboy Star ★★ (Downtown, $$$, p. 100)

Crest Cafe (Hillcrest/Uptown, $, p. 109)

Danny's Palm Bar & Grill (Coronado, $, p. 104)

The Green Flash (Pacific Beach, $$, p. 115)

Hash House a Go Go ★ (Hillcrest/Uptown, $$, p. 105)

Hodad's (Ocean Beach, $, p. 104)

Karl Strauss Brewery & Grill (Downtown, La Jolla, and Carlsbad, $$, p. 103)

Kemo Sabe (Hillcrest/Uptown, $$$, p. 102)

Kensington Grill ★★ (Kensington, $$$, p. 126)

Living Room Cafe & Bistro (Old Town and other locations, $, p. 111)

Lucky Buck's (Hillcrest/Uptown, $, p. 104)

Neighborhood ★ (Downtown, $, p. 104)

Rainwater's on Kettner ★★ (Downtown, $$$, p. 102)

Rhinoceros Cafe & Grille ★ (Coronado, $$, p. 124)

Rocky's Crown Pub (Pacific Beach, $, p. 104)

South Beach Bar & Grill (Ocean Beach, $, p. 114)

Tioli's Crazee Burger ★ (North Park, $, p. 104)

The Tractor Room ★ (Hillcrest/Uptown, $$, p. 105)

Urban Solace ★ (North Park, $$, p. 126)

Breakfast

Bino's Bistro & Winebar (Coronado, $, p. 124)

Brockton Villa ★ (La Jolla, $$, p. 121)

Cafe 222 ★ (Downtown, $$, p. 99)

Clayton's Coffee Shop (Coronado, $, p. 124)

Coffee Cup ★ (La Jolla, $, p. 117)

The Cottage ★ (La Jolla, $, p. 123)

Crest Cafe (Hillcrest/Uptown, $, p. 109)

Hash House a Go Go ★ (Hillcrest/Uptown, $$, p. 105)

Isabel's Cantina ★ (Pacific Beach, $$, p. 112)

Kono's Surf Club Cafe (Pacific Beach, $, p. 112)

The Mission ★ (Mission Beach, North Park, Downtown, $, p. 117)

Richard Walker's Pancake House ★ (Downtown, $, p. 99)

Californian

Baleen ★★ (Mission Bay, $$$$, p. 112)

Bite ★★ (Hillcrest/Uptown, $$, p. 107)

Brockton Villa ★ (La Jolla, $$, p. 121)

California Cuisine ★★ (Hillcrest/Uptown, $$$, p. 106)

Confidential ★ (Downtown, $$$, p. 99)

Dobson's Bar & Restaurant ★ (Downtown, $$$, p. 101)

Georges California Modern ★★★ (La Jolla, $$$, p. 118)

Grant Grill ★ (Downtown, $$$, p. 99)

Hawthorn's ★ (Hillcrest/Uptown, $$, p. 108)

Indigo Grill (Little Italy, $$$, p. 102)

Jack's La Jolla ★★★ (La Jolla, $$$, p. 118)

The Linkery ★ (North Park, $$, p. 126)

The Marine Room ★★★ (La Jolla, $$$$, p. 117)

Mistral ★★ (Coronado, $$$$, p. 123)

Modus ★ (Hillcrest/Uptown, $$, p. 108)

Napa Valley Grille ★ (Downtown, $$, p. 103)

Nine-Ten ★★★ (La Jolla, $$$$, p. 118)

Stingaree ★ (Downtown, $$$, p. 99)

Whisknladle ★ (La Jolla, $$, p. 122)

1500 Ocean ★★ (Coronado, $$$, p. 123)

Chinese

China Max ★ (Kearny Mesa, $$, p. 126)

Jasmine ★ (Kearny Mesa, $$, p. 125)

Red Pearl Kitchen ★★ (Downtown, $$, p. 103)

Spicy City (Kearny Mesa, $$, p. 126)

Coffee & Tea

Living Room Cafe & Bistro (Old Town and other locations, $, p. 111)

Mrs. Burton's Tea Room (Old Town, $$, p. 109)

Desserts

Extraordinary Desserts ★★★ (Hillcrest/Uptown, Little Italy, $, p. 109)

Michele Coulon Dessertier ★★ (La Jolla, $, p. 117)

French

Bleu Bohème ★ (Kensington, $$, p. 126)

Cafe Chloe ★★ (Downtown, $$, p. 102)

Chez Loma ★ (Coronado, $$$, p. 124)

El Bizcocho ★★★ (Rancho Bernardo, $$$$, p. 126)

Laurel Restaurant & Bar ★★ (Hillcrest/Uptown, $$$, p. 106)

The Marine Room ★★★ (La Jolla, $$$$, p. 117)

Sky Room ★★ (La Jolla, $$$$, p. 117)

Tapenade ★★★ (La Jolla, $$$, p. 120)

Thee Bungalow ★★ (Ocean Beach, $$$, p. 114)

The 3rd Corner ★★ (Ocean Beach, Encinitas, $$, p. 116)

International

Bandar ★ (Downtown, $$, p. 99)

Café Sevilla ★ (Downtown, $$, p. 99)

Costa Brava (Pacific Beach, $$, p. 112)

Isabel's Cantina ★ (Pacific Beach, $$, p. 112)

Parallel 33 ★★ (Hillcrest/Uptown, $$$, p. 106)

Rice ★★ (Downtown, $$$, p. 99)

Italian

Bronx Pizza ★ (Hillcrest/Uptown, $, p. 108)

Buon Appetito ★ (Little Italy, $$, p. 99)

Caffé Bella Italia ★★ (Pacific Beach, $$, p. 115)

Filippi's Pizza Grotto (Downtown, Pacific Beach, and other locations, $, p. 105)

Jack's La Jolla ★★★ (La Jolla, $$$, p. 118)

Piatti ★ (La Jolla, $$, p. 121)

Po Pazzo ★ (Little Italy, $$$, p. 99)

Sogno DiVino ★ (Little Italy, $, p. 99)

Solare (Point Loma, $$, p. 115)

Trattoria Acqua ★★ (La Jolla, $$$, p. 120)

Zagarella II at Cafe Pacifica (Old Town, $$, p. 110)

Latin American

Berta's Latin American Restaurant ★ (Old Town, $$, p. 110)

Light Fare

Bino's Bistro & Winebar (Coronado, $, p. 124)

Bread & Cie. ★★ (Hillcrest/Uptown, $, p. 108)

The Cottage ★ (La Jolla, $, p. 123)

The Mission ★ (Mission Beach, North Park, Downtown, $, p. 117)

Mediterranean

Bertrand at Mister A's ★★★ (Hillcrest/Uptown, $$$, p. 105)

Bread & Cie. ★★ (Hillcrest/Uptown, $, p. 108)

Laurel Restaurant & Bar ★★ (Hillcrest/Uptown, $$$, p. 106)

Mistral ★★ (Coronado, $$$, p. 123)

Napa Valley Grille ★ (Downtown, $$, p. 103)

Piatti ★ (La Jolla, $$, p. 121)

Sally's ★★ (Downtown, $$$, p. 99)

Trattoria Acqua ★★ (La Jolla, $$$, p. 120)

Mexican

Calaco Grill (Downtown, $, p. 104)

Candelas ★★ (Downtown, Coronado, $$$, p. 100)

Casa Guadalajara (Old Town, $$, p. 110)

El Agave Tequileria ★★ (Old Town, $$$, p. 109)

El Zarape ★ (Hillcrest/Uptown, $, p. 114)

Gringo's ★ (Pacific Beach, $$, p. 116)

Mamá Testa ★ (Hillcrest/Uptown, $, p. 114)

Miguel's Cocina (Coronado, $$, p. 123)

Old Town Mexican Café (Old Town, $, p. 112)

Pokez Mexican Restaurant (Downtown, $, p. 99)

Ranchos Cocina ★ (North Park, Ocean Beach, $$, p. 126)

Rubio's Fresh Mexican Grill (throughout the city, $, p. 114)

Su Casa (La Jolla, $$, p. 117)

Wahoo's Fish Taco (La Jolla, Mission Valley, and other locations $, p. 114)

Pacific Rim/Asian Fusion

Nobu ★★ (Downtown, $$$$, p. 99)

Red Pearl Kitchen ★★ (Downtown, $$, p. 103)

Roppongi ★ (La Jolla, $$$, p. 120)

Wa Dining Okan ★★ (Kearny Mesa, $$, p. 126)

Seafood

Baleen ★★ (Mission Bay, $$$$, p. 112)

Bay Park Fish Co. ★ (Bay Park, $$, p. 114)

Blue Water Seafood Market and Grill ★ (Mission Hills, $$, p. 114)

The Brigantine (Coronado and other locations, $$$, p. 123)

The Fishery ★ (Pacific Beach, $$, p. 115)

The Fish Market/Top of the Market ★ (Downtown, Del Mar, $$, p. 103)

Island Prime ★★ (Harbor Island, $$$, p. 102)

JRDN ★ (Pacific Beach, $$$, p. 112)

The Oceanaire Seafood Room ★★ (Downtown, $$$, p. 102)

Point Loma Seafoods ★ (Point Loma, $, p. 114)

Zagarella II at Cafe Pacifica (Old Town, $$$, p. 110)

Zenbu ★★ (La Jolla, $$$, p. 121)

Sushi

The Fish Market/Top of the Market ★ (Downtown, $$, p. 103)

Harney Sushi (Old Town, $$, p. 109)

Nobu ★★ (Downtown, $$$$, p. 99)

Sushi Ota ★★★ (Pacific Beach, $$, p. 116)

Zenbu ★★ (La Jolla, $$$, p. 121)

Thai

Rama ★ (Downtown, $$, p. 99)

Saffron ★ (Mission Hills, $$, p. 105)

Spice & Rice Thai Kitchen ★ (La Jolla, $$, p. 122)

Vegetarian

Jyoti Bihanga (Normal Heights, $, p. 126)

Pokez Mexican Restaurant (Downtown, $, p. 99)

Ranchos Cocina ★ (North Park, Ocean Beach, $$, p. 126)

Spread ★ (North Park, $$, p. 126)

3 DOWNTOWN, GASLAMP QUARTER & LITTLE ITALY

You can grab breakfast at a quirky stalwart such as **Cafe 222** ★, 222 Island Ave. (✆ **619/ 236-9902;** www.cafe222.com), or sit down to some gourmet pancakes at **Richard Walker's Pancake House** ★, 520 Front St. (✆ **619/231-7777;** www.richardwalkers. com); then have lunch with the artists and musicians at **Pokez Mexican Restaurant,** 947 E St. (✆ **619/702-7160;** www.pokezsd.com), where they offer more than 30 vegetarian dishes. Come the evening, you can dine with the party crowd at sexy supper clubs including **Stingaree** ★, 454 Sixth Ave. (✆ **619/544-9500;** www.stingsandiego.com), and **Confidential** ★, 901 Fourth Ave. (✆ **619/696-8888;** www.confidentialsd.com). International choices include Thai at **Rama** ★, 327 Fourth Ave. (✆ **619/501-8424;** www. ramarestaurant.com), tapas at **Café Sevilla** ★, 555 Fourth Ave. (✆ **619/233-5979;** www.cafesevilla.com), and Persian at **Bandar** ★, 825 Fourth Ave. (✆ **619/238-0101;** www.bandarrestaurant.com).

Downtown encompasses many more options beyond the 16½-block Gaslamp Quarter, and hotel restaurants in the area make an especially strong showing. Highlights include the Manchester Grand Hyatt's (p. 65) bayside **Sally's** ★★ (✆ **619/358-6740;** www.sallyssandiego.com), the US Grant's (p. 66) reinvented **Grant Grill** ★ (✆ **619/ 744-2077;** www.grantgrill.com), and **Rice** ★★ (✆ **619/398-3082;** www.whotels.com/ sandiego) at the W Hotel (p. 67).

Little Italy is home to various eateries including, of course, fine Italian at **Po Pazzo** ★, 1917 India St. (✆ **619/238-1917;** www.popazzo.signonsandiego.com), and **Buon Appetito** ★, 1609 India St. (✆ **619/238-9880;** www.buonappetito.signonsandiego. com). The owners of Buon Appetito also operate a sister property next door, the wine bar **Sogno DiVino** ★, 1607 India St. (✆ **619/531-8887;** www.sogno-divino.com), and a gourmet Italian market adjacent to that.

A word on parking: On evenings when the Padres are playing or when a big convention fills area hotels, you'll compete for parking downtown. Fortunately, pedicabs—three-wheeled bikes that carry two passengers each—are easy to hire. But if you take a taxi or the trolley downtown on game nights, you'll find most restaurants easy to get into once the baseball crowd has made its way into the ballpark and the first pitch is thrown.

VERY EXPENSIVE

Nobu ★★ SUSHI/PACIFIC RIM/ASIAN FUSION Chef Nobu Matsuhisa has earned a devoted worldwide following for his creative, celebrity-approved sushi and Asian fusion cuisine. Following a 3-year stint in Peru (hence the seviche and Pisco sours on the

Nobu menu), Matsuhisa found himself in Los Angeles, where he became friends with actor Robert De Niro, now one of his partners for the Nobu franchise installed at the **Hard Rock Hotel** (p. 67). You may hear complaints about the restaurant's pricey fare, lean portions, and full-volume ambience, but you'll be hard-pressed to argue with the textures, flavors, and beautiful presentations. House specialties include the broiled black cod with miso and the Sino-Latino scallops tiradito; when in doubt, entrust yourself to the chef with the *omakase* tasting menu.

207 Fifth Ave. (at L St.), Gaslamp Quarter. ✆ **619/814-4124.** www.noburestaurants.com. Reservations recommended. Main courses $29–$54; sushi $6–$14. AE, DC, DISC, MC, V. Mon–Thurs 5:30–10:30pm; Fri–Sat 5:30–11:30pm; Sun 5–10pm. Lounge/bar Mon–Sat 5pm–midnight; Sun 5–11pm. Valet parking $20 with validation. Bus: 3, 11, or 120. Trolley: Gaslamp Quarter.

EXPENSIVE

Anthology ★★★ AMERICAN   San Diego has a proliferation of supper clubs. No spot in the county, though, can compare with the smashing success that is Anthology. Featuring a modern American menu created by James Beard–award winner Bradley Ogden (mastermind behind Northern California's acclaimed Lark Creek Inn and his own eponymous eatery at Caesar's Palace in Las Vegas, among others), Anthology is also a sophisticated, acoustically excellent concert hall. The music is eclectic, with an emphasis on jazz, world music, and blues. The music won't drown out the food, though—in fact, you'll know the band onstage is really jamming when you're able to tear your attention away from your meal.

1337 India St. (btw. A and Ash sts.), downtown. ✆ **619/595-0300.** www.anthologysd.com. Reservations recommended. Main courses $19–$28. AE, DISC, MC, V. Tues–Sat 5pm–1:30am; Sun 5–11:30pm. Valet parking $7. Bus: 83.

Candelas ★★ MEXICAN   If you're in the mood for a sophisticated, romantic fine-dining experience, look no further than Candelas. Owner Alberto Mestre and executive chef Eduardo Baeza are both natives of Mexico City and brought with them that city's culinary influences, which often blend Mexican and European elements. The chef's signature creation is *langosta Baeza:* fresh lobster in its shell, stuffed with mushrooms, chilies, onions, bacon, and tequila. Candelas also has a sexy lounge next door. The restaurant has given sleepy Coronado a jolt, as well, opening a view-enhanced location at the Ferry Landing, 1201 First St. (✆ **619/435-4900**).

416 Third Ave. (at J St.), Gaslamp Quarter. ✆ **619/702-4455.** www.candelas-sd.com. Reservations recommended. Main courses $22–$53 dinner. AE, DC, DISC, MC, V. Daily 5–11pm. Valet parking Fri–Sat $15. Bus: 11 or 120. Trolley: Convention Center.

Cowboy Star ★★ AMERICAN   This restaurant and butcher shop celebrates the Old West as seen through the squint of a celluloid cowboy. It's an unabashed homage to the Hollywood westerns of the 1930s and 1940s, combined with an unstinting commitment to the finest products available. Specializing in dry-aged meats and game fowl, all products come from sustainable sources; everything is organic, hormone-free, grass-fed, or free-range. The adjacent butcher shop stocks the same cuts you get at the restaurant, and sells house-made sauces and rubs, too. The decor features exposed wood beams and cow skulls, but never dips into kitsch.

640 10th Ave. (btw. G and Market sts.), East Village. ✆ **619/450-5880.** www.thecowboystar.com. Reservations recommended. Main courses $10–$21 lunch, $19–$82 dinner. AE, DISC, MC, V. Lunch Tues–Fri 11:30am–2:30pm; dinner Tues–Thurs 5–10pm, Fri–Sat 5–10:30pm, Sun 5–9pm; bar menu Tues–Sun from 4pm. Butcher shop Tues–Sat noon–7pm, Sun 10am–3pm. Bus: 3, 5, 11, 901, or 929. Trolley: Park & Market.

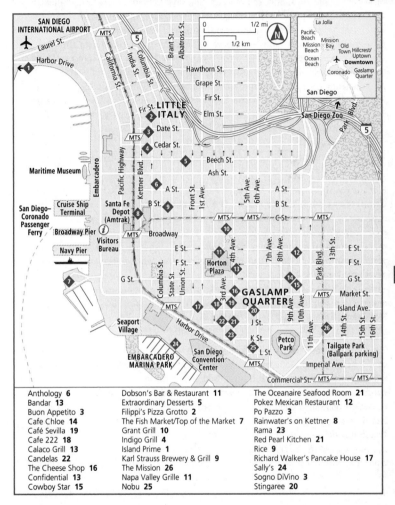

Anthology **6**
Bandar **13**
Buon Appetito **3**
Cafe Chloe **14**
Café Sevilla **19**
Cafe 222 **18**
Calaco Grill **13**
Candelas **22**
The Cheese Shop **16**
Confidential **13**
Cowboy Star **15**

Dobson's Bar & Restaurant **11**
Extraordinary Desserts **5**
Filippi's Pizza Grotto **2**
The Fish Market/Top of the Market **7**
Grant Grill **10**
Indigo Grill **4**
Island Prime **1**
Karl Strauss Brewery & Grill **9**
The Mission **26**
Napa Valley Grille **11**
Nobu **25**

The Oceanaire Seafood Room **21**
Pokez Mexican Restaurant **12**
Po Pazzo **3**
Rainwater's on Kettner **8**
Rama **23**
Red Pearl Kitchen **21**
Rice **9**
Richard Walker's Pancake House **17**
Sally's **24**
Sogno DiVino **3**
Stingaree **20**

WHERE TO DINE

6

DOWNTOWN, GASLAMP QUARTER & LITTLE ITALY

Dobson's Bar & Restaurant ★ CALIFORNIAN   No restaurant in San Diego has been more adept at mixing business and pleasure than Dobson's. Since 1984 it's been synonymous with the power lunch, a place where local executives and politicos come to break bread and make deals. By day it buzzes with the energy of movers and shakers; in the evening it segues from happy-hour watering hole to sophisticated pre- and post-theater American bistro. Look for menu entries such as oven-roasted wild salmon; chicken in Marsala, black fig, and thyme *jus;* and the signature mussel bisque.

956 Broadway Circle (at Broadway), downtown. ✆ **619/231-6771.** www.dobsonsrestaurant.com. Reservations recommended. Main courses $10–$18 lunch, $16–$39 dinner. AE, MC, V. Mon–Wed 11:30am–10pm; Thurs–Fri 11:30am–11pm; Sat 4–11pm; happy hour Mon–Fri 4–7pm. Valet parking $8/hour or $28 maximum. 3 hr. free parking at Horton Plaza. Bus: Numerous downtown routes including 7, 929, and 992.

Island Prime ★★ SEAFOOD   With its over-the-water dining, patio with fireplace, plentiful free parking, and spectacular bay and skyline views, Island Prime offers a wonderful setting for executive chef Deborah Scott. With dishes such as hazelnut-crusted diver scallops; cedar plank-roasted salmon with cucumber salsa and black linguini; and porcini-dusted rack of Colorado lamb with Moroccan-spiced tomato jam, the views actually have some competition. The restaurant's **C-Level Lounge** serves lunch and has a bar menu of both food and specialty cocktails. *Tip:* If you're stuck at Lindbergh Field, Island Prime is only a 10- to 15-minute walk from Terminal 1. Scott is also the mastermind behind the successful eateries **Kemo Sabe** and **Indigo Grill.** Both serve a culinary mishmash of Pacific Coast and Mexican/Southwestern cuisines to good effect and are worth a visit. Kemo Sabe is at 3958 Fifth Ave., Hillcrest (© **619/220-6802**); Indigo Grill is at 1536 India St., Little Italy (© **619/234-6802**).

880 Harbor Island Dr., Embarcadero. © 619/298-6802. www.cohnrestaurants.com. Reservations recommended. Main courses $11–$29 lunch, $25–$49 dinner. AE, DC, DISC, MC, V. Sun–Thurs 11:30am–10pm; Fri–Sat 11:30am–11pm. Free parking. Bus: 923 or 992.

The Oceanaire Seafood Room ★★ SEAFOOD   As you sweep up the dramatic staircase of the Oceanaire, the retro-nautical decor may evoke the grand elegance of a *Titanic*-style luxury liner. A Minneapolis-based chain that opened here in 2004, the popular Oceanaire features top local products as well as fish brought in daily from around the globe. Executive chef Brian Malarkey's preparations incorporate elements of Pacific Rim, Italian, classic French, and Asian cuisine; or you can have your catch-of-the-day simply grilled or broiled. Non-fish eaters can enjoy top-quality prime beef, chicken, and pork.

400 J St. (at Fourth Ave.), Gaslamp Quarter. © 619/858-2277. www.theoceanaire.com. Reservations recommended. Main courses $15–$50. AE, DISC, MC, V. Sun–Thurs 5–10pm; Fri–Sat 5–11pm. Valet parking from 6pm $10–$20. Bus: 3, 11, or 120. Trolley: Convention Center.

Rainwater's on Kettner ★★ AMERICAN   Venerable, locally owned, and the power-lunch choice of more than a few downtown business types and politicians, Rainwater's breaks no new ground in the steakhouse wars; but that's one of the reasons this spot is dependable. Lunch options include expectedly robust sandwiches and burgers, but you'll also find a good selection of entree salads. The restaurant's claim to fame is as an East Coast–style chophouse. For dinner check out the big hitters: prime rib-eye, prime T-bone, and even a prime New York strip for two, all expertly chosen and grilled to your specifications. The dinner menu also includes rack of lamb, pork chops, a selection of seafood, and pasta entrees. The spectacular wine list specializes in large-bottle formats and trophy labels, but still finds room for eclectic picks under $50.

1202 Kettner Blvd. (at B St., next to the Santa Fe depot), downtown. © 619/233-5757. www.rainwaters. com. Reservations recommended. Main courses $10–$32 lunch, $25–$95 dinner. AE, DISC, MC, V. Mon–Fri 11:30am–10pm; Sat 5–11pm; Sun 5–9pm Valet parking $10. Bus: 83. Trolley: America Plaza.

MODERATE

Cafe Chloe ★★ FRENCH   Creative, whimsical touches (such as a children's play area, a retail space, and a patio built for two) abound at this bistro infused with the refined tastes and *joie de vivre* of its proprietors. Cafe Chloe is small, it's loud when at capacity, and its tiny kitchen can get backed up. But the neighborly conviviality—combined with a short-but-sweet French-inspired menu covering breakfast, lunch, dinner, and weekend brunch—makes for a winning dining experience, and one unique enough to create a stir in ever-morphing San Diego.

721 Ninth Ave. (at G St.), East Village. © **619/232-3242.** www.cafechloe.com. Reservations for parties of 5 or more only. Main courses $8–$13 breakfast, $9–$13 lunch, $14–$23 dinner. AE, MC, V. Mon–Fri 7:30am–10:30pm; Sat 8:30am–10:30pm; Sun 8:30am–9:30pm. Bus: 3, 5, 11, 901, or 929.

The Fish Market/Top of the Market ★ SEAFOOD/SUSHI The bustling Fish Market at the end of the G Street Pier on the Embarcadero is a San Diego institution. Touristy, but an institution. Chalkboards announce the day's catches, which are sold by the pound or available in a number of classic, simple preparations in the casual, always-packed restaurant. Upstairs, the fancy offshoot **Top of the Market** offers sea fare with souped-up presentations (and jacked-up prices). I recommend having a cocktail in Top's plush, clubby atmosphere to enjoy the panoramic bay views, and then heading downstairs for more affordable fare or treats from the sushi and oyster bars. There's another Fish Market in Del Mar at 640 Via de la Valle (© **858/755-2277**), and a counter outlet in Mission Valley at 2401 Fenton Pkwy. (© **619/280-2277**).

750 N. Harbor Dr., Embarcadero. © **619/232-3474.** www.thefishmarket.com. Reservations not accepted. Main courses $10–$63 lunch, $13–$71 dinner. Top of the Market main courses $12–$75 lunch, $17–$95 dinner. AE, DC, DISC, MC, V. Daily 11am–9:30pm (till 10pm Fri–Sat). Valet parking $6. Trolley: Seaport Village.

Karl Strauss Brewery & Grill AMERICAN Brewmaster Karl Strauss put San Diego on the microbrewery map with this attractive factory setting, now all but engulfed by the adjacent W Hotel. The smell of hops and malt wafts throughout, and the stainless-steel tanks are visible from the bar. Brews on tap range from pale ale to amber lager. Five-ounce samplers are $1.75 each (or six for $6.95); if you like what you taste, 12-ounce glasses, pints, and hefty schooners stand chilled and ready. Nonalcoholic beer and wine are available by the glass. They've dressed up the lunch and dinner menu (Cajun fries, hamburgers, German sausage, and other bar foods) with items such as mango chicken salad and top sirloin. Beer-related memorabilia and brewery tours are available. Other locations include La Jolla, 1044 Wall St. (© **858/551-2739**), and Carlsbad, 5801 Armada Dr. (© **760/431-2739**).

1157 Columbia St. (at B St.), downtown. © **619/234-2739.** www.karlstrauss.com. Main courses $9–$30. AE, MC, V. Kitchen Sun–Thurs 11am–10pm, Fri–Sat 11am–11pm. Bar Mon–Thurs till 11pm, Fri–Sat till midnight. Bus: 83. Trolley: America Plaza.

Napa Valley Grille ★ CALIFORNIAN/MEDITERRANEAN Proving that a shopping mall doesn't have to be a wasteland when it comes to dining, Napa Valley Grille is a popular, moderately upscale lunch spot for downtown workers, where entree-size salads, sandwiches, and pasta dishes are rolled out. Come back at dinner when the atmosphere is often subdued, and you'll find a satisfying, seasonal selection of grilled items such as herb-rubbed filet mignon, grilled Chinook salmon, or citrus-glazed pork chops. Despite the mall bustle outside, the dining room is pleasant and appealing.

Horton Plaza (top floor), downtown. © **619/238-5440.** www.napavalleygrille.com. Main courses $9–$22 lunch, $18–$32 dinner. AE, DC, DISC, MC, V. Mon–Thurs 11:30am–9pm; Fri–Sat 11:30am–10pm; Sun 11:30am–9:30pm. Bus: Numerous downtown routes including 2, 7, 210, and 992. Trolley: Civic Center.

Red Pearl Kitchen ★★ CHINESE/ASIAN FUSION Specializing in dim sum dishes with a contemporary, Pan-Asian flair, this sexy Gaslamp Quarter restaurant is decorated in hues of deep red and features stone and tile accents, a cool pebbled floor, some nice deep booths, and two private dining areas. At Red Pearl, you may see a kung fu flick on one of the flatscreens over the bar while dining on your strawberry-cinnamon short ribs, duck lettuce wraps, or wok-fired Kobe beef with papaya and mint. For dessert,

Attack of the Killer Burgers

Burgers, it seems, are the new black. Upscale hamburger spots are popping up all around town, putting fast-food joints to shame with their chic surroundings; grass-fed, organic beef; and snazzy beer and wine menus.

Sleekly industrial **Burger Lounge** (www.burgerlounge.com) has three locations: La Jolla, 1101 Wall St. (📞 **858/456-0196**); Coronado, 922 Orange Ave. (📞 619/435-6835); and Kensington, 4116 Adams Ave. (📞 **619/584-2929**). The 10-item menu cuts right to the chase, featuring natural beef (as well as turkey and veggie) burgers, salads, milkshakes, and wine and beer. The amazing skyline mosaic on the back wall is reason enough to pay a visit to **Neighborhood** ★, 777 G St., downtown (📞 **619/446-0002;** www.neighborhoodsd.com). The 27 beers on tap (including plenty of local brews), sophisticated wine list, gourmet takes on burgers and classic bar food (Kosher hot dogs with chipotle purée), and creative salads will give you all the incentive you need to stay. In Hillcrest, **Lucky Buck's,** 1459 University Ave. (📞 619/297-0660), has a sidewalk patio and full bar; be sure to go for the waffle fries.

The don't-miss spot for burger aficionados is **Tioli's Crazee Burger** ★, 4201 30th St., North Park (📞 **619/282-6044;** www.tioliscrazeeburger.com). This eatery isn't hip or modern, but it takes a truly fine-dining approach toward its more than 30 burger offerings. Go crazy and order an ostrich, buffalo, or alligator burger; the German owners also take justifiable pride in the bratwurst. **Hodad's,** 5010 Newport Ave., Ocean Beach (📞 **619/224-4623;** www.hodadies. com), isn't new or urbane, either, but many locals insist it has the city's best burgers. If you want a big, messy burger in a classic beach environment, here's your place.

Dive bar connoisseurs can get their burger on at **Rocky's Crown Pub,** 3786 Ingraham St., Pacific Beach (📞 858/273-9140), and **Danny's Palm Bar & Grill,** 965 Orange Ave., Coronado (📞 **619/435-3171**). Rocky's is another longtime contender for the best-burger-in-town title; Danny's, which dates to 1908, also has a legion of fans. Kids are welcome at Danny's while the grill is open.

don't miss the airy *andagi,* the Japanese version of a doughnut hole. Get a glimpse of professionals in action; Red Pearl has an in-kitchen chef's table seating 4 to 12 people. Like any Chinese restaurant worth its noodles, Red Pearl also has takeout.

440 J St. (btw. Fourth and Fifth aves.), Gaslamp Quarter. 📞 **619/231-1100.** www.redpearlkitchen.com/sandiego. Reservations recommended. Main courses $8–$20. AE, MC, V. Daily 5pm–2am; kitchen Sun–Wed till 10pm, Thurs–Sat till 11pm. Valet parking $15. Bus: 3, 11, or 120. Trolley: Convention Center or Gaslamp Quarter.

INEXPENSIVE

Calaco Grill MEXICAN Open until 3am Thursday through Saturday, this is a great, casual spot in the Gaslamp Quarter for after-hours food; in fact, it's a great choice any time of day. There are traditional entrees such as tamales and fajitas, but it's the a la carte tacos that really shine, featuring the usual chicken, beef, and pork suspects, as well as more unique fare including salmon and beef tongue. For those who like to live on the edge, there's the TJ hot dog, which comes wrapped in bacon and is topped with mayo and mustard. Wash it down with a michelada, a beer and lime-juice concoction served in a glass with a salted rim. There's nothing like it on a hot day.

732 Fourth Ave. (btw. F and G sts.), Gaslamp Quarter. © **619/269-8032.** www.calacogrill.com. Main courses $10–$17; a la carte $3–$4.50. AE, DISC, MC, V. Mon–Wed 11am–10pm; Thurs–Sat 11am–3am; Sun 11am–9pm. Bus: Numerous downtown routes including 3, 120, and 992. Trolley: Civic Center.

Filippi's Pizza Grotto (**Value**) ITALIAN   When longtime locals think "Little Italy," Filippi's often comes to mind. To get to the dining area decorated with chianti bottles and red-checked tablecloths, you walk through a "cash and carry" Italian grocery store and deli stocked with cheeses, pastas, wines, bottles of olive oil, and salamis. The intoxicating smell of pizza wafts into the street; Filippi's has more than 15 varieties (including vegetarian). They also offer huge portions of spaghetti, lasagna, and other pasta; children's portions are available. On Friday and Saturday night, the lines to get in can look intimidating, but they move quickly. The original of a dozen branches throughout the county, this Filippi's has free parking. Other locations include 962 Garnet Ave. in Pacific Beach (© **858/483-6222**).

1747 India St. (btw. Date and Fir sts.), Little Italy. © **619/232-5094.** www.realcheesepizza.com. Reservations Mon–Thurs for groups of 8 or more. Main courses $6–$13. AE, DC, DISC, MC, V. Sun–Mon 11am–10pm; Tues–Thurs 11am–10:30pm; Fri–Sat 11am–11:30pm; deli opens daily at 8am. Free parking. Bus: 83. Trolley: Little Italy.

---

4 HILLCREST & UPTOWN

Whether it's ethnic food, bistro fare, retro comfort food, or specialty cafes and bakeries, Hillcrest and the other gentrified uptown neighborhoods to its west and east are jam-packed with great eateries catering to any palate and any wallet.

Hash House a Go Go ★, 3628 Fifth Ave. (© **619/298-4646;** www.hashhouseagogo. com), offers a menu of upscale comfort food; it serves three meals a day, but breakfast is the most popular choice. *Tip:* Portions are mountainous. Get one meal and pay $5 for a split order—you'll probably still leave with leftovers. Nearby is the Hash House's sister restaurant, **The Tractor Room** ★, 3687 Fifth Ave. (© **619/543-1007;** www.thetractor room.com). Dark and woody, with a touch of industrial design, this place bills itself as a "hunting lodge on Fifth." It prominently features game meats such as bison, rabbit, venison, and boar, as well as a huge selection of bourbon, rye, scotch, and whiskey.

Another spot favored by locals is **Saffron** ★, 3731 and 3737 India St. (© **619/574-0177** or 574-7737; www.sumeiyu.com), two low-key storefront spaces on the west side of Mission Hills. One spot serves noodles and saté; the other specializes in Thai-style grilled chicken. Also note that the popular **Whole Foods** supermarket, 711 University Ave. (© **619/294-2800;** www.wholefoodsmarket.com), has a mouthwatering deli and a robust salad bar—you can pack for a picnic or eat at the tables up front.

EXPENSIVE

Bertrand at Mister A's ★★★ AMERICAN/MEDITERRANEAN   Since 1965, San Diegans have come to high-rise Mister A's for proms, anniversaries, power meals, and other special occasions. A reported $1-million makeover turned the original Mister A's into Bertrand at Mister A's—an elegant, bright, sophisticated space with an array of modern art. The seasonal menu is modern American with a French/Mediterranean twist (think veal medallions, bouillabaisse, and Maine lobster strudel). A bar/patio menu gives diners on a budget access to the unsurpassed vistas. Bertrand at Mister A's has an equally impressive sister restaurant in the North County neighborhood of Rancho Santa Fe, romantic **Mille Fleurs** (p. 247).

2550 Fifth Ave. (at Laurel St.), Hillcrest. (℡ **619/239-1377.** www.bertrandatmisteras.com. Reservations recommended. Main courses $13–$30 lunch, $29–$50 dinner. AE, DC, MC, V. Mon–Fri 11:30am–2:30pm and 5:30–9:30pm; Sat–Sun 5–9:30pm. Valet parking $7.50 (after 6pm). Bus: 3 or 120.

California Cuisine ★★ CALIFORNIAN This long-popular restaurant has with-stood the test of time, offering a fresh and contemporary menu. The spare, understated dining room sets the stage as a smoothly professional and respectful staff proffers fine din-ing at fair prices to a casual crowd. The menu is a seasonal, market-driven affair that changes regularly. You may find jumbo lump crab cake with red-pepper coulis and mango salsa or Niman ranch pork chops in an apple compote and bourbon glacé. Whatever you order, just make sure you leave enough room for the scintillating desserts whipped up on a daily basis. The restaurant's back patio has been re-branded as the **CC Lounge,** offering a menu of creative cocktails ($5 before 7pm) and small-plate offerings. Allow time to find parking, which can be scarce along this busy stretch of University Avenue.

1027 University Ave. (east of 10th St.), Hillcrest. (℡ **619/543-0790.** www.californiacuisine.cc. Reserva-tions recommended. Main courses $14–$32 dinner. AE, DC, DISC, MC, V. Daily 5–10pm. Bus: 1, 10, or 11.

Laurel Restaurant & Bar ★★ FRENCH/MEDITERRANEAN In 2004, restaura-teur Tracy Borkum took ownership of Laurel and daringly reinvented what had already been one of the city's bright foodie lights. The gamble paid off, and Laurel remains one of San Diego's premier dining destinations. Laurel offers a seven-course chef's tasting meal (the whole table has to play along); a daily three-course, prix-fixe meal from 5 to 6:30pm for $35; and half-price discounts on many bottles of wine on Sundays. The quirky interior design features bold black-and-white patterns, punctuated by highlights of chartreuse, Kelly green, and lipstick red. Mirrored walls with arabesque and Joan Miró–inspired pat-terns reflect Swarovski crystal chandeliers, and bouquets of roses are suspended in large cylindrical vases like lab experiments—the place is an eyeful. Located adjacent to Balboa Park, Laurel offers complimentary shuttles to the nearby Old Globe Theatre.

505 Laurel St. (at Fifth Ave.), Balboa Park. (℡ **619/239-2222.** www.sdurbankitchen.com. Reservations recommended. Main courses $20–$36. AE, DC, DISC, MC, V. Sun–Thurs 5–9:30pm; Fri–Sat 5–10:30pm. Valet parking $7. Bus: 3 or 120.

Parallel 33 ★★ (Finds) INTERNATIONAL What do Morocco, Lebanon, India, China, Japan, and San Diego all have in common? They're all intersected by the same latitude—the 33rd parallel. Bringing together the unique flavors of those far-flung locales is the inspired idea behind Parallel 33, located in the upscale neighborhood of Mission Hills. The menu leaps enthusiastically from fragrant Moroccan lamb tagine to ginger-sautéed udon noodles with roasted artichoke hearts. The decor is a hodgepodge, too: a touch of Hinduism, a dash of Islam, a little bit of Buddhism—all contemporized by cement floors and iron accents. Next door is the restaurant's intimate, very chill lounge, **Blue Lotus,** which serves food from the same menu.

741 W. Washington St. (at Falcon), Mission Hills. (℡ **619/260-0033.** www.parallel33sd.com. Reservations recommended. Main courses $25–$34. AE, DISC, MC, V. Tues–Thurs 5:30–10pm; Fri–Sat 5:30–11pm. Bus: 10 or 83.

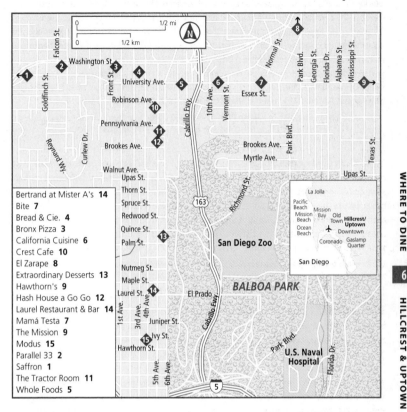

Bertrand at Mister A's **14**
Bite **7**
Bread & Cie. **4**
Bronx Pizza **3**
California Cuisine **6**
Crest Cafe **10**
El Zarape **8**
Extraordinary Desserts **13**
Hawthorn's **9**
Hash House a Go Go **12**
Laurel Restaurant & Bar **14**
Mamá Testa **7**
The Mission **9**
Modus **15**
Parallel 33 **2**
Saffron **1**
The Tractor Room **11**
Whole Foods **5**

MODERATE

Bite ★★ (Finds) CALIFORNIAN   San Diego gourmands are devoted to chef Chris Walsh. After his most recent tenure at the glitzy downtown supper club **Confidential** (p. 99), fans are relieved to find him in the friendly confines of his own neighborhood restaurant. Stylishly modern with a hint of industrial lounge (Walsh is responsible for the design, as well), Bite features a tapas-style roster of small plates that encourages grazing and sharing. The menu is seasonally driven and influenced by Northern Italian and French bistro fare (such as potato pancakes with smoked trout or bacon-wrapped dates stuffed with Gorgonzola); the wine list has nearly 30 interesting, reasonably priced wines by the glass. If you're feeling inspired, Bite allows you to invent your own cocktail; you can select mixers from a lineup of specialty sodas (pomegranate, pear, and so on), fresh juices, and house-infused sakes. Champagne fans can indulge in a daily bubbly happy hour from 5 to 7pm.

1417 University Ave. (at Richmond St.), Hillcrest. (C) **619/299-2483.** www.bitesd.com. No reservations, but call ahead to be placed on a priority-seating list. Small plates $5–$16. AE, DISC, MC, V. Mon–Thurs 5–10:30pm; Fri–Sat 5–11pm; Sun 5–10pm. Bus: 1, 10, or 11.

Hawthorn's ★ CALIFORNIAN   This longtime local favorite was forced from its previous location by impending redevelopment. It now finds itself inside the loving embrace of the North Park Theatre, a magnificently rehabilitated 1928 vaudeville house located just east of Hillcrest. The move has been a boon to both the restaurant and to North Park, which has become one of San Diego's most vibrant neighborhoods. The California fusion–style menu features items such as roasted chicken breast filled with goat cheese and artichoke stuffing, and barbecued pork chops served with your choice of either a smoky chipotle sauce or a cranberry-port wine reduction. Sunday brunch is served from 10am to 4pm; happy hour lasts all night Sunday and Monday (5–7pm the rest of the week, except on show nights).

2895 University Ave. (at 29th St.), North Park. ✆ **619/295-1688.** www.hawthornssandiego.com. Main courses $17–$32 dinner. AE, MC, V. Sun–Wed 5–9pm; Thurs–Sat 5–11pm; Sun brunch 10am–4pm. Paid parking across the street. Bus: 7 or 10.

Modus ★ (Finds) CALIFORNIAN   Livening up sedate Bankers Hill, this cool little "gastro-lounge" has been a hit since opening in 2006. It features mood lighting, a zigzagging bar, a mod fireplace, DJs, and a patio with a water-wall feature. The modern European bistro cuisine has a California flair, incorporating fresh, local, organic products. Look for classics such as onion soup and confit of duck, as well as vegetarian items, cheese and charcuterie plates, and a killer hamburger. Modus also takes its wine and cocktail program very seriously.

2202 Fourth Ave. (at Ivy St.), Bankers Hill. ✆ **619/236-8516.** www.modusbar.com. Reservations recommended Fri–Sat. Main courses $14–$24. AE, DISC, MC, V. Kitchen Tues–Sun 5–10pm, Fri–Sat 5pm–midnight. Bar Tues–Sun 5pm–1:30am. Free street parking after 6pm. Bus: 3 or 120.

INEXPENSIVE

Bread & Cie. ★★ LIGHT FARE/MEDITERRANEAN   The traditions of European artisan bread-making and attention to the fine points of texture and crust quickly catapulted Bread & Cie. to local stardom—they now supply bread to more than 75 local restaurants. Some favorites are available daily, including anise and fig, black olive, and jalapeño and cheese; others are available just 1 or 2 days a week. Ask for a free sample or order one of the many Mediterranean-inspired sandwiches. A specialty coffee drink perfectly accompanies a light breakfast of fresh scones, muffins, and homemade granola with yogurt. Seating is at bistro-style tables in full view of the busy ovens.

350 University Ave. (at Fourth St.), Hillcrest. ✆ **619/683-9322.** www.breadandcie.com. Reservations not accepted. Sandwiches and light meals $4–$9. DISC, MC, V. Mon–Fri 7am–7pm; Sat 7am–6pm; Sun 8am–6pm. Bus: 1, 3, 10, 11, or 120.

Bronx Pizza ★ (Finds) ITALIAN   This pizzeria, serving up arguably San Diego's best pies, has two small dining areas separated by a covered patio. With its red vinyl booths, checkered curtains, and pictures of boxers on the walls, the interior dining room looks as if it were airlifted straight out of the boroughs of New York. Bronx Pizza makes only pizzas and calzones—no salads, no chicken wings. And if there's a line out the door (a frequent occurrence), don't hesitate when you get to the counter to order, or you may find yourself living out the *Seinfeld* "Soup Nazi" episode. These guys will definitely drop a little New York attitude on you. Choices are simple, though. It's all thin-crust, 18-inch pies, or by the slice, with straightforward toppings (although Bronx Pizza has made concessions to the locals by including ingredients such as marinated artichokes and pesto).

111 Washington St. (at First Ave.), Hillcrest. ✆ **619/291-3341.** www.bronxpizza.com. Phone orders accepted for full pies. Pies $13–$19; $2.50 by the slice. Cash only. Sun–Thurs 11am–10pm; Fri–Sat 11am–11pm. Street parking. Bus: 3, 10, or 83.

The cheery pink interior of Crest Cafe announces 1940s style, and the room bubbles with upbeat waiters and comfort food doled out on Fiestaware. The church pew–like booths are comfortable, but the small stucco room doesn't mask the near constant clang of plates. No matter: Burger-lovers will fall in love with the spicy, rich "butter burger"—a dollop of herb butter is buried in the patty before cooking. The delicious East Texas–fried chicken breast crusted with hunks of jalapeño peppers is none too subtle either. A variety of sandwiches and salads, the steamed vegetable basket, and broiled chicken dishes are healthier options. A breakfast of omelets or crème brûlée French toast is a happy eye-opener.

425 Robinson Ave. (btw. Fourth and Fifth aves.), Hillcrest. ✆ 619/295-2510. www.crestcafe.net. Reservations not accepted. Main courses $7–$17 breakfast, $8–$17 lunch and dinner. AE, DISC, MC, V. Daily 7am–midnight. Bus: 1, 3, or 120.

Extraordinary Desserts ★★★ DESSERTS   Chef and proprietor Karen Krasne's talent surpasses the promise of her impressive pedigree, which includes a *Certificat de Patisserie* from Le Cordon Bleu in Paris. Dozens of divine creations are available daily, and many are garnished with edible gold or flowers. Among them: a passion-fruit ricotta torte bursting with kiwis, strawberries, and bananas, and a *gianduia* of chocolate cake lathered with hazelnut butter cream, chocolate mousse, and boysenberry preserves, sprinkled with shards of praline. She also sells her own exclusive line of jams, chutneys, syrups, spices, and confections, both at the original location and at an architecturally striking second space in Little Italy, 1430 Union St. (✆ 619/294-7001). The Little Italy location also serves paninis, salads, and artisan cheeses, as well as wine and beer; a light breakfast is offered Sundays from 11am to 2pm.

2929 Fifth Ave. (btw. Palm and Quince sts.) ✆ 619/294-2132. www.extraordinarydesserts.com. Desserts $2–$9. MC, V. Mon–Thurs 8:30am–11pm; Fri 8:30am–midnight; Sat 10am–midnight; Sun 10am–11pm. Street parking usually available. Bus: 3 or 120.

---

5 OLD TOWN & MISSION VALLEY

Visitors often have at least one meal in Old Town. Although this area is San Diego at its most touristy, I can't argue with the appeal of dining in California's charming original settlement. Mexican food and bathtub-size margaritas are the big draws. For a change of pace, stop by the hip sushi joint **Harney Sushi,** 3964 Harney St. (✆ 619/295-3272; www.harneysushi.com), or pop into **Mrs. Burton's Tea Room** in Heritage Park (✆ 619/294-4600; www.mrsburtons tearoom.com) for a spot of tea in a Victorian setting, 10am to 4pm.

Old Town is the gateway to the decidedly less historic Mission Valley. There are plenty of chain eateries, both good and bad—in the busy Fashion Valley Shopping Center complex (p. 211), you'll find the Cheesecake Factory, California Pizza Kitchen, and P.F. Chang's (expect waits for a table at each). In or near the Mission Valley Shopping Center (p. 212), you'll find an Outback Steakhouse, Hooters, and Mimi's Cafe, as well as Seau's, the sports bar and restaurant owned by beloved former San Diego Chargers football player Junior Seau.

EXPENSIVE
El Agave Tequileria ★★ MEXICAN   Don't be misled by this restaurant's less than impressive location above a liquor store on the outskirts of Old Town. This warm, bustling eatery continues to draw local gourmands for the regional Mexican cuisine and

rustic elegance that leave the touristy fajitas-and-*cerveza* joints of Old Town far behind. El Agave is named for the plant from which tequila and its cousin mescal are derived, and the restaurant boasts more than 850 tequilas and mescals. Needless to say, El Agave serves some of the best margaritas in town. But even teetotalers will enjoy the restaurant's authentically flavored mole sauces (from Taxco, rich with walnuts; tangy tomatillo from Oaxaca; and the more familiar dark mole flavored with chocolate and sesame), or El Agave's signature beef filet with goat cheese and dark tequila sauce. Inexpensive lunches are simpler affairs without the exotic sauces.

2304 San Diego Ave., Old Town. ℭ 619/220-0692. www.elagave.com. Reservations recommended. Main courses $8–$11 lunch, $16–$32 dinner. AE, MC, V. Daily 11am–10pm. Street parking. Bus: Numerous Old Town routes, including 8, 9, 10, 14, 28, and 30. Trolley: Old Town.

Zagarella II at Cafe Pacifica ITALIAN/SEAFOOD   Established in 1980, Cafe Pacifica was acquired in 2008 by the owners of an Italian restaurant near downtown, hence the awkward new name. Thankfully, signature Cafe Pacifica dishes such as the crab-stuffed portobello mushroom topped with grilled asparagus, griddled mustard catfish, and the "Pomerita," a pomegranate margarita, are still on the menu. Joining the old favorites are classic Italian specialties such as cioppino and various pasta creations. Also surviving the changeover is the early-bird special—arrive before 6:30pm to order an entree with soup or salad and dessert for $27. This unpretentious little casita has always been a pleasant escape from the Old Town rush, and if you really want a dose of history while you're eating in this neck of the woods, you're in luck—this place cozies right up to El Campo Santo, San Diego's first cemetery.

2414 San Diego Ave., Old Town. ℭ **619/291-6666.** www.cafepacifica.com. Reservations recommended. Main courses $13–$30. AE, DC, DISC, MC, V. Daily 5–10pm. Valet parking $5. Bus: Numerous Old Town routes including 8, 9, 10, 14, 28, and 30. Trolley: Old Town.

MODERATE

Berta's Latin American Restaurant ★ LATIN AMERICAN   Housed in a charming, basic cottage tucked away on a side street, Berta's faithfully re-creates the sunny flavors of Central and South America, where slow cooking mellows the heat of chilies and other spices. Everyone starts with a basket of fresh flour tortillas and mild salsa verde. Mouthwatering dishes include Guatemalan *chilemal*, a rich pork-and-vegetable casserole with chilies, cornmeal *masa*, coriander, and cloves; or try the Salvadoran *pupusas* (at lunch only)—dense corn-mash turnovers with melted cheese and black beans, their texture perfectly offset with crunchy cabbage salad and one of Berta's special salsas. You can also opt for a table full of Spanish-style tapas, grazing alternately on crispy *empanadas* (filled turnovers), strong Spanish olives, or *pincho moruno* (skewered lamb and onion redolent of spices and red saffron).

3928 Twiggs St. (at Congress St.), Old Town. ℭ **619/295-2343.** www.bertasinoldtown.com. Main courses $7–$12 lunch, $13–$17 dinner. AE, DISC, MC, V. Tues–Sun 11am–10pm (lunch menu till 3pm). Free parking. Bus: Numerous Old Town routes, including 8, 9, 10, 14, 28, and 30. Trolley: Old Town.

Casa Guadalajara Ⓚⁱᵈˢ MEXICAN   Bazaar Del Mundo Shops, a warren of mostly Latin-themed gift stores, operates this Mexican restaurant a block away from Old Town State Historic Park. Casa Guadalajara is both better and less crowded than options in the park, although waits of 30 minutes or more are not unusual here on Friday and Saturday. Mariachi tunes played by strolling musicians enliven the room nightly, and you can dine alfresco in a picturesque courtyard occupied by a 200-year-old pepper tree. Birdbath-size margaritas start most meals. Dining ranges from simple south-of-the-border fare to more

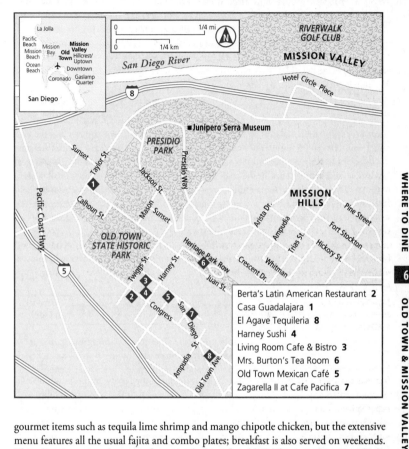

La Jolla
Pacific
Beach
Mission
Beach
Ocean
Beach
Coronado
San Diego

Mission
Bay
Old
Town
**Mission
Valley**
Hillcrest/
Uptown
Downtown
Gaslamp
Quarter

0   1/4 mi
0   1/4 km

San Diego River

**RIVERWALK
GOLF CLUB**

MISSION VALLEY

Hotel Circle Place

8

■Junípero Serra Museum

**PRESIDIO
PARK**

Sunset
Taylor St.
Jackson St.
Presidio Way
Mason
Sunset
Calhoun St.

**MISSION
HILLS**

Arista Dr.
Ampudia
Tribs St.
Hickory St.
Fort Stockton
Pine Street

Pacific Coast Hwy.

**OLD TOWN
STATE HISTORIC
PARK**

Heritage Park Row
Crescent Dr.
Whitman

5

Twiggs St.
Harney St.
Congress
San Diego St.
Juan St.
Ampudia
Old Town Ave.

1
2
3
4
5
6
7
8

Berta's Latin American Restaurant **2**
Casa Guadalajara **1**
El Agave Tequileria **8**
Harney Sushi **4**
Living Room Cafe & Bistro **3**
Mrs. Burton's Tea Room **6**
Old Town Mexican Café **5**
Zagarella II at Cafe Pacifica **7**

gourmet items such as tequila lime shrimp and mango chipotle chicken, but the extensive menu features all the usual fajita and combo plates; breakfast is also served on weekends. This place is touristy, but out-of-towners looking for old California ambience and reliable Mexican food will find it here.

4105 Taylor St. (at Juan St.), Old Town. ✆ **619/295-5111.** www.bazaardelmundo.com. Reservations recommended. Main courses $8–$12 breakfast, $9–$18 lunch and dinner. AE, DC, DISC, MC, V. Mon–Thurs 11am–10pm; Fri 11am–11pm; Sat 7am–11pm; Sun 7am–10pm. Free parking. Bus: Numerous Old Town routes, including 8, 9, 10, 14, 28, and 30. Trolley: Old Town.

INEXPENSIVE

Living Room Cafe & Bistro COFFEE & TEA/AMERICAN   Once a humble coffeehouse, the Living Room has added "cafe and bistro" to its name and expanded its menu. Covering breakfast, lunch, and dinner, the Living Room features omelets and waffles, hearty sandwiches, burgers, salads, quiches, and personal-size pizzas. In a nod to the neighborhood, there are also Mexican staples including fajitas, burritos, and fish tacos. Keeping true to its roots, though, plenty of specialty coffee drinks are still available, in addition to beer, wine, margaritas, and martinis. Grab a patio table in the courtyard of this lovely old house and enjoy the people-watching; indoors you'll find faux antiques, appropriately weathered for a lived-in feel. There's delivery service from 10am to 4pm, Monday through Saturday. Other locations are in La Jolla at 1010 Prospect St. (© **858/ 459-1187**); in Point Loma at 1018 Rosecrans St. (© **619/222-6852**); and in the College area near San Diego State University, at 5900 El Cajon Blvd. (© **619/286-8434**).

2541 San Diego Ave., Old Town. © **619/325-4445**. www.livingroomcafe.com. Most menu items $6–$10. AE, DISC, MC, V. Sun–Thurs 7am–10pm; Fri–Sat 7am–midnight. Bus: Numerous Old Town routes, including 8, 9, 10, 14, 28, and 30. Trolley: Old Town.

Old Town Mexican Café (Overrated) MEXICAN   This place is so popular that it's become an Old Town tourist attraction in its own right. Proceed with caution, though. The original structure is wonderfully funky and frayed, but the restaurant long ago expanded into additional, less appealing dining rooms and outdoor patios—and the wait for a table is often 30 minutes or longer. You can pass the time by gazing in from the sidewalk as tortillas are hand-patted the old-fashioned way, soon to be a hot-off-the-grill treat accompanying every meal. But the place is loud and crowded, and the food usually fails to impress. The best things here are the margaritas, served neat in a shaker for two; the deliciously simple rotisserie chicken accompanied by tortillas, guacamole, sour cream, beans, and rice; and the cheap breakfasts, when the place is pleasantly sleepy and throng-free.

2489 San Diego Ave., Old Town. © **619/297-4330**. www.oldtownmexcafe.com. Reservations accepted only for parties of 10 or more. Main courses $6–$9 breakfast, $9–$17 lunch and dinner. AE, DC, DISC, MC, V. Sun–Thurs 7am–11pm; Fri–Sat 7am–midnight (bar until 1am nightly). Bus: Numerous Old Town routes, including 8, 9, 10, 14, 28, and 30. Trolley: Old Town.

6 MISSION BAY & THE BEACHES

Restaurants at the beach exist primarily to provide an excuse for sitting and gazing at the water. Because this activity is most commonly accompanied by steady drinking, it stands to reason the food often isn't remarkable. Happily, the past few years have seen an influx of places bucking the trend, or at least raising the level of sophistication.

The beautiful party people get their groove and their feed bag on in Pacific Beach at **JRDN** ★ (pronounced "Jordan") in the swank Tower 23 hotel (p. 79), 723 Felspar St. (© **866/869-3723**; www.jrdn.com). The creator of **The Mission** (p. 117) is proprietor of hip **Isabel's Cantina** ★, 966 Felspar St. (© **858/272-8400**; www.isabelscantina. com), an Asian-Latino fusion cafe serving breakfast, lunch, and dinner in the remnants of an old bakery. Or start your day at the beach at **Kono's Surf Club Cafe,** 704 Garnet Ave., Pacific Beach (© **858/483-1669**), a Hawaiian-themed boardwalk breakfast shack that's cheap and delicious. A plump Kono's breakfast burrito provides enough fuel for a day of surfing or sightseeing; a side order of savory "Kono Potatoes" is a meal in itself. For lunch or dinner, **Costa Brava,** 1653 Garnet Ave. (© **858/273-1218**; www. costabravasd.com), serves traditional Spanish tapas.

VERY EXPENSIVE

Baleen ★★ SEAFOOD/CALIFORNIAN   This attractive waterfront eatery is located right in the middle of Mission Bay at the Paradise Point Resort (p. 78)—the patio dining is sublime here. With its lush bayfront view, it's easy to miss the design details indoors—from a monkey motif that includes simians hanging off chandeliers to specialized serving platters for many of Baleen's artistically arranged dishes. Ocean fare takes

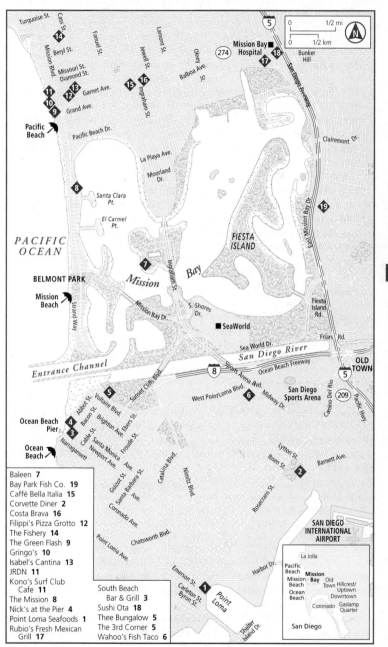

Turquoise St.
Cass St.
Mission Blvd.
Beryl St.
Famuel St.
Missouri St.
Diamond St.
Garnet Ave.
Grand Ave.
Lamont St.
Jewell St.
Ingraham St.
Olney Ave.
Balboa Ave. St.

14
11 **12** **13**
10 **15** **16**
9

Mission Bay
Hospital ■
17 **18**
Bunker
Hill

5
274

0 · 1/2 mi
0 · 1/2 km
N

**Pacific
Beach** ➚
Pacific Beach Dr.
La Playa Ave.
Moorland
Dr.
Clairemont Dr.

8
Santa Clara
Pt.
El Carmel
Pt.

FIESTA
ISLAND

East Mission Bay Dr.

19

**PACIFIC
OCEAN**

BELMONT PARK
**Mission
Beach** ➚
Strand Way

7
Mission Bay
Ingraham St.
Mission Bay Dr.
S. Shores
Dr.

■ SeaWorld

Fiesta
Island
Rd.

Friars Rd.

Entrance Channel
San Diego River
Sea World Dr.
Ocean Beach Freeway

8
Sports Arena Blvd.
Midway Dr.

**OLD
TOWN**
5
209
Pacific Hwy.

**Ocean Beach
Pier** ➚
5
Voltaire Blvd.
Abbot St.
Bacon St.
Brighton Ave.
West Point Loma Blvd.
6
**San Diego
Sports Arena**

Camino Del Rio

**Ocean
Beach** ➚
Narragansett
Cable St.
Santa Monica Ave.
Froude St.
Ebers St.
Newport Ave.

4
3

Lytton St.
Ibsen St.
Barnett Ave.

2

Catalina Blvd.
Nimitz Blvd.
Guizot St.
Santa Barbara St.
Coronado Ave.

Rosecrans St.

**SAN DIEGO
INTERNATIONAL
AIRPORT**

Point Loma Ave.
Chatsworth Blvd.

Emerson St.
Carleton St.
Byron St.
1
**Point
Loma**

Harbor Dr.

Shelter
Island Dr.

La Jolla
Pacific
Beach
Mission
Mission **Bay** Old
Beach Town Hillcrest/
Uptown
Ocean Downtown
Beach
Coronado Gaslamp
Quarter

San Diego

Baleen **7**
Bay Park Fish Co. **19**
Caffé Bella Italia **15**
Corvette Diner **2**
Costa Brava **16**
Filippi's Pizza Grotto **12**
The Fishery **14**
The Green Flash **9**
Gringo's **10**
Isabel's Cantina **13**
JRDN **11**
Kono's Surf Club
Cafe **11**
The Mission **8**
Nick's at the Pier **4**
Point Loma Seafoods **1**
Rubio's Fresh Mexican
Grill **17**

South Beach
Bar & Grill **3**
Sushi Ota **18**
Thee Bungalow **5**
The 3rd Corner **5**
Wahoo's Fish Taco **6**

WHERE TO DINE

6

MISSION BAY & THE BEACHES

Baja Fish Tacos

One of San Diego's culinary ironies is that despite its rich Hispanic heritage and proximity to the Mexican border, it's hard to find anything other than gringo-ized combo plates in many local Mexican restaurants. But one item you'll see on plenty of menus here is the fish taco—a native of Baja California. Consisting of batter-dipped, deep-fried filets wrapped in a corn tortilla with shredded cabbage, salsa, and a tangy sauce, fish tacos were popularized in San Diego by **Rubio's Fresh Mexican Grill** in the early 1980s. Rubio's has since grown into a sizable chain, and it's a good option if you're on the go—the original stand is still operating at the east end of Pacific Beach, 4504 E. Mission Bay Dr., at Bunker Hill Street (© **858/272-2801;** www.rubios.com).

Fish tacos are a casual food, served in casual settings. Here are some of the best places to taste one: **Bay Park Fish Co.** ★, 4121 Ashton St., Bay Park (© **619/276-3474;** www.bayparkfishco.com); **Blue Water Seafood Market and Grill** ★, 3667 India St., Mission Hills (© **619/497-0914**); **The Brigantine** (p. 123); **The Fishery** ★ (p. 115); **Mamá Testa** ★, 1417A University Ave., Hillcrest (© **619/298-8226;** www.mamatestataqueria.com); **Point Loma Seafoods** ★, 2805 Emerson St., Point Loma (© **619/223-1109;** www.pointlomaseafoods.com); **South Beach Bar & Grill,** 5059 Newport Ave., Ocean Beach (© **619/226-4577;** www.southbeachob.com); and **El Zarape** ★, 4642 Park Blvd., University Heights (© **619/692-1652**). Another worthy chain is **Wahoo's Fish Taco** (www.wahoos.com), with locations including La Jolla (639 Pearl St.; © **858/459-0027**), Encinitas (1006 N. El Camino Real; © **760/753-5060**), Mission Valley (2195 Station Village Way; © **619/299-4550**), and the Sport Arena area (3944 W. Point Loma Blvd.; © **619/222-0020**).

precedence, and local fish and shellfish are featured in a chef's tasting menu. There's also classic surf and turf or a selection of simply wood-roasted meats and seafood. *Note:* This is a family-oriented resort, so knee-high types may be sharing the space; a children's menu goes beyond the usual burgers and fries option and includes items such as shrimp scampi and petit filet.

1404 Vacation Rd. (Paradise Point Resort), Mission Bay. © **858/490-6363.** www.paradisepoint.com. Reservations recommended. Main courses $22–$78. AE, DC, DISC, MC, V. Sun–Thurs 5–9pm; Fri–Sat 5–10pm. Free parking. Bus: 8 or 9.

EXPENSIVE

Thee Bungalow ★★ FRENCH   For some 35 years this small cottage, standing alone at the edge of Robb Field near the Ocean Beach channel, has been a romantic hideaway beckoning diners for consistently rewarding French country cuisine. By far the fanciest restaurant in laid-back Ocean Beach, Thee Bungalow has endeared itself with its excellent wine list and house specialties such as bouillabaisse, Angus filet *au poivre* in a brandy-pepper sauce, *osso buco*–style lamb shank in a burgundy reduction, and decadent made-to-order dessert soufflés for two (chocolate or orange liqueur). This place is old school for sure, but it's run by the city's top restaurant group (whose holdings include **115** Island Prime and Corvette Diner, p. 102 and 116, respectively)—trust them; they know what they're doing.

4996 W. Point Loma Blvd. (at Bacon St.), Ocean Beach. ℂ 619/224-2884. www.cohnrestaurants.com. Reservations recommended. Main courses $23–$31. AE, DC, DISC, MC, V. Mon–Thurs 5:30–9:30pm; Fri–Sat 5–10pm; Sun 5–9pm. Free parking. Bus: 35 or 923.

MODERATE

Caffé Bella Italia ★★ ITALIAN   It's well away from the surf, has a rather odd-looking exterior, and is in a less-than-inspiring section of P.B., but this place is lovely inside, and the food can knock your socks off. It's the best spot in the area for shellfish-laden pasta, wood-fired pizzas (a selection of more than 30), and management that welcomes guests like family. Romantic lighting, sheer draperies, and warmly earthy walls create a Mediterranean ambience, assisted by the lilting Milanese accents of the staff (when the din of a few dozen happy diners doesn't drown them out, that is). Every item on the menu bears the unmistakable flavor of freshness and homemade care. Even the simplest curled-edge ravioli stuffed with ricotta, spinach, and pine nuts is elevated to culinary perfection. A sister restaurant, the stylish **Solare,** is located at Liberty Station in Point Loma, 2820 Roosevelt Dr. (ℂ **619/270-9670;** www.solarelounge.com).

1525 Garnet Ave. (btw. Ingraham and Haines sts.), Pacific Beach. ℂ 858/273-1224. www.caffebellaitalia. com. Reservations suggested for dinner. Main courses $13–$27. AE, DC, DISC, MC, V. Daily 4:30–10pm. Free (small) parking lot. Bus: 8, 9, or 27.

The Fishery ★ (Finds) SEAFOOD   You're pretty well guaranteed to get fresh-off-the-boat seafood at this off-the-beaten-track establishment: It's really a wholesale ware-house and retail fish market with a casual restaurant attached. The owners work with local, national, and global suppliers, and the wide range of bounty is reflected in an eclectic menu that ranges from sushi rolls and clam chowder to Scottish salmon and Mexican lobster. The Fishery makes an effort to offer sustainable product, so look for owner-caught harpooned swordfish in season. In spite of its informal air, there's a surpris-ingly impressive wine list, including some 35 vinos served by the glass; belly up to the restaurant's Fish Bar for some Prosecco and mussels.

5040 Cass St. (at Opal St.), ³⁄₄-mile north of Garnet Ave.), Pacific Beach. ℂ 858/272-9985. www.pacshell. com. Reservations recommended for dinner. Main courses $9–$28 lunch, $10–$35 dinner. AE, DC, DISC, MC, V. Daily 11am–10pm. Street parking usually available. Bus: 30.

The Green Flash AMERICAN   Known throughout Pacific Beach for its location and local clientele, the Green Flash serves adequate (and typically beachy) food at decent prices. The menu includes plenty of grilled and deep-fried seafood, straightforward steaks, and giant main-course salads. You'll also find appetizer platters of shellfish (oys-ters, clams, shrimp) and jalapeño "poppers" (cheese-stuffed fried peppers). The glassed-in patio is one of P.B.'s best places for people-watching, and locals congregate at sunset to catch a glimpse of the optical phenomenon for which this boardwalk hangout is named. It has something to do with the color spectrum at the moment the sun disappears below the horizon, but the scientific explanation becomes less important—and the decibel level rises—with every round of drinks.

701 Thomas Ave. (at Mission Blvd.), Pacific Beach. ℂ **858/270-7715.** www.greenflashrestaurant.com. Reservations not accepted. Main courses $5–$9 breakfast, $9–$15 lunch, $10–$43 dinner. AE, DC, DISC, MC, V. Daily 8am–10pm (bar till 2am). Bus: 8, 9, or 30.

Gringo's ★ MEXICAN   This upscale space may have a downscale name, but it bears little resemblance to typical Mexican restaurants. Warm woods, cool flagstone, and trendy lighting providing a modern feel; the large patio is primed with heaters and blazing fire pits most evenings. Although the menu offers a tip of the hat to dishes the average gringo will recognize (quesadillas, fajitas, burritos), flip it over and you'll see the focus is on regional specialties from all over Mexico—the food of Oaxaca, the Yucatan, and Mexico's Pacific Coast. So, a chicken breast is stuffed with goat cheese and corn and then lathered in a sauce of *huitlacoche* (a delicious fungus that grows on corn); a poblano chili is stuffed with picadillo and draped in a walnut cream sauce and a drizzle of pomegranate reduction. The margarita options are well worth inspection (with more than 100 tequilas available), as is the selection of Mexican wines. Sunday all-you-can-eat brunch is served from 9am to 2pm.

4474 Mission Blvd. (at Garnet Ave.), Pacific Beach. © **858/490-2877.** www.gringoscantina.com. Reservations suggested for weekends. Main courses $6–$14 lunch, $8–$31 dinner, $17–$20 brunch. AE, DC, DISC, MC, V. Mon–Sat 11am–11pm; Sun 9am–11pm. Free (small) parking lot. Bus: 8, 9, 27, or 30.

Sushi Ota ★★★ SUSHI   Masterful chef-owner Yukito Ota creates San Diego's finest sushi. This sophisticated, traditional restaurant is a minimalist bento box with stark white walls and black furniture, softened by indirect lighting. The sushi menu is short, because discerning regulars look first to the daily specials posted behind the counter. The city's most experienced chefs, armed with nimble fingers and seriously sharp knives, turn the day's fresh catch into artful little bundles accented with mounds of wasabi and ginger. The rest of the varied menu features seafood, teriyaki-glazed meats, feather-light tempura, and a variety of small appetizers perfect to accompany a large sushi order. This restaurant is difficult to find, mainly because it's hard to believe that such outstanding dining would hide behind a laundromat and convenience store in the rear of a minimall. It's also in a nondescript part of Pacific Beach—a stone's throw from I-5.

4529 Mission Bay Dr. (at Bunker Hill), Pacific Beach. © **858/270-5670.** Reservations strongly recommended on weekends. Main courses $6–$14 lunch, $9–$22 dinner; sushi $4–$13. AE, MC, V. Tues–Fri 11:30am–2pm and 5:30–10:30pm; Sat–Sun 5–10:30pm. Free parking (additional lot behind the mall). Bus: 30.

The 3rd Corner ★★ FRENCH   I love this place, set in an old beach bungalow on the outskirts of Ocean Beach. Part wine shop, part bistro, part neighborhood bar—it's intimate, convivial, and unique. You can wander through racks of wine (about 1,000 bottles are available at any given time), pick the one you like, and find yourself a spot to enjoy a menu of small plates and entrees with a French-Mediterranean flair ($5 corkage). Seating for dining is limited, but there's a full bar, lounge, and patio. Look for wine-friendly fare such as charcuterie plates, an array of cheeses, and pâté, as well as black truffle risotto and duck confit; Sunday brunch is served 11am to 3pm. Best of all, 3rd Corner serves food and drinks late—until 1am (except Mon). There's also an outpost in Encinitas at the Lumberyard shopping center, 897 S. Coast Hwy. (© **760/942-2104**).

2265 Bacon St. (at W. Point Loma Blvd.), Ocean Beach. © **619/223-2700.** www.the3rdcorner.com. Main courses $10–$21. AE, DISC, MC, V. Kitchen Tues–Sun 11:30am–1am. Wine shop Tues–Sun 10am–1:30am. Free parking. Bus: 35 or 923.

INEXPENSIVE

Corvette Diner ⓚⓘⓓⓢ AMERICAN   This family-friendly time warp serves burgers, sandwiches, appetizer munchies, blue-plate specials, and salads, along with a *very* full page of fountain favorites; beer, wine, and cocktails are also available. As of this writing,

Corvette Diner was in the process of relocating from Hillcrest to Liberty Station, the massive redevelopment project that was once the U.S. Naval Training Center in Point Loma. The new spot is twice the size of the original and is set in what was once the NTC officers' club. There will be three themed rooms: the Corvette Room, the '70s Blacklight Room, and the Diner Car; the Gamer's Garage will be stocked with arcade games. The huge parking lot (a big improvement over parking-challenged Hillcrest) will host classic car shows and auto rallies.

2965 Historic Decatur Rd. (in Liberty Station, off Rosecrans St.), Point Loma. (*) 619/542-1476. www. cohnrestaurants.com. Reservations not accepted. Main courses $9–$15; kids' plates $7. AE, DC, DISC, MC, V. Sun–Thurs 11am–10pm; Fri–Sat 11am–11pm. Free parking. Bus: 28 or 923.

The Mission ★ (**Value**) BREAKFAST/LIGHT FARE   Located alongside the funky surf shops and bikini boutiques of bohemian Mission Beach, the Mission is the neighborhood's central meeting place. The menu features all-day breakfasts, from traditional pancakes and nouvelle egg dishes to burritos and quesadillas. Standouts include chicken-apple sausage with eggs and a mound of rosemary potatoes, and cinnamon French toast with blackberry purée. At lunch, the menu expands for sandwiches, salads, and a few Chino-Latino items such as ginger-sesame chicken tacos. Seating is casual, comfy, and conducive to lingering (tons of students, writers, and surfers hang out here), if only with a soup bowl–size latte. Expect waits of half an hour or more on weekends. Other locations: 2801 University Ave., in North Park ((*) 619/220-8992), and 1250 J St., downtown ((*) 619/232-7662); both have similar menus and hours.

3795 Mission Blvd. (at San Jose), Mission Beach. (*) 858/488-9060. www.themission1.signonsandiego. com. All items $7–$11. AE, MC, V. Daily 7am–3pm. Bus: 8 or 9.

7 LA JOLLA

As befits an upscale community with time (and money) on its hands, La Jolla has more than its fair share of good restaurants, and thankfully not all of them are expensive. While many dining spots are clustered in the village, on Prospect Street and the few blocks directly east, you can also cruise down La Jolla Boulevard or up by the La Jolla Beach & Tennis Club for additional choices.

There are old-school favorites that still impress, such as the 11-table, utterly romantic **Sky Room** ★★ at the La Valencia Hotel (p. 84), 1132 Prospect St. ((*) 858/454-0771; www.lavalencia.com), which features fabulous views and French-inspired cuisine. There are more Gallic goings-on at **Michele Coulon Dessertier** ★★, 7556D Fay Ave. ((*) 858/456-5098; www.dessertier.com); this small cafe and bakery specializes in decadent desserts, but also serves very good light lunches (quiches, salads, sandwiches). For lunch or breakfast, the **Coffee Cup** ★, 1109 Wall St. ((*) 858/551-8514; www.isabels-cantina.com), is a spot popular with locals; Isabel's Cantina (p. 112) in Point Loma is this joint's sister restaurant. For traditional Mexican, head down La Jolla Boulevard to **Su Casa,** 6738 La Jolla Blvd. ((*) 858/454-0369; www.sucasarestaurant.com), a family-friendly place that's been here forever (well, since 1967 anyway).

VERY EXPENSIVE

The Marine Room ★★★ (**Moments**) FRENCH/CALIFORNIAN   Since 1941, San Diego's most celebrated dining room has been this shorefront institution. Executive Chef Bernard Guillas of Brittany and Chef de Cuisine Ron Oliver work with local produce, but never hesitate to pursue unusual flavors from other corners of the globe—pomegranate- and macadamia-coated Scottish salmon with red quinoa, bok choy, and lemon verbena essence, or nectarine-glazed pompano with crab risotto and a sake emulsion. The Marine Room ranks as one of San Diego's most expensive venues, but it's usually filled to the gills on weekends; weekdays it's much easier to score a table. Ideally, schedule your reservation a half-hour or so before sunset; if you can't get in at that magic hour, experience sundown by the bar—a more wallet-friendly lounge and happy-hour menu are available.

2000 Spindrift Dr., La Jolla. ℂ **866/644-2351.** www.marineroom.com. Reservations recommended, especially weekends. Main courses $27–$48. AE, DC, DISC, MC, V. Sun–Thurs 5:30–9:30pm; Fri–Sat 5:30–10pm Lounge daily from 4pm. Valet parking $6. Bus: 30.

Nine-Ten ★★★ CALIFORNIAN   This warmly stylish space is the place for market-fresh cuisine, prepared by Jason Knibb, another member of San Diego's cadre of skilled young chefs. Knibb, who was mentored by such culinary figures as Wolfgang Puck, Roy Yamaguchi, and Hans Rockenwanger, presides over a shifting, seasonal menu that's best enjoyed via small-plate grazings. Past offerings have included espresso and chocolate-braised boneless short ribs, Maine scallops with apple risotto, and harissa-marinated shrimp. Or better yet, turn yourself over to the "Mercy of the Chef," a five-course tasting menu for $80, or $120 with wine pairings (your whole table has to participate, though). When you're looking for a classy fine-dining experience without the old-guard attitude, Nine-Ten, located at the Grande Colonial hotel (p. 82), fits the bill very nicely. Breakfast and lunch are served, too.

910 Prospect St. (btw. Fay and Girard aves.), La Jolla. ℂ **858/964-5400.** www.nine-ten.com. Reservations recommended. Main courses $6–$18 breakfast, $11–$18 lunch, $13–$40 dinner. AE, DC, DISC, MC, V. Daily 6:30–11am (Sun breakfast until 12:30pm), 11:30am–2:30pm, and 6–10pm. Valet parking $2. Bus: 30.

EXPENSIVE

Georges California Modern ★★★ (Moments) CALIFORNIAN   This is perhaps La Jolla's signature restaurant. It has it all: stunning ocean views, style, impeccable service, and above all, a world-class chef. Not resting on its considerable laurels, however, Georges closed briefly in early 2007, undergoing a $2.5-million renovation. It reemerged with a slightly new name and a new design-forward environment. Most importantly, though, Trey Foshee can still be found in the kitchen. Foshee, named one of America's top 10 chefs by *Food & Wine,* has been set loose stylistically; there's a larger, more adventurous menu than before, incorporating more cross-cultural influences and still driven by the freshest local ingredients available. Fine food and incomparable views at more modest prices are upstairs at the **Ocean Terrace** and **George's Bar.** These two spaces offer indoor and outdoor seating, as well as food from the same kitchen as the pricey main dining room; lunch is served here daily. Georges also has complimentary car service, subject to availability, within an 8-mile radius. Classy.

1250 Prospect St., La Jolla. ℂ **858/454-4244.** www.georgesatthecove.com. Reservations strongly recommended. Main courses $28–$90. AE, DC, DISC, MC, V. Sun–Thurs 5:30–10pm; Fri–Sat 5–10:30pm. Ocean Terrace Bistro main courses $10–$15 lunch, $17–$25 dinner. Daily 11am–10pm (Fri–Sat till 10:30pm). Valet parking $7. Bus: 30.

Jack's La Jolla ★★★ CALIFORNIAN/ITALIAN   This multistory epicurean fun house rises from sidewalk coffee stop to third-floor sushi bar, with a fine-dining component and a handful of bars and lounges (with live music and DJs) thrown in for good measure. Jack's is built around an open-air courtyard that can take full advantage of

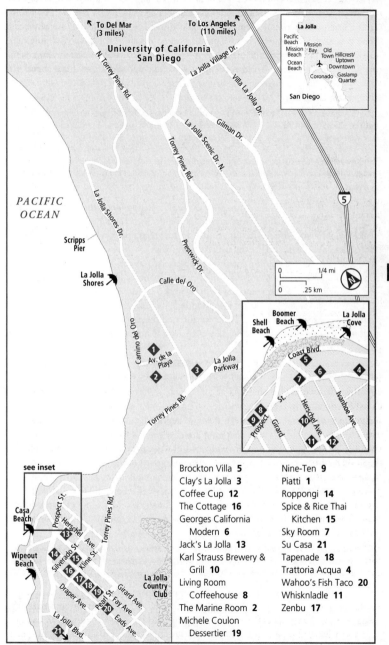

Brockton Villa **5**
Clay's La Jolla **3**
Coffee Cup **12**
The Cottage **16**
Georges California
    Modern **6**
Jack's La Jolla **13**
Karl Strauss Brewery &
    Grill **10**
Living Room
    Coffeehouse **8**
The Marine Room **2**
Michele Coulon
    Dessertier **19**

Nine-Ten **9**
Piatti **1**
Roppongi **14**
Spice & Rice Thai
    Kitchen **15**
Sky Room **7**
Su Casa **21**
Tapenade **18**
Trattoria Acqua **4**
Wahoo's Fish Taco **20**
Whisknladle **11**
Zenbu **17**

sunny days and mild nights; it's also built around the talents of chef Tony DiSalvo, formerly chef de cuisine at Jean-Georges in New York City. Jack's middle level features the chic **Wall Street Bar,** the most sedate of Jack's lounge areas, and **Viaggio.** This formal dining space is modern but warm, serving pasta dishes, steaks, and chops; on the ground floor is snazzy **Jack's Grille,** which provides more casual, less expensive dining. The **Ocean Room** offers lunch and dinner (and has private cabanas with ocean views), while the **Sidewalk Cafe** serves baked goods, pizzas, panini, smoothies, and salads. **Level 3** is Jack's alfresco rooftop nightclub; Thursday through Saturday it's where you will find the village's most Gaslamp Quarter–like experience.

7863 Girard Ave., La Jolla. ℂ **858/456-8111.** www.jackslajolla.com. Reservations recommended. Viaggio main courses $18–$47. AE, DC, DISC, MC, V. Tues–Sat 5:30–10pm. Jack's Grille main courses $11–$29. Sun–Wed 5–9:30pm; Thurs–Sat 5–11pm. Ocean Room main courses $11–$14 lunch, $23–$43 dinner. Daily 11:30am–2:30pm; Sun–Wed 5:30–9:30pm; Thurs–Sat 5:30–11pm. Sidewalk Cafe Sun–Tues 8am–8pm; Wed–Thurs 8am–10pm; Fri–Sat 8am–11pm. Bars and lounges daily for happy hour 5:30–6:30pm and until 2am Thurs–Sat (Wall St. Bar and Level 3 closed Mon). Valet parking Tues–Sun 11:30am–close $8. Bus: 30.

Roppongi ★ PACIFIC RIM/ASIAN FUSION   At Roppongi, the cuisines of Japan, Thailand, China, Vietnam, Korea, and India collide, sometimes gracefully, in a vibrant explosion of flavors. You might not get past the first menu page, a long list of small tapas dishes designed for sharing; each table is preset with a tall stack of plates that quietly encourage a communal meal of successive appetizers. You can jump from Thai satay and Chinese pot stickers to a Mongolian duck quesadilla and Indonesian spicy shrimp without missing a beat. When you order right, it works. (A number of the dishes are sweet, so ask your waiter for a good balance.) Options increase exponentially when you start considering the sushi bar menu. There are also traditionally sized main courses featuring seafood, meat, and game, all colorfully prepared; at lunch there's a selection of bento boxes.

875 Prospect St. (at Fay Ave.), La Jolla. ℂ **858/551-5252.** www.roppongiusa.com. Reservations recommended. Tapas $9–$19 tapas; main courses $10–$15 lunch, $23–$48 dinner. AE, DC, DISC, MC, V. Sun–Thurs 11:30am–9:30pm; Fri–Sat 11:30am–10:30pm. Valet parking $7; garage parking available for dinner. Bus: 30.

Tapenade ★★★ FRENCH   This elegant and distinguished restaurant is the poster child for the giant leap forward the local dining scene has taken over the last decade. A labor-of-love endeavor operated by husband-and-wife team Sylvie and Jean-Michel Diot, Tapenade is a showcase for Jean-Michel's light, creative touch in the kitchen—a talent he honed at a series of Michelin two- and three-star restaurants in his native France. He moved to San Diego in 1998 after establishing a series of successful bistros in New York. The Big Apple's loss has been San Diego's gain; Tapenade's fresh, sunny fare has helped redefine French cuisine here. Lunch and early-bird prix-fixe menus, as well as selections for vegetarians and children, are served; happy hour is Sunday to Thursday at 5pm.

7612 Fay Ave. (btw. Kline and Pearls sts.), La Jolla. ℂ **858/551-7500.** www.tapenaderestaurant.com. Dinner reservations recommended. Main courses $14–$19 lunch, $26–$38 dinner. AE, MC, V. Mon–Fri 11:30am–2:30pm; Sun–Thurs 5:30–9:30pm; Fri–Sat 5:30–10pm. Parking in lot behind the building. Bus: 30.

Trattoria Acqua ★★ ITALIAN/MEDITERRANEAN   Nestled on tiled terraces that look out over the sweeping coastline, this spot has a relaxed, Tuscan ambience, but serves Italian coastal cuisine. A mixed crowd of suits, couples, and families gathers to enjoy expertly prepared seasonal dishes; every table starts with bread served with an indescribably pungent Mediterranean spread. Acqua's pastas are luscious—rich, heady flavor combinations such as orecchiette with spicy shrimp, ham, broccoli, white beans, and wine, or lobster ravioli with tomato-and-chive beurre blanc. Other specialties include gourmet pizzas, scallops and shrimp in a spicy lobster sauce, and *quaglie a beccafico* (roasted quail with Italian bacon, spinach, raisins, and pine nuts).

1298 Prospect St. (on Coast Walk), La Jolla. © **858/454-0709.** www.trattoriaacqua.com. Reservations recommended. Main courses $9–$20 lunch, $16–$35 dinner. AE, DC, MC, V. Mon–Fri 11:30am–2:30pm; Mon–Thurs 5–9pm; Fri–Sat 5–10:30pm; Sun 5–9:30pm. Validated self-parking. Bus: 30.

Zenbu ★★ SUSHI/SEAFOOD   La Jolla native Matt Rimel loved fishing so much he bought a commercial fishing boat. "Nobody buys local fish, so in order to keep doing it, I had to open a restaurant," he says. He now operates three restaurants and still owns that local boat—not to mention an international fleet that trawls for his eateries as well as select clients. You can order something from the sushi bar, such as exquisite toro, creamy uni, or one of the specialty rolls. You could try an entree such as steak of locally harpooned swordfish or grilled local fish of the day. The fabulous lobster dynamite, a half lobster (local, naturally) and crab baked in a special sauce, is given a dramatic, flaming presentation. Next door, intimate **Zenbu Lounge** (Thurs–Sat) has a sushi bar and DJs.

7660 Fay Ave. (at Kline St.), La Jolla. © **858/454-4540.** www.zenbusushi.com. Reservations not accepted. Main courses $22–$30. AE, DC, DISC, MC, V. Sun–Wed 5–9:30pm; Thurs–Sat 5–10:30pm. Happy hour all night Sun–Mon; Tues–Thurs 5–7pm. Lounge Thurs–Sat 8pm–1am. Free parking. Bus: 30.

MODERATE

Brockton Villa ★ BREAKFAST/CALIFORNIAN   A restored 1894 beach bungalow, this charming cafe is named for an early resident's hometown (Brockton, Massachusetts) and occupies a breathtaking perch overlooking La Jolla Cove. The biggest buzz is at breakfast, when you can enjoy such inventive dishes as soufflé-like "Coast Toast" and Greek "steamers" (eggs scrambled with an espresso steamer, and then mixed with feta cheese, tomato, and basil). Breakfasts are served until noon weekdays, until 3pm weekends. Lunch highlights include house-made soups, salads, and sandwiches including the grilled organic salmon BLT. The somewhat less successful supper menu includes seafood and steak dishes, plus paella, pastas, and grilled meats. But any time you can actually enjoy this spectacular sea view, Brockton's food tastes good. *Note:* Steep stairs from the street limit wheelchair access.

1235 Coast Blvd. (across from La Jolla Cove), La Jolla. © **858/454-7393.** www.brocktonvilla.com. Reservations recommended. Main courses $7–$15 breakfast, $11–$18 lunch, $16–$30 dinner. AE, DISC, MC, V. Sun–Wed 8am–4pm; Thurs–Sat 8am–9pm. Bus: 30.

Piatti ★ ITALIAN/MEDITERRANEAN   La Jolla's version of the reliable neighborhood hangout is this pasta-centric trattoria, a couple blocks inland from La Jolla Shores. You're likely to be surrounded by a crew of regulars that pop in weekly and know the staff by name. You won't feel left out, however, and the food is well priced. The lemon herbroasted chicken and *bistecca* (rib-eye) are fantastic, but it's the pastas that parade out to most tables. Try orecchiette bathed in Gorgonzola, grilled chicken, and sun-dried tomatoes, or pappardelle—shrimp-crowned ribbons of saffron pasta, primed with garlic, tomato, and white wine. Those who are concerned with carbo-loading can substitute spinach for pasta. Beneath the romantic sprawl of an enormous ficus tree, the outdoor patio is always ideal, thanks to the cozy heaters.

2182 Av. de la Playa, La Jolla. © **858/454-1589.** www.piatti.com. Reservations recommended. Main courses $13–$29; Sat–Sun brunch $9–$13. AE, DC, MC, V. Mon–Thurs 11:30am–10pm; Fri 11:30am–11pm; Sat 11am–11pm; Sun 11am–10pm. Street parking usually available. Bus: 30.

(Moments) **Appetizing Views**

Incredible ocean vistas, a glittering skyline, and sailboats slicing through the water offshore—it's the classic backdrop for a memorable meal. So where can you find the best views?

Downtown, the **Fish Market** and its pricier cousin **Top of the Market** (p. 103) overlook San Diego Bay, and the management even provides binoculars for getting a good look at aircraft carriers and other vessels. With its over-the-water setting on Harbor Island, near the airport, **Island Prime** (p. 102) is another visual overachiever (with plenty of outdoor seating). Across the harbor in Coronado, **Il Fornaio,** 1333 First St. ((C) 619/437-4911; www.ilfornaio.com), **Peohe's,** 1201 First St. ((C) 619/437-4474; www.peohes.com), and **Candelas** (p. 100) offer gorgeous views of the San Diego skyline; tony **Mistral** (p. 123), at Loews Coronado Bay Resort, provides a unique north-facing look across the bay.

In Ocean Beach, **Nick's at the Pier,** 5083 Santa Monica Ave. ((C) 619/222-7437; www.nicksatthepier.com), sits on a second-floor perch right across the street from the beach; in Pacific Beach, the **Green Flash** (p. 115) is just 5 feet from the sand (although the year-round parade of bodies may prove a distraction from the ocean). In La Jolla, the **Sky Room** (p. 117) and **Georges California Modern** (p. 118) offer sweeping, elevated views of the coast, but **Brockton Villa** (p. 121) actually offers the La Jolla Cove perspective as advertised on every postcard stand in town. If you want to get up close and personal with the oceanic scene, head to the **Marine Room** (p. 117). Located right on La Jolla Shores beach, the restaurant's windows utilize SeaWorld technology to withstand the seasonal tides that crash into the glass. Somewhat inland, but 11 stories up atop the Hotel La Jolla, is **Clay's La Jolla** (p. 86).

Uptown, **Bertrand at Mister A's** (p. 105) sits on the 12th floor at Fifth and Laurel, and the panorama here encompasses Balboa Park (as well as the living rooms of some ritzy condo towers) to the east, downtown to the south, and San Diego Harbor and Point Loma to the west. The vistas here are unsurpassed.

Spice & Rice Thai Kitchen ★ THAI The lunch crowd at this attractive Thai restaurant consists of shoppers and tourists, while dinner is quieter. The covered front patio has a secluded garden feel, perfect for a romantic evening. The food is excellent, with polished presentations and expert renditions of classics such as pad Thai, curry, and glazed duck. Consider making a meal of appetizer specialties including "gold bags" (minced pork, vegetables, glass noodles, and herbs wrapped in crispy rice paper and served with earthy plum sauce) or prawns with yellow curry lobster sauce. Despite the passage of time, this all-around satisfier remains something of an insider's secret.

7734 Girard Ave., La Jolla. (C) 858/456-0466. www.spiceandricethaikitchen.com. Reservations recommended. Main courses $9–$11 lunch, $11–$17 dinner. AE, DC, DISC, MC, V. Mon–Fri 11am–3pm and 5–10pm (Fri until 11pm); Sat 11:30am–3:30pm and 5–11pm; Sun 5–10pm. Bus: 30.

Whisknladle ★ CALIFORNIAN Forging on through a transfer of ownership and an awkward series of name changes, Whisknladle (once known as **Fresh,** then **Fresher**) has proven to be remarkably resilient. Serving a menu of gourmet comfort food created from top-quality products at modest sums, Whisknladle also passes along retail pricing on wine. Chef Ryan Johnston, a protégé of French Laundry's Thomas Keller, is fanatical about making things from scratch, doing everything from curing and smoking meats to baking the bread and churning the ice cream in-house. The restaurant's covered patio segues into a down-tempo lounge on Friday and Saturday, offering another much-needed late-night alternative in sleepy La Jolla. Brunch is served on the weekends.

1044 Wall St. (at Hershel), La Jolla. © **858/551-7575.** www.whisknladle.com. Reservations recommended. Main courses $11–$32 lunch, $15–$32 dinner. AE, DISC, MC, V. Sun–Thurs 11:30am–9pm; Fri–Sat 11:30am–10pm (lounge until 1:30am). Free 2-hr. validated parking at Hotel Parisi. Bus: 30.

INEXPENSIVE

The Cottage ★ BREAKFAST/LIGHT FARE La Jolla's best—and friendliest— breakfast is served at this turn-of-the-20th-century bungalow. The cottage is light and airy, but most diners opt for tables outside, where a charming white picket fence encloses the trellis-shaded brick patio. Omelets and egg dishes feature Mediterranean, Cal-Latino, and classic American touches. Homemade granola is a favorite, as well (it's even packaged and sold to take home). The Cottage also bakes its own muffins, rolls, and coffeecakes. While breakfast dishes are served all day, toward lunchtime the kitchen begins turning out freshly made, healthful soups, light meals, and sandwiches. Dinners (served in summer only) are a delight, particularly when you're seated before dark on a balmy night.

7702 Fay Ave. (at Kline St.), La Jolla. © **858/454-8409.** www.cottagelajolla.com. Reservations accepted for dinner only. Main courses $8–$12 breakfast, $9–$15 lunch, $11–$23 dinner. AE, DISC, MC, V. Daily 7:30am–3pm; dinner (June–Aug only) Tues–Sat 5–9:30pm. Bus: 30.

---

8 CORONADO

Rather like the conservative aura that pervades the entire "island," Coronado's dining options are reliable, but the restaurants aren't exactly breaking new culinary ground. A couple of exceptions are the resort dining rooms, which seem to be waging a rivalry over who can set the bar highest. If you're in the mood for a special-occasion meal that'll knock your socks off, consider **Mistral** ★★ (© **619/424-4000;** www.loewshotels.com), at Loews Coronado Bay Resort (p. 91). With its plushly upholstered, gilded, and view-endowed setting, this stylish dining room wins continual raves from deep-pocketed San Diego foodies willing to cross the bay for inventive and artistic California-Mediterranean creations. Meanwhile, the Hotel del Coronado (p. 89) unveiled its signature restaurant, **1500 Ocean** ★★ (© **619/522-8490;** www.dine1500ocean.com), in 2006 to enthusiastic reviews. This smart, contemporary space eschews Victoriana for a stylish California Craftsman look. The menu is California-oriented as well, featuring a Southland coastal cuisine that draws inspiration—and top-quality products—from throughout the region. The fabulous patio dining offers views of the ocean and Point Loma in the distance.

Mexican fare (gringo-style, but well practiced) is served at popular **Miguel's Cocina** at El Cordova Hotel (© **619/437-4237;** www.brigantine.com), but if you seek ethnic food or designer spaces, head back across the bridge.

EXPENSIVE

The Brigantine AMERICAN/SEAFOOD The Brigantine is best known for its oyster-bar happy hour (3–6pm Mon–Fri; 4:30pm–close Sun). Beer, margaritas, and food are heavily discounted, and you can expect standing room only. Early-bird specials include a seafood, steak, or chicken entree served with soup or salad, a side of veggies, and bread for $19 (5–6:30pm Sun–Thurs). The food is good, not great, but the congenial atmosphere is a certifiable draw. Inside, the decor is upscale and resolutely nautical; outside, there's a pleasant patio with heaters to take the chill off the night air. At lunch, you can get everything from crab cakes or fish and chips to fresh fish or pasta. There are several other Brig locations, including Point Loma (the original), 2725 Shelter Island Dr. (© **619/224-2871**), and Del Mar, 3263 Camino del Mar (© **858/481-1166**).

1333 Orange Ave., Coronado. © 619/435-4166. www.brigantine.com. Reservations recommended on weekends. Main courses $10–$18 lunch, $16–$48 dinner. AE, DC, MC, V. Mon–Thurs 11:30am–10pm; Fri–Sat 11:30am–10:30pm; Sun 4:30–10pm. Small parking lot. Bus: 901 or 904.

Chez Loma ★ FRENCH This intimate Victorian cottage filled with antiques and subdued candlelight makes for romantic dining. The house dates from 1889, the French restaurant from 1975. Tables are scattered throughout the house and on the enclosed garden terrace; an upstairs wine salon, reminiscent of a Victorian parlor, is a cozy spot. Among the entrees are roast duck with lingonberry, port, and burnt-orange sauce. Follow dinner with a cheese platter with berries and port sauce or a dessert sampler. California wines and American microbrews are available, in addition to a full bar. Early birds enjoy specially priced meals: $25 for a three-course meal before 6pm and all night on Tuesday.

1132 Loma (off Orange Ave.), Coronado. © 619/435-0661. www.chezloma.com. Reservations recommended. Main courses $24–$37. AE, DC, DISC, MC, V. Tues–Sun 5–10pm. Bus: 901 or 904.

MODERATE

Rhinoceros Cafe & Grille ★ AMERICAN This light, bright bistro is more casual than it looks from the street and offers large portions, though the kitchen can be a little heavy-handed with sauces and spices. At lunch, try the popular penne à la vodka in creamy tomato sauce; favorite dinner specials are Italian cioppino, Southwestern-style meatloaf, and salmon poached and crusted with herb sauce. Plenty of crispy fresh salads balance out the menu. For drinks, choose from the fair wine list or try a Rhino Chaser's American Ale.

1166 Orange Ave., Coronado. © 619/435-2121. www.rhinocafe.com. Main courses $7–$12 lunch, $12–$27 dinner. AE, DC, DISC, MC, V. Daily 11am–2:30pm; Sun–Thurs 5–9pm; Fri–Sat 5–10pm. Street parking usually available. Bus: 901 or 904.

INEXPENSIVE

Bino's Bistro & Winebar (Finds) BREAKFAST/LIGHT FARE This casual, Euro-style spot near the Hotel Del serves sweet and savory crepes and fresh-baked pastries and bread that keep the regulars coming back for more. Owned by a husband-and-wife team with solid culinary creds (she's a native of Austria, where she attended culinary school; he's a veteran of one of San Diego's finest hotel dining rooms), the menu also includes creative omelets, deli sandwiches, and salads. Specialty coffees, wine, champagne, and beer are also on hand. Service can be spotty, but you'll be happy once you get your Nutella-banana crepe.

1120 Adella St., Coronado. © 619/522-0612. Main courses $6–$11. AE, DISC, MC, V. Daily 7am–5pm. Bus: 901 or 904.

Clayton's Coffee Shop (Value) AMERICAN/BREAKFAST The Hotel Del isn't the only relic of a bygone era in Coronado—just wait until you see this humble neighborhood favorite. Clayton's has occupied this corner spot forever, or at least since *everyone's* menu was full of plain American good eatin' for around $5. Now the horseshoe counter, chrome bar stools, and well-worn pleather-lined booths are "retro," but the burgers, fries,

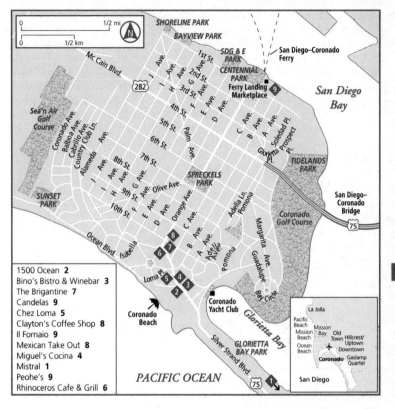

1500 Ocean **2**
Bino's Bistro & Winebar **3**
The Brigantine **7**
Candelas **9**
Chez Loma **5**
Clayton's Coffee Shop **8**
Il Fornaio **9**
Mexican Take Out **8**
Miguel's Cocina **4**
Mistral **1**
Peohe's **9**
Rhinoceros Cafe & Grill **6**

WHERE TO DINE

6

OFF THE (TOURIST) BEATEN PATH

and turkey noodle soup are timeless and quite good—plus you can still play three oldies for a quarter on the table-side jukebox. Behind the coffee shop is Clayton's *hermana* restaurant, **Mexican Take Out,** 1107 10th St. (*©* **619/437-8811**). This closet-size, no-frills spot does a brisk business in tamales and other Mexican staples. As the straightforward name implies, it's takeout only.

979 Orange Ave., Coronado. *©* **619/435-5425.** All menu items under $9. No credit cards. Mon–Sat 6am–8pm; Sun 6am–2pm. Bus: 901 or 904.

9 OFF THE (TOURIST) BEATEN PATH

Don't limit your dining experience in San Diego to the main tourist zones outlined above. Five minutes north of Mission Valley is the mostly business neighborhood of Kearny Mesa, home to San Diego's best Asian venues. One to try is **Jasmine** ★, 4609 Convoy St. (*©* **858/268-0888**; www.jasminerestaurants.com), which, at lunch, showcases wonderful Hong Kong–style dumplings that are wheeled around the room on carts; dinners are more elaborate—seafood dishes and the Peking duck are good choices.

Service here can range from gruff to incomprehensible, though. Nearby is **China Max** ★, 4698 Convoy St. (© **858/650-3333;** www.chinamaxsandiego.com), which occupies a nondescript building near the junction of the 805 and 163 freeways; the room is spare, but the kitchen exhibits finesse with southern Chinese delicacies and always has excellent (sometimes pricey) live fish specials. Another place easy to miss thanks to its inconspicuous locale is **Spicy City,** 4690 Convoy St. (© **858/278-1818**). This is Szechuan food, the real deal (though regulars bemoan changes that have occurred since a new owner has taken over). For a dining experience that will transport you straight to Japan, seek out tiny **Wa Dining Okan** ★★, 3860 Convoy St. (© **858/279-0941**). This friendly, hard-to-find spot has become a sensation (you'll need reservations); it serves traditional, home-style delicacies just like your mother would make, if she were Japanese ("okan" translates as "mom"). It's tucked into a shopping mall next to a Japanese market and has little signage.

Just east of Hillcrest (south and parallel to Mission Valley) is Adams Avenue. Here you'll find the **Kensington Grill** ★★, 4055 Adams Ave. (© **619/281-4014;** www. sdurbankitchen.com), next to the Ken Cinema. It's owned by the same crew in charge of the dining hot spot **Laurel** (p. 106) and features contemporary American cuisine in a chic setting that draws lots of neighborhood types. Across the street is the lively, authentically rustic **Bleu Bohème** ★, 4090 Adams Ave. (© **619/255-4167;** www.bleuboheme. com). This boisterous bistro is known for its mussels, meat and cheese platters, and French onion soup. In nearby Normal Heights, **Jyoti Bihanga,** 3351 Adams Ave. (© **619/282-4116;** www.jyotibihanga.com), delivers a vegetarian menu of Indian-influenced salads, wraps, and curries; the "neatloaf," made with grains and tofu, is a winner. Entrees are priced under $12.

South of Adams Avenue, University Avenue runs through North Park (p. 54). This working-class neighborhood has been infused with new life and new development, most notably the resurrected North Park Theatre, a performing arts venue originally built in 1928. Next door to the theater is **Spread** ★, 2879 University Ave. (© **619/543-0406;** www.spreadtherestaurant.com), where the "nouveau comfort food" menu is vegetarian/ vegan, relying on a daily influx of seasonal, organic products. Excellent health-conscious Mexican food (yes, it does exist) is found at **Ranchos Cocina** ★, 3910 30th St. (© **619/ 574-1288;** www.ranchosnaturalfoods.com), just off University Avenue. This popular eatery will even prepare you something vegan—try asking for *that* in Old Town. There is also an outlet in Ocean Beach at 1830 Sunset Cliffs Blvd. (© **619/226-7619**).

Some of the newer eateries making noise in North Park include **Urban Solace** ★, 3823 30th St. (© **619/295-6464;** www.urbansolace.net), **The Linkery** ★, 3794 30th St. (© **619/255-8778;** www.thelinkery.com), and **Jayne's Gastropub** ★, 4677 30th St. (© **619/563-1011;** www.jaynesgastropub.com). Urban Solace provides just that, serving contemporary comfort food such as lamb meatloaf; there's a live bluegrass brunch on Sundays, too. The Linkery is a meat-lover's paradise, featuring gourmet sausages and charcuterie, plus an amazing selection of beer; vegans and vegetarians will find something to their liking on the menu, too. Jayne's reflects the neighborhood's casual cool, featuring a sophisticated beer and wine list, and a menu that runs from mussels with chorizo to a stupendous burger.

Out in the far-flung 'burb of Rancho Bernardo awaits one of San Diego's most memorable dining experiences. **El Bizcocho** ★★★ is the fine-dining restaurant at the golf and tennis resort Rancho Bernardo Inn, 17550 Bernardo Oaks Dr. (© **858/675-8550;** www.ranchobernardoinn.com). It's one of the last of San Diego's formal, gourmet experiences, serving classic French dishes with a California twist in a tasting-menu-only style. No tennis shoes or denim are allowed; jackets suggested for men.

What to See & Do

You won't run out of things to see and do in San Diego, especially if outdoor activities are high on the agenda. The San Diego Zoo, SeaWorld, and the Wild Animal Park are the city's three top attractions, but there are also Balboa Park's museums, downtown's Gaslamp Quarter, the beaches, and shopping in Old Town. You can catch a performance at one of our prized live theaters or a Padres game at downtown PETCO Park, as well. See chapter 4 for itineraries and advice on how to organize your time.

1 THE THREE MAJOR ANIMAL PARKS

If you're looking for wild times, San Diego supplies them. The world-famous **San Diego Zoo** is home to more than 800 animal species, many of them rare and exotic. A sister attraction, the **Wild Animal Park,** offers 430 species in an *au naturel* setting. And Shamu and his friends form a veritable chorus line at **SeaWorld San Diego**—waving their flippers, waddling across an ersatz Antarctica, and blowing killer-whale kisses—in various shows throughout the day.

San Diego's "Big Three" family attractions are joined by **LEGOLAND California** (p. 237).

San Diego Wild Animal Park ★★★ (Kids) Thirty-four miles north of San Diego, outside of Escondido, this "zoo of the future" will transport you to the African plains and other faraway landscapes. Originally a breeding facility for the San Diego Zoo, the 1,800-acre Wild Animal Park now holds 3,500 animals representing some 430 different species. What makes the park unique is that many of the animals roam freely in vast enclosures, allowing giraffes to interact with antelopes, much as they would in Africa. You'll find the largest crash of rhinos at any zoological facility in the world, an exhibit for the endangered California condor, and a mature landscape of exotic vegetation from many corners of the globe. Although the San Diego Zoo may be "world famous," it's the Wild Animal Park that many visitors celebrate as their favorite.

The park's "Journey into Africa" tour aboard the **African Express** replaces the old monorail ride as the easiest way to see critters. The African Express is an open-air, soft-wheeled tram that runs on biodiesel. Although it visits less park space than the previous tour, the 2½-mile circuit (which takes about 30 min.) brings guests much nearer to the animals, in some places up to 300 feet closer. Depending on crowd size, trams leave about every 10 minutes. Lines build up by late morning, so make this your first or last attraction of the day (the animals are more active then, anyway).

There are also several self-guided **walking tours** that visit various habitats, including **Elephant Overlook** and **Lion Camp,** but why walk when you can tool around the park on Segway personal transporters ($75, minimum age 13)? The commercial hub of the park is **Nairobi Village,** but even here animal exhibits are interesting—check out the **nursery area,** where irresistible young'uns can be seen frolicking, bottle-feeding, and sleeping; a **petting station;** the **lowland gorillas;** and the **African Aviary.** There are

⬤ Moments   **Things That Go Bump in the Night**

The Wild Animal Park's **Roar & Snore sleepover programs,** which are held year-round on most Fridays and Saturdays—except in December and January, and with extended dates in summer—let you camp out next to the animal compound and observe the nocturnal movements of rhinos, lions, and other creatures. There are family and adults-only dates available. To request information by mail or to make reservations, call ✆ **800/407-9534** or 619/718-3000.

amphitheaters for shows scheduled two or three times daily. Visitors should be prepared for sunny, often downright hot weather; it's not unusual for temperatures to be 5° to 10°F warmer here than in San Diego.

If you want to get up-close-and-personal with the animals, take one of the park's **Photo Caravans,** which shuttle groups in flatbed trucks out into the open areas that are inaccessible to the general public. There are a variety of itineraries (some are seasonal and have varying age requirements); prices start at $69 for the 1-hour caravan (you'll need to make reservations ahead of your visit; ✆ **619/718-3000**). The **Savanna Safari** is a deluxe, 50-minute tour for up to 10 people; it visits the same places as the "Journey into Africa," but also includes places not on the regular tour; tickets are $35 (not including admission), and no reservations are necessary. The **Cheetah Run Safari** allows a limited number of guests to watch the world's fastest land mammal in action, sprinting after a mechanical lure (reservations required; ✆ **619/718-3000**). Cost is $69 per person, excluding park admission. You can also get unique aerial perspectives of the park from the **Balloon Safari,** a tethered hot-air balloon that soars to 400 feet, and **Flightline,** a zip-line ride that scoots above the African and Asian enclosures.

15500 San Pasqual Valley Rd., Escondido. ✆ 760/747-8702. www.wildanimalpark.org. Admission $29 adults, $19 children 3–11, free for children 2 and under and active-duty military (U.S. and foreign); "Best Value" package (includes "Journey into Africa" tour) $35 adults, $26 children 3–11; free for children 11 and under in Oct. AE, DISC, MC, V. Daily 9am–4pm (grounds close at 5pm); extended hours during summer and Festival of Lights (2 weekends in Dec). Parking $9, $14 RVs. Bus: 386 (Mon–Sat). Take I-15 to Via Rancho Pkwy.; follow signs for about 3 miles.

San Diego Zoo ★★★ Kids   More than 4,000 creatures reside at this celebrated, influential zoo, started in 1916 and run by the Zoological Society of San Diego. In the early days, the zoo's founder, Dr. Harry Wegeforth, traveled around the world and bartered native Southwestern animals such as rattlesnakes and sea lions for more exotic species. The zoo is also an accredited botanical garden, lavished with more than 700,000 plants; "Dr. Harry" brought home plants from every location where he acquired animals, ensuring what would become the zoo's naturalistic and mature environment.

The zoo is one of only four in the United States with giant pandas—including the most recent arrival, Zhen Zhen, who was born here in 2007. Many other rare species are here as well, including Buerger's tree kangaroos of New Guinea, long-billed kiwis from New Zealand, wild Przewalski's horses from Mongolia, lowland gorillas from Africa, and giant tortoises from the Galapagos.

Monkey Trails and Forest Tales is the largest, most elaborate habitat in the zoo's history, re-creating a wooded forest full of endangered species such as the mandrill monkey,

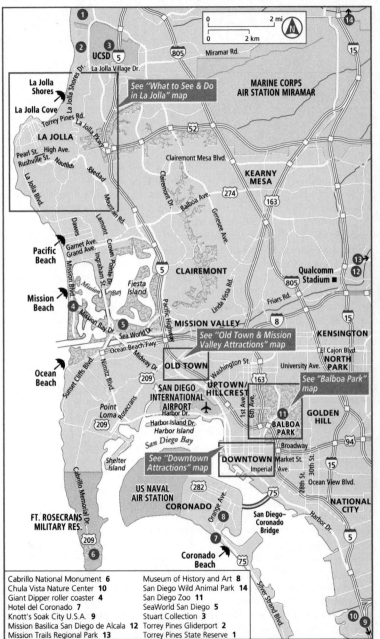

Scale
0 — 2 mi
0 — 2 km

MARINE CORPS AIR STATION MIRAMAR

Miramar Rd.

See "What to See & Do in La Jolla" map

La Jolla Shores

La Jolla Cove

Torrey Pines Rd.

LA JOLLA

Pearl St. High Ave.
Rushville St.
Nautilus
La Jolla Blvd.

Biledad

Clairemont Mesa Blvd.

KEARNY MESA

Clairemont Dr.

Balboa Ave.

Genesee Ave.

Pacific Beach
Garnet Ave.
Grand Ave.
Ingraham St.
Crown Pointe Dr.
Lamont
Dawes

Mission Beach
Mission Blvd.

Fiesta Island

CLAIREMONT

Linda Vista Rd.

Qualcomm Stadium ■

Friars Rd.

Sea World Dr.

MISSION VALLEY

See "Old Town & Mission Valley Attractions" map

KENSINGTON

El Cajon Blvd.

University Ave.

NORTH PARK

Ocean Beach
Sunset Cliffs Blvd.
Nimitz Blvd.

Ocean Beach Fwy.
Midway Dr.

OLD TOWN

Washington St.

UPTOWN/ HILLCREST

See "Balboa Park" map

Point Loma
Rosecrans

SAN DIEGO INTERNATIONAL AIRPORT
Harbor Dr.

Harbor Island Dr.
Harbor Island
San Diego Bay

Shelter Island

See "Downtown Attractions" map

DOWNTOWN Market St.
Imperial Ave.

BALBOA PARK

GOLDEN HILL

Broadway

Ocean View Blvd.

FT. ROSECRANS MILITARY RES.

Cabrillo Memorial Dr.

US NAVAL AIR STATION

CORONADO

Orange Ave.

San Diego– Coronado Bridge

Harbor Dr.

NATIONAL CITY

Coronado Beach

Silver Strand Blvd.

Cabrillo National Monument **6**	Museum of History and Art **8**
Chula Vista Nature Center **10**	San Diego Wild Animal Park **14**
Giant Dipper roller coaster **4**	San Diego Zoo **11**
Hotel del Coronado **7**	SeaWorld San Diego **5**
Knott's Soak City U.S.A. **9**	Stuart Collection **3**
Mission Basilica San Diego de Alcala **12**	Torrey Pines Gliderport **2**
Mission Trails Regional Park **13**	Torrey Pines State Reserve **1**

clouded leopard, and pygmy hippopotamus. An elevated trail through the treetops allows for close observation of the primate, bird, and plant life that thrive in the forest canopy. **Absolutely Apes** showcases orangutans and siamangs (black-furred gibbons) of Indonesia, while next door is **Gorilla Tropics,** where two troops of Western lowland gorillas roam an 8,000-square-foot habitat. Despite the hype, I find the **Giant Panda Research Center** *not* worth the hassle when there's a long line (lines are shortest first thing in the morning or toward the end of the day). More noteworthy is **Ituri Forest,** which simulates a central African rainforest with forest buffalos, otters, okapis, and hippos, which are viewed underwater from a glassed-in enclosure. At the **Polar Bear Plunge** you'll find a 4¹/₂-acre summer tundra habitat populated by Siberian reindeer, yellow-throated martens, and diving ducks, as well as polar bears. The **Children's Zoo** features a nursery with baby animals and a petting area where kids can cuddle up to sheep, goats, and the like; there's also a **sea lion show** at the 3,000-seat amphitheater (easy to skip if you're headed to SeaWorld). Opening summer 2009 is **Elephant Odyssey,** which will feature a herd of Asian elephants as well as life-size replicas of prehistoric animals.

If a lot of walking—some of it on steep hills—isn't your passion, a 35-minute **Guided Bus Tour** provides a narrated overview and covers about 75% of the facility. It costs $10 for adults, $7 for children 3 to 11; it's included in the so-called "Best Value" admission package. Since you get only brief glimpses of the enclosures, and animals won't always be visible, you'll want to revisit some areas. Included in the bus ticket is access to the unnarrated **Express Bus,** which allows you to get on and off at one of five different stops along the same route. You can also get an aerial perspective from the **Skyfari,** which costs $4 per person each way, though you won't see many creatures. An ideal plan is to take the complete bus tour first thing in the morning, when the animals are more active (waits for the bus tour can be long on a busy day); after the bus tour, take the Skyfari to the far side of the park and wend your way back on foot or by Express Bus to revisit animals you missed.

2920 Zoo Dr., Balboa Park. ✆ **619/234-3153** (recorded info), or 231-1515. www.sandiegozoo.org. Admission $29 adults, $19 children 3–11, free for children 2 and under and active-duty military (U.S. and foreign); "Best Value" package (includes guided bus tour, round-trip Skyfari aerial tram) $35 adults, $31 seniors, $26 children; free for children 11 and under in Oct. AE, DISC, MC, V. Sept to mid-June daily 9am–4pm (grounds close at 5 or 6pm); mid-June to Aug daily 9am–8pm (grounds close at 9pm). Bus: 7. I-5 S. to Pershing Dr.; follow signs.

SeaWorld San Diego ★★ (Kids)   One of California's most heavily marketed attractions, SeaWorld, which opened here in 1964, is a big draw for a number of visitors coming to San Diego. With each passing year the educational pretext increasingly takes a back seat to slick shows and rides, but the park—owned by the Anheuser-Busch Corporation—is still perhaps the country's premier showplace for marine life, made politically correct with a nominally informative atmosphere. At its heart, SeaWorld is a shoreside family entertainment center where the performers are dolphins, otters, sea lions, orcas, and seals. The 20-minute shows run several times each throughout the day, with visitors rotating through the various open-air amphitheaters and aquarium features.

Believe, starring Shamu, is SeaWorld's most popular show. Performed in a 5,500-seat stadium, the stage is a 7-million-gallon pool lined with Plexiglas walls that magnify the huge performers. But think twice before you sit in the seats down front—a high point of the act is multiple drenchings of the first 12 or so rows of spectators. A seasonal nighttime show (spring and summer), **Shamu Rocks,** features concert lighting, animation, and a rock soundtrack; most days, the venue fills before the two or three performances

(Value) Now That's a Deal!

San Diego's three main animal attractions offer combo tickets that can save you some cash. Here's how it works: If you plan to visit both the zoo and the Wild Animal Park, a two-park ticket (the "Best Value" zoo package, plus Wild Animal Park admission) is $60 for adults, $43 for children 3 to 11. You get unlimited visits to each attraction, to be used within 5 days of purchase. Or throw in SeaWorld within the same 5 days, and the combo works out to $115 for adults, $92 children ages 3 to 9.

Other value options include the **Southern California CityPass** (© 888/330-5008; www.citypass.com), which covers the zoo or Wild Animal Park, plus SeaWorld, Disneyland Resorts, and Universal Studios in Los Angeles. Passes are $259 for adults, and $219 for kids age 3 to 9 (a savings of about 30%), valid for 14 days. The **Go San Diego Card** (© 866/628-9032; www.gosandiegocard.com) offers unlimited general admission to more than 55 attractions. One-day packages start at $60 for adults and $40 for children (ages 3–12). The **San Diego Passport** ($89 adults, $45 children 3–11) includes zoo admission, an Old Town Trolley city tour, Hornblower bay cruises, and more. Call © 800/213-2474, or check out www.trustedtours.com.

even start, so arrive early to get the seat you want. The slapstick **Clyde and Seamore's Risky Rescue** (sea lions and otters), the fast-paced **Dolphin Discovery,** and **Pets Rule!** are other performing animal routines, each in arenas seating more than 2,000. During the summer, human acrobats are added to the mix with **Cirque de la Mer.**

The collection of rides is led by **Journey to Atlantis,** which combines a roller coaster and log flume with Atlantis mythology and a simulated earthquake. **Shipwreck Rapids** is a splashy adventure on raftlike inner tubes through caverns, waterfalls, and wild rivers; and **Wild Arctic** is a motion simulator helicopter trip to the frozen north. The **Skytower** and **Skyride** each cost an additional $3 to ride. There's also a passel of *Sesame Street*-related attractions, including rides and a "4-D" interactive movie experience.

SeaWorld's real specialties are simulated marine environments, such as the **arctic research station,** surrounded by beautiful beluga whales, walruses, and polar bears. Other animal environments worth seeing are **Manatee Rescue, Shark Encounter,** and the **Penguin Encounter.** Each of these attractions exits into a gift shop selling theme merchandise.

The **Dolphin** and **Wild Arctic Interaction programs** allow people to meet bottlenose dolphins and beluga whales up close. Although the programs stop short of allowing you to swim with these animals, they do offer the opportunity to wade waist-deep with them and try giving training commands. These programs include some classroom time before you wriggle into a wet suit and climb into the water for 20 minutes. The cost is $170 per person (not including park admission); minimum age for participants is 6 for the dolphin program, 10 for the arctic. One step further is the **Trainer for a Day** program, a 5-hour work shift with an animal trainer. Food preparation, feeding, a training session with a dolphin, and lunch are included; the price is $545 per person ($200 to be an observer). It's limited to three participants daily, and the minimum age is 13. Advance reservations are required for all programs (© 800/257-4268, press 7).

Although SeaWorld is best known as the home to pirouetting dolphins and fluke-flinging killer whales, it also plays a role in rescuing and rehabilitating beached animals found along the West Coast. Still, there is a troubling aspect to this kind of facility—for another point of view, check out the **Whale and Dolphin Conservation Society** at www.wdcs.org.

500 SeaWorld Dr., Mission Bay. (C) **800/257-4268** or 619/226-3901. www.seaworld.com. Admission $65 adults, $55 children 3–9, free for children 2 and under. AE, DISC, MC, V. Hours vary seasonally, but always at least daily 10am–5pm; most weekends and during summer 9am–11pm. Parking $12, $17 RVs. Bus: 8 or 9. From I-5, take SeaWorld Dr. exit; from I-8, take W. Mission Bay Dr. exit to SeaWorld Dr.

2 SAN DIEGO'S BEACHES

San Diego County is blessed with 70 miles of sandy coastline and more than 30 individual beaches. A word (rather, four) to the wise: **May Gray** and **June Gloom.** They're both names for a local weather pattern that can be counted on to foil sunbathing most mornings (and sometimes all day) from mid-May to mid-July. Overcast skies appear as the desert heats up at the end of spring, sucking the marine layer—a thick bank of fog—inland for a few miles each night. Be prepared for moist mornings and evenings (and sometimes afternoons) at the beaches this time of year. *But remember:* The sun may not be shining brightly, but that doesn't mean you're not being exposed to harmful UV rays; always wear sunscreen during prolonged outdoor exposure. Another beach precaution worth remembering is the "stingray shuffle." At beaches where the water is calm, such as Mission Bay and La Jolla Shores, it's a good idea to shuffle your feet as you walk through the surf—it rousts any stingrays that might be in your path. They can inflict an extremely painful, but nonlethal, wound.

Another sting to beware of is the pain you might feel if you're caught drinking alcohol on any San Diego beach, bay shore, or at coastal parks. In 2008, voters made permanent what originally had been a 1-year trial **ban on alcohol** at the beach. First offense has a maximum fine of $250.

Exploring **tide pools**—potholed, rocky shores that retain ponds of water after the tide has gone out, providing homes for a plethora of sea creatures—is a time-honored coastal pleasure (with or without alcohol). You can get a tide chart free or for a nominal charge from many surf and diving shops. Among the best places for tide-pooling are Cabrillo National Monument, at the oceanside base of Point Loma; Sunset Cliffs in Ocean Beach; and along the rocky coast immediately south of the cove in La Jolla.

Here's a list of San Diego's most noteworthy beaches, each with its own personality and devotees. They're listed geographically from south to north. All California beaches are open to the public to the mean high-tide line, and you can check **www.sannet.gov/ lifeguards/beaches** for descriptions and water quality. Beach closures due to bacterial contamination are a modern-day fact of life, especially following storms when runoff from city streets makes its way to the ocean—check for posted warnings, or call the county's Beach and Bay Status hot line ((C) **619/338-2073**) for the latest info. For the daily beach, tide, dive, and surf report, call (C) **619/221-8824**. *Note:* All beaches are good for swimming except as indicated. For a map of San Diego's beaches, see the color map at the beginning of this book.

IMPERIAL BEACH

Imperial Beach is just a half-hour south of downtown San Diego by car or trolley, and only a few minutes from the Mexican border. It's popular with surfers and local youth, who can be somewhat territorial about "their" beach in summer. There are 3 miles of surf breaks plus a guarded "swimmers only" stretch; check with lifeguards before getting wet, though, since sewage runoff from nearby Mexico can sometimes foul the water. I.B. also plays host to the annual **U.S. Open Sandcastle Competition** in late July—the best reason to come here—with world-class sand creations ranging from sea life to dinosaurs.

CORONADO BEACH

Lovely, wide, and sparkling, this beach is conducive to strolling and lingering, especially in the late afternoon. At the north end, you can watch fighter jets in formation flying from the Naval Air Station, while just south is the pretty section fronting Ocean Boulevard and the Hotel del Coronado. Waves are gentle here, so the beach draws many Coronado families—and their dogs, which are allowed off-leash at the most northwesterly end. South of the Hotel Del, the beach becomes the beautiful, often deserted **Silver Strand.** The islands visible from here, Los Coronados, are 18 miles away and belong to Mexico.

OCEAN BEACH

The northern end of Ocean Beach Park, officially known as **Dog Beach,** is one of only a few in the county where your pooch can roam freely on the sand (and frolic with several dozen other people's pets). Surfers generally congregate around the O.B. Pier, mostly in the water but often at the snack shack on the end. Rip currents can be strong here and sometimes discourage swimmers from venturing beyond waist depth (check with the lifeguard stations). Facilities at the beach include restrooms, showers, picnic tables, volleyball courts, and plenty of metered parking lots. To reach the beach, take West Point Loma Boulevard all the way to the end.

MISSION BAY PARK

This 4,600-acre aquatic playground contains 27 miles of bayfront, picnic areas, children's playgrounds, and paths for biking, in-line skating, and jogging. This man-made bay lends itself to windsurfing, sailing, water-skiing, and fishing. There are dozens of access points; one of the most popular is off I-5 at Clairemont Drive. Also accessed from this spot is **Fiesta Island,** where the annual **World Championship Over the Line Tournament** is held to raucous enthusiasm in July (see "Calendar of Events," in chapter 3). A 4-mile road loops around the island. Parts of the bay have been subject to closure over the years due to high levels of bacteria, so check for posted warnings. Personally, I'd rather sail on Mission Bay than swim in it.

BONITA COVE/MARINER'S POINT & MISSION POINT

Also enclosed in Mission Bay Park (facing the bay, not the ocean), this pretty and protected cove's calm waters, grassy picnic areas, and playground equipment make it perfect for families—or as a paddling destination if you've rented kayaks elsewhere in the bay. The water is cleaner for swimming than in the northeastern reaches of Mission Bay. Get to Bonita Cove from Mission Boulevard in south Mission Beach; reach Mariner's Point via Mariner's Way, off West Mission Bay Drive.

While Mission Bay Park is a body of salt water surrounded by land and bridges, Mission Beach is actually a beach on the Pacific Ocean, anchored by the **Giant Dipper** roller coaster. Always popular, the sands and wide cement "boardwalk" sizzle with activity and people-watching in summer; at the southern end, a volleyball game is always underway. The long beach and path extend from the jetty north to Belmont Park and Pacific Beach Drive. Parking is often tough, with your best bets being the public lots at Belmont Park or at the south end of West Mission Bay Drive; this street intersects with Mission Boulevard, the centerline of a 2-block-wide isthmus that leads a mile north to . . .

PACIFIC BEACH

There's always action here, particularly along **Ocean Front Walk,** a paved promenade featuring a human parade akin to that at L.A.'s Venice Beach boardwalk. It runs along Ocean Boulevard (just west of Mission Blvd.) to the pier. Surfing is popular year-round here, in marked sections; and the beach is well staffed with lifeguards. You're on your own to find street parking. Pacific Beach is also the home of **Tourmaline Surfing Park,** a half-mile north of the pier, where the sport's old guard gathers to surf waters where swimmers are prohibited; reach it via Tourmaline Street, off Mission Boulevard.

WINDANSEA BEACH

The fabled locale of Tom Wolfe's *Pump House Gang,* Windansea is legendary to this day among California's surf elite and remains one of San Diego's prettiest strands. Reached by way of Bonair Street (at Neptune Place), Windansea has no facilities, and street parking is first-come, first-served. It's not ideal for swimming, so come to surf, watch surfers, or soak in the camaraderie and party atmosphere.

CHILDREN'S POOL

Think clothing-optional Black's Beach is the city's most controversial sun-sea-sand situation? Think again—the Children's Pool is currently home to the biggest man-vs.-beast struggle since *Moby-Dick.* A seawall protects this pocket of sand, originally intended as a calm swimming bay for children. Since 1994, when a rock outcrop off the shore was designated as a protected mammal reserve, the beach has been cordoned off for the resident **harbor seal** population. On an average day you'll spot dozens lolling in the sun. Some humans did not take kindly to their beach banishment, and the fight was on. After much heated debate (and even acts of civil disobedience), swimming was reinstated—to the displeasure of many. So while it is possible to now swim at the Children's Pool, keep in mind those are federally protected *wild* animals and it is illegal to approach them or harass them in any way. Volunteers, with speed dials set to "lifeguard," keep watch to make sure bathers don't interfere with the colony—scofflaws will get arrested. The beach is at Coast Boulevard and Jenner Street; there's limited free street parking.

LA JOLLA COVE

The cove's protected, calm waters—celebrated as the clearest along the coast—attract snorkelers and scuba divers, along with a fair share of families. The stunning setting offers a small sandy beach, as well as, on the cliffs above, the **Ellen Browning Scripps Park.** The cove's "look but don't touch" policy protects the colorful garibaldi, California's state fish, plus other marine life, including abalone, octopus, and lobster. The unique Underwater Park stretches from here to the northern end of Torrey Pines State Reserve and incorporates kelp forests, artificial reefs, two deep canyons, and tidal pools. The cove is

terrific for swimming, cramped for sunbathing, and accessible from Coast Boulevard;
parking nearby is scarce.

LA JOLLA SHORES

The wide, flat mile of sand at La Jolla Shores is popular with joggers, swimmers, kayakers, novice scuba divers, and beginning body- and board-surfers, as well as families. It looks like a picture postcard, with fine sand under blue skies, kissed by gentle waves. Weekend crowds can be enormous, though, quickly claiming fire rings and occupying both the sand and the metered parking spaces in the lot. There are restrooms, showers, and picnic areas here, as well as the grassy, palm-lined Kellogg Park across the street.

BLACK'S BEACH

The area's unofficial nude beach (though technically nude sunbathing is illegal), 2-mile-long Black's lies between La Jolla Shores and Torrey Pines State Beach, at the base of steep, 300-foot-high cliffs. The beach is out-of-the-way and not easy to reach, but it draws scores with its secluded beauty and good swimming and surfing conditions—the graceful spectacle of paragliders launching from the cliffs above adds to the show. To get here, take North Torrey Pines Road, watch for signs for the Gliderport (where you can park), and clamber down the makeshift path, staying alert to avoid veering off to one of several false trails. To bypass the cliff descent, you can walk to Black's from beaches north (Torrey Pines) or south (La Jolla Shores). *Note:* There's no permanent lifeguard station, though lifeguards are usually present from spring break to October, and no restroom facilities. The beach's notoriety came about when, from 1974 to 1977, swimsuits *were* optional—the only such beach in the U.S. to be so designated at the time. Rich neighbors on the cliffs above complained enough to the city about their property being denigrated that the clothing-optional status was reversed. Still, citations for nude sunbathing are rarely issued—lifeguards will either ignore it or just ask you to cover up. Tickets *will* be written if you disregard their request.

TORREY PINES BEACH

The north end of Black's Beach, at the foot of Torrey Pines State Park, is this fabulous, underused strand, accessed by a pay parking lot at the entrance to the park. In fact, combining a visit to the park with a day at the beach makes for the quintessential San Diego outdoor experience. It's rarely crowded, though you need to be aware of high tide (when most of the sand gets a bath). In almost any weather, it's a great beach for walking. *Note:* At this and any other bluff-side beach, never sit at the bottom of the cliffs. The hillsides are unstable and could collapse.

DEL MAR BEACH

The Del Mar Thoroughbred Club's slogan, as famously sung by DMTC founder Bing Crosby, is "where turf meets the surf." This town beach represents the "surf" portion of that phrase. It's a long stretch of sand backed by grassy cliffs and a playground area. This area is not heavily trafficked, and you can dine right alongside the beach at **Jake's** (p. 235) or **Poseidon** (p. 234). Del Mar is about 15 miles from downtown San Diego; see "North County Beach Towns: Spots to Surf & Sun" in chapter 11 on p. 230.

NORTHERN SAN DIEGO COUNTY BEACHES

Those inclined to venture farther north in San Diego County won't be disappointed—Pacific Coast Highway leads to a string of inviting beaches. In Encinitas there are peaceful

Boneyards Beach, Swami's Beach for surfing, and Moonlight Beach, popular with families and volleyball buffs. Farthest north is Oceanside, which has one of the West Coast's longest wooden piers, wide sandy beaches, and several popular surfing areas. See "North County Beach Towns: Spots to Surf & Sun" in chapter 11 on p. 230 for more information.

3 ATTRACTIONS IN BALBOA PARK

San Diego's crown jewel is Balboa Park, a 1,174-acre city-owned playground and the largest urban cultural park in the nation. The park was established in 1868 in the heart of the city, bordered by downtown to the southwest and fringed by the early communities of Hillcrest and Golden Hill to the north and east. Originally called City Park, the name was eventually changed to commemorate the Spanish explorer Balboa. Tree plantings started in the late 19th century, while the initial buildings were created to host the 1915–16 Panama-California Exposition. Another expo in 1935–36 brought additional developments.

The park's most distinctive features are its mature landscaping, the architectural beauty of the Spanish Golden Age buildings lining El Prado (the park's east-west pedestrian thoroughfare), and the engaging and diverse museums contained within it. You'll also find eight different gardens, walkways, 4.5 miles of hiking trails in Florida Canyon, an ornate pavilion with the world's largest outdoor organ, an IMAX domed theater, the acclaimed Old Globe Theatre (p. 217), and the San Diego Zoo (p. 128).

The park is divided into three distinct sections, separated by Hwy. 163 and Florida Canyon. The narrow western wing of the park consists of largely grassy open areas that parallel Sixth Avenue; there are no museums in this section, but it's a good place for picnics, strolling, sunning, and dog-walking. The eastern section is also devoid of cultural attractions, but has the Balboa Park Municipal Golf Course (p. 170). The central portion of the park, between Hwy. 163 and Florida Drive, contains the zoo and all of the museums.

If you really want to visit the zoo and a few of the park's museums, don't try to tackle them both the same day. Allow at least 5 hours to tour the zoo; the amount of time you spend in the 15 major museums will vary depending on your personal interests. I've also mapped out a walking tour that takes in most of the park's highlights (p. 193). There are informal restaurants serving sandwiches and snacks throughout the park. For breakfast, Tobey's 19th Hole at the municipal golf course is a find (p. 170); try lunch at the Japanese Friendship Garden's Tea Pavilion (p. 197) or in the San Diego Museum of Art's sculpture garden (p. 194). The Prado Restaurant is also a San Diego favorite for lunch or dinner.

There are two primary road entrances into the heart of the park. The most distinctive is from Sixth Avenue and Laurel Street: Laurel turns into El Prado as it traverses the beautiful Cabrillo Bridge ★ across Hwy. 163. You can also enter via Presidents Way from Park Boulevard. Major parking areas are at Inspiration Point just east of Park Boulevard at Presidents Way; in front of the zoo; and along Presidents Way between the Aerospace Museum and Spreckels Organ Pavilion. Other lots, though more centrally located, are small and in high demand, especially on weekends.

Public bus no. 7 runs along Park Boulevard; for the west side of the park, nos. 1, 3, and 120 run along Fourth and Fifth avenues (except for the Marston House, all museums

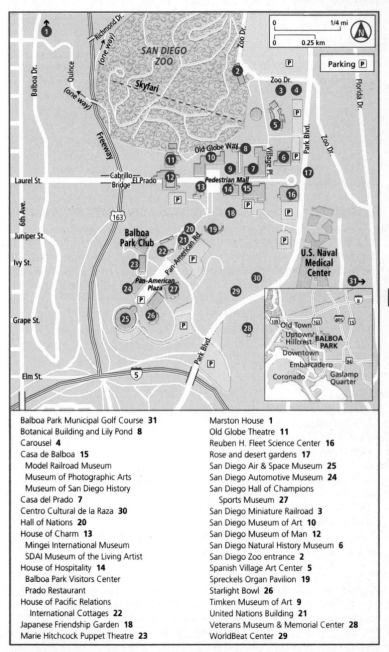

Balboa Park Municipal Golf Course **31**
Botanical Building and Lily Pond **8**
Carousel **4**
Casa de Balboa **15**
  Model Railroad Museum
  Museum of Photographic Arts
  Museum of San Diego History
Casa del Prado **7**
Centro Cultural de la Raza **30**
Hall of Nations **20**
House of Charm **13**
  Mingei International Museum
  SDAI Museum of the Living Artist
House of Hospitality **14**
  Balboa Park Visitors Center
  Prado Restaurant
House of Pacific Relations
  International Cottages **22**
Japanese Friendship Garden **18**
Marie Hitchcock Puppet Theatre **23**

Marston House **1**
Old Globe Theatre **11**
Reuben H. Fleet Science Center **16**
Rose and desert gardens **17**
San Diego Air & Space Museum **25**
San Diego Automotive Museum **24**
San Diego Hall of Champions
  Sports Museum **27**
San Diego Miniature Railroad **3**
San Diego Museum of Art **10**
San Diego Museum of Man **12**
San Diego Natural History Museum **6**
San Diego Zoo entrance **2**
Spanish Village Art Center **5**
Spreckels Organ Pavilion **19**
Starlight Bowl **26**
Timken Museum of Art **9**
United Nations Building **21**
Veterans Museum & Memorial Center **28**
WorldBeat Center **29**

(Value) **Balboa Park Money-Savers**

Most Balboa Park attractions are open free of charge one Tuesday each month; there's a rotating schedule so two or more participate each Tuesday. (See "Free of Charge & Full of Fun," later in this chapter.) If you plan to visit more than three of the park's museums, buy the **Passport to Balboa Park**—it allows entrance to 13 major museums (the rest are always free) and is valid for 1 week. It's $39 for adults, $21 for children 3 to 12. If you plan to spend a day at the zoo and return for the museums another day, buy the **Deluxe Passport,** which provides one ticket to the zoo (including guided bus tour and Skyfari aerial tram ride) and 7 days' admission to the 13 museums for $65 adults, $36 children. The passports can be purchased at any participating museum (but not the zoo), at the visitor center, or online at www.balboapark.org.

are closer to Park Blvd.). Free **tram** transportation within the park runs daily from 8:30am to 6pm, with extended hours in summer months. The red trolley trams originate at the Inspiration Point parking lot to circuit the park, arriving every 8 to 10 minutes and stopping at designated pickup areas. Stop by the **Balboa Park Visitors Center,** in the House of Hospitality (© **619/239-0512;** www.balboapark.org), to learn about walking and museum **tours,** or to pick up a brochure about the **gardens** of the park. The visitor center is open daily, 9:30am to 4:30pm, with extended summer hours. *Note:* Some museums are closed on Mondays.

Botanical Building and Lily Pond ★ This serene park within the park is one of my favorite hide-outs. Ferns, orchids, impatiens, begonias, and other plants—about 2,100 tropical and flowering varieties, plus rotating exhibits—are sheltered beneath a domed lath house. The graceful 250-foot-long building, part of the 1915 Panama-California Exposition, is one of the world's largest wood lath structures. Kids love the "touch and smell" garden and the smelly bog of carnivorous plants. The lily pond out front attracts sun worshipers, painters, and buskers.

El Prado. © **619/235-1100.** Free admission. Fri–Wed 10am–4pm; closed Thurs and major holidays. Bus: 7.

Centro Cultural de la Raza (Finds) This building has a less glamorous provenance than most other park facilities—it's an old water storage tank built during World War II. The circular structure is now festooned with colorful murals and hosts performances, art exhibits, and classes in support and celebration of Mexican, Chicano, and indigenous art and culture. Folkloric dances are presented every second Sunday and visual artists gather to sell their creations every third Sunday.

2125 Park Blvd. © **619/235-6135.** www.centroculturaldelaraza.org. Gallery admission $3–$5 donation suggested. Tues–Sun noon–4pm. Bus: 7.

House of Pacific Relations International Cottages This cluster of 17 charming one- and two-room cottages disseminates information about the culture, traditions, and history of more than 30 countries. Light refreshments are served, and outdoor lawn programs are presented by one of the nations every Sunday, 2 to 3pm, March through October. The adjacent **United Nations Building** houses an international gift shop where you can buy jewelry, toys, books, and UNICEF greeting cards (© **619/233-5044;** www.unasd.org); it's open daily from 10am to 4:30pm.

Japanese Friendship Garden (Finds) Of the 12 acres designated for the garden, only 2 acres have been developed. Still to come are herb and tea gardens, a cherry tree grove, a lily pond, and an amphitheater. What is here, though, is beautifully serene and is referred to as *San-Kei-En,* or "three-scene garden." It represents ties to San Diego's sister city of Yokohama, which has a similarly named garden. From the main gate, a crooked path (to confound evil spirits, who move only in a straight line) threads its way to the information center in a traditional Japanese-style house. Here you can view the most ancient kind of garden, the *sekitei,* made only of sand and stone (a self-guided tour is available). Teas, sushi, noodles, and more are served on a deck to the left of the entrance; imported gifts are also for sale. Japanese holidays are celebrated here, and the public is invited.

2125 Park Blvd., adjacent to the Organ Pavilion. ✆ **619/232-2721**. www.niwa.org. Admission $3 adults, $2.50 seniors, $2 students and military, free for children 6 and under. Free 3rd Tues of each month. Tues–Sun 10am–4pm; daily 10am–4pm in summer. Bus: 7.

Mingei International Museum ★★ This captivating museum (pronounced "*Min*-gay," meaning "art of the people" in Japanese) offers changing exhibitions generally describable as folk art. The exhibits—usually four at a time—encompass artists from countries across the globe; displays include textiles, costumes, jewelry, toys, pottery, paintings, and sculpture. The permanent collection features whimsical contemporary sculptures by the late French artist Niki de Saint Phalle, who made San Diego her home in 1993. Martha Longenecker, a potter and professor emeritus of art at San Diego State University, opened the museum in 1978. It is one of only a few major museums in the United States devoted to folk crafts on a worldwide scale and well worth a look. Allow up to an hour to view the exhibits; there's also a wonderful gift store that's worth a visit on its own. An Escondido branch has additional exhibits (p. 248).

1439 El Prado, in the House of Charm. ✆ **619/239-0003**. www.mingei.org. Admission $7 adults; $5 seniors; $4 children 6–17, students, and military with ID; free for children 5 and under. Free 3rd Tues of each month. Tues–Sun 10am–4pm. Bus: 7.

Museum of Photographic Arts ★★ If the names Ansel Adams and Edward Weston stimulate your fingers to do the shutterbug, then don't miss a taste of the 7,000-plus collection of images housed here. This is one of the few museums in the country devoted exclusively to the photographic arts (which, at MoPA, encompasses cinema, video, and digital photography). A 1999 expansion allowed the museum to display even more of the permanent collection, while leaving room for provocative traveling exhibits that change every few months. Photos by Alfred Stieglitz, Margaret Bourke-White, Imogen Cunningham, and Manuel Alvarez Bravo are all in the permanent collection, and the plush cinema illuminates classic films on an ongoing basis. Allow 30 to 60 minutes to see the collection.

1649 El Prado. ✆ **619/238-7559**. www.mopa.org. Admission $6 adults; $4 seniors, students, and military; free for children 11 and under with adult. Free 2nd Tues of each month. Tues–Sun 10am–5pm. Bus: 7.

Museum of San Diego History Operated by the San Diego Historical Society, this museum offers permanent and changing exhibits on topics related to the history of the region. Past shows have examined subjects ranging from San Diego's role as a Hollywood film location to the city's architectural heritage. Many of the museum's photographs depict Balboa Park and the growth of the city. Plan to spend about 30 to 45 minutes

WHAT TO SEE & DO

7

ATTRACTIONS IN BALBOA PARK

here. Books about San Diego's history are available in the gift shop, and the research library downstairs is open Wednesday through Saturday (9:30am–1pm).

1649 El Prado, in Casa del Balboa. ✆ **619/232-6203.** www.sandiegohistory.org. Admission $5 adults; $4 students, seniors, and military with ID; $2 children 6–17; free for children 5 and under. Free 2nd Tues of each month. Tues–Sun 10am–5pm. Bus: 7.

Reuben H. Fleet Science Center ★ (Kids A must-see for kids of any age is this tantalizing collection of interactive exhibits and rides designed to provoke the imagination and teach scientific principles. The Virtual Zone features a 23-passenger motion simulator that offers a virtual-reality experience with a scientific bent. The Fleet also houses an IMAX Dome Theater (the world's first) showing films on such a grand scale that ocean footage can actually give you motion sickness. Every Friday evening, four different IMAX films are shown in succession. The Fleet also has a spiffy planetarium simulator powered by computer graphics; planetarium shows are the first Wednesday of each month at 7pm ($11 adults, $9 seniors and kids 3–12). With all the interactive attractions, you'll need at least 90 minutes here.

1875 El Prado. ✆ **619/238-1233.** www.rhfleet.org. Fleet Experience admission includes an IMAX film and exhibit galleries: $15 adults, $12 seniors and children 3–12 (exhibit gallery can be purchased individually). Free 1st Tues of each month (exhibit galleries only). Hours vary but always daily 9:30am–5pm; later closing times possible. Bus: 7.

San Diego Air & Space Museum ★★ (Kids The other big kid-pleaser of the museums (along with the Reuben H. Fleet Science Center, above), this popular facility has more than 60 aircraft on display, providing an overview of aeronautical history from hot-air balloons to spacecraft. It emphasizes local aviation history, particularly the construction here of the *Spirit of St. Louis;* there's also a motion simulator ride that puts you at the controls of an F-22 fighter jet. The museum is housed in a cylindrical hall built by the Ford Motor Company in 1935 for the park's second international expo. The imaginative gift shop stocks items such as old-fashioned leather flight hoods and new-fashioned freeze-dried astronaut ice cream. Allow at least an hour for your visit.

2001 Pan American Plaza. ✆ **619/234-8291.** www.sandiegoairandspace.org. Admission $15 adults, $12 seniors and students with ID, $6 children 3–11, free for active military with ID and children 2 and under. Free 4th Tues of each month. Sept–May daily 10am–4:30pm; June–Aug daily 10am–5:30pm. Bus: 7.

SDAI Museum of the Living Artist Established in 1941, the San Diego Art Institute exhibits new pieces by local artists. The 10,000-square-foot municipal gallery rotates juried shows in and out every 4 to 6 weeks, ensuring a variety of mediums and styles. It's a good place to see what the San Diego art community is up to; young artists from area schools exhibit here, too. Local artisans sell their wares in the gift store. Plan to spend about half an hour here.

1439 El Prado. ✆ **619/236-0011.** www.sandiego-art.org. Admission $3 adults; $2 seniors, students, and military; free for children 12 and under. Free 3rd Tues of the month. Tues–Sat 10am–4pm; Sun noon–4pm. Bus: 7.

San Diego Automotive Museum ★ Even if you don't know a distributor from a dipstick, you're bound to ooh and aah over the more than 80 classic, antique, and exotic cars here. Each one is so pristine you'd swear it just rolled off the line, from an 1886 Benz to a 1931 Rolls-Royce Phaeton to the 1981 DeLorean. Most of the time, temporary shows take over the facility, so check ahead to see if it's one you're interested in. Some days you can take a peek at the ongoing restoration program, and the museum sponsors many car rallies and other special events. Allow 30 to 45 minutes for your visit.

ⓣⓘⓟⓢ Balboa Park Guided Tours

In addition to the walking tour I map out in chapter 8, guided tours of the park cater to a wide variety of interests (all tours start from the visitor center, ℰ **619/239-0512**). There are free rotating tours on Saturdays at 10am that highlight either the palm trees and vegetation or park history. Park rangers lead free 1-hour tours focusing on the park's history, architecture, and botanical resources every Tuesday and Sunday at 1pm. The Committee of 100 (ℰ **619/223-6566;** www.c100.org), an organization dedicated to preserving the park's Spanish Colonial architecture, offers a free exploration of the Prado's structures on the first Wednesday of the month at 9:30am. A self-guided audio tour is available at the visitor center costing $5 for adults; $4 for seniors, students, and military; and $3 for children 3 to 11.

The 90-minute Old Globe Theatre Tour visits the three performance venues and backstage areas on most Saturdays and Sundays at 10:30am; the tour costs $5 for adults and $3 for seniors and students (ℰ **619/231-1941;** www.theold globe.org). Plant Day at the San Diego Zoo is held the third Friday of each month and features self-guided and guided horticultural tours and functions. The orchid house is open to the public 10am to 2pm on Plant Day, as well as for Orchid Odyssey on the first Sundays of March, June, September, and December (zoo admission required; call ℰ **619/231-1515** for more details, or go to www. sandiegozoo.org).

2080 Pan American Plaza. ℰ **619/231-2886.** www.sdautomuseum.org. Admission $8 adults, $6 seniors and active military, $5 students, $4 children 6–15, free for children 5 and under. Free 4th Tues of each month. Daily 10am–5pm (last admission 4:30pm). Bus: 7.

San Diego Hall of Champions Sports Museum   From Padres great Tony Gwynn and skateboard icon Tony Hawk to legendary surfer Skip Frye and Hall of Fame quarterback Dan Fouts, this slick museum celebrates San Diego's best-ever athletes and the sports they played. This three-level, 68,000-square-foot facility features more than 25 exhibits, including memorabilia from around the world of sports (the biggies and the niche ones), rotating art shows, and interactive stations where you can try out your play-by-play skills. One particularly interesting exhibit is devoted to athletes with disabilities. You can see it all in under an hour.

2131 Pan American Plaza. ℰ **619/234-2544.** www.sdhoc.com. Admission $8 adults; $6 seniors 65 and older, students, and military; $4 children 7–17; free for children 6 and under. Free 4th Tues of each month. Daily 10am–4:30pm. Bus: 7.

San Diego Miniature Railroad and Carousel ⓚⓘⓓⓢ   Just east of the zoo entrance, these antiquated enticements never fail to delight the preteen set. The open-air railroad takes a 3-minute journey through a grove of eucalyptus trees, while the charming carousel is one of the last in the world to still offer a ring grab (free ride if you seize the brass one). The carousel, built in 1910, is a classic, with hand-carved wood frogs, horses, and pigs.

Zoo Dr., next to San Diego Zoo entrance. Railroad ✆ **619/231-1515**. www.sandiegozoo.org. Summer daily 11am–6:30pm; Sept–May weekends and holidays only 11am–4:30pm. Carousel ✆ **619/239-0512**. www. balboapark.org. Summer daily 11am–5:30pm (till 6:30pm on Sun); Sept–May weekends and holidays only 11am–4:30pm. Admission $2 Railroad (free for children 11 months and under), $2 Carousel. Bus: 7.

San Diego Model Railroad Museum ★ Kids

Okay, so it's not exactly high culture, but this museum is worth your time, especially if you have kids in tow. Four permanent, scale-model railroads depict Southern California's transportation history and terrain with an astounding attention to miniature details. The exhibits occupy a 27,000-square-foot space, making it the world's largest indoor model railroad display. Children will enjoy the hands-on Lionel trains, and train buffs of all ages will appreciate the interactive multimedia displays. Allow a half-hour to an hour for your visit.

1649 El Prado (Casa de Balboa), under the Museum of Photographic Arts. ✆ **619/696-0199**. www. sdmrm.com. Admission $6 adults, $5 seniors, $3 students, $2.50 military, free for children 14 and under. Free 1st Tues of each month. Tues–Fri 11am–4pm; Sat–Sun 11am–5pm. Bus: 7.

San Diego Museum of Art ★

Opened in 1926, this is the oldest and largest art museum in San Diego. It's known in the art world for its collection of Spanish baroque painting and possibly the most extensive horde of Asian Indian paintings outside India; the museum's holdings of Latin American work have grown significantly in recent years, as well. The American collection, which features paintings and decorative arts, includes works by Georgia O'Keeffe, Mary Cassatt, and Thomas Eakins. Only a small percentage of the 12,000-piece permanent collection is on display at any given time, though, in favor of varied—often prestigious—touring shows. SDMA also has an ongoing schedule of concerts, films, and lectures, usually tied thematically to a current exhibition.

1450 El Prado. ✆ **619/232-7931**. www.sdmart.org. Admission $10 adults, $8 seniors and military, $7 students, $4 children 6–17, free for children 5 and under. Admission to traveling exhibits varies. Free 3rd Tues of each month. Tues–Sat 10am–5pm; Sun noon–5pm. Bus: 7.

San Diego Museum of Man ★

The iconic California building, with its amazing tiled dome and signature bell tower, is where you will find this museum devoted to anthropology. Exhibits emphasize the peoples of North and South America, and also include life-size replicas of a dozen types of *Homo sapiens* (from Cro-Magnon and Neanderthal to Peking Man) and Egyptian mummies and artifacts. Don't overlook the annex across the street, which houses more displays; the museum store, with its selection of books, clothing, and folk art, is worth a peek, too. The museum's annual Indian Fair, held in June, features Native Americans from the Southwest demonstrating tribal dances and selling food, arts, and crafts. About once a month the museum celebrates a different culture with its Tower After Hours soiree ($20 adults, $15 students), featuring music, food, and special exhibits. Allow at least an hour for your visit.

1350 El Prado. ✆ **619/239-2001**. www.museumofman.org. Admission $19 adults; $7.50 seniors, students, and active-duty military; $5 children 3–12; free for children 2 and under. Free 3rd Tues of the month. Daily 10am–4:30pm. Bus: 3, 7, or 120.

San Diego Natural History Museum

Founded in 1874, the Natural History Museum is one of the oldest scientific institutions in Southern California. It focuses on the flora, fauna, and mineralogy of the region, including Mexico; as a binational museum, research is done on both sides of the border and most exhibits are bilingual. You can see them all in about an hour. There's a 300-seat large-format movie theater, and two films are included in the price of admission. The interactive installation *Fossil Mysteries* is the museum's largest, most detailed exhibit; it includes life-size models of prehistoric

animals such as the Megalodon shark, the largest predator the world has ever known.
SDNHM also leads free nature hikes and has a full schedule of classes, lectures, and overnight expeditions for both families and adults.

1788 El Prado. ☏ **619/232-3821.** www.sdnhm.org. Admission $13 adults; $11 seniors; $8 students, youth age 13–17, and active-duty military; $7 children 3–12; free for children 2 and under. Free 1st Tues of each month. Daily 10am–5pm. Bus: 7.

Spreckels Organ Pavilion   Presented to the citizens of San Diego in 1914 by brothers John D. and Adolph Spreckels, the ornate, curved pavilion houses a magnificent organ with 4,530 individual pipes. They range in length from the size of a pencil to 32 feet, making it one of the largest outdoor organs in the world. With only brief interruptions, the organ has been in continuous use. Today visitors can enjoy free hour-long concerts on Sundays at 2pm, given by civic organist Carol Williams; free concerts are also held in the evening during the summer months. There's seating for 2,400 but little shade, so bring some sunscreen.

South of El Prado. ☏ **619/702-8138.** www.sosorgan.com. Free 1-hr. organ concerts Sun 2pm year-round; free organ concerts late June to Aug Mon 7:30pm (see website for a schedule); free Twilight in the Park concerts Tues–Thurs mid-June to Aug (call ☏ **619/239-0512** for schedule). Bus: 7.

Timken Museum of Art ★ (Finds)   How many art museums invite you to see great works of art for free? The Timken houses the Putnam Foundation's collection of 19th-century American paintings and works by European old masters, as well as a worthy display of Russian icons. Yes, it's a small collection, but the marquee attractions include a Peter Paul Rubens, *Portrait of a Young Man in Armor;* San Diego's only Rembrandt, *St. Bartholomew;* and a masterpiece by Eastman Johnson, *The Cranberry Harvest.* Since you can tour all of the museum in well under an hour, the Timken also makes for an easy introduction to fine art for younger travelers; docent tours are available Tuesday through Thursday from 10am to noon, the third Tuesday of the month from 1 to 3pm, or by appointment.

1500 El Prado. ☏ **619/239-5548.** www.timkenmuseum.org. Free admission. Tues–Sat 10am–4:30pm; Sun 1:30–4:30pm. Bus: 7.

WorldBeat Center (Finds)   Located in a former water storage tank on Park Boulevard, the WorldBeat Center is on a mission to "heal the world through music, dance, art, technology, and culture." They start by bringing in some of the biggest names in reggae and African music, and follow up by holding weekly drum and dance classes. Special events, lectures, and roots-conscious celebrations are all part of the mix; musical instruments, textiles, decorative accessories, and other fair-trade items made by indigenous cultures from around the globe are on sale at the gift store. Are you feeling irie?

2100 Park Blvd. ☏ **619/230-1190.** www.worldbeatcenter.org. Admission price to events varies. Mon–Fri 11am–6:30pm; Sat–Sun noon–6pm. Bus: 7.

4 MORE ATTRACTIONS

DOWNTOWN & BEYOND

Wander from the turn-of-the-20th-century **Gaslamp Quarter** ★★ to the joyful, modern architecture of the **Horton Plaza** ★ shopping center. (See "Walking Tour 1: The Gaslamp Quarter," in chapter 8.) Adjacent to the Gaslamp is East Village, which, thanks to the opening of **PETCO Park** ★ (p. 176) in 2004, has extended downtown a few blocks farther east.

Seaport Village is a shopping and dining complex on the waterfront (p. 201); it was incongruously designed to look like a New England seaport community. If you find the views across the water alluring, another way to experience San Diego's waterfront is with one of several harbor tours (see "Organized Tours," later in this chapter).

Cabrillo National Monument ★★★ (Moments) Breathtaking views mingle with the history of San Diego, starting with the arrival of Juan Rodríguez Cabrillo in 1542. His statue dominates the tip of Point Loma, 422 feet above sea level; this is also a vantage point for watching migrating Pacific gray whales en route from the Arctic Ocean to Baja California (and back again) December through March. A self-guided tour of the restored lighthouse, built in 1855, illuminates what life was like here more than a century ago (fog and low clouds made the lighthouse ineffective, so another was built close to the water in 1891). National Park Service rangers lead walks at the monument, and there are tide pools to explore at the base of the peninsula. On the other side of the point is the Bayside Trail, a 3-mile round-trip down to a lookout over the bay. Free 25-minute videos and slide shows on Cabrillo, tide pools, and the whales are shown on the hour daily from 10am to 4pm. *Tip:* Even on a sunny day, temperatures here can be cool, so bring a jacket; and pack a lunch—the site has great picnicking spots but no food facilities. You should plan on a minimum of 90 minutes here.

1800 Cabrillo Memorial Dr., Point Loma. ✆ 619/557-5450. www.nps.gov/cabr. Admission $5 per vehicle, $3 for walk-ins (valid for 7 days from purchase). Daily 9am–5pm. Bus: 84. By car, take I-8 W. to Rosecrans St., turn right on Canon St., left on Catalina, and follow signs.

Firehouse Museum (Kids) Appropriately housed in San Diego's oldest firehouse, the museum features shiny fire engines, including hand-drawn and horse-drawn models, a 1903 steam pumper, and memorabilia such as antique alarms, fire hats, and foundry molds for fire hydrants. There's also a small gift shop. Allow about half an hour for your visit.

1572 Columbia St. (at Cedar St.). ✆ 619/232-3473. www.sandiegofirehousemuseum.com. Admission $3 adults; $2 seniors, military in uniform, and youths 13–17; free for children 12 and under. Thurs–Fri 10am–2pm; Sat–Sun 10am–4pm. Bus: 83. Trolley: County Center/Little Italy.

Maritime Museum ★★ (Kids) This flotilla of classic ships is led by the full-rigged merchant vessel *Star of India* (1863), a National Historic Landmark and the world's oldest ship that still goes to sea. The gleaming white San Francisco–Oakland steam-powered ferry *Berkeley* (1898) worked round-the-clock to carry people to safety following the 1906 San Francisco earthquake; it now pulls duty as a museum with fine ship models on display. The elegant *Medea* (1904) is one of the world's few remaining large steam yachts, and the *Pilot* (1914) was San Diego Bay's official pilot boat for 82 years. Among the more recent additions are a 300-foot-long Cold War–era B-39 Soviet attack submarine and the HMS *Surprise*. This painstakingly accurate reproduction of an 18th-century Royal Navy frigate played a supporting role to Russell Crowe in the film *Master and Commander: Far Side of the World*. You can board and tour each vessel; give yourself 90 minutes.

1492 N. Harbor Dr. ✆ 619/234-9153. www.sdmaritime.org. Admission $14 adults, $11 seniors 63 and over and active military with ID, $8 children 6–17, free for children 5 and under. Daily 9am–8pm (till 9pm in summer). Bus: 2, 210, 810, 820, 850, 860, 923, or 992. Trolley: County Center/Little Italy.

Museum of Contemporary Art San Diego Downtown ★★★ The city's latest cultural icon is the Museum of Contemporary Art's downtown space, opened in 2007 and known as the Jacobs and Copley Buildings. The annex is boldly grafted onto the end of the

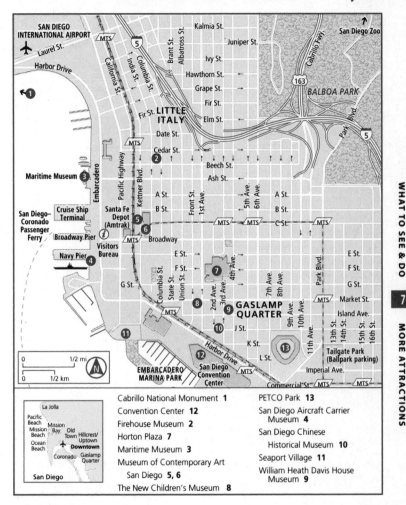

Cabrillo National Monument **1**	PETCO Park **13**
Convention Center **12**	San Diego Aircraft Carrier Museum **4**
Firehouse Museum **2**	San Diego Chinese Historical Museum **10**
Horton Plaza **7**	
Maritime Museum **3**	Seaport Village **11**
Museum of Contemporary Art San Diego **5, 6**	William Heath Davis House Museum **9**
The New Children's Museum **8**	

historic Santa Fe Depot, built in 1915; it transforms what had been the train station's baggage building into a state-of-the-art museum and educational facility. Designed by the architect responsible for the Warhol museum in Pittsburgh and the Museo Picasso in Málaga, Spain, the new wing provides an additional 30,000 feet of programming space. The expansion also features permanent, site-specific work by artists Richard Serra, Jenny Holzer, and others. Across the street at America Plaza are MCASD's original downtown galleries (MCASD's flagship museum is in La Jolla, p. 153). Lectures and special events for adults and children are presented, and the first Thursday evening of every month is "TNT" (Thursday Night Thing), an engaging music and arts program that's part cocktail party, part concert, part gallery opening. Free tours are given every third Thursday at 6pm and weekends at 2pm. Depending on the exhibits, allow yourself an hour.

1100 and 1001 Kettner Blvd. (btw. B St. and Broadway). ℂ **858/454-3541.** www.mcasd.org. Admission $10 adults, $5 seniors and military, free for anyone 25 and under, free admission every 3rd Thurs 5–7pm; paid ticket good for admission to MCASD La Jolla within 7 days. Thurs–Tues 11am–5pm; 3rd Thurs 11am–7pm; closed Wed. Bus: 83 and numerous Broadway routes. Trolley: America Plaza.

The New Children's Museum Ⓚⓘⓓⓢ Have some restless kids on your hands? Turn them loose in the pillow fight room, enroll them in a theater improv class, or perhaps some yoga or a photography workshop will pique their interest. San Diego's new, high-style children's museum is a $25-million facility designed by one of the city's most acclaimed architects. It's industrially modern and angular, which has led to wasted, underused space, but youngsters are sure to get a kick out of the rock climbing wall, hands-on art projects, and play areas. While there are activities scheduled for teens, this museum will appeal more to the under-13 set; give your family at least an hour here (or more if they want to start browsing for cool toys at the Gizmo Garage gift shop).

200 W. Island Ave. (at Front St.). ℂ 619/233-8792. www.thinkplaycreate.org. Admission $10, seniors and military $5, free for children 11 months and under; free admission the 2nd Sun of the month. Mon–Tues and Fri–Sat 10am–4pm; Thurs 10am–6pm; Sun noon–4pm (2nd Sun of the month 10am–4pm); closed Wed. Parking $10. Bus: 3, 11, 120, or 992. Trolley: Convention Center.

San Diego Aircraft Carrier Museum On January 10, 2004, the USS *Midway* made its final voyage into San Diego Bay. The aircraft carrier had a 47-year military history that began a week after the Japanese surrender of World War II in 1945. By the time the *Midway* was decommissioned in 1991, the warship had patrolled the Taiwan Straits in 1955, operated in the Tonkin Gulf, served as the flagship from which Desert Storm was conducted, and evacuated 1,800 people from volcano-threatened Subic Bay Naval Base in the Philippines. In all, more than 225,000 men served aboard the *Midway.* The carrier is now moored at the Embarcadero and has become the world's largest floating naval-aviation museum. A self-guided audio tour takes visitors to several levels of the ship while recounting the story of life on board; the highlight is climbing up the superstructure to the bridge and gazing down on the 1,001-foot-long flight deck, which holds various aircraft poised for duty. ***Note:*** Be prepared to climb some stairs and ladders; allow 90 minutes for your visit.

910 Harbor Dr. (at Navy Pier). ℂ **619/544-9600.** www.midway.org. Admission $17 adults, $13 seniors, $10 retired military, $9 children 6–17, free for children 5 and under and active-duty military. Daily 10am–5pm. Limited parking on Navy Pier, $7 for 4 hr.; metered parking available nearby. Bus: 2, 210, or 992.

San Diego Chinese Historical Museum In the former Chinese Mission, where Chinese immigrants learned English and adapted to their new environment, this small museum contains antique Chinese lottery equipment, a series of panels documenting the gold rush, and artifacts unearthed from San Diego's old Chinatown (south of Market, btw. Third and Fifth aves.). A nice gift shop and a pleasant garden in back with a bronze statue of Confucius complete the experience. Allow about half an hour for your visit. Walking tours of the Asian Pacific Historic District start here on the second Saturday of the month at 11am; the cost is $2.

404 Third Ave. (at J St.). ℂ **619/338-9888.** www.sdchm.org. Admission $2 adults, free for children 11 and under. Tues–Sat 10:30am–4pm; Sun noon–4pm. Bus: 3, 11, or 120. Trolley: Convention Center.

William Heath Davis House Museum Shipped by boat to San Diego in 1850 from Portland, Maine, this is the oldest structure in the Gaslamp Quarter. It is a well-preserved example of a prefabricated "saltbox" family home and has remained structurally unchanged for more than 150 years (although it originally stood at another location). A

museum on the first and second floors documents life in "New Town" and profiles some **147**
of the city's early movers and shakers. A small, shady park is adjacent to the house; the
Gaslamp Quarter Historical Foundation also makes its home here, and it sponsors walking tours of the neighborhood for $10 ($8 for seniors, students, and military) every
Saturday at 11am. The foundation has a nice gift store here, too, located in the basement;
you can tour the house in 30 minutes.

410 Island Ave. (at Fourth Ave.). ✆ 619/233-4692. www.gaslampquarter.org. Admission $5 adults and
children; $4 seniors, military, and students. Tues–Sat 10am–6pm; Sun 9am–3pm. Bus: 3, 11, or 120. Trol-
ley: Gaslamp Quarter or Convention Center.

OLD TOWN & MISSION VALLEY

The birthplace of San Diego—indeed, of California—Old Town takes you back to the
Mexican California of the mid-1800s. "Walking Tour 3: Old Town" in chapter 8 covers
Old Town's historic sights.

Mission Valley, which starts just north of Presidio Park and heads straight east, is
decidedly more modern; until I-8 was built in the 1950s, it was little more than cow
pastures with a couple of dirt roads. Shopping malls, motels, a golf course, condos, car
dealerships, and a massive sports stadium fill the expanse today. Farther upstream along
the San Diego River is the **Mission Basilica San Diego,** and just a few miles beyond lies
an outstanding park with walking trails. Few visitors make it this far, but **Mission Trails
Regional Park** reveals what San Diego looked like before the Spanish (and the car dealers) arrived.

El Campo Santo   Behind an adobe wall along San Diego Avenue is San Diego's first
cemetery, established in 1850. This small plot is the final resting place for Yankee Jim
Robinson, a local troublemaker who was hanged for stealing a rowboat in 1852. Some
say he still hangs around at the **Whaley House** (p. 149). Of more historical note is the
grave of Antonio Garra, chief of the Cupeño Indians, who led an uprising of dispossessed
tribes after a tax was levied against their livestock; it seems the Mission-educated Garra
had learned that taxation without representation is tyranny. He was executed by a firing
squad at his graveside in 1852, his final words: "Gentlemen, I ask your pardon for all my
offenses; I expect yours in return." *Note:* The small brass markers on the sidewalk and in
the street indicate the still-buried remains of some of the city's earliest residents, paved
over by the tide of progress.

2410 San Diego Ave. (btw. Conde and Arista sts.). Free admission. Daily 24 hr. Bus: 8, 9, 10, 14, 28, 30, 35,
44, 105, or 150. Trolley: Old Town.

Heritage Park   This 8-acre county park, dedicated to preservation of Victorian architecture, contains seven original 19th-century houses moved here from other parts of the
city and given new leases on life. The structures now serve as a bed-and-breakfast, a doll
shop, and a lingerie store, among other things. The small, charming synagogue at the
entrance, Temple Beth Israel, was built in 1889 in Classic Revival style and relocated here
in 1989. The San Diego County Parks department operates an information and reservation center out of the Sherman-Gilbert House; it's open Monday through Friday, 9am to
5pm. Allow 30 minutes for your visit.

2450 Heritage Park Row (corner of Juan and Harney sts.). ✆ 877/565-3600 or 619/291-9784. www.
sdparks.org. Free admission. Daily 24 hr. Bus: 8, 9, 10, 14, 28, 30, 35, 44, 105, or 150. Trolley: Old Town.

Mission Basilica San Diego de Alcalá   Established in 1769 above Old Town, this
was the first link in a chain of 21 California missions founded by Spanish missionary

WHAT TO SEE & DO

7

MORE ATTRACTIONS

Junípero Serra. In 1774, the mission was moved from Old Town to its present site for agricultural reasons—and to separate the indigenous converts from the fortress that included the original building. The mission was sacked by the local tribe a year after it was built, leading Father Serra to reconstruct it using 5- to 7-foot-thick adobe walls and clay tile roofs, rendering it harder to burn. In the process, he inspired a bevy of 20th-century California architects. A few bricks belonging to the original mission can be seen in Presidio Park in Old Town. Mass is said daily in this active Catholic parish. Other missions in San Diego County include **Mission San Luis Rey de Francia** in Oceanside, **Mission San Antonio de Pala** near Mount Palomar, and **Mission Santa Ysabel** near Julian. Known as "the King of Missions," the San Luis Rey is the largest of California's missions and one of its most beautiful (see "North County Beach Towns: Spots to Surf & Sun," in chapter 11). You can tour the church and grounds in about 45 minutes.

10818 San Diego Mission Rd., Mission Valley. ℂ **619/281-8449.** www.missionsandiego.com. Admission $3 adults, $2 seniors and students, $1 children 11 and under. Free Sun and for daily Masses. Museum and gift shop daily 9am–4:45pm; Mass daily 7am and 5:30pm, with additional Sun Mass at 8, 10, 11am, and noon. Bus: 14. Trolley: Mission San Diego. Take I-8 to Mission Gorge Rd. to Twain Ave., which turns into San Diego Mission Rd.

Mission Trails Regional Park ★ ⓕFindsⒻ   Well off the beaten track for tourists, but only 8 miles from downtown San Diego, this is one of the nation's largest urban parks. Encompassing more than 5,800 acres, it includes abundant bird life, two lakes, a picturesque stretch of the San Diego River, the Old Mission Dam (probably the first irrigation project in the West), and 1,592-foot Cowles Mountain, the summit of which reveals outstanding views over much of the county. The park boasts trails up to 4 miles in length, including a 1.5-mile interpretive trail; some are designated for mountain bike use. There's also a 46-space campground (ℂ **619/668-2748**). Mission Trails was founded in 1974, when the area surrounding Cowles Mountain began to experience a housing boom, leading city and county representatives—working with community planners—to make an initial purchase of land. In 1989 the first park ranger was hired; in 1995 the slick visitor center opened, cementing a place for Mission Trails in the hearts of outdoor-loving San Diegans.

1 Father Junípero Serra Trail, Mission Gorge. ℂ **619/668-3281.** www.mtrp.org. Free admission. Daily sunrise–sundown (visitor center 9am–5pm). Take I-8 to Mission Gorge Rd.; follow for 4 miles to entrance.

Old Town State Historic Park ★   Dedicated to re-creating the early life of the city from 1821 to 1872, this is where San Diego's Mexican heritage shines brightest. The community was briefly Mexico's informal capital of the California territory; the Stars and Stripes were eventually raised over Old Town in 1846. Of the park's 20 structures, 7 are original, including homes made of adobe; the rest are reconstructed. The park's headquarters is at the Robinson-Rose House, 4002 Wallace St., where you can pick up a map and peruse a model of Old Town as it looked in 1872. Among the park's attractions is La Casa de Estudillo, which depicts the living conditions of a wealthy family in 1872, and Seeley Stables, named after A. L. Seeley, who ran the stagecoach and mail service in these parts from 1867 to 1871. The stables have two floors of wagons, carriages, stagecoaches, and other memorabilia, including washboards, slot machines, and hand-worked saddles. On Wednesdays from 10am to 2pm, costumed park volunteers reenact life in the 1800s with cooking and crafts demonstrations, a working blacksmith, and parlor singing. Free 1-hour walking tours leave daily at 11am and 2pm from the Robinson-Rose House. Plan on 90 minutes here; more if you want to dine or seriously shop.

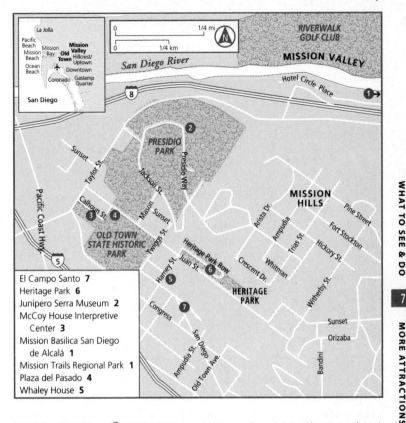

El Campo Santo **7**
Heritage Park **6**
Junípero Serra Museum **2**
McCoy House Interpretive
 Center **3**
Mission Basilica San Diego
 de Alcalá **1**
Mission Trails Regional Park **1**
Plaza del Pasado **4**
Whaley House **5**

WHAT TO SEE & DO

7

MORE ATTRACTIONS

4002 Wallace St., Old Town. ℰ **619/220-5422.** www.parks.ca.gov. Free admission (donations welcome). Museums daily 10am–5pm; most restaurants until 9pm. Bus: 8, 9, 10, 14, 28, 30, 35, 44, 105, or 150. Trolley: Old Town. Take I-5 to the Old Town exit and follow signs.

Whaley House   In 1856, this striking two-story house (the first in these parts to be constructed with brick) was built for Thomas Whaley and his family. It's probably an urban legend that this house is "officially" designated as haunted, but 100,000 people visit each year to see for themselves. Up to four spirits are said to haunt the grounds, including the ghost of Yankee Jim Robinson, who was hanged in 1852 on the site where the house now stands. Exhibits include a life mask of Abraham Lincoln, one of only six made, and the spinet piano used in the movie *Gone With the Wind*. The Whaley complex includes several other historic structures, including the Verna House and two false-front buildings, both dating from the 1870s. The Verna House is now an excellent little gift shop run by the Save Our Heritage Organisation, selling beautiful Arts and Crafts pottery, architecture-themed books, and crafts, as well as your admission tickets; you can tour the house in about 30 minutes. With 2 weeks' notice, you can also arrange a private, after-hours visit to the Whaley House.

2476 San Diego Ave. © **619/297-7511.** www.whaleyhouse.org. Admission before 5pm $6 adults, $5 seniors 55 and older, $4 children 3–12; admission after 5pm $10 adults, $5 children 3–12. Free for children 2 and under. Sept–May Sun–Tues 10am–5pm, Thurs–Sat 10am–10pm, closed Wed; summer daily 10am–10pm. Bus: 8, 9, 10, 14, 28, 30, 35, 44, 105, or 150. Trolley: Old Town.

MISSION BAY & THE BEACHES

Opened to the public in 1949, **Mission Bay** is a man-made, 4,600-acre aquatic playground created by dredging tidal mud flats and opening them to seawater. Today, this is a great area for walking, jogging, in-line skating, biking, and boating. For all of these activities, see the appropriate headings in "Outdoor Activities," later in this chapter. For **SeaWorld San Diego,** see p. 130.

For a **spectacular view,** drive north on Mission Boulevard, past Turquoise Street, where it turns into La Jolla Mesa Drive. Proceed up the hill ³/₄ mile and turn around. From here you'll see the beaches and Point Loma in front of you, Mission Bay and San Diego Bay, downtown, the Hillcrest/Uptown area, and (on a clear day) the hills of Tijuana, and to the east, San Diego's backcountry.

Belmont Park (Kids) This seaside amusement park was opened in 1925 by business tycoon John D. Spreckels. No, it wasn't quite the magnanimous gesture it seems; it was actually a real estate scheme to lure people to what was then a scarcely populated area. Today, Belmont Park's star attraction is the **Giant Dipper roller coaster** ★, one of two surviving fixtures from the original park and a registered national historic landmark; the other holdover is the **Plunge,** Southern California's largest (175 ft./53m) indoor swimming pool. There are a variety of carnie-style rides at Belmont Park, but something more unique awaits next door at the **Wavehouse** ★ (© **866/843-9283** or 858/228-9300; www.sd.wavehouse.com). This self-described "royal palace of youth culture" has as its centerpiece **Bruticus Maximus** ★, a wave machine designed to create stand-up rides; you have to get certified (about a 1-hr. process) before attempting "B-Max." The **Flow-Rider** provides a less gnarly wave-riding experience.

3190 Mission Blvd., corner of W. Mission Bay Dr. © **858/488-1549.** www.giantdipper.com. Ride on the Giant Dipper $6, unlimited rides $23; FlowRider starts at $25 for 1 hr., B-Max starts at $40 for 1 hr. Belmont Park daily 11am–8pm (weekend and summer hours later; closed Mon–Thurs Jan and Feb); Wavehouse Mon–Fri noon–8pm, Sat–Sun from 11am. Bus: 8 or 9. Take I-5 to the SeaWorld exit, and follow W. Mission Bay Dr. to Belmont Park.

LA JOLLA

One of San Diego's most scenic spots—the star of postcards for more than 100 years—is **La Jolla Cove** ★★★ and **Ellen Browning Scripps Park** ★★ on the bluff above it. The walk through the park, along Coast Boulevard (start from the north at Prospect St.), offers some of California's finest coastal scenery. Just south is the **Children's Pool** ★, a beach where dozens of harbor seals can be spotted lazing in the sun. The 6,000-acre **San Diego–La Jolla Underwater Park** ★★★, established in 1970, stretches for 10 miles from La Jolla Cove to the northern end of Torrey Pines State Reserve, and extends from the shoreline to a depth of 900 feet. The park is a boat-free zone. Its undersea flora and fauna draw scuba divers and snorkelers, many of them hoping for a glimpse of the brilliant orange garibaldi, California's state fish.

La Jolla has architectural treasures as well; highlights include **Mary Star of the Sea,** 7727 Girard Ave., a small Roman Catholic church with some stylish art; and **La Valencia Hotel,** 1132 Prospect St., a fine Spanish Colonial–style structure. The **La Jolla Woman's Club,** 7791 Draper Ave.; the adjacent **Museum of Contemporary Art San Diego** ★★★;

To Del Mar (3 miles)

To Los Angeles (110 miles)

University of California San Diego

N. Torrey Pines Rd.

La Jolla Village Dr.

Villa La Jolla Dr.

Gilman Dr.

La Jolla Scenic Dr. N.

Torrey Pines Rd.

La Jolla Shores Dr.

Scripps Pier

La Jolla Shores

Prestwick Dr.

Calle del Oro

Camino del Oro

Av. de la Playa

PACIFIC OCEAN

La Jolla Parkway

Torrey Pines Rd.

see inset

Prospect St.

Torrey Pines Rd.

Casa Beach

Wipeout Beach

Silverado St.

Kline St.

Girard Ave.

Pearl St.

Eads Ave.

Fay Ave.

Draper Ave.

La Jolla Blvd.

La Jolla Country Club

La Jolla

Pacific Beach
Mission Beach
Ocean Beach
Mission Bay
Old Town
Hillcrest/ Uptown
Downtown
Coronado
Gaslamp Quarter

San Diego

0   1/4 mi
0   .25 km

Shell Beach

Boomer Beach

La Jolla Cove

Coast Blvd.

Prospect St.

Girard

Herschel Ave.

Ivanhoe Ave.

Athenaeum Music & Arts Library **13**
Birch Aquarium at Scripps **4**
The Bishop's School **11**
Ellen Browning Scripps Park **15**
La Jolla Recreation Center **10**
La Jolla Woman's Club **9**
La Valencia Hotel **14**
Mary Star of the Sea church **8**
Mount Soledad **5**
Museum of Contemporary Art
    San Diego La Jolla **12**
Salk Institute for Biological Studies **2**
San Diego–La Jolla Underwater Park **6**
University of California San Diego **3**
        Geisel Library
        La Jolla Playhouse
        Stuart Collection
Sunny Jim Cave **7**
Torrey Pines Golf Course **1**
Torrey Pines State Reserve **1**

the **La Jolla Recreation Center;** and the **Bishop's School** are all the handiwork of famed architect Irving Gill.

At La Jolla's north end, you'll find the 1,200-acre, 22,000-student **University of California, San Diego (UCSD),** which was established in 1960 and represents the county's largest single employer. The campus features the **Geisel Library ★★**, a striking and distinguished contemporary structure, as well as the **Stuart Collection ★** of public sculpture and the **Birch Aquarium at Scripps ★★** (see individual listings, to follow). One of celebrated architect Louis I. Kahn's masterpieces is the **Salk Institute for Biological Studies ★★★**, 10010 N. Torrey Pines Rd., a research facility named for the creator of the polio vaccine. (For tours, see "For Architecture Buffs," later in this chapter.) Farther north is an ersatz jewel, the **Lodge at Torrey Pines** (p. 85), a modern, 175-room luxury resort in the guise of an early-20th-century Craftsman-style manse. It overlooks the revered **Torrey Pines Golf Course** (p. 171).

For a fine scenic drive, follow La Jolla Boulevard to Nautilus Street and turn east to get to 800-foot-high **Mount Soledad ★**, which offers a 360-degree view of the area. The appropriateness of the 43-foot-tall cross on top, erected in 1954 in this public park, has been the subject of 20 years of legal jousting (religious symbols are prohibited on public land). In 2008, a federal judge ruled the cross could stay.

Athenaeum Music & Arts Library ★★ (Finds) Founded in 1899, this is one of only 16 nonprofit, membership libraries in the United States. Year-round, it hosts exceptional art exhibits, intimate concerts (from jazz and classical to more experimental new music), lectures, special events, and classes that are open to the general public. An incredible collection of books, music, and more makes for fascinating browsing, but only members can check something out. The Athenaeum has been located at this site from the very beginning and over the years has expanded into adjacent buildings, including the beautiful Spanish Renaissance–style rotunda, designed by renowned architect William Templeton Johnson and dating to 1921. Free tours are conducted every third Saturday at 11am.

1008 Wall St. (at Girard Ave.) ℂ **858/454-5872.** www.ljathenaeum.org. Gallery and library admission free; various prices for concerts, classes, and lectures. Tues and Thurs–Sat 10am–5:30pm; Wed 10am–8:30pm; closed Sun–Mon. Bus: 30. Take Torrey Pines Rd. to Prospect Place and turn right. Prospect Place becomes Prospect St.; turn left on Girard Ave.

Birch Aquarium at Scripps ★★ (Kids) This beautiful facility is both an aquarium and a museum, operated as the interpretive arm of the world-famous Scripps Institution of Oceanography. The aquarium affords close-up views of the Pacific Northwest, the California coast, Mexico's Sea of Cortés, and the tropical seas, all presented in more than 60 marine-life tanks. The giant kelp forest is particularly impressive; other exotic highlights include a variety of sharks and ethereal moon jellies. The outdoor demonstration tide pool not only displays marine coastal life but also offers an amazing view of Scripps Pier, La Jolla Shores Beach, the village of La Jolla, and the ocean. The museum section has numerous interpretive exhibits on current and past research at the Scripps Institution, which was established in 1903 and became part of the University of California system in 1912. The bookstore is well stocked with textbooks, science books, educational toys, gifts, and T-shirts. Off-site adventures, such as tide-pooling, scouting for grunion runs (p. 228), and whale-watching, are also conducted year-round (call for more details). Give yourself at least 90 minutes here.

2300 Expedition Way. ℂ **858/534-3474.** www.aquarium.ucsd.edu. Admission $11 adults, $9 seniors, $8 college students with ID, $7.50 children 3–17, free for children 2 and under. Daily 9am–5pm. Free 3-hr. parking. Bus: 30. Take I-5 to La Jolla Village Dr. exit, go west 1 mile, and turn left at Expedition Way.

Museum of Contemporary Art San Diego La Jolla ★★★ Focusing on work
produced since 1950, this museum is internationally recognized for its permanent collection and thought-provoking exhibitions. MCASD's holdings include more than 4,000 paintings, sculptures, photographs, videos, and multimedia and installation pieces, with a strong showing by California artists. The museum itself is perched on a cliff overlooking the Pacific Ocean; the views from the galleries are gorgeous. The original building on the site was the residence of the legendary Ellen Browning Scripps and was designed by Irving Gill in 1916; the outdoor sculptures were designed specifically for this location. It became an art museum in 1941, and the Gill building facade was uncovered and restored in 1996. More than a dozen exhibitions are scheduled each year, and MCASD also offers lectures, cutting-edge films, and special events on an ongoing basis; depending on the show, you should plan on at least an hour here. The bookstore is also a great place for contemporary gifts, and the cafe is a pleasant stop before or after your visit. Free docent tours are available the third Thursday of the month at 6pm and weekends at 2pm.

700 Prospect St. ℂ **858/454-3541.** www.mcasd.org. Admission $10 adults, $5 seniors and military, free for anyone 25 and under; free admission every 3rd Thurs 5–7pm; paid ticket good for admission to MCASD downtown within 7 days. Thurs–Tues 11am–5pm; 3rd Thurs 11am–7pm; closed Wed. Bus: 30. Take I-5 N. to La Jolla Pkwy. or take I-5 S. to La Jolla Village Dr. W. Take Torrey Pines Rd. to Prospect Place and turn right; Prospect Place becomes Prospect St.

Stuart Collection ★ Consider the Stuart Collection a work in progress on a large scale. Through a 1982 agreement between the Stuart Foundation and UCSD, the still-growing collection consists of site-related sculptures by leading contemporary artists. Start by picking up a map from the information booth, and wend your way through the 1,200-acre campus to discover the 17 highly diverse artworks. Among them is Niki de Saint Phalle's *Sun God,* a jubilant 14-foot-high fiberglass bird on a 15-foot concrete base. Nicknamed "Big Bird," it's been made an unofficial mascot by the students, who use it as the centerpiece of their annual celebration, the Sun God Festival. Alexis Smith's *Snake Path* is a 560-foot-long slate-tile pathway that winds up the hill from the Engineering Mall to the east terrace of the spectacular Geisel Library (breathtaking architecture that's a fabulous sculpture itself). Terry Allen's *Trees* comprises three eucalyptus trees encased in lead. One tree emits songs, and another poems and stories, while the third stands silent in a grove of trees the students call "the Enchanted Forest." Allow at least 2 hours to tour the entire collection.

University of California, San Diego. ℂ **858/534-2117.** http://stuartcollection.ucsd.edu. Free admission. Bus: 30, 41, 48, 49, 101, 150, or 921. From La Jolla, take Torrey Pines Rd. to La Jolla Village Dr., turn right, go 2 blocks to Gilman Dr. and turn left into the campus; in about 1 block the information booth will be visible on the right.

Torrey Pines State Reserve ★★★ (**Moments**) The rare Torrey pine tree grows in only two places in the world: Santa Rosa Island, 175 miles northwest of San Diego, and here, at the north end of La Jolla. Even if the twisted shape of these awkwardly beautiful trees doesn't lure you to this spot, the equally scarce undeveloped coastal scenery should. The city first donated 369 acres as a public park, and the 1,750-acre reserve was established in 1921 from a gift by Ellen Browning Scripps. The reserve encompasses the beach below, as well as a lagoon immediately north, but the focus is the 300-foot-high, water-carved sandstone bluffs that provide a precarious footing for the trees. In spring, the wildflower show includes bush poppies, Cleveland sage, agave, and yucca. A half-dozen trails, all under 1.5 miles in length, travel from the road to the cliff edge or down to the beach. A small visitor center, built in the traditional adobe style of the Hopi Indians, features a lovely 12-minute video about the park. Watch for migrating gray whales in winter or dolphins that patrol these shores year-round. This delicate spot is one of San Diego's unique treasures, a taste of what Southern California's coast looked like a couple hundred years ago. Interpretive nature walks are held weekends and holidays at 10am and 2pm. *Note:* No facilities for food or drinks are available in the park. You can bring a picnic lunch, but you have to eat it on the beach; food and drink (other than water) are not allowed in the upper portion of the reserve. You could spend your whole day here, 90 minutes at least.

Hwy. 101, La Jolla. © **858/755-2063.** www.torreypine.org. Admission $8 per car, seniors $7. Daily 8am–sunset. Bus: 101. From I-5, take Carmel Valley Rd. west; turn left at Hwy. 101.

CORONADO

It's hard to miss San Diego Bay's most noteworthy landmark: the **San Diego–Coronado Bay Bridge** ★. Completed in 1969, this graceful five-lane bridge spans 2¼ miles and links the city and the "island" of Coronado. At 246 feet in height, the bridge was designed to be tall enough for the Navy's aircraft carriers to pass beneath. Heading to Coronado by car is a thrill because you can see Mexico and the shipyards of National City to the left, the San Diego skyline to the right, and Coronado, the naval station, and Point Loma in front of you (designated drivers have to promise to keep their eyes on the road). When the bridge opened, it put the antiquated commuter ferries out of business (though in 1986 passenger-only ferry service restarted—see "By Water" in the "Getting Around" section in chapter 3). Bus no. 901 from downtown will also take you across the bridge.

Hotel del Coronado ★★   Built in 1888, this turreted Victorian seaside resort (p. 89) remains an enduring, endearing national treasure. Whether you are staying here, dining here, or simply touring the grounds and photo gallery, prepare to be enchanted.

1500 Orange Ave., Coronado. © **800/468-3533** or 619/435-6611. www.hoteldel.com. Free admission. Parking $15 1st hour, $10 for each additional hour. Bus: 901 or 904. Ferry: Broadway Pier, and then a half-hour walk, or take a bus or the Coronado trolley, or rent a bike. From I-5 take the Coronado Bridge and make a left on Orange Ave.

Museum of History and Art   This museum features archival materials about the development of Coronado, as well as tourist information. Exhibits include photographs of the Hotel Del in its infancy, the old ferries, Tent City (a seaside campground for middle-income vacationers from 1900–39), and notable residents and visitors. You'll also learn about the island's military aviation history during World Wars I and II. Plan to spend up to half an hour here. The museum has a gift store with Coronado-themed items and offers guided and self-guided walking tours of the area. Guided tours of the Hotel Del are scheduled for Tuesdays at 10:30am, and Friday through Sunday at 2pm ($15); an architectural tour departs from the museum on Wednesdays at 2pm ($10).

1100 Orange Ave. © **619/435-7242.** www.coronadohistory.org. Suggested donation $4 adults, $3 seniors and military, $2 youths 9–18, free for children 8 and under. Mon–Fri 9am–5pm; Sat–Sun 10am–5pm. Bus: 901 or 904. From I-5 take the Coronado Bridge and make a left on Orange Ave.

FARTHER AFIELD

Chula Vista Nature Center ★ (Finds) (Kids)   Overshadowed by SeaWorld and the zoo, this wonderful interactive nature center highlights the plants and animals native to San Diego Bay and the surrounding wetlands. Featuring exhibits of stingrays and small sharks in kid-level open tanks, the center's most recent addition is its $3-million Discovery Center, which is home to **Turtle Lagoon,** San Diego's only habitat for endangered green sea turtles. There are also large tanks with moon jellyfish, eels, and rainbow trout. CVNC is located in Sweetwater Marsh, one of San Diego's top bird-watching spots. The nature center has walking trails and a facility for experiencing the bird life (including aviaries with shorebirds and raptors). The parking lot is located away from the center, and a shuttle bus ferries guests between the two points every 10 to 15 minutes.

1000 Gunpowder Point Dr., Chula Vista. (C) **619/409-5900.** www.chulavistanaturecenter.org. $6 adults, $5 seniors and students, $4 youth 12–17, $3 children 4–11, free for children 3 and under. Tues–Sun 10am–5pm (last shuttle at 4pm). Free parking. Bus: 932. Trolley: Bayfront/E St. (Request shuttle at trolley info center.) From I-5 S., take the E St. exit.

Knott's Soak City U.S.A. (**Kids**) Themed to replicate Southern California's surfer towns of the 1950s and 1960s, this 32-acre water park has 22 slides of all shapes and sizes, a 500,000-gallon wave pool, a ¹/₄-mile lazy river, and assorted snack facilities. The park is about 25 minutes south of downtown, just north of the border.

2052 Entertainment Circle, Chula Vista. (C) **619/661-7373.** www.knotts.com. Admission $30 adults, $20 seniors and children ages 3–11; reduced admission after 3pm. Late May to Aug daily 10am–6pm or later; weekends in Sept. Parking $9, $13 RVs. Take I-5 or I-805 to Main St.; turn right on Entertainment Circle.

---

5 FREE OF CHARGE & FULL OF FUN

Check out this summary of free San Diego activities, most of which are described in detail earlier in this chapter. In addition, scan the lists of "Special-Interest Sightseeing," below; "Outdoor Activities" and "Spectator Sports," later in this chapter; and the "San Diego Calendar of Events" in chapter 3. Many events listed in these sections, such as the U.S. Open Sandcastle Competition, are no-charge affairs. Also note that the walking tours outlined in chapter 8 are free to anyone.

DOWNTOWN & BEYOND

It doesn't cost a penny to stroll around the **Gaslamp Quarter,** which brims with restaurants, shops, and historic buildings, along the Embarcadero (waterfront), or around the shops at Seaport Village or Horton Plaza. And don't forget: **Walkabout International** offers free guided walking tours (described in "Organized Tours," later in this chapter), and Centre City Redevelopment Corporation's **Downtown Information Center** (p. 162) gives bus tours two Saturdays a month.

If you'd rather drive around, ask for the map of the **52-mile San Diego Scenic Drive** when you're at the International Visitor Information Center.

The **murals** in **Chicano Park** ((C) 619/563-4661; www.chicano-park.org), painted on the support system of the San Diego–Coronado Bay Bridge, are a colorful road map through Mexican and Chicano history. South of downtown (exit Cesar Chavez Pkwy. from I-5), the 70-plus murals represent some of San Diego's most important pieces of public art. For visibility and safety's sake, plan your visit during the day. The **Museum of Contemporary Art San Diego**'s two downtown spaces are free to everyone 25 and under; for those who have to pay, your ticket will get you into MCA's La Jolla museum for free, if you visit within 7 days. Both the La Jolla and downtown museums are also free every third Thursday from 5 to 7pm.

You can fish free of charge from any municipal pier (that is, if you bring your own pole). Fishing license is not required.

All the **museums** in Balboa Park are open to the public without charge one Tuesday a month. Here's a list of the free days:

> **First Tuesday of each month:** Natural History Museum, Reuben H. Fleet Science Center, Model Railroad Museum, Centro Cultural de la Raza
>
> **Second Tuesday:** Museum of Photographic Arts, Museum of San Diego History, Veterans Museum & Memorial Center
>
> **Third Tuesday:** Museum of Art, Museum of Man, Mingei International Museum, Japanese Friendship Garden, Museum of the Living Artist
>
> **Fourth Tuesday:** Air & Space Museum, Automotive Museum, Hall of Champions Sports Museum

These Balboa Park attractions are always free: The Botanical Building and Lily Pond, House of Pacific Relations International Cottages, the Timken Museum of Art, and the San Diego Museum of Art's Sculpture Garden. The **Spreckels Organ Pavilion** hosts free 1-hour Sunday afternoon organ concerts at 2pm year-round, and free concerts Monday through Thursday evenings in summer. Several free **tours** of the park are available; they leave from in front of the visitor center. See "Balboa Park Guided Tours" earlier on p. 141 for more information. The **San Diego Zoo** is free to all on the first Monday of October (Founders Day), and children 11 and under enter free every day during October.

OLD TOWN & MISSION VALLEY

Explore **Heritage Park, Presidio Park, Old Town State Historic Park,** or **El Campo Santo.** A 1-hour walking tour of the state park is conducted twice daily, and frontier reenactments are staged Wednesdays from 10am to 2pm. There's free entertainment (mariachis and folk dancers) at **Plaza del Pasado** (p. 204) on Saturdays and Sundays, and the **Old Town Market** (San Diego Ave. and Twiggs St.) has costumed storytellers. The free **San Diego County Sheriff's Museum,** 2384 San Diego Ave. (© **619/260-1850;** www.sheriffmuseum.org), traces the evolution of the department and its equipment since the first San Diego officer pinned on a badge in 1850. **Mission Trails Regional Park,** which offers hiking trails and an interpretive center, is reached by following Hwy. 8 east to Mission Gorge Road.

MISSION BAY, PACIFIC BEACH & BEYOND

Walk along the **beach,** the boardwalk, or around the bay—it's good exercise and there's a nonstop parade of colorful characters. Bring a picnic lunch to enjoy on the **Ocean Beach Pier** or the **Crystal Pier** in Pacific Beach.

LA JOLLA

The half-mile **Coast Walk** between the La Jolla Cove and Children's Pool is San Diego at its most beautiful. Dabble in the tide pools along the way and enjoy the harbor seal colony at Seal Rock and the Children's Pool.

It's also fun to meander around the campus of the University of California, San Diego, and view the **Stuart Collection** (bring a pocketful of quarters for the hungry parking meters). The main branch of the **Museum of Contemporary Art San Diego** is always free to those 25 and under; a paid ticket will get you into the downtown spaces for free (within 7 days). MCASD's museums are also free every third Thursday from 5 to 7pm.

Watching the hang gliders and paragliders launching from the **Gliderport** near Torrey Pines is always a blast (p. 172). For a **great vista,** follow the SCENIC DRIVE signs from La

Jolla Boulevard to Nautilus Street, leading up to Mount Soledad and its 360-degree view of the area.

CORONADO

Drive across the toll-free San Diego–Coronado Bay Bridge and take a self-guided tour of the **Hotel del Coronado**'s grounds and photo gallery. A walk on beautiful Coronado **beach** costs nothing—nor does a lookie-loo tour of the neighborhood's restored Victorian and Craftsman homes.

FARTHER AFIELD

At the **U.S. Olympic Training Center** in Chula Vista (© **619/656-1500** or 482-6222; www.usoc.org), you'll find some of the world's top amateur athletes honing their skills in nine different sports, including soccer, tennis, and track and field. Located on the western shore of Lower Otay Reservoir in Chula Vista, this is one of three United States Olympic training centers. It's open year-round and self-guided tours are available daily, 9am to 5pm; guided tours are offered Tuesday through Saturday at 1:30pm. Visitors can see a 10-minute film about the Olympic movement, shop in the gift store, and then check out the highlights of the 150-acre center. To get there, take I-805 S. to the Olympic Parkway exit, and then go east about 8 miles until you reach a sign directing you to the Copley Visitor Center.

6 ESPECIALLY FOR KIDS

Dozens of public parks, 70 miles of beaches, and numerous museums are just part of what awaits kids and families. For current information about activities for children, pick up a free copy of the monthly *San Diego Family Magazine,* or check it out online at www.sandiegofamily.com; its calendar of events is geared toward family activities and kids' interests. The **International Visitor Information Center,** 1040¹/₃ W. Broadway at Harbor Drive (© **619/236-1212**), is also a great resource.

THE TOP FIVE ATTRACTIONS FOR KIDS

- **Balboa Park** (p. 136) has street entertainers and clowns that always rate high with kids. They can usually be found around El Prado on weekends. The **Natural History Museum,** the **Model Railroad Museum,** the **Air & Space Museum,** and the **Reuben H. Fleet Science Center** (with its hands-on exhibits and IMAX theater) draw kids like magnets.
- The **San Diego Zoo** (p. 128) appeals to children of all ages, and the double-decker bus tours bring all the animals into easy view of even the smallest visitors. There's a Children's Zoo within the zoo, and kids adore the performing sea lion show.
- **SeaWorld San Diego** (p. 130), on Mission Bay, entertains everyone with killer whales, pettable dolphins, and plenty of penguins. There are also wet and wild thrill rides and a collection of *Sesame Street*–related attractions, including rides and a "4-D" interactive movie experience.
- The **San Diego Wild Animal Park** (p. 127) delivers a memorable wildlife experience, re-creating the savannas of Africa with free-roaming animals. For visitors age 3 and up, the Roar & Snore sleepover program—held year-round on weekends (except Dec and Jan)—is immensely popular.

• **LEGOLAND California** (p. 237), in Carlsbad, features impressive models built entirely with LEGO blocks. There are also rides, special events, and contests; a new sea-life aquarium has been added, too (with real fish). The park advertises itself as a "country just for kids"—need I say more?

OTHER TOP ATTRACTIONS

- **Birch Aquarium at Scripps** (p. 152), in La Jolla, is an aquarium that lets kids explore the realms of the deep and learn about life in the sea.
- **The New Children's Museum** (p. 146), in downtown, is a $25-million, modern space where kids can indulge in educational and cultural playtime, including hands-on art projects and storytelling.
- **Maritime Museum** (p. 144), along the Embarcadero, will have kids unleashing their inner Capt. Jack Sparrow, as they swashbuckle their way through this collection of classic sailing vessels.
- **Seaport Village** (p. 201) has an old-fashioned carousel for kids, lots of shops and outdoor eateries that children enjoy, and harbor views of some very impressive ships.
- **Whale-Watching Tours** (p. 165) offer a chance to spot 40-foot gray whales that migrate past San Diego each winter.
- **Old Town State Historic Park** (p. 148) has a one-room schoolhouse that rates high with kids. They'll also enjoy the freedom of running around the safe, parklike compound to discover their own fun.
- **The Gliderport** (p. 172) will transfix kids as they watch aerial acrobats swoop through the skies of La Jolla.
- **Chula Vista Nature Center** (p. 154) is a small facility near the southern end of San Diego Bay that has open tanks for getting up close to turtles, stingrays, and small sharks; there's also a walk-through aviary.

THAT'S ENTERTAINMENT

The **Old Globe Theatre** (© **619/234-5623;** www.theoldglobe.org) in Balboa Park showcases Dr. Seuss's *How the Grinch Stole Christmas!* each year during the holidays. Performances are scheduled late November through December. Tickets are priced $29 to $79 for adults, $19 to $59 for kids 3 to 17, free for children 2 and under. The **San Diego Junior Theatre** (© **619/239-8355;** www.juniortheatre.com) is the oldest continuing children's theater program in the country, operating since 1948. The productions (shows such as *Cats* and *Little Women*) are acted and crewed by kids 8 to 18 and are staged at two different theaters: Balboa Park's Casa del Prado Theatre and the YMCA Firehouse in La Jolla. Ticket prices are $10 to $13 for adults, $8 to $11 for seniors and children (ages 2–14). Nearly a dozen shows are staged each season, with performances held on Friday evenings and Saturday and Sunday afternoons.

Sunday afternoon is a great time for kids in **Balboa Park.** They can visit both the outdoor Spreckels Organ Pavilion for a free concert (the mix of music isn't too highbrow for a young audience) and the House of Pacific Relations to watch folk dancing on the lawn and taste food from many nations. Or try the **Marie Hitchcock Puppet Theatre,** in Balboa Park's Palisades Building (© **619/544-9203;** www.balboaparkpuppets.com). Individual shows might feature marionettes, hand puppets, or ventriloquism; the stories range from classic *Grimm's Fairy Tales* and *Aesop's Fables* to more obscure yarns. Performances are Wednesday through Friday at 10 and 11:30am, and Saturday and Sunday at 11am, 1, and 2:30pm (additional showtimes are added in summer). The cost is $5 for adults, $4 for seniors, and $3 for children 2 and older; free for children 1 and under.

7 SPECIAL-INTEREST SIGHTSEEING

FOR ARCHITECTURE BUFFS

San Diego's historical architecture often features the Spanish mission style introduced to California by Father Junípero Serra at the **Mission Basilica San Diego.** Ostensibly, the adobe walls and tile roofs made it harder for Native Americans to burn down his churches. Spanish Colonial style was revived gloriously for the 1915–16 **Panama-California Exposition** in Balboa Park by New York architect Bertram Goodhue, who oversaw the creation of a fantastically romantic landscape abounding with Mediterranean flourishes.

But San Diego's first important architect was Irving Gill, who arrived in the city in 1893 and soon made his mark by designing buildings to integrate into the desertlike landscape. Gill's structures include numerous homes in Uptown and La Jolla. Gill's **First Church of Christ Scientist** building, 2444 Second Ave. (at Laurel) in Hillcrest, is on the National Historic Landmark list. Following the Expo, prolific local architects such as William Templeton Johnson and Richard Requa integrated the Spanish/Mediterranean concept into their structures around the city—most famously the **Serra Museum** at Presidio Park, the Embarcadero's **County Administration Center,** the **Plaza del Pasado** (formerly the Casa de Pico Motel), and the **Torrey Pines Visitors Center.**

Modernism swept through the city after World War II, championed by Lloyd Ruocco; his office, built in 1949, can be found at 3611 Fifth Ave. (it still operates as a design center). The city's steady growth after the war allowed many inspired architects to leave their handprint on San Diego; more recently, though, unchecked development has led to more than a few blunders along the way. The expansion of the **San Diego Convention Center,** for instance, proves most effective as a ludicrous barrier to any view of the waterfront from downtown.

Historic buildings of particular interest include houses such as the Craftsman-style **Marston House** and Victorian **Villa Montezuma.** Located southeast of downtown, Villa Montezuma has been closed to visitors for renovation—check with the San Diego Historical Society (✆ **619/239-2211;** www.sandiegohistory.org) for its current status. The **Gaslamp Quarter** walking tour (see chapter 8) will lead you past the area's restored Victorian commercial buildings; a stroll along Balboa Park's **El Prado** (also described in chapter 8) is a must, while turn-of-the-20th-century neighborhoods such as **Bankers Hill** (just west of Balboa Park) and **Mission Hills** (west of Hillcrest) are feasts of Victorian mansions and Craftsman abodes. In **La Jolla,** you'll find the classic buildings created by Irving Gill (see "More Attractions," earlier in this chapter).

Downtown blends old and new with mixed results, though no one can deny the value of saving the **Gaslamp Quarter** from probable demolition in the 1970s. **Little Italy,** the hot business and residential district along India Street (btw. Ash and Laurel sts.), has been endangered by the building craze in recent years. Still, it's thriving amid some of the city's most progressive architecture. While you're in the central business district, take a look at the sprawling scale model of the city at the Centre City Development Corporation's **Downtown Information Center,** 225 Broadway (✆ **619/235-2222;** www.ccdc.com); it gives a taste of where the city is headed. It's open Monday through Saturday, 9am to 5pm.

A splendid corridor of contemporary architecture has sprouted around the University of California, San Diego, including the campus's spacecraft-like **Geisel Library,** by William Pereira. Nearby are the Louis I. Kahn–designed **Salk Institute** and the **Neurosciences**

Institute, a 1996 creation by Tod Williams Billie Tsien Architects. A free tour of the Salk Institute, one of Kahn's masterpieces, is held Monday, Wednesday, and Friday at noon. Reservations are required (© **858/453-4100,** ext. 1287; www.salk.edu).

For more information on San Diego architecture, call the local branch of the **American Institute of Architects** (© **619/232-0109;** www.aiasandiego.org). And for a self-guided tour of the city's highlights, Dirk Sutro's *San Diego Architecture* (San Diego Architectural Foundation, 2002; $25) is indispensable, with maps, addresses, and descriptions of hundreds of important structures throughout the city and county. Midcentury fans should check out the **Modern San Diego** website, www.modernsandiego.com.

FOR GARDENERS

Although most years we struggle with too little rain, San Diego is a gardener's paradise. A big inspiration for San Diego gardeners is Kate Sessions, who planted the initial trees that led to today's mature landscapes in **Balboa Park** (p. 136). While in the park, be sure to visit the **Japanese Friendship Garden,** the **Botanical Building and Lily Pond,** and the **rose and desert gardens** (across Park Blvd. from Plaza de Balboa). And you'll notice both the **San Diego Zoo** (p. 128) and **Wild Animal Park** (p. 127) are outstanding botanical gardens. Many visitors who admire the landscaping at the zoo don't realize the plantings have been carefully developed over the years. The 100 acres were once scrub-covered hillsides with few trees. Today, towering eucalyptus and graceful palms, birds of paradise, and hibiscus are just a few of the 6,500 botanical species from all over the world that flourish here.

Garden enthusiasts will also want to stop by the 35-acre **Quail Botanical Gardens** in Encinitas (see "North County Beach Towns: Spots to Surf & Sun," in chapter 11). If you'd like to take plants home with you, visit some of the area's nurseries. Start with the charming neighborhood one founded in 1910 by Kate Sessions herself, the **Mission Hills Nursery,** 1525 Fort Stockton Dr. (© **619/295-2808;** www.missionhillsnursery. com). **Walter Andersen Nursery,** 3642 Enterprise St. (© **619/224-8271;** www.walter andersen.com), is also a local favorite, located not far from Old Town. See chapter 11 for information on nurseries in North County; flower growing is big business in this area, and plant enthusiasts could spend a week just visiting the retail and wholesale purveyors of everything from pansies to palm trees.

Founded in 1907 by Kate Sessions, the **San Diego Floral Association** is the oldest garden club in Southern California. It's based in the Casa del Prado in Balboa Park (© **619/232-5762;** www.sdfloral.org) and offers workshops and exhibits, as well as day tours to places of horticultural interest.

FOR MILITARY BUFFS

San Diego's military history dates to the U.S. Navy's aviation achievements at Coronado in the 1910s. Today, one-third of the Navy's Pacific Fleet is home ported in the city's natural harbor. San Diego salutes its armed forces during **Fleet Week,** which lasts throughout the month of October. It's headlined by the popular Miramar Air Show, with aerial performances by the Blue Angels. For more information, see www.fleetweeksan diego.org or www.miramarairshow.com.

The city's flagship (pardon the pun) military attraction is the USS *Midway,* making its final tour of duty as the **San Diego Aircraft Carrier Museum.** The *Midway* served from the end of World War II until the first Gulf War, and it's now docked along the

Embarcadero (p. 146). The **San Diego Air & Space Museum** in Balboa Park (p. 140) celebrates the history of flight, and has a strong focus on aviation's military heroes and heroines. The park is also the location of the **Veterans Museum & Memorial Center,** 2115 Park Blvd. (© 619/239-2300; www.veteranmuseum.org), a resource center with a small museum that has holdings dating back to the Civil War.

Both **San Diego Harbor Excursion** and **Hornblower Cruises** tour San Diego Bay, providing a glimpse of naval activities (p. 162); and **Old Town Trolley Tours** offers an amphibious Sea and Land (SEAL) tour of the bay (p. 163). At **Cabrillo National Monument** in Point Loma, visitors gain an excellent view of the harbor, including the nuclear submarine base; and a museum installation tells about the gun batteries established on the peninsula during World War II.

Just before you reach the gates of Cabrillo National Monument, you can pay your respects at **Fort Rosecrans National Cemetery** (© 619/553-2084; www.cem.va.gov) to those who served. It didn't officially become a National Cemetery until 1934, but remains interred here date back to 1846 and the Battle of San Pasqual (p. 11). With its row upon row of gleaming white headstones and sweeping ocean views, this is a very moving and inspirational spot. It's open Monday through Friday 8am to 4:30pm, Saturday and Sunday 9:30am to 5pm.

The public is invited to the **recruit graduation** at the Marine Corps Recruit Depot, off Pacific Coast Highway (near Barnett St.), held most Fridays at 10am (© 619/524-8383; www.mcrdsd.usmc.mil). The **Command Museum** on the base (© 619/524-4426; www.mcrdmuseumhistoricalsociety.org) has a huge collection of Marine memorabilia; it was updated and expanded in 2007 and includes a new gallery devoted to the Vietnam experience. Hours are Monday through Saturday, 8am to 4pm (4:30pm Thurs); it's free, but admittance to the base requires a photo ID.

FOR WINE LOVERS

Visit **Orfila Vineyards,** 13455 San Pasqual Rd., Escondido (© **800/868-9463** or 760/738-6500; www.orfila.com), on the way to or from the **Wild Animal Park** (p. 127). Besides producing excellent chardonnay and merlot, the winery also makes several Rhône and Italian varietals. The tasting room is open daily from 10am to 6pm; guided tours are offered at 2pm. The property also features a parklike picnic area and a gift shop. Another tasting room is located about 2 miles outside the mountain town of Julian, 4470 Hwy. 78 (near Wynola Rd.); hours are Wednesday through Monday, 10am to 5pm.

Bernardo Winery, 13330 Paseo del Verano N., Escondido (© **858/487-1866;** www. bernardowinery.com), has an assortment of shopping and dining options on-site. Founded in 1889, it survived Prohibition by making grape juice and sacramental wine. The tasting room is open Monday through Friday 9am to 5pm, Saturday and Sunday 10am to 6pm; the shops and bistro are closed on Mondays. **Fallbrook Winery,** 2554 Via Rancheros, Fallbrook (© **760/728-0156;** www.fallbrookwinery.com), produces award-winning sauvignon blancs and Syrahs; a tasting room is set up in the aging cellar, but you need to call ahead to let them know you're coming.

If you have time, the wineries along Rancho California Road in **Temecula,** just across the San Diego County line, are open for tours and tastings; see p. 249. Mexico's wineries in the Valle de Guadalupe are also within reach; they are east of Ensenada, about a 90-minute drive from downtown (p. 289).

8 ORGANIZED TOURS

Centre City Development Corporation's **Downtown Information Center,** 225 Broadway, Ste. 160 (✆ **619/235-2222;** www.ccdc.com), offers free downtown bus tours the first Saturday of the month at 10am and noon. Reservations are required for the 90-minute tour, which is aimed at prospective home-buyers in the downtown area, as well as curious locals trying to stay abreast of developments. Go inside the information center to see models of the Gaslamp Quarter and the downtown area. The office is open Monday through Saturday from 9am to 5pm.

WATER EXCURSIONS

The Gondola Company   This unique business operates from Loews Coronado Bay Resort, plying the canals and marinas of a luxury, waterside community. The gondolas are crafted according to centuries-old designs from Venice and feature all the trimmings, right down to the striped-shirt gondolier with ribbons waving from his or her straw hat. Mediterranean music plays while you and up to five friends recline with snuggly blankets, and the company will even provide antipasti or chocolate-covered strawberries, along with chilled wineglasses and ice for the beverage of your choice (BYOB). You can also arrange to have dinner at the resort's stylish Mistral restaurant or have an onboard mandolin or violin player serenade you.

4000 Coronado Bay Rd., Coronado. ✆ 619/429-6317. www.gondolacompany.com. 1-hr. cruise $85 per couple, $20 for each additional passenger (up to 6 total); free for children 2 and under. Reservations required. Mon–Fri 3pm–midnight; Sat–Sun 11am–midnight. Bus: 901.

Hornblower Cruises   These 1-hour or 2-hour narrated tours lead passengers through San Diego harbor on one of seven different yachts, from a 61-passenger antique yacht to a three-deck, 800-passenger behemoth. You'll see the *Star of India,* cruise under the San Diego–Coronado Bridge, and swing by a submarine base and an aircraft carrier or two. Guests can visit the captain's wheelhouse for a photo op, and harbor seals and sea lions on buoys are a regular sighting. Whale-watching trips (mid-Dec to late Mar) are a blast. A 2-hour Sunday champagne-brunch cruise departs at 11am, and there are dinner/dance cruises nightly.

1066 N. Harbor Dr. ✆ 888/467-6256 or 619/686-8715. www.hornblower.com. Harbor tours $20–$25 adults, $2 off for seniors and military, half-price for children 4–12. Free for children 3 and under. Dinner cruises start at $67; brunch cruise $50; whale-watching trips $30–$35 ($5 off for seniors and military), $15 children. Bus: 2, 210, or 992. Trolley: America Plaza.

San Diego Harbor Excursion   This company also offers daily 1- and 2-hour narrated tours of the bay, using its fleet of eight boats that range from a 1940s passenger launch to plush, modern vessels. There are two 1-hour itineraries, each covering about 12 miles. The south bay tour includes the San Diego–Coronado Bridge and Navy shipyards; the north bay route motors past Naval Air Station North Island and Cabrillo National Monument. The 25-mile, 2-hour tour encompasses the entire bay. In winter, whale-watching excursions feature naturalists from the Birch Aquarium. The 2-hour Sunday brunch cruise aboard a sleek yacht is popular; dinner cruises embark nightly. A 5¹/₂-hour nature cruise navigates international waters around the Coronado Islands (Dec–June).

1050 N. Harbor Dr. (foot of Broadway). ✆ 800/442-7847 or 619/234-4111. www.sdhe.com. Harbor tours $20–$25, $2 off for seniors and military, half-price for children 4–12. Dinner cruises start at $66 adults, $38 children; brunch cruise $55 adults, $38 children; whale-watching trips $30–$35 adults, $25–$30 seniors and military, $15 children; nature cruise $50 adults, $45 seniors and military, $40 children. Bus: 2, 210, or 992. Trolley: America Plaza.

Xplore Offshore ★★ (Finds)   There are only two small boats in this fleet, and the one to ride is the tricked-out RIB (rigid-inflatable boat), similar to the crafts used by the U.S. Navy SEALS. Capable of cruising at up to 45 mph, the RIB is built for speed and comfort; there's lots of padding and straddle seating up front, and even a surprisingly roomy head—not bad for a 24-foot vessel. Other special features include hot water for showering after a swim and an underwater camera for those who want to look but not get wet. Trips are unscripted; you can do what you want to do and go wherever you want to go. You can do some rip-roaring wave riding or serene pleasure boating, go whale-watching or night diving, take a booze cruise to bayside restaurants and concerts, or camp on a remote Catalina beach—it's your call.

Pickup points are flexible, but usually Dana Landing in Mission Bay. ℂ **858/456-1636.** www.xplore offshore.com. 3-hr. rates start at $49 per person. Bus: 8 or 9 (for Dana Landing).

BUS TOURS

Gray Line (ℂ **800/331-5077** or 619/266-7365; www.sandiegograyline.com), has a plethora of outings, including a daylong Grand Tour that covers San Diego, Tijuana, and a 1-hour harbor cruise. There are also trips to the San Diego Zoo, Wild Animal Park, LEGOLAND, SeaWorld, Disneyland, Universal Studios, Tijuana, Rosarito Beach, and Ensenada. Prices range from $35 for the 4-hour City Tour to $64 for the Grand Tour (prices range $18–$31 for children 3–11). Multiple tours can be combined for discounted rates, and passengers can be picked up at most area hotels.

Not to be confused with the public transit trolley, the narrated **Old Town Trolley Tours** (ℂ **619/298-8687;** www.historictours.com) offer an easy way to get an overview of the city. You can tie together visits to several major attractions without driving or

---

Tours with a Twist

If you can't decide between a bus tour or a bay cruise, opt for both—an amphibious tour on Old Town Trolley Tour's **Sea and Land Adventures.** The 90-minute SEAL tour departs from Seaport Village and motors along the Embarcadero until splashing into San Diego Bay. This specially built craft holds 46 passengers, and the narrated tour gives you the maritime and military history of San Diego from the right perspective. Trips are scheduled daily April through October from 10am to 5pm, and Friday through Sunday 10am to 4pm the rest of the year. The cost is $32 for adults and $16 for kids 4 to 12. Free for children 3 and under. For information and tickets, call ℂ **619/298-8687,** or visit www.historictours.com.

Another novel way to see the sights is via **GoCar Tours** (ℂ **800/914-6227;** www.gocartours.com), small, three-wheeled vehicles that zip around town at about 35 mph (56kmph). These two-person open-air minicars are equipped with GPS technology that not only gives directions, but also indicates points of interest and narrates San Diego history (in five languages). Don't feel like listening to a talking car? Just pop a disc into the CD player. GoCar Tours is at 2100 Kettner Blvd. in Little Italy and is open daily from 8:30am to 5pm. Rates start at $44 for the first hour, and you must be 18 to rent; it's suggested you reserve 24 hours in advance.

resorting to pricey cabs. These vehicles, gussied up like old-time trolleys, do a 30-mile circular route; and you can hop off at any one of 10 stops, explore at leisure, and re-board when you please (the trolleys run every half-hour). Stops include Old Town, the Gaslamp Quarter and downtown area, Coronado, the San Diego Zoo, and Balboa Park. You can begin wherever you want, but you must purchase tickets before boarding (most stops have a ticket kiosk). The tour costs $32 for adults ($16 for kids 4–12, free for children 3 and under) for one complete circuit; the route by itself takes about 2 hours. The trolleys operate daily from 9am to 5pm in winter, and from 9am to 6pm in summer.

City Sightseeing (© **619/296-2400;** www.citysightseeing-sd.com), which operates in dozens of cities around the world, provides a similar service April through October (charters run year-round). Narrated tours are conducted aboard open-top, double-decker buses that continuously traverse the city, offering on-and-off privileges at Old Town, Balboa Park, the Gaslamp Quarter, and seven other spots. There are two loop tours, each about an hour long, and your ticket is good for 48 hours; tours commence in Old Town, from City Sightseeing's office at 2415 Old Town Ave., and depart about every 30 minutes. Day tours are $25 to $30 for adults, $15 to $20 for children age 4 to 12, and free for children 3 and under. Night tours are also available ($20 adults, $12 children). Coronado is not included in these tours, but passes for the Coronado ferry are included in some ticket prices.

WALKING TOURS

Walkabout International, 2825 Dewey Rd., Ste. 202, Point Loma (© **619/231-7463;** www.walkabout-int.org), sponsors more than 100 free walking tours every month that are led by local volunteers, listed in a monthly newsletter and on the website. Walking tours hit all parts of the county, including the Gaslamp Quarter, La Jolla, and the beaches. A wilderness hike takes place most Wednesdays and Saturdays.

Urban Safaris (© **619/944-9255;** walkingtoursofsandiego.com) provides walking tours of 10 San Diego neighborhoods, including Ocean Beach and Hillcrest. Tours depart from designated meeting places in the neighborhood where the walk takes place. All tours are $10.

Where You Want to Be Tours (© **619/917-6037;** www.wheretours.com) puts a lighthearted touch on its offerings, which include a walking (or biking) tour of San Diego's beach Tiki culture. Other itineraries include an Old Town power walk, a La Jolla gallery stroll, and a downtown nightlife primer. Prices start at $20.

The **Gaslamp Quarter Historical Foundation** offers 2-hour tours that focus on the Gaslamp's 19th-century history, every Saturday at 11am. Tours depart from the William Heath Davis House museum, 410 Island Ave., and cost $10 for adults, $8 for seniors (age 55 and above), students, and military (museum admission is included); free for children age 12 and under. For more information, contact the foundation directly at © **619/233-4692** or www.gaslampquarter.org.

Volunteers from the Canyoneer group of the **San Diego Natural History Museum** (© **619/255-0203;** www.sdnhm.org/canyoneers) lead free guided nature walks throughout San Diego County. The walks are held every Saturday and Sunday (except July–Aug), and usually focus on the flora and fauna of a particular area, which might be a city park or as far away as Anza-Borrego Desert.

At the **Cabrillo National Monument** on the tip of Point Loma (p. 58), rangers often lead free walking tours. Docents at **Torrey Pines State Reserve** in La Jolla (p. 153) lead interpretive nature walks at 10am and 2pm on weekends and holidays. And guided walks are often scheduled at **Mission Trails Regional Park** (p. 148).

Touring San Diego Haunts

Those who want to take a walk on the supernatural side can stroll through Old Town with self-proclaimed "ghost hunter" Michael Brown (📞 **619/972-3900;** www.oldtownsmosthaunted.com). He leads tours in search of real paranormal activity Thursday through Sunday at 8 and 10pm, and midnight. The early tour costs $19 adults, $10 children 6 to 12, and is free for children 5 and under. It's an anecdotal walking tour of Old Town; the two later tours are "ghost hunts," during which the spirits of the dearly departed will be asked to join the group. Plan accordingly. Ghost hunt tickets are $39; reservations required. **Ghostly Tours in History** (📞 **877/220-4844;** www.ghostlytoursinhistory.com) leads walking tours through both Old Town (Thurs–Sat 7 and 8:30pm) and the Gaslamp Quarter (Fri and Sat at 7:30pm). The cost is $10, free for children 4 and under (the Gaslamp tour may be inappropriate for small children). There's also a 3-hour limo tour to haunted sites around the city ($50).

Also see "Balboa Park Guided Tours" (p. 141) for organized walks through Balboa Park and "Hiking & Walking," later in this chapter, for unguided trail options.

WHALE-WATCHING

Along the California coast, whale-watching is an eagerly anticipated wintertime activity, particularly in San Diego where Pacific gray whales pass close by Point Loma on their annual migratory trek. Local whaling in the 1870s greatly reduced their numbers, but federal protection has allowed the species to repopulate; current estimates put the number of grays at about 20,000. When they approach San Diego, the 40- to 50-foot gray whales are more than three-quarters of the way along their nearly 6,000-mile journey from Alaska to breeding lagoons in the Sea of Cortés, around the southern tip of Baja California. After mating and calving they will pass by again, calves in tow, heading back to the rich Alaskan feeding grounds. From mid-December to mid-March is the best time to see the migration, and there are several ways to view the procession.

The easiest (and cheapest) is to grab a pair of binoculars and head to a good land-bound vantage point. The best is **Cabrillo National Monument,** at the tip of Point Loma, where you'll find a glassed-in observatory and educational whale exhibits 400 feet above sea level. When the weather cooperates, you can often spot the whales as they surface for breathing—as many as eight grays per hour at peak commute (mid-Jan). Each January the rangers conduct a special "Whale Watch Weekend" featuring presentations by whale experts, children's programs, and entertainment. For more information on Cabrillo National Monument, see p. 58.

If you want to get a closer look, head out to sea on one of the excursions that locate and follow gray whales, taking care not to disturb their journey. **Classic Sailing Adventures** (📞 **800/659-0141** or 619/224-0800; www.classicsailingadventures.com) offers two trips per day (8:30am and 1pm); each lasts 4 hours and carries a maximum of six passengers. Sailboats are less distracting to the whales than motorized yachts, but more expensive; the cruises are $75 per person (minimum two passengers), including beverages and snacks. **OEX Dive & Kayak Centers** (📞 **858/454-6195;** www.oexcalifornia.com) leads guided kayak tours in search of passing whales. It's about a 1-mile paddle that departs daily at 1pm from La Jolla Shores and lasts 2¹/₂ hours. The cost is $60 for a single kayak, $110 for double.

Companies that offer traditional, engine-driven expeditions include **Hornblower Cruises** and **San Diego Harbor Excursion** (see "Water Excursions," above). Excursions are 3 or 3¹/₂ hours, and fares run $30 to $35 for adults, with discounts for kids. **H&M Landing,** 2803 Emerson St., Point Loma (✆ **619/222-1144;** www.hmlanding.com), has 3- and 5-hour trips, starting at $25 for adults, $20 for those ages 13 to 17, and $18 for ages 2 to 12.

In La Jolla, the **Birch Aquarium at Scripps** celebrates gray whale season with classes, educational activities, and exhibits, and the outdoor terrace offers another vantage point for spotting the mammals from shore. Multiday trips to San Ignacio in Baja California, where the whales mate and calve, are offered in February and March, and Birch provides naturalists to accompany the whale-watching done by San Diego Harbor Excursion (see "Water Excursions," above). Call ✆ **858/534-7336,** or go to www.aquarium.ucsd.edu for more information.

The **San Diego Natural History Museum** also offers multiday, naturalist-led whale-watching trips to Baja. For a schedule and preregistration information, call ✆ **619/255-0203,** or check www.sdnhm.org/education.

9 OUTDOOR ACTIVITIES

See section 2 of this chapter for a complete rundown of San Diego's beaches. To find the locations of the following outdoor activities, see the color map at the beginning of this book.

BALLOONING & SCENIC FLIGHTS

A peaceful dawn or dusk balloon ride reveals sweeping vistas of the Southern California coast, wine country, rambling estates, and golf courses. For a sunrise or sunset flight, followed by a traditional champagne toast, contact **Skysurfer Balloon Company** (✆ **800/660-6809** or 858/481-6800; www.sandiegohotairballoons.com). The rate for a 40- to 60-minute flight is $175 to $185 per person for the sunset excursion in Del Mar (25 min. from downtown) and $165 for the sunrise flight in Temecula (70 min. north of downtown). Or float up, up, and away with **California Dreamin'** (✆ **800/373-3359** or 951/699-0601; www.californiadreamin.com). They charge $128 to $138 per person for a sunrise flight in Temecula (continental breakfast included), and $168 for sunset flights in Del Mar; both last about an hour and both include champagne. California Dreamin' also has various **biplane adventures** over Temecula's wine country, starting at $248 for two people. You may also be interested in the **Temecula Balloon & Wine Festival** held in early June; call ✆ **951/676-6713,** or visit www.tvbwf.com for information.

You can do just about everything but wing-walking with **Biplane, Air Combat & Warbird Adventures** (✆ **800/759-5667;** www.barnstorming.com). Vintage biplane flights leave from Montgomery Field in Kearny Mesa, taking up to two passengers per plane on scenic flights along the coast; rates start at $199 for two-person, 20-minute rides. Air Combat flights, most piloted by active-duty fighter pilots, offer simulated dogfights (these are not recommended for the weak of stomach). If you're bringing your own adversary, you need to reserve space 1 to 2 weeks in advance; if you need your target assigned, call 3 weeks in advance. Rates start at $298. You can also opt for a flight—with at the controls—no pilot's license necessary ($345 and up).

BIKING

With its impeccable weather and varied terrain, San Diego is one of the nation's preeminent bicycling destinations—the city was even named "one of the top 10 cities in the U.S. to bicycle" by *Bicycling* magazine. Many major thoroughfares offer bike lanes, but downtown is definitely a challenge. To obtain a detailed map by mail of San Diego County's bike lanes and routes, call **RideLink Bicycle Information** (© 511 or 619/699-1900), or go to www.511sd.com (there's also a downloadable version). You might also want to talk to the **San Diego County Bicycle Coalition** (© 858/487-6063; www.sdcbc.org). For information on taking your bike onto public transportation, see "By Bicycle," in the "Getting Around" section on p. 36 in chapter 3. Bicycle helmets are legally required for those 17 and under.

The paths around Mission Bay, in particular, are great for leisurely rides; the oceanfront boardwalk between Pacific Beach and Mission Beach can get very crowded, especially on weekends (but that's half the fun). The Bayshore Bikeway around San Diego Bay is one of the region's most popular rides. This 16-mile round-trip bike trail starts at the Ferry Landing Marketplace in Coronado and follows a well-marked route down to Imperial Beach, along the Silver Strand. The road out to Point Loma (Catalina Dr.) offers moderate hills and wonderful scenery. Traveling old State Route 101 (aka the Pacific Coast Hwy.) from La Jolla north to Oceanside offers terrific coastal views, along with plenty of places to refuel with coffee, a snack, or a swim. The 13-mile climb up steep switchbacks to the summit of 6,140-foot Mt. Palomar is perhaps the county's most invigorating challenge and offers its most gleeful descent.

Cycling San Diego by Nelson Copp and Jerry Schad is a good resource for bicyclists and is available at most local bike shops.

Rentals, Organized Bike Tours & Other Two-Wheel Adventures

Downtown, call **Bike Tours San Diego,** 509 Fifth Ave. (© 619/238-2444; www.bike-tours.com), which offers delivery as far north as Del Mar. Rates for a city/hybrid bike start at $22 for a day, and include helmet, lock, maps, and roadside assistance. Other downtown spots include **San Diego Bike Shop,** 619 C St. (© 619/237-1245; www.sdbikeshop.com), and across the street, **Pennyfarthing's Bicycle Store,** 630 C St. (© 619/233-7696); hourly rates are about $4, $25 for a 24-hour rental, or $150 for a full week.

In Mission Beach, there's **Cheap Rentals,** 3689 Mission Blvd. (© 800/941-7761 or 858/488-9070; www.cheap-rentals.com), which has everything from beach cruisers ($12 per day) to tandems ($24 per day) and baby trailers ($12 per day), as well as skates, surfboards, and even chairs, umbrellas, and coolers. Or try **Mission Beach Surf & Skate,** 704 Ventura Place, off Mission Boulevard at Ocean Front Walk (© 858/488-5050), for classic beach cruisers and more. In Coronado there are two great places for rentals (both owned by the same folks), **Holland's Bicycles,** 977 Orange Ave. (© 619/435-3153; www.hollandsbicycles.com), and **Bikes and Beyond,** 1201 First St. at the Ferry Landing Marketplace (© 619/435-7180). They've got beach cruisers and hybrids, mountain bikes, pedal surreys, and skate rentals; expect to pay $7 per hour for a basic cruiser, $30 for 24 hours.

For organized bike tours, **Hike Bike Kayak San Diego,** 2246 Av. de la Playa, La Jolla (© **866/425-2925** or 858/551-9510; www.hikebikekayak.com), has a variety of offerings, including a La Jolla coastal ride and a family excursion around Mission Bay, but the big draw is the plunge down La Jolla's Mount Soledad. It's a 3.5-mile descent through luxury neighborhoods with scintillating vistas (ages 14 and up; $50).

BIRD-WATCHING

The birding scene is huge: More than 480 species have been observed in San Diego County, more than in any other county in the United States. The area is a haven along the Pacific Flyway—the migratory route along the Pacific Coast—and the diverse range of ecosystems also helps to lure a wide range of winged creatures. It's possible for birders to enjoy four distinct bird habitats in a single day.

Among the best places for bird-watching is the **Chula Vista Nature Center** at Sweetwater Marsh National Wildlife Refuge (© **619/409-5900;** www.chulavistanaturecenter. org). You may spot rare residents such as the light-footed clapper rail and the western snowy plover, as well as predatory species including the American peregrine falcon and northern harrier. In addition, the nature center has aquariums for turtles, sharks, and rays; aviaries featuring raptors and shorebirds; and a garden with native plants (p. 154). Also worth visiting is the **Kendall-Frost Reserve** in Mission Bay. Most of this 30-acre area is off-limits to the public, but you can get close to it via the pathway that extends north from Crown Point or by kayak. The reserve draws skimmers, shorebirds, brants, and, in winter, the large-billed savannah sparrow. The **Torrey Pines State Reserve** (p. 153), north of La Jolla, is a protected habitat for swifts, thrashers, woodpeckers, and wren tits. Inland, **Mission Trails Regional Park** (p. 148) is a 5,800-acre urban park that is visited by orange-crowned warblers, swallows, raptors, and numerous riparian species; and the **Anza-Borrego Desert State Park** (see chapter 11) makes an excellent day trip from San Diego—268 species of birds have been recorded here.

Birders coming to the area can obtain a copy of the free brochure ***Birding Hot Spots of San Diego,*** available at the Port Administration Building, 3165 Pacific Hwy., and at the San Diego Zoo, Wild Animal Park, San Diego Natural History Museum, and Birch Aquarium. It's also posted online at www.portofsandiego.org/environment; click on "Birds of San Diego Bay," and you'll find the PDF file on the right-hand side. The **San Diego Audubon Society** is another great source of birding information (© **619/682-7200;** www.sandiegoaudubon.org).

FISHING

The sportfishing fleet consists of more than 75 large commercial vessels and several dozen private charter yachts; a variety of half-, full-, and multiday trips are available. The saltwater fishing season kicks off each spring with the traditional **Port of San Diego Day at the Docks,** held the last weekend in April or at the beginning of May at Sportfishing Landing, near Shelter Island; for more information, call © **619/234-8793,** or see www. sportfishing.org. Anglers of any age can fish free of charge without a license off any municipal pier in California. Public fishing piers are on Shelter Island (where there's a statue dedicated to anglers), Ocean Beach, and Imperial Beach.

An ideal time for fishing is summer or fall, when the waters around Point Loma are brimming with bass, bonito, and barracuda. The Islas los Coronados, which belong to Mexico but are only about 18 miles from San Diego, are popular for yellowtail, yellowfin, and big-eyed tuna. Some outfitters will take you farther into Baja California waters on multiday trips. Fishing charters depart from Harbor and Shelter Islands, Point Loma, the

Participants 17 and over need a California fishing license.

Rates for trips on a large boat average $42 for a half-day trip or $95 for a three-quarter-day trip, or you can spring $135 to $195 for a 20-hour overnight trip to the Islas los Coronados—call around and compare prices. Discounts are offered for kids and for twilight sailings; charters or "limited load" rates are also available. The following outfitters offer short or extended outings with daily departures: **H&M Landing,** 2803 Emerson St. (© 619/222-1144; www.hmlanding.com); **Point Loma Sportfishing,** 1403 Scott St. (© 619/223-1627; www.pointlomasportfishing.com); and **Seaforth Sportfishing,** 1717 Quivira Rd. (© 619/224-3383; www.seaforthlanding.com). Check in with **Lee Palm Sportfishers,** 2801 Emerson St. (© 619/224-3857; www.redrooster3.com), if you want to hit the high seas for a 3- to 16-day outing. All of these shops rent tackle.

For freshwater fishing, San Diego's lakes and rivers are home to bass, channel and bullhead catfish, bluegill, trout, crappie, and sunfish. Most lakes have rental facilities for boats, tackle, and bait, and they also provide picnic and (usually) camping areas. A 1-day California State Fishing License costs $13, a 2-day is $21, and a 10-day, nonresident license is $41. For information on lake fishing, call the city's **Lakes Line** © 619/465-3474.

For information on fishing at **Lake Cuyamaca,** 1 hour from San Diego near Julian, see "Julian: Apple Pies & More" in chapter 11. For more information on fishing in California, contact the **California Department of Fish and Game** (© 858/467-4201; www.dfg.ca.gov). For fishing in Mexican waters, including the area off the Coronado Islands, angling permits are required. Most charter companies will take care of the details, but if not, contact the **Mexican Department of Fisheries,** 2550 Fifth Ave., Ste. 15, San Diego, CA 92103-6622 (© 619/233-4324; www.conapescasandiego.org).

GOLF

With 90-plus courses, more than 50 of them open to the public, San Diego County offers golf enthusiasts innumerable opportunities to play their game. Courses are diverse: Some have vistas of the Pacific, others views of country hillsides or desert landscapes. For a full listing of area courses, including fees, stats, and complete score cards, visit www.golfsd.com, or request the *Golf Guide* from the **San Diego Convention and Visitors Bureau** (© 619/236-1212; www.sandiego.org).

In addition to the well-established courses listed below, other acclaimed links include **Maderas Golf Club** (© 866/413-5634 or 858/451-8100; www.maderasgolf.com), **Barona Creek Golf Club** (© 619/387-7018; www.barona.com), **Steele Canyon Golf Club** (© 619/441-6900; www.steelecanyon.com), **Salt Creek Golf Club** (© 619/482-4666; www.saltcreekgc.com), the **Grand Del Mar Golf Club** (p. 232), and **La Costa Resort and Spa** (p. 240).

San Diego Golf Reservations (© 866/701-4653 or 858/964-5980; www.sandiegogolf.com) can arrange tee times for you at San Diego's premier golf courses. There's no charge for the service, except for Torrey Pines reservations (up to 90 days in advance; $25 per person). And when you just want to practice your swing, head to **Stadium Golf Center & Batting Cages,** 2990 Murphy Canyon Rd., in Mission Valley (© 858/277-6667; www.stadiumgolfcenter.com). It's open daily from 7am to 10pm, with 72 artificial turf and natural grass hitting stations, plus greens and bunkers to practice your short game. A complete pro shop offers club rentals; a bucket of balls costs $7.50 to $18. Golf instruction and clinics are also available.

Balboa Park Municipal Golf Course   Everybody has a humble municipal course like this at home, with a bare-bones 1920s clubhouse where old guys hold down lunch-counter stools for hours after the game and players take a few more mulligans than they would elsewhere. Surrounded by the beauty of Balboa Park, this 18-hole course features fairways sprinkled with eucalyptus leaves and distractingly nice views of the San Diego skyline. It's so convenient and affordable that it's the perfect choice for visitors who want to work some golf into their vacation rather than the other way around. The course even rents clubs ($20). Nonresident greens fees are $36 weekdays ($15 for 9 holes), $45 weekends ($19 for 9 holes); the 18-hole twilight rate is $22 weekdays, $27 weekends. Cart rental is $26. Reservations are suggested at least a week in advance; first-come, first-served tee times are offered from 6:30 to 7am.

You don't have to be a golfer to enjoy **Tobey's 19th Hole,** the clubhouse's simple cafe, offering splendid views of Point Loma, downtown, and the park from its deck. The food is cheap and diner-esque—omelets, biscuits and gravy, corned beef hash for breakfast; chili burgers and sandwiches for lunch—but this local hangout is a nice find for visitors.

2600 Golf Course Dr. (off Pershing Dr. or 26th St. in the southeast corner of the park), San Diego. (*) **619/570-1234** (automated reservation system) or 239-1660 (pro shop). www.sandiego.gov/golf.

Coronado Municipal Golf Course   Opened in 1957, this course is mostly for the locals—and visitors—who just can't bear to leave the "island" of Coronado. It's an 18-hole, par-72 course with distractingly beautiful views of San Diego Bay, the Coronado Bridge, and the downtown skyline beyond; there are also a coffee shop, pro shop, and driving range. It's tough to get a tee time here, so 2-day prior reservations are strongly recommended (you can make a reservation up to 2 weeks in advance); call after 7am. (There's a $38 nonrefundable advance registration charge.) Greens fees are $25 for 18 holes; cart fees are $16 per person. For twilight play (2pm winter, 4pm summer), greens fees are $13; cart rates are $11 per person. Club rental is $50, $30 twilight rate.

2000 Visalia Row, Coronado. (*) **619/435-3121.** www.golfcoronado.com.

Four Seasons Resort Aviara Golf Club ★★★   Designed by Arnold Palmer, this uniquely landscaped course incorporates natural elements that blend in neatly with the protected Batiquitos Lagoon nearby. The course is 7,007 yards from the championship tees, laid out over rolling hillsides with plenty of bunker and water challenges; casual duffers may be frustrated here. Greens fees are $215 (including mandatory cart) Monday through Thursday, and $235 Friday through Sunday; afternoon rates start at 1:30pm in winter, 3pm in summer ($140 weekday, $145 weekend). There are practice areas for putting, chipping, sand play, and driving, and the pro shop and clubhouse are fully equipped. Golf packages are available for guests of the Four Seasons.

7447 Batiquitos Dr., Carlsbad. (*) **760/603-6900.** www.fourseasons.com. From I-5 N., take the Aviara Pkwy. exit east to Batiquitos Dr. Turn right and continue 2 miles to the clubhouse.

Mt. Woodson Golf Club ★   One of San Diego County's most dramatic golf courses, Mt. Woodson is a par-70, 6,180-yard course on 150 beautiful acres. The award-winning 18-hole course meanders up and down hills, across bridges, and around granite boulders. Elevated tees provide striking views of Ramona and Mount Palomar, and on a clear day you can see for almost 100 miles. It's easy to combine a game of golf with a weekend getaway to Julian (see chapter 11). Nonresident greens fees for 18 holes (including mandatory cart) are $72 Monday through Thursday, $82 Friday, $97 Saturday, and $92

Sunday. Early-bird and twilight rates are available, and seniors get a discount. Mt. Woodson is about 40 minutes north of San Diego.

16422 N. Woodson Dr., Ramona. ✆ **760/788-3555.** www.mtwoodson.com. Take I-15 N. to Poway Rd. exit; at the end of Poway Rd., turn left (north) onto Rte. 67 and drive 3³/₄ miles to Archie Moore Rd.; turn left. Entrance is on the left.

Rancho Bernardo Inn ★ Rancho Bernardo has a mature 18-hole, 72-par championship course with different terrains, water hazards, sand traps, lakes, and waterfalls. It was recently renovated and now plays to more than 6,600 yards; there are also four sets of tees for all level of play. Stay-and-play golf packages are available. Greens fees are $100 Monday through Thursday, $115 Friday, and $135 weekends, including a cart. Twilight rates (after 1pm winter, 2pm summer) are available.

17550 Bernardo Oaks Dr., Rancho Bernardo. ✆ **858/675-8470.** www.ranchobernardoinn.com or www.jcgolf.com. From I-15 N., exit at Rancho Bernardo Rd. Head east to Bernardo Oaks Dr., turn left, and continue to the resort entrance.

Riverwalk Golf Club ★ Completely redesigned, these links wander along the Mission Valley floor and are the most convenient courses for anyone staying downtown or near the beaches. Replacing the private Stardust Golf Club, the course reopened in 1998 sporting a slick, upscale new clubhouse; four lakes with waterfalls (in play on 13 of the 27 holes); open, undulating fairways; and one peculiar feature: trolley tracks. The bright red trolley speeds through now and then but doesn't prove too distracting. Nonresident greens fees, including cart, are $99 Monday through Thursday, $125 Friday through Sunday; senior, twilight, and early-bird rates are available.

1150 Fashion Valley Rd., Mission Valley. ✆ **619/296-4563.** www.riverwalkgc.com. Take I-8 to Hotel Circle south, and turn on Fashion Valley Rd.

Sycuan Resort & Casino ★ Offering 54 holes of golf (two championship courses and a 2,500-yd., par-54 executive course), Sycuan takes advantage of the area's natural terrain. Mountains, natural rock outcroppings, and aged oaks and sycamores add character to individual holes. The course also has a golf school for women taught by women. Greens fees are $57 Monday through Thursday, $62 Friday, $79 weekends for the two par-72 courses, and $19 to $26 on the shorter course; cart rental costs $13. Twilight rates are available. The course, formerly known as Singing Hills, is part of an Indian gaming resort (p. 229), which offers a variety of good-value packages; it's about 30 minutes from downtown San Diego.

3007 Dehesa Rd., El Cajon. ✆ **800/457-5568** or 619/442-3425. www.sycuanresort.com. Take Calif. 94 to the Willow Glen exit. Turn right and continue to the entrance.

Torrey Pines Golf Course ★★★ These two gorgeous municipal 18-hole championship courses are on the coast between La Jolla and Del Mar, only 20 minutes from downtown San Diego. Home of the Buick Invitational Tournament, and the setting for the 2008 U.S. Open, Torrey Pines is second only to Pebble Beach as California's top golf destination. Situated on a bluff overlooking the ocean, the north course has the postcard-perfect signature hole (no. 6), but the south course is more challenging, has more sea-facing play, and benefits from a $3.5-million overhaul in 2002. In summer, course conditions can be less than ideal due to the sheer number of people lined up to play, and "tee scalpers" aren't uncommon. Tee times are taken up to 90 days in advance by automated telephone system ($39 booking fee). Golf professionals are available for lessons (which assure you a spot on the course), and the pro shop rents clubs. Greens fees on the south course are $160 weekdays, $200 weekends; the north course is $90 weekdays and $113 weekends. Cart rentals are $40, and twilight and senior rates are available. *Tip:* First-come, first-served tee times are available from sunup to 7:30am. Single golfers also stand a good chance of getting on the course if they just turn up and get on the waiting list for a threesome.

11480 Torrey Pines Rd., La Jolla. ⓒ **877/581-7171** (option 3 for automated reservations 8–90 days in advance), 619/570-1234 (for automated reservations up to 7 days in advance), or 800/985-4653 for the pro shop and lessons. www.torreypinesgolfcourse.com or www.sandiego.gov/torreypines. From I-5, take Genesee Ave. exit west, and go left on N. Torrey Pines Rd. Bus: 101.

HANG GLIDING & PARAGLIDING

Since 1928, the **Torrey Pines Gliderport** ★★★, 2800 Torrey Pines Scenic Dr., La Jolla (ⓒ **858/452-9858;** www.flytorrey.com), has been one of the world's top spots for non-motorized flight. Set on a windy cliff top above Black's Beach, it draws legions of hang-gliding and paragliding enthusiasts, as well as hobbyists with radio-control aircraft. A 20- to 30-minute tandem flight with a qualified instructor costs $150 for paragliding and $175 for hang gliding. The difference between the two sports? Hang gliders are suspended from a fixed wing, while paragliders are secured to a parachute-like nylon wing. If you've ever dreamed of soaring like a bird, this is your opportunity. Even if you don't muster the courage to try a tandem flight—and there is something rather nerve-racking about stepping off a 300-foot cliff—sitting at the cafe here and watching the graceful acrobatics is a treat in itself.

If you already have experience, you can rent or buy equipment from the shop at the Gliderport—note that the conditions here are considered "P3"—or take lessons from the crew of able instructors. A 5- to 7-day beginning paragliding package is $1,095; advanced hang-gliding lessons run $195 per day and must be scheduled ahead of time. Winds in December and January are slightest (that is, least conducive for the activities here), while March through June is best. Peak flying time is in the early afternoon, so call in the morning to check on conditions; reservations are not accepted. The Gliderport is open daily from 9am to sunset.

HIKING & WALKING

Walking along the water is particularly rewarding. The best **beaches** for walking are Coronado, Mission Beach, La Jolla Shores, and Torrey Pines, but pretty much any shore is a good choice. You can also walk around most of Mission Bay on a series of connected footpaths. If a four-legged friend is your walking companion, head for Dog Beach in Ocean Beach or Fiesta Island in Mission Bay; they're two of the few areas where dogs can legally go unleashed. The **Coast Walk** in La Jolla offers supreme surf-line views.

The **Sierra Club** sponsors regular hikes in the San Diego area, and nonmembers are welcome to participate. A Wednesday mountain hike usually treks in the Cuyamaca Mountains, sometimes in the Lagunas; there are also outings for singles, families, and gays and lesbians. Call the office at ⓒ **858/569-6005** weekdays from noon to 5pm, or consult the website, www.sandiego.sierraclub.org. Volunteers from the **Natural History Museum** (ⓒ **619/232-3821;** www.sdnhm.org) also lead free nature walks throughout San Diego County.

Marian Bear Memorial Park (ⓒ **858/581-9961** for park ranger; www.sandiego.gov/park-and-recreation) in San Clemente Canyon has a 7-mile round-trip trail that runs directly underneath Hwy. 52. Most of the trail is flat, hard-packed dirt, but some areas are rocky. Benches and places to sit allow you to have a quiet picnic. From Hwy. 52 W., take the Genesee South exit; at the stoplight, make a U-turn and an immediate right into the parking lot. From Hwy. 52 E., exit at Genesee and make a right at the light, and then an immediate right into the parking lot.

Lake Miramar Reservoir has a 3.5-mile paved trail with a wonderful view of the lake and mountains. Take I-15 N. and exit on Mira Mesa Boulevard. Turn right on Scripps Ranch Boulevard, then left on Scripps Lake Drive, and make a left at the Lake Miramar sign. Hours are sunrise to sunset, 7 days a week; parking is free. There's also a pleasant path around **Lake Murray.** Take the Lake Murray Boulevard exit off I-8 and follow the signs. See www.sandiego.gov/water/recreation for information on both locations.

Other places for scenic hikes listed earlier in this chapter include **Torrey Pines State Reserve** (p. 153), **Cabrillo National Monument** (p. 58), and **Mission Trails Regional Park** (p. 148). Guided walks are also offered at each of these parks.

JOGGING

An invigorating route downtown is along the wide sidewalks of the Embarcadero, stretching around the bay. A locals' favorite place to jog is the sidewalk that follows the east side of Mission Bay. Start at the Visitor Information Center and head south past the Hilton to Fiesta Island. A good spot for a short run is La Jolla Shores Beach, where there's hard-packed sand even when it isn't low tide. The beach at Coronado is also a good place for jogging, as is the shore at Pacific Beach and Mission Beach.

Safety note: When jogging alone, be wary of secluded areas in Balboa Park, even during daylight hours.

SAILING & MOTOR YACHTS

There are some 55,000 registered watercraft docked at more than 25 marinas throughout San Diego County. Sailors have a choice of the calm waters of 4,600-acre **Mission Bay,** with its 26 miles of shoreline; **San Diego Bay,** one of the most beautiful natural harbors in the world; or the **Pacific Ocean,** where you can sail south to the Islas los Coronados (the trio of uninhabited islets on the Mexico side of the border). Joining a chartered sailing trip is easy.

The **Maritime Museum of San Diego** (*©* **619/234-9153;** www.sdmaritime.org) offers half-day and 3- to 6-day sailing adventures aboard the *Californian,* the official tall ship of the state. This ship is a replica of an 1847 cutter that sailed the coast during the gold rush. Half-day sails depart select Saturdays and Sundays at 1pm from the Maritime Museum downtown and are priced $42 for adults, $34 for seniors 63 and older and active military, and $31 for kids 17 and under. Reservations are required for multiday trips that make for Catalina Island and points as far north as San Francisco; fares start at $475. Forty-five-minute bay cruises are also available (Fri–Sun) aboard *Pilot,* the bay's official pilot boat for 82 years. Tickets are $3 plus regular museum admission price.

Based at Shelter Island Marina, **Classic Sailing Adventures** (*©* **800/659-0141** or 619/224-0800; www.classicsailingadventures.com) offers a 4-hour sailing trip daily aboard the *Soul Diversion,* a 38-foot Ericson. The afternoon cruise leaves at 1pm; in summer there's also a champagne sunset sail that departs at 5pm. The yacht carries a maximum of six passengers (minimum two), and the $75-per-person price includes beverages and snacks.

You can pretend you're racing for your country's honor with **Next Level Sailing** (*©* **800/644-3454;** www.nextlevelsailing.com), which offers bay sails aboard one of two 80-foot International America's Cup Class racing yachts. The 2-hour excursions, either on the *Stars and Stripes* or the *Abracadabra,* are $99 and depart from the Embarcadero.

If you have sailing or boating experience, go for a nonchartered rental. **Seaforth Boat Rental** (✆ **888/834-2628;** www.seaforthboatrental.com) has a wide variety of boats for bay and ocean, from kayaks ($12 per hour) to 240-horsepower cabin cruisers ($395, 2-hr. minimum). Sailboats start at $35 an hour; jet skis begin at $90 an hour. Half- and full-day rates are available. Canoes, catamarans, and pedal boats are also available, as well as fishing boats and equipment. Seaforth has three locations: Mission Bay, 1641 Quivira Rd. (✆ **619/223-1681**); downtown at the Marriott San Diego Hotel & Marina, 333 W. Harbor Dr. (✆ **619/239-2628**); and in Coronado at 1715 Strand Way (✆ **619/437-1514**).

Mission Bay Sportcenter, 1010 Santa Clara Place (✆ **858/488-1004;** www.mission baysportcenter.com), is located on an isthmus extending into the bay and is adjacent to basketball courts, a baseball field, and picnic areas. It rents sailboats (from $18 per hour), catamarans (from $30 per hour), sailboards ($18 per hour), kayaks (from $13 per hour), jet skis ($95 per hour), pedal boats ($17 per hour), and powerboats (from $105 per hour). There are discounts for 4-hour and full-day rentals. In summer, a variety of youth programs (ages 4–16) teach watersports such as surfing and sailing.

SCUBA DIVING & SNORKELING

San Diego's underwater scene ranges from the magnificent giant kelp forests of Point Loma to the nautical graveyard off Mission Beach called Wreck Alley. At the aquatic Ecological Reserve off La Jolla Cove, fishing and boating activity has been banned since 1929. Diving and snorkeling, though, are welcome in the 533-acre reserve; and it's a reliable place to spot garibaldi, California's state fish, as well as endangered giant black sea bass. Shore diving here or at nearby La Jolla Shores is common, and there are dive shops to help you get set up.

But boat dives are the rule. Check out the Islas los Coronados, a trio of uninhabited islets off Mexico (a 90-min. boat ride from San Diego), where seals, sea lions, eels, and more cavort against a landscape of boulders (watch for swift currents). There's also the *Yukon,* a 366-foot Canadian destroyer that was intentionally sunk in 2000. It's part of Wreck Alley, an artificial reef less than 1 mile out from Mission Beach that includes several other vessels and the remains of a research platform toppled by a storm in 1988. Water visibility is best in the fall; water temperatures are cold year-round.

The **San Diego Oceans Foundation** (✆ 619/523-1903; www.sdoceans.org) is a local nonprofit organization devoted to the stewardship of local marine waters. The website features good information about the local diving scene; **SanDiegoDiving.com** (www.sandiegodiving.com, naturally) is another great resource. Notable dive outfits include **Ocean Enterprises,** 7710 Balboa Ave. (✆ 858/565-6054; www.oceanenterprises.com); **Lois Ann Dive Charters,** 1717 Quivira Way (✆ 800/201-4381; www.loisann.com); and **Scuba San Diego** (✆ 800/586-3483 or 619/260-1880; www.scubasandiego.com). **OEX Dive & Kayak Centers** (www.oexcalifornia.com) has a handful of locations in the county, including La Jolla, 2158 Av. de la Playa (✆ 858/454-6195); Mission Bay, 1617 Quivira Rd. (✆ 619/224-6195); Point Loma, 1453 Rosecrans St. (✆ 619/758-9531); and Oceanside, 236 S. Coast Hwy. (✆ 760/721-6195).

SKATING

Gliding around San Diego, especially the Mission Bay area, on in-line skates is the quintessential Southern California experience. In Mission Beach, rent a pair of in-line skates or a skateboard ($5 per hour) from **Cheap Rentals,** 3689 Mission Blvd. (✆ 800/941-7761 or 858/488-9070; www.cheap-rentals.com). In Coronado, go to **Bikes and Beyond,** 1201

First St. at the Ferry Landing (© **619/435-7180;** www.hollandsbicycles.com); rates are $6 **175**
per hour.

If you'd rather ice-skate, try **Ice Town** at University Towne Center, 4545 La Jolla Village Dr., at Genesee Avenue (© **858/452-9110;** www.icetown.com). During the winter holidays, outdoor skating rinks open at the Hotel del Coronado (p. 89) and downtown at Horton Square (© **858/966-5887;** www.fantasyonice.kintera.org); proceeds from the downtown rink benefit a local children's hospital.

SURFING

Some of the best surf spots include Windansea, La Jolla Shores, Pacific Beach, Mission Beach, Ocean Beach, and Imperial Beach. In North County, you might consider Carlsbad State Beach and Oceanside. The best waves are in late summer and early fall; but winter storms bring big surf, too. Even in summer, you'll probably need a wet suit. For surf reports, check out www.surfingsandiego.com or www.surfline.com. A word of advice: Don't get in over your head; hazards include strong riptides and territorial locals.

Boards are available for rent at stands at many popular beaches. Many local surf shops also rent equipment and provide lessons, including **La Jolla Surf Systems,** 2132 Av. de la Playa, La Jolla Shores (© **858/456-2777;** www.lajollasurfsystems.com), and **Ocean Beach Surf & Skate,** 4885 Newport Ave. (© **619/225-0674;** www.oceanexperience. net). In Coronado, you can rent boards at **Emerald City: The Boarding Source,** 1118 Orange Ave. (© **619/435-6677;** www.emeraldcitysurf.com).

For surfing lessons in the North County, check with **Kahuna Bob's Surf School** (© **800/524-8627** or 760/721-7700; www.kahunabob.com), based in Encinitas; **San Diego Surfing Academy** (© **800/447-7873** or 760/230-1474; www.surfsdsa.com), which offers lessons at South Carlsbad State Beach; and **Surf Diva,** 2160 Av. de la Playa (© **858/454-8273;** www.surfdiva.com), a surfing school for women and girls, based in La Jolla. Surf Diva has become so popular it now does lessons for guys, too; in summer there are coed surf camps for kids ages 5 to 17.

SWIMMING

Most San Diego hotels have pools, but there are plenty of other swimming options for visitors. The centrally located Mission Valley **YMCA,** 5505 Friars Rd. (© **619/298-3576;** www.missionvalley.ymca.org), has two pools available daily (and nightly), including a new outdoor facility—call for schedule information. The nonmember fee is $5 for adults, $1.50 for seniors and children 15 and under. In Balboa Park, you can swim in the **Kearns Memorial Swimming Pool,** 2229 Morley Field Dr. (© **619/692-4920;** www. sandiego.gov/park-and-recreation/aquatics). The fee for using the public pool is $5 for adults, $1.50 for seniors and children 15 and under; call for seasonal hours and laps-only restrictions.

In Mission Beach, you'll find Southern California's largest indoor pool, the **Plunge,** 3115 Oceanfront Walk (© **858/228-9300;** www.wavehouseathleticclub.com), part of Belmont Park since 1925. This huge pool is 60×175 feet and was recently renovated; it also has a full gym facility. Nonmember swim hours are Monday through Friday 5:30 to 8am and noon to 8pm, Saturday and Sunday 8am to 4pm. Admission is $7 adults, $6 seniors and children; discounted family nights ($4 per person) are held Tuesday, Friday, and Sunday 4 to 8pm.

In La Jolla, you can swim at the **Lawrence Family Jewish Community Center,** 4126 Executive Dr. (© **858/457-3030;** www.lfjcc.org). This heated Olympic outdoor pool

WHAT TO SEE & DO

7

OUTDOOR ACTIVITIES

(with an ozone filter; no chlorine) is open to the public Monday through Thursday from 6am to 7:30pm, Friday from 6am to 5pm, Saturday from 11am to 5pm, and Sunday from 8:30am to 5pm. Admission is $10 adults, $5 for ages 14 and under.

TENNIS

At the **La Jolla Tennis Club,** 7632 Draper, at Prospect Street (© **858/454-4434;** www. ljtc.org), there are nine public courts, the oldest of which have been here since 1915, a gift from the ubiquitous Ellen Browning Scripps. It costs $5 for adults and is free for those 18 and under; it's open daily from dawn until the lights go off around 9pm. The **Balboa Tennis Club,** 2221 Morley Field Dr., in Balboa Park (© **619/295-9278;** www. balboatennis.com), has more than two dozen courts, including a stadium court. Day passes are $5 adults, $3 seniors 65 and above, $2 for 17 and under; reservations are for members only. The courts are open weekdays from 8am to 8pm, weekends from 8am to 6pm. The ultramodern **Barnes Tennis Center,** 4490 W. Point Loma Blvd., near Ocean Beach and SeaWorld (© **619/221-9000;** www.tennissandiego.com), has 20 lighted hard courts and 4 clay courts. They're open Monday through Friday from 8am to 9pm, Saturday and Sunday 8am to 7:30pm. Court rental is $6 to $10 per person for all-day usage (upon availability); a $2 light fee may apply for night play. Those 17 and under play free.

10 SPECTATOR SPORTS

BASEBALL & SOFTBALL

The **San Diego Padres** play April through September at downtown's $474-million **PETCO Park** ★, 100 Park Blvd. Mired in litigation and controversy, the 42,000-seat ballpark finally opened in 2004 to enthusiastic acclaim from baseball fans and civic boosters. Other San Diegans are still wondering when their promised new downtown library will be built.

A total of seven historic buildings were incorporated into the stadium, most prominently the Western Metal Supply building, a four-story brick structure dating to 1909 that now sprouts left field bleachers. The restaurant and bar here are hot spots during the game. Another unique feature is the Park at the Park, a grassy area beyond center field where kids can romp and watch the game at the same time; the area has its own playground and concession stands, as well as a bronze statue of Padre Hall of Famer Tony Gwynn.

This ballpark isn't the first to offer sushi alongside the usual franks and fries, but you'll find plenty of dining options. La Cocina, a Mexican food court, serves up grilled ahi sandwiches and Rubio's fish tacos; at Pacific Wok you can munch on spring rolls and Asian salads, while the barbecue stand is run by former Padres pitcher Randy Jones. PETCO parking is limited and can be costly; expect to pay anywhere from $8 to $20, depending on how close to the stadium you get. Less expensive lots are found around Santa Fe depot at Kettner Boulevard and Broadway—a 15- to 20-minute walk from the ballpark. Better yet, take the San Diego Trolley, which has three stops near the park. For Padres information and tickets (ranging in price from $5–$69), call © **877/374-2784** or 619/795-5000, or visit www.padres.com.

The highlight of many San Diegans' summer is the racy softball event known as the
World Championship Over-the-Line Tournament, held on Fiesta Island in Mission
Bay on the second and third weekends of July. For more information, see the "San Diego
Calendar of Events" on p. 19.

BOATING EVENTS

San Diego has probably played host to the America's Cup for the last time, but several
other boating events of interest are held here. Check with the **San Diego Association of
Yacht Clubs** (© 619/282-5050; www.sdayc.org) for information on races and other
boating to-dos. Yearly happenings include **America's Schooner Cup,** held every March
or April (© 619/222-1214; www.sgyc.org), and the **Annual San Diego Crew Classic,**
held on Mission Bay the first weekend in April (© 619/225-0300; www.crewclassic.
org). The Crew Classic rowing competition draws teams from throughout the United
States. The **Wooden Boat Festival** is held on Shelter Island every June over Father's Day
weekend (© 619/222-9051; www.koehlerkraft.com). More than 80 boats—from rowboats to schooners—participate in the festival, which features nautical displays, seminars,
food, music, and crafts. Admission is $5 adults, $3 children 6 to 12, free for children 5
and under.

FISHING TOURNAMENTS

Enthusiasts will want to attend the **Day at the Docks** event, held every April at the San
Diego Sportfishing Landing, at Harbor Drive and Scott Street in Point Loma. See the
"San Diego Calendar of Events" on p. 19; for more information, call © 619/234-8793,
or go to www.sportfishing.org.

FOOTBALL

San Diego's professional football team, the **Chargers,** has been shopping for another city
(including others within the county) since failing to generate interest—and lots of public
funding—for an audacious plan to create a huge urban village around a new stadium in
Mission Valley. With the current economic downturn, it's unlikely the Chargers will find
many takers willing to commit to a sweetheart deal like the one the Padres received for
their downtown stadium. So for now, the **Chargers** (© 619/220-8497 for single tickets,
877/242-7437, or 619/280-2121; www.chargers.com) play at **Qualcomm Stadium**
("the Q"), 9449 Friars Rd., Mission Valley. The season runs from August to December;
single tickets are $54 to $98. The **Chargers Express bus** (© 619/233-3004 for information) costs $10 round-trip and picks up passengers at five different locations throughout
the city, beginning 2 hours before the game; the stadium is also easily reached via the San
Diego Trolley. General parking is $25; the parking hot line is © 619/281-7275.

GOLF TOURNAMENTS

One of the country's biggest golf tournaments, the **Buick Invitational,** takes place in
early February at Torrey Pines Golf Course in La Jolla (© 619/281-4653; www.buick
invitational.com). The weeklong event draws the PGA Tours' top players and features a
number of special events, including clinics and pro-ams. Single-day tickets are $21 to
$32, and $21 for seniors; tournament passes are $120. Monday, when the PGA players
do their practice rounds, is free. Parking and round-trip shuttle service are offered from
Qualcomm Stadium in Mission Valley and the Del Mar Show Park, located off I-5 at Via
de la Valle; cost is $15 per vehicle.

Live thoroughbred racing takes place at the **Del Mar Race Track** (© 858/755-1141 for information and racing schedules; www.delmarracing.com) from mid-July to early September. Post time for the nine-race program is 2pm (except for Fri, when it's 4pm; 3:30pm on the final three Fri); there's no racing on Tuesdays. Admission to the clubhouse is $10, including program. Stretch-run admission is $6 with program and infield access; reserved seats are $5 to $15. Free for children 17 and under. Tables for four with food service run $60 to $100 (excluding admission). The infield area has a jungle gym where kids can play or watch shows put on by BMX riders and skateboarders; there's also a day camp offered for kids ages 5 to 12 ($23 per child). Party crowds are lured by post-race concerts by major artists and other special events. General parking is $8; valet parking is $20. Year-round, satellite wagering is available at the fairgrounds' race book, **Surfside Race Place** (© 858/755-1167; www.surfsideraceplace.com). It's open Wednesday through Sunday for both day and evening racing; $5 admission.

The **Del Mar National Horse Show** takes place at the Del Mar Fairgrounds from mid-April to early May. Olympic-caliber and national championship riders participate. For information, call © 858/755-1161 or 793-5555, or check www.sdfair.com.

POLO

The North County community of Rancho Santa Fe is one of the wealthiest enclaves in the country, so it's no wonder this upper-crust sport (with roots in ancient Persia) is played here. Staging one of the longest seasons in the United States, the **San Diego Polo Club,** 14555 El Camino Real (© 858/481-9217; www.sandiegopolo.com), has Sunday matches from May to October (with a summer break mid-July to mid-Aug) at 1:30 and 3pm. The scene is casual and convivial, with a touch of class (like the gourmet lunch buffet, $35). Even if you don't know a chukker from a ride-off, watching these skilled horsemen is plenty exciting. Tickets are $10, or $25 for preferred seating (free for children 12 and under); parking is $5. And FYI: A chukker is a period of play, and a ride-off is the polo equivalent of a hockey body-check.

City Strolls

From the history-heavy Gaslamp Quarter to idyllic Balboa Park, San Diego easily lends itself to the long, leisurely stroll. The four walking tours in this chapter will give you a special sense of the city, as well as a look at some of its most appealing sights and structures.

WALKING TOUR 1   THE GASLAMP QUARTER

START:	Fourth Avenue and E Street, at Horton Plaza.
FINISH:	Fourth Avenue and F Street.
TIME:	Approximately 1½ hours, not including shopping and dining.
BEST TIMES:	During the day.
WORST TIMES:	Evenings, when the area's popular restaurants and nightspots attract big crowds.

A National Historic District covering 16½ city blocks, the Gaslamp Quarter contains many Victorian and Edwardian commercial buildings built between the Civil War and World War I. The quarter—featuring electric versions of old gas lamps—lies between Fourth Avenue to the west, Sixth Avenue to the east, Broadway to the north, and L Street and the waterfront to the south. The blocks are not large; developer Alonzo Horton knew corner lots were desirable to buyers, so he created more of them. This tour hits some highlights along Fourth and Fifth avenues; if it whets your appetite for more, the **Gaslamp Quarter Historical Foundation,** 410 Island Ave. (© **619/233-4692;** www. gaslampquarter.org), offers walking tours every Saturday at 11am ($10, including museum admission, or $8 for seniors, students, and military; free for children 11 and under). The book *San Diego's Gaslamp Quarter,* jointly produced by the GQHF, the San Diego Historical Society, and the Gaslamp Quarter Association, makes an excellent, lightweight walking companion. It has then-and-now photos, historical background, and a self-guided tour.

The tour begins at:

❶ Horton Plaza

It's a colorful conglomeration of shops, eateries, and architectural flourishes—and a tourist attraction. Ernest W. Hahn, who planned and implemented the redevelopment and revitalization of downtown San Diego, built the plaza in 1985. This core project, which covers 12 acres and 6½ blocks in the heart of downtown, represents the successful integration of public and private funding.

The ground floor at Horton Plaza is home to the Jessop Street Clock. The timepiece has 20 dials, 12 of which tell the time in places throughout the world. Designed by Joseph Jessop, Sr., and built primarily by Claude D. Ledger, the clock stood outside Jessop's Jewelry Store on Fifth Avenue from 1907 until being moved to Horton Plaza in 1985. It has reportedly stopped only three times in its history: once after being hit by a team of horses, once after an earthquake, and again on the day in 1935 when Mr. Ledger died.

Exit Horton Plaza on the north side, street level, near Macy's. At the corner of Fourth and Broadway is:

② Horton Plaza Park

Its centerpiece is a fountain designed by well-known local architect Irving Gill and modeled after the monument of Lysicrates in Athens. Dedicated October 15, 1910, it was the first successful attempt in the United States to combine electric lights with flowing water. On the fountain's base are bronze medallions of San Diego's "founding fathers": Juan Rodríguez Cabrillo, Father Junípero Serra, and Alonzo Horton.

Walk south along Fourth Avenue to the:

③ Balboa Theatre

Constructed in 1924, the Spanish Renaissance–style building, at the southwest corner of Fourth Avenue and E Street, has a distinctive tile dome, striking tile work in the entry, and two 20-foot-high ornamental waterfalls inside. In the theater's heyday, plays and vaudeville took top billing. After years of sitting dormant and decrepit, the renovated Balboa is hosting live performances once again.

Cross Fourth Avenue and proceed along E Street to Fifth Avenue. The tall, striking building to your left at the northeast corner of Fifth and E is the:

④ Watts-Robinson Building

Built in 1913, this was one of San Diego's first skyscrapers. It once housed 70 jewelers and is now a boutique hotel (see the review for Gaslamp Plaza Suites on p. 69). Take a minute to look inside at the marble wainscoting, tile floors, ornate ceiling, and brass ornamentation.

Return to the southwest corner of Fifth Avenue and E Street. On the opposite side of the street, at 837 Fifth Ave., is the unmistakable "grand old lady of the Gaslamp," the twin-towered baroque revival:

⑤ Louis Bank of Commerce

You can admire the next few buildings from the west side of the street and then continue south from here. Built in 1888, this proud building was the first in San Diego made of granite. It once housed the city's first ice-cream parlor; an oyster bar

frequented by legendary lawman Wyatt Earp (of OK Corral shootout fame); and the Golden Poppy Hotel, a brothel run by a fortuneteller, Madame Coara. After a fire in 1904, the original towers of the building were removed, and the iron eagles perched atop them disappeared. A 2002 renovation installed a new pair of eagles, cast at the same English foundry as the originals.

On the west side of Fifth Avenue, at no. 840, near E Street, you'll find the:

⑥ F. W. Woolworth Building

Built in 1910, this building had been the site of San Diego Hardware since 1922. Sadly, the store relocated to friendlier confines in 2006, and the space is now an outlet for American Apparel. Thankfully, the amazing hammered-tin ceiling and the rounded glass display windows survived the changeover.

Across the street, at 801 Fifth Ave., stands the two-story:

⑦ Marston Building

This Italianate Victorian-style building dates from 1881 and housed businessman and philanthropist George W. Marston's department store for 15 years. In 1885, San Diego Federal Savings' first office was here, and the Prohibition Temperance Union held its meetings here in the late 1880s. Ironically, the site was later occupied by a series of bars and strip clubs. After a fire in 1903, the building was remodeled extensively.

The redbrick, Romanesque revival on the northwest corner of Fifth Avenue and F Street is the:

⑧ Keating Building

A San Diego landmark dating from 1890, this structure was nicknamed the "marriage building." It was developed by businessman George Keating, who died halfway through construction. His wife, Fannie, finished the project, changing some of the design along the way. She had her husband's name engraved in the top cornice as a tribute to him. Originally heralded as one of the

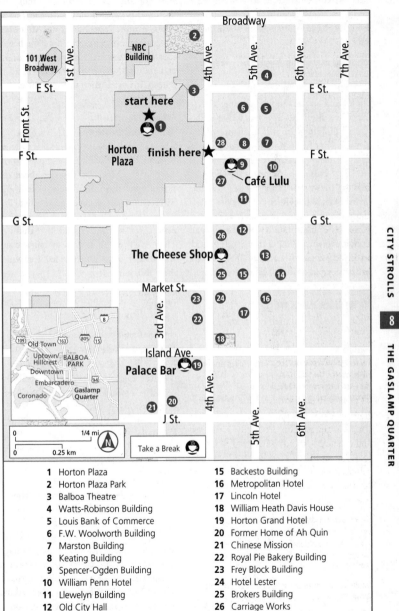

1	Horton Plaza	**15**	Backesto Building
2	Horton Plaza Park	**16**	Metropolitan Hotel
3	Balboa Theatre	**17**	Lincoln Hotel
4	Watts-Robinson Building	**18**	William Heath Davis House
5	Louis Bank of Commerce	**19**	Horton Grand Hotel
6	F.W. Woolworth Building	**20**	Former Home of Ah Quin
7	Marston Building	**21**	Chinese Mission
8	Keating Building	**22**	Royal Pie Bakery Building
9	Spencer-Ogden Building	**23**	Frey Block Building
10	William Penn Hotel	**24**	Hotel Lester
11	Llewelyn Building	**25**	Brokers Building
12	Old City Hall	**26**	Carriage Works
13	Yuma Building	**27**	Labor Temple Building
14	I.O.O.F. Building	**28**	Ingle Building

city's most prestigious office buildings, it featured conveniences such as steam heat and a wire-cage elevator. A sleek boutique hotel, the Keating House, is now ensconced here (p. 74).

Continuing south on Fifth Avenue, cross F Street and stand in front of the:

⑨ Spencer-Ogden Building

It's located on the southwest corner at 770 Fifth Ave. Built in 1874, this is one of the oldest buildings in the Gaslamp Quarter—and it's lucky to still be standing. It escaped major damage after an explosion in 1887 caused by a druggist who was making fireworks. Other tenants over the years included realtors, an import business, a home-furnishings business, and a "Painless Parker" dental office. Edgar Parker owned a chain of dental offices and legally changed his name to "Painless" in order to avoid claims of false advertising.

Directly across the street stands the:

⑩ William Penn Hotel

Built in 1913, it started out as the elegant Oxford Hotel; a double room with private bathroom and toilet cost $1.50. Note the restored glasswork that wraps around the building.

On the west side of the street, at 726 Fifth Ave., you'll find the:

⑪ Llewelyn Building

Built in 1887 by William Llewelyn, his family shoe store was here until 1906. Of architectural note are its arched windows, molding, and cornices. Through the decades, it has been home to a series of hotels, none of which had a particularly high standing among those in proper society; in 1917 charges were brought against the proprietor for operating a "cat house." Today the Llewelyn is a colorful hostel.

On the southwest corner of Fifth Avenue and G Street is the:

⑫ Old City Hall

Dating from 1874, when it was a bank, this Florentine Italianate building features 16-foot ceilings, 12-foot windows framed with brick arches, antique columns, and a wrought-iron cage elevator. Notice the windows on each floor are different. (The top two stories were added in 1887, when it became the city's public library.) Incredibly, in a 1950s attempt at modernization, this beauty was completely encased in stucco. It was restored in the 1980s.

Across the street in the middle of the block, at 631–633 Fifth Ave., is the:

⑬ Yuma Building

The striking edifice was built in 1888 and was one of the first brick buildings downtown. The brothel at the Yuma was the first to be closed during the infamous 1912 cleanup of the area. In the end, 138 women (and no men) were arrested. They were given a choice: Join the Door of Hope charity and reform or take a one-way train ride to Los Angeles. One hundred thirty-six went to L.A. (many were back within days), one woman was pronounced insane, and the last became San Diego's first telephone operator.

Go left on Market Street; at no. 526 is the:

⑭ I.O.O.F. Building

Finally finished in 1882 after 9 years of construction, this handsome building served as a joint lodge for the Masons and Odd Fellows. Gaslamp lore has it that while watching a parade from the balcony, Kalakaua, Hawaii's last reigning king, caught cold and died shortly thereafter in San Francisco in 1891.

Head back toward Fifth Avenue. On the northwest corner of Fifth Avenue and Market Street is the:

⑮ Backesto Building

Built in 1873, this classical revival and Victorian-style building fills most of the block. Originally a one-story structure on the corner, it expanded to its present size and height over its first 15 years. At the turn of the 20th century, this part of the Gaslamp was known as the Stingaree, the city's notorious red-light district. Gambling, opium dens, and wild saloons were all part of the mix.

Across Market Street, on the east side of the street, is the former:

16 Metropolitan Hotel

This building had bay windows and a cupola when it was built in 1886; now it looks decidedly contemporary—until you spot the rugged 19th-century columns still visible on the street level. The Metropolitan also features arrestingly realistic *trompe l'oeil* effects painted on the facade. When the building was being renovated in the '80s, it was determined a faithful restoration would be too costly, so the owner was permitted to do the faux finish. Today the Metropolitan is another of San Diego's well-located hostels.

In the middle of the block, at 536 Fifth Ave., is the small but distinctive:

17 Lincoln Hotel

It dates from 1913—the date is cast in a grand concrete pediment two stories up. An equally grand stone lion's head once reigned atop the parapet, but tumbled to the street during an earthquake in 1986 and was quickly snatched by a passerby. The building's unusual green-and-white ceramic tile facade is thankfully intact. At one time, the block was comprised of primarily Japanese-owned businesses. Japanese residents ended up being held in the hotel during World War II before being sent to internment camps.

Proceed to Island Avenue and turn right. The saltbox house at the corner of Fourth Avenue is the:

18 William Heath Davis House

Downtown's oldest surviving structure, this prefabricated lumber home was shipped to San Diego around Cape Horn from New England in 1850. Alonzo Horton lived in the house in 1867, at its original location at the corner of Market and State streets. Around 1873 it was moved to 11th Avenue and K Street, where it served as the county hospital. It was relocated to this site in 1984 and completely refurbished. The entire house, now a museum and gift shop, and the small

park next to it are open to the public (p. 146). The Gaslamp Quarter Historical Foundation is also headquartered here.

At the southwest corner of Island and Fourth avenues you'll see the bay windows of the winsome:

19 Horton Grand Hotel

Two 1886 hotels were moved here—very gently—from other sites, and then renovated and connected by an atrium; the original Grand Horton is to your left, the Brooklyn Hotel to your right. Now it's all one: the Horton Grand hotel (p. 68). The life-size papier-mâché horse (Sunshine), in the sitting area near reception, stood in front of the Brooklyn Hotel when the ground floor was a saddlery. Wyatt Earp lived upstairs at the Brooklyn for most of his 7 years in San Diego. The reception desk is a recycled pew from a choir loft, and old post-office boxes now hold guests' keys. In the Palace Bar, look for the portrait of Ida Bailey, a local madam whose establishment, the Canary Cottage, once stood nearby.

> **TAKE A BREAK**
> The **Cheese Shop,** 627 Fourth Ave. (☏ **619/232-2303**), is open for breakfast or lunch with house-made corned beef hash, blueberry pancakes, fresh soups, and tasty pork sandwiches. After 4pm, try the **Palace Bar** (☏ **619/544-1886**) in the Horton Grand Hotel; it's a good place to relax while surrounded by a bit of history. The bar is part of the same choir-loft pew that has been turned into the reception desk.

Around the corner from the Horton Grand, at 433 Third Ave., stands the:

20 Former Home of Ah Quin

One of the first Chinese merchants in San Diego, Ah Quin arrived in the 1880s and became known as the "Mayor of Chinatown" (an area bound by Market and J sts., and Third and Fifth aves.). He helped hundreds of Chinese immigrants find work on the railroad and owned a general merchandise store on Fifth Avenue. He was a respected father (of 12 children), and a leader and spokesperson for the city's Chinese population.

The Ah Quin home is not open to the public, but across the street at 404 Third Ave. is the:

㉑ Chinese Mission

Originally located on First Avenue, this charming brick building, built in 1927, was a place where Chinese immigrants (primarily men) could learn English and find employment. Religious instruction and living quarters were also provided. The building was rescued from demolition and moved to its present location, where it now contains the San Diego Chinese Historical Museum (p. 146). There's a gift shop with Chinese wares, a small Asian garden with a gate memorializing the father of modern China, Sun Yat-sen, and a statue of Confucius. Admission is $2.

When you leave the museum, retrace your steps back to Fourth and Island and walk north; in the middle of the block on the west side you will come to the:

㉒ Royal Pie Bakery Building

Erected in 1911, this building was a bakery for most of its existence. Something else was cooking upstairs, though—the second floor housed the Anchor Hotel, which was eventually closed because of "rampant immorality."

At the southwest corner of Fourth Avenue and Market Street stands the:

㉓ Frey Block Building

Built in 1911, this was first a secondhand store, then a series of Chinese restaurants. But real fame arrived in the 1950s when it became the Crossroads, one of San Diego's most important jazz clubs. It was a venue for local and touring African-American artists.

Across the street on the southeast corner, at 401–417 Market St., is the:

㉔ Hotel Lester

This hotel dates from 1906. It housed a saloon, pool hall, and hotel of ill repute when this was a red-light district. It's still a hotel (cheap but not tawdry) upstairs, while the ground level supports retail businesses, including an upscale pet boutique.

On the northeast corner of Fourth Avenue and Market Street, at 402 Market St., stands the:

㉕ Brokers Building

Constructed in 1889, this building has 16-foot wood-beam ceilings and cast-iron columns. In recent years it was converted to artists' lofts, with the ground floor dedicated to the downtown branch of the Hooters chain. Due to the failure of many previous ventures here, as well as a fire and a structural collapse, this was thought of as a "cursed corner."

At the north end of this block, you will find the:

㉖ Carriage Works

Established in 1890, it once served as storage for wagons and carriages. It then segued to horseless carriages, serving as a Studebaker showroom and repair shop. The building now features restaurants and clubs.

Cross G Street and walk to the middle of the block to the:

㉗ Labor Temple Building

Dating from 1907, it has striking arched windows on the second floor. The inside was once used as a meeting hall for unions representing everyone from cigar makers to theatrical employees. Le Travel Store, which has an STA Travel outlet, is now located here.

Continue north; at 801 Fourth Ave. is the:

㉘ Ingle Building

It dates from 1906 and now houses the Hard Rock Cafe. The mural on the F Street side of the building depicts a group of deceased rock stars (Janis Joplin, Jimi

Hendrix, John Lennon, Jim Morrison, and Elvis) lounging at sidewalk tables. Original stained-glass windows from the old Golden Lion Tavern (1907–32) front Fourth Avenue. Inside, the colorful stained-glass ceiling was taken from an Elks Club in Stockton, California, and much of the floor is original.

WINDING DOWN
Walk to bohemian **Café Lulu,** 419 F St. (*©* **619/238-0114**), near Fourth Avenue, for coffee and sweets; or head back into **Horton Plaza,** where you can choose from many kinds of cuisine, from Chinese to Indian, along with good old American fast food.

WALKING TOUR 2   THE EMBARCADERO

START:	The Maritime Museum, at Harbor Drive and Ash Street.
FINISH:	The Convention Center, at Harbor Drive and Fifth Avenue.
TIME:	1½ hours, not including museum and shopping stops.
BEST TIMES:	Weekday mornings (when it's less crowded and easier to park).
WORST TIMES:	Weekends, especially in the afternoon, when the Maritime Museum and Seaport Village are crowded; also when cruise ships are in port (days vary).

San Diego's colorful Embarcadero, or waterfront, cradles a bevy of seagoing vessels—frigates, ferries, yachts, cruise ships, a merchant vessel, an aircraft carrier, and even a Soviet submarine. You'll also find the equally colorful Seaport Village, a shopping and dining center with a nautical theme. It's not all about the water, though—you'll also find the two downtown wings of the Museum of Contemporary Art San Diego, including a spectacular annex that opened in 2007.

Start at the:

❶ Maritime Museum

Not a building, but a collection of ships, the Maritime Museum is located at Harbor Drive at Ash Street (see the review on p. 144). The main attraction is the magnificent *Star of India*—the world's oldest ship that still goes to sea—built in 1863 as the *Euterpe*. The ship, whose billowing sails are a familiar sight along Harbor Drive, once carried cargo to India and immigrants to New Zealand, and it braved the arctic ice in Alaska to work in the salmon industry. Another component of the museum is the 1898 ferry *Berkeley,* built to operate between San Francisco and Oakland. In service through 1958, it carried survivors to safety 24 hours a day for 4 days after the 1906 San Francisco earthquake. You can also check out the HMS *Surprise,* which had a star turn in the film *Master and Commander: The Far*

Side of the World; a Soviet-era B-39 attack submarine; the *Californian,* a replica of a 19th-century revenue cutter; the *Medea,* a 1904 steam yacht; and the *Pilot,* which served as San Diego Bay's official pilot boat for 82 years.

From this vantage point, you get a fine view of the:

❷ County Administration Center

This complex was built in 1936 with funds from the Works Progress Administration, and was dedicated in 1938 by President Franklin D. Roosevelt. The 23-foot-high granite sculpture in front, *Guardian of Water,* was completed by Donal Hord—San Diego's most notable sculptor—in 1939. It depicts a stoic woman shouldering a water jug. The building is even more impressive from the other side because of the carefully tended gardens; it's well worth the effort and extra few minutes to walk around to Pacific

185

CITY STROLLS

8

THE EMBARCADERO

Highway for a look. On weekdays, the building is open from 8am to 5pm; there are restrooms and a cafeteria inside.

> **TAKE A BREAK**
> The cafeteria on the fourth floor of the **County Administration Center,** 1600 Pacific Coast Hwy. ((C) **619/ 515-4258**), has lovely harbor views; it serves breakfast and lunch weekdays from 7am to 2:30pm. The salads, panini, and burgers are all modestly priced. If you can't pass up the chance to have some seafood, return to the waterfront to **Anthony's Fishette,** 1360 N. Harbor Dr. ((C) **619/232-5105**), a simple eatery with a simply marvelous location. It serves fish and chips, shrimp, and other snacks alfresco.

Continue south along the Embarcadero. The large carnival-colored building on your right is the:

❸ San Diego Cruise Ship Terminal

Located on the B Street Pier, it has a large nautical clock at the entrance. Unless you're catching a cruise, there's not much reason to go in, but the flag-decorated terminal's interior is light and airy, and there are also a snack bar and gift shop.

Farther along is the location for the:

❹ Harbor Cruises

They depart from sunup to sundown on tours of San Diego's harbor; there are evening dinner cruises, too. Ticket booths are right on the water. See "Organized Tours" in chapter 7 for more details.

A little farther south, near the Broadway Pier, is the:

❺ Coronado Ferry

It makes hourly trips between San Diego and Coronado. Buy tickets from the Harbor Excursion booth—you can make the round-trip in about 50 minutes. See "By Ferry" within the "Getting Around" section in chapter 3 for more information.

To your left as you look up Broadway, you'll see the two gold mission-style towers of the:

❻ Santa Fe Depot

This mosaic-draped railroad station was built in 1915 and provides one of the city's best examples of Spanish Colonial Revival style. It's only 1¹/₂ blocks away, so walk over and look inside at the vaulted ceiling, wooden benches, and walls covered in striking green-and-gold tiles. A scale model of the aircraft carrier USS *Midway* is on display inside.

Continue to the north end of the station where you will find the:

❼ Museum of Contemporary Art San Diego

What was once the station's baggage building is now the Museum of Contemporary Art San Diego's dynamic new space (p. 144). Designed by the architect responsible for the Warhol museum in Pittsburgh and the Picasso museum in Spain, this is one of the city's new cultural flagships. The original downtown annex is across the street.

Return to Harbor Drive and head south; you'll stroll through a small tree- and bench-lined park and suddenly encounter the:

❽ USS Midway

This aircraft carrier had a 47-year military history that started 1 week after the Japanese surrender of World War II in 1945. By the time the *Midway* was decommissioned in 1991, more than 225,000 men had served aboard. The carrier is now a naval museum, telling the story of life on board the ship, of the wars it fought, and of the records it set. (The *Midway* was tasked with setting new standards throughout much of its career.) For more information, see p. 146.

South of the *Midway,* at Pier 11, is the:

❾ "Unconditional Surrender" Statue

Kitsch with a capital K. This 25-foot, full-color statue re-creates an iconic American image: Alfred Eisenstaedt's 1945 photo of a sailor and nurse in passionate embrace

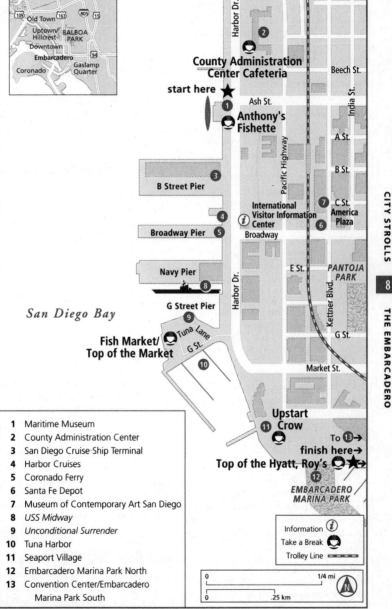

CITY STROLLS

8

THE EMBARCADERO

1   Maritime Museum
2   County Administration Center
3   San Diego Cruise-Ship Terminal
4   Harbor Cruises
5   Coronado Ferry
6   Santa Fe Depot
7   Museum of Contemporary Art San Diego
8   *USS Midway*
9   *Unconditional Surrender*
10 Tuna Harbor
11 Seaport Village
12 Embarcadero Marina Park North
13 Convention Center/Embarcadero
    Marina Park South

Information 🛈
Take a Break 🍴
Trolley Line ▬ ▬ ▬

following the news of Japan's surrender in World War II. You have to see this one to believe it. Nearby are several other pieces of patriotic art, including a salute to another American icon, Bob Hope. Featuring a cast of 15 bronze statues, this most recent addition to the Embarcadero art collection depicts the comedian entertaining the troops.

Continue along the walkway to:
⑩ Tuna Harbor

This is where the commercial fishing boats congregate. San Diego's tuna fleet is based here but is a shadow of its former self—it was once the world's largest.

 TAKE A BREAK
The red building on the peninsula to your right houses the **Fish Market,** 750 N. Harbor Dr. (℗ 619/232-3474), a market and casual restaurant, and its upscale counterpart, **Top of the Market,** just upstairs. A meal here is fresh off the boat. Both serve lunch and dinner, and the Fish Market has a children's menu and an oyster and sushi bar. It's acceptable to drop in just for a drink and to savor the mighty view. Prices are moderate downstairs, expensive upstairs. For dessert or coffee, go inside Seaport Village, 849 W. Harbor Dr., to **Upstart Crow** (℗ 619/232-4855), a bookstore and coffeehouse.

Keep walking south, where you can meander along the winding pathways of:
⑪ Seaport Village

This outdoor shopping center contains myriad boutiques and restaurants. The carousel is pure nostalgia—Charles Looff of Coney Island carved the animals out of poplar in 1895. You will no doubt notice the official symbol of Seaport Village: a 45-foot-high detailed replica of the famous Mukilteo Lighthouse in Everett, Washington.

From Seaport Village, continue your waterfront walk southeast to the:
⑫ Embarcadero Marina Park North

Jutting out into the bay, Embarcadero Marina Park North is a lovely patch of green, well used by San Diegans for strolling and jogging. It features expansive views and is often fairly deserted. The four hotel towers here that wall you off from the rest of the city belong to the Manchester Grand Hyatt and the Marriott San Diego Hotel & Marina. A concession at the marina rents boats by the hour, and arranges diving, water-skiing, and fishing outings.

The waterfront walkway continues to the:
⑬ Convention Center/ Embarcadero Marina Park South

This building is another striking piece of architecture hugging the city's waterfront. When it was first completed in late 1989, its presence on the Embarcadero was a major factor in the revitalization of downtown San Diego. It was later enlarged to an even more imposing size, to less acclaim. Embarcadero Marina Park South stretches out into the bay from here; you'll find a restaurant, basketball courts, concession stand, and fishing pier. You can also catch a ferry to Coronado from the park.

To access the Gaslamp Quarter or San Diego Trolley, you'll need to head back to Seaport Village or cut through the lobbies of the Hyatt or Marriott hotels.

WINDING DOWN
There's no better place in San Diego to catch a sunset than the **Top of the Hyatt,** 1 Market Place (℗ 619/232-1234), a 40th-floor lounge with sweeping views of the city and harbor. It's located in the eastern tower of the Manchester Grand Hyatt and opens at 3pm daily. For those afraid of heights, there's a branch of the popular Pacific Rim–fusion eatery **Roy's,** 333 W. Harbor Dr. (℗ 619/239-7697), on the marina side of the Marriott, perched right above the action along the pedestrian pathway.

START: The McCoy House, overlooking the San Diego Trolley's Old Town station.
FINISH: Heritage Park.
TIME: 2 hours, not including shopping or dining.
BEST TIMES: Weekdays; there are daily 1-hour free tours at 11am and 2pm; on Wednesdays, from 10am to 2pm, costumed park volunteers reenact life in the 1800s.
WORST TIMES: Weekends, especially if you want to dine at one of the restaurants, where waits can be long. Of special note is Cinco de Mayo weekend (the first weekend in May)—Old Town is a madhouse, so plan accordingly. The holiday celebrates Mexico's defeat of the French on May 5, 1862, in the Battle of Puebla, and there are a number of special events held.

When you visit Old Town, you go back to a time of one-room schoolhouses and village greens, when many of the people who lived, worked, and played here spoke Spanish. Inside the state park the buildings are old or built to look that way, making it easy to let the modern world slip away—you don't have to look hard or very far to see yesterday. The time warp is especially palpable at night, when you can stroll along the unpaved streets and look up at the stars. Begin your tour at the McCoy House, at the northwestern end of this historic district, which preserves the essence of the small Mexican and fledgling American communities that existed here from 1821 to 1872. The core of Old Town State Historic Park is a 6-block area with no vehicular traffic and a collection of restaurants and retail shops; the commercial district of Old Town continues for several blocks, with San Diego Avenue as the main drag.

Start at the intersection of Wallace and Calhoun, the location of the:

❶ McCoy House

This is the interpretive center for the park and is a historically accurate replication of the home of James McCoy, a lawman/legislator who lived on this site until the devastating fire of 1872. With exhibits, artifacts, and visitor information, the house gives a great overview of life in San Diego in the 19th century.

After checking in here and getting your bearings, head to the neighboring:

❷ Robinson-Rose House

Built in 1853 as a family home, it also served as a newspaper and railroad office; now, it's the visitor center for the park. Here you'll see a large model of Old Town the way it looked prior to 1872, the year a large fire broke out (or was set). The blaze

destroyed much of the town and initiated the population exodus to New Town, now downtown San Diego. Old Town State Historic Park contains seven original buildings, including the Robinson-Rose House, and replicas of other buildings that once stood here.

From here, turn left and stroll into the colorful world of Mexican California called:

❸ Plaza del Pasado

Located at 2754 Calhoun St., this is where colorful shops and restaurants spill into a flower-filled courtyard. Costumed employees and weekend entertainment create an early California atmosphere throughout what was once a 1930s motel (albeit one designed by acclaimed architect Richard Requa). See p. 204 for additional information.

CITY STROLLS

8

OLD TOWN

From Plaza del Pasado, stroll into the grassy plaza, where you'll see a:

❹ Large Rock Monument

This monument commemorates the first U.S. flag raised in Southern California. After Northern California had been wrested from Mexico by invading U.S. forces in July 1846, the USS *Cyane* sailed into San Diego Bay to lay claim to the southern portion of the state. Aboard ship were John C. Frémont (who would go on to become one of California's first senators and the first Republican candidate for president) and legendary frontiersman and scout Kit Carson. On July 29, 1846, a detail raised the Stars and Stripes on this spot. When Frémont rode off with his battalion 10 days later, though, the town was left to its own devices and loyal *Californios* hoisted the Mexican flag again. A sailmaker, Albert B. Smith, eventually nailed Old Glory permanently in place to the flagpole.

Straight ahead, at the plaza's eastern edge, is:

❺ La Casa de Estudillo

An original adobe building dating from 1827, the U-shaped house has covered walkways and an open central patio. The patio covering is made of corraza cane, the seeds for which were brought by Father Junípero Serra in 1769. The walls are 3 to 5 feet thick, holding up the heavy beams and tiles, and they work as terrific insulators against summer heat. In those days, the thicker the walls, the wealthier the family. The furnishings in this "upper-class" house are representative of the 19th century (note the beautiful four-poster beds); the original furniture came from as far away as Asia. The Estudillo family, which then numbered 12, lived in the house until 1887; today family members still live in San Diego.

After you exit La Casa de Estudillo, turn right. Here you'll find the:

❻ Casa de Bandini

Now home to a so-so restaurant, the Casa de Bandini was completed in 1829. It was the home of Peruvian-born Juan Bandini, who arrived in California in 1818 and became one of early San Diego's most prominent citizens. The 14-room home was the hub of the small town's social and political life. When U.S. troops invaded in 1846, Bandini welcomed them and appealed to others to do the same. In fact, the commander of the U.S. force, Samuel DuPont, was a guest in the Bandini home, where there was music and dancing every night during his stay. In 1869, the building, with a second story added, became the Cosmopolitan Hotel.

Walk back across the plaza to the:

❼ Colorado House

Built in 1851, it was destroyed by fire in 1872—as were most buildings on this side of the park. Today it's the home of the Wells Fargo Historical Museum, but the original housed San Diego's first two-story hotel. The museum features an original Wells Fargo stagecoach, numerous displays of the overland-express business, and a video presentation. Next door to the Wells Fargo museum, and cater-cornered to La Casa de Estudillo, is the small, redbrick San Diego Court House & City Hall.

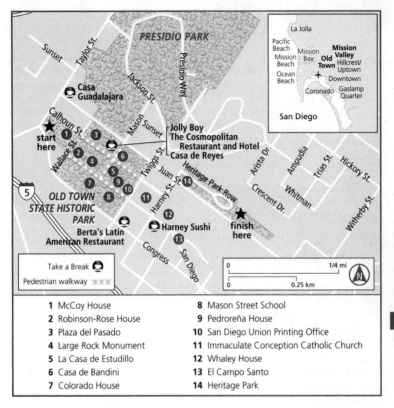

1	McCoy House	**8**	Mason Street School
2	Robinson-Rose House	**9**	Pedroreña House
3	Plaza del Pasado	**10**	San Diego Union Printing Office
4	Large Rock Monument	**11**	Immaculate Conception Catholic Church
5	La Casa de Estudillo	**12**	Whaley House
6	Casa de Bandini	**13**	El Campo Santo
7	Colorado House	**14**	Heritage Park

From here, continue along the pedestrian walkway 1 short block, turn right, and walk another short block to a reddish-brown building on your right. This is the one-room:

❽ Mason Street School

This is an original building dating from 1865. If you look inside, you'll notice that the boards that make up the walls don't match; they were leftovers from the construction of San Diego homes. The school was commissioned by San Diego's first mayor, Joshua Bean, whose brother was the notorious Roy Bean, who would go on to become an eccentric judge in Texas. Before Roy Bean became known as "the law west of the Pecos," though, he had to escape a San Diego jail by digging his way through the adobe walls with a knife that had been hidden in a tamale (he had been jailed for wounding a man in a duel).

When you leave the schoolhouse, retrace your steps to the walkway (which is the extension of San Diego Ave.) and turn right. On your left, you'll see two buildings with brown shingle roofs. The first is the:

❾ Pedroreña House

No. 2616 is an original Old Town house built in 1869, with stained glass over the doorway. The shop inside now sells fossils, minerals, and gems. The original owner was Miguel Pedroreña, a Spanish-born merchant and local bigwig. He also owned the house next door, which became the:

❿ San Diego Union Printing Office

The newspaper was first published here in 1868. This house arrived in Old Town after being prefabricated in Maine in 1851 and shipped around the Horn (it has a distinctly New England appearance). Inside you'll see the original hand press used to print the paper, which merged with the *San Diego Tribune* in 1992. The offices are now in Mission Valley, about 3 miles away.

At the end of the pedestrian part of San Diego Avenue stands a railing; beyond it is Twiggs Street, dividing the historic park from the rest of Old Town, which is more commercial, with shops, galleries, and restaurants.

At the corner of Twiggs Street and San Diego Avenue stands the Spanish mission–style:

⓫ Immaculate Conception Catholic Church

The cornerstone was laid in 1868, making it the first church built in California that was not part of the mission system. With the movement of the community to New Town in 1872, though, it lost its parishioners and was not dedicated until 1919. Today the church serves about 300 families in the Old Town area.

Continue along San Diego Avenue 1 block to Harney Street. On your left is the restored:

⓬ Whaley House

The first two-story brick structure in Southern California, it was built between 1856 and 1857. The house is said to be haunted by several ghosts, including that of Yankee Jim Robinson, who was hanged on the site in 1852—for stealing a *rowboat*. The house is beautifully furnished with period pieces and features the life mask of Abraham Lincoln, the spinet piano used in the film *Gone With the Wind*, and the concert piano that accompanied Swedish soprano Jenny Lind on her final U.S. concert tour in 1852. See p. 149.

Continue down San Diego Avenue 2 short blocks to:

⓭ El Campo Santo

This is San Diego's first cemetery, established in 1850. The small plot is home to several notable characters, including the hanged boat thief Yankee Jim Robinson and Antonio Garra, who led the Southland's last Native American uprising. The small brass plaques you see on the sidewalk and in the street indicate where the remains of some of San Diego's earliest citizens are still interred. Stories float through Old Town about cars that are unable to start after parking over these markers, or whose alarms go off for no reason. See p. 147.

Return down Old Town Avenue and make a right on Harney Street. Head up the hill 1½ blocks to the collection of Victorian jewels known as:

⓮ Heritage Park

The seven buildings in this grassy finger canyon were moved here from other parts of the city and are now used in a variety of ways. Among them are a charming bed-and-breakfast inn (in the Queen Anne shingle–style Christian House, built in 1889; see p. 75), a doll shop, a teahouse, a lingerie store, and offices. Toward the bottom of the hill is the classic revival Temple Beth Israel, dating from 1889. On Sundays, local art is often exhibited in the park. If you've brought picnic supplies, enjoy them under the sheltering coral tree at the top of the park.

> **WINDING DOWN**
> You've been immersed in California's Mexican culture, but two of Old Town's best restaurants don't follow suit, serving sushi and South American fare. At the end of your walk, make your way back down Harney Street, past San Diego Avenue to **Harney Sushi,** 3964 Harney St. ((© 619/295-3272). If this hip and lively sushi joint isn't your style, continue to Congress Street, make a right, and head 1 block to **Berta's Latin American Restaurant,** 3928 Twiggs St. ((© 619/295-2343). This unassuming eatery offers a travelogue of dishes that roams from El Salvador to Argentina.

START:	Cabrillo Bridge, entry at Laurel Street and Sixth Avenue.
FINISH:	San Diego Zoo.
TIME:	2½ hours, not including museum or zoo stops. If you get tired, hop on the free park tram.
BEST TIMES:	Anytime. If you want to get especially good photographs, come in the afternoon, when the sun lends a glow to the already photogenic buildings. Most museums are open until 4 or 5pm (many are closed on Mon), and several are free every Tuesday.
WORST TIMES:	More people (especially families) visit the park on weekends. But there is a festive—rather than overcrowded—spirit even then, particularly on Sunday afternoons when you can catch a free organ concert at the outdoor Spreckels Organ Pavilion at 2pm.

Established in 1868, Balboa Park is the second-oldest city park in the United States, after New York's Central Park. Much of its striking architecture was the product of the 1915–16 Panama-California Exposition and the 1935–36 California Pacific International Exposition. The structures now house a variety of museums and contribute to the overall beauty of the park. But what makes Balboa Park truly unique is the extensive botanical collection, thanks largely to Kate Sessions, a horticulturalist who devoted her life to transforming the barren mesas and scrub-filled canyons into the oases they are today. Originally called "City Park," it was renamed in 1910 when Mrs. Harriet Phillips won a contest, naming it in honor of the Spanish conquistador Vasco Núñez de Balboa, who in 1513 was the first European to see the Pacific Ocean.

CITY STROLLS

8

BALBOA PARK

Take bus no. 3 or 120 along Fifth Avenue to Laurel Street, which leads into Balboa Park through its most dramatic entrance, the:

❶ Cabrillo Bridge

It has expansive views of downtown San Diego and straddles scenic, sycamore-lined Hwy. 163 (which John F. Kennedy proclaimed as "the most beautiful highway I've ever seen," during his 1963 visit to San Diego). Built in 1915 for the Panama-California Exposition and patterned after a bridge in Ronda, Spain, the dramatic cantilever-style bridge has seven pseudo-arches. As you cross the bridge, to your left you'll see the yellow cars of the zoo's aerial tram and, directly ahead, the distinctive California Tower of the Museum of Man. The delightful sounds of the 100-bell Symphonic Carillon can be heard every quarter-hour. Sitting atop this San Diego landmark is a weather vane shaped like the ship in which Cabrillo sailed to California in 1542. The city skyline lies to your right.

Once you've crossed the bridge, go through the:

❷ West Gate

The heart of Balboa Park is accessed through this ceremonial arch. Built for the 1915 expo, the gateway's two reclining figures hold flowing water jugs and represent the Atlantic and Pacific oceans. The park's cornucopia of attractions lies just beyond. For now, just view the museums from the outside. (Read more about them, and all the park's museums, in chapter 7.)

You have entered the park's major thoroughfare, El Prado—if you're driving a car, you'll want to find a parking space (the map on p. 195 shows all public lots) and go to the:

❸ San Diego Museum of Man

Architect Bertram Goodhue designed this structure, originally known as the California Building, in 1915—it now houses an anthropological museum. Goodhue, considered the world's foremost authority on Spanish Colonial architecture, was the master architect for the 1915–16 exposition. The exterior doubled as part of

Kane's mansion in the 1941 Orson Welles classic *Citizen Kane;* historical figures carved on the facade include conquistador Juan Rodríguez Cabrillo, Spanish kings Charles I and Phillip III, and, at the very top, Father Junípero Serra. See p. 142.

Just beyond and up the steps to the left is the nationally acclaimed:

❹ Old Globe Theatre

This is actually a three-theater complex that includes the Old Globe, an outdoor stage, and a small theater-in-the-round. The Old Globe was built for the 1935 exposition as a replica of Shakespeare's Globe Theatre; it was meant to be demolished at the conclusion of the expo but was saved by a group of dedicated citizens. In 1978, an arsonist destroyed the theater, which was rebuilt into what you see today. It's California's oldest professional theater. If you have the opportunity to go inside, you can see the bronze bust of Shakespeare that miraculously survived the fire, battered but unbowed. See p. 158 and 217 for more information.

Beside the theater is the:

❺ Sculpture Garden of the Museum of Art

The San Diego Museum of Art Sculpture Garden features works by Joan Miró and Alexander Calder, as well as a signature piece, *Reclining Figure: Arch Leg,* by Henry Moore. *Reclining Figure* was damaged by a falling tree branch several years ago, but it was seamlessly repaired and reclaimed its spot in the garden. Admission is free.

Across the street, to your right as you stroll along the Prado, is the:

❻ Alcazar Garden

It was designed in 1935 by Richard Requa and W. Allen Perry. They patterned it after the gardens surrounding the Alcazar Castle in Sevilla, Spain. The garden is formally laid out and trimmed with low clipped hedges; in the center walkway are two star-shaped yellow-and-blue tile fountains. The

large tree at the rear is an Indian laurel fig, planted by Kate Sessions when the park was first landscaped.

Exit to your left at the opposite end of the garden, and you'll be back on El Prado. Proceed east to the corner; on your right is the:

❼ House of Charm

This is the site of the San Diego Art Institute gallery (p. 140) and the Mingei International Museum (p. 139). The Art Institute is a nonprofit space that primarily exhibits works by local artists; the Mingei offers changing exhibitions that celebrate human creativity expressed in textiles, costumes, jewelry, toys, pottery, paintings, and sculpture.

To your left is the imposing:

❽ San Diego Museum of Art

This exquisite facade was patterned after the famous university building in Salamanca, Spain. The three life-size figures over the scalloped entryway are the Spanish painters Bartolomé Murillo, Francisco de Zurbarán, and Diego Velázquez. The museum holds San Diego's most extensive collection of fine art; major touring shows are presented, as well. There's also an ongoing schedule of concerts, films, and lectures, usually themed with a current exhibition. See p. 142 for more information.

Across the street are the House of Hospitality and the park's:

❾ Visitor Center

Pick up maps, souvenirs, and discount tickets to the museums here. In the central courtyard behind the visitor center is the beautiful *Woman of Tehuantepec* fountain sculpture by Donal Hord, as well as the attractive **Prado** restaurant (p. 136).

Head back toward the House of Charm, passing the statue of the mounted:

❿ El Cid Campeador

Created by Anna Hyatt Huntington and dedicated in 1930, this sculpture of the 11th-century Spanish hero was made from a mold of the original statue in the court

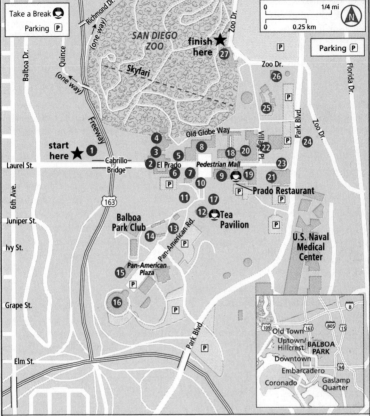

1 Cabrillo Bridge
2 West Gate
3 San Diego Museum of Man
4 Old Globe Theatre
5 Sculpture Garden
6 Alcazar Garden
7 House of Charm
8 San Diego Museum of Art
9 Visitor Center
10 El Cid Campeador
11 Palm Canyon
12 Spreckels Organ Pavilion
13 United Nations Building
14 House of Pacific Relations
   International Cottages

15 San Diego Automotive Museum
16 San Diego Air & Space Museum
17 Japanese Friendship Garden
18 Botanical Building & Lily Pond
19 Casa de Balboa
20 Casa del Prado
21 Reuben H. Fleet Science Center
22 San Diego Natural History Museum
23 Bea Evenson Fountain
24 Gardens
25 Spanish Village Art Center
26 Miniature Railroad and Carousel
27 San Diego Zoo entrance

of the Hispanic Society of America in New York. A third version is in Sevilla, Spain. A decidedly more modern sculpture is found outside the entrance to the Mingei Museum. Created by Niki de Saint Phalle, a French artist who made San Diego her home until her death in 2002, the colorful mosaic alligator is a favorite with kids, who love to clamber over it.

Continue to your left toward the ornamental outdoor Organ Pavilion. Before reaching the pavilion, the wooden bridge above the ravine on your right will take you into:

⓫ Palm Canyon

Fifty species of palm, plus magnolia trees and a Moreton Bay fig tree provide a tropical canopy here. It's secluded, so care should be exercised if you're walking solo, but you can get a good sense of its beauty by venturing only a short distance along the path. The walkway dead-ends, so you must exit from where you entered.

From the top of Palm Canyon, continue to the ornate:

⓬ Spreckels Organ Pavilion

Donated to San Diego by brothers John D. and Adolph B. Spreckels, the pavilion was dedicated on December 31, 1914. A brass plaque honors her charity and patriotism. Free, lively recitals featuring one of the largest outdoor organs in the world (its vast structure contains 4,530 pipes) are given Sundays at 2pm, with additional concerts and events scheduled in the summer. See p. 143.

As you continue on, you'll see the Hall of Nations on your right, and beside it, the:

⓭ United Nations Building

This building also houses the United Nations International Gift Shop, a favorite for its diverse merchandise, much of it handmade around the world. You'll recognize the shop by the United States and United Nations flags out front. Check the bulletin board, or ask inside, for the park's calendar of events. If you need to rest, there's a pleasant spot with a few benches opposite the gift shop.

You will notice a cluster of small houses with red-tile roofs. They are the:

⓮ House of Pacific Relations International Cottages

These charming dollhouse cottages promote ethnic and cultural awareness and are open to the public on Sunday afternoons year-round. From March to October, there are lawn programs with folk dancing. See p. 138.

Take a quick peek into some of the cottages, and then keep heading south to see more of the park's museums; to your right is the notable:

⓯ San Diego Automotive Museum

Whether you're a gear-head into muscle cars or someone who appreciates the sculptural beauty of fine design, this museum has something for everyone. It features a changing roster of exhibits, as well as a permanent collection of fabulous wheels. See p. 140 for more information.

And the cylindrical:

⓰ San Diego Air & Space Museum

The museums in this part of the park operate in structures built for the 1935–36 Exposition. It is not necessary to walk all the way to the Air & Space Museum (located appropriately enough under the flight path to San Diego's airport), but it's one of San Diego's finest examples of Art Deco architecture. Across the parking lot on the left is the Hall of Champions Sports Museum, with another fun Niki de Saint Phalle sculpture in front. See p. 140 and 141.

Go back past the parking lot and the Organ Pavilion. Take a shortcut through the pavilion, exit directly opposite the stage, and follow the sidewalk to your right. Almost immediately, you'll come to the:

⓱ Japanese Friendship Garden

Only a small portion of this 12-acre canyon has been developed, but the part that has been incorporates beautifully serene, traditional Japanese elements. At the entrance is an attractive teahouse whose deck overlooks the entire ravine; there is a small meditation garden beside it. See p. 139.

Return to El Prado, which becomes a pedestrian mall
to the east of the El Cid sculpture. Set your sights on
the fountain at the end of the broad walkway and
head toward it. Stroll down the middle of El Prado to
get the full benefit of the lovely buildings on either
side. On weekends, you'll pass street musicians, artists, and clowns—one of their favorite haunts is
around the fountain.

The latticework building you see to the left is the:

18 Botanical Building & Lily Pond

An open-air conservatory, this delicate
wood lath structure dates to the 1915–16
Exposition, and is filled with 2,100 permanent plants, plus seasonal displays. Particularly noteworthy is the collection of cycads
and ferns. Admission is free, and the gardens are a cool retreat on a hot day. Directly
in front is the Lily Pond. See p. 138.

Back on El Prado, left of the Lily Pond, you'll see the:

19 Casa de Balboa

Inside, you'll find the Museum of Photographic Arts (p. 139), the Model Railroad
Museum (p. 142), and the Museum of San
Diego History (p. 139). Note the realistic-
looking bare-breasted figures atop the
Casa de Balboa. These shameless caryatids
were the perfect complement to the nudist
colony that temporarily sprouted as an
attraction in Zoro Garden—the canyon
immediately east of the building—during
the 1935–36 Exposition.

On the other side of El Prado, on your left, note the
ornate work on the:

20 Casa del Prado

While it doesn't house a museum, it's one
of the best—and most ornate—of the El
Prado buildings, featuring baroque Spanish Golden Age ornamentation.

At the end of El Prado, on either side of the fountain,
are two museums particularly appealing to children;
the first, on the right, is the:

21 Reuben H. Fleet Science Center

This science fun house has plenty of hands-
on attractions, as well as a giant-screen
IMAX theater. See p. 140 for a complete
review of this popular attraction.

To the left is the:

22 San Diego Natural History Museum

The original building that stood on this
spot burned to the ground in 1925—
hours before local firefighters were to
gather there for their annual gala. A new
structure, funded by the ever-generous
Ellen Browning Scripps, rose in 1933. In
2001, the museum more than doubled in
size with the completion of an ultramodern wing that springs from the building's
north side. See p. 142.

In the center of the Plaza de Balboa is the
high-spouting:

23 Bea Evenson Fountain

This fountain was added to the park in
1972, and was later named in honor of the
woman who formed the Committee of
100, a group dedicated to preserving the
park's architecture. It spouts water almost
60 feet into the air, but what makes it truly
unique is a wind regulator on top of the
Natural History Museum—as the wind
increases, the fountain's water pressure is
lowered so the water doesn't spray over the
edges. The 200-foot-wide fountain is especially beautiful at night when it's illumi-
nated by colored lights.

From here, use the pedestrian bridge to cross the
road and visit the nearly secret:

24 Gardens

They are tucked away on the other side of
the boulevard: to your left, a Desert Garden for plants at home in an arid landscape; to your right, the Inez Grant Parker

Memorial Rose Gardens, home to 2,400 roses. The World Rose Society voted the latter as one of the top 16 rose gardens in the world. Blooms peak March through May, but there are almost always some flowers visible, except in January and February when they are pruned. After you've enjoyed the flowers and plants, return to El Prado.

Just past the Natural History Museum, take a right. Behind the museum is another voluptuous Moreton Bay fig tree, planted in 1915 for the exposition; it's now more than 62 feet tall, with a canopy 100 feet in diameter.

Straight ahead is the quiet:

25 Spanish Village Art Center

Artists are at work here daily from 11am to 4pm. They create jewelry, paintings, and sculptures in tile-roofed studios around a courtyard. There are restrooms here, too.

Exit at the back of the Spanish Village Art Center and take the paved, palm-lined sidewalk that will take you past the:

26 Miniature Railroad and Carousel

The tiny train makes a 3-minute loop through the eucalyptus trees, while the charming 1910 carousel offers a ride atop hand-carved wood frogs, horses, and pigs. The train and carousel are open daily in summer, weekends the rest of the year.

To the left is the entrance to the world-famous:

27 San Diego Zoo

You can also retrace your steps and visit some of the tempting museums you just passed, saving the zoo for another day.

Bus tip: From here, you can walk out past the zoo parking lot to Park Boulevard; the bus stop (a brown-shingled kiosk) is on your right. The no. 7 bus will take you back to downtown San Diego.

WINDING DOWN
Back on El Prado (in the House of Hospitality), the **Prado Restaurant** (© **619/557-9441**) has a handsome view of the park from oversize windows and a great patio for outdoor dining. Far from your average park concession, the Prado boasts a zesty menu with colorful ethnic influences—plus inventive margaritas and Latin cocktails. Lunch starts daily at 11:30am (Sat–Sun at 11am), and a festive (expensive) dinner menu takes over at 5pm (daily except Mon; reservations advisable). In between, a long list of tapas will satisfy any hunger pangs.

Shopping

Whether you're looking for a souvenir, a gift, or a quick replacement for an item inadvertently left at home, you'll find no shortage of stores in San Diego. This is, after all, Southern California, where looking good is a high priority and shopping in sunny outdoor malls is a way of life.

---

1 THE SHOPPING SCENE

Okay, so San Diegans have embraced the suburban shopping mall with vigor. Many do the bulk of their shopping at two massive complexes in Mission Valley where every possible need is represented; downtown has even adopted the mall concept at whimsical Horton Plaza.

Local neighborhoods, on the other hand, offer specialty shopping that meets the needs—and mirrors the personality—of that part of town. For example, hip Hillcrest and Uptown neighborhoods are the place to go for offbeat boutiques, while conservative La Jolla offers many upscale traditional shops, especially jewelers. And don't forget that Mexico is only 20 minutes away; *tiendas* (stores) in Tijuana, Rosarito Beach, and Ensenada stock colorful crafts perfectly suited to the California lifestyle. Visitors head across the border each weekend in search of bargains and cheap margaritas.

Sales tax in San Diego is 7.75%; savvy out-of-state shoppers have larger items shipped directly home at the point of purchase, avoiding the tax.

---

2 THE TOP SHOPPING NEIGHBORHOODS

DOWNTOWN, THE GASLAMP & LITTLE ITALY

In the Gaslamp Quarter, high rents have led to the influx of deep-pocketed chains and brand names, such as **Adidas,** 926 Fifth Ave. (© 619/615-0287; www.shopadidas.com), **Urban Outfitters,** 665 Fifth Ave. (© 619/231-0102; www.urbanoutfitters.com), **Quiksilver,** 402 Fifth Ave. (© 619/234-3125; www.quiksilver.com), **American Apparel,** 840 Fifth Ave. (© 619/696-3409; www.americanapparel.net), and **G-Star,** 470 Fifth Ave. (© 619/238-7088; www.g-star.com). A few intrepid boutiques can still be found among the big retailers and the area's multitudinous eateries, though.

For hip and glamorous women's clothing and a great selection of jewelry, **Villa Moda,** 363 Fifth Ave. (© **619/236-9068;** www.villamoda.com), is a Gaslamp standout; **Bubbles Boutique,** 226 Fifth Ave. (© **619/236-9003;** www.bubblesboutique.com), is where you'll find all manner of handmade soap products, from Mary Jane hemp soap bars to banana shake–flavored bath "bombs." For an unusual gift for yourself or someone back home, pop into **Scott James,** 915 E St. (© **619/696-0910;** www.scottjameseastvillage. com); it's got everything from fashion accessories such as the very cool Harvey's seatbelt handbags to martini glasses. **HatWorks,** 433 E St. (© **619/234-0457**), has had a presence in downtown since 1922; if you've got a head, they have something to fit your style, from Stetson to Kangol. You can pamper your pooch with something from **Lucky Dog Pet Boutique,** 415 Market St. (© **619/696-0364;** www.shopluckydog.com), where you'll find supplies swank and chic: collars, snacks, soaps, and bowls.

Kita Ceramics & Glassware, 517 Fourth Ave. (© **619/239-2600;** www.kitaceramics glass.com), stocks fine Japanese pottery and colorful Italian glass products; **Vitreum,** 917 E St. (© **619/237-9810;** www.vitreum-us.com), is an artfully Zen shop that also sells glassware, as well home decor, tea sets, tableware, and jewelry. Although it can be found in many cities, **Design Within Reach,** 393 Seventh Ave. (© **619/744-9900;** www.dwr. com), is just too cool to pass by. DWR offers modern furniture and accessories from names including Knoll, Miller, and Eames.

You can continue your search for serious art, design, and home furnishings in Little Italy. The conglomeration of cool stores and galleries along Kettner Boulevard and India Street, from Laurel to Date streets, has become known as the **Kettner Art & Design District.** Throughout the year, Friday evening open-house events known as Kettner Nights are scheduled; for information, check www.littleitalysd.com/events. Among the district's highlights for modern furnishings and accessories are **Boomerang for Modern,** 2475 Kettner Blvd. (© **619/239-2040;** www.boomerangformodern.com); **Mixture,** 2210 Kettner Blvd. (© **619/239-4788;** www.mixturedesigns.com); and **DNA European Design Studio,** 1900 Columbia St. (© **619/235-6882;** www.dnaeuropeandesign. com). Look for fine art at **Scott White Contemporary Art,** 939 W. Kalmia St. (© **619/ 501-5689;** www.scottwhiteart.com), and **Noel-Baza Fine Art,** 2165 India St. (© **619/ 876-4160;** www.noel-bazafineart.com).

The nearby Fir Street Cottages are a quaint cluster of festively painted stores where the highlights include **Carol Gardyne,** 1840 Columbia St. (© **619/233-8066;** www.carol gardyne.com), which has hand-painted, one-of-a-kind silk scarves and wall hangings; and **Rosamariposa,** 611 W. Fir St. (© **619/237-8064;** www.rosamariposasd.com), stocking exotic (but responsibly crafted) baubles and bangles from Indonesia.

Downtown's two destination shopping centers are:

Horton Plaza ★ The Disneyland of shopping malls, Horton Plaza is the heart of the revitalized city center, bounded by Broadway, First and Fourth avenues, and G Street. Covering 6¹/₂ city blocks, the multilevel shopping center has more than 130 specialty shops and kiosks—there are clothing and shoe stores, fun shops for kids, and a bookstore. There's a performing arts venue (the Lyceum Theatre, home to the San Diego Repertory Theatre, p. 217), a 14-screen cinema, two major department stores, and a variety of restaurants and short-order eateries. Horton Plaza opened in 1985 to rave reviews and provided an initial catalyst for the Gaslamp Quarter's redevelopment. It's almost as much an attraction as SeaWorld or the San Diego Zoo, transcending its genre with a conglomeration of crisscrossing paths, bridges, towers, and piazzas.

Anchor stores are Macy's and Nordstrom, while name outlets such as Abercrombie & Fitch, Victoria's Secret, and Louis Vuitton are also in the mix; the top-level food court has a good variety of meal options. Three hours of free parking are available from 7am to 9pm; there are machines scattered throughout the mall where you can self-validate (validation in food court offered until 11pm). The lot is open 24 hours and costs $8 per hour. The parking levels are confusing, and temporarily losing your car is part of the Horton Plaza experience; if you need help or information, you can find a plaza concierge on the first level (Mon–Sat 11am–7pm, Sun 11am–6pm). Macy's also has a Visitor Information Center on the third floor, open daily 10am to 6pm. 324 Horton Plaza.

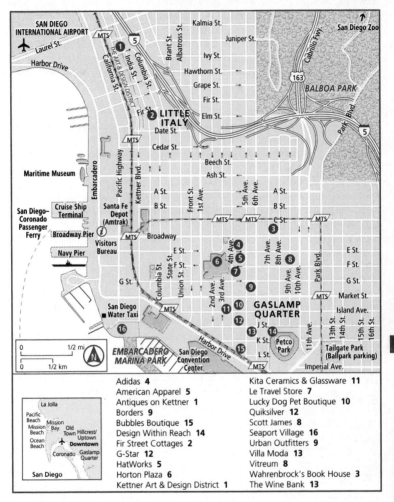

Adidas **4**
American Apparel **5**
Antiques on Kettner **1**
Borders **9**
Bubbles Boutique **15**
Design Within Reach **14**
Fir Street Cottages **2**
G-Star **12**
HatWorks **5**
Horton Plaza **6**
Kettner Art & Design District **1**

Kita Ceramics & Glassware **11**
Le Travel Store **7**
Lucky Dog Pet Boutique **10**
Quiksilver **12**
Scott James **8**
Seaport Village **16**
Urban Outfitters **9**
Villa Moda **13**
Vitreum **8**
Wahrenbrock's Book House **3**
The Wine Bank **13**

© **619/239-8180.** www.westfield.com/hortonplaza. Bus: 2, 3, 5, 7, 11, 15, 20, 30, 50, 120, 150, 210, 850, 860, 901, 923, 929, or 992. Trolley: Civic Center.

Seaport Village (**Kids**)   Designed as an ersatz Cape Cod community, this choice, 14-acre bayfront outdoor mall provides an idyllic setting that visitors love. Many of the more than 50 shops are of the Southern California cutesy variety, but the atmosphere is pleasant, and there are a few gems. Favorites include the **Tile Shop,** featuring hand-painted tiles from Mexico and beyond; **Best of San Diego,** where you can stock up on all your city-themed souvenir needs; and the **Upstart Crow** bookshop and coffeehouse, with the Crow's Nest children's bookstore inside. Other stores specialize in Scandinavian items, hammocks, travel accessories, and more. There are four sit-down restaurants and a variety of sidewalk eateries, and live music is often scheduled for weekend afternoons; the carousel, with its hand-carved menagerie dating from 1895, is a popular draw with families. You get 2 hours of free parking with purchase ($3 per hour thereafter). Open daily 10am to 9pm; restaurants have extended hours. 849 W. Harbor Dr. (at Kettner Blvd.). ℂ **619/235-4014.** www.seaportvillage.com. Trolley: Seaport Village.

HILLCREST & UPTOWN

Compact Hillcrest is an ideal shopping destination. As the hub of San Diego's gay and lesbian community, hip fashion and chic housewares are the order of the day here. There are plenty of establishments selling cool trinkets, used books, vintage clothing, and memorabilia; you'll also find a plethora of modestly priced globe-hopping dining options, too.

There's no defined zone in which shops are found, so you may as well start at the neighborhood's axis, the busy intersection of University and Fifth avenues. From this corner the greatest concentration of boutiques spreads for 1 or 2 blocks in each direction, but farther east on University—between 10th Avenue and Vermont Street—you'll find another aggregation of good options, especially in the home furnishing category. **Pomegranate Home,** 1037 University Ave. (ℂ 619/220-0225; www.pomegranate.signon sandiego.com), has got you covered for modern home accessories; **Co-Habitat,** 1433 University Ave. (ℂ **619/688-1390;** www.cohabitathome.com), has colorful decor and textiles from India; and **Nativa,** 1003 University Ave. (ℂ **619/299-4664;** www.nativa-online.com), has a huge showroom with sumptuous furniture made mostly from plantation-grown South American wood. On the other side of University Avenue is a small shopping complex where the highlight is the contemporary clothing store **Studio 1220,** 1220 Cleveland Ave. (ℂ **619/220-7344;** www.studio1220.com).

Street parking is available; most meters run 2 hours and devour quarters at a rate of one every 12 minutes, so be armed with plenty of change. You can also park in a lot—rates vary, but you'll come out ahead if you're planning to stroll for several hours.

If you're looking for postcards or provocative gifts, step into wacky **Babette Schwartz,** 421 University Ave. (ℂ **619/220-7048;** www.babette.com), a pop-culture emporium named for a local drag queen and located under the can't-miss HILLCREST street sign. You'll find books, clothing, and kitsch accessories. A couple of doors away, **Cathedral,** 435 University Ave. (ℂ **619/296-4046;** www.shopcathedral.com), is stocked with candles of all scents and shapes, plus unusual holders.

If all this walking is wearing a hole in your shoes, you can get a pair of urban-fabulous sneakers at **Mint,** 525 University Ave. (ℂ **619/291-6468**); then march yourself over to **Kingdom,** 3696 Fifth Ave. (ℂ **619/298-5464;** www.kingdomsandiego.com), for some trendy threads to go along with your new shoes. Headgear—from straw hats to knit caps to classy fedoras—fills the **Village Hat Shop,** 3821 Fourth Ave. (ℂ **619/683-5533;** www. villagehatshop.com); there's also a mini-museum of stylishly displayed vintage hats.

Lovers of rare and used books will want to poke around the **used bookstores** on Fifth Avenue, between University and Robinson avenues. Though their number has decreased with the advent of online shopping, you can always find something to pique your interest. This block is also home to **Wear It Again Sam,** 3823 Fifth Ave., north of Robinson (ℂ **619/299-0185;** www.wearitagainsamvintage.com). This classy step back in time sells quality vintage clothing—for both men and women—from the 1920s through the 1950s.

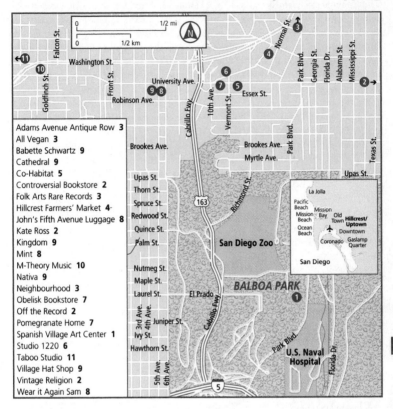

Adams Avenue Antique Row **3**
All Vegan **3**
Babette Schwartz **9**
Cathedral **9**
Co-Habitat **5**
Controversial Bookstore **2**
Folk Arts Rare Records **3**
Hillcrest Farmers' Market **4**
John's Fifth Avenue Luggage **8**
Kate Ross **2**
Kingdom **9**
Mint **8**
M-Theory Music **10**
Nativa **9**
Neighbourhood **3**
Obelisk Bookstore **7**
Off the Record **2**
Pomegranate Home **7**
Spanish Village Art Center **1**
Studio 1220 **6**
Taboo Studio **11**
Village Hat Shop **9**
Vintage Religion **2**
Wear it Again Sam **8**

To the north and east of Hillcrest are University Heights and North Park, which are brimming with interesting shops. You'll find independent-minded boutiques such as **Neighbourhood,** 4496 Park Blvd. (© **619/296-2100;** www.neighbourhoodboutique. com), **Kate Ross,** 3013 University Ave. (© **619/688-1088;** www.shopkateross.com), and **All Vegan,** 4669 Park Blvd. (© **619/299-4669;** www.allveganshopping.com), which offers cruelty-free clothing and accessories; there are also unusual gift stores such as **Vintage Religion,** 3821 32nd St. (© **619/280-8408;** www.vintagereligion.com), selling jewelry, apparel, and collectibles inspired by global religions and cultures.

Running east from where Park Boulevard T-bones Adams Avenue is **Adams Avenue Antique Row.** It doesn't have the concentration of antiques stores it once had, but along with vintage-clothing boutiques and dusty used book and record shops, there are plenty of coffeehouses, pubs, and small restaurants to enliven the excursion. The district stretches a couple miles from Arizona Street to Normal Heights, so it's best tackled by car. For more information, contact the **Adams Avenue Business Association** (© **619/282-7329;** www.adamsaveonline.com).

Old Town State Historic Park features restored historic sites and adobe structures, a number of which now house shops that cater to tourists. Many have a "general-store" theme and carry gourmet treats and inexpensive Mexican crafts alongside the obligatory T-shirts, baseball caps, and other San Diego–emblazoned souvenirs. **Plaza del Pasado,** 2754 Calhoun St. (℗ **619/297-3100;** www.plazadelpasado.com), maintains the park's old *Californio* theme, and features nearly a dozen specialty shops, and three restaurants. Costumed employees, special events and activities, and strolling musicians add to the festive flavor. *Note:* As of this writing, Plaza del Pasado was undergoing a change of ownership; it's unknown which stores will stay and which will go. Regardless, this quaint courtyard with its shady arcades is worth a peek.

There's also plenty of shopping outside the park, too. **Bazaar del Mundo,** 4133 Taylor St. (℗ **619/296-3161;** www.bazaardelmundo.com), has a collection of stores featuring Mexican and Latin American folk art, accessories, and clothing; Old Town's best spot for Mexican collectibles, though, is **Miranda's Courtyard,** 2548 Congress St. (℗ **619/296-6611**). For a huge selection of Southwestern art, jewelry, and fashion, make a bead for **Apache,** 2425 San Diego Ave. (℗ **619/296-9226**). Photography is strongly represented in Old Town at **Gallery Old Town,** 2513 San Diego Ave. (℗ **619/296-7877**), and **Chuck Jones' Studio Gallery Old Town,** 2501 San Diego Ave. (℗ **619/294-9880;** www.chuckjones.com). Gallery Old Town deals in limited-edition photos from the archives of *LIFE* magazine; Chuck Jones' Gallery features classic Hollywood glamour shots and animation cels by the likes of Dr. Seuss and Jones himself, who was creator of Bugs Bunny.

Mission Valley is home to two giant malls, **Fashion Valley Center** (p. 211) and **Mission Valley Center** (p. 212), with more than enough stores to satisfy any shopper, and free parking—both can be reached via the San Diego Trolley from downtown. Book lovers will find local outposts of **Barnes & Noble,** 7610 Hazard Center Dr. (℗ **619/220-0175;** www.barnesandnoble.com), and **Borders,** 1072 Camino del Rio N. (℗ **619/295-2201;** www.borders.com).

MISSION BAY & THE BEACHES

The beach communities offer laid-back shopping, with plenty of surf shops, recreational gear, and casual garb. If you're looking for something more distinctive than T-shirts and shorts, you'd best head east to Mission Valley or north to La Jolla.

For women in need of a new bikini, the best selection is at **Pilar's,** 3745 Mission Blvd., Pacific Beach (℗ **858/488-3056;** www.pilarsbeachwear.com), where choices range from stylish designer numbers to suits inspired by surf- and skate-wear. Across the street is **Liquid Foundation Surf Shop,** 3731 Mission Blvd. (℗ **858/488-3260**), which specializes in board shorts for guys. For affordable shoes, check out the **Skechers Footwear Outlet,** 4475 Mission Blvd. (℗ **858/581-6010;** www.skechers.com), at the corner of Garnet Avenue.

In Pacific Beach, **Pangaea Outpost,** 909 Garnet Ave. (℗ **858/581-0555;** www.pangaeaoutpost.com), gathers more than 60 diverse shops under one roof; while San Diego's greatest concentration of antiques stores is found in the **Ocean Beach Antique District** (www.obantiquedistrict.com), along the 4800 block of Newport Avenue, the community's main drag. Several of the stores are mall-style, featuring dozens of dealers under one roof, and although you won't find a horde of pricey, centuries-old European antiques, the overall quality is high enough to make it interesting for any collector. Most of the O.B. antiques stores are open daily from 10am to 6pm, with somewhat reduced hours Sunday.

If you've come to O.B. for that hippie vibe, you can find it alive and well at **The Black,** 5017 Newport Ave. (© **619/222-5498**), an old-fashioned head shop that's a local institution, and **Falling Sky Pottery,** 1951 Abbott St. (© **619/226-6820**), a collective of potters that's been around since the late 1960s.

LA JOLLA

It's clear from the look of La Jolla's village that shopping is a major pastime in this upscale community. Precious gems and pearl necklaces sparkle in their cases, luxurious Persian rugs await your caress, crystal goblets prism the light—even if you're not in the market for any of it, it makes for great window-shopping.

The clothing boutiques tend to be conservative and costly (and mostly geared toward women), like those lining Girard and Prospect streets, such as **Ann Taylor, Armani Exchange, Polo Ralph Lauren, Nicole Miller,** and **Sigi Boutique.** But you'll also find less pricey venues including **Talbots, Banana Republic,** and **American Apparel.**

Laura Gambucci, 7629 Girard Ave., Ste. C3 (© **858/551-0214**), bucks the staid trend with contemporary apparel for women; and **La Jolla Fiber Arts,** 7644 Girard Ave. (© **858/454-6732;** www.lajollafiberarts.com), features hand-woven creations that make the store something of an art gallery and a fashion outlet. A sexy, glamorous local line of bathing suits (for her and him) is at **Sauvage,** 1025 Prospect St. (© **858/729-0015;** www.sauvagewear.com); **Blondstone Jewelry Studio,** 925 Prospect St. (© **858/456-1994;** www.blondstone.com), has locally made designs as well, producing adornments that incorporate seashells and tumbled sea-glass "mermaid tears." **Emilia Castillo,** 1273 Prospect St. (© **858/551-9600;** www.emiliacastillolajolla.com), is where you'll find the work of a silversmith based in Taxco, Mexico, who forges one-of-a-kind pieces of jewelry and home decor.

Midcentury modernism meets Hello Kitty at **My Own Space,** 7840 Girard Ave. (© **866/607-7223** or 858/459-0099; www.mosmyownspace.com); **Ligne Roset,** 7726 Girard Ave. (© **858/454-3366;** www.ligne-roset-usa.com), features minimalist furniture in a showroom that had previously been one of the last single-screen theaters in San Diego; and **Vetro Collections,** 7605 Girard Ave. (© **858/729-0045;** www.vetrocollections. com), has a rainbow collection of vintage, handblown glass from America, Italy, and Scandinavia. History buffs should not miss **Ruderman Antique Maps,** 1298 Prospect St., Ste. 2C (© **858/551-8500;** www.raremaps.com), which sells maps, atlases, and books that date from the 15th through 19th centuries.

There are also more than 20 art galleries in La Jolla village. Although most won't appeal to serious collectors, there are plenty of crowd-pleasers such as the rock photography at **Morrison Hotel Gallery,** 1230 Prospect St. (© **858/551-0835;** www.morrison hotelgallery.com); the sensuous landscape photography at **Peter Lik Gallery,** 1205 Prospect St. (© **858/200-0990;** www.peterlik.com); and **Africa & Beyond,** 1250 Prospect St. (© **800/422-3742** or 858/454-9983; www.africaandbeyond.com), with its contemporary and traditional African sculpture, textiles, jewelry, and furnishings. Off the beaten tourist path is **Quint Contemporary Art,** 7739 Fay Ave. (entrance on Drury Lane; © **858/454-3409;** www.quintgallery.com), one of the best contemporary art galleries in the city.

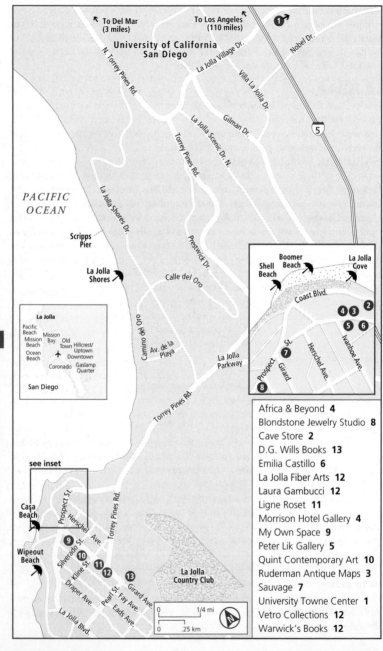

SHOPPING

9

THE TOP SHOPPING NEIGHBORHOODS

Africa & Beyond **4**
Blondstone Jewelry Studio **8**
Cave Store **2**
D.G. Wills Books **13**
Emilia Castillo **6**
La Jolla Fiber Arts **12**
Laura Gambucci **12**
Ligne Roset **11**
Morrison Hotel Gallery **4**
My Own Space **9**
Peter Lik Gallery **5**
Quint Contemporary Art **10**
Ruderman Antique Maps **3**
Sauvage **7**
University Towne Center **1**
Vetro Collections **12**
Warwick's Books **12**

A unique experience awaits at the **Cave Store,** 1325 Coast Blvd., just off Prospect Street (© **858/459-0746;** www.cavestore.com). This cliff-top shop is equal parts art gallery and antiques store, but the main attraction is the **Sunny Jim Cave,** a large sea cave reached by a steep, narrow staircase that was tunneled through the rock more than 100 years ago; admission is $4 for adults, $3 for kids 3 to 16, free for 2 and under.

CORONADO

This rather insular, conservative Navy community doesn't have many stellar shopping opportunities; the best of the lot line Orange Avenue at the southwestern end of the island. You'll find some scattered housewares and home-decor boutiques, several small women's boutiques, and the gift shops at Coronado's major resorts.

There is an excellent independent bookshop, **Bay Books,** 1029 Orange Ave. (© **619/435-0070;** www.baybookscoronado.com), which carries a selection in many categories, plus volumes of local historical interest, books on tape, and Mexican and European magazines. **La Provençale,** 1126 Orange Ave. (© **619/437-8881**), is a little shop stocked with fabric, tablecloths, pottery, and tableware items from the French countryside; nearby **In Good Taste,** 1146 Orange Ave. (© **619/435-8356**), has a small but choice selection of gourmet gift items—in addition to a tempting display of luscious truffles and sweets. And, if you're in pursuit of swimwear, poke your head into **Dale's Swim Shop,** 1150 Orange Ave. (© **619/435-7301**), a tiny boutique jampacked with suits to fit all bodies, including styles from European makers seldom available in this country.

Ferry Landing Marketplace Approached by ferry, the entrance is impressive— turreted red rooftops with jaunty blue flags that draw closer to you as the boat pulls in. As you stroll up the pier, you'll find yourself in the midst of about 20 souvenir shops and galleries filled with gifts, jewelry, and crafts. You can get a quick bite to eat or have a leisurely dinner with a view, wander along landscaped walkways, or laze on a beach or grassy bank. Open daily 10am to 7pm or later. There's also a farmers' market every Tuesday from 2:30 to 6pm. 1201 First St. (at B Ave.), Coronado. © **619/435-8895.** www.coronado ferrylandingshops.com. Bus: 904. Ferry: From Broadway Pier. Take I-5 to Coronado Bay Bridge, to B Ave., and turn right.

ELSEWHERE IN SAN DIEGO COUNTY

The **Cedros Design District** ★★, along the 100 and 200 blocks of South Cedros Avenue in Solana Beach, is an outstanding place for designer interior decorating goods. Many of the shops are housed in a row of Quonset huts that were once used by a company that made photographic equipment for spy planes. Today, you can find more than two dozen chic shops selling furniture, original art, imported goods, home decor, antiques, and clothing, plus a couple of good cafes. The strip is located just north of the Del Mar racetrack; reach it by taking the Via de la Valle exit off I-5 and going right on Cedros Avenue. The Coaster commuter train stops at the Solana Beach station next to the district.

Garden fanciers will find North County the best hunting grounds for bulbs, seeds, and starter cuttings. **North County nurseries** are known throughout the state for rare and hard-to-find plants—notably begonias, orchids, bromeliads, succulents, ranunculuses, and unusual herbs. For more information on the area's largest growers, the **Flower Fields at Carlsbad Ranch,** and **Weidners' Gardens,** see chapter 11.

Large stores and shops in malls tend to stay open until about 9pm on weekdays, 6pm on weekends. Smaller businesses usually close at 5 or 6pm or may keep odd hours. When in doubt, call ahead.

ANTIQUES

See also the "Hillcrest & Uptown" and "Mission Bay & the Beaches" sections in "The Top Shopping Neighborhoods," earlier in this chapter.

Antiques on Kettner　Nearly 30 individual dealers share this space, offering a wide selection of antiques and collectibles, including artwork, pottery, and glassware. Open daily 10am to 6pm (closed Tues). 2400 Kettner Blvd., Ste. 106, Little Italy. ✆ **619/234-3332.** www.antiquesonkettner.com. Bus: 83.

Newport Avenue Antique Center & Coffee House　With 18,000 square feet of retail, this is the big daddy of the Ocean Beach Antique District malls—it even has a small espresso bar. One corner is a haven for collectors of 1940s and 1950s kitchenware; there's also a fine selection of vintage linens and chinoiserie. Open daily 10am to 6pm; reduced hours on Sunday. 4864 Newport Ave., Ocean Beach. ✆ **619/222-8686.** www.obantique district.com. Bus: 35 or 923.

ART & CRAFTS

While San Diego is not known as a powerhouse art city, you'll find some 25 galleries in La Jolla village alone; downtown, Little Italy, and North Park also offer a concentration of galleries. To get an overview of North Park's alternative art spaces, consider the **North Park Nights** gallery crawl, scheduled the third Saturday of every month (www.north parknights.org).

Four Winds Trading Company　Located in the heart of Old Town, this shop has a bevy of authentic Native American crafts. Browse among pottery (including the sought-after Mata Ortiz), oil and watercolor paintings (originals and prints), silversmith products (Zuni, Kumeyaay, Navajo, Isleta Pueblo), rugs, kachinas, and baskets. Open daily 10am to 9pm. 2448 San Diego Ave., Old Town. ✆ **619/692-0466.** www.fourwinds.signonsan diego.com. Bus: Numerous Old Town routes, including 8, 9, 10, 14, 28, or 30. Trolley: Old Town.

Joseph Bellows Gallery ★★　Devotees of photography will want to check out this gallery showcasing both contemporary and vintage work. Solo and group shows are presented on an ongoing basis. Open Tuesday to Friday 10am to 5pm, Saturday 11am to 5pm. 7661 Girard Ave., La Jolla. ✆ **858/456-5620.** www.josephbellows.com. Bus: 30.

Spanish Village Art Center ★　Spanish Village is a collection of 37 charming and historic casitas set around a colorful courtyard in Balboa Park. Dating from the 1935–36 California-Pacific Exposition, the structures today are home to more than 250 artists specializing in various mediums, including oil and watercolor painting, pottery, jewelry, metal art, origami, fused and blown glass, woodcarving, and wearable art. Many of the artists work on-site, allowing you to see their products in the making. Open daily 11am to 4pm. 1770 Village Place, Balboa Park. ✆ **619/233-9050.** www.spanishvillageart.com. Bus: 7.

Taboo Studio ★★★　This impressive gallery exhibits and sells the work of jewelry designers from throughout the United States. Focusing on jewelry as wearable art, these are one-of-a-kind pieces and limited editions, made from a variety of materials. Four

major exhibitions are usually held each year. Open Tuesday through Friday, 11am to
6pm, Saturday 10am to 5pm. 1615½ W. Lewis St., Mission Hills. © **619/692-0099.** www.
taboostudio.com.

Tasende Gallery ★★   You probably won't walk away with a newly purchased Louise
Nevelson or Fernando Botero, but a detour into this museum-like sculpture gallery is
well worth your time. The calm and serenity, coupled with the modern architecture,
provide a great respite from the commercial hubbub nearby. Open Tuesday to Friday
10am to 6pm, Saturday 11am to 5pm. 820 Prospect St., La Jolla. © **858/454-3691.** www.
tasendegallery.com. Bus: 30.

BOOKS

For travel-related books, also note the shops listed under "Travel Accessories," below.

Barnes & Noble   The main San Diego branch of this book discounter sits amid one
of Mission Valley's smaller malls, Hazard Center, just off Friar's Road (east of Hwy. 163).
Besides a wide selection of paperback and hardcover titles, it offers a comprehensive
periodicals rack. Open daily 10am to 9pm. 7610 Hazard Center Dr., Mission Valley. © **619/
220-0175.** www.bn.com. Trolley: Hazard Center.

Borders   This full-service bookstore offers discounts on many titles. Borders also
stocks a stylish line of greeting cards and encourages browsing; there's an adjoining coffee
lounge. Of the two locations, the Mission Valley store is slightly larger. The downtown
location is open Monday to Thursday 10am to 9pm, Friday to Saturday 10am to 10pm,
Sunday 11am to 8pm; the Mission Valley store has slightly longer hours. 668 Sixth Ave.,
downtown. © **619/702-4200.** 1072 Camino del Rio N., Mission Valley. © **619/295-2201.** www.
borders.com. Bus: 3, 11, or 992 (downtown). Trolley: Gaslamp Quarter (downtown); Mission
Valley Center (Mission Valley).

Controversial Bookstore ★   San Diego's oldest metaphysical and spiritual bookstore started out in 1963, originally heavy on conspiracy and political tomes, as far right
and far left as possible—hence the moniker. The store has evolved to embrace books on
healing and alternative medicine, magic and witchcraft, astrology, UFO studies, women's
issues, and spiritual pathways. It also stocks crystals, New Age music, incense, and jewelry.
Open Monday to Friday 10am to 7pm, Saturday 10am to 6pm, Sunday 11am to 5pm.
3063 University Ave., North Park. © **619/296-1560.** www.controversialbookstore.com. Bus: 7.

D.G. Wills Books ★★   This bookstore has tomes stacked to its wood rafters—if
you're looking for something scholarly, offbeat, or esoteric, this place is for you. Over the
years this charmingly musty La Jolla treasure has hosted readings by such powerhouses as
Norman Mailer, Gore Vidal, Allen Ginsberg, and Maureen Dowd. Open Monday to
Saturday 10am to 7pm, Sunday 11am to 6pm. 7461 Girard Ave., La Jolla. © **858/456-1800.**
www.dgwillsbooks.com. Bus: 30.

Obelisk Bookstore   This is San Diego's main gay and lesbian bookstore. You'll find
just about every gay magazine there is, as well as gay-themed movies for rent on DVD
and video. It's also a clearinghouse for info on local LGBT events. Open Monday to
Thursday 10am to 9pm, Friday and Saturday 10am to 10pm, Sunday 11am to 9pm.
1029 University Ave., Hillcrest. © **619/297-4171.** www.obeliskbookstore.com. Bus: 1, 10, or 11.

Wahrenbrock's Book House ★★★   If you live for the thrill of the hunt, love to
lose yourself in a maze of books covering almost every conceivable topic, you'll want to
spend some time at Wahrenbrock's. This is San Diego's oldest and largest independent

bookseller—a three-story playground for bibliophiles. It's especially known for its collection of first editions. Open Tuesday through Saturday 9:30am to 5:30pm. 726 Broadway, downtown. ℰ 800/315-8643 or 619/232-0132. Bus: Numerous downtown routes, including 2, 7, or 923. Trolley: Fifth Avenue.

Warwick's Books ★ This popular family-run bookstore is a browser's delight, with more than 40,000 titles, a large travel section, gifts, cards, and stationery. The Warwick family has been in the book and stationery business since 1896. The La Jolla store was established in the mid-1930s, and the fourth generation is now involved with the store's day-to-day operation. Authors come in for readings several times a month. Open Monday to Saturday 9am to 6pm, Sunday 11am to 5pm. 7812 Girard Ave., La Jolla. ℰ 858/454-0347. www.warwicks.com. Bus: 30.

DEPARTMENT STORES

You'll find plenty of major retailers in large shopping centers that provide ample opportunity to browse for gifts, mementos, or necessities.

Bloomingdale's This venerable department store, founded in 1872, made its way to San Diego and the upscale Fashion Valley mall in 2006. Designers such as Tommy Hilfiger, Donna Karan, and Ralph Lauren got their first big exposure through the chain, which operates 40 stores around the country. The store's cafe, **59th & Lex,** offers a full menu. Hours may vary, but usually Monday to Saturday 10am to 9pm, Sunday 11am to 7pm. Fashion Valley Center, Mission Valley. ℰ 619/610-6400. www.bloomingdales.com. Bus: 6, 14, 20, 25, 41, 120, or 928. Trolley: Fashion Valley.

Macy's This comprehensive store has a number of local branches, carrying clothing for women, men, and children, as well as housewares, electronics, and luggage. Besides downtown at Horton Plaza, Macy's also has stores at Fashion Valley Center, two in Mission Valley Center (including a housewares-only store), University Towne Center La Jolla, Carlsbad, and North County Fair (Escondido). Open Monday to Friday 10am to 9pm, Saturday 10am to 8pm, Sunday 11am to 7pm. Horton Plaza, downtown. ℰ 619/231-4747. www.macys.com. Bus: 2, 3, 7, 11, 15, 20, 30, 50, 120, 150, 210, 850, 860, 901, 923, 929, or 992. Trolley: Civic Center.

Nordstrom A San Diego favorite, Nordstrom is best known for its outstanding customer service and fine selection of shoes. It features a variety of stylish fashions and accessories for women, men, and children. Tailoring is done on the premises, and there's a full-service restaurant on the top floor. Nordstrom also has stores at Fashion Valley Center, University Towne Center, and North County Fair (Escondido), and there's an outlet store—Nordstrom Rack—in the Mission Valley Shopping Center. Open Monday to Friday 10am to 9pm, Saturday 10am to 8pm, Sunday 11am to 7pm. Horton Plaza, downtown. ℰ 619/239-1700. www.nordstrom.com. Bus/Trolley: Same as Macy's above.

FARMERS' MARKETS

We love our open-air markets. Throughout the county more than two dozen regularly scheduled street fests are stocked with the freshest fruits and vegetables from Southern California farms, augmented by crafts, fresh-cooked ethnic foods, flower stands, and other surprises. San Diego County produces more than $1 billion worth of fruits, flowers, and other crops each year. Avocados, known locally as "green gold," are the most profitable crop and have been grown here for more than 100 years. Citrus fruit follows close behind, and flowers are the area's third most important crop; ranunculus bulbs from here are sent all over the world, as are the famous Ecke poinsettias.

Here's a schedule of noteworthy farmers' markets—you can also check with the San Diego Farm Bureau (✆ 760/745-3023; www.sdfarmbureau.org).

There are four farmers' markets **downtown.** One is a seasonal affair, held in the square just north of Horton Plaza, running March through October on Thursdays from 11am to 3pm; call ✆ 760/741-3763 for information. The East Village market, Eighth Avenue and Market Street, is every Saturday from 8am to 2pm; ✆ 619/232-1480 or www. evfarmersmarket.com. The Third Avenue market, specializing in Asian goods, takes place between Island Avenue and J Street. It runs throughout the year on Sundays from 9am to 1pm; call ✆ 619/279-0032 for details. The Little Italy Mercato (✆ 619/233-3769; www.littleitalymercato.com) is on Saturdays, 9am to 1:30pm, along Date Street, between India and Columbia streets.

In **Hillcrest,** the market runs Sundays from 9am to 1pm at the corner of Normal Street and Lincoln Avenue, 1 block north of University Avenue. The atmosphere is festive, and exotic culinary delights reflect the eclectic neighborhood. For more information, call ✆ 619/237-1632.

La Jolla also has a Sunday market. It's held on the playground at La Jolla Elementary School, 7335 Girard Ave., from 9am to 1pm. Call ✆ 858/454-1699 for more information, or go to www.lajollamarket.com.

In **Ocean Beach,** a fun-filled market is held Wednesday evenings between 4 and 7pm (until 8pm in summer) along the 4900 block of Newport Avenue. In addition to fresh-cut flowers, produce, and exotic fruits and foods laid out for sampling, the market features art and entertainment. For more information, call ✆ 619/279-0032, or check www.oceanbeachsandiego.com.

Head to **Pacific Beach** on Saturday from 8am to noon, when Mission Boulevard between Reed Avenue and Pacific Beach Drive is transformed into a bustling marketplace. Call ✆ 760/741-3763 for more information.

In **Coronado,** every Tuesday afternoon the Ferry Landing hosts a produce and crafts market from 2:30 to 6pm; call ✆ 760/741-3763 for more details.

FLEA MARKETS

Kobey's Swap Meet (Value) Since 1976, this gigantic open-air market positioned at the west end of the San Diego Sports Arena parking lot has been a bargain-hunter's dream come true. Some 1,000 vendors fill row after row with new and used clothing, jewelry, electronics, hardware, appliances, furniture, collectibles, crafts, antiques, auto accessories, toys, and books. There's produce, too, along with food stalls and restrooms. Although Kobey's is open Friday, the weekend is when the good stuff is out—and it goes quickly, so arrive early. Open Friday to Sunday 7am to 3pm. San Diego Sports Arena, 3500 Sports Arena Blvd. ✆ 619/226-0650. www.kobeyswap.com. Admission Fri 50¢; Sat and Sun $1, free for children 11 and under. Take I-8 W. to Sports Arena Blvd. turnoff, or I-5 to Rosecrans St. and turn right on Sports Arena Blvd.

MALLS

See p. 200 for details on **Horton Plaza;** also see "Outlet Malls," p. 213.

Fashion Valley Center The Mission Valley corridor, running east-west about 2 miles north of downtown along I-8, is where you'll find San Diego's major shopping centers. Fashion Valley is the most attractive and most upscale, with six anchor stores: **Saks Fifth Avenue, Neiman Marcus, Nordstrom, Bloomingdale's, Macy's,** and **JCPenney** (most of which keep extended hours). There are also some 200 specialty shops and eateries, and an 18-screen AMC movie theater. Other noteworthy shops include **H&M, Jimmy Choo, M.A.C, Louis Vuitton, Michael Kors, Tiffany & Co.,** and **Bose.** Open Monday to Saturday 10am to 9pm and Sunday 11am to 7pm. 7007 Friars Rd. ✆ 619/688-9113. www.simon.com. Bus: 6, 14, 20, 25, 41, 120, or 928. Trolley: Fashion Valley. Hwy. 163 to Friars Rd. W.

Mission Valley Center This old-fashioned outdoor mall predates sleek Fashion Valley and has found a niche with budget-minded stores such as **Loehmann's, Nordstrom Rack,** and **Target;** you'll also find **Macy's Home & Furniture, West Elm, Sport Chalet,** and **Bed Bath & Beyond.** There's a 20-screen AMC movie theater and 150 other stores and places to eat. Across from the center to the north and west are separate complexes that feature Saks Fifth Avenue's **Off Fifth** (an outlet store), **Borders,** and more. Open Monday to Saturday 10am to 9pm and Sunday 11am to 6pm. 1640 Camino del Rio N. ✆ 619/296-6375. www.westfield.com/missionvalley. Bus: 6 or 14. Trolley: Mission Valley Center. I-8 to Mission Center Rd.

University Towne Center (UTC) This outdoor shopping complex is in La Jolla, east of the university. It has a landscaped plaza and more than 150 stores and dining spots, including some big ones such as **Nordstrom, Sears,** and **Macy's.** It is also home to an **Apple Store;** a year-round ice-skating rink, **Ice Town;** and an outlet of Encinitas-based **Chuao Chocolatier,** a fabulous artisan chocolate shop. It's open Monday through Friday 10am to 9pm, Saturday 10am to 8pm, and Sunday 11am to 7pm. 4545 La Jolla Village Dr. ✆ 858/546-8858. www.westfield.com/utc. Bus: 30, 31, 48, 49, 50, 89, 101, 105, 150, 310, 921, or 960. I-5 to La Jolla Village Dr. and go east, or I-805 to La Jolla Village Dr. and go west.

MUSIC

Folk Arts Rare Records ★★★ Nirvana for serious jazz, folk, blues, and country collectors. Operated since 1967 by local legend Lou Curtiss, it offers a huge selection of 78s and first-edition rarities on vinyl, most of them fairly priced. If you're not a collector or don't have a turntable, the store specializes in creating custom recordings of the vintage music on CD or cassette. Monday to Friday 9am to 5pm, Saturday and Sunday 10am to 6pm. 2881 Adams Ave., Normal Heights. ✆ 619/282-7833. www.folkartsrarerecords.com. Bus: 11.

Lou's Records ★★★ A mind-blowing place for collectors or anyone just seriously into music or movies. Located in Encinitas, about 30 minutes north of downtown, Lou's has a building devoted to new and import CDs, one to used CDs and vinyl, and yet another catering to DVD and VHS fanatics. You can even buy turntable styluses and cartridges here. Open Monday to Thursday 10am to 7pm, Friday 10am to 10pm, Saturday 10am to 9pm, Sunday 11am to 7pm. 434 Hwy. 101, Encinitas. ✆ 888/568-7732 or 760/753-1382. www.lousrecords.com. Bus: 101.

M-Theory Music ★ Offers CDs and vinyl (as well as DVDs) in an eclectic range of genres, from indie rock to old-school R&B. M-Theory also hosts lots of in-store band appearances. Open Monday to Saturday 10am to 10pm, Sunday 11am to 7pm. 915 W. Washington St., Mission Hills. ✆ 619/220-0485. www.mtheorymusic.com. Bus: 10 or 83.

Off the Record This small independent shop is a longtime San Diego fixture. It relocated several years ago to the up-and-coming neighborhood of North Park. You'll find a good selection of new and used CDs and vinyl; plus there's lots of other fun stuff in the surrounding blocks. Daily 11am to 8pm. 2912 University Ave., North Park. ✆ 619/298-4755. www.offtherecordmusic.com.

Carlsbad Premium Outlets ★★★   With some 90 stores, this mall includes favorites such as **Barneys New York, Crate & Barrel, Converse, Juicy Couture,** and **Swarovski.** The mall also has several specialty shops, including locally based **Thousand Mile Outdoor Wear;** there's also a fine-dining restaurant on-site. These outlets are located 32 miles north of downtown San Diego, close to LEGOLAND. Open Monday to Saturday 10am to 9pm, Sunday 10am to 7pm. 5600 Paseo del Norte. ℂ **888/790-7467** or 760/804-9000. www.premiumoutlets.com. I-5 N. to Palomar Rd. exit; the mall is next to the freeway.

Las Americas ★   This outlet mall, San Diego's largest, is located in San Ysidro, immediately north of the Tijuana border crossing. Currently home to more than 125 stores, including **Neiman Marcus, Nike, Banana Republic, Guess, bebe,** and the **Disney Store,** it's located 16 miles south of downtown. Open Monday to Saturday 10am to 9pm and Sunday 10am to 7pm. 4211 Camino de la Plaza ℂ **619/934-8400.** www.lasamericas. com. Trolley: San Ysidro. I-5 S. to Camino de la Plaza, the last U.S. exit; go right at the light.

Viejas Outlet Center ★★   More discount name-brand shopping is found at the Viejas Casino, east of El Cajon. Here you'll find **Vans, Eddie Bauer, Gap, Nike, Perry Ellis,** and **Polo Ralph Lauren**—40-plus stores in all. Tuesdays are Senior Citizen Days, with additional discounts at some stores. There is also nightly entertainment at the Showcourt with pyrotechnics, music, and an interactive fountain—and if that's not enough, there's a casino next door. Viejas is about 30 miles east of downtown. Open Monday to Saturday 10am to 8pm and Sunday 11am to 7pm. 5005 Willows Rd., Alpine. ℂ **619/659-2070.** www.shopviejas.com. Bus: 864 or 888. I-8 E. to Willows Rd. exit; turn left and follow the signs to Viejas Casino.

TOYS

Apple Box Toys ★   Batteries are not included here. Apple Box, one of the original stores at downtown's Seaport Village, specializes in wooden toys. You'll find everything from puzzles and pull toys to rocking horses and toy chests. The items can be personalized with names, slogans, whatever you want (they can even do it in Hebrew). Open daily 10am to 9pm. 837 W. Harbor Dr., Ste. C, Embarcadero. ℂ **800/676-7529.** www.appleboxtoys. com. Trolley: Seaport Village.

TRAVEL ACCESSORIES

John's Fifth Avenue Luggage ★★   This San Diego institution carries just about everything you can imagine in the way of luggage, travel accessories, computer cases, handbags, and wallets; there's on-premises luggage repair, too. Open Monday to Friday 9am to 5:30pm, and Saturday 9am to 4pm. There are also two mall outlets with extended hours: Fashion Valley (ℂ **619/574-0086**) and University Towne Center (ℂ **858/458-0700**). 3833 Fourth Ave., Hillcrest. ℂ **619/298-0993.** www.johnsluggage.com. Bus: 1, 3, or 120.

Le Travel Store ★★   In business since 1976, Le Travel Store has a good selection of soft-sided luggage (particularly the Eagle Creek brand), travel books, language tapes, maps, and lots of travel accessories. The Gaslamp Quarter location makes this spot extra handy. Open Monday to Saturday 10am to 6pm, Sunday noon to 6pm. 745 Fourth Ave. (btw. F and G sts.). ℂ **800/713-4260** or 619/544-0005. www.letravelstore.com. Bus: 3, 120, or 992. Trolley: Civic Center.

Traveler's Depot ★★ Around since 1983, this family-run shop offers an extensive selection of travel books and maps, plus a great array of travel gear and accessories, backpacks, and luggage. Open Monday to Friday 10am to 7pm, Saturday 10am to 5pm, and Sunday 11am to 5pm. 1655 Garnet Ave., Pacific Beach. ✆ **858/483-1421.** www.travelersdepot. com. Bus: 8, 9, or 27.

WINE

3rd Corner ★★ Relaxed and sophisticated, this old beach bungalow is now part wine store, part casual eatery. You can browse for a bottle of wine and then settle into a leather couch or enjoy a mild evening on the patio with a platter of cheese ($5 corkage). It serves late and has become popular with local bar and restaurant workers. There's also an outpost in Encinitas at the Lumberyard shopping center, 897 S. Coast Hwy. (✆ **760/ 942-2104**). Open Tuesday to Sunday 10am to 1:30am. 2265 Bacon St., Ocean Beach. ✆ **619/223-2700.** www.the3rdcorner.com. Bus: 35 or 923.

The Wine Bank ★★★ This wonderful wine shop features a great selection from around the world, as well as spirits and liqueurs. You'll find rare wines from France, Italy, and Spain, and bottles from seemingly every winery in California, plus a small trove of Mexican wines. Wine tastings ($20 per person) are held Fridays (5–7pm) and Saturdays (3–5pm). Open daily 10am to 10pm. 363 Fifth Ave. (at J St.), downtown. ✆ **619/234-7487.** www.sdwinebank.com. Bus: 992. Trolley: Gaslamp Quarter.

WineSellar & Brasserie ★★★ You'll feel like you've really accomplished something when you finally locate this place in its odd business-park setting, about 15 miles north of downtown. It started out as a wine storage facility, hence the strange locale; not only has it grown into one of the area's best wine stores, but there's also an excellent French-inspired restaurant upstairs. Pick a bottle and head on up (reservations definitely recommended). Store hours are Monday 9am to 6pm, Tuesday to Saturday 9am to 9pm, Sunday 11am to 6pm; lunch is served Thursday to Saturday, dinner is Tuesday to Saturday. 9550 Waples St., Ste. 115, Sorrento Mesa. ✆ **888/774-9463** or 858/450-9557. www.wine sellar.com. Bus: 921.

10

San Diego After Dark

Historically, San Diego's cultural scene has languished in the shadows cast by those in Los Angeles and San Francisco. The go-go '90s, though, brought new blood and money into the city, and arts organizations felt the impact. The biggest winner was the San Diego Symphony, which in 2002 received the largest single donation to a symphony anywhere, ever—$120 million. More recently, individual donors have lavished big bucks on other arts groups: The Old Globe Theatre received $20-million and $10-million gifts, while the Museum of Contemporary Art San Diego was bestowed with a $3-million donation. But don't think "after dark" in this city is limited to high-falutin' affairs for the Lexus crowd—rock and pop concerts, bars (both swank and dive), and nightclubs crank up the volume on a nightly basis.

Thankfully, San Diego's orgy of development over the past decade has included more than just luxury condos and hotels. The **NTC Promenade** in Point Loma ((C) **619/573-9260;** www.ntcpromenade. org) consists of 26 historic buildings on 28 bayfront acres. It's the remnants of a huge Navy base transformed into a flagship hub of creative activity, housing museums and galleries, educational facilities, and arts groups. The **Birch North Park Theatre,** 2891 University Ave. ((C) **619/239-8836** or 231-5714; www.birchnorthparktheatre. net), is a 1928 vaudeville and movie house resurrected to its original glory. It's now the home base for Lyric Opera San Diego, and plays host to numerous other groups throughout the year. The **Balboa Theatre,** 868 Fourth Ave. ((C) **619/858/760-570-1100** or 619/615-4000; www.sdbalboa. org), is another gilded beauty given a new lease on life. Originally built in 1924, the Balboa sat empty and decaying for years, barely avoiding several brushes with the wrecking ball. This Gaslamp Quarter icon reopened in 2008 and is once again presenting music, dance, theater, and films. **Sushi Performance & Visual Art,** 390 11th Ave. ((C) **619/235-8466;** www.sushi art.org), was homeless for several years but has now settled into a cool, industrial space in the East Village. Although it's ensconced on the ground floor of a new condo tower, Sushi remains uncompromised. Since 1980, Sushi has been presenting brave, fierce, brazen, and provocative works of art, dance, and performance. If any group in the city deserves the mantle of "cutting edge," this is the one.

FINDING OUT WHAT'S ON

For a rundown of the week's performances, gallery openings, and other events, check the listings in the free, weekly alternative publications *San Diego CityBeat* (www.sdcitybeat. com), published on Wednesday, and the *San Diego Weekly Reader* (www.sdreader.com), which comes out on Thursday (also distributed in hotels and tourist areas in a slimmed-down version known as *The Weekly*). The *San Diego Union-Tribune's* entertainment section, "Night and Day," also appears on Thursday (www.signonsandiego.com). For what's happening at the gay clubs, get the weekly *San Diego Gay & Lesbian Times* (www. gaylesbiantimes.com).

The local convention and visitors bureau's *Art + Sol* campaign provides a calendar of events covering the performing and visual arts, and more; see www.sandiegoartandsol.com. The San Diego Performing Arts League produces the performing arts guide *What's Playing?* every 2 months; you can pick one up at the ARTS TIX booth in Horton Plaza, or check the schedule online (© **619/238-0700;** www.sandiegoperforms.com).

GETTING TICKETS

Half-price tickets to theater, music, and dance events are available at the **ARTS TIX** booth in Horton Plaza Park, at Broadway and Third Avenue. It opens Tuesday through Thursday at 11am, and Friday through Sunday at 10am. The booth stays open till 6pm daily except Sunday, when it closes at 5pm. Half-price tickets are available only for same-day shows except for Monday performances, which are sold on Sunday. For a daily listing of offerings, call © **619/497-5000,** or check www.sandiegoperforms.com; the website also sells half-price tickets for some shows. There is also an ARTS TIX North, at the San Diego North Convention & Visitors Bureau in Escondido, 360 N. Escondido Blvd. (© **800/848-3336** or 760/745-4741). Hours are Monday through Friday, 8:30am to 5pm; the Escondido location accepts credit cards (American Express, MasterCard, Visa) only.

For full-price advance tickets, the Horton Plaza kiosk doubles as a Ticketmaster outlet (© **619/220-8497;** www.ticketmaster.com), selling seats to concerts throughout California. Although Ticketmaster sells seats for a majority of local events, you'll avoid bruising "convenience" fees by purchasing directly from the venue's box office.

1 THE PERFORMING ARTS

THEATER

These listings focus on the best known of San Diego's many talented theater companies, but don't hesitate to try a less prominent troupe if the show appeals to you. Smaller companies doing notable work include **Cygnet Theatre** (© 619/337-1525; www.cygnettheatre.com), **Sledgehammer Theatre** (© 619/544-1484; www.sledgehammer.org), **North Coast Repertory Theatre** (© 858/481-1055; www.northcoastrep.org), and **Moxie Theatre** (© 858/598-7620; www.moxietheatre.com). The **California Center for the Performing Arts** in Escondido also books major productions of all types (see "North County Inland," in chapter 11). For shows oriented toward kids, see "That's Entertainment," in chapter 7.

Diversionary Theatre ★ Diversionary was founded in 1985 and focuses on plays with gay and lesbian themes. The 104-seat theater is in the charming neighborhood of University Heights, 2 blocks north of El Cajon Boulevard. Box office hours vary, but are usually Wednesday through Saturday from noon to 8pm (when shows are playing); discounts are available for students, seniors, and military. It's a parking-challenged area, so it's a good idea to come early and have dinner at one of the neighborhood eateries. 4545 Park Blvd. © 619/220-0097. www.diversionary.org. Tickets $29–$33, $10 student rush 1 hr. prior to curtain. Bus: 11.

La Jolla Playhouse ★★★ The Playhouse boasts a Hollywood pedigree (it was founded in 1947 by Gregory Peck, Dorothy McGuire, and Mel Ferrer) and a 1993 Tony Award for outstanding regional theater. The Playhouse is known for its contemporary takes on classics and commitment to commedia dell'arte style, as well as producing Broadway-bound blockbusters such as Billy Crystal's *700 Sundays*. This three-theater complex is also the site of Wolfgang Puck's new Asian fusion restaurant, **Jai**. Subject to availability, discounted tickets ($15–$20) are available for students and seniors (62 and over) in a "public rush" sale 10 minutes before curtain; for seniors the rush is on for the first six performances of a show, and student rush is for all performances. There's also a "pay-what-you-can" performance one Saturday matinee per production. Box office hours are daily from noon to 7pm on nonperformance days, noon to curtain when shows are playing. 2910 La Jolla Village Dr. (at Torrey Pines Rd.). (℃ **858/550-1010**. www.lajollaplayhouse. org. Tickets $25–$75. Parking $2, free on weekends. Bus: 30, 41, 48, 49, 101, 150, or 921.

Lamb's Players Theatre ★ One of the few professional companies in the country with a true resident ensemble, Lamb's was established in 1971. It features five shows annually at its 350-seat main stage in Coronado's historic Spreckels Building (where no seat is more than seven rows from the stage), plus a show at the Horton Grand Theatre (444 Fourth Ave.) in the Gaslamp Quarter. Additionally, Lamb's produces two Christmas productions, one of which is a dinner theater extravaganza at the Hotel del Coronado. You'll see well-acted, well-designed plays, both premières and classics. The box office is open Tuesday through Saturday from noon to 7pm, Sunday from noon to 2pm; senior, military, and student discounts available. 1142 Orange Ave., Coronado. (℃ **619/437-0600**. www.lambs players.org. Tickets $22–$58. Street parking or pay parking garage nearby. Bus: 901 or 904.

The Old Globe Theatre ★★★ This Tony Award–winning, three-theater complex is in Balboa Park, behind the Museum of Man. Though best known for the 581-seat Old Globe—fashioned after Shakespeare's wooden-O theater—there's also a 612-seat open-air theater and a new 251-seat arena stage. More than a dozen plays are scheduled here year-round, from world premières (and subsequent Broadway hits) to the excellent summer Shakespeare festival. Dr. Seuss's *How the Grinch Stole Christmas!* has been a popular family draw during the holidays since 1997. As of this writing, the Globe grounds are undergoing a massive renovation, scheduled to be completed in time for the theater's 75th anniversary in 2010. Backstage tours are offered most weekends at 10:30am and cost $5 for adults, $3 for students, seniors, and military. The box office is open Monday (and other nonperformance days) noon to 6pm, and noon to curtain on performance days. Balboa Park. (℃ **619/234-5623**. www.theoldglobe.org. Tickets $29–$89. Senior, student, and military discounts available. Free parking in the park's public lots; valet parking located at the Prado restaurant. Bus: 3, 7, or 120.

San Diego Repertory Theatre ★ Founded in 1976, the Rep mounts plays and musicals at the Lyceum Theatre in Horton Plaza, which consists of the 545-seat Lyceum Stage and the 260-seat Lyceum Space. The theater acts as a "cultural town hall," hosting nearly daily events, exhibits, and shows, in addition to the Rep's work. The Rep has a strong multicultural bent—it has had a long association with Chicano playwright Luis Valdez, and produces the annual African-American Kuumba Fest and the Jewish Arts Festival. A tiled obelisk marks the spot where you'll find the theater, situated at the entrance to Horton Plaza, in a sunken courtyard. The box office is open Tuesday through Sunday from noon to 6pm (or curtain time). 79 Broadway Circle, in Horton Plaza. (℃ **619/ 544-1000**. www.sdrep.org. Tickets $25–$53. Student discounts available. Free validated parking at Horton Plaza Shopping Center. Bus: All Broadway routes. Trolley: Civic Center.

La Jolla Music Society ★★ This well-respected organization has been bringing marquee names to San Diego since 1968. About half of the 40-plus annual shows are held October through May in the 500-seat Sherwood Auditorium at the Museum of Contemporary Art in La Jolla; others are presented at the acoustically excellent Neurosciences Institute, downtown's Copley Symphony Hall, and the restored North Park Theatre. The annual highlight is SummerFest, a 3-week series of concerts, forums, open rehearsals, talks, and artist encounters—it's held in August and is perhaps San Diego's most prestigious musical event. Box office: 7946 Ivanhoe Ave., Ste. 103, La Jolla. ☎ **858/459-3728.** www.ljms.org. Tickets $25–$95. Bus: 30.

San Diego Symphony ★ The symphony's home, Copley Symphony Hall, is a baroque jewel dating from 1929, swallowed whole by a downtown financial tower; the building's modern exterior gives no hint of the plush theater inside. The season runs October through May; a Summer Pops series, with programs devoted to big band, Broadway, and Tchaikovsky, is held weekends from July to early September on the Embarcadero—always bring a sweater for these pleasantly brisk evenings on the water. The box office is open Monday through Thursday from 10am to 6pm, Friday 10am to 5pm, and Saturday from noon to 3pm; on performance days from noon until through intermission. Select performances have a $10 student rush 1 hour prior to curtain. 750 B St., at Seventh Ave. ☎ **619/235-0804.** www.sandiegosymphony.com. Tickets $20–$100. Bus: Numerous Broadway routes. Trolley: Fifth Ave.

OPERA

San Diego Opera ★★★ One of the community's most successful arts organizations, San Diego Opera has been presenting work here since 1965. The annual season runs from late January to mid-May, with five offerings at downtown's 3,000-seat Civic Theatre, as well as occasional recitals at smaller venues. The productions range from well-trod warhorses such as *Carmen* to edgier works such as Alban Berg's *Wozzeck,* all performed by name talent from around the world, as well as local singers. To purchase tickets in person, visit patron services at the opera offices (Civic Center Plaza, 18th floor, directly across from the theater), Monday through Friday 8:30am to 4:30pm; rush tickets ($20–$50) become available 2 hours before curtain at the theater. Civic Theatre, 1200 Third Ave. ☎ **619/533-7000** (box office) or 232-7636 (admin.). www.sdopera.com. Tickets $35–$200. Bus: Numerous Broadway routes. Trolley: Civic Center.

DANCE

Dance Place at NTC Promenade has become the heart of the city's dance scene, providing studio, performance, and educational space for several of San Diego's leading companies, including **San Diego Ballet** (☎ **619/294-7378;** www.sandiegoballet.org), **Malashock Dance** (☎ **619/260-1622;** www.malashockdance.org), and **Jean Isaacs San Diego Dance Theater** (☎ **619/225-1803;** www.sandiegodancetheater.org).

Other major dance companies include **California Ballet** (☎ **858/560-5676;** www.californiaballet.org), a classical company that produces four shows annually at the Civic Theatre downtown and elsewhere (*The Nutcracker* is a Christmas tradition); and **City Ballet** (☎ **858/272-8663;** www.cityballet.org), which is officially sanctioned by the George Balanchine Foundation to perform that choreographer's work. Turning hearts and minds (but hopefully not ankles) is the socially conscious modern-dance troupe **Eveoke Dance Theatre** (☎ **619/238-1153;** www.eveoke.org). Their studio space is in the heart of North Park at 2811 University Ave.

2 LIVE ENTERTAINMENT

LIVE MUSIC

Maddeningly, some artists bypass San Diego, but on the plus side—especially when it comes to acts that haven't pushed through to the mainstream—if they do play locally, chances are it's in a venue smaller than what you'd find them in up north. *Note:* If you're under 21, much of the city's nightlife will be off-limits to you.

Small- & Medium-Size Venues

Acoustic Music San Diego (Finds)　One of San Diego's most unique venues is a nearly 100-year-old church in Normal Heights, which hosts shows presented by Acoustic Music San Diego. Programming ranges from Americana and blues to bluegrass and Celtic. Many artists sign autographs and hawk merchandise between sets in the church's adjacent auditorium. 4650 Mansfield St., Normal Heights (south of Adams Ave.). **☏ 619/303-8176.** www.acousticmusicsandiego.com. Bus: 11.

Anthology ★★★　This is a fine-dining establishment masquerading as a top-notch music venue. Or is it the other way around? However you want to describe it, this acoustically excellent and architecturally alluring supper club lures big-name jazz, blues, world, and rock musicians, as well as local talent. You don't have to eat here to see a show, but diners get the best seats—and the food is as much of an attraction as the artists (p. 100). 1337 India St. (btw. A and Ash sts.), downtown. **☏ 619/595-0300.** www.anthologysd.com. Bus: 83.

The Belly Up Tavern ★★ (Finds)　This club in Solana Beach, a 30-minute drive from downtown, has played host to critically acclaimed and international artists of all genres. The eclectic mix ranges from Lucinda Williams and Toots & The Maytals to Frank Black and The Roots. A funky setting in recycled Quonset huts underscores the venue's uniqueness. Look into advance tickets, if possible, though you can avoid excessive Ticketmaster fees by purchasing your tickets at the box office. You can also dine before the show at the BUT's Wild Note Cafe. 143 S. Cedros Ave., Solana Beach (1½ blocks from the Coaster stop). **☏ 858/481-9022** (recorded info) or 481-8140 (box office). www.bellyup.com. Bus: 101.

The Casbah ★　It may have a total dive ambience, and passing jets overhead sometimes drown out ballads, but this rockin' Little Italy 200-plus capacity club has a well-earned rep for showcasing bands that either are, were, or will be famous. Look into advance tickets if possible (**☏ 888/512-7469;** www.casbahtickets.com); live music can be counted on at least 6 nights a week. Doors open 8:30pm. 2501 Kettner Blvd., at Laurel St., near the airport. **☏ 619/232-4355.** www.thecasbah.com. Cover charge usually under $15. Bus: 83.

Croce's Restaurant & Jazz Bar ★　Croce's is a cornerstone of Gaslamp Quarter nightlife: a loud, crowded, and mainstream gathering place where you'll find a variety of jazz and rhythm 'n' blues stylings 7 nights a week (Sun–Thurs starting at 7pm; Fri–Sat at 8:30pm); there's also a jazz brunch on Sunday from 11:30am to 2pm. The venue is named for the late Jim Croce and is owned by his widow, Ingrid, who was a vital component of the Gaslamp's revitalization. The cover charge is waived if you eat at the pricey restaurant (from where you can see and hear the music from most tables). 802 Fifth Ave. (at F St.). **☏ 619/233-4355.** www.croces.com. Cover $5–$10. Bus: 3, 120, or 992.

Dizzy's ★　When this place first opened downtown, it served up its jazz straight, no chaser—as in no alcohol was available. With its relocation to the San Diego Wine & Culinary Center . . . well, the name says it all. In fact the space Dizzy's occupies features a wall installation of wine bottles, but it's still an all-ages venue with a great location. And the jazz is just as uncompromising as ever. 200 Harbor Dr. (at Second Ave. and J St.), Gaslamp Quarter. ℂ **858/270-7467.** (Tickets available at the door; cash only.) www.dizzyssandiego.com. Bus: 992. Trolley: Convention Center.

4th & B   In a former bank building downtown, 4th & B received a $4.5-million sprucing in 2006, giving this formerly no-frills venue a bit more panache. The back of the room, which had previously been bleacher-type seating, now features VIP boxes and lounges. The genre is barrier-free, including live music, DJs, and comedy shows. The box office is open Monday, Wednesday, and Friday, 10am to 2pm, and 1 hour prior to show-time. 345 B St., downtown. ℂ **619/231-4343.** www.4thandbevents.com. Bus: 3, 120, 850, or 860. Trolley: Civic Center.

House of Blues ★★   Whatever your feelings about corporate music entities, there's no denying House of Blues knows how to do things right. A visual feast of amazing outsider art fills this multiroom venue. There's a restaurant serving Southern-inspired cuisine (and the Sun gospel brunch is a definite hoot—though be prepared to praise Jesus); there are also a swag store, a bar, and two stages, including an 1,100-person capacity concert space. HOB's booking power brings in an eclectic range of music, from world beat to punk (and yes, blues, too). VIP dinner packages are available. 1055 Fifth Ave., downtown. (btw. Broadway and C St.). ℂ **619/299-2583.** www.hob.com/sandiego. Bus: 3, 120, and numerous Broadway routes. Trolley: Fifth Ave.

Humphrey's ★   This locally beloved 1,300-seat outdoor venue is set alongside the bay, next to bobbing yachts. The annual lineup covers the spectrum of entertainment—rock, jazz, blues, folk, and comedy. You can often snag a seat in the first seven rows by buying the dinner/concert package ($63 extra); there are also packages with the adjacent hotel that can get you in the first four rows. Concerts are held from mid-May to October only, and most shows go on sale in early April (seats are also available through Ticketmaster). The hotel's indoor lounge, **Humphrey's Backstage,** also has music nightly. 2241 Shelter Island Dr., Point Loma. ℂ **619/523-1010** (general info) or 224-3577 (package reservations). www.humphreysconcerts.com.

Large Venues

Built in 1967, the **San Diego Sports Arena,** 3500 Sports Arena Blvd. ((ℂ **619/224-4171;** www.sandiegoarena.com), is a 15,000- to 18,000-seat indoor venue with middling acoustics. Located west of Old Town, several big-name concerts are held here every year because of the seating capacity and availability of paid parking. **Qualcomm Stadium** ((ℂ **619/641-3131**), in Mission Valley, is a 71,000-seat outdoor stadium mainly occupied by football (Chargers and San Diego State University).

The **Open Air Theatre** ((ℂ **619/594-6947;** www.as.sdsu.edu), on the San Diego State University campus, northeast of downtown along I-8, is a 4,000-seat outdoor amphitheater. It has great acoustics—if you can't get a ticket, you can sit outside on the grass and hear the entire show. Also located at SDSU is **Cox Arena** (same contact info as above); it has equally superb acoustics in an indoor, 12,000-seat facility that is used for bigger draws. Both these venues are easily accessed by the San Diego Trolley. **Cricket Wireless Amphitheatre,** 2050 Entertainment Circle ((ℂ **619/671-3600;** www.cricketwireless amphitheatre.com), is a slick facility in Chula Vista, a stone's throw north of the Mexican border. Built in 1999, the venue has a capacity of 20,000 (10,000 in festival seating in a grassy area) and boasts excellent acoustics and good sightlines; many of the big summer tours play here. The drawbacks: overpriced snacks and drinks, and a location 25 to 45 minutes south of downtown (depending on traffic).

The **Spreckels Theatre,** 121 Broadway (✆ **619/235-9500;** www.spreckels.net), and **Copley Symphony Hall,** 750 B St. (✆ **619/235-0804;** www.sandiegosymphony.com), are wonderful old vaudeville houses located downtown, used by touring acts throughout the year.

COMEDY CLUBS

The Comedy Store   Yes, it's a branch of the famous Sunset Strip club in Los Angeles, and yes, plenty of L.A. comics make the trek to headline Friday and Saturday shows here. Local comedians perform Wednesday, Thursday, and Sunday; the Sunday show is kicked off at 6:45pm by an open-mic "potluck" that can be hilarious, horrendous—or both (but, hey, there's no cover that night). Shows start at 8pm, with later shows on weekends. 916 Pearl St., La Jolla. ✆ **858/454-9176.** www.thecomedystore.com. Cover $8–$20 (plus 2-drink minimum). Bus: 30.

National Comedy Theatre   Two teams of professional comedians square off in a 90-minute improv competition to see which can make you laugh hardest. The action is all based on your suggestions—you call it out, they make it funny. Thursdays are collegiate night, when teams from schools around the state go at it. 3717 India St. (at W. Washington St.), Mission Hills. ✆ **619/295-4999.** www.nationalcomedy.com. Cover $8–$15. Bus: 10 or 30. Trolley: Washington Street.

---

3 THE BAR & COFFEEHOUSE SCENE

BARS, COCKTAIL LOUNGES & DANCE CLUBS
Downtown

Downtown is the busiest place for nightlife—you'll find something going on nightly. The best nights (or worst, depending on your tolerance for crowds) are Thursday through Saturday, when the 20-somethings pour in and dance clubs spring into action. Keep in mind that many clubs have "city style" dress codes—no tank tops, sports jerseys, tennis shoes, and the like.

Airport ★★★   This sexy, minimalist gem on the northern edge of Little Italy has one of the best shows in town. From its very cool interior patio, you can almost touch the planes as they come roaring in for a landing at nearby Lindbergh Field. Keeping to the theme, bartenders are in pilots' uniforms, and waitresses are in classic flight attendant miniskirts. Open Thursday to Saturday 8pm to 2am; dinner is served until 1am. 2400 India St. (just south of Laurel St.), Little Italy. ✆ **619/685-3881.** www.airportsd.com. Cover: $10–$20. Bus: 83.

Altitude Skybar ★★   Twenty-two stories up in the Gaslamp Quarter Marriott (p. 65), this long, narrow open-air space looks down on PETCO Park and the Convention Center. The best view of downtown is curiously walled off by a water sculpture that backs the bar. No worries—there's still lots to look at, as well as fire pits and DJ-spun grooves. And in a Gaslamp rarity, there's no cover charge. Open daily 5pm to 1:30am. 660 K St. (btw. Sixth and Seventh aves.), Gaslamp Quarter. ✆ **619/696-0234.** www.altitudeskybar. com. Bus: 3, 11, 120, or 992. Trolley: Gaslamp Quarter.

The Beach ★★ The Beach is the open-air, rooftop bar of the W hotel (p. 67). What makes it truly unique is that most of the floor is sand—you can kick off your shoes even in winter when the sand is heated. A gas fire pit adds to the ambience, as do the cabanas lining one wall. The hotel's two other bars, Living Room and Magnet, are also stylish venues. Beach is open Monday to Thursday 2:30pm to 2am, Friday to Sunday from 10:30am to 2am; no cover charge. 421 B St. (at State St.), downtown. ⓒ 619/398-3100. www. wbeachbar.com. Bus: All Broadway routes. Trolley: America Plaza or Civic Center.

The Bitter End ★ With three floors, this Gaslamp Quarter hot spot manages to be a sophisticated martini bar, dance club, concert venue, and relaxing cocktail lounge all in one. On weekends, you're subject to the velvet rope treatment, and there's always a strict dress code in play—no shorts, no tennis shoes. Don't miss the plush upstairs bar. Open daily from 3pm to 2am. 770 Fifth Ave. (at F St.), Gaslamp Quarter. ⓒ 619/338-9300. www. thebitterend.com. Cover Fri–Sat $10 after 9pm. Bus: 3, 120, or 992. Trolley: Fifth Ave.

Confidential ★★ This glamorous nightspot sports smart, contemporary design and a global tapas menu designed for sharing. The food here is the best of any served by dance clubs pulling double duty as restaurants. It's compact in size and has a smoking patio directly across the street from Horton Plaza. Open Tuesday to Saturday 5pm to 2am; happy hour (5–7pm) is a good way to sample the food. 901 Fourth Ave. (at E St.), Gaslamp Quarter. ⓒ 619/696-8888. www.confidentialsd.com. Cover: $10–$15. Bus: 3, 120, or 992. Trolley: Civic Center.

East Village Tavern & Bowl Whether you bowl passionately or ironically, this raucous spot has you covered. Featuring 12 colorfully lit bowling lanes, as well as a separate bar area with outdoor seating, there's classic bar food (limited menu served until 1am), a good selection of beer on tap, and billiards. Open daily 11:30am to 2am; kids are allowed in until 9pm. 930 Market St. (btw. Ninth and 10th aves.), East Village. ⓒ 619/677-2695. www. bowlevt.com. Bus: 3 or 11. Trolley: Gaslamp Quarter or Park and Market.

Envy/Ivy Rooftop ★★★ These are the hip and very happening clubs located in the ultra-stylish Ivy Hotel (p. 64). Multilevel Envy is chic and sexy, with a definite A-lister vibe; Ivy Rooftop is an open-air bar where beautiful people prove a distraction to the beautiful views. Envy is open Thursday to Saturday 9pm to 2am; Ivy Rooftop's hours are Sunday to Wednesday 10am to midnight, Thursday to Saturday 10am to 2am. 600 F St. (btw. Sixth and Seventh aves.), Gaslamp Quarter. ⓒ 619/814-2055. www.envysandiego.com. Cover $10–$20. Bus: 3 or 120. Trolley: Gaslamp Quarter.

Lounge Six ★ Considerably more earthbound than Altitude (see above), Lounge Six is on the fourth-floor pool deck of the Hotel Solamar (p. 64). Let's see: fire pits, check. Cabanas, check. Comfy lounges, check. A menu of small-plate edibles from the first-floor restaurant, check. Cool music playing overhead, check. Excellent views of the Gaslamp Quarter action, check. Yup, everything you need for a great afternoon or evening. Open daily 11:30am to midnight. 616 J St. (at Sixth Ave.), Gaslamp Quarter. ⓒ 619/ 531-8744. www.hotelsolamar.com. Bus: 3 or 120. Trolley: Gaslamp Quarter.

On Broadway ★ This retro swanky hangout is a converted 1925 bank building. It has five rooms covering the musical gamut: house, techno, hip-hop, R&B—using a 90,000-watt sound system—plus a sushi bar with live music (reservations suggested) and a billiards room in the former bank vault. Dress to impress. Open Friday and Saturday from 8pm (dinner from 7pm) to 2am. 615 Broadway (at Sixth Ave.), downtown. ⓒ 619/231-0011. www.obec.tv. Cover $15–$25. Bus: All Broadway routes. Trolley: Fifth Ave.

The Onyx Room/Thin ★★★ This upstairs/downstairs combo makes for a nightlife twofer that can't be beat. At street level is hyper-modern Thin, where specialty cocktails and chill music make for a relaxed atmosphere; subterranean Onyx is more classic lounge, and every Tuesday trumpeter Gilbert Castellanos takes the stage for a jazz jam (no cover). The Onyx Room and Thin are open Tuesday and Thursday through Saturday from 9pm; the cover charge gets you into both clubs. 852 Fifth Ave., Gaslamp Quarter. ✆ **619/235-6699.** www.onyxroom.com. Cover Thurs–Fri $10, Sat $15. Bus: 3, 120, 992, or any Broadway route. Trolley: Fifth Ave.

Sevilla ★★ This Spanish-themed club is the spot for salsa and merengue lessons Tuesday through Thursday (8:30pm) and Sunday (6:45pm), followed by live bands at 10pm (8pm Sun). Friday and Saturday, DJs take over for hip-hop, reggaeton, and other sounds with a Latin vibe; Monday features live rock en Español. Sevilla also has a tapas bar and dining room, open from 5pm (till 11pm Sun–Thurs, till midnight Fri–Sat). Live flamenco and Gypsy music dinner shows are staged Friday and Saturday (7:30pm). 555 Fourth Ave., Gaslamp Quarter. ✆ **619/233-5979.** www.sevillanightclub.com or www.cafesevilla. com (restaurant). Cover $5–$15. Bus: 3, 11, 120, or 992. Trolley: Convention Center.

Stingaree ★★ This $6-million, three-level club has been a hot destination in the Gaslamp Quarter since opening in 2005. It has more than 22,000 square feet of space, a fine-dining component, a handful of bars and private nooks, and a rooftop deck with cabanas and fire pit. The decor is chicly mod and retro; the name is a throwback to San Diego's Wild West days when this area was known as the Stingaree. Open Tuesday through Saturday 6pm to 2am (restaurant till 10pm). 454 Sixth Ave. (btw. Island Ave. and J St.), Gaslamp Quarter. ✆ **619/544-9500.** www.stingsandiego.com. Cover $20. Bus: 992. Trolley: Gaslamp Quarter.

Top of the Hyatt ★★★ ⓂMoments This is San Diego's ultimate bar with a view, the 40th floor of the West Coast's tallest waterfront building, the Manchester Grand Hyatt (p. 65). You'll get a wide view of the city, harbor, and Coronado. The bar is open 3pm to 1:30am daily and is an unparalleled spot from which to watch the sunset. No cover charge. 1 Market Place. (at Harbor Dr.), Embarcadero. ✆ **619/232-1234.** www.manchestergrand. hyatt.com. Trolley: Seaport Village.

Elsewhere in San Diego

Beauty Bar ★ The indie set that eschews the glitz of the Gaslamp Quarter flocks to this club, located in a rather sketchy part of town. Part of a minichain that includes outlets in New York, San Francisco, and Austin, it presents live music, as well as special events such as burlesque and fashion shows. Martini manicures are available, too. Open daily from 8pm to 2am. 4746 El Cajon Blvd. (at Euclid Ave.), City Heights. ✆ **619/516-4746.** Cover free–$20, depending on what's happening that night. www.beautybar.com. Bus: 1 or 15.

Lips ★ This drag revue supper club has a different show nightly, such as Bitchy Bingo on Wednesday and celebrity impersonations on Thursday. Dinner seating is at 7pm Sunday, Tuesday, and Wednesday; Thursday through Saturday it's at 6:30pm, with an additional 9pm seating on Friday and Saturday. Sunday gospel brunch begins at 11:30am. Weekend late shows are 21 and over only; reservations are recommended. 3036 El Cajon Blvd. (at 30th St.), North Park. ✆ **619/295-7900.** www.lipsshow.biz. Cover $3–$5, food minimum $10–$18. Bus: 1 or 15.

Nunu's Cocktail Lounge You'll find lots of 1960s Naugahyde-style, cheap drinks, and an eclectic crowd at this classic Hillcrest dive, plus a kitchen that whips up specialties

Brewpubs & Wine Bars

Over the last 10 years, San Diego has been making a name for itself in the beer world, with local brewers earning props at the World Beer Cup and Great American Beer Festival. While San Diego's regional wineries (p. 161) haven't earned the same respect, whether you are a beer drinker or a wine sipper, there are plenty of great places to quaff local (and international) libations. If you'd like someone else to do the driving, check out the beer tours run by **Brew Hop** (© **858/361-8457;** www.brewhop.com) and **Brewery Tours of San Diego** (© **619/961-7999;** www.brewerytoursofsandiego.com).

Pizza Port Brewing Company (www.pizzaport.com), 135 N. Hwy. 101, Solana Beach (© **858/481-7332**), and 571 Carlsbad Village Dr., Carlsbad (© **760/720-7007**), has creative pizzas and giant pretzels to go along with award-winning beers, including the signature Sharkbite Red ale. Kids can enjoy the house-made root beer.

San Diego's most acclaimed brewery, **Stone Brewery World Bistro and Gardens,** 1999 Citracado Pkwy., Escondido (© **760/471-4999;** www.stone brew.com), is the maker of Arrogant Bastard Ale. Lunch is served at this elegant, beautifully landscaped indoor/outdoor eatery Monday to Saturday, dinner nightly, with brunch offered on Sunday.

Pacific Beach AleHouse, 721 Grand Ave. (© **858/581-2337;** www.pbale house.com), has a rooftop deck where you can sip a Pacific Sunset IPA while you actually watch a Pacific sunset. With its multitude of flatscreen TVs, it's a great place to catch a sporting event, too.

Coronado Brewing Company, 170 Orange Ave., Coronado (© **619/437-4452;** www.coronadobrewingcompany.com), is a family-friendly restaurant and brewery that has a happy hour from 2 to 6pm (Mon–Fri). Their brews include the Point Loma Porter and the Islandweizen.

Karl Strauss Brewing Company & Grill is Southern California's largest distributing microbrewery and has four San Diego locations (p. 103).

Wine and beer drinkers can find common ground at **The Vine,** 1851 Bacon St., Ocean Beach (© **619/222-8463;** www.theobvine.com), which serves quality wines by the glass and by the flight, and also has an excellent selection of

such as the Jack Daniel's burger with breaded artichoke hearts. It's open daily from 6am to 2am; kitchen is closed on Mondays. 3537 Fifth Ave. (at Ivy Lane), Hillcrest. © **619/295-2878.** www.nunuscocktails.com. Bus: 3 or 120.

Ould Sod Irish through and through, this little gem sits in a working-class neighborhood northeast of Hillcrest, hosting a very local crowd. There's an Irish jam session on Tuesday, more live music on Friday, and karaoke on Thursday and Saturday. Open Monday to Friday 2pm to 2am, weekends from 10am to 2am. 3373 Adams Ave. (at 34th St.), Normal Heights. © **619/284-6594.** www.theouldsod.com. Cover for bands $3. Bus: 11.

Starlite ★★ (Finds) Local musician Steve Poltz and the mastermind behind the Casbah (p. 219) joined forces to create this great little drinking and dining spot. It has sophisticated design sense, a lounge vibe (including a roster of DJs), and fine food; there's beer. Located a block from the O.B. pier, the Vine also has an eclectic menu of small-plate offerings.

The **3rd Corner** multi-tasks as a bistro and a wine shop. There are locations in Ocean Beach and Encinitas (p. 116).

In Hillcrest, there is a passel of fine establishments from which to choose. **Wine Steals,** 1243 University Ave., Hillcrest (© **619/295-1188;** www.wine stealssd.com), has a casual, neighborhood feel and includes a wine-shop component. It's also conveniently attached to a cheese store. (Additional Wine Steals are in Point Loma, 2970 Truxton Rd., © **619/221-1959;** and Cardiff, 1953 San Elijo Ave., © **760/230-2657**). **The Wine Lover,** 3968 Fifth Ave. (© **619/294-9200;** www.thewinelover.us), is intimate and romantic, and features more than a dozen wine flights. It also has truffles, cheeses, and imported charcuterie. And don't let the nondescript strip-mall setting dissuade you from checking out **The Wine Encounter,** 690 University Ave. (© **619/543-9463;** www. thewineencounter.com), where you'll find probably the city's largest by-the-glass selection, with more than 150 wines available, along with nearly 30 flights. **Bamboo Lounge,** 1475 University Ave. (© **619/291-8221**), doesn't have a great selection of wines by the glass, but the Asian-influenced back patio is so awesome, it deserves a mention.

Downtown is another hot spot for wining. **The Grape,** 823 Fifth Ave., Gaslamp Quarter (© **619/238-8010;** www.thegrapebar.com), was San Diego's first wine bar, opening in 1996. A newer arrival is **The Cask Room,** 550 Park Blvd., East Village (© **619/822-1606;** www.caskroom.com), located near PETCO Park; it features nice touches such as comfy club chairs and sofas, free Wi-Fi, a selection of cheeses and appetizers, and plenty of beer selections. The **San Diego Wine & Culinary Center,** 200 Harbor Dr., Gaslamp Quarter (© **619/231-6400;** www.sdwineculinary.com), is directly across the street from the Convention Center, and there's even a trolley stop steps away from the door. SDWCC also offers classes and food/wine excursions, and is the home of the jazz venue **Dizzy's** (p. 219).

also a sweet outdoor patio. Open Monday through Saturday 5pm to 2am, and Sunday 6pm to 2am; a limited late-night menu kicks in at 10pm. 3175 India St. (at Spruce St.), Mission Hills. © 619/358-9766. www.starlitesandiego.com. Bus: 83. Trolley: Middletown.

Turf Supper Club ★★ (Finds   The gimmick at this retro steakhouse is all about cheap, "grill your own" dinners. Steaks ($7–$16) are delivered raw, but seasoned, on a paper plate with sides—you do the rest. If red meat isn't your thing, there are seafood, veggie, and chicken dishes. The decor is pure 1950s and approved by the cocktail crowd; the volume level is not always conducive to intimate dining, though. Monday to Thursday 5pm to 2am, Friday to Sunday 1pm to 2am. 1116 25th Ave. (at C St.), Golden Hill. © 619/234-6363. www.turfsupperclub.com. Bus: 2.

Universal ★ This multispace, "omnisexual" restaurant and club opened in 2008, adding a shot of Gaslamp-style glamour to this stretch of University Avenue in Hillcrest. The outdoor lounge area features a fire pit, and offers a refuge to sweat-soaked dancers who want to cool down or have a smoke. The restaurant, **Dish,** also serves a Sunday brunch. Open Thursday to Saturday, 9pm to 2am; Dish opens at 5pm, 9am on Sunday. 1202 University Ave. (at Vermont St.), Hillcrest. ℭ **619/692-1900.** www.universalhillcrest.com. Cover: $10. Bus: 1, 10, or 11.

COFFEEHOUSES WITH PERFORMANCES

Claire de Lune Coffee Lounge (Finds) Housed in a handsome building dating from 1929, this coffeehouse has helped create a happening little scene in the neighborhood. There's usually entertainment Friday and Saturday, ranging from world-beat music to belly dancing. Open Monday to Thursday 5am to 11:30pm, Friday and Saturday 6am to 2am, and Sunday 5am to midnight. 2906 University Ave. (at Kansas St.), North Park. ℭ **619/688-9845.** www.clairedelune.com. Bus: 7 or 10.

Lestat's Coffee House ★ This local's favorite is open 24/7. There's entertainment nightly, everything from guitar-strumming troubadours (some of the city's best) and rock bands to comics and open-mic hopefuls (Mon). 3343 Adams Ave. (at Felton St.), Normal Heights. ℭ **619/282-0437.** www.lestats.com. Bus: 11.

---

4 GAY & LESBIAN NIGHTLIFE

HILLCREST & UPTOWN

Bourbon Street ★ This bar has several spaces, including an outdoor patio meant to evoke jazzy New Orleans, a game room for darts or pool, a performance area (karaoke, Guitar Hero contests), and a lounge where DJs spin house music. Open daily from 5pm to 2am; Friday is ladies' happy hour (5–10pm) in the front bar and Sunday is all about the girls. 4612 Park Blvd. (near Adams Ave.), University Heights. ℭ **619/291-4043.** www. bourbonstreetsd.com. Bus: 11.

The Brass Rail San Diego's oldest gay bar (open since 1960) has been remodeled, refreshed, and given a jolt of new energy. It now features VIP rooms, bottle service, and upgraded sound and lighting. The popular Manic Monday features '80s music; Thursday is karaoke night; Saturday features Latin grooves. Open daily 2pm to 2am. 3796 Fifth Ave. (at Robinson St.), Hillcrest. ℭ **619/298-2233.** www.thebrassrailsd.com. Cover Fri–Sat $7–$15. Bus: 1, 3, or 120.

The Flame ★ For 20 years, it was the city's top lesbian hangout; now, the Flame sits mostly idle except for weekends. It's usually boys' night on Friday, girls on Saturday. It's a great space with cool neon out front, and new ownership has locals hoping for a Flame resurgence. 3780 Park Blvd. at Robinson Ave. www.theflamesd.com. Bus: 1, 7, 10, or 11.

Flicks ★ Since 1983, this video bar has featured VJs drawing from a database of 15,000 music and comedy clips. There are also various weekly special events, including karaoke on Sunday and Monday, and poker tournaments (for fun only) on Tuesday and Thursday. Open 2pm to 2am daily. 1017 University Ave., Hillcrest. ℭ **619/297-2056.** www. sdflicks.com. Bus: 1, 10, or 11.

Numbers ★ Across the street from the Flame, it's a predominantly male crowd at this busy dance emporium, with three bars, two dance floors, and go-go boy dancers. Friday is ladies' night. Open Tuesday through Friday 4pm to 2am, Saturday and Sunday from 1pm to 2am. 3811 Park Blvd. (at University Ave.), Hillcrest. ℂ **619/294-7583.** www.numberssd. com. Cover $3–$10. Bus: 1, 7, 10, or 11.

Rich's ★ This mega-dance club in the heart of Hillcrest has been an institution for years. A variety of special events are scheduled, including ladies' nights on Thursdays and a "bear" dance party the third Saturday of every month. A recent renovation has opened the space up with windows and a sidewalk patio. It's open Wednesday to Sunday 9pm to 2am. 1051 University Ave. (btw. Vermont St. and 10th Ave.), Hillcrest. ℂ **619/295-2195.** www. richssandiego.com. Cover $5–$10. Bus: 1, 10, or 11.

Top of the Park ★★ The penthouse bar of the Park Manor Hotel, offering spectacular views of Balboa Park and beyond, is a very popular social scene on Friday evenings from 5 to 10pm. The weekend party scene officially begins here. 525 Spruce St. (at Fifth Ave.), Hillcrest. ℂ **619/291-0999.** www.parkmanorsuites.com. Bus: 3 or 120.

5 MORE ENTERTAINMENT

EVENING BAY CRUISES

Hornblower Cruises Aboard the 151-foot antique-style yacht *Lord Hornblower,* you'll be entertained—and encouraged to dance—by a DJ playing a variety of music. The three-course meal is standard-issue banquet style, but the scenery is marvelous. Boarding is at 6:30pm, and the cruise runs from 7 to 10pm. 1066 N. Harbor Dr. (at Broadway Pier). ℂ **888/467-6256** or 619/686-8715. www.hornblower.com. Tickets Sun–Fri $67, Sat $73 adults, $65/$71 seniors (55 and above) and military, $40/$44 children ages 4–12, free for children 3 and under; drinks cost extra. Bus: 2, 210, or 992. Trolley: America Plaza.

San Diego Harbor Excursion This company offers nightly dinner packages, with choice of four entrees, dessert, and cocktails. For an additional $50 per couple, you can guarantee yourself a private table with window, plus a bottle of champagne, wine, or cider. A DJ plays dance music during the $2^{1}/_{2}$-hour outing. Boarding is at 7pm, and the cruise lasts from 7:30 to 10pm. 1050 N. Harbor Dr. (at Broadway Pier). ℂ **800/442-7847** or 619/234-4111. www.sdhe.com. Tickets $66 adults ($88 with fully hosted bar), $38 children ages 4–12, free for children 3 and under; all prices $5 higher on Sat. Bus: 2, 210, or 992. Trolley: America Plaza.

CINEMA

A variety of multiscreen complexes around the city show first-run films; for showtimes, call ℂ **619/444-3456.** In the heart of the Gaslamp Quarter, you'll find the **Gaslamp Stadium,** 701 Fifth Ave., featuring 15 screens and stadium seating; and the **Horton Plaza 14,** on the top level of the mall. The AMC chain operates swarming complexes in both the **Mission Valley** and **Fashion Valley** shopping centers; both have free parking, but popular films sell out early on weekends. The other Mission Valley movieplex is the **Ultrastar** at the Hazard Center, 7510 Hazard Center Dr.

Current American independent and foreign films play at Landmark's five-screen **Hillcrest Cinema,** 3965 Fifth Ave., Hillcrest, which offers 3 hours of free parking (ℂ **619/ 819-0236**); the **Ken Cinema,** 4061 Adams Ave., Kensington (ℂ **619/819-0236**); and the four-screen **La Jolla Village,** 8879 Villa La Jolla Dr., La Jolla, also with free parking (ℂ **619/819-0236**).

(Finds) Running with the Grunion

The **Grunion Run** is a local tradition—so if someone invites you down to the beach for a late-night fishing expedition, armed only with a sack and flashlight, don't be afraid. Grunion are 5- to 6-inch silvery fish that wriggle out of the water to lay their eggs in the sand. Found only in Southern and Baja California, they make for decent eating, coated in flour and cornmeal, and then fried. April to early June is peak spawning season, but they may only be caught—by hand—during the months of March and June through August; a fishing license is required for those 16 and older. Grunion runs happen twice a month, after the highest tides, 2 to 5 nights after a full or new moon; anywhere from a few dozen to thousands of grunion can appear during a run. They prefer wide, flat, sandy beaches (such as the Coronado Strand, Mission Beach, and La Jolla Shores); you'll spot more grunion if you go to a less-populated stretch of beach, with a minimum of light. For details, go to the little critters' website, **www. grunion.org**, or check with the Department of Fish and Game at **www.dfg. ca.gov**.

The **Museum of Photographic Arts** in Balboa Park (© **619/238-7559;** www.mopa. org) and the **Museum of Contemporary Art San Diego** in La Jolla (© **858/454-3541;** www.mcasd.org) both have ongoing film programs that are worth investigating. The **IMAX Dome Theater** at the Reuben H. Fleet Science Center (© **619/238-1233;** www. rhfleet.org), also in Balboa Park, features movies projected onto an enormous tilted dome screen (films are shown in the early evening, with later screenings on weekends). Planetarium shows are held the first Wednesday of the month.

CASINOS

San Diego County has 18 Native American tribes—more than any other county in the nation. Half of them operate casinos in east and north San Diego County, and the **Convention & Visitors Bureau** (© **619/232-3101;** www.sandiego.org) has comprehensive listings and discount coupons on its website. Locations are shown on the "Eastern San Diego County" map on p. 265.

The most easily accessible casino from the downtown area is **Viejas Casino,** 5000 Willows Rd. in Alpine (© **800/847-6537** or 619/445-5400; www.viejas.com)—it's a straight shot out I-8 (exit Willows Rd.), less than a half-hour's drive away. Besides the usual table games, slots, bingo, and satellite wagering, Viejas presents an outdoor summer concert series that draws major artists; there is also an outlet center with more than 50 brand-name retailers. In 2006, the casino added 48,000 square feet of new space, encompassing a VIP lounge and high-end bar, the V Lounge.

The **Barona Valley Ranch Resort & Casino** is at 1932 Wildcat Canyon Rd., Lakeside (© **888/722-7662** or 619/443-2300; www.barona.com). Take I-8 East to Route 67 North; at Willows Road, turn right and continue to Wildcat Canyon Road; turn left and continue 6 miles to the 7,500-acre Barona Reservation (allow 40 min. from downtown). The casino features 2,000 Vegas-style slots, 70 table games, and an off-track betting area.

The resort, which includes 400 guest rooms, a spa, and an 18-hole championship golf course, restricts alcohol consumption (limited to the hotel, steakhouse, and golf course), but allows smoking (the Indian reservations are exempt from California's nonsmoking laws).

Sycuan Resort & Casino is outside El Cajon, at 5469 Casino Way (© **800/279-2826** or 619/445-6002; www.sycuan.com). Follow I-8 East for 10 miles to the El Cajon Boulevard exit. Take El Cajon 3 blocks to Washington Avenue, turning right and continuing on Washington as it turns into Dehesa Road. Stay on Dehesa for 5 miles, and follow the signs (allow 30 min. from downtown). Sycuan features more than 2,000 slots, 60 gaming tables, a 24-table poker room, a 1,200-seat bingo palace, and a 450-seat theater that books name touring acts. A nonsmoking boutique casino, complete with separate entrance, opened in 2008. The nearby resort offers 100 rooms and 54 holes of golf.

To bet on the ponies, go to the **Del Mar** racetrack during the local racing season (mid-July to early Sept); see p. 231 for more details. At any time of the year, you can also bet on races being run far and wide at **Surfside Race Place,** at the Del Mar fairgrounds (© **858/755-1167;** www.surfsideraceplace.com).

6 ONLY IN SAN DIEGO

San Diego's top three attractions—the **San Diego Zoo, Wild Animal Park,** and **Sea-World**—all keep extended summer hours; SeaWorld caps off its "Summer Nights" at 9:30pm with a **fireworks** display that's visible from anywhere around Mission Bay.

San Diego's most unique movie venue is experienced at **Movies Before the Mast** (© **619/234-9153;** www.sdmaritime.org), aboard the *Star of India* at the waterfront Maritime Museum. During July and August, nautically themed movies are shown on a special "screensail" Fridays and Saturdays at 8pm. Fridays are "date" night; Saturdays are for families ($13 adults, $8 children 12 and under).

In Balboa Park, **Starlight Theatre** presents Broadway musicals in the Starlight Bowl from June through September (© **619/544-7827;** www.starlighttheatre.org). What's unusual, though, is that the venue is under the flight path to Lindbergh Field, and when planes pass overhead, singers stop in midnote and wait for the roar to cease.

Side Trips from San Diego

Popular day trips include the beaches and inland towns of **"North County"** (as locals call the part of San Diego County north of the I-5/I-805 junction), as well as our south-of-the-border neighbor, **Tijuana.** All are less than an hour away.

If you have time for a longer trip, you can explore some distinct areas (all within 2 hr. of the city), such as the **Disneyland Resort** in Anaheim; the wine country of **Temecula;** the gold-mining town of **Julian,** known for its apple pies; and the vast **Anza-Borrego Desert.** Whichever excursion you choose, you're in for a treat.

1 NORTH COUNTY BEACH TOWNS: SPOTS TO SURF & SUN

The string of picturesque beach towns that dot the coast of San Diego County from Del Mar to Oceanside make great day-trip destinations for sun worshipers and surfers. *Be forewarned:* You'll be tempted to spend the night.

ESSENTIALS

GETTING THERE **Del Mar** is only 18 miles north of downtown San Diego, **Carlsbad** about 33 miles, and **Oceanside** approximately 36 miles. If you're driving, follow I-5 N.; Del Mar, Solana Beach, Encinitas, Carlsbad, and Oceanside all have freeway exits. The northernmost point, Oceanside, will take about 45 minutes. The other choice by car is to wander up the old coast road, known as Camino del Mar, "PCH" (Pacific Coast Hwy.), Old Hwy. 101, and County Hwy. S21.

From San Diego, the **Coaster** commuter train provides service to Solana Beach, Encinitas, Carlsbad, and Oceanside; and **Amtrak** stops in Solana Beach—just a few minutes north of Del Mar—and Oceanside. The Coaster makes the trip a number of times (6:30am–7pm) on weekdays and four times on Saturday; Amtrak passes through about 11 times daily each way. For the Coaster, call © **800/262-7837** or 511, or visit www.transit.511sd.com; check with Amtrak at © **800/872-7245** or www.amtrak.com. United Express departs from Los Angeles and flies into the **McClellan Palomar Airport** (© **760/431-4646;** www.sdcounty.ca.gov), 3 miles east of I-5 in Carlsbad.

VISITOR INFORMATION The **San Diego North Convention and Visitors Bureau,** based in Escondido (© **800/848-3336** or 760/745-4741; www.sandiegonorth.com), can answer your questions about North County as well as the Anza-Borrego desert.

DEL MAR ★★

A small community, Del Mar is home to just more than 4,500 inhabitants in a 2-square-mile municipality. The town has adamantly maintained its independence, eschewing incorporation into the city of San Diego. It's one of the most upscale communities in the

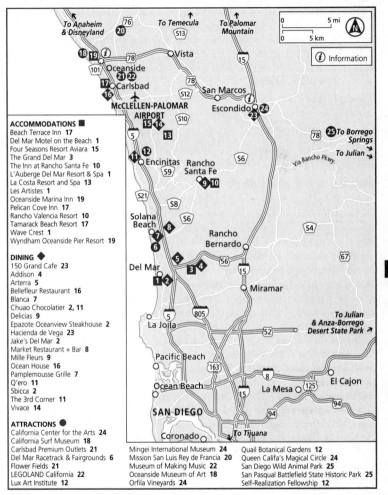

To Anaheim & Disneyland
To Temecula
To Palomar Mountain
0   5 mi
0   5 km

(i) Information

To Borrego Springs
To Julian
Via Rancho Pkwy.

Vista
Oceanside
Carlsbad
San Marcos
Escondido
McCLELLEN-PALOMAR AIRPORT
Encinitas
Rancho Santa Fe
Solana Beach
Del Mar
Rancho Bernardo
Miramar
La Jolla
Pacific Beach
Ocean Beach
SAN DIEGO
Coronado
La Mesa
El Cajon
To Tijuana
To Julian & Anza-Borrego Desert State Park

ACCOMMODATIONS ■
Beach Terrace Inn **17**
Del Mar Motel on the Beach **1**
Four Seasons Resort Aviara **15**
The Grand Del Mar **3**
The Inn at Rancho Santa Fe **10**
L'Auberge Del Mar Resort & Spa **1**
La Costa Resort and Spa **13**
Les Artistes **1**
Oceanside Marina Inn **19**
Pelican Cove Inn **17**
Rancho Valencia Resort **10**
Tamarack Beach Resort **17**
Wave Crest **1**
Wyndham Oceanside Pier Resort **19**

DINING ◆
150 Grand Cafe **23**
Addison **4**
Arterra **5**
Bellefleur Restaurant **16**
Blanca **7**
Chuao Chocolatier **2, 11**
Delicias **9**
Epazote Oceanview Steakhouse **2**
Hacienda de Vega **23**
Jake's Del Mar **2**
Market Restaurant + Bar **8**
Mille Fleurs **9**
Ocean House **16**
Pamplemousse Grille **7**
Q'ero **11**
Sbicca **2**
The 3rd Corner **11**
Vivace **14**

ATTRACTIONS ●
California Center for the Arts **24**
California Surf Museum **18**
Carlsbad Premium Outlets **21**
Del Mar Racetrack & Fairgrounds **6**
Flower Fields **21**
LEGOLAND California **22**
Lux Art Institute **12**

Mingei International Museum **24**
Mission San Luis Rey de Francia **20**
Museum of Making Music **22**
Oceanside Museum of Art **18**
Orfila Vineyards **24**

Quail Botanical Gardens **12**
Queen Califa's Magical Circle **24**
San Diego Wild Animal Park **25**
San Pasqual Battlefield State Historic Park **25**
Self-Realization Fellowship **12**

SIDE TRIPS FROM SAN DIEGO

11

NORTH COUNTY BEACH TOWNS: SPOTS TO SURF & SUN

greater San Diego area, yet Del Mar somehow manages to maintain a casual, small-town ambience that radiates personality and charm. Come summer, the town swells as visitors flock in for the thoroughbred horse-racing season and the county's San Diego Fair.

The history and popularity of Del Mar are inextricably linked to the **Del Mar Racetrack & Fairgrounds,** 2260 Jimmy Durante Blvd. ((C) **858/755-1161** or 793-5555; www.sdfair.com). In 1933, actor/crooner Bing Crosby developed the Del Mar Turf Club, enlisting the help of Hollywood celebrity friends including Lucille Ball, Desi Arnaz, Betty Grable, and Bob Hope. Soon the good times were off and running around Del Mar; racing season is mid-July through early September. The expansive complex also hosts San Diego's largest annual event, the **San Diego County Fair** (mid-June to early July), still referred to by most locals as the Del Mar Fair.

Two excellent beaches flank Del Mar: **Torrey Pines State Beach** and **Del Mar State Beach.** Both are wide, well-patrolled strands popular for sunbathing, swimming, and surfing (in marked areas). The sand stretches north to the mouth of the San Dieguito Lagoon, where people bring their dogs for a romp in the sea. Beyond the surf and the turf, the hub of activities for most residents and visitors is **Del Mar Plaza,** 1555 Camino del Mar (www.delmarplaza.com), an open-air shopping center with fountains, sculptures, and palazzo-style terraces. It has good restaurants and shops, and wonderful views to the sea, especially at sunset.

Essentials

For more information about Del Mar, contact or visit the **San Diego Coastal Chamber of Commerce,** 1104 Camino del Mar, Del Mar (© **858/755-4844;** www.delmarchamber. org). The hours of operation vary according to volunteer staffing but usually approximate weekday business hours. There's also a city-run website at **www.delmar.ca.us**.

Fun On & Off the Beach

Torrey Pines State Beach is accessed from I-5 via Carmel Valley Road; take a left on McGonigle Road to a large parking area to the south. For **Del Mar State Beach,** take 15th Street west to Seagrove Park, where you can usually find volleyballs and Frisbees in flight. Just past this cliff-side park is the sand; be aware parking spaces here are in short supply on weekends and any day in summer. There are **free concerts** at adjacent Power-house Park during the summer; for information, call © **858/635-1363,** or go to www. delmarfoundation.org. This grassy expanse extends right to the shore and gets its name from the distinctive building at its north end—a power plant built in 1928. It's now a community center with restrooms, showers, meeting space, and lovely verandas. *Note:* Del Mar's beaches and parks are smoke-free.

Beyond the surf and the turf is **Del Mar Plaza,** a multistory structure at the corner of Camino Del Mar and 15th Street. This is one stylish shopping center; its collection of restaurants and shops, coupled with the ocean views, make it a great place to while away an afternoon. Also check out the **Del Mar Library,** 1309 Camino del Mar (© **858/755-1666**), built in 1914 as St. James Catholic Church and restored in the 1990s by the city.

Most evenings near dusk, brightly colored **hot-air balloons** punctuate the skies just east of the racetrack; they're easily enjoyed from the racetrack area (and by traffic-jammed drivers on I-5). See "Outdoor Activities" in chapter 7 for more details.

Where to Stay
Very Expensive

The Grand Del Mar ★★★   Resembling a Tuscan villa transported to the foothills of Del Mar, this luxury resort boasts a Las Vegas–like opulence, from its marbled lobby to its manicured croquet lawn. Paying homage to the Spanish Revival creations of architect Addison Mizner, the Grand Del Mar features fragrant landscaping, Mediterranean-style courtyards, terraces and walkways with sweeping views of the Tom Fazio–designed golf course, as well as outdoor fireplaces and fountains. Other amenities include tennis courts, four swimming pools, a teen activity center, and a 21,000-square-foot spa. The signature restaurant, **Addison,** is one of San Diego's most refined dining rooms, and is the county's only AAA 5 Diamond restaurant. The resort's name is truly no idle boast; this is one grand hotel. *Note:* Gay rights activists have called for a boycott of this property in response to the owner's $125,000 contribution to Proposition 8 which, as of this writing, has outlawed same-sex marriage in California; see www.boycottmanchesterhotels.com.

5300 Grand Del Mar Court, San Diego, CA 92130. © **888/314-2030** or 858/314-2000. Fax 858/314-2001. www.thegranddelmar.com. 249 units. From $395 double; from $695 suites. Children 17 and under stay free in parent's room. AE, DC, DISC, MC, V. Valet parking. From I-5 merge onto Hwy. 56 E., exit Carmel Country Rd. and turn right, left at Grand Del Mar Way. Packages available. **Amenities:** 4 restaurants, including Addison (p. 234); 5 bars; live entertainment; kids' activity center; concierge; exercise room; 18-hole championship golf course; Jacuzzi; 4 swimming pools; room service; spa; 2 tennis courts. *In room:* A/C, TV/DVD, CD player, hair dryer, minibar, free Wi-Fi.

L'Auberge Del Mar Resort & Spa ★★★ Sporting a French beach-château look, this classy property is fresh off a top-to-bottom, $25-million renovation, completed in 2009. The most noticeable difference is the handsome new pool area with its lattice deck, chill-out fire pit area, and dramatic one-story water-wall feature. Guest rooms are casually sophisticated, and are given a homey touch by fireplaces and bureaus topped with shelves stocked with coffee-table books and decorative seashells. Not all are rooms-with-a-view, but many feature balconies or patios. Unchanged, of course, is the hotel's prime location—the beach is a 3-minute walk away down a private pathway, and Del Mar's main shopping and dining scene is just across the street. Fine dining has always been one of the resort's priorities, and the new signature eatery **Kitchen 1540** doesn't miss a beat. Serving a seasonal California cuisine that utilizes organic, sustainable products, Kitchen 1540 also has a charcuterie bar and lots of raw food designed for sharing. This is one of North County's destination dining spots; it offers some very cool outdoor dining opportunities, too.

1540 Camino del Mar (at 15th St.), Del Mar, CA 92014. © **800/245-9757** or 858/259-1515. Fax 858/755-4940. www.laubergedelmar.com. 120 units. From $350 double; from $600 suite. AE, DC, MC, V. Valet parking $25. Take I-5 to Del Mar Heights Rd. west, and then turn right onto Camino del Mar Rd. **Amenities:** Restaurant; 2 bars; concierge; access to nearby health club; Jacuzzi; 2 outdoor pools; room service; full-service spa; 2 tennis courts. *In room:* A/C, TV, CD player, hair dryer, minibar, MP3 docking station, free Wi-Fi.

Expensive

Del Mar Motel on the Beach (Finds) The only property in Del Mar right on the beach, this simply furnished little white-stucco motel has been here since 1946. All of the well-kept rooms are of good size; upstairs units have one king-size bed, and downstairs rooms have two double beds. Most of them don't have much in the way of a view, but two oceanfront rooms sit right over the sand (and are dressed up with fake plants and larger bathrooms). This is a good choice for beach lovers because you can walk along the shore for miles. Families can be comfortable knowing a lifeguard station is right next door, as are the popular seaside restaurants Poseidon and Jake's. The motel has a newly renovated deck with barbecue and picnic table for guests' use.

1702 Coast Blvd. (at 17th St.), Del Mar, CA 92014. © **800/223-8449** for reservations or 858/755-1534. www.delmarmotelonthebeach.com. 44 units (upper units with shower only). $269–$344 double; call for heavily reduced Oct–May rates. AE, DC, DISC, MC, V. Free parking. Take I-5 to Via de la Valle exit. Go west, and then south on Hwy. 101 (Pacific Coast Hwy.); veer west onto Coast Blvd. **Amenities:** Picnic and barbecue area; free use of boogie boards, beach chairs, and sand toys. *In room:* A/C, TV, fridge, hair dryer.

Wave Crest ★★ On a bluff overlooking the Pacific, these gray-shingled bungalow condominiums are beautifully maintained and wonderfully private—from the street it looks nothing like a hotel. The studios and suites surround a lovingly landscaped courtyard; each has a queen-size bed, sofa bed, reproduced artwork, stereo, full bathroom, and fully equipped kitchen with dishwasher. The studios sleep two people; the one-bedroom accommodates up to four; two-bedroom units can sleep six. Some units face the garden or shady street; rooms with ocean views are about $30 extra. In racing season (mid-July to early Sept), 90% of the guests are track-bound. It's a 5-minute walk to the beach, and shopping and dining spots are a few blocks away. There is an extra fee for maid service.

1400 Ocean Ave., Del Mar, CA 92014. ℂ **858/755-0100.** www.wavecrestresort.com. 31 units. $220–$260 studio; from $345 suite. Weekly rates available. MC, V. Free parking. Take I-5 to Del Mar Heights Rd. west, turn right onto Camino del Mar, and drive to 15th St. Turn left and drive to Ocean Ave., and turn left. **Amenities:** Jacuzzi; outdoor pool. *In room:* TV/DVD, kitchen.

Moderate

Les Artistes (Finds)   What do you get when you take a 1940s motel and put it in the hands of an architect with a penchant for prominent painters? The answer is an intriguingly funky, disarmingly informal hotel, just a few blocks from downtown Del Mar. None of the rooms at this nonsmoking property have an ocean view, but charming touches abound—a lily and koi pond, Asian chimes, and climbing bougainvillea. Ten rooms have been redone as tributes to favored artists; two more were given a Japanese makeover. Artists spotlighted include Diego Rivera, whose room gives you the feeling of stepping into a warm Mexican painting; the Japanese Furo room features a soaking tub carved into the bathroom floor. Downstairs rooms in the two-story structure have tiny private garden decks. A sister B&B, the 5-room **Secret Garden Inn,** is located adjacent to the owner's nearby **Cafe Secret Bistro,** 1140 El Camino Real (ℂ **858/481-4239**), a Euro-style bistro serving breakfast and lunch.

944 Camino del Mar, Del Mar, CA 92014. ℂ **858/755-4646.** www.lesartistesinn.com. 12 units. $105–$250 double. Rates include continental breakfast. DISC, MC, V. Free parking. From I-5 go west on Del Mar Heights Rd., and then left onto Camino Del Mar Rd. Pets accepted with $50 cash deposit plus $30 cleaning fee. *In room:* TV.

Where to Dine

Head to the upper level of the centrally located Del Mar Plaza, at Camino del Mar and 15th Street. You'll find **Il Fornaio Cucina Italiana** ★ (ℂ **858/755-8876;** www.ilfornaio.com), for moderately priced and pleasing Italian cuisine and an *enoteca* (wine bar) with great ocean views; **Pacifica Del Mar** ★★ (ℂ **858/792-0476;** www.pacificadelmar.com), which serves outstanding seafood; as well as **Epazote Oceanview Steakhouse** (see review below). Head west from the plaza on 15th Street, and you'll run into neighborhood favorite **Sbicca** ★★, 215 15th St. (ℂ **858/481-1001;** www.sbiccabistro.com), serving modern American cuisine sweetened with great wine deals; right on the beach is **Poseidon,** 1670 Coast Blvd. (ℂ **858/755-9345;** www.theposeidonrestaurant.com), good for California cuisine and fabulous sunsets.

The racetrack contingent congregates at **Bully's Restaurant,** 1404 Camino del Mar (ℂ **858/755-1660;** www.bullysprimerib.com), for burgers, prime rib, and crab legs. It's worth ducking into just to get a look at the fabulously carved front door. Also near the track, located in the Flower Hill Mall, is **Paradise Grille** ★, 2690 Via de la Valle (ℂ **858/350-0808;** www.paradisegrille.com), a casual-but-sophisticated spot for seasonal California cuisine. And if you're looking for fresh seafood—and lots of it—make a beeline to the Del Mar branch of San Diego's popular **Fish Market** ★, 640 Via de la Valle (ℂ **858/755-2277;** www.thefishmarket.com), near the racetrack (and reviewed on p. 178).

Addison ★★★ FRENCH   Set on a hillside overlooking a golf course, this standalone restaurant at the Grand Del Mar hotel is San Diego County's one and only AAA 5 Diamond dining establishment. Although it is named for Addison Mizner—the early-20th-century architect noted for his work in Florida—Palm Beach will be the last place on your mind when you arrive here. With its gaping fireplaces, plush draperies, carved

stone columns, and wrought-iron fixtures, this sumptuous dining destination is grandly
European. There's even a private banquet space that resembles a great room in a Spanish
castle. Featuring daily four- or seven-course tasting menus of modern French cuisine,
chef William Bradley incorporates the best local and seasonal ingredients. There's also a
jaw-dropping wine list that's more like a wine book; Addison has some 3,100 wine selections (and a knowledgeable staff to keep you from getting too overwhelmed by them).

5200 Grand Del Mar Way (from I-5 merge onto Hwy. 56 E., exit Carmel Country Rd. and turn right, then
left at Grand Del Mar Way). ℭ 858/314-1900. www.addisondelmar.com. Reservations recommended.
4-course menu $98; 7-course menu $140. AE, DC, DISC, MC, V. Tues–Sat 5:30–10pm. Bar Tues–Sat
5–11pm. Complimentary valet parking.

Arterra ★★ CALIFORNIAN   The name of this restaurant derives from "art of the
earth," and the moniker is no mere marketing gimmick. The menu is crafted based on
what's available at Chino or Be Wise, the local farms specializing in fine produce. Needless to say, the menu is regularly adapted to meet the schedule of Mother Earth. You'll
never eat rigid hothouse tomatoes—Arterra doesn't serve them in winter, when tomatoes
don't grow naturally in San Diego. Patrons can also sample a variety of chef's tasting
meals with wine pairings; there is a sushi bar, as well. Housed in a businesslike, modern
Marriott hotel, the broad dining room is impressive, cast in gold and purple tones, with
plush leather banquettes and accents of glass and copper. The stylish outdoor pool lounge
serves small plates and hosts DJs Thursday to Saturday.

11966 El Camino Real (next to I-5 in the Marriott Del Mar), Carmel Valley. ℭ 858/369-6032. www.arterra
restaurant.com. Reservations recommended. Main courses $12–$16 breakfast buffet, $14–$25 lunch,
$24–$60 dinner. AE, DC, DISC, MC, V. Breakfast Mon–Fri 6:30–10:30am and Sat–Sun 7–11:30am; lunch
Mon–Fri 11:30am–2pm; dinner Mon–Sat 5:30–9:30pm; lounge menu daily 11am–midnight. Free 3-hr.
parking with validation, or $7 for valet parking.

Epazote Oceanview Steakhouse ★ AMERICAN   This splendid perch sits a
couple of stories above Camino del Mar in the Del Mar Plaza, and although you're set
back a few blocks from the beach, the unimpeded sea views are regal. Epazote offers
contemporary steak and seafood that gets highlighted on a nightly three-course tasting
menu. The best bet, though, is to come for the long, daily happy hour (3–7pm) when
there's a selection of appetizers and drinks for $5. The lounge scene at Epazote's mood-lit
Z Ocean Bar includes live jazz on Thursday and Saturday, and a DJ on Friday—with
killer sunsets at no extra charge. This Del Mar favorite has long been known for its
wicked house margarita made with fresh lime and lemon juice, served in individual shakers over rocks; all in all, not a bad way to finish off a day of retail therapy at the shopping
center.

1555 Camino del Mar (at 15th St.), Del Mar Plaza. ℭ 858/259-9966. www.epazotedelmar.com. Reservations recommended on weekends. Main courses $9–$16 lunch, $16–$39 dinner. AE, DC, DISC, MC, V.
Lunch Mon–Sat 11:30am–3pm; dinner Sun–Thurs 5–9:30pm, Fri–Sat 5–10:30pm; bar menu daily from
3pm to close. Free 2-hr. parking in garage with validation. Bus: 101.

Jake's Del Mar ★ SEAFOOD/CALIFORNIAN   The spirit of "aloha" permeates this
Hawaiian-owned seafood-and-view outpost. Occupying a building originally constructed
in 1910, Jake's has a perfect seat next to the sand so that diners on a series of terraces
behind glass get straight-on views of the beach scene—sunbathers, surfers, and the occasional school of dolphins pass by. The predictable menu can't live up to the panorama,
but it's prepared competently and service is swift (too swift, actually—don't let them rush
you). At lunch you'll find a mixed seafood grill and pecan-crusted sea bass; sandwiches

and salads round out the offerings. Dinner brings in the big boys: Maine lobster tails, giant scampi, and rack of lamb, for example. To enjoy the scene without the wallet wallop, come for happy hour (Mon–Fri 4–6pm and Sat 2:30–4:30pm), when a shorter bar/bistro menu is up to half-off; mai tais are $3.50 on Wednesday.

1660 Coast Blvd. (at 15th St.), Del Mar. 📞 **858/755-2002.** www.jakesdelmar.com. Reservations recommended. Main courses $10–$16 lunch, $10–$53 dinner, $11–$17 brunch. AE, DISC, MC, V. Tues–Sat 11:30am–2:30pm; Sun brunch 10am–2pm; daily 5–9pm (Fri–Sat until 9:30pm). Valet parking $3. Bus: 101.

Market Restaurant + Bar ★★★ CALIFORNIAN Native San Diegan Carl Schroeder has made a major splash with this comfortably elegant restaurant in an off-the-beaten path location. Schroeder specializes in a regional San Diego cuisine, showcasing the best ingredients from the area's top farms, ranches, and fishmongers. The menu is printed daily, depending on what he finds at the produce stands; the weekly wine list is no less quality-obsessed, focusing on small and nontraditional wineries. Past Market menu items have included blue cheese soufflé with roasted pears, candied pecans, and fig-port reduction; tempura black sea bass; and a tasting of game hen served three ways. Market has also introduced a new sushi menu. This is truly fine dining in a relaxed atmosphere.

3702 Via de la Valle (at El Camino Real), Del Mar. 📞 **858/523-0007.** www.marketdelmar.com. Reservations recommended. Main courses $24–$35; sushi $4–$22. AE, MC, V. Daily 5–10pm. Free valet parking. Bus: 308.

Pamplemousse Grille ★★★ FRENCH The whimsical interior murals of pigs on parade and a slouched chef with a cigarette dangling from his lips might lead one to believe this isn't a serious restaurant. Even the name, which is French for grapefruit, is a bit silly. Yes, there is a lighthearted touch to the operation, but make no mistake—this is one of the county's upper-echelon dining destinations. The menu is contemporary French, and includes plentiful seafood options, as well as a vegetarian entree; you can also personalize your meal by creating your own main course of grilled meats (prime rib-eye, rack of lamb) with a choice of sauce (wild mushroom, peppercorn), and a side of veggies and potatoes (truffled Parmesan fries). You may be loath to order a burger at an upscale place like this, but there's a great one here.

514 Via de la Valle (across from the Del Mar Fairgrounds), Solana Beach. 📞 **858/792-9090.** www.pgrille.com. Dinner reservations recommended (and a necessity during race season). Main courses $20–$25 lunch (served Fri only), $24–$53 dinner. AE, MC, V. Daily 5–9pm; Fri lunch 11:30am–2pm. Bus: 308.

SOLANA BEACH, ENCINITAS & CARLSBAD ★

North of Del Mar and a 45-minute drive from downtown San Diego, the pretty communities of Solana Beach, Encinitas, and Carlsbad provide many reasons to linger on the California coast: good swimming and surfing beaches, small-town atmosphere, an abundance of antiques and gift shops, and a seasonal display of the region's most beautiful flowers.

Carlsbad was named after Karlsbad, Czechoslovakia, because of the similar mineral (some say curative) waters each produced. Carlsbad's once-famous artesian well was capped in the 1930s, but was redrilled in 1994—and the healthful water is flowing once more. Along with its neighbor Encinitas, Carlsbad is a noted commercial flower-growing region. A colorful display can be seen at **Carlsbad Ranch** (p. 238) each spring, when 50 acres of solid ranunculus fields bloom into a breathtaking rainbow visible even from the freeway. In December, the nurseries are alive with holiday poinsettias.

Visitor Information

The **Solana Beach Visitor Center** is near the train station at 103 N. Cedros (© **858/ 350-6006;** www.solanabeachchamber.com). The **Encinitas Visitors Center** is at 859 Second St. (corner of H St.) in downtown Encinitas (© **800/953-6041** or 760/753-6041; www.encinitaschamber.com). The **Carlsbad Visitor Information Center,** 400 Carlsbad Village Dr. (in the old Santa Fe Depot; © **800/227-5722** or 760/434-6093; www.carlsbadca.org), has information on flower fields and nursery touring.

Family Fun

LEGOLAND California ★ (Kids)   Opened in 1999, this 128-acre theme park is the ultimate monument to the world's most famous plastic building block. This is the world's third LEGOLAND, following branches in Denmark and Britain (and now Germany). Forty minutes north of downtown San Diego, the Carlsbad park offers a full day of entertainment for families. **Note:** LEGOLAND is geared toward children ages 2 to 12, and there's just enough of a thrill-ride component to amuse preteens, but teenagers will find it a bit of a snooze. There are more than 50 rides, shows, and attractions, including hands-on interactive displays; a life-size menagerie of tigers, giraffes, and other animals; and scale models of international landmarks (the Eiffel Tower, Sydney Opera House, and so on), all constructed of LEGO bricks. In addition to 5,000 LEGO models, the park is beautifully landscaped with bonsai trees and other plants from around the world. LEGO-LAND's latest draw is the Egyptian-themed **Land of Adventure,** where the signature ride takes you on a search for stolen treasure and tests your laser shooting skills; **Pirate Shores** features four water-based attractions—all designed to get you good and wet; and the **Wild Woods** miniature golf course plays through more than 40 LEGO forest animals. In 2008, a sister attraction opened just outside the LEGOLAND gates—**Sea Life Aquarium,** focusing on the creatures (real ones, not LEGO facsimiles) found in regional waters from the Sierra Mountains to the depths of the Pacific. The highlight of this interactive, educational aquarium experience is a 200,000-gallon tank with sharks, rays, and colorful tropical fish; a 35-foot acrylic tunnel takes you right into the depths of it. Separate admission is required; discounted two-park tickets are available.

1 Legoland Dr. © **877/534-6526** or 760/918-5346. www.legoland.com or www.sealifeus.com. LEGO-LAND $63 adults, $53 seniors and children 3–12, free for children 2 and under; Sea Life $19 adults, $16 seniors, $12 children; discounted 1- or 2-day park-hopper tickets available. AE, DISC, MC, V. July–Aug daily 10am–8pm; June daily 10am–5 or 6pm; off season Thurs–Mon 10am–5 or 6pm. Closed Tues–Wed Sept–May, but open daily during winter and spring vacation periods. Parking $10. From I-5 take the Cannon Rd. exit east ½ mile, following signs for Legoland Dr. Bus: 321.

Shoppers' Delight

From Adidas to Juicy, Bose to Swarovski, some of the biggest names in fashion and retail are elbow to elbow at **Carlsbad Premium Outlets,** Paseo del Norte, via Palomar Airport Road (© **888/790-7467** or 760/804-9000; www.premiumoutlets. com). This smart, upscale outlet mall features some 90 stores, including Crate & Barrel, Barney's New York, Nine West, and Harry & David. It even has a fine-dining component: Bellefleur Winery & Restaurant (p. 242).

Carlsbad and its neighbor Encinitas make up a noted commercial flower-growing region. The most colorful display can be seen each spring at the **Flower Fields at Carlsbad Ranch,** 5704 Paseo del Norte (© **760/431-0352;** www.theflowerfields.com), just east of I-5 on Palomar Airport Road; see p. 20 in chapter 3 for additional information on this seasonal event. Also popular is **Weidners' Gardens,** 695 Normandy Rd., Encinitas (© **760/436-2194;** www.weidners.com). Its field of 25,000 tuberous begonias blooms from mid-May to August; fuchsias and impatiens show their true colors between March and September; and the holiday season brings an explosion of pansies and poinsettias, as well as the opportunity to dig your own pansies. Touring the grounds is free; Weidners is open to the public November 1 to December 22 and March 1 through Labor Day, 9am to 5pm (4:30pm in winter), and closed Tuesdays.

Even if you don't visit during the spring bloom—or during December, when area nurseries shine with holiday poinsettias—there's plenty for the avid gardener to enjoy throughout the year. In fact, North County is such a popular destination for horticultural pursuits, there's a **North County Nursery Hoppers Guide** in Encinitas. It's a comprehensive leaflet describing all the area growers and nurseries, including a map that shows where to find flowers; it's available at local visitor centers, or contact Weidners' Gardens for more information. Also read about the gardens at the Self-Realization Fellowship below.

Quail Botanical Gardens ★

You don't have to possess a green thumb to be satisfied with an afternoon at this wonderful botanical facility. Boasting the country's largest bamboo collection, plus more than 35 acres of California natives, exotic tropicals, palms, cacti, Mediterranean, Australian, and other unusual collections, this serene compound is crisscrossed with scenic walkways and trails. The newest attraction is the Children's Garden, featuring a treehouse built into a 20-foot, climbable tree. Guided tours are given Saturdays at 10am, and there's a gift shop and nursery; a variety of special events and classes (including bird-watching, children's activities, and floral design) are scheduled throughout the year. The gardens are free to everyone on the first Tuesday of the month.

230 Quail Gardens Dr., Encinitas. © **760/436-3036.** www.qbgardens.com. Admission $10 adults; $7 seniors, students, and military; $5 children 3–12; free for children 2 and under. AE, MC, V. Daily 9am–5pm. Parking $1. From San Diego take I-5 N. to Encinitas Blvd.; go ¹/₂ mile east, left on Quail Gardens Dr.

More Fun Things to See & Do

The hub of activity for Solana Beach is South Cedros Avenue, 1 block east of and parallel to the Pacific Coast Highway. In a 2-block stretch (from the train station south) are many of San Diego's best furniture and home-design shops, antiques stores, art dealers, and boutiques selling imported goods. You'll also find **The Belly Up Tavern,** one of San Diego's most appealing concert venues (p. 219).

If you've ever wanted to get a glimpse into the artistic process, get yourself to the **Lux Art Institute** in Encinitas, 1550 S. El Camino Real (© **760/436-6611;** www.luxart institute.com). This unique facility, a work of art in itself, allows visitors to watch as an artist-in-residence paints, sculpts, or draws in a studio environment. It's open to the public Thursday and Friday 1 to 5pm, and Saturday from 11am to 5pm ($10, ticket good for two visits; free for those 20 and under). Every third Wednesday of the month is Lux@night, a free wine-and-cheese reception from 7 to 9pm.

If you've got something a little less lofty in mind, head to the beach. Everyone flocks to **Moonlight Beach** for good reason—it offers plenty of facilities, including free parking, free Wi-Fi, a children's playground, volleyball nets, restrooms, showers, picnic tables, and fire grates. The beach entrance is at the end of B Street (at Encinitas Blvd.). Also in Encinitas is the appropriately serene **Swami's Beach.** It's named for the adjacent Self-Realization Fellowship (see below), whose lotus-shaped towers are emulated in the pointed wooden stairway leading to the sand from First Street. This lovely little beach is surfer central; it adjoins little-known **Boneyard Beach,** directly to the north. Here, low-tide coves provide shelter for romantics and nudists; this isolated stretch can be reached only from Swami's Beach. There's a free parking lot at Swami's, plus restrooms and a picnic area.

The **Self-Realization Fellowship Hermitage and Meditation Gardens** (© 760/753-2888; www.yogananda-srf.org) was founded in 1920 by Paramahansa Yogananda, a guru born and educated in India. The exotic-looking domes are what remain of the retreat originally built in 1937 (the rest was built too close to the cliff edge and tumbled to the beach); today the site serves as a spiritual sanctuary for holistic healers and their followers. Serene meditation gardens, with their often-beautiful flower displays and koi ponds, line a cliff; they're a terrific place to cool off on a hot day, and no disciples will give you a sales pitch. The gardens are entered at 215 K St. and are open Tuesday through Saturday 9am to 5pm, and Sundays 11am to 5pm; admission is free. The **Hermitage,** where Yogananda lived and worked for many years, is also on-site and usually open Sundays from 2 to 5pm. A bookstore and gift shop that sells Fellowship publications and distinctive arts and crafts from India is nearby at 1150 S. Coast Hwy.

Carlsbad is a great place for antiquing. Whether you're a serious shopper or seriously window-shopping, park the car and stroll the 3 blocks of **State Street** between Oak and Beech streets. Two dozen shops occupy this part of town, where diagonal street parking and welcoming merchants lend a village atmosphere. Wares range from estate jewelry to country quilts, from inlaid sideboards to Depression glass. You never know what you'll find, but there's always something.

What about those therapeutic waters that put Carlsbad on the map? They're still bubbling at the **Carlsbad Mineral Water Spa,** 2802 Carlsbad Blvd. (© 760/434-1887; www.carlsbadmineralspa.com), an ornate European-style building on the site of the original well. Step inside for mineral baths ($65 for 30 min.), massages, or body treatments in the spa's exotic theme rooms—or just pick up a refreshing bottle of this "Most Healthful Water" to drink on the go.

Carlsbad State Beach (aka Tamarack Surf Beach) parallels downtown and has a wide concrete walkway that's a fine place to take a stroll. It attracts outdoor types for walking, jogging, and inline skating even at night (thanks to good lighting). Although the sandy strand is narrow, the beach is popular with bodysurfers, boogie boarders, and fishermen; surfers tend to stay away. Enter on Ocean Boulevard at Tamarack Avenue; there's an $8 fee per vehicle. About 4 miles south of town is **South Carlsbad State Beach** (© 760/438-3143; www.parks.ca.gov), with almost 3 miles of cobblestone-strewn sand. A state-run campground at the north end is immensely popular year-round; and if you're within 150 feet or so of the lifeguard headquarters, you'll be able to pick up the free Wi-Fi. There's a $10 per vehicle fee at the beach entrance, along Carlsbad Boulevard at Poinsettia Lane; area surfers favor the southern portion of the beach.

Just a stone's throw from LEGOLAND is a diversion for music lovers, the **Museum of Making Music,** 5790 Armada Dr. (© **877/551-9976** or 760/438-5996; www.museumofmakingmusic.org). Visitors go on a journey from Tin Pan Alley to MTV, stopping along the way to learn historic anecdotes about the American music industry; or try your hand at playing drums, guitars, or a digital keyboard. It's open Tuesday through Sunday from 10am to 5pm; admission is $7 for adults, $5 for military and children ages 6 to 18, free for children 5 and under.

Golfers might want to note San Diego's newest public course is the **Crossings at Carlsbad,** 5800 The Crossings Dr. (© **760/444-1800;** www.thecrossingsatcarlsbad.com). Located about 1 mile inland, this $70-million, 18-hole championship course features a 28,000-square-foot clubhouse, restaurant, bar, and ocean vistas.

Where to Stay
Very Expensive
Four Seasons Resort Aviara ★★★ (Kids)   In 1997, the top-drawer Four Seasons chain opened its first oceanview golf and tennis resort in the continental United States, and Aviara quickly overtook nearby La Costa (below) in the battle for high-end travelers. It also won over local residents, who now head here for summer jazz concerts and the exceptional signature restaurant, **Vivace.** When not wielding club or racquet, guests of this AAA 5 Diamond property can lie by the dramatically perched pool, relax in a series of carefully landscaped gardens, or luxuriate in the award-winning spa. A recreation center also offers everything from sand volleyball to bocce ball; there's even a surf concierge who can give lessons, and a beach butler who will arrange a perfect day at the beach for you. The ambience here is one of both privilege and comfort, but the rooms—with their passive pastel color schemes and nature prints—are beginning to feel dated. The hotel's Arnold Palmer–designed golf course maintains a harmony with the surrounding Batiquitos wetlands, incorporating native marshlike plants throughout its 18 holes. There's also a nature trail, perfect for a morning run or for keeping an eye for some of the 130 bird species that call the protected lagoon home.

7100 Four Seasons Point, Carlsbad, CA 92009. © **800/819-5053** or 760/603-6800. Fax 760/603-6801. www.fourseasons.com/aviara. 329 units. From $395 double; from $795 suite. Children 17 and under stay free in parent's room. AE, DC, DISC, MC, V. Valet parking $29. From I-5, take Poinsettia Lane east to Aviara Pkwy. S. **Amenities:** 4 restaurants (see Vivace review, p. 243); 2 bars; babysitting; bike rental; children's center and programs (age 4–12); concierge; golf course; health club; Jacuzzi; 2 outdoor pools; room service; spa; 6 lighted tennis courts; watersports equipment/rentals. *In room:* A/C, TV/DVD, CD player, fridge, hair dryer, minibar, Wi-Fi.

La Costa Resort and Spa ★★ (Kids)   Since 2001, La Costa has poured $140 million into a series of renovations, redefining the resort's California ranch–style motifs into a campuslike setting, with a 45-foot bell tower, white stucco walls, and red tile roofs. Rooms have been refashioned with leather headboards and beds trimmed in Egyptian-cotton linens, dark walnut desks, metal accents, and bathrooms with quaint pedestal sinks. A huge spa features 42 treatment rooms and neatly landscaped outdoor sunning areas, a sprawling gym, and the (Dr. Deepak) **Chopra Center,** with services and products relating to mind/body healing and transformation. The 400-acre property also boasts a 17-court racquet club and two championship 18-hole golf courses; the revamped golf clubhouse includes a state-of-the-art fitness center. **BlueFire Grill,** the stylish bar and signature restaurant, faces out onto a lovely plaza and has three distinctly different, chic spaces. Kids aren't overlooked here, either—La Costa has dedicated areas for everyone from toddlers to teens, featuring both high- and low-tech entertainments; the resort's Splash Landing even has theme park–style waterslides and play areas. La Costa recently added 149 privately owned luxury villas, which are available for rent, as well.

2100 Costa del Mar Rd., Carlsbad, CA 92009. ℂ **800/854-5000** or 760/438-9111. Fax 760/931-7585. www.lacosta.com. 610 units. From $264 double; from $349 suite; from $449 villa. Children 17 and under stay free in parent's room. $22/day resort fee. Golf, spa, and tennis packages available. AE, DC, DISC, MC, V. Valet parking $25 overnight; self-parking $12. From I-5 take La Costa Ave. east; left on El Camino Real. **Amenities:** 5 restaurants/cafes; 4 bars; bike rentals; children's center and programs (age 6 months–16); concierge; 2 golf courses; health club; 5 Jacuzzis; 8 outdoor pools; room service; spa; 17 tennis courts (7 lighted); Wi-Fi (free in lobby and other spaces). *In room:* A/C, TV, hair dryer, free Internet, minibar.

Expensive

Tamarack Beach Resort ★   Located in the village across the street from the beach, this resort property's rooms are restfully decorated with beachy wicker furniture. Privately owned suites—similar to Maui-style vacation condos—are also available, featuring stereos, full kitchens, washers, and dryers. The pretty Tamarack has a pleasant lobby and a sunny pool courtyard with barbecue grills. Popular with locals, the on-site restaurant, **Dini's by the Sea,** has an oceanview patio and is a good bet for steak and seafood.

3200 Carlsbad Blvd., Carlsbad, CA 92008. ℂ **800/334-2199** or 760/729-3500. Fax 760/434-5942. www. tamarackresort.com. 77 units. $210–$240 double (winter $149–$169); from $300 suite. Children 12 and under stay free in parent's room. Rates include continental breakfast. AE, MC, V. Free underground parking. **Amenities:** Restaurant; concierge; exercise room; 2 Jacuzzis; outdoor pool. *In room:* A/C, TV/DVD, fridge, hair dryer.

Moderate

Beach Terrace Inn ★   At Carlsbad's only beachside hostelry (others are across the road or a little farther away), almost all the rooms—as well as the pool and Jacuzzi—have ocean views. This downtown property is tucked between rows of high-rent beach cottages and touts its scenic location as its best quality. The rooms are extra-large, and some have balconies, fireplaces, and kitchenettes; suites make this a good choice for families. Plus you can walk everywhere from here—except LEGOLAND, which is a 5-minute drive away. *Note:* The entire property was renovated and reopened in June 2009.

2775 Ocean St., Carlsbad, CA 92008. ℂ **800/433-5415** or 760/729-5951. Fax 760/729-1078. www.beach terraceinn.com. 49 units. $185–$265 double; from $255 suite. Children 12 and under stay free in parent's room. Extra person $20. Rates include continental breakfast. AE, DC, DISC, MC, V. Free parking. **Amenities:** Jacuzzi; outdoor pool. *In room:* A/C, TV, fridge, hair dryer.

Pelican Cove Inn ★   Two blocks from the beach, this Cape Cod–style bed-and-breakfast hideaway combines romance with luxury. Your hosts see to your every need, from furnishing guest rooms with feather beds and down comforters to providing beach chairs and towels or preparing a picnic basket (with 24 hr. notice). Each room features a fireplace and private entrance; some have private spa tubs. The Pacific Room is most spacious, while the airy La Jolla Room has bay windows and a cupola ceiling. Courtesy transportation from the Carlsbad or Oceanside train stations is available.

320 Walnut Ave., Carlsbad, CA 92008. ℂ **888/735-2683** or 760/434-5995. www.pelican-cove.com. 10 units. $95–$215 double. Rates include full breakfast. Extra person $15. AE, MC, V. Free parking. From downtown Carlsbad, follow Carlsbad Blvd. south to Walnut Ave.; turn left and drive 2¹/₂ blocks. *In room:* TV, no phone, free Wi-Fi.

Where to Dine

Start your day with some carbo-loading at the **Potato Shack ★** in Encinitas, 120 W. I St. (ℂ **760/436-1282;** www.potatoshackcafe.com), or at other local hangouts such as

Swami's Cafe ★, also in Encinitas, 1163 S. Coast Hwy. 101 (© **760/944-0612;** www. swamis.signonsandiego.com), and the **Beach Grass Café** ★★, which also serves a great dinner. There are two Beach Grass locations: the original at 159 S. Coast Hwy. 101, Solana Beach (© **858/509-0632;** www.beachgrasscafe.com), and the newer, less stylish Encinitas branch at 1476 Encinitas Blvd. (© **760/942-2741**). Always crowded is **Fidel's Little Mexico** ★, known for reliably tasty Mexican food and kickin' margaritas. The restaurant is in Solana Beach at 607 Valley Ave. (© **858/755-5292**).

The architectural centerpiece of Carlsbad is **Ocean House,** 300 Carlsbad Village Dr. (© **760/729-4131;** www.oceanhousecarlsbad.com), a restored Victorian mansion complete with turrets and cupolas. The more formal dining area is in a fabulous 1920s-era pavilion where you can get items such as macadamia-crusted salmon or filet mignon; Sunday brunch is a tremendous buffet of breakfast and lunch items. There is also a casual cafe and bar where the menu includes burgers, pastas, and salads. Live music and DJs are regularly scheduled.

In Encinitas, look for **Vigilucci's Trattoria Italiana** ★, 505 S. Coast Hwy. 101 (at D St.; © **760/942-7332;** www.vigiluccis.com). This perennial favorite spawned a mini-empire of North County bistros, pizzerias, and steakhouses. Nearby **Siamese Basil** ★, 527 S. Coast Hwy. 101 (© **760/753-3940**), presents an innocuous facade and bland interior that belie a well-deserved reputation for fresh, zesty Thai food and a friendly attitude. You can even choose your spice quotient, from toddler-safe 1 to fire-alarm 10.

While in the North County, chocoholics must make a pilgrimage to **Chuao Choco-latier** (www.chuaochocolatier.com), one of the top artisan chocolate makers in the country. You'll find creative confections including dark chocolate bonbons laced with strawberry pulp and balsamic vinegar. Chuao has several locations, including the Lum-beryard shopping center, 937 S. Coast Hwy., Encinitas (© **760/635-1444**), and the Del Mar Heights Shopping Center, 3485 Del Mar Heights Rd., Del Mar (© **858/755-0770**).

Bellefleur Restaurant ★ CALIFORNIAN/MEDITERRANEAN
This busy restaurant boasts a "California winery" experience, although no wine country is evident among the surrounding outlet retailers and car dealerships. But its cavernous, semi-industrial dining room, coupled with the wood-fired and wine-enhanced aromas emanating from a clanging open kitchen, do somehow evoke the ambience of California wine-producing regions such as Santa Barbara and Napa. In addition to the main seating area, there are an open-air dining patio, a tasting bar, and a glassed-in barrel aging room. The place can be noisy and spirited, drawing exhausted shoppers for cuisine that incorporates North County's abundant produce with fresh fish and meats. It adds up to an experience that surpasses the shopping-mall standard. Sunday champagne brunch is served from 10am to 2pm.

5610 Paseo del Norte, Carlsbad. © **760/603-1919.** www.bellefleur.com. Reservations suggested. Lunch $9–$16; dinner $17–$35; brunch $22 adults, $10 children 2–11. AE, DC, DISC, MC, V. Mon–Thurs 11am– 9pm; Fri–Sat 11am–10pm; Sun 10am–9pm.

Blanca ★★★ CALIFORNIAN/FRENCH
Watch out, San Francisco. With a few more restaurants like Blanca, San Diego just might give the Golden Gate city a run for its foodie money. Despite its pedestrian, strip-mall location, this sleek, cosmopolitan space quickly ascended to the top of San Diego's food chain when it opened in 2006. Blanca uses only top seasonal products to prepare creative California cuisine with a modern French touch. Like several of the area's top restaurants, Blanca is only serving prix-fixe tasting menus; choose a three-, four-, or five-course dinner from fare such as duck breast

en sous vide with sweet potato purée, or Scottish halibut in burgundy demi-glace. The wine list will have connoisseurs cooing, too. The more casual lounge menu (happy hour Tues–Sun 5:30–7pm) includes truffled french fries, Jidori chicken satay, charcuterie, and artisan cheeses.

437 S. Hwy. 101 (north of Via de la Valle), Solana Beach. © 858/792-0072. www.dineblanca.com. Reservations recommended. 3-course menu $46; 4-course menu $56; 5-course menu $66. AE, DC, DISC, MC, V. Tues–Thurs 5:30–9:30pm; Fri–Sat 5:30–10:30pm; Sun 5:30–9pm. Valet parking $3. Bus: 101.

Q'ero ★★ LATIN AMERICAN (Finds The Q'ero are the isolated people of the Peruvian Andes who believe themselves to be the last descendants of the Inca, and the guardians of ancient knowledge. So thank your lucky mountain spirits that this tiny Encinitas restaurant has decided to share their food with us. Of course this is no ethnographical culinary survey; there's plenty of recognizable Latin American fare, from seviche and *papa relleno* (mashed potatoes stuffed with savory beef and raisins), to cheese-filled cornmeal-cake *arepas* and the melt-in-your mouth *tres leches* sponge cake. There are lots of exotic ingredients, too, from sweet *chancaca* glazes to the minty herb *huacatay,* so there's more than enough to keep adventurous eaters happy, as well. ***Note:*** This is a very small space; dinner reservations are a must. Also, if you nab one of the sidewalk tables, you will not be able to drink alcohol.

564 S. Coast Hwy. 101, Encinitas. © **760/753-9050.** Reservations recommended. Lunch $9–$18; dinner $19–$28. AE, DISC, MC, V. Tues–Sat 11:30am–3pm and 5–9pm (Fri–Sat till 10pm). Bus: 101.

Vivace ★★★ ITALIAN Romantically lit, plushly upholstered, and adorned with decorative glassware and elegant floral displays, Vivace is as striking a dining destination as San Diego has to offer. Located at the sumptuous Four Seasons Resort Aviara in Carlsbad, Vivace serves a seasonal, sophisticated menu of Italian fare, such as breast of guinea hen in butternut squash sauce; lamb *osso buco;* and rabbit with lentils, pancetta, and Brussels sprouts. If the weather is nice, request a table out on the terrace, which features ocean, lagoon, and golf course views; on a chilly evening, cozy up next to the fireplace. The Vivace experience is all about class and elegance.

7100 Four Seasons Point, Carlsbad. © **760/603-6999.** www.fourseasons.com/aviara. Reservations required. Main courses $32–$50. AE, DC, DISC, MC, V. Sun–Thurs 6–9:30pm; Fri–Sat 6–10pm. Validated valet parking only.

OCEANSIDE

For decades Camp Pendleton, the huge Marine base established in 1942, defined this northernmost community in San Diego County. Now a city of 170,000, Oceanside is forging an identity beyond the military, even to the point of nurturing a nascent artists' scene, anchored by the **Oceanside Museum of Art** (p. 244). Yes, this place still has an inordinate number of barbershops with Marines spilling out onto the sidewalk waiting to get their buzz cuts, but appealingly low-rise Oceanside has a welcoming, small-town feel. And it's caught the attention of restaurateurs and artists trying to find a place in the sun.

Oceanside claims almost 4 miles of beaches and has the West Coast's longest wooden pier, measuring 1,942 feet. The beach, pier (and its adjacent outdoor amphitheater), and downtown attractions are all within easy walking distance of the train station.

Visitor Information

Just north of downtown is the **California Welcome Center,** 928 N. Coast Hwy. (© **800/ 350-7873** or 760/721-1101; www.oceansidechamber.com). It provides information on local attractions, dining, and accommodations; it also has a gift shop.

One of the nicest things to do in Oceanside is to stroll around the city's upscale **harbor.** Surrounded by apartment complexes of unfortunate architecture, the harbor has a Cape Cod–themed shopping village with a rustic, if faux, charm; the marina bustles with pleasure craft, fishing boat charters, and sightseeing excursions. The **Harbor Days Festival,** held the third weekend in September, typically attracts 100,000 visitors for a crafts fair, entertainment, and food booths; call © 760/722-1534 for more details.

Probably the area's most important attraction is **Mission San Luis Rey de Francia ★**, 4050 Mission Ave. (© 760/757-3651; www.sanluisrey.org), located a few miles inland. Founded in 1798, it's known as the "King of the Missions," and is the largest of California's 21 missions. You can tour the mission, its impressive church, exhibits, and grounds; in the cemetery you'll find the names of some of California's most important early families (Pico, Alvarado, Bandini). The cost is $6 for adults, $5 seniors and military, $4 for ages 6 to 18, free for kids 5 and under. Hours are daily from 10am to 4pm; a gift shop and small bookstore/coffeehouse are also on-site.

For a wide selection of rental watercraft, head to **Boat Rentals of America,** 256 Harbor Drive S. (© 760/722-0028; www.boats4rent.com). It rents everything from kayaks, WaveRunners, and electric boats for relaxed harbor touring to 14- and 23-foot sailboats and powerboats. Even if you have no experience, the harbor provides plenty of room for exploration. Sample rates: single kayak, $15 per hour; powerboat, from $60 per hour; and WaveRunner, $105 per hour. Boat Rentals keeps seasonal hours, so call for specific information.

As of this writing, the **California Surf Museum ★** (© 760/721-6876; www.surf museum.org), is set to move into its new home, a slick, ocean-facing facility located at 312 Pier View Way. With its modern, wave-inspired facade, it will be a far cry from the museum's ramshackle former digs. Founded in 1985, the museum has an extensive collection that includes surfboards (everything from a 155-lb. redwood board to the motorized "Jet Board"), photos documenting surfing's early days, and other relics that chronicle the development of the sport. There's also a gift shop selling surf-themed music, T-shirts, and other items. The museum is open daily from 10am to 4pm; admission is free, but donations are welcomed.

Artists have begun converging in town over the last few years, drawn by cheaper rents and a slower pace than in San Diego. Art and commerce mash up nicely at **Swiv Tackle Circus ★**, 530 S. Coast Hwy. (© 760/439-3760; www.swivtacklecircus.com), a "gallertique" dealing in art and urban style. You'll find gallery shows, art supplies, books, DJs, and clothing inspired by surf, skate, and music culture. Galleries and studios are also found at the collective known as **Artists' Alley,** located behind the 200 block of North Coast Highway (btw. Mission Ave. and Pier View Way). Meanwhile, the **Oceanside Museum of Art ★**, 704 Pier View Way (© 760/435-3720; www.oma-online.org), presents contemporary artwork by both regional and international artists; past exhibits have included everything from pop surrealism to quilts. OMA's Central Pavilion, opened in 2008, is a cutting-edge glass-and-steel box space that links the museum complex's two other structures—Oceanside's old city hall, designed by Irving Gill in 1934, and a Gill-designed firehouse built in 1929. The museum also presents concerts, lectures, and films. OMA is open Tuesday through Saturday 10am to 4pm, Sunday 1 to 4pm; admission is $8 adults, $5 seniors, free for students.

Oceanside's string of beaches starts just outside Oceanside Harbor, and runs south to the border of Carlsbad. Along the way you can enjoy the **Strand,** a grassy park that begins just south of the jetty where the San Luis Rey River meets the ocean, and ends at **Wisconsin Street Beach.** The sandbar formed by the confluence of river and ocean makes **Breakwater Way** beach a popular spot for surfers. The beaches north of the pier are wide, sandy, and generally less crowded; **Pier View South** beach and **Tyson Street Park** are where you should go if you want to be in the thick of things. Between them, these two adjacent beaches offer restrooms, showers, picnic areas, fire rings, vendors, playgrounds, and surf lessons. Oceanside's world-famous surfing spots also attract competitions, including the **World Bodysurfing Championships** (p. 23) and **Longboard Surf Contest** (p. 23), both held in August. Parking is at metered street spaces or in pay lots, which can fill up on nice summer days. The most southern beaches have some free parking in lots or on the street.

Where to Stay & Dine

Book early for a summertime stay at the **Wyndham Oceanside Pier Resort,** 333 N. Myers St. (© **877/999-3223** or 760/901-1200; www.wyndham.com). The privately owned one- and two-bedroom suites at this new property look out over the pier and feature kitchens and sleeper sofas—and they book up fast. Beware of studio rooms with no view and train tracks for a neighbor. Rates vary by season and day of the week, ranging from moderate to expensive. The **Oceanside Marina Inn,** 2008 Harbor Dr. N. (© **800/252-2033** or 760/722-1561; www.omihotel.com), also has a scenic location, surrounded by water on three sides at the mouth of the harbor. The moderate-to-expensive rates will get you an exceptional view, but accommodations that are a bit on the dingy side. Plusses include an oceanview pool and spa, complimentary breakfast, and gas fireplaces; some rooms have fully equipped kitchens.

At the end of the long pier you'll find the 1950s-style diner **Ruby's** (© **760/433-7829;** www.rubys.com). This place can get crazy busy, but it's a great spot for burgers and fountain drinks, especially in the Tiki-inspired upstairs dining room and patio. Hipster sushi has debuted in Oceanside with the opening of **Harney Sushi,** 301 Mission Ave. (© **760/967-1820;** www.harneysushi.com). This is the sister restaurant of the Old Town favorite, and it features cool design, mood lighting, and DJs adding some grooves to go along with the rolls.

Several surf-and-turf harborside restaurant stalwarts are close by, too, including **Joe's Crab Shack** (© **760/722-1345;** www.joescrabshack.com), **Jolly Roger** (© **760/722-1831;** www.jollyrogerrestaurants.com), and **Monterey Bay Canners** (© **760/722-3474;** www.montereybaycanners.com).

Elsewhere in Oceanside, you can get a side helping of history with your burger and fries at the original **101 Cafe,** 631 S. Coast Hwy. (© **760/722-5220;** www.101cafe.net). This humble diner dates from the earliest days of the old coast highway, the only route between Los Angeles and San Diego until 1953 brought the interstate.

2 NORTH COUNTY INLAND

The coastal and inland sections of North County are as different as night and day. Inland you'll find beautiful scrub hills, citrus groves, and conservative ranching communities where agriculture plays an important role.

Rancho Santa Fe is about 27 miles north of downtown San Diego; from there the scenic Del Dios Highway (S6) leads to Escondido, 32 miles north of San Diego. Nearly

70 miles from the city is Palomar Mountain in the Cleveland National Forest, which spills over the border into Riverside County.

RANCHO SANTA FE

Exclusive Rancho Santa Fe was once the property of the Santa Fe Railroad, but the area was "discovered" in the early 1900s by movie director Theodore Reed, who encouraged his friends Douglas Fairbanks and Mary Pickford to purchase property as an investment; they bought 800 acres in 1924. After just a few minutes in town today, you'll notice that Rancho Santa Fe is a playground for the über wealthy, though not in the usual pretentious sense—this upscale slice of North County is a sweet little town that's enjoyed by everyone. Primarily residential, Rancho Santa Fe has just two hotels that blend into the stately eucalyptus groves surrounding the town. Shopping and dining—both refined and quite limited—revolve around a couple of understated blocks known locally as "the Village." There are more real estate businesses here than anything else, and the homes advertised all list for well into the seven digits. This is one of the most affluent communities in the United States.

Essentials

GETTING THERE   From San Diego, take I-5 N. to Lomas Santa Fe (County Hwy. S8) east; it turns into Linea del Cielo and leads directly into the Village. If you continue through town on Paseo Delicias, you'll pick up the Del Dios Highway (County Hwy. S6), the scenic route via Lake Hodges to Escondido and the **Wild Animal Park.**

Where to Stay

The Inn at Rancho Santa Fe ★★   Most of the accommodations at this 23-acre resort are tile-roofed Spanish Colonial Revival–style cottages, nestled throughout the property's beautifully landscaped grounds. It's an idyllic, community-like setting with chirping birds, flowering plants, and towering eucalyptus trees; and the Village is directly accessed from the inn's front door via a pathway surrounded by a manicured lawn and colorful garden. There are a variety of room styles (as well as one-, two-, and three-bedroom suites), ranging from rather austere digs with tile floors and vaulted ceilings to ones with a warmer, English country flavor; there are also generously sized rooms in the original 1920s lodge building. Some rooms have kitchenettes, modern marble bathrooms with tricked-out showers, and wood-burning fireplaces; others have secluded patios with outdoor fireplaces. The **Inn Fusion** restaurant serves classic steak and seafood fare, as well as Asian-inspired dishes; the lounge features a roaring fireplace and live piano music.

5951 Linea del Cielo (P.O. Box 869), Rancho Santa Fe, CA 92067. ⓒ **800/843-4661** or 858/756-1131. Fax 858/759-1604. www.theinnatrsf.com. 87 units. From $285 double; from $600 suite. Extra person $25. AE, DC, MC, V. Free parking. From I-5, take the Lomas Santa Fe exit, following signs to Rancho Santa Fe. The Inn is in the center of town. Pets accepted. **Amenities:** Restaurant; bar; babysitting; exercise room; nearby golf course; Jacuzzi; outdoor pool; room service; 3 tennis courts. *In room:* A/C, TV/DVD, hair dryer, free Wi-Fi.

Rancho Valencia Resort & Spa ★★★   Sister property of the La Valencia Hotel (p. 84) in La Jolla, Rancho Valencia is a luxurious tennis-resort hideaway set on 40 beautifully landscaped acres. It features 49 stand-alone, hacienda-style accommodations, all with fireplaces, custom furniture, and colorful tilework. The impressive $12-million spa facility, completed in 2006, encompasses 2½ acres; it has five pools—including a designated Watsu pool—indoor/outdoor treatment rooms, and couples rooms with fireplaces and private outdoor showers and tubs. Rancho Valencia's main dining room, with its oak-beamed ceilings, fireplace, and large picture windows, is at once rustic and sophisticated. Ask for table 42; you'll have unobstructed sunset vistas and be able to watch hot-air balloons drift by. Outdoor dining is available on the patio overlooking the tennis courts and the valley beyond, or in the old-world courtyard anchored by a small fountain and framed in bougainvillea. Playing privileges are offered at four nearby golf courses.

5921 Valencia Circle (P.O. Box 9126), Rancho Santa Fe, CA 92067. (📞 **800/548-3664** or 858/756-1123. Fax 858/756-0165. www.ranchovalencia.com. 49 units. From $450 double; from $550 suite. AE, DC, MC, V. Free parking. From I-5 take the Del Mar Heights exit heading east, go left on El Camino Real, right on San Dieguito Rd., right on Rancho Digueño Rd., and make an immediate left onto Rancho Valencia Dr. Pets $75 per day. **Amenities:** Restaurant; bar; bikes; concierge; exercise room; golf courses nearby; Jacuzzi; pool; ; pro shop; room service; spa; 17 tennis courts. *In room:* A/C, TV/DVD, CD player, CD library, fridge, hair dryer, free Internet, minibar.

Where to Dine

If you're looking for a casual lunch, breakfast, or snack, seek out **Thyme in the Ranch** ★★, 16905 Av. de Acacias (📞 **858/759-0747;** www.thymeintheranch.com), a bakery/cafe that's open Tuesday through Saturday from 7am to 3pm. Hidden on a small plaza behind chic Mille Fleurs, this tiny treasure is well known (as evidenced by constant lines at the counter). Salads, sandwiches, soup, and quiche are the menu mainstays—all delicious—but the baked treats are extra-special.

Delicias ★★ CALIFORNIAN   Refined but relaxed, with a welcoming, comfortable interior featuring a stone fireplace as its centerpiece, this cozy restaurant also has outdoor dining available on its patio and fireplace-warmed courtyard. Delicias is equally appropriate for a casual meal or special occasion; service is attentive and personable, and the food is delicious. The California cuisine menu includes appetizers such as wood-fire roasted mussels with chorizo, and maple-glazed pork belly; there's a main course vegetarian plate, as well as fine steaks. Classic comfort foods are also served, such as excellent burgers, pizzas, and mac-and-cheese (albeit primped with prosciutto, peas, and shaved truffles). Happy hour is scheduled Tuesday through Friday from 4 to 6pm.

6106 Paseo Delicias. (📞 **858/756-8000.** www.deliciasrestaurant.com. Reservations recommended on weekends. Main courses $11–$16 lunch, $25–$50 dinner. AE, DC, MC, V. Tues–Fri 11:30am–2:30pm; Tues–Sun 5:30–10pm.

Mille Fleurs ★★★ CALIFORNIAN/FRENCH   Chef Martin Woesle has been wowing critics and patrons for years at this landmark restaurant, owned by the same restaurateur who operates **Bertrand at Mister A's** (p. 105). Although Mille Fleurs has a French name and a Gallic country-cottage atmosphere, Woesle mixes in elements of American and Californian cuisine, along with tastes from his native Germany. Every dish, every dessert is a special here; the menu changes daily, highlighted by whatever Woesle has found during his morning sojourn to nearby Chino Farm. Expect something along the lines of squab breast and foie gras salad with arugula in a black truffle vinaigrette, or venison chop with potato noodles, fresh cherries, and asparagus flan in port-wine sauce. The sky's the limit with the dizzying wine list, one of the best in San Diego. The piano lounge features a nightly bistro menu, featuring more casual service and prices ($18–$30); Sunday through Tuesday you can take advantage of a three-course prix-fixe meal ($40). If you want to have a really private dinner, ask for the "Booth," a very intimate space that seats up to eight.

6009 Paseo Delicias. (📞 **858/756-3085.** www.millefleurs.com. Reservations recommended. Main courses $18–$29 lunch, $23–$42 dinner. AE, DC, MC, V. Thurs–Fri 11:30am–1:45pm; daily 6–9:30pm (from 5:30pm Sat).

Best known as the home of the San Diego Wild Animal Park (p. 127), Escondido is a city of 138,000, founded near the site of a historic battlefield where U.S. forces were routed during the Mexican-American War. Escondido is surrounded by agriculture, particularly citrus and avocado (neighboring Fallbrook is known as the avocado capital of the world). Grand Avenue, old Escondido's main drag, is experiencing a well-conceived renewal, with historic storefronts filled by new restaurants and an antiques district with a mother lode of finds. Two of the biggest are **Escondido Antique Mall,** 135 W. Grand (© 760/743-3210), and **Hidden Valley Antique Emporium,** 333 E. Grand (© 760/737-0333), each holding dozens of individual dealers.

This is also the site of the **California Center for the Arts ★**, 340 N. Escondido Blvd., an attractive 12-acre campus with postmodern architecture and two theaters, an art museum, and a conference center. Renowned symphonies, eclectic musical artists, Broadway roadshows, and national dance companies are regularly scheduled here, often making the 45-minute drive from downtown to Escondido (along I-15 N. to the Valley Pkwy. exit) worth the effort. To find out what's playing and to get tickets, call © **800/988-4253,** or visit www.artcenter.org.

Kids and their art-loving chaperones will want to check out the amazing **Queen Califia's Magical Circle ★★** (© 760/839-4691; www.queencalifia.org) at Kit Carson Park; the entrance to the park is at the corner of Bear Valley Parkway and Mary Lane (you can pick up pre-printed directions from the Mingei Museum; see below). This wildly fanciful creation is the only American sculpture garden by acclaimed artist Niki de Saint Phalle, who in the years before her death in 2002, called San Diego her home. This brilliantly imaginative work features 10 sculptures and totems—the tallest standing 24 feet—encircled by an undulating, 400-foot-long wall of mosaic snakes. Comprised of glass, stone, and tile, it's a riot of color and shape. Entrance is free, but it's closed on Mondays.

As this is a major agricultural area, the **farmers' market** on Tuesday afternoons is unsurprisingly one of the county's best. It's held on Grand Avenue, between Juniper and Kalmia streets (© 760/745-8877; www.sdfarmbureau.org), from 4 to 7pm in summer and 2:30 to 6pm the rest of the year. Another attraction is **Orfila Vineyards** on the way to the Wild Animal Park (see "Special-Interest Sightseeing," in chapter 7).

Two miles east of the Wild Animal Park is the **San Pasqual Battlefield State Historic Park** (© 760/737-2201; www.parks.ca.gov); there's a picnic area, a .5-mile loop trail, and a small museum that details the bloody clash of 1846 in which *Californios* loyal to Mexico, armed only with lances, were able to repulse—at least temporarily—invading U.S. troops. It's open weekends only, 10am to 5pm.

Visitor information is available at the **San Diego North Convention and Visitors Bureau,** 360 N. Escondido Blvd. in Escondido (© **800/848-3336** or 760/745-4741; www.sandiegonorth.com), open Monday through Friday 8:30am to 5pm.

Mingei International Museum ★   An offshoot of the wonderful Balboa Park museum (p. 139) devoted to "art of the people," this 21,000-square-foot Escondido branch opened in 2003 at the site of an abandoned JCPenney's department store. Rotating exhibitions offer folk art, crafts, and design from countries around the world; displays might encompass textiles, costumes, jewelry, toys, pottery, paintings, or sculpture. Permanent highlights include Niki de Saint Phalle's literally soaring *Angel of Temperance* sculpture and an insanely intricate Dale Chihuly glass chandelier with tendrils that float

ⓕFinds Grape Escape: Temecula Wineries

Over the line in Riverside County, 60 miles north of San Diego via I-15, **Temecula** is known for its 20-plus wineries and the increasingly noteworthy vintages they produce. The town's very name (pronounced "ta-*meck*-you-la") provides the first clue to this valley's success in the volatile winemaking business/art. It translates (from a Native American language) as "where the sun shines through the mist," identifying two climatological factors necessary for viticulture. A third component is Rainbow Gap, an opening to the south through the Agua Tibia Mountains that funnels cool afternoon sea breezes to the valley, which sits at an elevation of 1,500 feet. Some believe Franciscan friars from Mission San Luis Rey planted the first grapevines here in the early 1800s, but this was cattle country—the 87,000-acre Vail Ranch operated from 1904 until it was sold in 1964. Orange groves followed, but they gave way to grapevines; the first commercial vineyard was planted in 1968.

Most of the wineries are strung along Rancho California Road, and harvest time is generally from mid-August to September. But visitors are welcome year-round to tour, taste, and stock up. Among the more notable are **Callaway Vineyard & Winery** (ⓒ 800/472-2377 or 951/676-4001; www.callawaywinery.com), the biggest winery in the region and also the best known. In-depth tours are offered throughout the day between 11am and 3pm (4pm weekends), and they have a casual bistro. Across the street from Callaway stands another old-timer, **Thornton Winery** (ⓒ 951/699-0099; www.thorntonwine.com), which makes a good choice if you visit only one location—Thornton provides an all-in-one overview of Temecula's wine country. It has a striking setting, fragrant herb garden, extensive gift shop, and award-winning restaurant, and tours are offered on weekends, between 11am and 4pm. Jazz concerts are also presented from April to October.

Mount Palomar Winery (ⓒ 800/854-5177 or 951/676-5047; www.mount palomar.com) specializes in bordeaux-style blends, as well as port and sherry. Mount Palomar has big plans for the future, too, including enlarging its facilities and developing a wine country resort and spa. Perhaps the most welcoming tasting room is the yellow farmhouse of the **Maurice Car'rie Winery** (ⓒ 800/716-1711 or 951/676-1711; www.mauricecarriewinery.com), famous for its baked brie and sourdough bread. Farther up the road is a sister winery, **La Cereza Vineyard and Winery** (ⓒ 951/699-6961), which features a cigar lounge. Both wineries are open daily from 10am to 5pm, and each has gourmet deli items for composing a picnic to enjoy in Maurice Car'rie's rose-filled front garden and patio.

For detailed information on Temecula wine touring, contact the **Temecula Valley Winegrowers Association** (ⓒ 800/801-9463 or 951/699-6586; www. temeculawines.org) and request the *Wine Country* pamphlet, a guide with winery locations, hours, and a brief description of each. The **Temecula Valley Convention and Visitors Bureau,** 42031 Main St. (ⓒ 888/363-2852 or 951/ 506-0056; www.temeculacvb.com), has info on accommodations, golf, fishing, and the region's famous **Temecula Balloon & Wine Festival,** held in June (p. 166). Your best call, though, might be to **Grapeline** (ⓒ 888/894-6379 or 951/693-5755; www.gogrape.com), which can pick you up from your hotel and shuttle you on a wine country tour.

through the air like an alien jellyfish. The wonderful gift shop has books, toys, and doo-dads from around the world.

Where to Stay & Dine

Accommodations in Escondido are pretty much limited to economy chains, though the city will hopefully see the completion of a Marriott and a Candlewood Suites by 2010. The **Welk Resort Center,** 8860 Lawrence Welk Dr. (© **800/932-9355** or 760/749-3000; www.welksandiego.com), is an expensive-to-very-expensive, 600-room resort about 10 miles north of town. Lodging is in one- and two-bedroom condo-style "villas," and the 600-acre property offers golf, tennis, and live theatrical entertainment.

Hacienda de Vega ★★ (Finds) MEXICAN   San Diego County has an abundance of Mexican restaurants but a shortage of places that specialize in *Mexican* Mexican—food one would encounter in an upscale Mexico City venue. Hacienda de Vega is a 1930s adobe home whose grounds spread over 1 1/2 acres and feature a lovely garden with a large pond and waterfall. This oasis-like escape is located just south of downtown Escondido. You can start with one of several margarita options—the tamarind-flavored variety offers a vibrant twist on this classic—and move on to an appetizer sampler that will prime your taste buds with potato/chorizo quesadillas, *sopes,* and seviche. Entrees include robust dishes such as chicken in mole sauce, seared pork loin lathered in a beer-and-potato sauce, and zesty pork *carnitas* wrapped up like an enchilada.

150 Grand Cafe ★★ AMERICAN   Just around the corner from the performing arts center on a charming stretch of Grand Avenue, 150 Grand serves sophisticated, contemporary American cuisine using top local products. The restaurant embraces an Americana vibe—patrons are greeted by a bold, room-length mural that pays homage to artist Edward Hopper; the main dining room is as comfy as a living room and, in fact, actually looks like one (fireplace, bookshelves, and all). The ever-evolving menu may include items such as pecan-crusted pork in a brandy-maple reduction, sautéed Idaho trout, or braised short ribs with a mocha-espresso demi-glace. There's also a bar and patio seating; a three-course prix-fixe menu ($35) is served nightly.

PALOMAR MOUNTAIN

At an elevation of 5,600 feet, **Palomar** is a tiny mountain community 70 miles north of downtown San Diego. The village probably wouldn't be here today but for its famous observatory, which escaped unscathed from the severe scorching the mountain took in the 2007 fires. From San Diego, take I-15 N. to Hwy. 76 E. and turn left onto County

Hwy. S6—a serpentine road climbs to the summit. Even if you don't want to inch your way to the top, drive the 3 miles to the lookout or just beyond it to the campground, grocery store, restaurant, and post office.

For many years home to the largest telescope in the world, **Palomar Observatory** ★ (© 760/742-2119; www.astro.caltech.edu/palomar) has kept silent watch over the heavens since 1949. The project was proposed and funded with $6 million from the Rockefeller Foundation in 1928, but it took another 2 decades to find a suitable site, build the 135-foot-high dome, perfect the massive mirror—made from the then-new glass blend Pyrex—and build a road to the summit. Owned by the California Institute of Technology, the Hale telescope's 200-inch mirror weighs 530 tons—it took 2 days to haul the mirror up the Palomar road. Now completely computerized, the telescope is still actively searching the skies.

The visitor center is open daily from 9am to 3pm November through March, till 4pm April through October. The gift shop is open weekends only, daily during the summer. Palomar is primarily a research facility, and you'll only be able to look at (not through) the mammoth telescope. Behind-the-scenes tours are offered Saturdays, April through October, at 11:30am and 1:30pm. Tickets ($5 adults, $3 seniors, $2.50 children) are available at the gift shop. Tours are limited to a maximum of 25 people, and reservations are not accepted; podcasts of a self-guided tour can be downloaded from the website. Evening tours are offered through the Reuben H. Fleet Science Center (p. 140). *Note:* The interior of the dome is kept at nighttime temperature—dress accordingly.

3 THE DISNEYLAND RESORT & KNOTT'S BERRY FARM

95 miles N of San Diego

The sleepy Orange County town of Anaheim grew up around Disneyland. Sprawling suburbs have become a playground of family-oriented hotels, restaurants, and unabashedly tourist-oriented attractions, including Knott's Berry Farm theme park in nearby Buena Park.

ESSENTIALS

GETTING THERE From San Diego, take I-5 N. For the Disneyland Resort, exit at Disney Way; dedicated offramps from both the right-hand lane *and* the left-hand commuter lane lead into the attractions' parking lots and surrounding streets. The drive from downtown San Diego takes approximately 1 hour and 45 minutes in average traffic.

Ten or so **Amtrak** (© 800/872-7245; www.amtrak.com) trains go to Anaheim daily from San Diego. The one-way fare is $20, and the trip takes about 2 hours. From Anaheim station, take a 10-minute taxi ride (budget around $15) to the Disneyland Resort.

VISITOR INFORMATION The **Anaheim/Orange County Visitor & Convention Bureau,** 800 W. Katella Ave. (© 888/598-3200 or 714/765-8888; www.anaheimoc. org), can fill you in on area activities and shopping shuttles. It's across the street from the Disneyland Resort, inside the convention center. It's open Monday through Friday from 8am to 5pm. The **Buena Park Convention & Visitors Office,** 6601 Beach Blvd., Ste. 200 (© 800/541-3953 or 714/562-3560; www.visitbuenapark.com), provides specialized information on the neighboring area, including Knott's Berry Farm.

"The Happiest Place on Earth," Disneyland was the world's first family-oriented mega-theme park. Founder Walt Disney opened it in 1955, and since then it has sprouted siblings in Florida, Tokyo, Hong Kong, and France. But nothing compares to the original.

In 2001, Disney unveiled an additional theme park (California Adventure), a shopping/dining/entertainment district (Downtown Disney), and more on-site hotels (Disney's Grand Californian and Disney's Paradise Pier). Although Disneyland is still considerably smaller than Walt Disney World Resort in Orlando, Fla., the head Mouseketeers changed the name of the Anaheim branch to "The Disneyland Resort," reflecting a greatly expanded array of entertainment options within the complex. It's no longer a (long) day trip from San Diego—you'll want to think seriously about budgeting more time (and yes, more money) for your Disney visit. You'll need at least 48 hours to see it all. If you have less time, plan carefully so you don't skip what's important to you.

ADMISSION, HOURS & INFORMATION Admission to *either* Disneyland or California Adventure, including unlimited rides and all festivities and entertainment, is $69 for adults and children ages 10 and up, $59 for children 3 to 9, and free for children 2 and under; parking is $12 ($17 for RVs). There are various types of ticket combos available—everything from 1- and 2-day park-hopping passes to weeklong visas (and even a 365-day passport). The 2-day ticket is $143, or $123 for children ages 3 to 9. Additionally, some area accommodations offer lodging packages that include admission for 1 or more days. Another option worth investigating is the **Southern California CityPass** (p. 131), which incorporates a 3-day Disneyland/California Adventure ticket, plus 1-day tickets to Universal Studios Hollywood, SeaWorld, and the San Diego Zoo or Wild Animal Park. They cost $259 for adults, $219 for children 3 to 9, and are valid for 2 weeks. Residents of Southern California are also usually offered off-season (nonsummer/holiday) discounts, provided they can show a driver's license with a Southern California zip code.

Disneyland and California Adventure are open every day of the year, but operating hours vary daily. Call for information that applies to the specific day(s) of your visit (✆ **714/781-4565**), particularly if you're doing Disneyland as a day trip from San Diego. (You'll need at least 10–12 hr. to see most of this park.) The same information, including ride closures and show schedules, can also be found online at www.disneyland. com. Generally speaking, Disneyland opens at 9am and closes around 9pm, with extended hours on weekends, holidays, and during the summer. California Adventure, which requires less time to tour, is open from 10am to 6pm, and longer hours also apply many days.

If you plan to arrive when the ticket booths are busiest—from when the park gates open until about noon—purchase your tickets in advance and get a jump on the crowds. Advance tickets may be purchased through Disneyland's website (www.disneyland.com), at Disney stores in the United States, or by calling the ticket mail-order line (✆ **714/ 781-4043**).

DISNEY TIPS The theme parks are busiest from mid-June to mid-September and on weekends and school holidays year-round. Peak touring hours are from 11am to 5pm; visit the most popular rides before and after these hours, and you'll cut your waiting times substantially. Disneyland still draws the lion's share of the visitors, so by all means try to see it on a weekday. Since its opening in 2001, California Adventure has been a bit of an underachiever, making it relatively easy to conquer, even on weekends. However, that may soon change. Disney has announced a major overhaul of the park at a cost

(Value) **The Art of the (Package) Deal**

If you intend to spend 2 or more days in Disney territory, it pays to investigate the bevy of packaged vacation options available. Start by contacting your hotel (even those in Los Angeles or San Diego). Many vacation packages include Disneyland and/or California Adventure (and other attractions) with their inclusive packages. Also, put a call in to the official Disney travel agency, **Walt Disney Travel Co.** (© **800/225-2024** or 714/520-5050). You can request a glossy catalog by mail, or log onto www.disneyland.com to peruse package details, take a virtual tour of participating hotel properties, and get online price quotes for customized, date-specific packages. Their packages are value-packed time-savers with abundant flexibility. Hotel choices range from the official Disney hotels to one of more than 35 "good neighbor hotels" in every price range and category. A wide range of available extras includes admission to other Southern California attractions and tours (such as Universal Studios or a Tijuana shopping excursion), and behind-the-scenes Disneyland tours, all in limitless combinations. Rates are highly competitive, considering that each package includes multiday admission, early park entry, free parking (at the Disney hotels), souvenirs, and coupon books.

estimated to be in excess of $1 *billion*. Attractions that failed to catch on will be scrapped in favor of ones that will incorporate the latest in high-tech imagineering.

Many visitors tackle the parks systematically, beginning at the entrance and working their way clockwise around the park. But a better plan of attack is to arrive early and dash to the most popular rides: Indiana Jones Adventure, Star Tours, Space Mountain, Big Thunder Mountain Railroad, Splash Mountain, Haunted Mansion, Finding Nemo Submarine Voyage, Many Adventures of Winnie the Pooh, and Pirates of the Caribbean in Disneyland; and Soarin' Over California, Grizzly River Run, Twilight Zone Tower of Terror, and California Screamin' in California Adventure. Lines for these rides can last more than an hour in the middle of the day.

However, this time-honored plan of attack is increasingly obsolete thanks to the **FASTPASS** system. Here's how it works: Say you want to ride Splash Mountain (probably the top draw of both parks), but the line is long—*so* long that the wait sign indicates a 90-minute crawl. Now you can head to the automated FASTPASS ticket dispensers, through which you swipe the magnetic strip of your entrance ticket. The machine spits out a FASTPASS that denotes a time to return later that day. When you come back you'll use the FASTPASS entrance, which bypasses most of the queue. Essentially, you're reserving a place in line, and the beauty of the system is that it evens out the flow of traffic. Note, however, that the most popular attractions can "sell out" of FASTPASS slots by early afternoon. Also, craft your itinerary carefully: You cannot obtain a FASTPASS for a second attraction until the window for the first ride has opened. At least 10 rides between the two parks are equipped with FASTPASS; for a complete list, check your official map/guide when you enter.

Since many of the more popular rides have a set number of seats, Disney tries to fill unused single seats on some rides with a line bypass for **solo riders.** At the FASTPASS distribution area, ask the attendant for a single rider's pass (a coupon that advances you to the front of the line to await the first single seat available).

Parents should note that a number of rides have minimum height requirements of 32 inches or more. Couples touring with someone under the height requirement can perform the **"baby pass"** at many attractions: Both parents get in line and one is allowed to wait while the other rides; then they trade the child for the other to ride (so that parents don't have to wait in the line separately). The majority of attractions favored by preteens are found in Disneyland but, following some criticism that it wasn't kid-friendly enough, A Bug's Land was added to California Adventure and seems to be keeping the moppets happy.

Touring Disneyland ★★★

The Disneyland complex is divided into eight theme "lands," each of which has rides and attractions related to that land's theme. You'll find the practical things you might need, such as stroller and wheelchair rentals and storage lockers, just outside the park's main gate.

MAIN STREET, U.S.A.   At the park's entrance, Main Street, U.S.A. is a cinematic version of turn-of-the-20th-century small-town America. The whitewashed Rockwellian fantasy is lined with gift shops, candy stores, a soda fountain, and a silent theater that continuously runs early Mickey Mouse films.

Because there are no big-ticket rides, it's best to tour Main Street during the middle of the afternoon, when lines for popular attractions are longest, or in the evening, when you can go for a ride in a horse-drawn streetcar. There's always something happening on Main Street; stop in at the information booth to the left of the main entrance for a schedule of the day's events. The **Disneyland Railroad** starts its circular journey around the park here, with stops at New Orleans Square, Mickey's Toontown, and Tomorrowland; but you can reach all of these places on foot just about as fast, so don't use it as a shortcut to the other side of the park.

ADVENTURELAND   Inspired by exotic Asia, Africa, and South America, the central icon of Adventureland is a giant tree, home to **Tarzan's Treehouse,** a stagnant attraction based on the animated film. Its safari-themed neighbor is the **Jungle Cruise,** where passengers board *African Queen*–style riverboats and explore the animal "life" along an Amazon-like river. A spear's throw away is the **Enchanted Tiki Room,** where you can sit down and watch an 18-minute musical comedy featuring electronically animated tropical birds, flowers, and "Tiki gods."

The **Indiana Jones Adventure ★★** is Adventureland's marquee attraction. Based on the Steven Spielberg films, this ride takes you into the Temple of the Forbidden Eye aboard joltingly realistic all-terrain vehicles. *Note:* The volume on this ride is ear-splitting.

NEW ORLEANS SQUARE   Overlooking the "Rivers of America" and Tom Sawyer Island, New Orleans Square is a beautifully detailed re-creation of the Crescent City. There are just two rides here, but both are popular classics. The **Haunted Mansion ★★** is a high-tech ghost house; the clever events inside are as funny as they are scary.

Even more fanciful is the epic **Pirates of the Caribbean ★★★**, one of Disneyland's best-loved attractions. Visitors float on boats through underground caves to the Spanish Main, entering a story of swashbuckling, cannon-fire battles, and buried treasure. The **Blue Bayou** restaurant (p. 261) is situated in the middle of the ride itself.

FRONTIERLAND   Inspired by 19th-century America, the centerpiece of Frontierland is the Rivers of America. Here, you can set sail on the **Mark Twain Riverboat,** a detailed re-creation of a Mississippi-style paddle-wheel steamer, and the **Sailing Ship Columbia,** a three-masted replica of the windjammer that first sailed the American flag around the world (both travel the same route). The river circles **Pirate's Lair on Tom Sawyer Island,** which is reached by a brief raft ride. Revamped in 2007, this play area now features pirate-themed games and characters. The **Big Thunder Mountain Railroad** ★★ is a runaway roller coaster that races through a deserted 1870s gold mine. It's a relatively moderate coaster.

CRITTER COUNTRY   An ode to the backwoods, Critter Country is a corner of Frontierland without those pesky settlers. **The Many Adventures of Winnie the Pooh** ★ is a gentle excursion through the Hundred Acre Wood. Everyone loves **Splash Mountain** ★★★, an immensely popular log flume ride. Be prepared to get wet, especially if someone sizable is in the front seat of your log. There's also **Davy Crockett's Explorer Canoes** ★, where you can paddle free-floating, steady canoes around Tom Sawyer Island.

On weekends and holidays, and daily during summer, head to Frontierland after dark to see **FANTASMIC!** ★. This show mixes magic, music, more than 50 live performers, and sensational special effects. Best viewing is directly in front of Pirates of the Caribbean, but this is also the most crowded area (get there early).

MICKEY'S TOONTOWN   This is a colorful, whimsical land inspired by the film *Who Framed Roger Rabbit?*—a wacky, gag-filled land populated by 'toons. There are several rides, including **Roger Rabbit's Car Toon Spin** and a miniature roller coaster with just a 35-inch height requirement, **Gadget's Go Coaster.**

FANTASYLAND   With its storybook theme, this is the catchall land for stuff that doesn't quite fit anywhere else, much of it based on Walt Disney's animated classics. Most of the rides are geared to the under-6 set, including the **King Arthur Carrousel, Dumbo the Flying Elephant,** and the **Casey Jr. Circus Train.** Some, like **Mr. Toad's Wild Ride** and **Peter Pan's Flight** ★, appeal to grown-ups as well.

The most famous lure is **It's a Small World** ★, an indoor river ride through a Gen-Xer's saccharine nightmare of all the world's children singing the song everybody loves to hate. Fantasyland's biggest thrill is the **Matterhorn Bobsleds** ★★, a zippy roller coaster through chilled caverns and drifting fog banks. It's one of the park's classics (and not found in Disney's sibling parks).

TOMORROWLAND   Conceived as an optimistic look at the future, Tomorrowland employs an angular, metallic look popularized by futurists such as Jules Verne.

After nearly 10 years, the subs are back. The original bright-yellow submarines have been restored and are once again tooling around the Disney lagoon, this time in search of a certain clown fish, in the **Finding Nemo Submarine Voyage** ★★. *Note:* Due to the slow on- and off-load time, this popular ride endures some of the longest lines. The **House of the Future** gives a peek at the technology and digital lifestyle that may someday be coming to a home near you.

The jet-propelled, longtime favorite **Space Mountain** ★★★ offers a pitch-black indoor roller coaster that assaults your equilibrium. **Buzz Lightyear Astro Blasters** ★ takes you through an interactive, moving arcade game aboard your own Star Cruiser. **Star Tours** ★★ is a Disney–George Lucas joint venture that spins off the *Star Wars* myth in a flight simulator. The **Astro Orbitor** is a kid-friendly spinning spacecraft ride, while

Autopia offers every under-16-year-old's fantasy: driving gas-powered cars along a scenic track. The attraction **"Honey, I Shrunk the Audience"** ★ is an eye-popping presentation by the "Imagination Institute" that rides on the characters and plot from the hit film *Honey, I Shrunk the Kids.*

The **Disneyland Monorail** ★ stops in Tomorrowland, transporting passengers to and from a stop outside the park, between the Disney resorts and Downtown Disney. You don't have to get off at this stop, and the ride offers a good scenic overview of the entire resort complex.

Touring California Adventure ★★

California Adventure experienced a lukewarm reception when it opened in 2001. Initial visitors complained the park didn't offer enough to do (yet admission was priced the same as Disneyland); there wasn't enough for preteens; and half the rides were dressed-up, carny-style attractions that could be found at your average county fair. Disney responded to the criticisms by adding a number of shows and attractions, including a half-dozen kiddie rides and the elaborate **Twilight Zone Tower of Terror.** Now Disney is seriously shaking things up, embarking on a 5-year renovation that estimates put at $1.1 billion—a cost higher than what it took to build the park in the first place.

Thus far, the multiyear makeover has included the dismantling of unpopular draws, a redesign of the park grounds, and a whole new slew of rides, including an interactive gaming-meets-storytelling attraction based on the *Toy Story* films. **Toy Story Midway Mania** ★★, which debuted in June 2008, is the first Disney ride to incorporate industrial Ethernet, and set Disney back a reported $80 million to design and build. Wearing 3-D glasses, riders board spinning vehicles that travel through virtual carnival games. Other changes will include a new entrance (goodbye postcard letters, hello 1920s Art Deco); a brand-new, 12-acre **Cars Land,** themed after the hit animated feature *Cars;* a nighttime show, **World of Color,** incorporating water effects, lighting, music, and images from classic and contemporary Disney flicks; and a handful of new dining options. The work is expected to be completed by 2012; check the website to see what new attractions have been rolled out.

Whether or not California Adventure continues to draw small crowds (which on the plus side makes it easier to tour), one thing won't change: You will still be able to get a cold beer, glass of wine, or cocktail here, as opposed to alcohol-free Disneyland.

THE GOLDEN STATE This multidimensional area represents California's history, heritage, and physical attributes. Sound boring? Actually, two of the park's biggest crowd-pleasers are here. Inside a weathered corrugated test pilots' hangar is **Soarin' Over California** ★★, the ride that immediately rose to the top of everyone's run-to-get-in-line-first list (it's equipped with FASTPASS but often sells out by midday anyway). It uses cool technology to combine suspended, hang glider–style seats with a spectacular IMAX movie experience—riders literally "soar over" California's scenic wonders.

Nearby, the park's iconic Grizzly Peak towers over the **Grizzly River Run** ★★, a splashy, gold-country ride through caverns and along craggy slopes. It culminates with a wet plunge into a bubbling geyser field. Kids can cavort nearby on the **Redwood Creek Challenge Trail,** a forest playground with smoke-jumper cable slides, net climbing, and swaying bridges.

On the backside of Grizzly Peak is the Robert Mondavi–sponsored **Golden Vine Winery,** which boasts a demonstration vineyard, a mission-style "aging room" (with a back-to-basics presentation on the art of winemaking), tastings, and the park's most upscale eatery, the **Vineyard Room; Pacific Wharf Cafe** was inspired by Monterey's Cannery Row and features various food counters.

A BUG'S LAND   The Golden State blends seamlessly into this pint-size section of the park. At its entrance, **Bountiful Valley Farm** pays tribute to California's rich agriculture industry and demonstrates cultivation techniques. The 3-D attraction **"It's Tough To Be A Bug"** ★ uses advanced film technology to expand on *A Bug's Life* characters Flik and Hopper, who lead the audience on a slap-happy underground romp that keeps everyone hopping, ducking, and laughing.

Just beyond is **A Bug's Land,** featuring five smaller amusements that are perfect for younger visitors. The set is an amusingly detailed backyard garden with a leaky spigot and towering clover, allowing visitors to view the world from a bug's perspective.

PARADISE PIER   Journey back to the glory days of California's beachfront amusement attractions on this fantasy boardwalk. Highlights include **California Screamin'** ★★, a classic roller coaster that replicates the whitewashed wooden white-knucklers of the past—but with state-of-the-art steel construction and a smooth, computerized ride. The 0-to-50 mph takeoff packs quite a thrill. There's also the **Maliboomer,** a trio of towers (modeled after He-Man sledgehammer tests) that catapults riders to the tiptop bell before letting them down bungee-style; **Mulholland Madness,** a wacky trip along L.A.'s precarious hilltop street; and **Toy Story Midway Mania.** The **Orange Stinger,** a whooshing swing ride inside an enormous orange, and the **Sun Wheel Carousel** (to be reborn as Mickey's Fun Wheel) have been sidelined due to the renovation, but should be back in action in 2010.

Most of the rides in Paradise Pier have minimum height requirements, but younger tykes can content themselves with the undersea-themed **King Triton's Carousel.**

HOLLYWOODLAND   If you've visited Disney World in Florida, you'll recognize many elements of this ersatz Hollywood movie lot (neé Hollywood Pictures Backlot). Pass through a classic studio archway flanked by gigantic golden elephants, and you'll find yourself on a surprisingly realistic "Hollywood Boulevard." In the **Disney Animation** building, visitors can participate in six different interactive galleries. Learn how to draw Disney characters at the Animation Academy; listen to a Disney illustrator invent "Crush," the surfin' sea turtle dude from *Finding Nemo;* and even take a computerized personality test to see which Disney character you most resemble.

At the end of the street, the replica movie palace **Hyperion Theater** presents the live-action musical show **Disney's *Aladdin,*** a large-scale 40-minute musical production performed several times daily. The lot includes **Jim Henson's MuppetVision 3D** ★, an on-screen blast from the past featuring Kermit, Miss Piggy, Gonzo, Fozzie Bear, and even hecklers Waldorf and Statler. Saving the best for last, California Adventure's big tingle is **The Twilight Zone Tower of Terror** ★★★—another import from Orlando. Guests board a possessed elevator that travels through the bowels of a creepy hotel; you'll witness a parade of spiffy effects before making a sudden plunge down the 13-story shaft.

Downtown Disney ★

Borrowing another page from Central Florida's successful Disney compound, **Downtown Disney** is a district filled with spots for a quick bite, snacks, or casual and fine dining. There are also more than 20 shops and several entertainment venues for all ages. It's not a theme park, so you can visit admission-free, but note this isn't a place for bargain hunting—whether it's a cup of coffee or a choice bit of Disneyana, nothing is cheap.

The promenade begins at the amusement park gates and stretches toward the Disneyland Hotel. Highlights include the **House of Blues,** a restaurant/club that features Delta-inspired cuisine and big-name music; **ESPN Zone,** a dining and entertainment spot for sports fans; **World of Disney,** the largest Disney shopping experience in the West; and a 12-screen stadium-seating movie theater. Sating the too-old-for-Goofy-hats set is **Disney Vault 28,** a 1,000-square-foot contemporary boutique featuring both custom cutesy lines (Harajuku Lovers, Mighty Fine) and urban-artsy duds (Betsey Johnson, local fave Harveys). Parking is free for 3 hours (2 hr. more with restaurant or theater validation), $6 per hour thereafter; valet available from 5pm to 2am ($6). Downtown Disney is also accessible via the monorail.

KNOTT'S BERRY FARM ★

Like Disneyland, Knott's Berry Farm is not without historical background. In 1933, Buena Park farmer Walter Knott planted 10 acres of boysenberry on leased land and launched Knott's Berry Farm. When things got tough during the Depression, Mrs. Knott set up a roadside stand to sell pies, preserves, and home-cooked chicken dinners. Within a year she was selling 90 meals a day. Lines became so long that Walter decided to create an Old West Ghost Town as a diversion for waiting customers.

Today the amusement park offers a whopping 165 shows, attractions, and high-tech rides that are far more thrilling than most of the rides at the Disneyland Resort. Granted, it doesn't have anywhere near the magical appeal of Disneyland; but if you're more into fast-paced amusement rides than swirling teacups, spend your money here.

GETTING THERE   Knott's Berry Farm is at 8039 Beach Blvd. in Buena Park, about 10 minutes north of Disneyland. From I-5 N., exit south onto Beach Boulevard and follow the signs.

ADMISSION, HOURS & INFORMATION   Admission to the park, including unlimited access to all rides, shows, and attractions, is $52 for those ages 3 to 61, 48 inches or taller (save $7 by printing tickets at home); and $23 for seniors 62 and over and for children 3 and up, under 48 inches. Children 2 and under are admitted free. After 4pm, admission is $25 for adults. Parking is $12, $17 RVs. Like Disneyland, Knott's offers discounted admission for Southern California residents during much of the year, so if you're bringing local friends or family members along, be sure to take advantage of the bargain. Knott's Berry Farm's hours vary both during the week and week to week, so call ahead. The park is always open 10am to 6pm weekdays, until 10pm Saturdays, and until 7pm Sundays; during the summer peak season and holidays, hours are extended. Knott's is closed Christmas Day. Special hours and prices are in effect during the hugely popular Knott's Scary Farm in late October. Stage shows and special activities are scheduled throughout the day. Pick up a schedule at the ticket booth. For more information, call ✆ **714/220-5200,** or log onto www.knotts.com.

Touring the Park

Despite all the high-tech, multimillion-dollar rides, Knott's Berry Farm still maintains much of its original Old West motif and is divided into six themed areas spread across 160 acres. **Rip Tide** is a floorless gondola ride featuring 13 full 360-degree vertical arcs, the **Xcelerator** launches you from 0 to 82 mph (132kmph) in 2.3 seconds, and the **Silver Bullet** is a 55-mph (89kmph) roller coaster with six inversions. The park's newest coaster, **Pony Express,** opened in 2008; other attractions include the **California MarketPlace,** the Farm's version of Downtown Disney, and **Knott's Soak City U.S.A.,** a 21-ride water-adventure park right next door (open seasonally, separate admission required).

OLD WEST GHOST TOWN   The park's original attraction is a collection of refurbished 19th-century buildings relocated from deserted Old West towns. You can pan for gold, ride an authentic stagecoach, take rickety train cars through the Calico Mine, get held up aboard the Denver and Rio Grande Calico Railroad, and watch the stunt spectacular at the Wagon Camp Theatre. If you love wooden roller coasters, don't miss the clackety **GhostRider.**

FIESTA VILLAGE   Here you'll find a south-of-the-border theme. That means festive markets, strolling mariachis, and wild rides such as **Montezooma's Revenge** and **Jaguar,** a roller coaster that includes two heart-in-the-mouth drops and a loop that turns you upside down.

WILD WATER WILDERNESS   This 3^1/$_2$-acre attraction is styled like a turn-of-the-20th-century California wilderness park. The top ride is a white-water adventure called **Bigfoot Rapid,** the longest ride of its kind in the world. Don't miss the wonderful multimedia theater piece **Mystery Lodge**—it's a truly amazing high-tech attraction based on the legends of local Native Americans.

CAMP SNOOPY   This will probably be the youngsters' favorite area. It's meant to re-create a wilderness camp in the picturesque High Sierras. Its 6 rustic acres are the playgrounds of Charles Schulz's beloved beagle and his pals, Charlie Brown and Lucy, who greet guests and pose for pictures. The 30 rides here, including the **Charlie Brown Speedway** and **Lucy's Tugboat,** are tailor-made for the 6-and-under set.

INDIAN TRAILS   This interpretive center on the outskirts of Ghost Town is a nod to Native Americans. Exhibits include authentic tepees, hogans, and big houses. There are also daily educational events such as craft-making, storytelling, music, and dance.

THE BOARDWALK   This theme area is a salute to Southern California's beach culture. The main attractions are the **Xcelerator, RipTide, Boomerang,** the 30-story **Supreme Scream,** and a white-water adventure called **Perilous Plunge,** the world's tallest, steepest (think four-story waterfall), and wettest water ride.

WHERE TO STAY IN THE ANAHEIM AREA
Very Expensive

Disneyland Hotel ★★ (Kids)   The "Official Hotel of the Magic Kingdom" features a monorail connection via Downtown Disney, allowing for a quick trip back to your room anytime. The hotel is an attraction unto itself, and the best choice for families with small children. The rooms aren't fancy, but they're comfortably furnished and all have balconies. In-room amenities include movie channels (with free Disney Channel, naturally) and cute-as-a-button Disney-themed toiletries and accessories. The hotel has every kind of service desk imaginable, a pool area complete with a white-sand beach, and a game arcade. The complex includes Disney's adjoining 489-room **Paradise Pier Hotel** with a whimsical beach boardwalk theme that ties in with the Paradise Pier section of California Adventure across the street. A bonus is the private entrance to that park, accessed with your hotel room key. Although the hotel was remodeled and received a new pool in 2004, it is still fairly generic compared with the other two Disney hotels.

1150 Magic Way, Anaheim, CA 92802. (C) **714/956-6425.** Fax 714/956-6582. www.disneyland.com. 990 units. $310–$520 double, plus $14 per night resort fee; from $650 suite. AE, DC, DISC, MC, V. Free parking. **Amenities:** 6 restaurants; 2 bars; babysitting; children's programs; concierge; exercise room; Jacuzzi; 3 outdoor pools; room service. *In room:* A/C, TV, fridge, hair dryer, minibar, Wi-Fi.

Disney's Grand Californian Hotel & Spa ★★ (Kids) Taking inspiration from California's redwood forests, Mission pioneers, and plein-air painters, Disney designers created a nostalgic yet state-of-the-art high-rise hotel. The centerpiece of this Arts and Crafts lodge is a six-story "living room" with a three-story walk-in "hearth" whose fire warms Stickley-style rockers and plush leather armchairs. The hotel opens onto a landscaped area with a pair of swimming pools; guest rooms are spacious and smartly designed (the best ones overlook the parks). Despite the sophisticated air of the Grand Californian, this is a hotel that truly caters to families, offering a bevy of room configurations (including one with a double bed plus bunk beds with trundle). Since the hotel provides sleeping bags rather than rollaways for kids, this standard-size room will sleep a family of six. Guests of the hotel can enter California Adventure through a private entrance, avoiding the crush at the main gate, and another entrance leads directly into Downtown Disney.

1600 S. Disneyland Dr., Anaheim, CA 92802. ℂ **714/956-6425** (central reservations) or 714/635-2300. Fax 714/956-6099. www.disneyland.com. 745 units. $425–$665 double, plus $14 per night resort fee; from $985 suite. AE, DC, DISC, MC, V. Free parking. **Amenities:** 3 restaurants; bar; children's center (evenings only); concierge; concierge-level rooms; exercise room; Jacuzzi; 2 outdoor pools; room service; spa. *In room:* A/C, TV, hair dryer, minibar, Wi-Fi.

Moderate

Candy Cane Inn ★★ (Value) Take your standard U-shaped motel court with outdoor corridors, spruce it up with cobblestone drives and walkways, old-time streetlamps, and flowering vines engulfing the balconies of attractively painted rooms, and you have the Candy Cane. The face-lift worked, making this nonsmoking hotel near Disneyland's main gate a treat for the stylish bargain hunter. The rooms are decorated in bright floral motifs with comfortable furnishings, including queen-size beds, custom duvets, and a separate dressing and vanity area. Premium rooms include a microwave and DVD/VCR (with a complimentary movie library). Breakfast is served in the courtyard, where you can also splash around in a year-round heated pool.

1747 S. Harbor Blvd., Anaheim, CA 92802. ℂ **800/345-7057** or 714/774-5284. Fax 714/772-5462. www.candycaneinn.net. 171 units. $95–$189 double. Rates include expanded continental breakfast. AE, DC, DISC, MC, V. Free parking. **Amenities:** Exercise room; Jacuzzi; outdoor pool. *In room:* A/C, TV, fridge, hair dryer, Wi-Fi.

Knott's Berry Farm Resort Hotel ★ (Kids) Within easy walking distance of Knott's Berry Farm and adjacent to the shopping and dining at Knott's Marketplace, this spit-shined hotel knows who the big dog is in town and offers a free shuttle to Disneyland, 7 miles away. The pristine lobby has the look of a business-oriented hotel, and that it is, but vacationers can also benefit from the elevated level of service. Ask about "Super Saver" rates (as low as $79), plus a variety of stay-and-play package deals. The rooms in the nine-story tower are tastefully decorated, and doting parents can even treat their kids to a Peanuts-themed room where you can get turndown service from Snoopy himself, as well as telephone bedtime stories.

7675 Crescent Ave. (at Grand), Buena Park, CA 90620. ℂ **866/752-2444** or 714/995-1111. Fax 714/828-8590. www.knottshotel.com. 320 units. $99–$120 double; from $150 suite. AE, DC, DISC, MC, V. Parking $12. **Amenities:** Restaurant; bar; concierge; exercise room; Jacuzzi; outdoor pool; room service; lighted tennis and basketball courts. *In room:* A/C, TV, hair dryer, Wi-Fi.

Portofino Inn & Suites ★ (Kids) This complex of low- and high-rise buildings sports a cheery yellow exterior and family-friendly interior. The location couldn't be better: It's directly across the street from California Adventure's backside, and they'll shuttle you straight to the front gate. Designed to work as well for business travelers from the nearby Convention Center as for Disney-bound families, the Portofino offers contemporary, stylish furnishings, as well as rates and suites for any family configuration. You may want to consider one of the many "Kids Suites," which have bunk beds and a sleeper sofa, plus TV, fridge, and microwave—and that's just in the kids' room. Mom and dad have a separate bedroom with grown-up comforts including a double vanity and shower massage.

1831 S. Harbor Blvd. (at Katella), Anaheim, CA 92802. ⓒ **800/398-3963** or 714/782-7600. Fax 714/782-7619. www.portofinoinnanaheim.com. 190 units. $59–$130 double; from $160 suite. AE, DC, DISC, MC, V. Free parking. **Amenities:** Restaurant; health club; Jacuzzi; outdoor pool. *In room:* A/C, TV, hair dryer, Wi-Fi.

Inexpensive

Howard Johnson Hotel ★ This nonsmoking hotel occupies an enviable location directly opposite Disneyland. Accommodations are divided among six low-profile buildings, all with balconies opening onto a central garden; during the summer you can see the nightly fireworks display at Disneyland from the upper balconies of the park-side rooms. Try to avoid the rooms in the rear buildings, though, which get some freeway noise. Kids can frolic at an elaborate water-themed play area with water slides, splash fountains, and a toddler wading pool; adults can relax around a more sedate pool area. Services and facilities include family lodging/Disney admission packages; the hotel is also in the process of building kids' suites. All in all, it's pretty classy for a HoJo.

1380 S. Harbor Blvd., Anaheim, CA 92802. ⓒ **800/422-4228** or 714/776-6120. Fax 714/533-3578. www.hojoanaheim.com. 316 units. $99–$149 double. AE, DC, DISC, MC, V. Free parking. **Amenities:** Restaurant; concierge; Jacuzzi; 2 outdoor pools; room service. *In room:* A/C, TV, fridge, hair dryer.

WHERE TO DINE IN THE ANAHEIM AREA

If you're visiting the Disneyland Resort, chances are good you'll probably eat at one of the many choices inside the theme parks or at Downtown Disney; there are plenty of restaurants to choose from, catering to all tastes. At Disneyland, in the Creole-themed **Blue Bayou,** you can sit under the stars inside the Pirates of the Caribbean ride. California Adventure features several sit-down options, including **Ariel's Grotto,** where Disney characters serve casual fare in a faux-1920s beachfront setting, and the **Vineyard Room,** which offers upscale prix-fixe wine-country cuisine matched to California pours. Make reservations early in the day for dinner—priority seating can be arranged by calling ⓒ **714/781-3463.** At Knott's Berry Farm, try the fried chicken dinners and boysenberry pies at historic **Mrs. Knott's Chicken Dinner Restaurant** (see below for full review).

A newcomer muscling in on Downtown Disney's shopping and dining turf is **Anaheim GardenWalk,** 321 W. Katella Ave. (ⓒ **714/635-7410;** www.anaheimgardenwalk.com). Located a block away from Disneyland and the Convention Center, it has more than 50 retailers and restaurants including such chain eateries as **P.F. Chang's China Bistro, Roy's Hawaiian Fusion Cuisine,** and **McCormick & Schmick's.** You can also enjoy flights of wine and small-plate tastings at **Pop the Cork;** or for a "strikingly different" experience, check out **300 Anaheim,** a bar, bistro, and 41-lane bowling alley.

Listed below are some of the best bets in the surrounding area, including nearby **Orange** (a 10–15 min. drive), whose historic downtown is home to several of the region's best dining options.

Anaheim White House ★★ FRENCH/ITALIAN   Once surrounded by orange groves, this stately 1909 colonial-style mansion now sits on a wide industrial street just 5 minutes from Disneyland. Set back and framed by lawns and gardens, it exudes gentility and nostalgia. Owner Bruno Serato maintains this architectural treasure, serving Northern Italian cuisine (with a French accent) in elegant white-on-white rooms on the main and second floors. Dinner courses are whimsically named for fashion giants (sand dabs Dolce Gabbana, rack of lamb Prada). Prices tend to reflect the expense-account and well-heeled-retiree crowds, but lunch prices deliver the same bang for fewer bucks; there's also a Sunday brunch. *Tip:* Ask about free shuttle service from area hotels.

887 S. Anaheim Blvd. (north of Ball Rd.), Anaheim. © **714/772-1381.** www.anaheimwhitehouse.com. Reservations recommended at dinner. Main courses $12–$30 lunch, $26–$50 dinner; $39 brunch. AE, MC, V. Mon–Fri 11:30am–2:30pm and 5–10pm; Sat 5–10pm; Sun 11am–3pm and 5–10pm. Valet parking $4.

Napa Rose ★★ CALIFORNIAN   Those who scoff at the idea that one of the Southern California's finest dining options might just exist within a Disney resort clearly haven't tried the Gulf of California rock scallops at Napa Rose. Wine Country cuisine gets the all-star treatment (minus the snobbery) courtesy of Napa-bred chef Andrew Sutton, who highlights the seasonal-best of the state, from both land and sea. The Glasgow-styled spot is nestled inside the Disney Grand Californian, and serves up Craftsman romance by the plateful (special occasions call for the four-course, wine-paired tasting menu at the Chef's Table). The wine selection is exactly what you'd expect from a restaurant that takes its name from the land of vines: expertly chosen and Golden State heavy. Snag a table with a view of the enormous exhibition kitchen, and enjoy the show.

1600 S. Disneyland Dr., Anaheim, inside the Grand Californian Hotel. © **714/300-7170.** www.disneyland.com. Reservations recommended. Main courses $30–$60 dinner. AE, MC, V. Daily 5:30–9:30pm. Validated parking up to 5 hr. at the Grand Californian Hotel.

Moderate

Citrus City Grille ★★ CALIFORNIAN   Though housed in Orange's second-oldest brick building, this crowd-pleaser is furnished without an antique in sight. Instead, it pays homage to the town's agricultural legacy with a casual, industrial chic. World-inspired appetizers range from Hawaiian-style ahi *poke* (raw tuna salad) to Southeast Asian coconut-shrimp tempura accented with spiced apricots. Main courses come from the Mediterranean (pasta, risotto, and gourmet pizza) and mom's kitchen (wild mushroom meatloaf and pot roast). Gleaming bar shelves house myriad bottles for the extensive martini menu, and outdoor foyer tables are nicely protected from the street.

122 N. Glassell St. (½ block north of Chapman), Orange. © **714/639-9600.** www.citruscitygrille.com. Reservations recommended. Main courses $9–$28 lunch, $11–$40 dinner. AE, DC, MC, V. Daily 11am–10pm.

Gabbi's Mexican Kitchen ★★ MEXICAN   There's no sign outside Gabbi's Mexican Kitchen, but the Old Towne Orange restaurant is easy to spot—just look for the swarms of people waiting 2 hours for a table. Make reservations far in advance for this blend of regional cuisine and Tex-Mex standards. The narrow space is well appointed with loads of south-of-the-border furnishings and the best tequila selection this side of Jalisco; the menu is a culinary world tour of Spanish, Indian, and Euro influences, though the Mexican mestizo dishes are especially popular with locals. Everything from the mini-mole tostaditas to the traditional tacos is superb—just watch out for the habañero salsa, which lulls taste buds into a sense of false safety before unleashing its fury.

Main courses $10–$25 lunch, $11–$30 dinner. AE, DC, MC, V. Daily 11am–11pm.

Inexpensive

Felix Continental Cafe ★ CUBAN/SPANISH If you like the re-created Main Street in the Magic Kingdom, you'll love the city of Orange's historic 1886 town square on view from the cozy sidewalk tables outside the Felix Continental Cafe. Dining on traditional Cuban specialties (such as citrus-marinated chicken, black beans and rice, and fried plantains) and watching traffic spin around the magnificent fountain and rose-bushes of the plaza evokes old Havana or Madrid rather than the cookie-cutter Orange County communities just blocks away. The food is praised by restaurant reviewers and loyal locals alike.

36 Plaza Sq. (at the corner of Chapman and Glassell), Orange. ☎ **714/633-5842.** www.felixcontinental cafe.com. Reservations recommended for dinner. Main courses $3–$11 breakfast (Sat–Sun), $5–$14 lunch, $8–$14 dinner. AE, DC, MC, V. Mon–Fri 11am–10pm; Sat–Sun 8am–10pm.

Mrs. Knott's Chicken Dinner Restaurant ★ **Kids** AMERICAN The restaurant that launched Knott's Berry Farm descended from Cordelia Knott's Depression-era farm-land tearoom, opened in 1934. It stands just outside the park's entrance, with plenty of free parking for patrons. Looking just as you'd expect—country-cute, with window shut-ters and paisley aplenty—the restaurant's featured attraction is the original fried chicken dinner. Country-fried steak, pot roast, roast turkey, and pork ribs are also options, as well as sandwiches, salads, and a terrific chicken potpie. Boysenberries abound (of course), from breakfast jam to traditional double-crust pies; and there's even an adjacent takeout shop that's always crowded.

8039 Beach Blvd. (near La Palma), Buena Park. ☎ **714/220-5080.** Reservations for parties of 12 or more only. Main courses $5–$10; complete dinners $15. DC, DISC, MC, V. Daily 7am–8:30pm (until 9pm Fri, 9:30pm Sat).

---

4 JULIAN: APPLE PIES & MORE

---

60 miles NE of San Diego; 31 miles W of Anza-Borrego Desert State Park

A trip to Julian (pop. 3,000) is a trip back in time. The old gold-mining town, now best known for its apples, has a handful of cute B&Bs; its popularity is based on the fact that it gives city-weary folks a chance to get away from it all, especially on weekdays, when things are a little quieter here.

Prospectors first ventured into these fertile hills—elevation 4,225 feet—in the late 1860s. They struck gold in 1870 near where the Julian Hotel stands today, and 18 mines sprang up like mushrooms. During all the excitement, four cousins—all former Confed-erate soldiers from Georgia, two with the last name Julian—founded the town. The mines produced up to an estimated $13 million worth of gold in their day.

In October 2003, Julian was virtually engulfed by the devastating Cedar Fire, and firefighters made a valiant stand to protect the town against what seemed insurmountable odds. For several days it was touch-and-go, and some 800 homes in the surrounding hillsides were lost. The central historic part of Julian was saved, though, along with all of the town's famed apple orchards. Today, you can stand on Main Street again without knowing a catastrophe visited just a few hundred yards away. Most of Julian's residents do live on the outskirts of town, though, and more than a third lost their homes and livelihoods; many left and never returned. A 15-mile stretch of State Route 79 is known as the Steven Rucker Memorial Highway in honor of a firefighter who died battling the blaze—one of the inferno's 15 victims.

ESSENTIALS

GETTING THERE   You can make the 90-minute trip on Hwy. 78 or I-8 to Hwy. 79. You can take one route going and the other on the way back. Hwy. 79 winds through Rancho Cuyamaca State Park. Hwy. 78 traverses countryside and farmland severely burned by the Witch Fire, one of Southern California's epic wildfires in 2007. If you come via Cuyamaca, you'll still see residual damage from the 2003 fire.

VISITOR INFORMATION   The **Julian Chamber of Commerce** is at the corner of Main and Washington streets (© 760/765-1857; www.julianca.com). Staffers always have enthusiastic suggestions for local activities. The office is open daily from 10am to 4pm. Main Street in Julian is only 6 blocks long, and shops, cafes, and some lodgings are on it or a block away. Town maps and accommodations fliers are available from Town Hall; public restrooms are located here as well. There's no self-service laundry (so come prepared), but you'll find a post office, a liquor store, and a few grocery stores.

SPECIAL EVENTS   **Apple Harvest Days** take place mid-September through mid-November and include lots of special events, including an **Arts and Crafts Show,** the **Grape Stomp Festa, Bluegrass Festival,** and even an **old-time melodrama.** There are also plenty of cider and apple pie, plus brilliant fall foliage. The **Wildflower Show,** sponsored by the local Women's Club, features displays of native plants; it was begun in 1926 and is held in early May at the historic Town Hall. During the second half of August, the **Julian Weed Show** displays and sells artwork and arrangements of wildflowers and indigenous plants. And year-round (weather permitting), **Doves & Desperados**—performers in Old West costume—present skits and stroll the streets on Sunday from noon to 4pm.

TOURING THE TOWN

Radiating the aura of the Old West, Julian offers an abundance of early California history, quaint Victorian streets filled with apple-pie shops and antiques stores, fresh air, and friendly people. While Wal-Mart and McDonald's have invaded formerly unspoiled mountain resorts such as Big Bear and Mammoth, this 1880s gold-mining town has managed to retain a rustic, woodsy sense of its historic origins, despite the arrival of a Subway sandwich shop.

Be forewarned, however, that downtown Julian can be exceedingly crowded during the fall harvest season. Consider making your trip during another season (or midweek) to enjoy this unspoiled relic with a little privacy. Rest assured, apple pies are baking around town year-round. But autumn is perfect; the air is crisp and bracing. Julian gets dusted (sometimes pounded) by snow during the winter; spring prods patches of daffodils into bloom.

The best way to experience Julian is on foot. Two or 3 blocks of Main Street offer plenty of diversions for an afternoon or longer, depending on how much pie you stop to eat. And don't worry, you'll grow accustomed to constant apple references very quickly here—the fruit has proven to be more of an economic boon than gold ever was.

After stopping in at the chamber of commerce in the old Town Hall—don't miss the vintage photos in the auditorium—cross the street to the **Julian Drug Store & Miner's Diner,** 2130 Main St. (© 760/765-3753). This old-style soda fountain serves sparkling

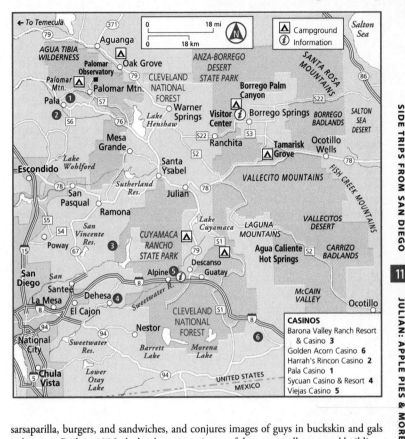

sarsaparilla, burgers, and sandwiches, and conjures images of guys in buckskin and gals in bonnets. Built in 1886, the brick structure is one of the many well-preserved buildings in town on the National Historic Register; it's jampacked with local memorabilia.

The **Eagle and High Peak Mines,** built around 1870, at the end of C Street (© **760/765-0036**), may seem to be a tourist trap, but they offer an interesting and educational look at the town's one-time economic mainstay. Tours take you underground to the 1,000-foot hard-rock tunnel to see the mining and milling process; antique engines and authentic tools are on display. Tours are usually given beginning at 10am, but hours vary so it's best to call ahead. Admission is $10 for adults, $5 for children 6 to 16, $1 for children 5 and under.

There's more local history on view at the **Julian Pioneer Museum,** 2811 Washington St. (© **760/765-0227**). It's open April through November, Wednesday through Sunday 10am to 4pm; weekends only 10am to 4pm the rest of the year. The "soul of Julian" is presented by the **Julian Black Historical Society** at its museum and gift shop, 2024 Third St. (© **760/765-1120;** www.julianblackhistoricalsociety.org). African-American roots are deep in Julian (it was a black settler who originally found gold here in 1869), and the society offers walking tours on Saturday and Sunday at 2pm ($5). And no historic survey of Julian is complete without a visit to **Pioneer Cemetery,** a hilltop grave-yard straight out of *Our Town* or *Spoon River Anthology.* It can be accessed by a stairway on Main Street (which becomes Farmer Rd.), just past A Street; at one time this steep climb was the only entrance, but now you can also get there by car via A Street.

A ride from **Country Carriages** (✆ **760/765-1471;** www.southwestblend.com/country carriages) is a quintessential Julian experience. Even the locals get into the act, snuggling under a blanket for romantic horse-drawn carriage rides to celebrate anniversaries and birthdays. You can make reservations or find your carriage on Main Street across from Town Hall. A 30-minute rambling drive down country roads and through town starts at $30 for two people. Hours are Monday, Thursday, and Friday (usually no rides Tues–Wed, but it can be arranged) 11am to 4pm, and weekends 11am to 7pm; hours are extended for summer.

Animal lovers might also want to look into the **California Wolf Center** ★, 18457 Hwy. 79 (✆ **760/765-0030** or 619/234-9653; www.californiawolfcenter.org), located about 4 miles from town. This educational and conservation facility offers public pro-grams on Saturday and Sunday at 10am and 1:30pm (reservations required; $10–$20), which include a visit with the resident wolf pack. Private tours can be arranged Tuesday through Friday ($25 per person).

APPLE PIES

Before you leave, you must try Julian's apple pies. You'll need to sample them all to judge whether the best pies come from **Mom's Pies** ★, 2119 Main St. (✆ **760/765-2472;** www.momspiesjulian.com), the **Julian Pie Company** ★, 2225 Main St. (✆ **760/765-2449;** www.julianpie.com), **Apple Alley Bakery** ★, a nook on Main Street between Washington and B streets (✆ **760/765-2532**), or the **Julian Café & Bakery** ★, 2112 Main St. (✆ **760/765-2712**).

The special attraction at Mom's Pies is a sidewalk plate-glass window through which you can observe the mom-on-duty rolling crust, filling pies, and crimping edges. The shop routinely bakes several varieties of apple pie and will, with advance notice, whip up apple-rhubarb, peach-apple crumb, or any one of a number of specialties. There's a coun-try cafe in the store, in case a cup of coffee and a slice of fresh pie prove irresistible. Mom's is open Monday through Friday from 8am to 5pm, 8am to 6pm on weekends.

The Julian Pie Company's blue-and-white cottage boasts a small front patio with umbrella tables, a no-frills indoor parlor, and a large patio deck in back where overhang-ing apples are literally up for grabs. The shop serves original-style, Dutch, apple-moun-tain berry, and no-sugar-added pies as well as walnut-apple muffins and cinnamon cookies made from pie-crust dough. Light lunches of soup and sandwiches are offered weekdays from 11am to 2pm; it's open daily from 9am to 5pm.

SHOPPING

One of the simple pleasures of any weekend getaway is window- or souvenir-shopping in unfamiliar little stores like those lining both sides of Main Street (most merchants are open daily 10am–5pm). Rickety old structures are filled with antiques and collectibles—including places such as **Antique Boutique,** 2626 Main St. (✆ 760/765-0541), and **A Rose Path,** 2229 Main St. (✆ **760/765-1551;** www.arosepath.net), a rustic hideaway with two small art galleries and a retail area selling antiques and scented candles made on-site. **Warm Hearth,** 2125 Main St. (✆ 760/765-1022), is a vintage barn housing country crafts, candles, and woven throws among the woodstoves, fireplaces, and barbe-cue grills that make up the shop's main business.

Nearby is the **Julian Cider Mill,** 2103 Main St. (© **760/765-1430**), where you can see cider presses at work October through March. It offers free tastes of the fresh nectar, and jugs to take home. Throughout the year, the mill also carries the area's widest selection of food products, from apple butters and jams to berry preserves, several varieties of local honey, candies, and other goodies.

You'll have to step uphill 1 block to find the charming **Julian Tea & Cottage Arts,** 2124 Third St. (© **866/765-0832;** www.juliantea.com), for afternoon tea served amid a treasure-trove of tea-brewing tools and other tea-themed paraphernalia (reservations required for weekends; closed Tues–Wed Jan–Aug). If that sounds too frilly, head upstairs to the **Culinary Cottage,** home to stylish housewares, fine cookbooks, and gourmet foods (some of which are often available for tastings). Book lovers will enjoy stopping into the **Old Julian Book House,** 2230 Main St. (© **760/765-1989**), purveyor of new and antiquarian volumes alike; it also carries a smattering of maps, sheet music, CDs, and ephemera.

Wineries have a presence in the area, too, including rustic **Menghini Winery,** 1150 Julian Orchards Dr. (© **760/765-2072;** www.menghiniwinery.com), and **Witch Creek Winery,** 2100 Main St. (© **760/765-2023;** www.witchcreekwinery.com). Menghini has a small tasting area and gift shop, with rolling picnic grounds that host special events throughout the year, while Witch Creek is a simple tasting room right in town.

A number of **roadside fruit stands and orchards** dot the Julian hills; during autumn they're open all day, every day, but in the off season some might open only on weekends or close entirely. Depending on the season, most stands sell apples, pears, peaches, cider, jams, jellies, and other homemade foodstuffs. Many are along Hwy. 78 between Julian and Wynola, 3 miles away; there are also stands along Farmers Road, a scenic country lane leading north from downtown Julian.

Ask San Diegans who regularly make excursions to Julian, and they'll concur: No trip would be complete without stopping for a loaf (or three) of bread from **Dudley's Bakery,** 30218 Hwy. 78, Santa Ysabel (© **760/765-0488;** www.dudleysbakery.com). Loaves are stacked high, and folks are often lined up at the counter clamoring for the nearly 20 varieties of bread baked fresh daily since 1963. Choices range from raisin-date-nut to jalapeño, with some garden-variety sourdough and wheat grain in between. There's also a deli and gift shop stocking jewelry, books, and crafts. Dudley's is open Thursday through Sunday from 8am to 5pm. If it's closed, never fear—**Don's Market** (© **760/ 765-3272**) next door stocks a good selection, as well as sweet treats from Mom's Pies. There's also a Julian Pie Company outpost here.

OUTDOOR PURSUITS IN & AROUND JULIAN

Within 10 miles of Julian are numerous hiking trails that traverse rolling meadows, high chaparral, and oak and pine forests. Fire damage is visible—oaks have recovered, but pine trees have not, though seedlings are springing up; hiking here makes for a fascinating look at how Mother Nature works, and the additional good news is that you can actually see more of the vistas than you could before. The most spectacular hike is at **Volcan Mountain Preserve,** an area not affected by the 2003 or 2007 fires. It's located north of town along Farmers Road; the trail to the top is a moderately challenging hike of about 5 miles round-trip, with a 1,400-foot elevation gain. From the top, hikers have a panoramic view of the desert, mountains, and sea. Free ranger-led hikes are offered monthly, spring through fall; for a schedule, call © **760/765-4098,** or check www.volcanmt.org.

The 26,000-acre **Cuyamaca Rancho State Park,** along Hwy. 79 between Julian and I-8, was badly burned during the October 2003 forest fires. It is regenerating nicely, but if you're looking for a conifer forest here you may be disappointed. There are creeks and wildflower-enhanced meadows, and more than 100 miles of trails for hikers, bikers, and horseback riders. For a map and further information about park status, stop in at **park headquarters** on Hwy. 79, or check in with the **Cuyamaca Rancho State Park Interpretive Association** (© 760/765-3020; www.cuyamaca.us). Outside of Pine Hills is 900-acre **William Heise County Park** (© 760/765-0650; www.co.san-diego.ca.us/parks), which has an easy .5-mile loop trail.

Eight miles south of Julian (and not part of the state park), **Lake Cuyamaca** has a tiny community at the 4,600-foot elevation that centers on lake activities—primarily boating and fishing for trout (stocked year-round), plus bass, catfish, bluegill, and sturgeon. There's a general store and restaurant at the lake's edge. The fishing fee is $6 per day, $3.50 per day for kids 8 to 15, free for children 7 and under. A California State fishing license is required and sold here ($13 for the day), and a tackle shop can outfit you with whatever you need, including rental rods and reels ($10). Rowboats are $15 per day, and motorboat rentals run $45 for the day ($35 after 1pm). In the summer, canoes and paddle-boats can be rented by the hour for $15. For boat rental, fishing information, and RV or tent sites, call © 877/581-9904 or 760/765-0515, or see www.lakecuyamaca.org.

For a different way to tour, try **Llama Trek** (© 800/694-5487; www.wikiupbnb.com). You'll lead the llama, which carries packs, for a variety of hikes that include a visit to a winery or a historic gold mine. Rates for a 4- to 5-hour trip run $95 per person ($75 for children 10 and under) and include a picnic lunch.

WHERE TO STAY

Julian is B&B country, and they fill up months in advance for the fall apple-harvest season. The **Julian Bed & Breakfast Guild** (© 760/765-1555; www.julianbnbguild.com) has more than 10 members and is a terrific resource for locating accommodations that suit your taste. **Pine Hills Lodge,** 2960 Posada Way (© 760/765-1100; www.pinehillslodge.com), is a rustic getaway about 2 miles from town that serves a Sunday brunch (9am–2pm) in a wonderfully knotty dining room; there's also a small pub (Fri–Sat from 5pm) and a great deck area.

Julian Gold Rush Hotel ★   Built in 1897 by freed slave Albert Robinson, this frontier-style hotel is a living monument to the area's boomtown days—it's one of the oldest continually operating hotels in Southern California. Centrally located at the crossroads of downtown, the Julian Gold Rush Hotel isn't as secluded or plush as the many B&Bs in town, but if you seek historically accurate lodgings in Queen Anne style to complete your weekend time warp, this is the place. The 14 rooms and two cottages have been authentically restored (with nicely designed private bathrooms added where necessary) and feature antique furnishings; some rooms are also authentically tiny, so claustrophobics should inquire when reserving. Upstairs rooms are engulfed by a mélange of colorful wallpapers; downstairs, an inviting private lobby is stocked with books, games, literature on local activities, and a wood-burning stove.

2032 Main St. (at B St.), Julian, CA 92036. © 800/734-5854 or 760/765-0201. Fax 760/765-0327. www.julianhotel.com. 16 units. $135–$165 double; $170–$210 cottages. Rates include full breakfast and afternoon tea. AE, MC, V. Take I-8 E. to Hwy. 79. *In room:* No phone.

Orchard Hill Country Inn ★★ (Value   This AAA 4 Diamond inn is the most upscale lodging in Julian—a surprisingly posh, two-story Craftsman lodge and 12 cottages on a hill overlooking the town. Ten guest rooms, a lovely dining room (serving a guests-only gourmet dinner 4 nights a week, reservations required), and a great room with a massive stone fireplace are in the lodge. The cottages are spread over 3 acres and offer romantic hideaways. All units feature contemporary, nonfrilly country furnishings and snacks. While rooms in the main lodge feel somewhat hotel-ish, the cottage suites are secluded and luxurious, with private porches, fireplaces, wet bars, and whirlpool tubs in most. Several hiking trails lead from the lodge into adjacent woods. Check for specials and packages on the website.

2502 Washington St., at Second St. (P.O. Box 2410), Julian, CA 92036. (©) **800/716-7242** or 760/765-1700. Fax 760/765-0290. www.orchardhill.com. 22 units. $195–$250 double; from $295 for cottages. 2-night minimum stay if including Sat. Rates include breakfast and afternoon hors d'oeuvres. AE, MC, V. From Calif. 79, turn left on Main St., and then right on Washington St. **Amenities:** Restaurant; bar; bikes. *In room:* A/C, TV/VCR, movie library, CD player, hair dryer.

WHERE TO DINE

Julian Grille ★ AMERICAN   Set in a cozy cottage festooned with lacy draperies, flickering candles, and a warm hearth, the Grille is the nicest eatery in town. Lunch here is an anything-goes affair, ranging from soups, sandwiches, and large salads to char-broiled burgers and hearty omelets. There are delectable appetizers such as baked brie with apples and pecans, and the "Prime Tickler" (chunks of prime rib served cocktail-style *au jus* with horseradish sauce). Dinner features grilled and broiled meats, seafood, and prime rib. If it's a nice day, enjoy your meal out on the shady patio.

2224 Main St. (at A St.). (©) **760/765-0173.** Reservations recommended Fri–Sun. Main courses $8–$13 lunch, $15–$28 dinner. AE, DISC, MC, V. Lunch Mon 11am–3pm, Tues–Sat 11am–4pm, Sun 10:30am–4pm; dinner Tues–Thurs 4:30–8pm, Fri–Sun 4:30–9pm, no dinner on Mon.

Romano's Dodge House ★ ITALIAN   Occupying a historic home just off Main Street (vintage photos illustrate the little farmhouse's past), Romano's is proud to be the only restaurant in town *not* serving apple pie. It's a home-style Italian spot, with red-checked tablecloths and straw-clad chianti bottles. Romano's offers pizzas and pastas, as well as more creative fare such as spicy apple-cider sausage, and pork loin in cinnamon, garlic, and whiskey sauce; the wine list features local vintages from nearby Menghini, Jenkins, and Orfila wineries. Seating is on a narrow shaded porch, in the wood-plank dining room, and in a little lounge in back (which sometimes stays open late).

2718 B St. (just off Main). (©) **760/765-1003.** www.romanosjulian.com. Reservations recommended. Main courses $8–$19. DISC, MC, V. Wed–Mon 11:30am–8:30pm.

5 ANZA-BORREGO DESERT STATE PARK ★★

90 miles NE of San Diego; 31 miles E of Julian

The sweeping 650,000-acre Anza-Borrego Desert State Park, the largest state park in California, lies mostly within San Diego County (in fact it makes up more than 20% of the county). For many city-weary residents, a couple of days here is just the ticket to rejuvenate overburdened minds.

A sense of timelessness pervades this landscape. The desert is home to fossils and rocks dating from 540 million years ago; human beings arrived about 12,000 years ago. The terrain ranges in elevation from 15 to 6,100 feet above sea level. It incorporates dry lake beds, sandstone canyons, granite mountains, palm groves fed by year-round springs, and more than 600 kinds of desert plants. After the winter rains, thousands of wildflowers burst into bloom, transforming the desert into a brilliant palette of pink, lavender, red, orange, and yellow. The giant ocotillo bushes flower extravagantly, hummingbirds fill the air, and an occasional migratory bird stops off en route to the Salton Sea. The park got its name from the rare bighorn sheep, or *borrego,* which can sometimes be spotted navigating rocky hillsides. The other half of the name comes from Spanish army officer Juan Bautista de Anza, who from 1774 to 1775 led back-to-back expeditions (including one with more than 200 men, women, and children, plus livestock), through the desert from the Gulf of Mexico to the California coast. Following his second journey to the ocean, he made his way north, laying the groundwork for the presidio and mission that would become the city of San Francisco.

Many people visit the area with little interest in the flora and fauna—they're here to relax and sun themselves in tiny Borrego Springs, a town surrounded by the state park. It is, however, somewhat remote, and its supporters proudly proclaim that Borrego Springs is and will remain what Palm Springs used to be: a small, charming resort community with more empty lots than built ones. Yes, there are a couple of country clubs, some chic fairway-view homes, a luxury resort, and a regular influx of vacationers, but it's still plenty funky. One of the valley's unusual sights is scattered patches of tall, lush palm tree groves, perfectly square in shape: Borrego Springs's tree farms are a major source of landscaping trees for San Diego and surrounding counties.

When planning a trip here, keep in mind that temperatures rise to as high as 125°F (52°C) in July and August. Winter days are very comfortable, with temperatures averaging around 70°F (21°C) December through January, but nighttime temps can drop to freezing. Hypothermia is as big a killer out here as the heat.

ESSENTIALS

GETTING THERE   The drive to Anza-Borrego Desert State Park is spectacular; the scenery ranges from rolling, pastoral landscapes to endless bird's-eye vistas from precarious dead-man's curves. It's about a 2-hour drive from San Diego; the fastest route is I-15 N. to the Poway (S4) exit to its end, left on 67 north to Ramona, which turns into 78 E., to Santa Ysabel. From here, go left on 79, right on S2, and left on S22. Alternatively, follow I-8 E. past Alpine to Hwy. 79. Follow 79 N. for 23 miles to Julian; take a right on 78, and then a left on S3 to Borrego Springs. Another (longer) option is to take I-8 to Ocotillo, and then San Diego's loneliest highway, Hwy. S2, north. Along this 40-mile stretch you'll follow the Southern Overland Stage Route of 1849 (be sure to stop and notice the view at the Carrizo Badlands Overlook) to 78 E. into Borrego Springs. The closest airport with scheduled service is Palm Springs, 75 minutes away by car.

GETTING AROUND   You don't need a four-wheel-drive vehicle to tour the desert, but you'll probably want to get off the main highways and onto the jeep trails. The Anza-Borrego Desert State Park Visitor Center staff (see below) can tell you which jeep trails are in condition for two-wheel-drive vehicles. The Ocotillo Wells area of the park has been set aside for off-road vehicles such as dune buggies and dirt bikes. To use the jeep trails, a vehicle has to be licensed for highway use.

ORIENTATION & VISITOR INFORMATION   In Borrego Springs, a town completely surrounded by the state park, Palm Canyon Drive is the main drag. Christmas Circle surrounds a grassy park at the entry to town; the "mall" is just west and contains many of the town's businesses. The architecturally striking **Anza-Borrego Desert State Park Visitor Center** (© **760/767-4205** or 767-5311; www.parks.ca.gov) lies 2 miles west of Borrego Springs; it's cut into the side of a hill and is totally invisible from the road. In addition to a small museum with interactive exhibits, it supplies information, maps, and two 15-minute audiovisual presentations, one on the bighorn sheep and the other on wildflowers; an interpreted loop trail is also on-site. The visitor center is open October through May daily from 9am to 5pm, June through September weekends from 9am to 5pm. You should also stop by the **Desert Natural History Association,** 652 Palm Canyon Dr. (© **760/767-3098;** www.abdnha.org), whose Borrego Desert Nature Center and Bookstore is open daily, 9am to 5pm. It features an impressive selection of guidebooks, educational materials for kids, native plants, regional crafts, and a mini-museum display that includes a pair of frighteningly real taxidermied bobcats. This is also your best source for information on the nearby Salton Sea.

For more details on the park, check in with the **Anza-Borrego Foundation Institute** (© 760/767-0446; www.theabf.org); for information on lodging, dining, and activities, contact the **Borrego Springs Chamber of Commerce,** 786 Palm Canyon Dr. (© **800/ 559-5524** or 760/767-5555; www.borregospringschamber.com).

EXPLORING THE DESERT

Remember when you're touring in this area, hydration is of paramount importance. Whether you're walking, cycling, or driving, always have a bottle of water at your side. The temperatures in the desert vary like the winds; do yourself a favor and dress in layers to protect yourself from the elements. If you will be out after dusk, or anytime during January and February, warm clothing is also essential.

You can explore the desert's stark terrain on one of its many trails or on a self-guided driving tour; the visitor center can supply maps. For starters, the **Borrego Palm Canyon self-guided hike** ★ starts at the campground near the visitor center, and is 1.5 miles each way. It's a beautiful, easy-to-moderately difficult hike (depending on what Mother Nature has been up to), winding around boulders and through dry washes to a waterfall and a native grove of massive fan palms. Keep an eye out for the rare bighorn sheep on the canyon walls above. If you've got some time and crave solitude, try **Hellhole Canyon** trail.

You can also take a guided off-road tour of the desert with **California Overland** (© **866/639-7567** or 760/767-1232; www.californiaoverland.com). Visit spectacular canyons, fossil beds, ancient Native American sites, caves, and more in military-style vehicles; you'll learn about the history and geology of the area along the way. There are 2-, 4-, 5-, 8-, and 10-hour (as well as overnight) excursions; you can also arrange for a private guided jeep tour. Tours include drinks and snacks (or box lunch on longer treks); prices start at $55 for the standard 2-hour adventure, $35 for children age 3 to 12.

Whether you tour with California Overland or on your own, don't miss the sunset view of the Borrego Badlands from **Font's Point.** Savvy travelers plan ahead and bring champagne and beach chairs for the nightly ritual. *Note:* The road to Font's Point—just past mile marker 29 on Palm Canyon Drive—is often suitable only for four-wheel-drive vehicles; check with the visitor center for current conditions.

If you have only 1 day to spend here, a good day trip from San Diego would include driving over on one route, going to the visitor center, hiking to Palm Canyon, having a picnic, and driving back to San Diego using another route.

GOLF

The **Borrego Springs Resort,** 1112 Tilting T Dr. (© **888/826-7734** or 760/767-3330; www.borregospringsresort.com), has three 9-hole courses—you'll play more than 6,700 yards over any 18 holes. There are four sets of tees to accommodate all levels of play, five lakes, a driving range, clubhouse, and pro shop; **The Arches Restaurant** and **Fireside**

Lounge and Bar are in the clubhouse. The greens fee for 18 holes (cart included) is $55 Monday to Thursday, $65 Friday to Sunday in the high season (Oct–May); in the off season (June–Sept), it's $40 Monday to Thursday, $45 Friday to Sunday. Discounts are available for afternoon play; the resort also offers stay-and-play packages.

WHERE TO STAY

Borrego Springs is small, but there are enough accommodations to suit all travel styles and budgets. Peak season—from November to April—corresponds with the most temperate weather and wildflower viewing. Most hotels also post lower midweek rates; substantially cheaper prices are available in summer. For basic, 1950s-style digs there's the conveniently located **Hacienda del Sol,** 610 Palm Canyon Dr. (© **760/767-5442;** www.haciendadelsol-borrego.com); another option is **Palm Canyon Resort,** 221 Palm Canyon Dr. (© **800/242-0044** or 760/767-5341; www.pcresort.com), a large complex that includes a moderately priced hotel, RV park, restaurant, and recreational facilities.

Very Expensive

Borrego Ranch Resort & Spa ★★   Formerly known as La Casa del Zorro, this clubby oasis is 5 miles southeast of Borrego Springs. Over time the property has evolved into a cohesive blend of discretely private cottages and luxurious one- and two-story hotel buildings; it's blessed with personalized service and unwavering standards that make this resort unequaled in Borrego Springs. The name change has brought along with it new landscaping and a much-appreciated high-end spa experience, as well as adoption of the nearby 18-hole, Tom Fazio–designed golf course. Most of the 19 casitas—part of a never-finished residential community—have up to four bedrooms and feature a fireplace and private pool or spa; they all have minifridges and microwaves. Standard rooms offer fireplaces and balconies or patios. On-site diversions include tennis, archery, a scenic jogging track, a life-size chess set, a climbing wall, and a labyrinth. The atmosphere here is conservative, and those 17 and under are not allowed.

3845 Yaqui Pass Rd., Borrego Springs, CA 92004. © **800/824-1884** or 760/767-5323. Fax 760/767-5963. www.borregoranchresort.com. 63 units. From $295 double; from $470 casitas (summer rates considerably less). AE, DC, DISC, MC, V. No children. **Amenities:** 3 restaurants; 2 bars; bikes; concierge; golf course; health club (w/classes and personal trainers); 4 Jacuzzis; 5 pools; room service; spa; 6 lighted tennis courts. *In room:* A/C, TV/DVD, hair dryer, Internet, minibar.

Expensive

Borrego Valley Inn ★★   Stepping into the courtyard here—with its adobe casitas, desert landscaping of agave and bougainvillea, clumps of chilies drying in the sun, an aviary of chirping birds—is an evocative experience. Perhaps an Ennio Morricone theme will whistle through your brain, as you study the Hollywood-perfect surroundings that lend the air of a charming Southwestern pueblo. Featuring private patios adorned with fruit trees and Mexican *chiminea* fireplaces, the meticulously maintained accommodations have Saltillo tile floors and a Southwest/Mex decor; larger rooms have a kitchenette. The La Casita suite has a full kitchen and a 500-square-foot patio with a propane barbecue grill. Opened in 1998, this nonsmoking hotel is close to town and has two pools, one of which—surrounded by a high fence—is clothing optional.

405 Palm Canyon Dr., Borrego Springs, CA 92004. © **800/333-5810** or 760/767-0311. www.borrego valleyinn.com. 15 units. From $215 double; from $280 suite (summer rates considerably less). Rates include continental breakfast. 2-night minimum seasonal weekends. AE, DISC, MC, V. No children 13 or under. Nonsmoking. **Amenities:** 2 Jacuzzis; 2 pools. *In room:* A/C, TV, CD player, fridge, hair dryer, Wi-Fi.

The Palms Hotel ★★ (Finds) This classic retro desert retreat originally opened in 1947, but was rebuilt after a fire in 1958. It was a favorite hideaway for San Diego and Hollywood elite, playing host to movie stars including Clark Gable and Marilyn Monroe. In 1993, new owners rescued it from extreme disrepair, clearing away the most dilapidated guest bungalows and restoring the resort to its midcentury modern glory. Ten rooms are in the main building, while two casitas close to the pool have a fireplace and wet bar, and offer a little more privacy. Staying here is comfortable and satisfying; the old glamour is tangible, and sweeping views across the undeveloped desert set an easygoing mood. The Palms also has one of the best restaurants in town, the **Krazy Coyote/Red Ocotillo** (see "Where to Dine," below), and a fabulous, completely restored Olympic-length pool.

2220 Hoberg Rd., Borrego Springs, CA 92004. ℂ **800/519-2624** or 760/767-7788. Fax 760/767-9717. www.thepalmsatindianhead.com. 12 units. $159–$229 double (summer rates considerably less). Rates include continental breakfast. 2-night minimum seasonal weekends. Extra person $20. AE, DISC, MC, V. No children 12 or under. **Amenities:** Restaurant; bar; Jacuzzi; pool; room service. *In room:* A/C, TV, fridge.

Camping

The park has two developed campgrounds. **Borrego Palm Canyon,** with 117 sites, is 2¹/₂ miles west of Borrego Springs, near the visitor center. **Tamarisk Grove,** at Hwy. 78 and County Road S3, has 27 sites. The overnight rate at both is $20 without a hookup, or $29 with a hookup (at Palm Canyon only); both have restrooms with pay showers (bring quarters) and a campfire program. Reservations are required in winter/spring high season; contact **Reserve America** (ℂ **800/444-7275;** www.reserveamerica.com). Primitive and backcountry camping are also allowed, making this one of the few parks in the country where you can just pull off the road and find yourself a spot to commune with nature (ground fires are not allowed, though). For more information, check with the visitor center (ℂ **760/767-4205** or 767-5311; www.parks.ca.gov).

WHERE TO DINE

Pickings are slim in Borrego Springs, but you can follow legions of locals into the downtown mainstay **Carlee's Place,** 660 Palm Canyon Dr. (ℂ **760/767-3262**), a casual bar and grill with plenty of neon beer signs, a well-worn pool table, and a fine trophy of a jackalope (the mythic creature that's part jack rabbit, part antelope) mounted over the bar. For Mexican food, look to **Carmelita's Mexican Grill & Cantina,** 575 Palm Canyon Dr. (ℂ **760/767-5666**); for a diner-esque breakfast there's **Kendall's Cafe,** 587 Palm Canyon Dr. in the mall (ℂ **760/767-3491**), where steaks, teriyaki, and Mexican combo platters are also available for lunch and dinner. French food has carved a niche here, as well, at **The French Corner,** 721 Av. Sureste (ℂ **760/767-5713;** www.thefrenchcorner. biz). You'll find quiches and crepes for breakfast (Fri–Sun) and lunch, plus heartier fare for dinner; antiques and decorative items are for sale here, too.

Krazy Coyote Bar & Grille/Red Ocotillo ★ AMERICAN/CALIFORNIAN Sharing a space overlooking the pool at the retro Palms Hotel, this two-for-one dining spot combines the hotel's seasonal, dinner-only restaurant with the popular comfort-food eatery that was formerly housed in a Quonset hut on the other side of town. Red Ocotillo serves breakfast, plus refreshing salads, creative burgers, and pastas from 7am to 9pm; beginning at 5:30pm, the more upscale Krazy Koyote menu joins the party, featuring prime steaks, fresh fish, and individual gourmet pizzas. The evening ambience is especially welcoming and romantic here, as the sparse lights of tiny Borrego Springs twinkle on the desert floor below; the classy cocktail menu adds to the allure.

In the Palms Hotel, 2220 Hoberg Rd. ☏ **760/767-7788**. www.thepalmsatindianhead.com. Dinner reservations highly recommended. Main courses $7–$15 breakfast and lunch, $10–$40 dinner. AE, DISC, MC, V. Daily 7am–9pm; Krazy Koyote closed in summer.

6 TIJUANA: GOING SOUTH OF THE BORDER

17 miles S of San Diego

First things first: The city's name is pronounced—at least in gringoized Spanish—"Tee-*wanna*," not "Tee-*uh*-wanna." And despite her presence in the wax museum (see below), there was no kindly rancho matriarch named Tía (aunt) Juana for whom the city was named. Tijuana derives its name from "tycuan," an indigenous word meaning "near the water," a reference to a broad, shallow river that is now little more than a trickle (except during storms) running down a concrete wash.

Vibrant, chaotic, colorful, and confounding, Tijuana has a population of more than two million people, making it Mexico's fourth-largest city (and the second largest on the West Coast—only Los Angeles is bigger). Although the majority of San Diegans are basically estranged from our neighbor to the south, the history of the two cities is inextricably linked—Tijuana exists because of San Diego. T.J., as San Diegans refer to it, was little more than a village at the turn of the 20th century. It grew explosively in response to the needs of San Diego and the rest of California, providing a workforce for factories and fields, especially during World War II. It also offered succor, becoming a decadent playground for Americans deprived of booze and gambling by Prohibition and moral reformers. The city's economic engine is now driven by free-trade policies that gave rise to the *maquiladoras*—foreign-owned factories where appliances, furniture, and other goods are assembled by poorly paid, often underage workers, with little environmental or labor oversight.

Architecturally, little remains of Tijuana's boomtown days. Most of the city is of a more modern vintage, and some structures are quite striking; but for the most part this is, sorry to say, not an attractive urban landscape. Tijuana's beauty lies within. The city has fabulous restaurants and a burgeoning art and music scene; yet many still visit solely for the two-for-one drink specials or photo ops with a zebra-striped burro. If you want to find the real treasures of Tijuana, you'll have to venture out of the main tourist zone of Avenida Revolución.

ESSENTIALS
Getting There
BY TROLLEY   The easiest way to get to Tijuana from downtown San Diego is to hop aboard the bright-red **San Diego Trolley.** Take the Blue Line headed for San Ysidro and get off there (it's the last stop). From the trolley, cross the street and head up the ramp that accesses the border-crossing bridge. Tijuana's shopping and nightlife district, Avenida Revolución, is a $5 taxi ride from the border, or you can walk the mile into the tourist area. The trolley is simple and inexpensive and takes about 40 minutes from downtown San Diego; the one-way fare is $2.50. The last trolley to San Ysidro departs downtown around midnight (3am on Sat); the last returning trolley from San Ysidro is at 1am (2am on Sat).

ACCOMMODATIONS ■
Baja Inn La Mesa **29**
Camino Real **17**
Fiesta Inn **24**
Grand Hotel Tijuana **26**
Hotel Hacienda del Rio **20**
Hotel Lucerna **19**
Hotel Pueblo Amigo **4**
Palacio Azteca Hotel **21**
Tijuana Marriott Hotel **28**

DINING ◆
Cafe La Especial **7**
Carnitas Uruapan **30**
Cheripan **22**
Chiki Jai **8**
Cien Años **18**
La Costa **9**
La Diferencia **23**
La Fonda de Roberto **25**
La Querencia **22**
Negai **22**
El Potrero **27**
Tepoznieves **22**
Villa Saverios **22**

ATTRACTIONS ●
Antigua Palacio Municipal **5**
Caliente Race & Sports Book **6**
Caliente Racetrack **31**
Centro Cultural Tijuana **13**
Cervecería Tijuana **33**
L.A. Cetto Winery **12**
Mercado de Artesanías **2**
Mercado Hidalgo **16**
Mercado el Popo **5**
Mundo Divertido **31**
Museo de Cera **1**
Palacio Frontón **10**
Plaza Fiesta **15**
Plaza Rio Tijuana **14**
Pueblo Amigo **3**
Sanborns **11**
Tijuana Country Club **32**

Tijuana Safety Alert

Violence has risen dramatically in Tijuana, mostly due to the presence of organized crime. In April 2008, the U.S. State Department heightened its travel alert after the city was rocked by a series of shootouts between drug cartels and the federal police, sent in by President Felipe Calderón. For the latest security advisories, go to http://travel.state.gov; you can also call toll-free ✆ **888/407-4747** Monday through Friday 5am to 5pm. From Mexico, dial 001-202-501-4444 (tolls apply).

Although a few tourists have been caught in the crossfire, they are not the targets—drug cartels wage turf wars, businessmen are extorted, political scores are settled, and wealthy *Tijuanenses* are kidnapped for ransom. There is petty crime, too, so don't flash a lot of cash and expensive jewelry, and stick to populated areas. *Mordida,* "the bite," is also still known to occur. That's when uniformed police officers extort money in exchange for letting you off some infraction, like a traffic ticket. If you do find yourself dealing with an official, never offer a bribe—you may find yourself in much more trouble than you bargained for. And if you do meet up with corruption, you have little recourse but to comply, and then report any incident to your consulate in Tijuana (be sure to note the officer's name, as well as badge and patrol car numbers). You can also file complaints about police or city officials in English at www.consulmexsd.org (click on the link "Complaints About Your Trip to Tijuana." Another option is the city of Tijuana Internal Affairs 24-hour hot line at ✆ **664/688-2810;** the San Diego Police Department will take crime reports and forward them to the proper agency, as well.

Coming home, the border crossing for pedestrians can require as little as a few minutes midweek, or more than 2 hours on weekend and holiday afternoons. This is, after all, possibly the busiest border crossing in the world. Travelers going no farther south than Ensenada for less than 72 hours do not need a Mexican tourist card. In order to cross back, U.S. citizens now need either: 1) **a passport,** passport card, or similarly secure document such as a SENTRI card (used by frequent border crossers), or 2) **two proofs of citizenship,** the most common option being a driver's license and a birth certificate. Those 18 and under must have a birth certificate. These rules apply to land, air, and sea arrivals. Non-U.S. citizens will need a passport, an I-94, a multiple-entry visa, or a Resident Alien Card to return to the U.S. Check with the **U.S. Department of State** (✆ **202/647-5225;** www.travel.state.gov) before your visit for more information.

BY CAR   Unless you want to explore more of Baja California, leave your car north of the border. If you do drive, take I-5 S. to the Mexican border at San Ysidro; the drive takes under a half-hour from downtown San Diego. Although the southbound border crossing rarely requires more than a few minutes, allow at least 1 hour to cross the border coming back to the U.S., or a minimum of 2 hours on weekends or holidays. An alternative option if you're going only to Tijuana is to drive to the border and park in one of the long-term parking lots on the U.S. side for about $6 to $10 a day; a shuttle can take you to Avenida Revolución for $4 ($6 round-trip). Once you're in Tijuana, it's easier to get around by taxi than to adapt to the local driving standards.

Many car-rental companies in San Diego, such as **Avis** (© **800/831-2847;** www.avis. com) and **West Coast Rent-a-Car** (© **619/544-0606;** www.westcoastrentacar.net), allow their cars to be driven into Baja California, at least as far as Ensenada. Mexican auto insurance of around $25 a day (depending on the value of your ride) is highly recommended. It's not compulsory; but if you're involved in an accident and don't have it, you may end up in police custody until the details are sorted out. Insurance is available from your car-rental agency in San Diego; at various outlets just north of the border in San Ysidro; or from a stateside AAA office, if you're a member.

BUS TOURS   **Baja California Tours** (© **800/336-5454** or 858/454-7166; www.baja specials.com), based in La Jolla, offers two daily tours to Tijuana ($36, $20 for ages 3–11), from 9am to 1pm and 2 to 5:30pm. Trips to Rosarito ($48, $29 ages 3–11) and Ensenada ($72, $43 ages 3–11) depart at 9am and head back to San Diego at 4:30pm and 3:30pm, respectively. The company picks up at many San Diego hotels from La Jolla south; it also offers overnight trips, Baja wine tasting tours, and other packages. **Gray Line San Diego** (© **800/331-5077** or 619/266-7365; www.sandiegograyline.com) also offers tours of Baja, including a Tijuana excursion for $36 per person ($20 for children 3–11, or up to two children 3–11 free with two paying adults); the twice-daily departures are at 8:30am and 1:30pm. **Five Star Tours** (© **800/553-8687** or 619/232-5040; www.sdsuntours.com) offers a $43 ($23 for children 3–11) tour into Tijuana from 11am to 5pm. Five Star also has a Baja winery tour that leaves Old Town on Saturdays at 9am ($93 adults, $43 children). Do-it-yourselfers who aren't interested in a narrated tour or rigid time constraints can grab a **Mexicoach** bus (© **619/428-9517;** www.mexicoach.com) for transportation to Tijuana ($6 round-trip) or Rosarito ($20 round-trip). You can find them at the Border Station parking lot or adjacent to the San Ysidro trolley stop. Trips to the heart of Avenida Revolución run daily from 8am to 9pm; the last Rosarito run is at 7pm (last return is at 8pm). Mexicoach has round-trip departures from Old Town, too. The company has also launched a city bus tour with (usually) bilingual guides; the loop tour departs from the CECUT cultural center and stops at 13 sites around Tijuana, allowing on-and-off privileges along the way ($10, $5 for seniors and children).

Getting Around

If you've come to Tijuana on the San Diego Trolley or if you leave a car on the U.S. side of the border, you will walk through the border crossing. The first structure you'll see on your left is a **Visitor Information Center** (© **664/607-3097**), open daily from 9am to 6pm; it has maps, safety tips, and brochures that cover the city's highlights. From here, you can easily walk into the center of town or take a taxi. If you're walking, a good landmark is the tall silver archway known as **Reloj Monumental;** it marks the intersection of First Street and Avenida Revolución, the main tourist strip that extends to the south. *Note:* If you head north from the monument, you'll enter the red-light district.

Taxicabs are easy to find; they queue up around most of the visitor hot spots, and drivers often solicit passengers. It's customary to agree upon the rate before stepping into the cab, whether you're going a few blocks or hiring a cab for the afternoon. One-way rides within the city cost $5 to $10, and a trip to Playas de Tijuana might be around $20; tipping is not expected. Some cabs are "local" taxis, frequently stopping to take on or let off other passengers during your ride; they are less expensive than private cabs. Metered taxis *(taxi libre)*—the cars are white with red stripes—are often a little cheaper than cabs with a negotiated rate. As opposed to places like Mexico City, there's no threat of crime from larcenous-minded cabbies.

The **Tijuana Convention & Visitors Bureau** has a website that will get you started: www.tijuanaonline.org. You can request a free visitors' guide by mail via the site; in Tijuana, the main office is across the street from the Centro Cultural, Paseo de los Héroes 9365, Ste. 201 (© **664/684-0537**), and is open Monday through Friday, 9am to 6pm. You can also request information and maps from the **Baja California Information Office** in San Diego (© **800/522-1516** in Calif., Ariz., or Nev.; 800/225-2786 in the rest of the U.S. and Canada; or 619/299-8518). It's in Mission Valley at 6855 Friars Rd., Ste. 26, and is open Monday through Friday from 9am to 5pm. If you are thinking about a longer trip to Baja, the **Discover Baja Travel Club** (© **800/727-2252** or 619/275-4225; www.discoverbaja.com) might be a worthwhile investment. For a $39 membership fee you can get discounted insurance; special offers from restaurants, hotels, and shops; and deals on an extensive inventory of books, maps, and other Baja-related goods. Non-members can purchase items at normal price, including online insurance. Discover Baja is at 3089 Clairemont Dr., east of Mission Bay; it's open Monday through Friday, 9am to 5pm, Saturday from 9am to 1pm.

If you run into problems in Tijuana, you can get English-speaking tourist assistance by dialing © **078;** it operates 24/7. For information on events or attractions, you can call © **664/683-1405.** Mexico's "911" is © **066.** The Convention & Visitors office can also help with legal assistance for visitors who encounter trouble while in Tijuana. The following countries have consulate offices in Tijuana: the **United States** (© **664/622-7400**), **Canada** (© **664/684-0461**), and the **United Kingdom** (© **664/681-7323**). If you need to find an MD or dentist, contact **MexDoctors** (© **664/634-3744,** or 619/378-0104 in San Diego; www.mexdoctors.com). More than a few San Diegans have medical procedures done in Tijuana to avoid the high cost of U.S. healthcare. *Note:* When calling from the U.S., dial 011-52 then the 10-digit number.

SOME HELPFUL TIPS The city does not take time for an afternoon siesta; you'll always find shops and restaurants open, as well as people in the streets. Most streets are safe for walking; observe the same precautions you would in any large city. Most people who deal with the traveling public speak English, often very well.

CURRENCY The Mexican currency is the peso, but you can easily visit Tijuana (and Rosarito and Ensenada) without changing money; dollars are accepted just about everywhere. Many prices are posted in American (indicated with the abbreviation "dlls.") and Mexican ("m.n.," *moneda nacional*) currencies—both use the "$" sign. Bring a supply of smaller-denomination ($1, $5, and $10) bills. Although change is readily given in American dollars, many merchants are reluctant to break a $20 bill for small purchases. Visa and MasterCard are accepted in many places, but never assume they will be; ask before dining or purchasing. When using credit cards at restaurants, it's a nice gesture to leave the tip in cash. As of this writing, the dollar is worth 15 pesos.

TAXES & TIPPING A sales tax of 10%, called an IVA, is added to most bills, including those in restaurants. This does not represent the tip; the bill will read *IVA incluído,* but you should add about 10% for the tip if the service warrants. Taxi drivers do not expect a tip.

EXPLORING TIJUANA

For many visitors, Tijuana's main event is bustling **Avenida Revolución,** the street whose reputation precedes it. Beginning in the 1920s, Americans flocked to this street for bawdy, illicit fun; but civic improvements have vanquished the girlie shows whose barkers once accosted passersby. Drinking and shopping are the main order of business these days. While young people from across the border knock back tequila shooters and dangle precariously at the upstairs railings of glaring neon discos, bargain-hunters peruse the never-ending array of goods (and not-so-goods) for sale. You'll find the action between *calles* 1 and 9; there's a visitor information booth at Revolución and Third on the east side of the street.

Among the numerous curio shops, bars, and restaurants are a few attractions, too. If you've made the 10-minute walk from the border, the first one you'll encounter is the **Museo de Cera (Wax Museum)**, 8281 Calle 1, between avenidas Revolución and Maderas (℃ **664/688-2478**). It's filled with characters from Mexican history and lore, and includes a few incongruous figures such as Bill Clinton and Whoopi Goldberg. This creepy sideshow is open daily from 10am to 6pm; admission is about $1. In an attractive, flagstone-fronted space on Revolución at Calle 4 is the **Caliente Race & Sports Book** (℃ **664/688-3425;** www.caliente.com.mx), which opened in 2006. Here you can bet on international sporting events including NFL, NBA, and soccer games; there's also electronic gaming. Caliente also operates the **Hipódromo Caliente (Caliente Racetrack),** Bulevar Agua Caliente and Tapachula (℃ **664/633-7300**), home of daily greyhound racing and another sports book. It's about a 10-minute cab ride from the tourist drag.

For something decidedly more cultural, head west down Calle 2. Just past Avenida Constitución is the **Palacio de la Cultura ★** (℃ **664/688-1721;** www.imac.tijuana.gob. mx), a multipurpose complex that opened in 2006, featuring galleries, a library, and event spaces. Showcasing the work of local artists, this complex is set in the **Antigua Palacio Municipal,** which served as a seat of government from 1921 to 1986 (it's one of the area's few remaining historical buildings). Adjacent to the Palacio on Calle 2, cater-cornered from the Cathedral, is **Mercado el Popo,** a quintessentially Mexican marketplace selling nuts, candy, and produce. One of the most ornate buildings in town is the **Palacio Frontón (Jai Lai Palace),** Revolución and Calle 7, where the fast-paced court game was once played. The facility is now used for concerts and special events.

A short cab ride away in the **Zona Río** is Tijuana's cultural icon, the **Centro Cultural Tijuana (CECUT) ★**, Paseo de los Héroes, at Avenida Independencia (℃ **664/687-9600;** www.cecut.gob.mx). You'll easily spot the ultramodern complex, which opened in 1982—its centerpiece is a gigantic sand-colored sphere, "La Bola," that houses an IMAX Dome Theater. At least two different 45-minute Spanish-language films are shown daily; on weekends there is usually an English-language screening. Joining La Bola is "El Cubo," the new $9-million, state-of-the-art gallery that hosts major touring exhibits; there's a cafe and a great museum bookshop, as well. CECUT (pronounced see-*coot*) also has a museum that covers the history of Tijuana and Baja, with a collection of artifacts from pre-Hispanic times through the modern political era (descriptions are in both Spanish and English); music, theater, and dance performances are held in the center's acoustically excellent concert hall. The center is open Tuesday through Sunday from 10am to 6:30pm; admission to the museum's permanent exhibit is about $1.60; tickets for the films and El Cubo are about $3 for adults and $1.60 for children.

CECUT also gets you away from the tourist kitsch and into the more sophisticated Zona Río, where you can admire the wide, European-style **Paseo de los Héroes.** The boulevard's intersections are marked by gigantic traffic circles, at the center of which stand statuesque monuments to leaders ranging from Aztec Emperor Cuauhtémoc to Abraham Lincoln. In the Zona Río you'll find some classier shopping, a colorful local marketplace, and some of Tijuana's best restaurants.

Mundo Divertido, Vía Rápida Poniente 15035 (© **664/701-7133;** www.mundo divertido.com.mx), is an ultimate destination for kids, featuring roller coasters, batting cages, miniature golf, go-carts, video games, and more. It's open daily from about noon to 9pm. There's also a movie theater at the Plaza Mundo Divertido, and Hollywood films are presented in English with Spanish subtitles.

Adult pleasures await at **L.A. Cetto Winery (Cava de Vinos)** ★, Av. Cañón Johnson 2108, at Avenida Constitución Sur (© **664/685-3031;** www.cettowines.com), where you can get an introduction to the Mexican winemaking industry, the heart of which is based in the Valle de Guadalupe, a fertile region southeast of Tijuana. Many of the local high-quality vintages are exported to Europe; most are unavailable in the United States due to high tariffs. Shaped like a wine barrel, L.A. Cetto's unique facade is made from old oak aging barrels; an impressive visitor center offers an array of treats, including not only the company's award-winning wines, but also its line of tequila, brandy, and olive oil. Admission is $2 for the tour (and tastings, for those 18 and above; kids 17 and under are admitted free with an adult), $5 with souvenir wineglass. It's open Monday through Saturday from 10am to 5pm.

About 6 miles west of the Zona Centro, off the scenic toll road that heads toward Rosarito and Ensenada (but before you reach the first tollbooth), is the beach community of **Playas de Tijuana.** The large, sandy beach is popular with families, and a line of ramshackle restaurants and cafes on a bluff overlooking the surf offers great spots for lunch and a cold beer. A stone's throw away is the bullring-by-the-sea known as **Plaza Monumental** (p. 281). Perhaps the most notable feature here, though, is an imposing fence, a parting gift from the Bush administration. The new barrier replaces an old, rusting fence with unevenly spaced girders that allowed divided families to meet and share stories, kisses, food, or money. When completed, the new triple fence will keep those on the U.S. side 90 feet away from the border.

SHOPPING

Tijuana's biggest attraction is shopping—ask any of the millions of people who cross the border each year to do it. They come to take advantage of reasonable prices on a variety of merchandise: colorfully glazed pottery, woven blankets and serapes, embroidered dresses and sequined sombreros, onyx chess sets, beaded necklaces and bracelets, silver jewelry (beware of fake gold, though), leather bags and *huarache* sandals, hammered-tin picture frames, thick drinking glasses, Cuban cigars, and Mexican liquors such as Kahlúa and tequila. You're permitted to bring $800 worth of purchases back across the border duty-free (but no Cuban cigars), including 1 liter of alcohol per person (for adults 21 and older). If your total purchases come anywhere near the $800 per-person limit, it's a good idea to have receipts on hand for the border crossing; Customs officers are familiar with the average cost of handcrafted items. Pharmacies in Tijuana also do a brisk business selling "controlled" medicines such as Viagra without a prescription. U.S. law allows for the importation of about 1 month's supply (50 dosages) of any medicine that requires a prescription in the states.

When most people think of Tijuana, they picture **Avenida Revolución,** which appears to exist solely for the extraction of dollars from American visitors. Dedicated shoppers quickly discover most of the curios spilling out onto the sidewalk look alike, despite the determined sellers' assurances that their wares are the best in town. Browse for comparison's sake, but duck into one of the many *pasajes,* or passageway arcades, for the best souvenir shopping. There you'll find merchants willing to bargain, and you'll get a pleasant respite from the quickly irritating tumult of Avenida Revolución.

Notable shops include **Casa Rodriguez,** 1080 Av. Revolución (☎ 664/685-9960), which is entered through an easily missed doorway that leads to a huge showroom of wrought iron and wood furnishings; **Hand Art,** 1040-B Av. Revolución (☎ **664/685-2642;** www.handartmx.com), featuring hand-embroidered tablecloths and dresses; **Casa de Arte,** 980-C Av. Revolución (☎ **664/685-1707**), where you can custom order stained- and blown-glass creations; and **Sara's London Shop,** 907 Av. Revolución (☎ **664/685-0622**), selling a vast array of perfumes, soaps, and body sprays. Sara's first opened for business in 1944, making it one of the oldest businesses on the street. One of the few places in Tijuana to find better-quality crafts from a variety of Mexican states is **Tolán,** Avenida Revolución between calles 7 and 8 (☎ **664/688-3637**). Look for blue glassware from Guadalajara, glazed pottery from Tlaquepaque, crafts from the Oaxaca countryside, and distinctive tile work from Puebla.

An alternative is to visit **Sanborns,** Avenida Revolución between calles 8 and 9 (☎ **664/688-1462;** www.sanborns.com.mx/sanborns), a branch of the Mexico City department store. It sells an array of regional folk art and souvenirs, books about Mexico in Spanish and English, and candies and bakery treats. You can have breakfast in the sunny cafe. There's another location in Zona Río.

If a marketplace atmosphere and spirited bargaining are what you're looking for, head to **Mercado de Artesanías (Crafts Market),** Calle 2 and Avenida Negrete. Vendors of pottery, clayware, clothing, and other crafts fill an entire city block.

Shopping malls are as common in Tijuana as in any big American city. You shouldn't expect to find typical souvenirs, but shopping alongside residents and other intrepid visitors is often more fun than feeling like a sitting-duck tourist. The biggest and most convenient is **Plaza Río Tijuana** (on Paseo de los Héroes at Av. Independencia). It's an outdoor plaza anchored by several department stores, with dozens of shops and casual restaurants. This is the place to buy shoes.

For a taste of everyday Mexico, join the locals at **Mercado Hidalgo** (1 block west at Av. Sánchez Taboada and Av. Independencia), a busy indoor-outdoor marketplace where vendors display fresh flowers and produce, sacks of dried beans and chilies by the kilo, and a few souvenir crafts, including some excellent piñatas. Morning is the best time to visit the farmers' market.

SPORTS

BULLFIGHTING Tijuana's downtown bullring, the **Toreo de Tijuana,** fell to the wrecking ball, but the city still has bullfighting. The impressive **Plaza Monumental** (☎ **664/680-1808;** www.plazamonumental.com), the bullring-by-the-sea in Playas de Tijuana, stages a season from about April to November. Contests are scheduled as often as every other Sunday (at 4pm). Ticket prices range from $11 to $55; premium seats are on the shady side of the arena. Tickets are for sale at the bullring or in advance in San Diego from **Five Star Tours** (☎ **619/232-5040;** www.sdsuntours.com). If you want to catch the bullfights but don't want to drive, Five Star offers bus trips that depart from downtown San Diego; the price is $24 round-trip, plus the cost of your bullfight ticket. Or you can take a taxi from the border (about $20). You can find a nice English-language primer on bullfighting, as well as scheduling info, at www.bullfights.org.

GOLF Once the favorite of golfing celebrities and socialites who stayed at the now-defunct Agua Caliente Resort, the **Club Campestre de Tijuana (Tijuana Country Club),** Bulevar Agua Caliente at Avenida Gustavo Salinas (☎ **888/217-1165** from the U.S., or 664/104-7545; www.tijuanacountryclub.com), is near the Caliente Racetrack and behind the Grand Hotel Tijuana. It's about a 10-minute drive from downtown. The course attracts mostly business travelers staying at nearby hotels, many of which offer golf packages (see Grand Hotel Tijuana in "Where to Stay," below). This course has quite a pedigree: It was designed by Alister MacKenzie, who along with Bobby Jones was the creator of the course at the Augusta National Golf Club. Weekday greens fees are $45 each for two players ($60 for solo player), including cart, and $69 per person on weekends for a duo ($80 for one person). Stop by the pro shop for balls, tees, and a limited number of other accessories; the clubhouse also has two restaurants with cocktail lounges.

Along the toll road to Rosarito, at Km 19.5, is the golf community of **Real Del Mar** (© **800/662-6180** from the U.S., or 664/631-3401; www.realdelmar.com.mx). Open to the public, this course has incredible ocean vistas, as well as plenty of wildlife playing through; stiff breezes, as well as rattlesnakes in the summer, make for some interesting challenges here. Rates are $69 weekday, $89 weekend; twilight rates are available. After your game you can repair to the wonderful on-site restaurant **Rincón San Román** (p. 285).

WHERE TO STAY

When calculating room rates, remember that hotel rates in Tijuana are subject to a 12% tax. Also note this guide uses the term "double" when listing rates, referring to the American concept of "double occupancy." However, in Mexico a single room has one bed, a double has two, and you pay accordingly.

Befitting Tijuana's prominence as an international commerce center (companies such as Sony and Sanyo have factories here), a selection of hotels caters to business travelers. **Camino Real,** Paseo de los Héroes 10305 (© **877/215-3051** from U.S., 800/025-6350, or 664/633-4000; www.caminoreal.com), is right in the heart of the Zona Río shopping and dining district; **Tijuana Marriott Hotel,** Blvd. Agua Caliente 11553 (© **888/748-8785** from U.S., 800/900-8800, or 664/622-6600; www.marriott.com), is adjacent to the golf course; and **Hotel Pueblo Amigo,** Vía Oriente 9211 (© **800/386-6985** from U.S., 800/026-3686, or 664/624-2700; www.hotelpuebloamigo.com), is in Zona Río's Plaza Pueblo Amigo, where several popular restaurants and clubs are clustered. **Fiesta Inn,** Paseo de los Héroes 18818, Zona Río (© **800/343-7821** from U.S., 800/504-5000, or 664/636-0000; www.fiestainn.com), has the in-house **Vita-Spa** (© **664/636-0016;** www.vitaspatijuana.com), where you can soak in the healthful, sulfurous—though disconcertingly brown—thermal waters that are tapped from directly beneath the hotel.

If you want to stay at Playas de Tijuana, solid choices are **Hacienda del Mar,** Paseo Playas 116 (© **888/675-2927** from U.S., or 664/630-8603), and **Jardines Monumental Motel,** Av. del Pacifico 884 (© **664/680-6775**).

Moderate

Grand Hotel Tijuana ★ These 28-story mirrored twin towers are visible from all over the city. Modern and sleek, the hotel opened in 1982 and is popular with business travelers, visiting celebrities, and for society events. The lobby has dark carpeting, 1980s mirrors, and neon accents that feel like a Vegas hotel/casino; rooms have spectacular views of the city from the top floors. There are several ballrooms and an airy atrium that serves elegant international cuisine at dinner and an extravagant Sunday brunch; next to it is a casual Mexican restaurant. The Vegas resemblance resumes with an indoor shopping arcade and a sports and race book. Golf packages with the adjacent Tijuana Country Club are available.

Agua Caliente 4500, Tijuana, BC 22440, Mexico. ✆ **866/472-6385** from U.S., 800/026-6007, or 664/681-7000. Fax 664/681-7016. www.grandhoteltij.com.mx. 422 units. From $119 double; from $196 suite. AE, MC, V. Covered parking. **Amenities:** 3 restaurants; 3 bars; babysitting; nearby golf course; exercise room; Jacuzzi; outdoor heated pool; room service; sauna; tennis courts. *In room:* A/C, TV, hair dryer, Internet, minibar.

Hotel Lucerna   Once the most chic hotel in Tijuana, the neoclassical Lucerna still offers hospitable accommodations with plenty of personality. The hotel is in the Zona Río, away from the noise and congestion of downtown, so a quiet night's sleep is easy. It's kept in great shape for the international visitors who enjoy Lucerna's proximity to the financial district, and the staff's friendly and attentive service reflects this clientele. The five-story hotel's rooms all have balconies or patios but are otherwise unremarkable. Sunday brunch is served outdoors by the swimming pool.

Av. Paseo de los Héroes 10902, Zona Río, Tijuana, BC 22320, Mexico. .www.lucerna.com.mx. ✆ **800/026-6300** or 664/633-3900. 168 units. $95–$131 double; from $165 suite. AE, MC, V. **Amenities:** 2 restaurants; 2 bars; exercise room; outdoor pool; room service. *In room:* A/C, TV, hair dryer, Wi-Fi.

Inexpensive

Hotel Hacienda del Río   Located in the Zona Río, this reliable hotel is close to Tijuana's fine-dining, commercial, and financial district. It's part of a small chain that includes two properties in Ensenada as well as the **Baja Inn La Mesa,** Blvd. Díaz Ordaz esq. Gardenias 50 (✆ **664/681-6522**), near the Tijuana racetrack (about a $7 cab ride from downtown). Rates are cheaper at the La Mesa property, topping out at about $70.

Blvd. Sanchez Taboada 10606, Tijuana, BC 22440, Mexico. ✆ **888/226-1033** from U.S., 800/026-6999, or 664/684-8644. Fax 664/684-8620. www.bajainn.com. 131 units. From $67 double; from $150 suite. Extra person $7. AE, MC, V. Parking. **Amenities:** Restaurant; bar; exercise room; pool; room service. *In room:* A/C, TV.

Palacio Azteca Hotel   Popular with businesspeople and airline flight crews, this seven-story hotel looks rather drab from the outside. The interior is modern and inviting, though, with gleaming marble, honey-blond wood, and a fireplace in the lobby lounge area. Located near where the downtown bullring once stood, it has a small-but-stylish bar, a pool area shaded by palms, and a restaurant that serves a daily breakfast buffet for $11 ($8 kids; $18 Sun). The rooms are simply and tastefully furnished, and the master suites have long balconies that afford an overview of the city.

Blvd. Cuauhtémoc Sur 213, Tijuana, BC 22400, Mexico. ✆ **888/901-3720** from U.S., 800/026-6660, or 664/681-8100. Fax 664/681-8160. www.hotelpalacioazteca.com. 200 units. $89–$123 double; $173–$193 suite. Extra person $10. AE, DISC, MC, V. Parking. **Amenities:** Restaurant; bar; free airport transfers; exercise room; pool; room service. *In room:* A/C, TV, hair dryer.

WHERE TO DINE

Although the irresistible aroma of street food—*carne asada* (marinated beef grilled over charcoal) tucked into corn tortillas, for starters—is everywhere, less well known is that Tijuana has restaurants of real quality, despite the presence of a Hard Rock Cafe that lures many of the visitors. The following places are worth the taxi trip. The main meal of the day is *la comida* (lunch); restaurants are busiest around 2:30pm.

   Note: Do not drink water unless it comes straight from a bottle (this includes ice, or uncooked vegetables, including lettuce, that have been washed), or you might leave Tijuana with a going-away gift; restaurants listed below generally have sanitary conditions, but it doesn't hurt to be cautious.

For breakfast (or lunch or dinner, for that matter), a local favorite not far from the Grand Hotel is **El Potrero,** Blvd. Salinas 4700 (© **664/686-3626**). Like Hollywood's old Brown Derby, this restaurant is shaped like a giant hat—a sombrero, to be exact. The interior is filled with cowboy memorabilia from the owner's days as a *charro* (horseman).

Tijuana is also home to outstanding restaurants representing international cuisines—just because you're in Mexico, doesn't mean you have to eat Mexican. There's award-winning Argentine food at **Cheripan** ★, Escuadrón 201 No. 3151 (© **664/622-9730;** www.cheripan.com); excellent Mediterranean-Baja fusion at **Villa Saverios** ★★, Blvd. Sánchez Taboada 10451 (© **664/686-6442;** www.villasaverios.com); sushi at **Negai** ★, Escuadrón 201 No. 3110-4 (© **664/971-0000;** www.negairestaurant.com); and the flavors of Spain at **Chiki Jai,** Av. Revolución 1388 (© **664/685-4955**). Except for Chiki Jai, the preceding eateries are all in the Zona Río's dining district.

For something really unusual, stop by **Tepoznieves** ★, Blvd. Sánchez Taboada 10737, Zona Río (© **664/634-6532**), an ice-cream parlor that serves a dizzying array of flavors it dubs the "ice cream of the gods." The treats here include wine- and spirits-infused sorbets (tequila, white wine, gin); poetically named concoctions such as *mil flores,* or "thousand flowers" (cream, almonds, and herbal tea); and traditional ice creams made with everything from rose petals to prunes. This gourmet spot will have you coming back for more, and yes, they do have chocolate, too.

Cafe La Especial ★ MEXICAN

Tucked away in a shopping *pasaje* at the bottom of some stairs (enter just south of Calle 3, on the east side of the street), this restaurant is a well-known shopper's refuge. It offers home-style Mexican cooking at reasonable (though not dirt-cheap) prices. The no-nonsense, efficient waitstaff carries out platter after platter of *carne asada* served with fresh tortillas, beans, and rice—it's La Especial's most popular item. Standard border dishes such as tacos, enchiladas, and burritos round out the menu, augmented by frosty cold Mexican beers.

Av. Revolución 718 (btw. calles 3 and 4), Zona Centro. © **664/685-6654.** www.cafelaespecial.com. Menu items $3–$14. No credit cards. Daily 9am–10pm.

Carnitas Uruapan ★ MEXICAN

Carnitas, a beloved dish in Mexico, consists of marinated pork roasted on a spit until it's falling-apart tender, and then served in chunks with tortillas, salsa, cilantro, guacamole, and onions. At Carnitas Uruapan, the meat is served by the kilo (or portion thereof) at long, communal wooden tables to a mostly local crowd, accompanied by mariachi music. A half-kilo of *carnitas* is plenty for two people and costs around $15, including beans and that impressive array of condiments. It's a casual feast without compare, but vegetarians need not apply.

Blvd. Díaz Ordaz 12650 (across from Plaza Patria), La Mesa. © **664/681-6181.** www.carnitasuruapantj. com. Menu items under $8. No credit cards. Daily 7am–3am. Follow Blvd. Agua Caliente south toward Tecate. It turns into Blvd. Díaz Ordaz, also known as Carretera Tecate and Hwy. 2.

Cien Años ★★ MEXICAN

Perhaps Tijuana's finest restaurant, this elegant Zona Río eatery offers the artfully blended Mexican flavors you expect (tamarind, poblano chilies, and mango), but with a host of traditional offerings that date back centuries, all stylishly presented. Go ahead and try something exotic such as the stingray tacos. Cien Años also serves breakfast, and the creativity is evident here, too, with dishes such as omelets stuffed with cactus, mushrooms, and cheese in a mango sauce. Though modestly priced, Cien Años is dressy by San Diego and Tijuana standards.

José María Velazco 1407, Zona Río. ☏ **664/634-3039,** or from U.S. 888/534-6088 or 619/819-5079. www. cien.info. Reservations recommended. Main courses $8–$21. AE, MC, V. Daily 8am–11pm (until midnight Fri–Sat, until 10pm Sun).

La Costa ★ MEXICAN   The oldest seafood restaurant in Tijuana, La Costa is a long-time favorite that lives up to its well-earned reputation. The menu overflows with the ocean's bounty, starting with the hearty seafood soup. Crustaceans (shrimp, crab, and lobster) and bivalves (mussels, oysters, and clams) dominate, or you can order up some squid or octopus; abalone, a rare find nowadays, also makes an occasional appearance. If you can't make up your mind, try a combination platter of grilled lobster, stuffed shrimp, and baked shrimp, or a fish filet stuffed with seafood and cheese.

Calle 7, no. 8131 (just off Av. Revolución), Zona Centro. ☏ **664/685-3124.** Reservations recommended. Main courses $9–$21. AE, MC, V. Daily 10am–11pm (until midnight Fri–Sat).

La Diferencia ★★ MEXICAN   This enchanting Zona Río restaurant has a delightful courtyard with a fountain, bird cages, and muraled walls. Even though it's a faux, indoor setting in a modern building, you'll swear you are dining at a rustic hacienda. After the salsa is handmade at your table, the creative appetizers are wheeled out—if you ever wanted to try fried crickets, this is the place. Most of the dishes are made with delicate sauces offering a variety of unusual spices and flavors from around Mexico. Entrees include steaks, seafood, duck, and chicken.

Blvd. Sanchez Taboada 10611-A, Zona Río. ☏ **664/634-3346.** www.ladiferencia.com.mx. Reservations recommended. Main courses $9–$22. AE, MC, V. Daily noon–11pm.

La Fonda de Roberto ★ MEXICAN   A short drive (or taxi ride) from downtown Tijuana, La Fonda's colorful dining room opens onto the courtyard of a kitschy 1960s motel, complete with retro kidney-shaped swimming pool. The festive atmosphere is perfect for enjoying a variety of regional Mexican dishes, including a decent chicken mole and generous portions of *milanesa* (beef, chicken, or pork pounded paper thin, and then breaded and fried). A house specialty is *queso fundido,* deep-fried cheese with chilies, and mushrooms served with freshly made corn tortillas.

In La Sierra Motel, Blvd. Cuauhtémoc Sur Oriente 2800 (on the old road to Ensenada). ☏ **664/686-4687.** Reservations recommended. Most dishes $7–$11. MC, V. Tues–Sun 9am–10pm.

La Querencia ★★ MEXICAN/MEDITERRANEAN   Chef Miguel Angel Yagües, a fourth-generation native of Baja, is at the forefront of a cuisine he calls Baja Med. He takes his inspiration from the cooking of Mediterranean cultures (noting that Baja shares a similar climate and also produces wine, dates, and olives), mixes in a hint of Asian flavor, and ties it all together with traditional Mexican style. An incredible range of fresh, local product is incorporated, including lobster, marlin, tuna, oysters, deer, quail, and lamb. Whether it's duck tacos, sashimi scallops, or venison cooked in the wood-burning stove, the results are memorable. The space is casual and modern, with concrete floors, exposed air-ducts, and steel beams, as well as a disconcerting array of stuffed animal trophies.

Escuadrón 201, No. 3110 (btw. Av. Sanchez Taboada and Blvd. Salinas), Zona Río. ☏ **664/972-9935** or 972-9940. www.laquerenciatj.com. Dinner reservations recommended. Menu items $1.50–$26. AE, MC, V. Mon–Thurs 1–11pm; Fri–Sat 1pm–midnight; Sun 1–8pm.

Rincón San Román ★★ FRENCH/MEXICAN   Along the scenic toll road on the way to Rosarito, at Km 19.5, is the golf resort **Real Del Mar.** Within this mini-community (it even has its own church), set in a small plaza, is this world-class restaurant. It's no fluke the cuisine mixes French and Mexican traditions—chef Martín San Román trained at the Academie Culinaire de France and is one of Baja's most acclaimed chefs. Upstairs is a sophisticated, upscale room with fine modern art on the walls and views of the Islas de Coronado; downstairs has a casual European bistro feel. Lunch and dinner are served, and it's worth the drive.

Km 19.5 Ensenada Cuota, Real Del Mar. ⓒ **664/631-2241** or 631-2242. Reservations recommended for parties of 3 or more. Menu items $13–$27. MC, V. Mon–Sat 1–10pm.

TIJUANA AFTER DARK

It won't be difficult to find the bars offering cheap drinks and loud music, but Tijuana offers much more than that, if you know where to look. Just off Revolución is the all-night joint **Dandy Del Sur,** Calle 6 Flores Magón No. 2030 (ⓒ **664/688-0052**). The tiny bar's status was secured when the Nortec Collective, the city's pioneering electronica band, named a song after the place. Across the street you'll find locals dancing away to salsa and other Latin rhythms at the dance-hall dive **La Estrella;** look for the neon star. In the Zona Río, a smorgasbord of clubs, bars, and restaurants is found in **Plaza Pueblo Amigo,** Vía Oriente and Paseo Tijuana, and **Plaza Fiesta,** Paseo de los Héroes 9415 (www.plazafiestatijuana.com), making it easy to pick and choose the venue that's right for you. In Pueblo Amigo, you'll find an ersatz Mayan temple that is home to the disco **Balak** (ⓒ **664/290-9383**); Spanish food and flamenco music at **Gypsys** (ⓒ **664/683-6006**); and an alternative dance party at **Mofo Bar** (ⓒ **664/683-5427**). There are more than a dozen choices at Plaza Fiesta, where top draws include **Sótano Suiza** (ⓒ **664/684-8834**), **Monte Picacho** (ⓒ **664/684-0705**), and **Ah Jijo! Bar** (ⓒ **664/684-0405**). You can also work up a sweat at the dance clubs **Tangaloo,** Av. Monterrey 3215 (ⓒ **664/681-8091;** www.tangaloo.com.mx), and **The Rock,** Av. Diego Rivera 1482, Zona Río (ⓒ **664/634-2404**). Tijuana's gay bars can be found along Avenida Constitución, north of Calle 1.

Brewery, restaurant, and nightclub **Cervecería Tijuana,** Blvd. Fundadores 2951 (ⓒ **664/638-8662;** www.tjbeer.com), will transport you to the beer halls of Prague, of all places. Everything in this wood-paneled tavern, located a few minutes' drive from the tourist zone, was imported from the Czech Republic. Upstairs is club space presenting a variety of live music Wednesday through Saturday. For salsa or *trova* (singer/songwriter balladeers), check out **Antigua Bodega de Papel,** Calle 11 No. 2012, Zona Centro (ⓒ **664/664-8246;** www.myspace.com/laantiguabodegadepapel); or, for a complete immersion in Tijuana arts and culture, go to **El Lugar del Nopal,** Callejón 5 de Mayo 1328, Zona Centro (ⓒ **664/685-1264;** www.lugardelnopal.com), a gallery, cabaret, and restaurant all in one. For something more traditional, you'll find mariachis blasting away at lively **La Cantina de los Remedios,** Diego Rivera 19, Zona Río (ⓒ **664/634-3065;** www.lacantinadelosremedios.com.mx). It has the cure for whatever ails you.

EXPLORING BEYOND TIJUANA

If you have a car, venture into Baja California for a long day trip or an overnight getaway. Beyond the border city of Tijuana are the seaside resort towns of **Rosarito,** just 18 miles south of Tijuana, and **Ensenada,** 42 miles farther south. About 10 miles south of Rosarito you'll find the former fishing hamlet of **Puerto Nuevo,** now a kind of lobster-meal Disneyland, with more than 30 restaurants—all serving the same thing; northeast of Ensenada is the **Valle de Guadalupe,** Mexico's wine country. VIP cards that offer discounts on lodging, dining, and shopping are available from both the Rosarito and

Ensenada visitor bureaus; contact them at www.rosarito.org (© **800/962-2252**) and www.enjoyensenada.com (© **800/310-9687** from the U.S., 800/025-3991, or 646/178-8578). **Note:** Most U.S. auto insurance policies don't cover drivers or their vehicles south of Tijuana. Mexican auto insurance is advised (see "Getting There & Getting Around," on p. 26 in chapter 3); avoid driving the highway at night when animals and other obstacles can't be seen. Also be aware that many businesses are cash only. You can visit Rosarito, Ensenada, and the wine country on a tour, as well (see "Bus Tours," p. 163).

Two well-maintained roads link Tijuana and Puerto Nuevo: the scenic, coast-hugging toll road (marked *cuota* or 1-D; $2.60 at each of the three tollbooths btw. Tijuana and Ensenada) and the free but slower public road (marked *libre* or 1). Start out on the toll road, but cut over to the free road at the first Rosarito Beach exit so that you can stop and enjoy the view at a leisurely pace. This coastal area was once sparsely populated, but developers began exploiting the world-class ocean vistas here, and luxury condominiums—mostly snapped up by Americans—cropped up everywhere. The ensuing real estate bust has led to a string of unsightly, unfinished projects, the most notable of which is Donald Trump's Ocean Resort Baja. Unfortunately for investors, the Donald has drained them of $32 million they'll never see again; for the rest of us, though, the demise of this project means one less ill-conceived development along what had been (and hopefully will stay) a pristine bay north of Ensenada.

Once a tiny resort town that remained a secret despite its proximity to Tijuana, Rosarito developed explosively in the 1980s; it's now garish and congested beyond recognition. But it remains popular for a couple of reasons: 1) It's the first beach resort town south of the border, and 2) its reputation continues to lure visitors. For years, the **Rosarito Beach Hotel** (© **866/767-2748** from the U.S., or 661/612-0144; www.rosarito beachhotel.com) was a hideaway for Hollywood celebrities, and it remains the most interesting place in town—check out its expert tile and woodwork, as well as the lobby's panoramic murals. The original owner's mansion is now home to a spa and a decadent gourmet restaurant, **Chabert's.** Not to be missed is the amazingly tiled **Salon Quijote,** where you can escape for a quiet drink (the chandelier is rumored to have been a gift from gangster Al Capone). Sadly, the hotel fell victim to the post-millennial building craze, too, and unleashed a 17-story, 271-unit condo hotel that is monstrously out of proportion to its surroundings.

If you don't mind being a little outside of town, **Las Rocas Resort & Spa,** Km 38.5 (© **866/445-8909** from the U.S., 800/788-5648, or 661/614-9850; www.lasrocas. com), is a sweet spot with killer views—minus the crowds. It sits under the watchful gaze of a 70-foot Jesus that was built on a hilltop on the other side of the highway.

Bulevar Benito Juárez is Rosarito's main drag. The southern end is anchored by the Rosarito Beach Hotel; this is where you'll find all things touristic, including the rustic shopping arcade **Pueblo Plaza,** home to one of the city's best restaurants, **Susanna's** (© **661/613-1187;** www.susannasinrosarito.com). Also nearby is **Bazar de las Artesanías,** where you can get lost among the stalls of souvenirs, clothing, and gewgaws. The best shopping, though, is south of town along the free road, where there are several quality art galleries, as well as sellers of ceramics, wood furniture, and wrought-iron goods.

The big draws for young people are the series of enormous, thumping, beachfront clubs: **Papas & Beer** (© **661/612-0444;** www.rosarito.papasandbeer.com), which also has a branch in Ensenada; **Iggy's; Club Maya;** and **Club Animale.** For dining, best bets include the very fun **El Nido,** Blvd. Benito Juárez 67 (© **661/612-1430**), and the French **Bistro le Cousteau,** Blvd. Benito Juárez 184 (© **661/612-2655**); for a quick taco, head east off Benito Juárez on Calle de la Palma to **Tacos el Yaqui.** A few minutes' drive south of town is the **Hotel Calafia,** Km 35.5 (© **661/612-1580** or 619/739-4343 from the U.S.; www.hotel-calafia.com). You can dine alfresco on tiered tables that overlook the ocean, but the surroundings outshine the food. There's also a chic wine bar, a small exhibit on Baja history, and a scale replica of a Spanish galleon for kids to clamber on.

A few miles south of Rosarito, at Km 32.5 on the free road, is the state-of-the-art production facility used for *Titanic, Pearl Harbor,* and *Master and Commander: The Far Side of the World.* It's still a working studio, as well as a movie theme-park known as **Foxploration** (© **866/369-2252** from the U.S., or 661/612-4294; www.foxploration. com). You can take a guided tour through a *Titanic* exhibit with partial sets (such as a first-class hallway) and numerous props; see displays highlighting the *X-Men* films; or tour an interactive gallery that demystifies moviemaking. It's not Universal or Disney, but it can be amusing for a couple hours. Admission is $12 for adults and $9 for children and seniors; it's open Wednesday through Friday 9am to 4:30pm, Saturday and Sunday from 10am to 5:30pm.

From Rosarito, drive south and stop at **Puerto Nuevo,** a tiny, portless fishing village with more than 30 restaurants—all serving lobster in the local style: halved, grilled, and slathered in butter. Around 1952, the wives of fishermen started serving local lobsters from the kitchens of their simple shacks; many eventually built small dining rooms onto their homes or constructed restaurants. The result is a crustacean lover's paradise, where a feast of lobster, beans, rice, salsa, limes, and fresh tortillas costs $15 to $25. **Ortega's** is probably the oldest restaurant and has expanded to five locations in the village, including **Villa Ortega's** (© **661/614-0706** or 619/632-4875 from the U.S.; www.puertonuevo-villaortega.com), the most upscale spot in town. Puerto Nuevo regulars prefer the smaller, family-run joints, though, such as **Sandra's** (© **661/614-1051**), **Puerto Nuevo Numero Uno** and **Dos** (© **661/614-1411** and **1454**), and **La Casa de la Langosta** (© **661/614-1072**), which also has an outpost in Rosarito. Alas, overfishing means there's now a lobster season, so if you come April through September you'll probably be eating imported crustaceans. The fishing town of **Popotla,** just past Foxploration and through the concrete arch, also serves lobster dinners, in somewhat less commercial trappings. *Note:* Many small restaurants are closed Tuesdays.

About 10 miles farther south, roughly halfway between Rosarito and Ensenada at Km 59.5, is **La Fonda,** a beloved hotel, restaurant, and spa (© **646/155-0307;** www.lafonda mexico.com). The Sunday brunch is an orgy of food, everything from "paella to pancakes," washed down with free-flowing bloody marys. You can sit under thatched umbrellas on the tiled terrace overlooking the breaking surf; there's also a bar and easy access to the sandy beach below.

Continue your journey for several more miles to **Ensenada**—the drive is flat-out breathtaking. This port city of 150,000 offers good shopping, a friendly atmosphere, and some of the best fishing around (but no beaches). Deep-sea charters take visitors out on cruises for a chance to catch albacore, barracuda, and bonito. Ensenada also purports to be the birthplace of the fish taco.

The tourist area is compact and walkable. Nearby is the harborside *malecón* (sea wall boardwalk), where you can rent fishing or sightseeing boats and grab a fish taco at the open-air fish market. You can put silver jewelry, leather goods, textiles, and folk art on your shopping list, too. The most interesting cultural attraction is the lovely **Riviera del Pacifico,** Blvd. Costero at Av. Riviera (© **646/176-4233**), a former gambling palace that's been converted into a cultural center and museum with beautiful gardens.

When you're ready to take a break from touring, stop by **Bodegas de Santo Tomás,** Av. Miramar 666 (© **646/174-0836;** www.santo-tomas.com), a historic winery open for tours and tastings. If you're in the mood for a beer—and even if you aren't—pay a visit to legendary **Hussong's Cantina,** Av. Ruiz 113 (© **646/178-3210**), which opened for business in 1892, reputedly making it the oldest bar in the Californias. For the nicest meal in town, **El Rey Sol,** Av. López Mateos 1000 (© **646/178-1733;** www.elreysol. com), has few competitors.

True to its name, **Hotel Misión Santa Isabel,** Blvd. Costero 1119 (© **646/178-3616**), is an attractive, mission-style lodging at the southern end of the tourist zone. It's affordably priced and within walking distance of all the action, but far away enough to be peaceful. **Las Rosas Hotel & Spa,** Km 105.5 (© **866/447-6727** or 646/174-4595; www.lasrosas.com), offers more luxury, and has an enviable setting on the edge of Ensenada's huge Todos Santos bay. The only drawback is that it's 2 miles north of town.

About 20 miles south of Ensenada is **La Bufadora.** This ocean blowhole sprays a torrent of water high into the air with amazing force, often showering giggling onlookers who watch from observation decks. There are also numerous curio stands, restaurants, and bars here; you can get a taste of rural Mexico, too, as you drive along the highway, where roadside vendors sell nuts, tamales, and olives. To the northeast of Ensenada is the **Valle de Guadalupe,** Mexico's most important wine region, where more than 10 wineries are making waves in the oenological world; tours and tastes are offered. It's also the site of one of the finest restaurants on either side of the border, **Laja** (reservations required; © **646/155-2556;** www.lajamexico.com). It's located at Km 83 along the Tecate-Ensenada highway.

Fast Facts, Toll-Free Numbers & Websites

1 FAST FACTS: SAN DIEGO

AMERICAN EXPRESS Traveler's checks are available from various banks, including **Bank of America,** 450 B St., downtown (© 858/452-8400). **Anderson Travel & Cruises,** 11952 Bernardo Plaza Dr., Rancho Bernardo (© 858/487-7722), is an independently operated American Express travel office. Or call **American Express** directly at © 800/221-7282.

AREA CODES San Diego's main area code is **619,** used primarily by downtown, uptown, Mission Valley, Point Loma, Coronado, La Mesa, El Cajon, and Chula Vista. The area code **858** is used for northern and coastal areas, including Mission Beach, Pacific Beach, La Jolla, Del Mar, Rancho Santa Fe, and Rancho Bernardo. Use **760** to reach the remainder of San Diego County, including Encinitas, Carlsbad, Oceanside, Escondido, Ramona, Julian, and Anza-Borrego.

AUTOMOBILE   ORGANIZATIONS Motor clubs will supply maps, suggested routes, guidebooks, accident and bail-bond insurance, and emergency road service. The **American Automobile Association (AAA)** is the major auto club in the United States. If you belong to a motor club in your home country, inquire about AAA reciprocity before you leave. The San Diego AAA office is at 2440 Hotel Circle N. (© 619/233-1000; www.aaa-calif.com).

BABYSITTERS Marion's Childcare (© 888/891-5029; www.hotelchildcare.com) has bonded babysitters available to come to your hotel room; rates start at $17 per hour with a 4-hour minimum. **Panda's Domestic Service Agency** (© 619/295-3800; www.sandiegobabysitters.com) and **Around Town Childcare** (© 619/283-2120; www.aroundtownchildcare.com) are also available.

BUSINESS HOURS Banks are open weekdays from 9am to 4pm or later, and sometimes Saturday morning. Stores in shopping malls tend to stay open until about 9pm weekdays and until 6pm weekends, and are open on secondary holidays.

DENTISTS For dental referrals, contact the **San Diego County Dental Society** at © 800/201-0244 (www.sdcds.org), or call © **1-800/DENTIST** (800/336-8478; www.1800dentist.com).

DOCTORS In a life-threatening situation, dial © **911.** For a doctor referral, contact the **San Diego County Medical Society** (© 858/565-8888; www.sdcms.org) or **Scripps Health** (© 800/727-4777; www.scripps.org).

DRINKING LAWS The legal age for purchase and consumption of alcoholic beverages in California is 21. Proof of age is a necessity—it's requested at bars, nightclubs, and restaurants, even from those well into their 30s and 40s, so always bring ID when you go out. Beer, wine, and hard liquor are sold daily from 6am to 2am and are available in grocery stores.

Do not carry open containers of alcohol in your car or at any public area not zoned

(Tips) It's Easy Being Green

Here are a few simple ways you can help conserve fuel and energy when you travel:

- Each time you take a flight or drive a car, greenhouse gases release into the atmosphere. You can help neutralize this danger to the planet through "carbon offsetting"—paying someone to invest your money in programs that reduce your greenhouse gas emissions by the same amount you've added. Before buying carbon offset credits, just make sure that you're using a reputable company, one with a proven program that invests in renewable energy. Reliable carbon offset companies include **Carbonfund** (www.carbon fund.org), **TerraPass** (www.terrapass.org), and **Carbon Neutral** (www.carbon neutral.com).

- Whenever possible, choose nonstop flights; they generally require less fuel than indirect flights that stop and take off again. Try to fly during the day—some scientists estimate that nighttime flights are twice as harmful to the environment. And pack light—each 15 pounds of luggage on a 5,000-mile flight adds up to 50 pounds of carbon dioxide emitted.

- Where you stay during your travels can have a major environmental impact. To determine the green credentials of a property, ask about trash disposal and recycling, water conservation, and energy use; also question if sustainable materials were used in the construction of the property. The website **www.greenhotels.com** recommends green-rated member hotels around the world that fulfill the company's stringent environmental requirements. Also consult **www.environmentallyfriendlyhotels.com** for more green accommodation ratings.

- At hotels, request that your sheets and towels not be changed daily. (Many hotels already have programs like this in place.) Turn off the lights and air-conditioner (or heater) when you leave your room.

- Use public transport where possible—trains, buses, and even taxis are more energy-efficient forms of transport than driving. Even better is to walk or cycle; you'll produce zero emissions and stay fit and healthy on your travels.

- If renting a car is necessary, ask the rental agent for a hybrid, or rent the most fuel-efficient car available. You'll use less gas and save money at the tank.

- Eat at locally owned and operated restaurants that use produce grown in the area. This contributes to the local economy and cuts down on greenhouse gas emissions by supporting restaurants where the food is not flown or trucked in across long distances. Visit **Sustain Lane** (www.sustainlane.org) to find sustainable eating and drinking choices around the U.S.; also check out **www.eatwellguide.org** for tips on eating sustainably in the U.S. and Canada.

for alcohol consumption—the police can fine you on the spot. **Alcohol is forbidden at all city beaches, boardwalks, and coastal parks.** Pay heed or pay the price: First-time violators face a $250 fine.

Nothing will ruin your trip faster than getting a citation for DUI ("driving under the influence"), so don't even think about driving while intoxicated.

DRUGSTORES Long's, Rite-Aid, and CVS sell pharmaceuticals and nonprescription products. Look in the phone book to find the one nearest you. If you need a pharmacy after normal business hours, the following branches are open 24 hours: **CVS,** 8831 Villa La Jolla Dr., La Jolla (© 858/457-4390), and 313 E. Washington St., Hillcrest (© 619/291-7170); and **Rite-Aid,** 535 Robinson Ave., Hillcrest (© 619/291-3703). Local hospitals also sell prescription drugs.

ELECTRICITY Like Canada, the United States uses 110–120 volts AC (60 cycles), compared to 220–240 volts AC (50 cycles) in most of Europe, Australia, and New Zealand. Downward converters that change 220–240 volts to 110–120 volts are difficult to find in the United States, so bring one with you.

Wherever you go, bring a **connection kit** of the right power and phone adapters, a spare phone cord, and a spare Ethernet network cable—or find out whether your hotel supplies them to guests.

EMERGENCIES Call © **911** for fire, police, and ambulance. The TTY/TDD emergency number is © **619/233-3323.** The main police station is at 1401 Broadway, at 14th Street (© **619/531-2000;** from North San Diego call © **858/484-3154**).

If you encounter serious problems, contact the San Diego chapter of **Traveler's Aid International** at © **619/295-8393,** or log on to www.travelersaid.org to help direct you to a local branch. This nationwide, nonprofit, social-service organization geared

to helping travelers in difficult straits offers services that might include reuniting families separated while traveling, providing food and/or shelter to people stranded without cash, or even emotional counseling. If you're in trouble, seek them out.

GASOLINE (PETROL) Petrol is known as gasoline (or simply "gas") in the United States, and petrol stations are known as both gas stations and service stations. The cost of gasoline can fluctuate wildly, but at press time, the price in San Diego is about $1.95 per gallon (taxes are included in the printed price). One U.S. gallon equals 3.8 liters or .85 imperial gallons. Most gas stations accept credit cards.

HOLIDAYS Banks, government offices, post offices, and many stores, restaurants, and museums are closed on legal national holidays. For more information on holidays, see "San Diego Calendar of Events" in chapter 3.

HOSPITALS Near downtown San Diego, **UCSD Medical Center-Hillcrest,** 200 W. Arbor Dr. (© **619/543-6222**), has the most convenient emergency room. In La Jolla, **UCSD Thornton Hospital,** 9300 Campus Point Dr. (© **858/657-7000**), has a good emergency room, and you'll find another in Coronado, at **Sharp Coronado Hospital,** 250 Prospect Place, opposite the Marriott Resort (© **619/522-3600**).

INSURANCE Although it's not required of travelers, health insurance is highly recommended. Most health insurance policies cover you if you get sick away from home—but check your coverage before you leave.

International visitors to the U.S. should note that unlike many European countries, the United States does not usually offer free or low-cost medical care to its citizens or visitors. Doctors and hospitals are expensive, and in most cases will require advance payment or proof of coverage before they render their services.

LEGAL AID If you are "pulled over" for a minor infraction (such as speeding), never attempt to pay the fine directly to a police officer; this could be construed as attempted bribery, a serious crime. Pay fines by mail, or directly into the hands of the clerk of the court. If accused of a more serious offense, say and do nothing before consulting a lawyer. Here the burden is on the state to prove a person's guilt beyond a reasonable doubt, and everyone has the right to remain silent, whether he or she is suspected of a crime or actually arrested. Once arrested, a person can make one telephone call to a party of his or her choice. International visitors should call their embassies or consulates.

LOST & FOUND Be sure to tell all of your credit card companies the minute you discover your wallet has been lost or stolen and file a report at the nearest police precinct. Your credit card company or insurer may require a police report number or record of the loss. Most credit card companies have an emergency toll-free number to call if your card is lost or stolen; they may be able to wire you a cash advance immediately or deliver an emergency credit card in a day or two.

MAIL At press time, domestic postage rates were 28¢ for a postcard and 44¢ for a letter. For international mail, a first-class letter of up to 1 ounce costs 98¢ (79¢ to Canada and Mexico); a first-class postcard costs the same as a letter. For more information, go to **www.usps.com** and click on "Calculate Postage."

San Diego's main post office is located in the boondocks, but the former main office, located just west of Old Town at 2535 Midway Dr., is a good alternative; it's open Monday from 7am to 5pm, Tuesday through Friday from 8am to 5pm, and Saturdays from 8am to 4pm. Post offices are downtown, at 815 E St. and at 51 Horton Plaza, next to the Westin Hotel. There is a post office in the Mission Valley Shopping Center, next to Macy's. These branch offices are generally open Monday through Friday during regular business hours, plus Saturday morning; for specific branch information, call ✆ **800/275-8777,** or log on to www.usps.com.

MEDICAL CONDITIONS If you have a medical condition that requires **syringe-administered medications,** carry a valid signed prescription from your physician; syringes in carry-on baggage will be inspected. Insulin in any form should have the proper pharmaceutical documentation. If you have a disease that requires treatment with **narcotics,** you should also carry documented proof with you—smuggling narcotics aboard a plane carries severe penalties in the U.S.

For **HIV-positive visitors,** requirements for entering the United States are somewhat vague and change frequently. For up-to-the-minute information, contact **AIDSinfo** (✆ **800/448-0440** or 301/519-6616 outside the U.S.; www.aidsinfo.nih.gov) or the **Gay Men's Health Crisis** (✆ **212/367-1000;** www.gmhc.org).

NEWSPAPERS & MAGAZINES The *San Diego Union-Tribune* is published daily, and its entertainment section, "Night & Day," is in the Thursday edition. The free *San Diego Weekly Reader* is published Thursdays and is available at many shops, restaurants, theaters, and public hot spots; it's the best source for up-to-the-week club and show listings (a visitor-friendly version called the *Weekly* is available in tourist areas). The free alternative weekly *San Diego CityBeat* is distributed on Wednesdays. It also has listings and can get you up to speed on local issues and local music. *San Diego* magazine has covered all aspects of the city since 1948, and is plumped with social news and dining listings. *San Diego Home/Garden Lifestyles* magazine highlights interior design and also includes articles about Southern California gardening and the local restaurant scene. Both magazines are published monthly and sold at newsstands. The *Los Angeles Times,* the *New York Times,* and *USA Today* are widely available.

PASSPORTS   The websites listed provide downloadable passport applications as well as the current fees for processing applications. For an up-to-date, country-by-country listing of passport requirements around the world, go to the "International Travel" tab of the U.S. State Department at **http://travel.state.gov**. International visitors to the U.S. can obtain a visa application at the same website. *Note:* Children are required to present a passport when entering the United States at airports. More information on obtaining a passport for a minor can be found at http://travel.state.gov. Allow plenty of time before your trip to apply for a passport; processing normally takes 4 to 6 weeks (3 weeks for expedited service) but can take longer during busy periods (especially spring). And keep in mind that if you need a passport in a hurry, you'll pay a higher processing fee.

For Residents of Australia   You can pick up an application from your local post office or any branch of Passports Australia, but you must schedule an interview at the passport office to present your application materials. Call the **Australian Passport Information Service** at (C) **131-232,** or visit the government website at www.passports.gov.au.

For Residents of Canada   Passport applications are available at travel agencies throughout Canada or from the central **Passport Office,** Dept. of Foreign Affairs and International Trade, Ottawa, ON K1A 0G3 ((C) **800/567-6868;** www.ppt.gc.ca). *Note:* Canadian children who travel must have their own passport. However, if you hold a valid Canadian passport issued before December 11, 2001, that bears the name of your child, the passport remains

valid for you and your child until it expires.

For Residents of Ireland   You can apply for a 10-year passport at the **Passport Office,** Setanta Centre, Molesworth Street, Dublin 2 ((C) **1/671-1633;** www.irlgov.ie/iveagh). Those under age 18 and over 65 must apply for a 3-year passport. You can also apply at 1A South Mall, Cork ((C) **21/494-4700**) or at most main post offices.

For Residents of New Zealand   You can pick up a passport application at any New Zealand Passports Office or download it from the website. Contact the **Passports Office** at (C) **0800/225-050** in New Zealand or 644/474-8100, or log on to www.passports.govt.nz.

For Residents of the United Kingdom   To pick up an application for a standard 10-year passport (5-year passport for children 15 and under), visit your nearest passport office, major post office, or travel agency. You can also contact the **Identity and Passport Service** at (C) **0300/222-0000,** or search its website at www.ips.gov.uk.

POLICE   The downtown police station is at 1401 Broadway ((C) **619/531-2000;** from North San Diego call (C) **858/484-3154**). Call (C) **911** in an emergency; the TTY/TDD emergency number is (C) **619/233-3323.**

SMOKING   Smoking is prohibited in nearly all indoor public places, including theaters, hotel lobbies, and enclosed shopping malls. In 1998, California enacted legislation prohibiting smoking in all restaurants and bars, except those with outdoor seating. San Diego has also banned smoking from all city beaches, boardwalks, piers, and parks, which includes Mission Bay Park and Balboa Park. *Be forewarned:* Fines start at $250.

TAXES   The United States has no value-added tax (VAT) or other indirect tax at the national level. Every state, county, and city may levy its own local tax on all purchases, including hotel and restaurant checks and airline tickets. These taxes will not appear on price tags. In San Diego, sales tax in restaurants and shops is 7.75%. Hotel tax is 10.5%, or 12.5% for lodgings with more than 70 rooms.

TELEGRAPH, TELEX & FAX Telegraph and telex services are provided primarily by **Western Union** (*C* **800/325-6000;** www.westernunion.com). You can telegraph (wire) money, or have it telegraphed to you, very quickly over the Western Union system, but this service can cost as much as 15% to 20% of the amount sent.

Most hotels have **fax machines** available for guest use (be sure to ask about the charge to use it). Many hotel rooms are wired for guests' fax machines. A less expensive way to send and receive faxes may be at businesses such as the **UPS Store.**

TIME The continental United States is divided into **four time zones:** Eastern Standard Time (EST), Central Standard Time (CST), Mountain Standard Time (MST), and Pacific Standard Time (PST). Alaska and Hawaii have their own zones. For example, when it's 9am in San Diego (PST), it's 7am in Honolulu (HST), 10am in Denver (MST), 11am in Chicago (CST), noon in New York City (EST), 5pm in London (GMT), and 2am the next day in Sydney.

San Diego, like the rest of the West Coast, is in the Pacific Standard Time zone, which is 8 hours behind Greenwich Mean Time. To check the time, call *C* **619/853-1212.**

Daylight saving time is in effect from 1am on the second Sunday in March to 1am on the first Sunday in November, except in Arizona, Hawaii, the U.S. Virgin Islands, and Puerto Rico. Daylight saving time moves the clock 1 hour ahead of standard time.

TIPPING Tips are a very important part of certain workers' income, and gratuities are the standard way of showing appreciation for services provided. (Tipping is certainly not compulsory if the service is poor.) In hotels, tip **bellhops** at least $1 per bag ($2–$3 if you have a lot of luggage) and tip the **chamber staff** $1 to $2 per day (more if you've left a disaster area for him or her to clean up). Tip the **doorman** or **concierge** only if he or she has provided you with some specific service (for example, calling a cab for you or obtaining difficult-to-get theater tickets). Tip the **valet-parking attendant** $1 every time you get your car.

In restaurants, bars, and nightclubs, tip **service staff** 15% to 20% of the check, tip **bartenders** 10% to 15%, tip **checkroom attendants** $1 per garment, and tip **valet-parking attendants** $1 per vehicle.

As for other service personnel, tip **cab-drivers** 15% of the fare; tip **skycaps** at airports at least $1 per bag ($2–$3 if you have a lot of luggage); and tip **hairdressers** and **barbers** 15% to 20%.

TOILETS You won't find public toilets or "restrooms" on the streets in most U.S. cities, but they can be found in hotel lobbies, bars, restaurants, museums, department stores, railway and bus stations, and service stations. Large hotels and fast-food restaurants are often the best bet for clean facilities. Restaurants and bars in resorts or heavily visited areas may reserve their restrooms for patrons.

Horton Plaza and Seaport Village downtown, Balboa Park, Old Town State Historic Park in Old Town, and the Ferry Landing Marketplace in Coronado all have well-marked public restrooms. In general, you won't have a problem finding one; they are usually clean and accessible.

USEFUL PHONE NUMBERS Transit information *C* **619/233-3004** (TTY/TDD 619/234-5005), or log onto **www.transit.511sd.com**. If you know your bus

San Diego arts and entertainment information ℂ **619/238-0700.**

ARTS TIX half-price day-of-performance tickets ℂ **619/497-5000.**

Beach and weather report ℂ **619/221-8824.**

U.S. Dept. of State Travel Advisory ℂ **202/647-5225** (manned 24 hr.).

U.S. Passport Agency ℂ **202/647-0518.**

U.S. Centers for Disease Control International Traveler's Hotline ℂ **404/332-4559.**

VISAS For information about U.S. visas, go to **http://travel.state.gov** and click on "Visas." Or go to one of the following websites:

Australian citizens can obtain up-to-date visa information from the **U.S. Embassy Canberra,** Moonah Place, Yarralumla, ACT 2600 (ℂ **02/6214-5600**), or by checking the U.S. Diplomatic Mission's website at **http://usembassy-australia.state.gov/consular.**

British subjects can obtain up-to-date visa information by calling the **U.S. Embassy Visa Information Line** (ℂ **09042/450-100;** *note:* This is a toll call.) or by visiting the "Visas to the U.S." section of the American Embassy London's website at **www.usembassy.org.uk.**

Irish citizens can obtain up-to-date visa information through the **Embassy of the USA Dublin,** 42 Elgin Rd., Dublin 4, Ireland (ℂ **353/1-668-8881;** or by checking the "Visas to the U.S." section of the website at **http://dublin.usembassy.gov.**

Citizens of **New Zealand** can obtain up-to-date visa information by contacting the **U.S. Consulate General Auckland,** Citigroup Centre, 23 Customs St. E., Auckland (ℂ **6409/303-2724**), or get the information directly from the website at **http://newzealand.usembassy.gov.**

VISITOR INFORMATION In downtown San Diego, the **Convention & Visitors Bureau (ConVis;** ℂ **619/236-1212; www.sandiego.org**) has an International Visitor Information Center located on the Embarcadero at 1040¹/₃ W. Broadway, at Harbor Drive. Daily summer hours are from 9am to 5pm; for the remainder of the year it's open daily from 9am to 4pm. ConVis offers great info and deals on its website, but you can also get your hands on the glossy *Official Visitors Planning Guide* from the information center. The guide includes information on member accommodations, dining, activities, attractions, tours, and transportation. ConVis also publishes *San Diego Travel Values,* featuring discounts on hotels, restaurants, and attractions (it's available online, too).

In La Jolla, ConVis operates a walk-up-only facility at 7966 Herschel Ave., near the corner of Prospect Street. This office is open daily in summer, from 11am to 7pm (Sun 10am–6pm); from September to May the center is open daily but with more limited hours.

If you're driving into town, the **San Diego Visitor Information Center,** 2688 E. Mission Bay Dr. (ℂ **800/827-9188** or 619/276-8200; www.infosandiego.com), is between Mission Bay and I-5, at the Clairemont Drive exit. This private facility books hotels and sells discounted admission tickets to a variety of attractions. There's plenty of parking; stop in between 9am and dusk.

The **Coronado Visitors Center,** 1100 Orange Ave. (ℂ **866/599-7242** or 619/437-8788; www.coronadovisitorcenter.com), dispenses maps, newsletters, and information-packed brochures. Inside the Coronado Museum, it's open Monday through Friday from 9am to 5pm, Saturday and Sunday from 10am to 5pm.

You can also find staffed information booths at the airport and the train station.

FAST FACTS, TOLL-FREE NUMBERS & WEBSITES

TOLL-FREE NUMBERS & WEBSITES

Browse for online information in advance of your trip at the following websites: **www.discoversd.com** and **www. infosandiego.com**, for general information; **www.lajollabythesea.com**, for details on La Jolla's offerings; and **www.sandiego north.com**, for information on excursion areas in northern San Diego County, including Del Mar, Carlsbad, Escondido, Julian, and Anza-Borrego Desert State Park. For more helpful websites, see "The Best of San Diego Online," on p. 50.

If you're thinking of attending a play or some other performance while you're in town, contact the **San Diego Performing Arts League** (✆ 619/238-0700; www. sandiegoperforms.com) for a copy of *What's Playing?*, which contains information on upcoming shows. The calendar is also available online. Half-price day-of-show tickets are available through the league's Arts Tix program.

San Diego Art + Sol (✆ **619/236-1212;** www.sandiegoartandsol.com) is a cultural marketing campaign guided by ConVis. The website lists performances and exhibits scheduled for any specific date, and you may also request a free copy of the biannual magazine, which contains a 6-month calendar of events and cultural itineraries.

San Diego has two major print publications: The daily *San Diego Union-Tribune* and the alternative (and free) *San Diego Weekly Reader.* "Night & Day," the *U-T*'s weekly entertainment supplement, which comes out on Thursdays, will give you the nuts and bolts of what's going on in town that week. For a more complete list of happenings, check the *Reader,* which also comes out on Thursdays, and can be found all over the city at bookstores, cafes, liquor stores, and other outlets; a condensed version called the *Weekly* is found in hotels and tourist areas. Check the free *San Diego CityBeat* for a truly alternative take on San Diego. It's distributed throughout the city on Wednesdays.

2 TOLL-FREE NUMBERS & WEBSITES

MAJOR U.S. AIRLINES
(*flies internationally as well)

Alaska Airlines/Horizon Air
✆ 800/252-7522
www.alaskaair.com

American Airlines*
✆ 800/433-7300 (in U.S. or Canada)
✆ 020/7365-0777 (in U.K.)
www.aa.com

Continental Airlines*
✆ 800/523-3273 (in U.S. or Canada)
✆ 084/5607-6760 (in U.K.)
www.continental.com

Delta Air Lines*
✆ 800/221-1212 (in U.S. or Canada)
✆ 084/5600-0950 (in U.K.)
www.delta.com

Frontier Airlines
✆ 800/432-1359
www.frontierairlines.com

Hawaiian Airlines*
✆ 800/367-5320 (in U.S. or Canada)
www.hawaiianair.com

JetBlue Airways
✆ 800/538-2583 (in U.S.)
✆ 080/1365-2525 (in U.K. or Canada)
www.jetblue.com

Northwest Airlines
✆ 800/225-2525 (in U.S.)
✆ 870/0507-4074 (in U.K.)
www.flynaa.com

Long-Haul Flights: How to Stay Comfortable

- Your choice of airline and airplane will definitely affect your legroom. Find more details about U.S. airlines at **www.seatguru.com**. For international airlines, the research firm Skytrax has posted a list of average seat pitches at **www.airlinequality.com**.

- Emergency exit seats and bulkhead seats typically have the most legroom. Emergency exit seats are usually left unassigned until the day of a flight (to ensure that someone able-bodied fills the seats); it's worth checking in online at home (if the airline offers that option) or getting to the ticket counter early to snag one of these spots for a long flight. Many passengers find that bulkhead seating offers more legroom, but keep in mind that bulkhead seats have no storage space on the floor in front of them.

- To have two seats for yourself in a three-seat row, try for an aisle seat in a center section toward the back of coach. If you're traveling with a companion, book an aisle and a window seat. Middle seats are usually booked last, so chances are good you'll end up with three seats to yourselves. And in the event that a third passenger is assigned the middle seat, he or she will probably be more than happy to trade for a window or an aisle.

- To sleep, avoid the last row of any section or the row in front of an emergency exit, as these seats are the least likely to recline. Avoid seats near highly trafficked toilet areas. Avoid seats in the back of many jets—these can be narrower than those in the rest of coach. Or reserve a window seat so you can rest your head and avoid being bumped in the aisle.

- Get up, walk around, and stretch every 60 to 90 minutes to keep your blood flowing. This helps avoid **deep vein thrombosis,** or "economy-class syndrome."

- Drink water before, during, and after your flight to combat the lack of humidity in airplane cabins. Avoid caffeine and alcohol, which will dehydrate you.

United Airlines*
✆ 800/864-8331 (in U.S. or Canada)
✆ 084/5844-4777 (in U.K.)
www.united.com

US Airways*
✆ 800/428-4322 (in U.S. or Canada)
✆ 084/5600-3300 (in U.K.)
www.usairways.com

Virgin America*
✆ 877/359-8474
www.virginamerica.com

MAJOR INTERNATIONAL AIRLINES

AeroMéxico
✆ 800/237-6639 (in U.S.)
✆ 020/7801-6234 (in U.K., information only)
www.aeromexico.com

Air Canada
✆ 888/247-2262 (in U.S. or Canada)
www.aircanada.com

American Airlines
☏ 800/433-7300 (in U.S. or Canada)
☏ 020/7365-0777 (in U.K.)
www.aa.com

Continental Airlines
☏ 800/523-3273 (in U.S. or Canada)
☏ 084/5607-6760 (in U.K.)
www.continental.com

Delta Air Lines
☏ 800/221-1212 (in U.S. or Canada)
☏ 084/5600-0950 (in U.K.)
www.delta.com

BUDGET AIRLINES

AirTran Airways
☏ 800/247-8726
www.airtran.com

Allegiant Air
☏ 702/505-8888
www.allegiantair.com

Frontier Airlines
☏ 800/432-1359
www.frontierairlines.com

JetBlue Airways
☏ 800/538-2583 (in U.S.)
☏ 801/365-2525 (in U.K. or Canada)
www.jetblue.com

CAR-RENTAL AGENCIES

Advantage
☏ 800/777-5500 (in U.S.)
☏ 021/0344-4712 (outside of U.S.)
www.advantage.com

Alamo
☏ 800/462-5266
www.alamo.com

Avis
☏ 800/331-1212 (in U.S.)
☏ 800/879-2847 (in Canada)
☏ 084/4581-8181 (in U.K.)
www.avis.com

Budget
☏ 800/527-0700 (in U.S.)
☏ 087/0156-5656 (in U.K.)
☏ 800/268-8900 (in Canada)
www.budget.com

Hawaiian Airlines
☏ 800/367-5320 (in U.S. or Canada)
www.hawaiianair.com

United Airlines*
☏ 800/864-8331 (in U.S. or Canada)
☏ 084/5844-4777 (in U.K.)
www.united.com

US Airways*
☏ 800/428-4322 (in U.S. or Canada)
☏ 084/5600-3300 (in U.K.)
www.usairways.com

Southwest Airlines
☏ 800/435-9792 (in U.S., U.K., or Canada)
www.southwest.com

Sun Country Airlines
☏ 800/359-6786
www.suncountry.com

WestJet
☏ 888/937-8538 (in U.S. or Canada)
☏ 800/5381-5696 (in U.K.)
www.westjet.com

Dollar
☏ 800/800-4000 (in U.S.)
☏ 800/848-8268 (in Canada)
☏ 080/8234-7524 (in U.K.)
www.dollar.com

Enterprise
☏ 800/261-7331 (in U.S. or Canada)
☏ 0870/350-3000 (in U.K.)
www.enterprise.com

Hertz
☏ 800/654-3131
☏ 800/654-3001 (for international reservations)
www.hertz.com

National
☏ 800/227-7368
www.nationalcar.com

Rent-A-Wreck
📞 800/944-7501
www.rentawreck.com

Thrifty
📞 800/847-4389 (in U.S. or Canada)
📞 918/669-2168 (international)
www.thrifty.com

MAJOR HOTEL & MOTEL CHAINS

Best Western International
📞 800/780-7234 (in U.S. or Canada)
📞 0845/773-7373 (in U.K.)
www.bestwestern.com

Clarion Hotels
📞 877/424-6423 (in U.S. or Canada)
📞 0800/444-444 (in U.K.)
www.clarionhotel.com

Comfort Inns
📞 877/424-6423 (in U.S. or Canada)
📞 0800/444-444 (in U.K.)
www.comfortinn.com

Courtyard by Marriott
📞 888/236-2427 (in U.S. or Canada)
📞 0800/221-222 (in U.K.)
www.marriott.com/courtyard

Crowne Plaza Hotels
📞 877/227-6963 (in U.S. or Canada)
📞 800/8222-8222 (in U.K.)
www.crowneplaza.com

Days Inn
📞 800/329-7466 (in U.S.)
📞 0800/280-400 (in U.K.)
www.daysinn.com

Doubletree Hotels
📞 800/222-8733 (in U.S. or Canada)
📞 087/0590-9090 (in U.K.)
www.doubletree.com

Econo Lodges
📞 877/424-6423 (in U.S. or Canada)
📞 0800/444-444 (in U.K.)
www.econolodge.com

Embassy Suites
📞 800/362-2779 (in U.S. or Canada)
📞 800/4445-8667 (in U.K.)
www.embassysuites.hilton.com

Four Seasons
📞 800/819-5053 (in U.S. or Canada)
📞 0800/6488-6488 (in U.K.)
www.fourseasons.com

Hampton Inn
📞 800/426-7866 (in U.S. or Canada)
📞 800/4445-8667 (in U.K.)
www.hamptoninn.hilton.com

Hilton Hotels
📞 800/445-8667 (in U.S. or Canada)
📞 800/4445-8667 (in U.K.)
www.hilton.com

Holiday Inn
📞 800/465-4329 (in U.S. or Canada)
📞 0800/405-060 (in U.K.)
www.holidayinn.com

Howard Johnson
📞 800/446-4656 (in U.S. or Canada)
www.hojo.com

ⓘTips   Need a Lift into Town?

Remember to ask your hotel whether it has an **airport shuttle** from Lindbergh Field. Hotels often offer this service—usually free, sometimes for a nominal charge—and some also provide complimentary shuttles from the hotel to popular shopping and dining areas. Make sure the hotel knows when you're arriving, and get precise directions on where it will pick you up.

Hyatt
☎ 888/591-1234 (in U.S. or Canada)
☎ 084/5888-1234 (in U.K.)
www.hyatt.com

InterContinental Hotels & Resorts
☎ 800/424-6835 (in U.S. or Canada)
☎ 0800/1800-1800 (in U.K.)
www.ichotelsgroup.com

La Quinta Inns and Suites
☎ 800/753-3757 (in U.S. or Canada)
www.lq.com

Loews Hotels
☎ 866/563-9792
www.loewshotels.com

Marriott
☎ 888/236-2427 (in U.S. or Canada)
☎ 0800/221-222 (in U.K.)
www.marriott.com

Motel 6
☎ 800/466-8356 (in U.S. or Canada)
☎ 614/601-4060 (international)
www.motel6.com

Omni Hotels
☎ 888/444-6664
www.omnihotels.com

Quality
☎ 877/424-6423 (in U.S. or Canada)
☎ 0800/444-444 (in U.K.)
www.qualityinn.com

Radisson Hotels & Resorts
☎ 888/201-1718 (in U.S. or Canada)
☎ 0800/374-411 (in U.K.)
www.radisson.com

Ramada Worldwide
☎ 800/272-6232 (in U.S. or Canada)
☎ 080/8100-0783 (in U.K.)
www.ramada.com

Residence Inn by Marriott
☎ 888/236-2427 (in U.S. or Canada)
☎ 800/221-222 (in U.K.)
www.marriott.com/residenceinn

Rodeway Inn
☎ 877/424-6423 (in U.S. or Canada)
☎ 0800/444-444 (in U.K.)
www.rodewayinn.com

Sheraton Hotels & Resorts
☎ 800/325-3535 (in U.S. or Canada)
☎ 0800/3253-5353 (in U.K.)
www.starwoodhotels.com/sheraton

Super 8 Motels
☎ 800/800-8000
www.super8.com

Travelodge
☎ 800/578-7878
www.travelodge.com

Vagabond Inn
☎ 800/522-1555
www.vagabondinn.com

Westin Hotels & Resorts
☎ 800-937-8461 (in U.S. or Canada)
☎ 0800/3259-5959 (in U.K.)
www.starwoodhotels.com/westin

Wyndham Hotels & Resorts
☎ 877/999-3223 (in U.S. or Canada)
☎ 0800/5551-2000 (in U.K.)
www.wyndham.com

INDEX

See also Accommodations and Restaurant indexes, below.

GENERAL INDEX

A
AAA (American Automobile Association), 29, 290
AARP, 42
A Bug's Land (Disneyland), 257
Accessible Journeys, 41
Accessible San Diego, 41
Accommodations, 1–2, 59–93. See also Accommodations Index
Anaheim area, 259–261
best, 5–6, 61–62
Borrego Springs, 272–273
Coronado, 89–92
Del Mar, 232–234
Downtown, The Gaslamp & Little Italy, 62–71
Ensenada, 289
Escondido, 250
Hillcrest and Uptown, 71–74
hostels, 60
Julian, 268–269
La Jolla, 82–89
Mission Bay and the Beaches, 76–81
near the airport, 93
northern San Diego County, 240–241
Oceanside, 245
Old Town and Mission Valley, 74–76
Rancho Santa Fe, 246–247
saving on, 59–60
Tijuana, Mexico, 282–283
tips on, 59–60
Accommodations Express, 60
Acoustic Music San Diego, 219
Adams Avenue Antique Row, 203
Adams Avenue Roots Festival, 20
Adventure and wellness trips, 47–48
Adventureland, 254

Ah Quin, former home of, 183–184
Air Ambulance Card, 41
Aircraft Carrier Museum, San Diego, 146
Airport (bar), 221
Air travel, 26–27
Alcazar Garden, 194
Altitude Skybar, 221
American Automobile Association (AAA), 29, 290
American Express, 38, 290
American Foundation for the Blind, 41
American Institute of Architects, 160
America's Schooner Cup, 177
America the Beautiful Access Pass, 41
America the Beautiful Senior Pass, 43
Amtrak, 28, 34
Anaheim, accommodations, 259–261
Anaheim GardenWalk, 261
Animal-rights issues, 47
Annual San Diego Crew Classic, 177
Anthology, 219
Antiques, 203–205, 208
Escondido, 248
Julian, 266
Antiques on Kettner, 208
Anza-Borrego Desert State Park, 168, 269–274
Apple Box Toys, 213
Apple Harvest Days (Julian), 264
Apple pies, Julian, 266
Architecture, La Jolla, 150, 152
Area codes, 290
Art galleries, 208–209
La Jolla, 205
Oceanside, 244
Tijuana, 279
Arts and crafts, 208–209

Art + Sol campaign, 43, 216
ARTS TIX, 216
ArtWalk, 20
Asian/Pacific Historic District, 44
Athenaeum Music & Arts Library, 152
ATMs (automated teller machines), 37
Auto insurance, 31–32
Automobile Club of Southern California, 32

B
Babysitters, 290
Backesto Building, 182
Backroads, 45
Baja Airventures, 47
Balboa Park, 52, 56
attractions in, 136–143
golf course, 170
sights and attractions, 156, 157
tours, 141
walking tour, 193–198
Balboa Park December Nights, 24
Balboa Park Food & Wine School, 48
Balboa Park Visitors Center, 138
Balboa Tennis Club, 176
Balboa Theatre, 180, 215
Ballooning, 166
Barnes & Noble, 209
Barnes Tennis Center, 176
Barona Creek Golf Club, 46
Barona Valley Ranch Resort & Casino (Lakeside), 228–229
Bar Pink, 55
Baseball, 176
The Beach (bar), 222
Beaches
northern San Diego County, 135–136, 232, 239
San Diego, 132–136

Tijuana, 280
walking, 172
Bea Evenson Fountain, 197
BearCom, 49
Beauty Bar, 223
Bed & breakfasts (B&Bs), 60
Beer, 15
The Belly Up Tavern, 219
Belmont Park, 150
Bernardo Winery (Escon-dido), 161
Biking, 36–37, 167–168
Biplane, Air Combat & War-bird Adventures, 166–167
Birch Aquarium at Scripps, 47, 152
whale-watching cruises, 166
Birch North Park Theatre, 215
Bird-watching, 168
Bishop's School, 152
The Bitter End, 222
Black Historical Society of San Diego, 44
Black's Beach, 135
Bloomingdale's, 210
Boating (boat rentals), Oceanside, 244
Boating events, 177
Boat tours and cruises, 29, 162–163, 173
evening bay cruises, 227
harbor cruises, 186
Boneyard Beach, 239
Bonita Cove, 133
Bookstores, 209–210
Borders, 209
Borrego Springs, 270
Botanical Building and Lily Pond, 138, 197
Bourbon Street, 226
The Brass Rail, 226
Brewery Tours of San Diego, 224
Brew Hop, 224
Brewpubs and wine bars, 224–225
Brokers Building, 184
Bruticus Maximus, 150
B Street Cruise Ship Terminal, 29
Buick Invitational, 19, 177
Bullfighting, Tijuana, 281
Business hours, 290
Bus tours, 163–164
Tijuana, 277
Bus travel, 27, 28, 34–35

Cabrillo Bridge, 193
Cabrillo National Monument, 58, 144, 164, 165
Cal-a-Vie, 87
Caliente Race & Sports Book (Tijuana), 279
California Adventure (Disneyland), 256–257
California Center for the Arts (Escondido), 248
California Dreamin', 166
California Overland, 47, 271
California Surf Museum (Oceanside), 244
California Wolf Center (near Julian), 266
Callaway Vineyard & Winery (Temecula), 249
Camping, Anza-Borrego Desert State Park, 273
Carlsbad, 236–238, 240–243
Carlsbad Fall Village Faire, 24
Carlsbad Marathon & Half Marathon, 19
Carlsbad Mineral Water Spa, 239
Carlsbad Premium Outlets, 213, 237
Carlsbad Ranch, 20, 236
Carlsbad Spring Village Faire, 21
Carlsbad State Beach, 239
Car rentals, 30–32
Carriage Works, 184
Car travel, 28–33
driving safety, 40
Tijuana, 276–277
Casa de Balboa, 197
Casa de Bandini, 190
Casa de Estudillo, 190
Casa del Prado, 197
Casa del Rey Moro African Museum, 44
The Casbah, 219
Casinos, 228–229
Cedros Design District, 207
Cellphones, 49
Centers for Disease Control and Prevention, 39
Centro Cultural de la Raza, 44, 138
Centro Cultural Tijuana (CECUT), 279
Chicano Park, 44, 155
Children, families with, 43
Children's Pool, 134
Chinese community, 44
Chinese Historical Museum, San Diego, 146

Chinese Mission, 184
Chopra Center for Wellbeing, 48, 87
Chuao Chocolatier (Encinitas and Del Mar), 242
Chula Vista Nature Center, 154–155, 168
Cinco de Mayo (May 5), 44
Cinemas, 227–228
City Sightseeing, 164
Claire de Lune Coffee Lounge, 226
Classical music, 218
Classic Sailing Adventures, 165, 173
Climate, 18–19
The Coaster, 33–34
Coast Walk, 172
Colorado House, 190
Comedy clubs, 221
The Comedy Store, 221
Comic-Con International, 22
Command Museum, 161
Confidential, 222
Controversial Bookstore, 209
Convention Center/Embarca-dero Marina Park South, 188
Cooking classes, 48
Copley Symphony Hall, 221
Coronado
accommodations, 89–92
restaurants, 123–125
shopping, 207, 211
sights and attractions, 154, 157
Coronado Beach, 133
Coronado Brewing Company, 224
Coronado Cab Company, 36
Coronado Ferry, 186
Coronado Flower Show weekend, 20
Coronado Municipal Golf Course, 170
Country Carriages (Julian), 266
County Administration Center, 185–186
Cox Arena, 220
Credit cards, 37
auto insurance and, 31
Cricket Wireless Amphi-theatre, 220–221
Critter Country (Disneyland), 255
Croce's Restaurant & Jazz Bar, 219
Currency and currency exchange, 37

Customs regulations, 26
Cuyamaca, Lake, 268
Cuyamaca Rancho State
    Park, 267–268
Cygnet Theatre, 216

Dance companies, 218
Day at the Docks, 20, 177
Day Trippers, 34
Debit cards, 38
Del Mar, 230–236
Del Mar Library, 232
Del Mar National Horse
    Show, 21, 178
Del Mar Plaza, 232
Del Mar Racetrack & Fair-
    grounds, 178, 231
Del Mar State Beach,
    135, 232
Deluxe Passport, 138
Department stores, 210
D.G. Wills Books, 209
Dining, 2, 94–126. *See also*
    Restaurants Index
    Anaheim area, 261–263
    best, 94–95
    Borrego Springs area,
        273–274
    Coronado, 123–125
    by cuisine, 96–99
    Del Mar, 234–236
    discount coupons, 94
    Downtown, Gaslamp
        Quarter and Little
        Italy, 99–105
    Escondido, 250
    hamburger, 104
    Hillcrest and Uptown,
        105–109
    Julian, 269
    La Jolla, 117–123
    Mission Bay and the
        Beaches, 112–117
    northern San Diego
        County, 241–243
    Oceanside, 245
    off the "tourist" beaten
        path, 125–126
    Old Town and Mission
        Valley, 109–112
    price categories, 94
    Rancho Santa Fe, 247
    San Diego Bay Wine &
        Food Festival, 24
    Tijuana, 283–286
    with views, 122
Disabilities, travelers with,
    40–41

Disneyland Railroad, 254
Disneyland Resort, 251–258
Diversionary Theatre, 216
Dizzy's, 219–220
Doctors and dentists, 290
Dog Beach, 45, 133
Dog Beach Dog Wash, 45
Doves & Desperados
    (Julian), 264
Downtown
    accommodations, 62–71
    attractions, 143–147
    nightlife, 221–223
    restaurants, 99–105
    shopping, 199–202
        farmers' markets, 211
    sights and attractions, 155
Downtown Disney, 257–258
Downtown Information
    Center, 155, 159, 162
Drinking laws, 290–291
Driving rules, 32
Driving safety, 40
Dr. Seuss' *How the Grinch
    Stole Christmas!*, 24
Drugstores, 292
Dudley's Bakery (Julian), 267

Eagle and High Peak Mines
    (Julian), 265
East Village, 52
East Village Tavern & Bowl,
    222
Eating and drinking, 14–15
Ecotourism, 46
El Campo Santo, 147, 192
El Cid Campeador, 194, 197
Elderhostel, 43
ElderTreks, 43
Electricity, 292
Electronic System for Travel
    Authorization (ESTA), 25
Ellen Browning Scripps Park,
    134–135
El Niño, 19
The Embarcadero, 58
    walking tour, 185–188
Embarcadero Marina Park
    North, 188
Emergencies, 292
Encinitas, 236–239, 241–243
Ensenada, 286, 288–289
Entry requirements, 25–26
Envy/Ivy Rooftop, 222
E-Passport, 25
Escondido, 248–250
Escorted tours, 48
Ethical tourism, 46

Fallbrook Winery, 161
Fall Flower Tour
    (Encinitas), 24
Families with children, 43
Fantasyland (Disneyland),
    255
Farmers' markets, 210–211
    Escondido, 248
Fashion Valley Center,
    211–212
FASTPASS system, 253–254
Ferries, 36
Ferry Landing Marketplace,
    207
Festival of Beer, 23
Fiesta Cinco de Mayo, 21
Fiesta Island, 133
52-mile San Diego Scenic
    Drive, 155
Films, 16–17
Firehouse Museum, 144
First Church of Christ
    Scientist, 159
Fishing, 168–169
    tournaments, 177
Fish tacos, 114
The Flame, 226
Flea markets, 211
Fleet Science Center, 140
Fleet Week, 23, 160
Flicks, 226
Flower Fields at Carlsbad
    Ranch, 238
The Flow-Rider, 150
Flying Wheels Travel, 41
Folk Arts Rare Records, 212
Font's Point, 271
Food and wine trips, 48
Food stores and markets
    farmers' markets, 210–211
    Julian, 267
Football, 177
Fort Rosecrans National
    Cemetery, 161
Four Points Communica-
    tions, 49
Four Seasons Resort Aviara
    Golf Club, 170
4th & B, 220
Four Winds Trading
    Company, 208
Foxploration, 288
Frey Block Building, 184
Frontierland (Disneyland),
    255
F. W. Woolworth
    Building, 180

Galleries, 208–209
  La Jolla, 205
  Oceanside, 244
  Tijuana, 279
Gardens, 160
  Balboa Park, 197–198
  Japanese Friendship
    Garden, 139, 196
Gaslamp Quarter, 52, 56,
  155, 159
  accommodations, 62–71
  restaurants, 99–105
  shopping, 199–202
  walking tour, 179–185
Gaslamp Quarter Historical
  Foundation, 164, 179
Gasoline, 292
Gator by the Bay, 21
Gays and lesbians
  information and
    resources, 42
  LGBT Pride Parade, Rally,
    and Festival, 22
  nightlife, 226–227
Geisel Library, 152, 159
Ghostly Tours in History, 165
Giant Dipper roller
  coaster, 150
Gliderport, 156
Go Baby Go!, 43
GoCar Tours, 163
Golden Door, 87
The Golden State (Disney-
  land), 256–257
Golf, 169–172
  Borrego Springs, 271
  Carlsbad, 240
  environmentally-
    friendly, 46
  Tijuana, 281–282
  tournaments, 177
The Gondola Company, 162
Go San Diego Card, 131
Gray Line, 163
Great News!, 48
Greyhound, 28
Grunion Run, 228
GSM (Global System for
  Mobile Communications)
  wireless network, 49

H&M Landing, 166
Hang gliding and paraglid-
  ing, 172
Harbor Days Festival (Ocean-
  side), 244
Health concerns, 39
Heritage Park, 147, 192

The Hermitage, 239
Hike Bike Kayak, 47
Hiking and walking,
  172–173. *See also*
  Walking tours
  Anza-Borrego, 271
Hillcrest and Uptown, 56
  accommodations, 71–74
  gay and lesbian nightlife,
    226–227
  restaurants, 105–109
  shopping, 202–203
    farmers' markets, 211
Hipódromo Caliente
  (Tijuana), 279
History of San Diego, 8–14
HIV-positive visitors, 292
Hollywoodland (Disneyland),
  257
Hornblower Cruises, 162, 227
Horse racing, 178, 231
  Tijuana, 279
Horton Grand Hotel, 183
Horton Plaza, 179, 200–201
Horton Plaza Park, 180
Hospitals, 39, 292
Hostels, 60
Hotel del Coronado, 154, 157
Hotel Discounts, 60
Hotel Lester, 184
Hotel Locators, 60
Hotels, 1–2, 59–93. *See also*
  Accommodations Index
  Anaheim area, 259–261
  best, 5–6, 61–62
  Borrego Springs, 272–273
  Coronado, 89–92
  Del Mar, 232–234
  Downtown, The Gaslamp &
    Little Italy, 62–71
  Ensenada, 289
  Escondido, 250
  Hillcrest and Uptown,
    71–74
  hostels, 60
  Julian, 268–269
  La Jolla, 82–89
  Mission Bay and the
    Beaches, 76–81
  near the airport, 93
  northern San Diego
    County, 240–241
  Oceanside, 245
  Old Town and Mission
    Valley, 74–76
  Rancho Santa Fe, 246–247
  saving on, 59–60
  Tijuana, Mexico, 282–283
  tips on, 59–60

House of Blues, 220
House of Charm, 194
House of Pacific Relations
  International Cottages,
  138–139, 196
Humphrey's, 220
Humphrey's Backstage, 220

Ice Town, 175
IMAX Dome Theater, 140, 228
Immaculate Conception
  Catholic Church, 192
Imperial Beach, 133
Indian Fair, 21
Influx Cafe, 55
Ingle Building, 184–185
Insurance, 292
  car-rental, 31–32
International Association for
  Medical Assistance to
  Travelers, 39
The International Ecotourism
  Society (TIES), 46
International Gay & Lesbian
  Travel Association, 42
International Student
  Identity Card (ISIC), 45
International Student Travel
  Confederation, 45
International Visitor Informa-
  tion Center, 32
International Youth Travel
  Card (IYTC), 45
Internet access, 50
InTouch USA, 49
I.O.O.F. Building, 182
Irish Festival, 20
Itineraries, suggested, 51,
  56–58

Japanese Friendship
  Garden, 139, 196
Jogging, 173
John's Fifth Avenue Luggage,
  213
Joseph Bellows Gallery, 208
Julian, 263–269
  apple harvest, 23
Julian Black Historical
  Society, 44, 265
Julian Cider Mill, 267
Julian Drug Store & Miner's
  Diner, 264–265
Julian Gold Rush Hotel, 44
Julian Pioneer Museum, 265
Julian Weed & Craft Show, 22
Julian Weed Show, 264
June Gloom, 132

Kahuna Bob's Surf School, 175
Karl Strauss Brewing Company & Grill, 224
Kearns Memorial Swimming Pool, 175
Keating Building, 180, 182
Kendall-Frost Reserve, 168
Kettner Art & Design District, 200
Kiwanis Ocean Beach Kite Festival, 20
Knott's Berry Farm, 258–259
Knott's Soak City U.S.A. (Chula Vista), 155
Kobey's Swap Meet, 211

Labor Temple Building, 184
La Bufadora, 289
La Cereza Vineyard and Winery (Temecula), 249
L.A. Cetto Winery (Tijuana), 280
La Jolla, 54–55, 58
   accommodations, 82–89
   restaurants, 117–123
   shopping, 205–207
      farmers' markets, 211
   sights and attractions, 150–154, 156–157
La Jolla Cove, 134
La Jolla Music Society, 218
La Jolla Playhouse, 216–217
La Jolla Recreation Center, 152
La Jolla Rough Water Swim, 23
La Jolla Shores, 135
La Jolla SummerFest, 22
La Jolla Tennis Club, 176
La Jolla Woman's Club, 150
Lake Miramar Reservoir, 173
Lake Murray, 173
Lakeside Rodeo, 21
Lamb's Players Theatre, 217
Large Rock Monument, 190
Las Americas, 213
La Valencia Hotel, 150
Lawrence Family Jewish Community Center, 175–176
Legal aid, 293
LEGOLAND California (Carlsbad), 158, 237
Lestat's Coffee House, 226
Le Travel Store, 213
Lily Pond, 138, 197

Lincoln Hotel, 183
Lips, 223
Literature, San Diego in, 16
Little Italy, 52, 159
   accommodations, 62–71
   restaurants, 99–105
   shopping, 199–202
Little Italy Festa, 23
Live-music clubs, 219–221
Live Wire, 55
Llama Trek, 268
Llewelyn Building, 182
Lost and found, 293
Louis Bank of Commerce, 180
Lounge Six, 222
Lou's Records, 212
Lux Art Institute (Encinitas), 238

McCoy House, 189
Macy's, 210
Mail, 293
Main arteries and streets, 33
Mainly Mozart Festival, 21
Main Street, U.S.A. (Disneyland), 254
Malls, 211–212
   outlet, 213, 237
Maps, 32–33
   biking, 36
Mardi Gras in the Gaslamp Quarter, 20
Marian Bear Memorial Park, 172–173
Marie Hitchcock Puppet Theatre, 158
Mariner's Point, 133
Maritime Museum, 144, 185
Maritime Museum of San Diego, 173
Marston Building, 180
Marston House, 159
Mary Star of the Sea, 150
Mason Street School, 191
MasterCard, 38
Maurice Car'rie Winery (Temecula), 249
May Gray, 132
Medical requirements for entry, 26
Metropolitan Hotel, 183
Metropolitan Transit System (MTS), 27
Mexico, driving to, 29
Mickey's Toontown (Disneyland), 255
Midway, USS, 146, 160–161, 186

Mingei International Museum
   Escondido, 248, 250
   San Diego, 139
Miniature Railroad and Carousel, 198
Mission Basilica San Diego de Alcalá, 147–148, 159
Mission Bay, 173
Mission Bay and the Beaches, 52, 54, 57
   accommodations, 76–81
   restaurants, 112–117
   shopping, 204–205
   sights and attractions, 150
Mission Bay Boat Parade of Lights, 24–25
Mission Bay Park, 133
Mission Bay Sportcenter, 174
Mission Beach, 134
Mission Hills, 52
Mission Hills Nursery, 160
Mission Point, 133
Mission San Antonio de Pala, 148
Mission San Luis Rey de Francia, 148, 244
Mission Santa Ysabel, 148
Mission Trails Regional Park, 147, 148, 156, 164, 168
Mission Valley
   accommodations, 74–76
   restaurants, 109–112
   shopping, 204
   sights and attractions, 147–150
Mission Valley Center, 212
Money and costs, 37–39
Moonlight Beach, 136, 239
MossRehab, 41
Mount Palomar Winery (Temecula), 249
Movies Before the Mast, 229
Moxie Theatre, 216
M-Theory Music, 212
MTS Transit Store, 28, 33, 34, 41
Mt. Woodson Golf Club, 170–171
Multicultural travelers, 43–45
Mundo Divertido (Tijuana), 280
Museo de Cera (Tijuana), 279
Museum of Contemporary Art San Diego Downtown, 144–146, 155, 186
Museum of Contemporary Art San Diego La Jolla, 150, 153, 155, 156

Museum of History and
Art, 154
Museum of Making
Music, 240
Museum of Photographic
Arts, 139
Museum of San Diego
History, 139–140
Music
classical, 218
live-music clubs, 219–221
Music stores, 212

Nate's Point, 45
National Comedy
Theatre, 221
Natural History Museum, 172
Neighborhoods, 51–55
shopping, 199–207
Neurosciences Institute,
159–160
The New Children's Museum,
146
New Orleans Square (Disney-
land), 254
Newport Avenue Antique
Center & Coffee House, 208
Newspapers and magazines,
293–294
Next Level Sailing, 173
Nightlife, 2, 215–229
bars, cocktail lounges and
dance clubs, 221–226
brewpubs and wine bars,
224–225
coffeehouses with perfor-
mances, 226
current listings, 215–216
performing arts, 216–218
Rosarito area, 287–288
tickets, 216
Nordstrom, 210
North Coast Repertory
Theatre, 216
Northern San Diego County
(North County), 230–251
beach towns, 135–136,
230–245
inland, 245–251
North Park, 54–55
North Park Nights, 208
NTC Promenade, 215
Numbers, 226–227
Nunu's Cocktail Lounge,
223–224
Nurseries, North County, 238

Obelisk Bookstore, 209
Obelisk bookstore, 42
Ocean Beach, 133
shopping, 211
Ocean Beach Antique
District, 204–205
Ocean Beach Christmas
Parade and Tree
Festival, 24
Ocean Beach Jazz Festival, 23
Ocean Front Walk, 134
Oceanside, 136, 243–245
Oceanside Museum of Art,
243, 244
OEX Dive & Kayak Centers,
165–166
Off the Record, 212
Old City Hall, 182
Old Globe Summer Shake-
speare Festival, 22
Old Globe Theatre, 158,
194, 217
Old Town, 56
accommodations, 74–76
restaurants, 109–112
shopping, 204
sights and attractions,
147–150
walking tour, 189–192
Old Town Market, 156
Old Town State Historic Park,
148–149, 204
Old Town Trolley Tours,
163–164
On Broadway, 222
The Onyx Room/Thin, 223
Open Air Theatre, 220
Opera, 218
Orange, 261
Orange Cab, 36
Orfila Vineyards (Escondido),
161
Ould Sod, 224
Outdoor activities, 166–176.
See also Beaches
Outlet malls, 213, 237

Pacific Beach, 134, 211
Pacific Beach AleHouse, 224
Palace Bar, 183
Palacio de la Cultura
(Tijuana), 279
Palm Canyon, 196
Palomar, 250–251
Palomar Mountain, 250–251
Palomar Observatory, 251
Panama-California Exposi-
tion, 159

Paradise Pier (Disneyland),
257
Paras Newsstand, 55
Parking, 30, 32–33
Passports, 25, 294
Passport to Balboa Park, 138
Pedroreña House, 191
Performing arts, 216–218
PETCO Park, 176
Petrol, 291
Pets, traveling with, 45–46
Pioneer Cemetery
(Julian), 266
Pizza Port Brewing
Company, 224
Playas de Tijuana, 280
Plaza del Pasado, 156,
189, 204
The Plunge, 150, 175
Poinsettia Festival Street Fair
(Encinitas), 24
Police, 294
Polo, 178
Port of San Diego Day at the
Docks, 168
Prescription medications, 39
Puerto Nuevo, 286–288

Quail Botanical Gardens
(Encinitas), 160, 238
Qualcomm Stadium, 177, 220
Queen Califia's Magical Circle
(Escondido), 248
Quikbook, 60

Rail travel, 28, 33–34
Rainfall, average monthly, 19
Rancho Bernardo Inn, 171
Rancho La Puerta, 48, 87
Rancho Santa Fe, 246–247
Red Fox Steak House, 55
Restaurants, 2, 94–126. See
also Restaurants Index
Anaheim area, 261–263
best, 94–95
Borrego Springs area,
273–274
Coronado, 123–125
by cuisine, 96–99
Del Mar, 234–236
discount coupons, 94
Downtown, Gaslamp
Quarter and Little
Italy, 99–105
Escondido, 250
hamburger, 104
Hillcrest and Uptown,
105–109

308 **Restaurants** *(cont.)*
Julian, 269
La Jolla, 117–123
Mission Bay and the Beaches, 112–117
northern San Diego County, 241–243
Oceanside, 245
off the "tourist" beaten path, 125–126
Old Town and Mission Valley, 109–112
price categories, 94
Rancho Santa Fe, 247
San Diego Bay Wine & Food Festival, 24
Tijuana, 283–286
with views, 122
Restaurant Week, San Diego, 19
Reuben H. Fleet Science Center, 140, 197
Rich's, 227
Riverwalk Golf Club, 171
Riviera del Pacifico (Ensenada), 288–289
Robinson-Rose House, 189
Rock 'n' Roll Marathon, 21
Rosarito, 286
Royal Pie Bakery Building, 184

Safety concerns, 39–40
Sailing and motor yachts, 173–174
Salk Institute, 159
Salk Institute for Biological Studies, 152
San Diego Air & Space Museum, 140, 161, 196
San Diego Aircraft Carrier Museum, 146, 160–161
San Diego Art + Sol, 43, 216
San Diego Association of Yacht Clubs, 177
San Diego Audubon Society, 168
San Diego Automotive Museum, 140–141, 196
San Diego Bay, 173
San Diego Bayfair, 23
San Diego Bay Wine & Food Festival, 24
San Diego Bed & Breakfast Guild, 60
San Diego Boat Parade of Lights, 25
San Diego Cab, 36
San Diego Chargers, 177

San Diego Chinese Historical Museum, 44, 146
San Diego Convention Center, 159
San Diego-Coronado Bay Bridge, 56, 154
San Diego County Fair, 21, 231
San Diego County Sheriff's Museum, 156
San Diego Crew Classic, 20, 177
San Diego Cruise Ship Terminal, 186
San Diego Film Festival, 23
San Diego Floral Association, 160
San Diego from Gay to Z, 42
San Diego Gay & Lesbian Chamber of Commerce, 42
San Diego Gay and Lesbian Times, 42
San Diego Gay Rodeo, 42
San Diego Hall of Champions Sports Museum, 141
San Diego Harbor Excursion, 162–163, 227
San Diego International Airport (Lindbergh Field), 26
San Diego Junior Theatre, 158
San Diego-La Jolla Underwater Park, 150
San Diego Latino Film Festival, 20
San Diego LGBT Pride Parade, Rally, and Festival, 22
San Diego Miniature Railroad and Carousel, 141–142
San Diego Model Railroad Museum, 142
San Diego Museum of Art, 142, 194
San Diego Museum of Man, 142, 193–194
San Diego Natural History Museum, 47, 142–143, 164, 166, 197
San Diego Oceans Foundation, 174
San Diego Opera, 218
San Diego Padres, 176
San Diego Passport, 131
San Diego Polo Club, 178
San Diego Repertory Theatre, 217
San Diego Restaurant Week, 19
San Diego Sports Arena, 220

San Diego Surfing Academy, 175
San Diego Symphony, 218
San Diego Symphony Summer Pops, 22
San Diego Thanksgiving Dixieland Jazz Festival, 24
San Diego Union Printing Office, 191–192
San Diego Wild Animal Park, 127–128, 157
San Diego Wine & Culinary Center, 48
San Diego Zoo, 57, 127, 128, 130, 156, 157, 198
San Pasqual Battlefield State Historic Park, 248
Santa Anas, 18
Santa Fe Depot, 186
Scenic flights, 166
Scuba diving, 174
Sculpture Garden of the Museum of Art, 194
SDAI Museum of the Living Artist, 140
Sea and Land Adventures., 163
Seaforth Boat Rental, 174
Seaport Village, 144, 188, 201–202
Seasons, 18–19
SeaWorld San Diego, 57, 127, 130–132, 157
Self-Realization Fellowship Hermitage and Meditation Gardens, 239
Sevilla, 223
Sharp Coronado Hospital, 39
Shopping, 199–214
top neighborhoods for, 199–207
Sierra Club, 172
Sights and attractions, 2, 127–166
for architecture buffs, 159–160
Balboa Park, 136–143, 156, 157
Coronado, 154, 157
Downtown, 143–147, 155
free, 6–7, 155–157
for gardeners, 160
for kids, 157–158
La Jolla, 150–154, 156–157
for military buffs, 160–161
Mission Bay and the Beaches, 150
Old Town and Mission Valley, 147–150, 156
for wine lovers, 161

Silver Strand, 52, 133
Singles Travel International, 45
Single travelers, 45
Skating, 174–175
Skysurfer Balloon Company, 166
Sledgehammer Theatre, 216
Smoking, 32, 294
Snorkeling, 174
Society for Accessible Travel & Hospitality, 41
Softball, 177
Solana Beach, 236–238
Soledad, Mount, 152
Soul of America, 45
South Carlsbad State Beach, 239
Southern California CityPass, 131, 252
Spanish Village Art Center, 198, 208
Spas, 48, 87
Spectator sports, 17, 176–178
Spencer-Ogden Building, 182
Spreckels Organ Pavilion, 143, 156, 196
Spreckels Theatre, 221
The Sprinter, 34
Stadium Golf Center, 169
Starlight Theatre, 229
Starlite, 224–225
Star of India, 185
State Street (Carlsbad), 239
STA Travel, 45
Steele Canyon Golf Club, 46
Stingaree, 223
Stone Brewery World Bistro and Gardens, 224
St. Patrick's Day Parade, 20
Street maps, 32–33
Street Scene, 23
Stuart Collection, 152, 153, 156
Student travel, 45
Super Shuttle, 28, 41
Surf Diva, 175
Surfing, 175
  competitions, 23
Surfside Race Place, 178
Sushi Performance & Visual Art, 215
Sustainable tourism, 46
Swami's Beach, 239
Swimming, 175–176
Sycuan Resort & Casino, 171, 229

Taboo Studio, 208–209
Tasende Gallery, 209
Taxes, 294–295
Taxis, 28, 36
Telegraph, telex and fax, 295
Telephones, 48–49
Temecula, 161
  wineries, 249
Temecula Balloon & Wine Festival, 166, 249
Temperatures, average monthly, 19
Tennis, 176
Theater, 17, 216–217
3rd Corner, 214
Thomas Guide, 33
Thornton Winery (Temecula), 249
Thoroughbred Racing Season, 22
Tide pools, 132
TIES (The International Ecotourism Society), 46
Tijuana, Mexico, 274–289
  accommodations, 282–283
  bullfighting, 281
  currency, 278
  exploring, 278–280
  getting around, 277
  golf, 281–282
  nightlife, 286
  restaurants, 283–286
  safety alert, 276
  shopping, 280–281
  traveling to, 274, 276–277
  visitor information, 278
Time zones, 295
Timken Museum of Art, 143
Tipping, 295
Toilets, 295
Tomorrowland (Disneyland), 255–256
Top of the Hyatt, 188, 223
Top of the Park, 227
Toronado, 55
Torrey Pines Beach, 135
Torrey Pines Gliderport, 172
Torrey Pines Golf Course, 171–172
Torrey Pines State Beach, 232
Torrey Pines State Reserve, 58, 153–154, 164, 168
Tourmaline Surfing Park, 134
Tours, 162–166
Toys, 213
Train travel, 28, 33–34
Transit information, 36
Transit Store, 28, 33, 34, 41

Transportation, 33–37
Travel accessories, 213
TravelChums, 45
Travel CUTS, 45
Traveler's checks, 38
Traveler's Depot, 214
Traveling to San Diego, 26
Trolleys, 34–36
Trolley tours, 163–164
Tuna Harbor, 188
Turtle Lagoon (Chula Vista), 155
Twilight in the Park Concerts, 21

UCSD Medical Center-Hillcrest, 39
UCSD Thornton Hospital, 39
"Unconditional Surrender" Statue, 186–187
United Kingdom
  for seniors, 41
  sustainable tourism, 47
United Nations Building, 138–139, 196
Universal, 226
University of California, San Diego (UCSD), 152
Uptown. See Hillcrest and Uptown
Urban Safaris, 164
USAHostels, 60
USA Rail Pass, 29
USA Sevens Rugby Tournament and International Festival, 19
USIT, 45
U.S. Olympic Training Center (Chula Vista), 157
U.S. Open Sandcastle Competition, 22
U-31, 55

Valle de Guadalupe, 286, 289
Veterans Museum & Memorial Center, 161
Viejas Casino (Alpine), 228
Viejas Outlet Center, 213
Villa Montezuma, 159
The Vine, 224–225
Visa, 38
Visas, 25–26, 296
Visitor information, 296–297
Visit USA, 27
Voice-over Internet Protocol (VoIP), 49

Volcan Mountain Preserve, 267
Volunteer travel, 47
Voz Alta, 44

Wahrenbrock's Book House, 209–210
Walkabout International, 155, 164
Walking tours
   guided, 164–165
   self-guided, 179–198
      Balboa Park, 193–198
      the Embarcadero, 185–188
      Gaslamp Quarter, 179–185
      Old Town, 189–192
Walter Andersen Nursery, 160
Warner Springs Ranch, 48, 87
Warwick's Books, 210
Water taxis, 36
Watts-Robinson Building, 180
The Wavehouse, 150
Weather, 18–19
Websites, best, 50
Weidners' Gardens (Encinitas), 238
West Gate, 193
Whale and Dolphin Conservation Society, 132
Whale-watching, 24, 165–166
Whaley House, 149–150, 192
Wheelchair accessibility, 40–41
Where You Want to Be Tours, 164
Whistle Stop Bar, 55
Wi-Fi access, 50
Wild Animal Park, 127–128
Wildflowers, 20, 23, 264, 269, 271
Wildflower Show (Julian), 264
William Heath Davis House, 183
William Heath Davis House Museum, 146–147
William Penn Hotel, 182
Windansea Beach, 134
The Wine Bank, 214
Wines and wineries, 15, 256–257, 289
   Julian, 267
   San Diego Bay Wine & Food Festival, 24

stores, 214
tours and classes, 48
WineSellar & Brasserie, 214
Wooden Boat Festival, 177
WorldBeat Center, 143
WorldBeat Cultural Center, 44
World Championship Over the Line Tournament, 133
World Championship Over-the-Line Tournament, 22, 177

Xplore Offshore, 163

Yellow Cab, 36
YMCA, 175
Yuma Building, 182

ACCOMMODATIONS

Balboa Park Inn, 73–74
Banana Bungalow, 60
The Beach Cottages, 80
Beach Terrace Inn (Carlsbad), 241
The Bed & Breakfast Inn at La Jolla, 88
Best Western Bayside Inn, 68
Best Western Blue Sea Lodge, 79
Best Western Inn by the Sea, 88
Best Western Seven Seas, 76
Borrego Ranch Resort & Spa (Borrego Springs), 272
Borrego Valley Inn (Borrego Springs), 272
Bristol Hotel, 62
Britt Scripps Inn, 71
Camino Real (Tijuana), 282
Candy Cane Inn (Anaheim), 260
Catamaran Resort Hotel, 79–80
Coronado Inn, 92
The Cottage, 71–72
Crone's Cobblestone Cottage Bed & Breakfast, 72
Crowne Plaza San Diego, 74–75
Crystal Pier Hotel, 78
The Dana on Mission Bay, 80–81
Del Mar Motel on the Beach, 233
Disneyland Hotel, 259

Disney's Grand Californian Hotel & Spa (Anaheim), 260
El Cordova Hotel, 90
Elsbree House, 81
Embassy Suites Hotel San Diego Bay-Downtown, 62
Empress Hotel of La Jolla, 88–89
Estancia La Jolla Hotel & Spa, 85–86
Fiesta Inn (Tijuana), 282
500 West, 62
Four Seasons Resort Aviara (Carlsbad), 240
Gaslamp Plaza Suites, 69–70
Glorietta Bay Inn, 90–91
The Grand Del Mar, 232–233
The Grande Colonial, 82
Grand Hotel Tijuana, 282–283
Hacienda del Sol (Borrego Springs), 272
Harbor View Days Inn Suites, 69
Hard Rock Hotel San Diego, 67
Heritage Park Bed & Breakfast Inn, 75–76
HI Downtown Hostel, 60
Hilton San Diego Airport/Harbor Island, 93
Hilton San Diego Gaslamp Quarter, 62–63
Holiday Inn Express-Old Town, 76
Holiday Inn on the Bay, 68–69
Hostelling International, 60
Hotel del Coronado, 89–90
Hotel Hacienda del Río (Tijuana), 283
Hotel La Jolla, 86
Hotel Lucerna (Tijuana), 283
Hotel Misión Santa Isabel (Ensenada), 289
Hotel Occidental, 70
Hotel Parisi, 82, 84
Hotel Pueblo Amigo (Tijuana), 282
Hotel Solamar, 64
Howard Johnson Hotel (Anaheim), 261
Hyatt Regency, 82
The Inn at Rancho Santa Fe, 246
Ivy Hotel, 64
Keating Hotel, 64–65
Keating House, 74
Knott's Berry Farm Resort Hotel (Buena Park), 260

La Costa Resort and Spa (Carlsbad), 240–241
La Jolla Beach & Tennis Club, 86
La Jolla Cove Suites, 86, 88
La Jolla Shores Hotel, 84
La Jolla Village Lodge, 89
La Pensione Hotel, 70
Las Rocas Resort & Spa (near Rosarito), 287
L'Auberge Del Mar Resort & Spa (Del Mar), 233
La Valencia Hotel, 84
Les Artistes (Del Mar), 234
Little Italy Hotel, 70
The Lodge at Torrey Pines, 85
Loews Coronado Bay Resort, 91–92
Manchester Grand Hyatt San Diego, 65
Marriott Coronado Island Resort, 90
Marriott San Diego Gaslamp Quarter, 65
Marriott San Diego Hotel & Marina, 65–66
Mission Valley Travelodge, 76
Motel 6 Hotel Circle, 76
Ocean Beach International Hostel, 60
Ocean Park Inn, 80
Oceanside Marina Inn, 245
Omni San Diego Hotel, 66
Pacific Terrace Hotel, 78
Palacio Azteca Hotel (Tijuana), 283
Palm Canyon Resort (Borrego Springs), 272
The Palms Hotel (Borrego Springs), 273
Paradise Point Resort & Spa, 78–79
Park Manor Suites, 72
The Pearl Hotel, 81
Pelican Cove Inn (Carlsbad), 241
Portofino Inn & Suites (Anaheim), 260–261
Ramada Plaza, 76
Rancho Valencia Resort & Spa (Rancho Santa Fe), 246–247
Residence Inn by Marriott, 82
Rodeway Inn & Suites Downtown, 71
Rosarito Beach Hotel, 287
Scripps Inn, 85
Sheraton San Diego Hotel & Marina, 93

The Sofia Hotel, 69
Sommerset Suites Hotel, 72–73
Tamarack Beach Resort (Carlsbad), 241
Tijuana Marriott Hotel, 282
Tower 23, 79
The US Grant, 66
Vagabond Inn-Hotel Circle, 76
The Village Inn, 92
Wave Crest (Del Mar), 233–234
Welk Resort Center (near Escondido), 250
The Westgate Hotel, 67–68
W San Diego, 67
Wyndham Oceanside Pier Resort, 245

RESTAURANTS
Addison (Del Mar), 234–235
Anaheim White House, 262
Anthology, 100
Anthony's Fishette, 186
Arterra (Del Mar), 235
Baleen, 112
Bandar, 99
Bay Park Fish Co., 114
Beach Grass Café (Encinitas), 242
Bellefleur Restaurant (Carlsbad), 242
Berta's Latin American Restaurant, 110
Bertrand at Mister A's, 105–106, 122
Big Kitchen, 55
Bino's Bistro & Winebar, 124
Bite, 107
Blanca (Solana Beach), 242–243
Bleu Bohème, 126
Blue Water Seafood Market and Grill, 114
Bread & Cie., 108
The Brigantine, 114, 123–124
Brockton Villa, 121, 122
Bronx Pizza, 108
Bully's Restaurant (Del Mar), 234
Buon Appetito, 99
Burger Lounge, 104
Cafe 222, 99
Cafe Chloe, 102–103
Cafe La Especial (Tijuana), 284
Café Lulu, 185

Café Sevilla, 99
Caffé Bella Italia, 115
Calaco Grill, 104–105
California Cuisine, 106
Candelas, 100, 122
Carlee's Place (Borrego Springs), 273
Carmelita's Mexican Grill & Cantina (Borrego Springs), 273
Carnitas Uruapan (Tijuana), 284
Casa de Reyes, 190
Casa Guadalajara, 110–111
Cheese Shop, 183
Chez Loma, 124
China Max, 126
Cien Años (Tijuana), 284–285
Citrus City Grille (Orange), 262
Clay's La Jolla, 122
Clayton's Coffee Shop, 124–125
Coffee Cup, 117
Confidential, 99
Corvette Diner, 116–117
Cosmopolitan Restaurant and Hotel, 190
Costa Brava, 112
The Cottage, 123
County Administration Center cafeteria, 186
Cowboy Star, 100
Crest Cafe, 109
Danny's Palm Bar & Grill, 104
Delicias (Rancho Santa Fe), 247
Dish, 226
Dobson's Bar & Restaurant, 101
El Agave Tequileria, 109–110
El Bizcocho, 126
El Zarape, 114
Epazote Oceanview Steakhouse (Del Mar), 235
Extraordinary Desserts, 109
Felix Continental Cafe (Orange), 263
Fidel's Little Mexico (Solana Beach), 242
1500 Ocean, 123
Filippi's Pizza Grotto, 105
The Fishery, 114, 115
Fish Market, 122, 188
Fish Market (Del Mar), 234
The Fish Market/Top of the Market, 103
The French Corner (Borrego Springs), 273

312 Gabbi's Mexican Kitchen (Orange), 262–263
Georges California Modern, 118, 122
Grant Grill, 99
Green Flash, 122
The Green Flash, 115
Gringo's, 116
Hacienda de Vega (Escondido), 250
Harney Sushi, 109
Harney Sushi (Oceanside), 245
Hash House a Go Go, 105
Hawthorn's, 108
Hodad's, 104
Il Fornaio, 122
Il Fornaio Cucina Italiana (Del Mar), 234
Isabel's Cantina, 112
Island Prime, 102, 122
Jack's La Jolla, 118, 120
Jake's Del Mar (Del Mar), 235–236
Jasmine, 125
Jayne's Gastropub, 126
Joe's Crab Shack (Oceanside), 245
Jolly Boy Restaurant & Saloon, 190
Jolly Roger (Oceanside), 245
JRDN, 112
Julian Gold Rush Hotel, 268
Julian Grille, 269
Jyoti Bihanga, 126
Karl Strauss Brewery & Grill, 103
Kendall's Cafe (Borrego Springs), 273
Kensington Grill, 126
Kitchen 1540 (Del Mar), 233
Kono's Surf Club Cafe, 112
Krazy Coyote Bar & Grille/ Red Ocotillo (Borrego Springs), 273–274
La Costa (Tijuana), 285
La Diferencia (Tijuana), 285
La Fonda de Roberto (Tijuana), 285
La Querencia (Tijuana), 285
Laurel, 126
Laurel Restaurant & Bar, 106
The Linkery, 126
Living Room Cafe & Bistro, 111–112
Lucky Buck's, 104
Mamá Testa, 114

Marine Room, 122
The Marine Room, 117–118
Market Restaurant + Bar (Del Mar), 236
McCormick & Schmick's Seafood Restaurant, 66
Mexican Take Out, 125
Michele Coulon Dessertier, 117
Miguel's Cocina, 123
Mille Fleurs (Rancho Santa Fe), 247
The Mission, 117
Mistral, 122, 123
Modus, 108
Monterey Bay Canners (Oceanside), 245
Mrs. Burton's Tea Room, 109
Mrs. Knott's Chicken Dinner Restaurant (Buena Park), 263
Napa Rose (Anaheim), 262
Napa Valley Grille, 103
Neighborhood, 104
Nick's at the Pier, 122
Nine-Ten, 118
Nobu, 99–100
The Oceanaire Seafood Room, 102
Ocean House (Carlsbad), 242
Old Town Mexican Café, 112
150 Grand Cafe (Escondido), 250
101 Cafe (Oceanside), 245
Orchard Hill Country Inn (Julian), 268–269
Pacifica Del Mar (Del Mar), 234
Pamplemousse Grille (Del Mar), 236
Paradise Grille (Del Mar), 234
Parallel 33, 106
Peohe's, 122
Piatti, 121
Pine Hills Lodge (Julian), 268
Point Loma Seafoods, 114
Pokez Mexican Restaurant, 99
Po Pazzo, 99
Poseidon (Del Mar), 234
Potato Shack (Encinitas), 241
Prado Restaurant, 198
Q'ero (Encinitas), 243
Rainwater's on Kettner, 102
Rama, 99
Ranchos Cocina, 126
Red Pearl Kitchen, 103–104

Rhinoceros Cafe & Grille, 124
Rice, 99
Richard Walker's Pancake House, 99
Rincón San Román (Tijuana), 285–286
Rocky's Crown Pub, 104
Romano's Dodge House (Julian), 269
Roppongi, 120
Roy's, 188
Rubio's Fresh Mexican Grill, 114
Ruby's (Oceanside), 245
Saffron, 105
Sally's, 99
Sbicca (Del Mar), 234
Siamese Basil (Encinitas), 242
Sky Room, 117, 122
Sogno DiVino, 99
South Beach Bar & Grill, 114
Spice & Rice Thai Kitchen, 122
Spicy City, 126
Spread, 126
Stingaree, 99
Su Casa, 117
Sushi Ota, 116
Swami's Cafe (Encinitas), 242
Tapenade, 120
Tea Pavilion, 197
Tepoznieves (Tijuana), 284
Thee Bungalow, 114–115
The 3rd Corner, 116
Thyme in the Ranch (Rancho Santa Fe), 247
Tioli's Crazee Burger, 104
Tobey's 19th Hole, 170
Top of the Market, 103, 122, 188
The Tractor Room, 105
Trattoria Acqua, 120–121
Upstart Crow, 188
Urban Solace, 126
Vagabond, 55
Vigilucci's Trattoria Italiana (Encinitas), 242
Vivace (Carlsbad), 243
Wa Dining Okan, 126
Wahoo's Fish Taco, 114
Whiskpladle, 122–123
Whole Foods, 105
Zagarella II at Cafe Pacifica, 110
Zenbu, 121
Zenbu Lounge, 121